Economic Development in Asia

SECOND EDITION

J. Malcolm Dowling
University of Hawaii

Ma. Rebecca Valenzuela
Monash University

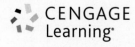
CENGAGE
Learning·

Andover • Melbourne • Mexico City • Stamford, CT • Toronto • Hong Kong • New Delhi • Seoul • Singapore • Tokyo

Economic Development in Asia, Second Edition
J. Malcolm Dowling,
Ma. Rebecca Valenzuela

Publishing Director:
Roy Lee

Senior Regional Director:
Janet Lim

Senior Product Manager:
Charles Ho

Regional Manager,
Production & Rights:
Pauline Lim

Senior Production Executive:
Cindy Chai

Copy Editor:
Roselie Chia

Cover Designer:
S. T. Leng

Cover Image:
Getty Images

Compositor:
Exemplarr Worldwide

For product information and technology assistance, contact us at
Cengage Learning Asia Customer Support, 65-6410-1200

For permission to use material from this text or product,
submit all requests online at **www.cengageasia.com/permissions**
Further permissions questions can be emailed to
asia.permissionrequest@cengage.com

ISBN-13: 978-981-4272-93-3
ISBN-10: 981-4272-93-0

Cengage Learning Asia Pte Ltd
151 Lorong Chuan
#02-08 New Tech Park
Singapore 556741

Cengage Learning is a leading provider of customized learning solutions with office locations around the globe, including Andover, Melbourne, Mexico City, Stamford (CT), Toronto, Hong Kong, New Delhi, Seoul, Singapore, and Tokyo. Locate your local office at **www.cengage.com/global**

Cengage Learning products are represented in Canada by Nelson Education, Ltd.

For product information, visit **www.cengageasia.com**

Printed in Singapore
5 6 7 8 16 15 14 13

Preface

The purpose of this book is to fill a gap in the existing range of books dealing with economic development and growth. Many books have been written on the general fields of economic development and growth. However, during the last decade, we have noticed both a need and desire by students in the Asian regiion to study and understand the growth and development experience in this particular part of the developing world, and from an Asian development perspective. None of the current books fulfill this need nor do they have a regional focus.

What we set out to do when we began assembling class notes as preparation for writing this book was to give the students a flavor of the individual experiences of different Asian countries as they have grown and developed since the 1960s. At the same time, we wanted to relate this development experience to the literature on economic growth and development. Therefore, we have structured each chapter by first introducing the general principles of development and growth that pertain to a particular subject, and then following it up with a detailed discussion of the Asian experience.

The coverage of the book is similar to that found in standard books dealing with economic development. What differentiates this book from others is the exclusive focus on the Asian economies and the balance of coverage between economic theory and institutional and empirical discussion of these theories. Care has been taken to adapt and adjust the theoretical material within the context of economic development in Asia. We draw on concrete examples, including case studies and the use of empirical data to enrich the discussion. Extensive use is made of boxes as well as charts, tables, and graphs to enhance and elaborate on particular aspects of the topic. In many Asian and industrial countries, the study of economic development in Asia has become quite popular. This is not only due to the interest in the conduct and formulation of economic policy, but also because the knowledge of issues pertaining to the economic development of the region is critical for many groups of students. Future teachers, government officials, and business students will all be interested in this course as it serves to provide a better understanding of the process of economic development.

APPROACH AND STRUCTURE

It is important that courses in economic development be grounded in the foundations and applications of development principles relevant to the Asian region. Because the Asian experience is fluid, dynamic, and rich with examples, it provides students with many insights that will be useful in their careers after they graduate. Apart from its focus on Asia, what distinguishes this book from others are the extensive discussions of institutions and the wide use of examples taken from individual Asian countries, as well as the cross-cultural analysis of the Asian experience. In this way, the richness and variety of the Asian economic development experience is brought out.

The book contains thirteen chapters and is designed to be used for a 13–15 week course. Chapter 2 may be covered in two weeks if time permits, while the rest of the chapters can be completed per week.

In Chapter 1, the general concept of economic development is discussed, including the concepts of income, income per capita, human development, and other indicators of economic growth and development. The emphasis is on the Asian experience and how it has evolved over the past several decades.

In Chapter 2, growth models are introduced, beginning with the Harrod–Domar model and proceeding to the Solow/Swan model, as well as the newer growth theories of Gregory N. Mankiw, Romer, and others. While technical material is provided, the thrust of the discussion is on the conclusions that the flow from the models and how empirical work has led to further refinement of these models. The experience of Asian economic growth since the 1950s and 1960s is then discussed in depth. The so-called "Asian miracle" is analyzed, as well as the sources of rapid growth during this period. Country examples, together with the extensive use of visual material (graphs, tables, and charts), are introduced to demonstrate particular points. The experience of South Asia is juxtaposed against the "miracle" economies. This chapter provides a summary of the Asian experience from a macroeconomic perspective and also points the way to further discussion later on in the book with particular issues in microeconomics, finance, international trade, human resource, environment, and welfare. The chapter concludes with a discussion of convergence theory.

In Chapter 3, the Asian financial crisis is discussed along with recent developments following the crisis. This period, from 1997 onwards, is given special treatment because it represents a time of intense study of the future of the Asian region and the policies that are being put into place as a result of the crisis. The causes of the crisis are discussed, drawing on recent research papers and commentaries by specialists in the Asian region. The roles of international institutions, such as the International Monetary Fund (IMF) and the World Bank in the crisis, are also analyzed. What emerges from this is a series of recommendations for policy and how they are being implemented.

In Chapters 4, 5, and 6, the emphasis shifts from macroeconomic analysis to sector issues such as agriculture, industrial and international trade, and financial sector developments. In agriculture, the role of the Green Revolution is highlighted along with the importance of irrigation and the use of fertilizers in raising productivity and output. The symbiosis between agriculture and industrial development is developed, including the importance of maintaining a policy of fostering agricultural growth and enhanced productivity, while at the same time using surpluses created in agriculture to fuel the process of industrialization. Examples from the Asian countries are used to illustrate where policies were successful and where they could have been improved.

The discussion of agriculture in Chapter 4 leads logically to the chapter on industrialization in Chapter 5, and the different approaches that policymakers have used to encourage the sector's development. Institutional and market factors are discussed from various points of view. The approach is not doctrinaire, but rather eclectic. In Chapter 6, the topic of international trade is addressed. After a discussion of the various theories of international trade and the gains from trade, the chapter moves on to a discussion of the important role that international trade has played in the growth of the Asian economies. The shift in export mix to manufactured goods is explored in some detail. For example, the theory of comparative advantage is used to show how and why the Asian economies have been able to shift their exports from primary products to labor-intensive, and further to skill- and capital-intensive goods.

Savings, financial sector development, and the banking system are examined in Chapter 7. The theory of saving behavior is discussed, beginning with the Keynesian theory of saving, followed by a discussion of the permanent income and life cycle hypotheses of saving. The Asian saving behavior is reviewed and the major determinants of saving outlined. This is followed by a discussion of the concept of financial repression, issues of financial liberalization, and the Asian experience. The Asian financial crisis of 1997 is analyzed from this perspective along with recent developments in financial sector restructuring.

Chapter 8 discusses the process of demographic transition that economies go through during the process of growth and development. It identifies the economic and social factors that help explain high fertility rates in developing countries by putting in these into a neat model using microeconomic tools of analysis. The last section of the chapter provides the student with a look into the future through the analysis of recent trends, including aging populations and the future implications of populations policies, such as those we see now in China (one-child policy) and Singapore (policies encouraging families to have more children).

Chapter 9 deals with several aspects on the issue of poverty and inequality in Asian countries. It begins by introducing various ways of measuring these phenomena, followed by a comprehensive analysis of recent trends in the world and the Asian region. Subsequent sections then discuss selected issues, including poverty income elasticities, factor relationships such as those between inequality and growth and between inequality and openness, the dichotomy of poverty into urban and rural poverty, and the policies that have been put in place to address these issues.

Chapter 10 deals with human capital formation and builds on directly from the knowledge and discussions in the preceding two chapters. Attention is first focused on education, followed by a discussion of health as it relates to development. The factors that influence public and private spending on these types of human "investment" are presented and analyzed. This is then followed by a critical analysis of the investment policies that Asian governments have adopted in more recent times in an effort to bolster growth and also mange rapidly rising population. A new section on HIV/AIDS in Asia is included in the last section.

Chapter 8, 9, and 10 are usually taken together to paint a coherent picture of the progress that has been made in these areas. By comparing the various aspects of human development and growth, insights into the reduction of poverty and improvement in income distribution are obtained. The emphasis is on understanding what has taken place, the major factors that have contributed to change, and the way forward in terms of policy prescriptions for the future. For example, analysis of the impact of the global financial crisis on poverty and education provide useful insights into the relationship between macroeconomic performance, social indicators, and microeconomic impacts.

In the last three chapters, several cross-border topics are discussed, including globalization, the environment, and ethics and governance. Globalization is given special treatment in Chapter 11 because it has become an extremely important issue for Asia. The region has thrived because it has become rapidly integrated into the global trading system and this has proceeded at a much faster rate than it has for other developing regions. A number of pertinent issues are discussed, including the possible risks created by globalization, such as volatile capital movements as well as the benefits that have come from the process of global integration. The Asian experience is particularly interesting given the current global financial crisis. In preparation for the discussion of globalization, international trade theory, which is introduced in Chapter 6, is used to further explore the integration of East and Southeast Asia and the prospects for further integration. The contrasting experiences of East and Southeast Asia with South Asia are particularly revealing and lead to a discussion of policy issues and prospects. The chapter also deals with the issues of regional integration and the role of institutions, such as the ASEAN and APEC, within the context of the World Trade Organization (WTO).

In discussing the environment (Chapter 12), both local and national problems and issues of pollution in Asia are covered, including cross-border environmental issues, and renewable and nonrenewable resources. The chapter begins with a discussion of the Coase theorem and the economic concepts and tools that can be applied in examining various problems affecting the environment. For example, environmental degradation—water and air pollution, deforestation, and land use—are extensively discussed, with several empirical examples provided. Climate change and its implications for the region are discussed and analyzed. This is followed by a discussion of the Kyoto Protocol and the role of international agencies and international cooperation in controlling pollution and environmental damage on a global scale.

Finally, in Chapter 13, some philosophical and governance issues are examined. We believe that these topics are particularly important in the light of developments in Asia and the rest of the world in recent years. These developments point to the need to consider deeply ethical and governmental issues. The chapter covers several topics, including a discussion of ethics and altruism that is not usually studied in development economic courses. The discussion highlights the welfare aspects of having a cooperative and altruistic view in contrast with a purely selfish perspective. The discussion moves on to consider governance issues and aspects of public choice. Asian examples are used to illustrate the major issues and challenges involved. The importance of establishing the rule of law and the role of ethics in business and government are examined with reference to the Asian economies. In particular, the chapter looks at social relationships that have given rise to corruption and graft, such as crony capitalism.

CHANGES IN THE SECOND EDITION

In the new edition, several new topics have been added, and examples, tables and charts have also been updated, improving the exposition of existing materials. The organization of the chapters has not changed much; only some reorganization of topics and extension of coverage where warranted. Chapter 3 has been expanded to include recent developments including a discussion of the global recession of 2008 and 2009, and its impact on the Asian region. Chapter 4 discusses recent applications of agricultural technology, including no-tillage farming methods and new drought- and flood-resistant crop varieties. It also examines their roles in increasing productivity and farm incomes. The role of agricultural extension in implementing the new development is also reviewed. In Chapter 5, recent industrial practices in innovation and technology transfer are explored, along with the important role of foreign direct investment. The role of labor migration in facilitating structural changes in industrial development is also discussed. In Chapter 6, recent shifts in comparative advantage and composition of international trade are reviewed. The increasing role of China in the Asian pattern of intraregional and international trade is reviewed and the implications for the region explored. Chapter 7 investigates the impact of the global financial and economic crisis of 2008 and 2009 on Asian financial systems. Fiscal stimulus measures implemented by policymakers to provide some offset to the slowdown in export growth and portfolio outflows are also analyzed.

In Chapters 8, 9 and 10, short sections were consolidated to make room for more detailed discussion on public policies on human capital formation. Unique institutional and social constraints faced by developing Asian nations that result in outcomes not seen in other parts of the world were discussed. New topics here include the latest educational trends and HIV/AIDS impact in Asia. In Chapter 11, the impact of recent developments on the process of globalization and the growing threat of protectionism are investigated. Recent trends in foreign direct investment and capital flows are reviewed with regard to their impact on globalization. Chapter 12 revises and updates coverage of the core material on market failures in the market for environmental goods. The latest developments in climate change are reviewed and analyzed implications for the Asian region explored. The Kyoto Protocol is discussed, along with the role of international agencies and international cooperation in controlling pollution and environmental damage on a global scale. In Chapter 13, the importance of the rule of law on economic development is discussed, along with recent development on progress in reducing corruption.

Overall, the major strength of this book is its firm theoretical foundation upon which a rich discussion of developments, issues, and challenges in the Asian region are built. Economic policy questions and issues arise from this discussion, bringing out various interpretations of the development experience of the different countries. This leads to a number of points for class discussion and reflection. The interrelationship between the topics covered in the various chapters is also highlighted, helping the student to recognize the interrelatedness of economic development and social change. Each chapter concludes with a summary of such policy issues, questions and challenges, as well notes and suggested references for further reading.

The narrative is up-to-date and topical. Current issues such as the perceived threat of China to the rest of the region, the impact of the WTO on the region, the ongoing response to the financial crisis of the late 1990s, the challenge to respond flexibly to the shifting import requirements of the industrial countries, the growing trend toward regional integration, and social issues related to HIV/AIDS and labor migration, both domestically and internationally, are all discussed and analyzed. Thus, the book will be especially useful to students as they move out of the academic and into government or business environment as their careers unfold.

INTENDED MARKET

The book is designed for use in courses that focus on the economics of development in the Asian region. It is structured and written for students who have had some basic training in economics, as well as for those with little or only informal economics background. The approach to economic analysis is basic and practical, with minimal use of mathematics. Each topic is discussed clearly using well-defined economic terms and concepts, and supported with well-illustrated charts and graphs, and stories of real situations in the world. Each chapter ends with notes and suggested references for further reading, and most chapters with some review questions. The book should be of special value to upper-division undergraduate development courses and students should find it very interesting and stimulating as they try to understand the many aspects of how Asian economies have evolved over time. It is also an invaluable resource for educators, policymakers, and other readers seeking to better understand the process of growth and economic development in the region.

ANCILLARIES

The PowerPoint Lecture and Exhibit Slides is available to instructors for classroom presentation who use this book. It is linked to the charts, graphs, and equations in the book. Instructors may adapt or add slides to customize for their lectures. It is available for download at www.cengageasia.com/dowling.

ACKNOWLEDGEMENTS

We owe our thanks to many individuals and institutions. First, we would like to thank the University of Melbourne, Monash University, and the Singapore Management University for providing research assistance for the projects that contributed to the material used in this book. In particular, the University of Melbourne rendered support for research on women's education and labor force participation, while the Singapore Management University provided a grant from the Office of Research, Wharton–SMU

Research Center, and Monash University funded the various Monash Research Grant schemes. Professor Dowling would also like to thank the Asian Development Bank where he worked for fifteen years carrying out research on the Asian development experience. He would also like to thank the University of Hawaii at Manoa for proving office and research facilities.

Secondly, we want to thank our students. Teaching and interacting with them has enabled us to refine and deepen our understanding of the growth process in Asia. Our colleagues and research collaborators have also given us much encouragement and stimulation throughout the project, especially Lisa Cameron, Chris Worswick, Chia T. Cheang, David Ray, Peter Lloyd, Peter Sheehan, M.G. Quibria, N. Rao, J. P. Verbiest, F. Harrigan, Medhi Krongkaew, Sugata Margit, Ifzal Ali, Jugong Zhuang, Ulrich Hiemens, Roberto Mariano, Hing-Man Leung, Lawrence Klein, Gerard Adams, Douglas Brooks, Joe Hirchberg, Donald McLaren, Jan Dutta, Mudrajad Kunchoro, Barry Poulson, Lata Gangadharan, John Freebairn, Seiji Naya, Peter Pauly, Ian MacDonald, Helen Hughes, Richard Hooley, Bob Rice, Ranjan Ray, Bill Griffiths, Prasada Rao, Tony Dingle, Mita Battacharya, Pushkar Maitra, Russell Smyth, Sisira Jayasuriya, Param Silvapulle, Duangkamon Chotikapanich, Jakob Madsen, Russell Symth, and Mita Bhattacharya. We are grateful to them.

Finally, we wish to record our appreciation to our research assistants, Yap Chin Fang, Leanna Ma, Mavy Piening, Michelle Lim, and Seema Narayan, who helped us to compile and organize the material on the Asian development experience that forms the heart of this book.

About the Authors

J. Malcolm Dowling has been living, working, and teaching in Asia and Australia for nearly three decades. Professor Dowling has held teaching positions at the University of Colorado, Boulder, Colorado; and University of Melbourne, Australia. He has also taught as a Fulbright Scholar at Tehran University in Iran, at Reading University in England, and as a Fulbright and Rockefeller Foundation scholar in Bangkok, Thailand. Currently, he is a visiting lecturer with the Department of Economics at the University of Hawaii. He is the author of numerous publications on economics and economic development in international scholarly journals, including *Economic Development and Cultural Change, Review of Economics and Statistics, Oxford Economic Papers, Southern Economic Journal, World Development, The Economic Record, Australian Economic Review, Journal of Asian Economics, The Developing Economies* and *Explorations in Economic History,* and has written and edited several books including *Modern Developments in Behavioral Economics: Perspectives on Choice and Decision Making* (with Yap Chin Fang) and *Future Perspectives on the Economic Development of Asia and South Asia: Rising to the Challenge of Globalization* (with P.B. Rana). His book on chronic poverty in Asia with Yap Chin Fang will be published in 2009. He has also benefited from working for the Asian Development Bank (ADB), Manila, for nearly fifteen years. Combined with his academic experience at the University of Colorado, the University of Melbourne, and Singapore Management University, his experience at the ADB has given him the opportunity to blend economic theory with practical development experience. The book draws heavily on this experience and the databases of the ADB, the World Bank, the IMF, and the United Nations.

Rebecca Valenzuela grew up in the Philippines before moving to Australia in the 1990s. Dr. Valenzuela holds a PhD in Econometrics from the University of New England and is currently a senior lecturer with the Department of Economics at Monash University. She has taught a wide range of subjects including introductory and intermediate microeconomics, quantitative methods, applied econometrics, postgraduate economics, environmental economics and development economics. Dr. Valenzuela's research interests cover the wide area of demand system analysis and the associated fields of consumer behavior, inequality, poverty, equivalence scales, and household living standards. Her work, which also involves research into welfare issues affecting developing countries, has been published in several international scholarly journals, including *Economic Development and Cultural Change*, *Empirical Economics*, *Review of Income and Wealth*, *Advances of Econometrics*, and *Journal of Quantitative Economics*. In Australia, she is a national expert in the measurement of living standards and the costs of raising children and has been a consultant to the Australian Institute of Family, Department of Human Services, and the Ronald Henderson Foundation.

Brief Contents

Brief Contents

Contents

CHAPTER

1

Introduction and Overview

1.1 INTRODUCTION

The enormous interest in the economic development of postwar East Asia has continued into the new millennium. The region's recent economic history has been marked by an "economic miracle" that spanned several decades followed by a severe financial and economic crisis. Problems of widespread poverty and economic inequality remain despite significant economic progress. Addressing these issues, as well as the impact of developments in the world economy, is a challenge the region's governments, international organizations, and the economics profession face as a whole. The region provides fertile ground for economists to study and address a wide variety of economic development issues.

East Asia stands out because of the dynamic economic growth and development it has achieved throughout the postwar period. The development process began in Japan when it opened its economy to increased trade and investment. The rapid industrialization that followed quickly spread to the neighboring economies of South Korea, Singapore, Taiwan, and Hong Kong. Economic growth in these newly industrialized economies (NIEs), sometimes called the Asian "tigers," averaged 8 percent a year in the three decades prior to the Asian financial crisis in 1997. This growth continued despite two oil crises in the 1970s, a sluggish world economy in the early 1980s, and rising protectionism and currency appreciation in the latter half of the eighties.

The industrialization experiences of Japan and these Asian "tigers" formed the basis of the "East Asian development model," which has now become an accepted part of economic development literature. Recent studies have used this model to characterize the growth and development in the neighboring ASEAN economies and China. Inspired by the success of Japan and the NIEs, Indonesia, Malaysia, Thailand, and the Philippines developed strategies that promoted the inflow of foreign capital and encouraged exports. These outward-oriented economic policies fuelled rapid growth during the 1980s. China's economic growth and development has likewise accelerated since the late 1970s when its government shifted to an open-door policy that promoted foreign investment and exports.

However, the remarkable economic record of the Asian economies was marred by the Asian financial crisis. Triggered by the collapse of the Thai baht in July 1997, equity markets and currencies throughout Southeast Asia came under great pressure and the ensuing currency devaluations led to foreign capital flight. Consequently, in a matter of two months or so, Asia's once vibrant economies were plunged into deep recession. This economic collapse forced an unprecedented reappraisal of policies ranging from corporate government to exchange rate management. It also forced a rethink of the prescriptive policies imposed on the ailing economies by international development institutions such as the International Monetary Fund (IMF) and the World Bank.

After the sharp economic contraction in 1998, the region rebounded rapidly. In South Korea, for example, year-on-year industrial production and gross domestic product (GDP) increased dramatically in 1999 while stock market values doubled in Thailand and Malaysia. The primary equity market indexes in Seoul and Singapore returned to their pre-crisis levels. However, as the U.S. economy slowed in 2001 and 2002, and war in Iraq and the spread of the SARS virus took place in 2003, prospects for the region were adversely affected and the future became uncertain.

The financial crisis also hampered progress in reducing poverty and addressing other social issues. The human development gains in health, education, poverty, and equality, and the distribution of income achieved by East Asia in the two decades prior to the crises was eroded to some degree, resulting in slower growth.

There is no doubt, however, that the economies of East Asia are in the process of recovering from the crisis and the region, as a whole, will play a major role in the global, high-tech world economy that we are moving towards in this new millennium.

In South Asia, where the impact of the financial crisis on the region was not as severe, economic progress has accelerated following a shift in policy in the late 1980s and early 1990s. Nevertheless, this region faces a number of challenges, including further progress in reducing poverty and the resolution of political disputes that have drawn resources away from economic development.

This book cannot tell you where Asia is going or exactly how it is going to get there. The dynamics of growth of the region and the world economy will determine this in the long run. What this book offers are tools of analysis and insights based on historical experiences so that the reader will be able to appreciate, understand, and evaluate economic development policy and issues in the region. This knowledge will enable the reader to better understand and participate more fully in the ongoing dialogue between policymakers, economists, business firms, and international agencies.

1.2   How is Development Economics Distinct from Other Aspects of Economics?

In today's classrooms, economic development concentrates on economies that have low per-capita incomes. These economies are set apart, for argument's sake, from the industrial economies of Europe, North America, Japan, and Australia/New Zealand. Economic development considers the experience of these industrial countries as relevant for analyzing the process of economic growth. In Asia, there are many poor countries, as well as some that have recently joined the group of industrialized countries, such as Singapore, Hong Kong, Korea, and Taiwan. We will study all of these Asian economies, particularly those that have been highly successful in achieving high growth and high levels of per-capita income. Many useful lessons can be learned from them by comparing their development experience with economies that have grown less rapidly. The book does not deal with the economies of Central Asia, but focuses on East and Southeast Asia (including the Mekong economies), and South Asia.

Development economists also make use of analytical tools and methods developed in a variety of other branches of economics, such as growth theory, macroeconomics, microeconomics, labor, industrial organization, international trade, and fiscal and monetary policies, to name just a few. They apply these tools of analysis to the problems and challenges of developing countries.

1.3 MEASURING GROWTH AND DEVELOPMENT

For many years, economic development was considered to be synonymous with economic growth—either total economic growth or economic growth in per-capita terms. The two concepts of economic growth and economic development are, however, not necessarily the same. The concept of economic development is a broader and much more encompassing view than economic growth, and relates to levels of social and humanitarian achievement and income distribution, as well as a narrower measure of per-capita income.

Using a measure of the amount of goods and services produced in an economy in a year, we can get some idea about the standard of living in that economy. When the value of these goods increases over time, there is economic growth. Gross domestic product (the total value of production in an economy) or gross national product (GNP—which is GDP plus net factor income from abroad) is used as a measure of the nation's income or production. The size of the total population can be used to deflate it to per-capita terms. An improvement in the living standards of the population is a natural consequence of economic growth over a period of time. Thus, by looking at GDP or GNP growth rates, we get some idea about living standards and how they change over time. Comparisons of these figures also allow us to relate the performances of countries or regions in terms of their growth.

Figure 1.1 shows GDP in constant 2000 U.S. dollars for selected Asian countries over the period 1960–2007. As you can see, some countries have grown very rapidly during this period while others have progressed very slowly. These comparisons may be somewhat misleading, particularly for countries where their currencies were devalued against the U.S. dollar during the period (more on this later). Nevertheless, they give some indication of the relative performance of different economies. By 2007, among the selected Asian countries, China, India, and Korea appear to have had the highest level of GDP (over US$400 billion) whereas Pakistan, Bangladesh, and Sri Lanka lagged behind, with their GDP less than US$100 billion. The GDP for Indonesia, Hong Kong, Singapore, and Malaysia lies between US$100 and US$200 billion. However, care should be exercised when interpreting the economic growth and standard of living in these countries based only on aggregate GDP levels since population levels are not taken into account here.

Table 1.1 shows a clearer picture of economic growth over time as it takes into account population changes by using data for GDP per capita for 1960 and 2007. Since GDP per capita measures the level of GDP for each country, it is an indication of the standard of living at the individual country level. As can be seen, GDP per capita in the NIEs, such as Singapore, Hong Kong, and Korea, grew rapidly while other countries such as India and Nepal grew at a slower rate. Current figures show that Singapore's GDP per capita is almost twice that of Korea, more than six times that of Malaysia, and more than sixteen times that of China (see last column of Table 1.1).

As noted above, when we speak of economic development, we usually mean economic growth accompanied by an improvement in the people's quality of life. To a large degree, economic development results from economic growth. However, the experiences of many economies have shown that economic growth can occur without any improvement in the quality of the lives of its people. A case in point is the resource-rich country of Papua New Guinea. Its mineral-based modern economic sector has grown quite rapidly in the past few decades, pushing up total income and income per capita. In spite of this, it is common to find households in the rural areas continuing to live at a subsistence level. The fruits of this economic growth have not been distributed throughout the society and the government still provides few opportunities for education and health. Human development indicators, such

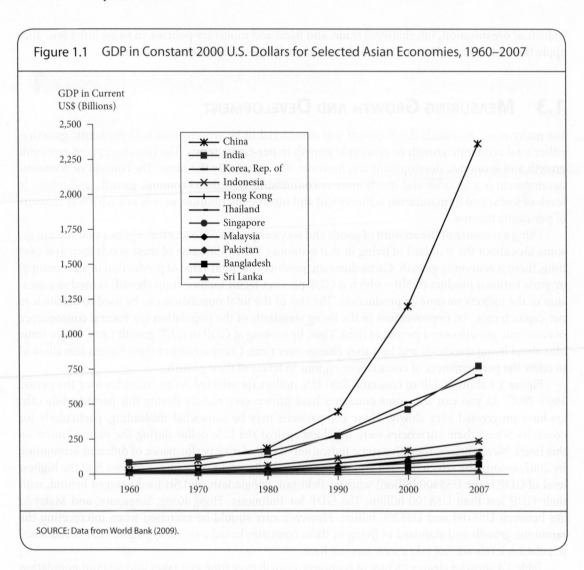

Figure 1.1   GDP in Constant 2000 U.S. Dollars for Selected Asian Economies, 1960–2007

GDP in Current
US$ (Billions)

Legend:
- China
- India
- Korea, Rep. of
- Indonesia
- Hong Kong
- Thailand
- Singapore
- Malaysia
- Pakistan
- Bangladesh
- Sri Lanka

SOURCE: Data from World Bank (2009).

as life expectancy, infant mortality, and the average level of educational attainment have lagged behind those of the other countries in the Asian region.

As a result, there is a growing awareness that the concepts of GDP (and GNP) need to be broadened in order to include other factors that measure economic development. As they stand, GDP and GNP are not sufficiently balanced to adequately capture the essence of economic development. Several additional indicators of growth and development have therefore been proposed in this book.

1.4   New Approaches to Measuring Economic Development

1.4.1   The Human Development Index (HDI)

The United Nations Development Program (UNDP) developed the HDI in the late 1980s and has been publishing it since 1990. This index has three components: per-capita income and two additional

Table 1.1   GDP Per Capita by Country in Constant 2000 U.S. Dollars[a]

	1960	2007
Japan	7,118	40,656
Singapore	2,251	28,964
Hong Kong	3,080	34,037
South Korea	1,110	14,540
Malaysia	784	4,715
Thailand	317	2,713
Philippines	612	1,216
Indonesia	196	1,034
China	105	1,791
Pakistan	188	660
India	181	686
Nepal	135	243

[a]However, figures for GDP per capita will not accurately reflect the standard of living when there exists a bias in income distribution, since it assumes that GDP is equally distributed among the population. This will be discussed in greater detail in Chapter 9.

SOURCE: Data from World Bank (2009).

measures—life expectancy at birth, and level of educational attainment that combines adult literacy and educational enrolment rates. These are added to per-capita income, which is adjusted to reflect the diminishing marginal use of money, to obtain HDI. The HDI is developed as a ratio of a particular country to the most developed country. It varies between zero and one. Both of these additional indicators are somewhat related to per-capita income. However, the HDI can be useful in recognizing that some countries may have rather low income levels, but still have achieved a lot in terms of satisfying human needs (see Table 1.2, ranked in terms of descending HDI values). Examples are Sri Lanka, China, and several countries in Central Asia. For other countries, such as Papua New Guinea and Pakistan, the HDI is much lower than we would expect by looking at per-capita income alone.

Several countries, such as Kuwait and Guatemala, rate much higher in per-capita income terms than they do with respect to human development. Within Asia, the rankings are more closely correlated.

1.4.2   Healthy Life Expectancy

A measure used by the World Health Organization (WHO) summarizes the expected number of years to be lived in "full health." The years of ill-health are weighted according to severity and subtracted from the overall life expectancy rate to give the equivalent years of healthy life. According to the latest data available from the WHO's Statistical Information System Online Database, Japanese men have the longest healthy life expectancy of 72 years among 191 countries, compared with 27 years for the lowest ranking country, Sierra Leone (see Table 1.3, arranged in descending order of healthy life expectancy values for 2003).

Table 1.2   GDP Per Capita versus HDI, 2000 and 2005

	2000		2005	
	GDP Per Capita (PPP$)	HDI Value	GDP Per Capita (PPP$)	HDI Value
Hong Kong	25,153	0.888	34,833	0.937
Singapore	23,356	0.885	29,663	0.922
Korea	17,380	0.882	22,029	0.921
Kuwait	15,799	0.813	26,321	0.891
Malaysia	9,068	0.782	10,882	0.811
Thailand	6,402	0.762	8,677	0.781
Philippines	3,971	0.754	5,137	0.771
Sri Lanka	3,530	0.741	4,595	0.743
China	3,976	0.726	6,757	0.777
Vietnam	1,996	0.688	3,071	0.733
Indonesia	3,043	0.684	3,843	0.728
Guatemala	3,821	0.631	4,568	0.689
India	2,358	0.577	3,452	0.619
Pakistan	1,928	0.499	2,370	0.551
Bangladesh	1,602	0.478	2,053	0.547
Uganda	1,208	0.444	1,454	0.505
Tanzania	523	0.440	744	0.467
Rwanda	943	0.403	1,206	0.452
World	7,446	0.772	9,543	0.743

SOURCES: United Nations Development Program, *Human Development Report* 2002; United Nations Development Program, *Human Development Report 2008*.

1.4.3   Green GNP

One of the more recent approaches developed to address the inherent shortcomings of GDP and GNP as growth and development measures is based on what is known as the "green" system of national accounting. Green GNP is the informal name given to national income measures that are adjusted to take into account the depletion of natural resources (both renewable and non-renewable) and environmental degradation. The types of adjustments made to standard GNP would include the cost of exploiting a natural resource and valuing the social cost of pollution emissions. Damages to the global environment, such as global warming and depletion of the ozone layer, should also be deducted; but these damages are hard to estimate. Others suggest that "defensive" expenditures, those for environmental protection and compensation for environmental damage, including medical expenses, should also be deducted. The argument here is that these costs would not have been incurred if the environment had not been damaged.

Table 1.3   Healthy Life Expectancy, 2003

	Number of Years	
	Male	**Female**
Japan	72	78
Singapore	69	71
Kuwait	67	67
Korea	65	71
China	63	65
Malaysia	62	65
Vietnam	60	63
Sri Lanka	59	64
Thailand	58	62
Indonesia	57	59
Philippines	57	62
Bangladesh	55	53
Pakistan	54	52
India	53	54
Uganda	42	44
Tanzania	40	41
Rwanda	36	40
Sierra Leone	27	30

SOURCE: World Health Organization, Statistical Information System (online database).

1.5   MAKING COMPARISONS BETWEEN COUNTRIES

There are two different methods currently in use for comparing income between countries using the GDP measure—the exchange rate method and the purchasing power parity (PPP) method. (Notice in Table 1.2 that a PPP measure was used to compare GDP per capita).

1.5.1   Exchange Rate Method

The exchange rate method uses the exchange rate between the local currency and the U.S. dollar to convert the currency into its U.S. dollar equivalent. A country's GDP and GDP per capita would then be valued accordingly, in U.S. dollars.

1.5.2   PPP Method

The purchasing power parity method develops a cost index for comparable baskets of consumption goods in the local currency and then compares this with prices in the United States for the same set of

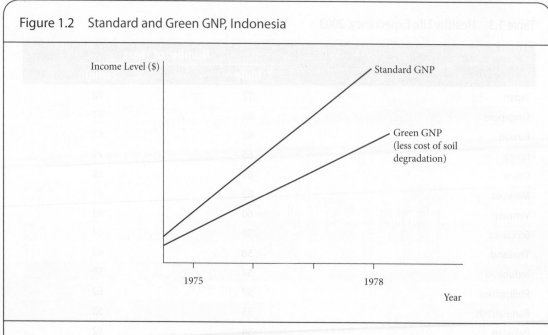

Figure 1.2   Standard and Green GNP, Indonesia

SOURCE: Robert Repetto, William Magrath, Michael Wells, Christine Beer, and Fabrizio Rossini, *Wasting Assets: Natural Resources in the National Income Accounts* (Washington, D.C.: World Resources Institute, 1989).

commodities. A country's PPP is defined as the number of units of the country's currency required to buy the same amount of goods and services that a dollar would buy in the United States. Because the PPP method uses a basket of many goods and calculates the relative price of these goods, many economists view this as a better measure of the relative standards of living than the conventional exchange rate method described above.

These two different methods can give widely varying estimates of GDP. In general, the PPP method gives higher estimates of living standards for developing countries compared with the exchange rate method. The reason is that calculations of GDP based on exchange rate values depend only on the relative prices of traded goods, whereas the PPP method considers a basket of goods that include both traded and nontraded goods. Nontraded goods[1] are generally much cheaper in developing countries and this helps to lift the estimate of GDP for these economies. A further advantage of the PPP method is that it is unaffected by exchange rate changes. As a result of these advantages, the PPP method has become the preferred measure of GDP for country comparisons. One difficulty with the PPP method, however, is that it is costly to maintain since price movements need to be updated on a regular basis. Figure 1.3 shows an alternate indicator of national income other than GDP and GNP, namely, gross national income (GNI), under both the PPP and exchange rates in 2007.

---

[1] Simply put, nontraded goods are those which do not leave their country of production, perhaps because of their nature (for example, domestic transport, and construction) or because of government-policy restrictions, or simply the lack of an international market.

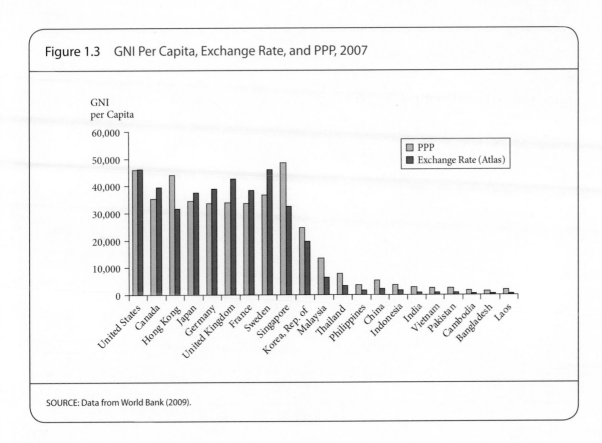

Figure 1.3   GNI Per Capita, Exchange Rate, and PPP, 2007

SOURCE: Data from World Bank (2009).

1.6 Summary

Economic development is a special field of economics which concentrates on the study of countries which are in the process of moving upward from low levels of income, and social progress. There are many features of an economy that are relevant for measuring its level of national well-being, including the annual production of goods and services (GDP/GNP/GNI) and social indicators, such as life expectancy, educational attainment, and environmental quality.

To compare and contrast the level of economic development in different economies, it is useful to consider all these factors. In particular, it is important to recognize that there are two popular ways to compare levels of income: the exchange rate and purchasing power parity methods. The exchange rate method has the advantage of simplicity and ease of calculation. The PPP method, while more costly to calculate and maintain over time, is a better measure of relative living standards since it is unaffected by exchange rate fluctuations and includes all goods produced rather than traded goods only.

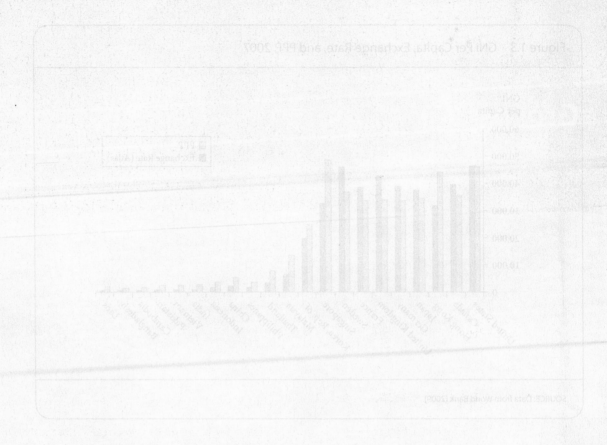

CHAPTER

2

Growth and the Asian Experience

2.1 INTRODUCTION

Why do economies grow? Why should they grow? Why do we want them to grow faster? These are the sorts of questions that economic development and macroeconomic subjects are concerned with. Of course, there are many other subjects that economists are interested in, but in this book we will be primarily looking at economic growth and economic development. Some economists like to distinguish between *growth* and *development*. As mentioned earlier, it is sometimes said that there can be growth without development. The cases of the oil sheikhdoms in the Middle East are good examples. Income and income per capita are much higher now than they were before the first oil shock, but the basic structure of these economies has not changed. Fortunately, because of small populations and high income, poverty is not a problem. In some other economies, there can be rapid growth of a mineral-based subsector, as in Papua New Guinea, and yet there are almost no signs of economic development. Often, growth without development occurs when there is *dualism* in the economy—that is, when one sector is growing strongly but it has no strong linkages with the rest of the economy. This is the case with the mining sector in Papua New Guinea. The strong sector is either capital-intensive or has linkages with overseas investors, while the rest of the economy is underdeveloped, depends on local markets, and has a large agricultural sector.

Recent rapid developments in technology may also lead to the growth of dualism across economies. Inevitably, there will be a dichotomy between those economies that are able to take advantage of technological developments and those who lag behind because of their inability to access computers, the Internet, and other technologies. This kind of duality can also occur at a global level.

2.2 IMPORTANT CONCEPTS FOR UNDERSTANDING GROWTH

In this chapter, we will study a number of theories that may explain the growth experiences of countries over time. To facilitate understanding of these theories, we first discuss some fundamental economic concepts.

2.2.1   Components of Income and Output

Output is derived by combining various factors of production, which include land, capital, and labor. Normally, we take the supply of land as fixed and assume that its productivity can be enhanced by the application of labor or capital, the two variable inputs which are combined in a standard production function.

The production function is a useful tool for analyzing the process of economic growth. A production function relates the inputs of the production process, such as labor (L) and capital (K), to the output/income (Y) from the process. This relationship can be stated in a number of ways. A general function (f) without any functional form can be stated as

$$Y = f(K, L) \tag{2.1}$$

As labor and capital grow over time, so will income. What are some of the attributes of this relationship?

To a large extent, the law of diminishing returns governs the growth process. As each worker acquires more capital, it follows that there would be diminishing returns to that capital. If this process were to continue for a long enough period, growth would slow to zero. However, this has not been the experience of the industrialized nations. Why? This is principally because of changes in the nature of the capital and labor and the way they are organized to produce output. The former is sometimes called embodied technical progress, and the latter disembodied technical progress.

Embodied technical progress is reflected by the fact that labor forces have tended to become more educated over time as more resources are spent on upgrading the skills of the existing labor force and also on educating the young. Technological developments also tend to increase the productivity of capital. These developments are the result of innovation and invention. In the last decade, advances in information and computer technology have been the most apparent sources of innovation. These have both changed the nature of capital and labor inputs and the way that they are combined to create output.

In terms of the kind of disembodied technical progress seen in applications in information and computer technology, there have been advances in management and industrial organization that have increased the level of output even when the amounts of labor and capital are fixed. The Internet as a tool for communication, information collection, and dissemination has increased in importance, and the use of computers to monitor and control production has become widespread. As a result, production processes have been streamlined, the need to keep large inventory of raw and semi-finished goods has been reduced, and the flexibility of production processes has increased.

To summarize, at any level of capital and labor inputs, there will be an associated level of output. When the output increases at the same rate as the inputs, we refer to the production function as having constant returns to scale. This means that in Equation 2.1, we could multiply each input by some constant and the output would increase by that constant amount.

In what follows, we will explore various aspects of the production function and technology that can change the relationship. For example, researchers have studied the rate of increase in labor, capital, and output. The evidence from these studies suggests that output increases more rapidly than inputs. If technology were fixed, this would imply that there would be increasing returns to scale, that is, that output would increase faster than inputs. However, as technology has changed, we have to interpret the difference between input and output growth in a slightly different way.

The size of the labor force will increase over time as a lagged consequence of the natural increase in population. The capital stock will also increase as a result of investment. While it depends on how these factors are combined and the shape of the production function, increases in labor and capital will result in an increase in output and income. Historically, there has been a significant rate of growth in per-capita income over time and this has resulted in higher standards of living—more goods and services per capita—for many regions of the world. The contribution of the two kinds of technological advance has also played a critical role in raising the standards of living. The next section will discuss how these two distinct contributing factors of embodied and disembodied technical progress can be measured.

2.2.2 Total Factor Productivity

By investigating the rate of growth of labor and capital together with income and output, economists have observed that there is some growth in output that is unaccounted for by the growth of labor and capital in the standard production functions, even when adjustments are made in the quality of the labor and capital inputs. In some cases, this discrepancy or residual is quite large. This residual has been called total factor productivity (TFP), or multifactor productivity.

TFP pertains to the efficiency with which the inputs are combined to produce output. These efficiency gains can be due to a number of factors, including greater economies of scale, better management, marketing or organizational abilities, shifts in production from low productivity activities to higher productivity activities with the same amount of labor and capital, or the impact of new technology which enables greater output to be obtained with the same capital and labor inputs.

If we call this TFP, or multifactor productivity, term A, and denote capital and labor by K and L respectively, then the production function can be rewritten as

$$Y = f(K, L, A). \tag{2.2}$$

Equation 2.2 is a general expression. Often, economists assume that competitive conditions exist in capital and labor markets and there are constant returns to scale. If this is the case, then we can show that the growth rate of income is equal to the growth rates of the capital and labor inputs weighted by their shares in national income:

$$g(Y) = g(K) \, W(K) + g(L) \, W(L) + A, \tag{2.3}$$

where $g(Y)$ is the growth rate of income, $g(K)$ is the growth rate of capital (investment), $g(L)$ is the growth rate of labor, and $W(K)$ and $W(L)$ are the weighted shares of capital and labor in the economy. The growth rate of income thus equals the sum of the three terms. The first term is the growth rate of capital multiplied by the ratio of capital to labor, and by a term that is the marginal product of capital. The second term is similar to the first term except that it is for labor. The third term involves the efficiency factor, A.

If we assume that labor and capital are paid the value of their marginal products, the result would be that the growth in output would be equal to the sum of three factors: the growth rate of capital multiplied by its share of output plus the growth rate of labor multiplied by labor's share in output plus a residual term. Notice that this residual term measures both embodied and disembodied technical progress. To the extent that we can adjust the labor and capital inputs to reflect changes in the level of skill of the labor force and the quality of capital inputs, we can incorporate embodied technical progress into the first two terms. However, to the extent that we miss out on some of this embodied technical progress, it will be included in the efficiency term A.

Working through an example, suppose a country has a growth rate of income of 6 percent, a growth rate of capital (net of depreciation) of 10 percent, and capital's share of income is 30-percent, labor's share is 70 percent and labor grows at 1 percent, then the sum of the terms on the right-hand side, apart from A, will be

$$0.06 = A + 0.3(0.10) + 0.7(0.01).$$

In this example, $A = 0.023$ and technical progress accounts for just a little less than 40 percent of the output growth of 6 percent. There are, of course, many assumptions in this model. The biggest assumption is that factors are paid the value of their marginal product and that the two factors, K and L, exhaust total output, in the sense that their coefficients add up to one. This is essentially a constant returns to scale argument so that we do not allow for output growth to exceed the rate of growth of labor and capital.

Notice also that the growth in income will be raised if the investment rate is increased or if the labor force increases more rapidly. Efficiency, meanwhile, is assumed to be unchanged.

2.2.3   Economic Efficiency

The production possibility frontier (PPF) is a curve depicting the best possible combination of goods that is produced in an economy—best in the sense that the combination utilizes all the available inputs efficiently and minimizes waste. The case for an economy that produces only two goods—cell phones and jeans—is shown in Figure 2.1. In Figure 2.1a, the point A on the y axis is the production option where all inputs are used to manufacture cell phones only, while the point D on the x axis is the production option that uses all available inputs for the productions of jeans alone. The points B and C are production options where all available inputs are used for the production of some cell phones and jeans. Each point—A, B, C, and D (as well as other combinations on the curve)—trace the PPF curve of the economy. Each point on this curve represents the maximum number of jeans and/or cell phones that can be produced according to the inputs to the production process. In this sense, these combinations are efficient and the PPF, therefore, represents the "best practice" firms in the economy. In contrast, a production combination represented by a point inside the PPF curve, say E, does not utilize all the available resources for economic production. With some resources remaining idle, this production option is considered inefficient.

Economic efficiency is boosted in a static sense (static efficiency) if firms move from inside the production possibility frontier, say point E, toward the frontier itself, to point E'. An improvement in economic efficiency of this type could lead to a one-time increase in income but it would not arrest the tendency toward decreasing returns. This drift toward decreasing returns is one reason that richer economies tend to grow more slowly than some poorer economies. There are, of course, many other factors involved in growth, which is why many poor countries, particularly in Africa and Latin America, have also experienced slow or even negative growth in per-capita income.

Improvements in economic efficiency can take place in a number of ways, including the move toward best practice through better management and organization. This could be done by implementing better inventory-control measures, better relations between management and labor, new methods of organizing the way products are assembled (within the existing capital structure and labor-force configurations), and so on.

By contrast with static efficiency, dynamic efficiency takes place when there is economic growth and the scale of production increases (scale efficiencies), or production shifts from a low productivity sector to a more productive sector. In Figure 2.1b, this is represented by an outward shift of the PPF curve (the dotted line).

In Asia, much of the dynamic efficiency resulted from a shift from the less efficient agricultural sector to a more efficient industry. Such inter-industry shifts usually take place quickly when an economy is growing rapidly. Dynamic efficiency can also result from new innovations and inventions which boost total factor productivity. It can also be due to more effective marketing and distribution arrangements, sometimes with foreign outlets. Large-scale operations also allow bulk purchasing and quantity discounts that are unavailable to smaller-scale operations. Many multinational firms also use different production sites to manufacture different components of a product in order to take advantage of lower costs. These components are then shipped to other locations where they are assembled and delivered to buyers. Since dynamic efficiency leads to an outward shift of the production possibility frontier, it

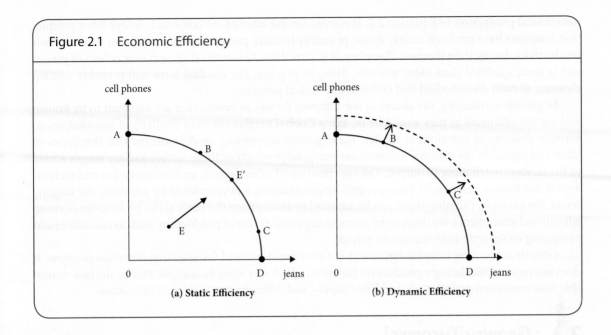

Figure 2.1 Economic Efficiency

(a) Static Efficiency

(b) Dynamic Efficiency

leads to a higher level of output for the same level of capital and labor inputs. Dynamic efficiency may also involve the use of new technology and innovations as old capital equipment is replaced and older workers are either replaced or retrained.

2.2.4 Technical Progress

As noted above, there are two kinds of technical progress or innovation that can be achieved by an economy. Embodied technical progress has to do with the changing nature of the inputs into the production process. These would include more highly skilled and computer-literate workers, or less stressed and more congenial workers, or the installation of new innovations in capital equipment. Disembodied technical progress, on the other hand, relates to the way factors are combined together in the workplace, such as management or organizational innovations. This type of technical progress would be contained in the residual, A, in Equation 2.2 and would arise from the way in which factors are combined together within the firm and the industry.

Practically, it is unlikely that all the embodied technical progress will be captured in the measures of labor and capital. Usually, it is hard to get good estimates of the capital stock as we tend to rely on investment figures to measure the increment to capital. These figures are measured in a monetary unit and therefore do not tell much about the amount of new innovation or technology contained in this new capital. Similarly, labor input is usually measured in terms of man-hours or man-years worked.

However, new, more highly trained and educated workers enter the workforce all the time and older workers retire. These figures are not ordinarily used to construct a new labor series each year that reflects this higher embodiment of education and skill into the hours or years worked. There are, nevertheless, attempts to use a range of educational attainment variables to measure these labor-force effects separately. There have also been attempts to measure what are called vintage production functions—that is, production functions which assume that each year has a new vintage of capital that has higher innate productivity than do capital investments in previous years. By constructing a vintage capital model, some economists have been able to reduce quite substantially the size of the residual, A, in the neoclassical production in Equation 2.2. However, similar attempts to construct vintage labor production functions have not been widely made, primarily because people, unlike capital, can increase their productivity during their lifetime. Therefore, it is unrealistic to assume that each new cohort of graduates is more qualified than older workers. Thus, in practice, the residual term will probably contain elements of both disembodied and embodied technical progress.

In growth accounting, the shares of the different factors of production are assumed to be known and are not estimated as they would be in, say, a Cobb–Douglas constant elasticity of substitution, or variable elasticity of substitution model. These growth accounting models assume that the shares of labor and capital in the national accounts are marginal products of these factors and are simply added to the factors contributing to output. The contribution of other factors, such as education and technological innovation, can also be incorporated by constructing a new series or by adjusting the existing series. For example, the labor input can be adjusted by multiplying the labor series by an index of rising educational attainment over time, or by introducing a new factor of production, such as education, and measuring its separate contribution to output.

Growth accounting is useful because it is a shorthand method for assessing technical progress. It does not require calculating a production function, which can often be complicated by the lack of reliable information on capital stock and labor supply, and difficulties in empirical estimation.

2.3   GROWTH THEORIES[1]

There are a number of theories on how the process of economic development takes place. A very broad interpretation of these theories could consider five alternative approaches.

KEYNESIAN THEORY   These models stress the accumulation of capital. They include Rostow's (1960) stages of growth model and the Harrod–Domar growth model (see Harrod, 1939; and Domar, 1946) which will be discussed below. Growth among countries using these models could easily diverge. The models do not explicitly consider the law of diminishing returns to capital which can take effect as growth proceeds. In this sense, they are not particularly realistic.

SOLOW OR NEOCLASSICAL THEORY   These models stress the neoclassical economic principle that factors of production should be paid the value of their marginal products. In these models, the law of diminishing returns can operate and there is mobility of factors to seek their highest return. These models have all been developed on the basis of the Solow–Swan (1956) model. They were favored by most mainstream economists for more than thirty years—from the early 1960s or late 1950s when the Solow model was first published until quite recently. These models show a convergence in growth among countries and also imply that there will be a slowdown in growth in the absence of technical progress as a result of diminishing returns.

POWER-BALANCE THEORY   These models stress international power balance as an important factor in development, including the terms and patterns of trade which tend to keep some countries poor while other countries get richer. In one sense, the international power-balance model can be considered as a subclass of the neoclassical model where there is a lack of factor mobility in international trade.

---

[1] The expositions in the sections on the Solow model and new growth theories have benefited from discussions with Mark Crosby at the University of Melbourne, Australia.

STRUCTURAL THEORY   These models emphasize the shifts in resources between different sectors on the supply side. These theories discuss the transition from labor-intensive agriculture, which relies on traditional, low-productivity farming techniques, to modern, high-productivity industries which have benefited from innovation and more intensive use of capital and technology.

NEW GROWTH THEORY   The most recent growth theories, simply called "new growth theories," try to endogenize technical progress and make use of assumptions of increasing returns to scale and positive externalities. These assumptions contrast sharply with the neoclassical model which stresses diminishing returns and a slowdown of growth to a steady-state rate.

Let us look briefly at the Keynesian and neoclassical theories and then examine the structuralist approach, and the power balance and new growth theories.

2.3.1   The Keynesian Growth Theory and the Harrod–Domar Model

The Harrod–Domar (1939, 1946) model is the simplest macroeconomic model. It begins with the assumption that saving is a constant proportion of income.[2] We first define income Y as the sum of consumption C and saving S, and that saving equals investment I. Thus, at any time t, it follows that

$$Y(t) = C(t) + S(t), \tag{2.4}$$

$$S(t) = I(t), \text{ and} \tag{2.5}$$

$$Y(t) = C(t) + I(t). \tag{2.6}$$

Then if we define investment as the change in the capital stock K, including a term for depreciation, δ, we get

$$K(t+1) = (1 - \delta) K(t) + I(t). \tag{2.7}$$

One of the key assumptions of the Harrod–Domar model is that saving is a constant proportion of income. The saving rate, s, is thus defined as

$$s = S(t) / Y(t). \tag{2.8}$$

We also define the capital–output ratio θ as

$$\theta = K(t) / Y(t), \tag{2.9}$$

which represents the amount of capital needed to produce a single unit of output.

Combining Equations 2.5 and 2.7 with 2.8 and 2.9, we get

$$\theta Y(t+1) = (1 - \delta) \theta Y(t) + s Y(t). \tag{2.10}$$

After some manipulation we obtain

$$\frac{Y(t+1) - Y(t)}{Y(t)} = \frac{s}{\theta} - \delta, \tag{2.11}$$

where the left-hand side of Equation 2.11 defines the growth rate of income g. According to this Harrod–Domar equation, the growth of income is a function of the depreciation rate of capital, the saving rate, and the capital–output ratio.

---

[2] Keynes (1936). In this assumption, the Harrod–Domar model is Keynesian in character and was, in fact, developed immediately following the publication of Keynes' *The General Theory of Employment, Interest, and Money*. This model features the Keynesian theory based on the consumption function but makes it more dynamic.

This is obviously a very simplistic yet powerful result. For example, in an economy with no depreciation, where the capital–output ratio is 3 and the saving rate is 6 percent, the growth in output is 6/3 = 2 percent per annum. The growth rate will be higher, the higher the saving and investment rates and the lower the capital–output ratio.

Notice the constant assumption of the ratio θ. Because of this, the Harrod–Domar formulation does not recognize that there may be diminishing returns: given increases in input lead to continually smaller increases in output. By assuming that the capital–output ratio is constant, this model assumes that there are constant returns to scale regardless of what the level of capital stock in the economy. This is unrealistic. The larger the capital stock, the more likely it is that there will be diminishing returns to the capital factor. The model in this form also does not specifically include labor or other inputs.

Nevertheless, the Harrod–Domar model does contain some important information, that

- saving and investment are very important in achieving higher growth.
- the efficiency with which capital is employed is very important in achieving higher growth.

The Harrod–Domar equations can be adjusted to account for population growth. Let us say that the population is growing at a constant rate of η. The population level at time $(t + 1)$ is thus represented as

$$P(t + 1) = P(t)(1 + \eta), \tag{2.12}$$

If per-capita income is defined as $y(t) = Y(t)/P(t)$, then by dividing Equation (2.10) by $P(t)$ and some manipulation, we have

$$\theta Y(t + 1)/\{P(t + 1)/P(t)\} = (1 - \delta)\,\theta y(t) + sy(t), \tag{2.13}$$

When we divide this by $\theta y(t)$, we get

$$\frac{y(t+1)}{y(t)} \cdot \frac{P(t+1)}{P(t)} = (1 - \delta) + \frac{s}{\theta}, \tag{2.14}$$

It follows that

$$\frac{s}{\theta} = (1+g^*)(1+\eta) - (1-\delta) \tag{2.15}$$

using Equation (2.10), and where g^* is the growth rate of per-capita income.[3] Expanding this expression further, we have

$$\frac{s}{\theta} = g^* + \eta + \delta + g^* \eta. \tag{2.16}$$

Since g^* and η are both small (in the range of 0.02 to 0.05) the last term can be ignored. Therefore,

$$g^* = \frac{s}{\theta} - \eta - \delta. \tag{2.17}$$

Comparing Equation (2.17) with (2.11), we can see that the addition of the population growth rate, η, is a factor reducing growth in per-capita income. This model specifically suggests that countries with low population growth will be better off, other things being equal.

---

[3] Note the difference between g and g^*, where g represents the growth rate of income while g^* represents the growth rate of per-capita income. The latter takes population growth into account.

The main weakness of the Harrod–Domar model is that it still incorporates the restrictive assumption about constant returns to scale and the constancy of the saving rate. In addition, the extended model fails to consider that population growth may be endogenous, depending on the stage of economic development.

2.3.2 The Solow (Neoclassical) Model

A more general model of growth incorporating the law of diminishing returns to factors of production was developed by Solow and Swan in 1956. The model assumes the endogeneity of the capital–output ratio—that is, the output of an economy depends crucially on its initial endowments of labor and capital, and that these factors work in tandem to produce the economy's level of output.

The Solow model thus starts from a production function, rather than a saving function. To fix ideas, we begin from Equations 2.5, 2.7, 2.8, and 2.10 of the Harrod–Domar model. We also denote population by $P(t)$ and assume that it grows at a constant rate as in Equation 2.12. Dividing Equation 2.13 by $P(t)$, we obtain the following fundamental Solow equation:

$$(1 + n)\, k(t + 1) = (1 - \delta)\, k(t) + sy(t), \tag{2.18}$$

where k and y denote the per-capita units of capital and output, respectively, that is, $k(t) = K(t)/P(t)$ and $y(t) = Y(t)/P(t)$. This fundamental Solow equation shows that the amount of per-capita capital in the current period depends upon the per-capita capital in the last period, the saving rate in the previous period, and the rate of population growth. If we assume a production function that has diminishing returns to per-capita capital, the output–capital ratio falls as capital increases because of a relative shortage of labor. This does not mean that output per person will decline; in fact, it continues to rise even as the labor shortfall causes a decline in the output–capital ratio. This relationship is shown in Figure 2.2.

In Figure 2.3, we plot the relationship derived in Equation 2.18 to help us determine what the per-capita stock might be at date $t + 1$ if the current per-capita stock is k. The RHS term is the production function multiplied by the saving rate, s, and then added to the depreciated capital stock. It will thus

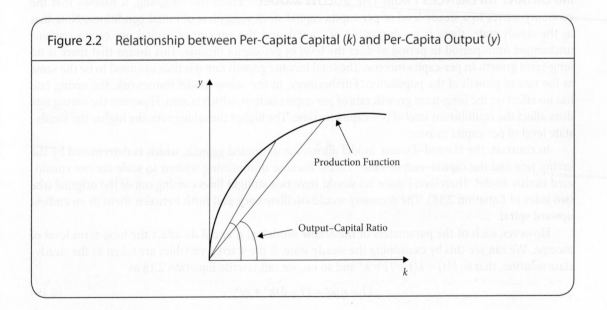

Figure 2.2 Relationship between Per-Capita Capital (k) and Per-Capita Output (y)

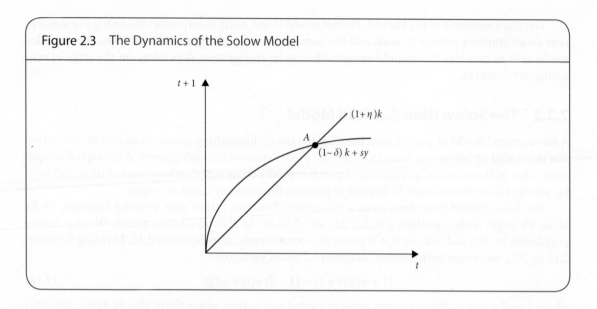

Figure 2.3   The Dynamics of the Solow Model

have the same shape as the production function, as shown in Figure 2.3. The LHS term is $(1 + \eta)k$, which is represented here by the straight line. There will be a tendency for the system to move to the place where the two curves cross, at A.

To the left of the intersection of the two curves, the capital stock per capita is small and returns to this capital are higher than required to service a constantly growing population's need for capital. Thus, the amount of capital per capita will tend to increase. To the right of this point, there is a large capital stock and the returns to capital are so low (due to diminishing returns to capital) that there is not enough being saved to provide the same amount of capital for all the new members of society and to cover the depreciation of the large capital stock. In both cases, the tendency is to return to the equilibrium point where the two lines intersect.

IMPORTANT INFERENCES FROM THE SOLOW MODEL   From the foregoing, it follows that the economy moves to a steady level of per-capita capital stock regardless of initial conditions. Note that in the steady state, there is no deepening of capital, and the amount of capital per capita remains unchanged from period to period as does the level of per-capita income. This means that there is no long-term growth in per-capita income. The total income growth rate η is thus assumed to be the same as the rate of growth of the population. Furthermore, in the Solow model framework, the saving rate has no effect on the long-term growth rate of per-capita output, which is zero. However, the saving rate does affect the equilibrium *level* of per-capita income. The higher the saving rate, the higher the steady-state level of per-capita income.

In contrast, the Harrod–Domar model allows for unlimited growth, which is determined by the saving rate and the capital–output ratio. This is because diminishing returns to scale are not considered in this model. Therefore, Figure 2.3 would have two straight lines coming out of the original (the two sides of Equation 2.18). The economy would oscillate back and forth between them in an endless upward spiral.

However, each of the parameters of the Solow model, η, s, and δ do affect the long-term level of income. We can see this by examining the steady state. If the starred variables are taken as the steady-state solution, that is, $k(t) = k(t + 1) = k^*$ and so on, we can rewrite Equation 2.18 as

$$(1 + \eta)k^* = (1 - \delta)k^* + sy^*.\qquad(2.19)$$

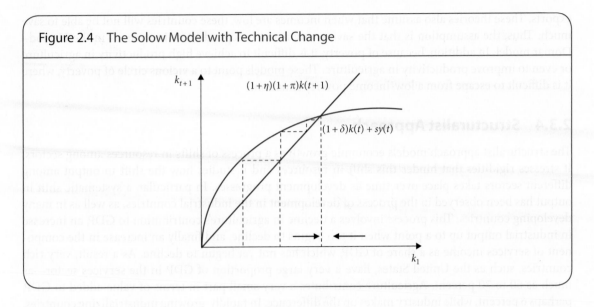

Figure 2.4   The Solow Model with Technical Change

Thus,

$$\frac{k^*}{y^*} = \frac{s}{(\eta + \delta)}. \tag{2.20}$$

The ratio of capital per capita to income per capita in the steady state will be a positive function of s and an inverse function of η and δ. In the steady state, the ratio k^*/y^* is a constant. This means that when saving increase, the ratio does not change—that is, both capital per capita and income per capita increase at the same rate. Conversely, both capital per capita and income per capita decrease at the same rate if the depreciation and population growth rates are higher.

SOLOW MODEL WITH TECHNOLOGICAL PROGRESS   If technical progress is introduced by increasing the efficiency of workers over time, then we can insert a new variable, π, into the fundamental Solow equation. Thus, π is the constant growth rate of worker efficiency and is entered on the left side of Equation 2.18. The right side remains unchanged. The phase diagram remains the same except for the intersection of the two curves (see Figure 2.4). A steady state remains but it relates to efficiency units of capital, which is the same as physical capital growing at the rate of technical progress, π. Of course, per-capita income has to grow at the same rate. Thus,

$$(1 + \eta)\,(1 + \pi)\,k(t + 1) = (1 - \delta)\,k(t) + sy(t). \tag{2.21}$$

2.3.3   Power Balance Theory

These theories, which were popular when North–South issues were being stressed, were based on the assumption that the poor "southern" economies were being exploited by the rich industrial "northern" countries. In these models, the poor countries export raw materials to the industrial countries in exchange for industrial goods. Because the terms of trade (that is, the price of raw materials *vis-à-vis* manufactured goods) tend to deteriorate over time, the power balance theories assert that the poor countries have to export more and more raw materials in order to keep from slipping backward. As a result, their development is retarded. The development of industrial capacity in East and Southeast Asia, and in some Latin American countries, has caused these theories to become discredited generally, although there are elements of truth in this paradigm in Africa, where raw materials are still the main exports. These theories also assume that when incomes are low, these countries will not be able to save much. Thus, the assumption is that the saving rate is not independent of income, as in the Harrod–Domar model. In addition, because of poverty, it is difficult to achieve high productivity in agriculture or even to improve productivity in agriculture. These models point to a vicious circle of poverty, where it is difficult to escape from a low-income poverty situation.

2.3.4   Structuralist Approach

The structuralist approach models economic growth as a process of shifts in resources among sectors. It stresses rigidities that hinder this shift in resources and it studies how the shift in output among different sectors takes place over time as development progresses. In particular, a systematic shift in output has been observed in the process of development in the industrial countries, as well as in many developing countries. This process involves a decline in agriculture's contribution to GDP, an increase in industrial output up to a point when it too begins to decline, and finally an increase in the component of services income as a share of GDP, which has not yet begun to decline. As a result, very rich countries, such as the United States, have a very large proportion of GDP in the services sector—as much as 60 to 70 percent. Agriculture contributes a very small part in terms of value added to GDP, perhaps 6 percent, while industry makes up the difference. In rapidly-growing industrializing countries, the share of industry would be larger and still growing, while agriculture would be large but falling. Although services would be rising, it would have a smaller share in GDP. A very poor country would have most of its resources in agriculture and very little in services or manufacturing (see Table 2.1).

Table 2.1   Share of Income by Sector (Percent)

	Agriculture				Industry				Services			
	1970	1980	2001	2007	1970	1980	2001	2007	1970	1980	2001	2007
China	42.2	25.6	11.3	9.7	44.6	51.7	64.6	59.0	13.2	22.7	24.0	31.4
Hong Kong[a]	n.a.	0.8	0.1[b]	0.1	n.a.	31.7	14.3[b]	8.2	n.a.	67.5	85.6[b]	91.7
Korea	29.8	14.2	5.1	3.6	23.8	37.8	44.0	44.4	46.4	48.1	50.9	52.0
Taiwan	17.3	8.4	2.4	1.3	32.3	42.8	32.1	31.4	50.4	48.8	65.5	67.2
Indonesia	35.0	24.4	16.2	13.8	28.0	41.3	36.0	43.0	37.0	34.3	47.8	43.1
Malaysia	n.a.	22.9	8.2	7.4	n.a.	35.8	43.1	40.5	n.a.	41.3	48.7	52.1
Philippines	28.2	23.5	20.1	18.4	33.7	40.5	34.0	32.5	38.1	36.0	46.0	49.1
Singapore	2.2	1.1	0.1	0.1	36.4	38.8	30.7	31.8	61.4	60.0	69.2	68.1
Thailand	30.2	20.2	8.0	8.7	25.7	30.1	44.0	47.5	44.1	49.7	48.0	43.8
Bangladesh	n.a.	56.7	49.4	21.4	n.a.	12.2	5.0	42.9	n.a.	31.1	45.6	49.2
India	44.5	38.1	24.3	17.8	23.9	25.9	26.8	26.5	31.6	36.0	49.0	55.7
Pakistan	40.1	30.6	24.7	21.8	19.6	25.6	25.1	26.1	40.3	43.8	50.3	52.1
Sri Lanka	30.7	26.6	20.4	11.9	27.1	27.2	27.4	28.5	42.2	46.2	52.1	59.6

[a]ADB, *Key Indicators* (2002).
[b]Refers to 2000.

SOURCES: Asian Development Bank, *Asian Development Outlook 2002, 2009*; Asian Development Bank, *Key Indicators of Developing Asian and Pacific Countries* (2002).

The source of rapid growth, from the structuralist point of view is manufacturing (see Chenery and Syrquin, 1975). Productivity increases faster in manufacturing and remains high for many years as technological developments are made or copied from other countries. The reason that industrial countries grow slowly, from this perspective, is that productivity in the services sector has historically been low and has not grown as fast as productivity in manufacturing.

Although this may be changing as a result of the technological revolution, leading to higher rates of growth, this "new productivity revolution" has not yet been firmly established. Lower growth in the services sector is still a drag on the economic performance of the industrial countries. Another contributing factor to slower growth in the industrial countries is that their rates of saving and investment are lower than in rapidly growing poorer countries. Therefore, the industrial countries have to depend to a greater extent on TFP and new innovations, as well as human capital development through education for their growth.

THE LEWIS–FEI–RANIS MODEL   A very well-known theory of development is the so-called Lewis–Fei–Ranis (LFR) model (see Lewis, 1954; and Fei and Ranis, 1961). There are elements of this model which are very important to understanding the pattern of development in many countries. It tries to explain how the process of industrialization takes place and how inefficiencies can arise. There are two sectors in the LFR model: a modern sector and a traditional sector. The former is primarily based in cities and the latter in the countryside. The rural sector has low capital accumulation and low labor skill. Its productivity and earnings capabilities are also very low. The modern sector has high productivity and pays higher wages. Labor thus moves from the countryside to the city to take advantage of wage differentials. The LFR model is discussed in further detail in Chapter 5.

2.3.5 New Growth Theory

The new growth theory has been developed in the last decade by a number of younger economists who became dissatisfied with the Solow–Swan (1956) model. The new growth theory attempts to endogenize technical change by using external economies and spillovers. These operate on the basis of beneficial effects which new technology and higher levels of education have on other sectors of the economy. These externalities help to generate increasing returns to scale and drives the growth process to higher levels of income, instead of slowing growth through diminishing returns. One of the important features of this model is the mechanism by which technology is transferred from one firm to another within an industry in a single country and then across international borders. One group of economists working on this model contends that the development of new technology in industrial countries is passed on to other countries quite slowly so that there is little tendency for convergence to take place. Others argue that the process is swifter (see Barro and Sala-i-Martin, 1995; and Grossman and Helpman, 1991). We will revisit this theory again in Chapter 6.

ASPECTS OF HUMAN CAPITAL IN THE NEW GROWTH THEORY   Let us start by assuming that there can be two types of saving in an economy. The first is the traditional form of saving for investment in physical capital. The second is saving for investment in human capital through education and training. If, for simplicity, we assume that the population growth rate is zero and ignore unskilled labor which does not benefit from education, then we can construct a simple Cobb–Douglas production function in per-capita magnitudes as

$$y = k^{\alpha} + h^{(1-\alpha)}, \tag{2.22}$$

where h is the amount of human capital created. A proportion of output is assumed to be saved in either of the two forms of saving. Denoting the proportion of output devoted to physical capital investments as s, and the proportion of output devoted to human capital investments as q, we can now summarize the process of physical and human capital formation with the following equations:

$$k(t+1) + k(t) = sy(t), \text{ and} \tag{2.23}$$

$$h(t+1) + h(t) = qy(t). \tag{2.24}$$

Equations 2.22, 2.23, and 2.24 together suggest that the growth of the economy is fuelled by the saving rate s, as well as the propensity to invest in human capital, measured by q. We then divide Equations 2.23 and 2.24 by $k(t)$ and $h(t)$, respectively, to obtain the rates at which physical and human capital grows. By assuming that, in the long run, the ratio of human capital to physical capital is the constant r, and using Equation 2.22, we obtain the following results:

$$\frac{k(t+1) - k(t)}{k(t)} = s \cdot r^{1-\alpha} \text{ and} \tag{2.25}$$

$$\frac{h(t+1) - h(t)}{h(t)} = q \cdot r^{-\alpha}. \tag{2.26}$$

These give us the growth rate of physical and human capital, respectively. Since these two growth rates are the same in the long run (so that the ratio r is constant), we can then equate both right-hand side terms and obtain the simple relationship of

$$r = \frac{q}{s}. \tag{2.27}$$

Intuitively, this implies that the larger the ratio of saving in the form of human capital to physical capital, the larger the value of this ratio in the long run.

From this, it is seen that all the variables must grow at the same rate in the long run. The long-run growth rate G can be derived from either growth rate equation and is given as

$$G = s^\alpha q^{1-\alpha}. \tag{2.28}$$

This equation looks suspiciously like the Cobb–Douglas function. In fact, it is! Equation 2.28 shows that it is unlikely that growth would be the same for all countries since s and q can differ between economies. It will depend upon the relative shares of saving for capital and human capital formation in each country. It may be that there are diminishing returns to physical capital *alone*. However, when both kinds of capital are considered, the model has strong implications for the overall constancy of returns. This is clearly suggested in Equation 2.28 that there may be broad constant returns to physical and human capital combined. Notice also that the saving rate and the human capital formation rate, s and q, have growth effects like the Harrod–Domar model. However, unlike the Harrod–Domar model where s is exogenous, these two parameters are determined inside the model. Since the decisions to save depend upon the behavior of agents in the model itself, this is an endogenous growth model.

This model further implies that even if countries enjoy the same rates of economic growth over a significant period of time, it does not necessarily follow that their per-capita incomes will converge. This is because initial disparities in both physical and human capital endowments make a significant difference and will, by and large, be maintained in the long term.

There are additional insights that such a model can provide. Where growth rates are plotted against per-capita income in a base period, the resulting curve picks up the net effect from two factors. The first effect is that high per-capita income alone does tend to slow down growth in the future. The second is that higher endowments of human capital tend to speed up the rate of growth. This is what the Solow model misses.

If the two factors offset each other, convergence is unlikely. Studies show that this proposition is more consistent with historical data for a group of both developing and industrial countries than the Solow model. There may be some convergence between the higher growth Asian economies and the industrial economies, but it is unlikely for the poorest countries to converge.

Even though there is some colinearity between the two opposing factors (rich countries also have a high per-capita income), there are some interesting cases which support inferences from the human capital model. The cases of Japan, Korea, and Taiwan tend to support the model. They had high stocks of human capital (suggesting high historical investment rates) and low levels of per-capita income when they began the process of industrialization. Because of this, they grew much faster than the average country at the same level of per-capita income during the postwar period.

2.4   THE ASIAN GROWTH MIRACLE

The pace of economic growth and structural change in many Asian countries in the past thirty to forty years ranks as one of the most outstanding features of recent world economic history. It has been termed the "Asian growth miracle." Why have the Asian economies flourished whilst other developing countries and regions have not? Incomes in developing Asia have grown much faster for a sustained period of time—up to four decades—than they have anywhere else in the world. These economies were able to move from a very low level of economic activity in the late 1950s and early 1960s, to fairly high levels of per-capita income, much faster than most of the industrial countries outside Japan were able to do during their rapid growth phases. This can be seen in Table 2.2 and from evidence of the growth of the United States and the United Kingdom in their high-growth phase in the nineteenth and early twentieth centuries. During that time, growth rarely exceeded 3 percent per year (see Maddison, 1995). What were some of the characteristics of this spectacular growth performance in Asia and what were the policies that contributed to it and supported it?

Many aspects of the growth theories described above do apply to the Asian experience, though each is not fully sufficient to adequately explain the "miracle." In the following section, we look at the various aspects that may have supported such rapid growth.

In what follows, we adopt the approach suggested by Quibria (2002), grouping the explanations for the Asian "miracle" into primary and secondary factors. The primary factors were present in all the "miracle" economies at the time of their economic takeoff. The World Bank (1993) study identified the countries falling into this classification to be Japan, the NIEs (Singapore, Hong Kong, Taiwan, and Korea), Indonesia, Malaysia, Thailand, and China. The primary factors in these countries form the common denominator of the Asian growth experience and they are the fundamental determinants of sustained rapid growth during the period. They are mutually reinforcing and therefore constitute a bundle of characteristics or factors that cannot be easily separated.

In addition, there were secondary factors that were sometimes present and sometimes not. They contributed to the "miracle" of rapid growth but they varied from country to country. They added richness and variety to the growth experience.

In analyzing the growth experience of the "miracle" economies, it is important to distinguish the policy environment that existed during the early stage of the economic takeoff to sustained high growth and the economic performance that resulted from the mix of policies. To do this, it is useful to describe the dynamics of the growth process that resulted in such outstanding growth performance.

Initially, the "miracle" economies had a policy matrix that stressed import substitution across a wide range of industries and products. Bhaghwati (1996) and Quibria (2002) note that the policy regime

Table 2.2   Decade Growth Rates for Selected Asian Economies, 1961–2007

	1961–1970	1971–1980	1981–1990	1991–2000	2001–2007
East Asia					
China	3.7	5.4	9.3	10.2	9.4
Hong Kong	9.9	9.2	6.6	4.4	4.6
Korea	8.3	7.8	8.7	6.3	4.6
Taiwan	11.3	9.0	8.0	6.4	3.4
Southeast Asia					
Indonesia	4.2	7.9	6.3	4.4	5.9
Malaysia	6.5	7.9	6.1	7.2	4.8
Philippines	4.9	6.0	1.8	2.9	4.5
Thailand	8.2	6.9	7.9	4.6	5.1
Singapore	10.0	9.1	7.4	7.8	4.3
South Asia					
Bangladesh	4.1	1.6	3.9	4.8	5.6
India	3.9	3.1	5.9	5.3	7.0
Pakistan	7.3	4.6	4.3	5.2	5.5
Sri Lanka	4.6	4.6	4.4	5.2	4.3

SOURCE: John Malcolm Dowling, *Future Perspectives on the Economic Development of Asia* (Singapore: World Scientific Publishing, 2008).

and development strategy of the "miracle" economies and India were similar until the beginning of the 1960s. However, in that decade, the "miracle" economies, particularly those in East Asia, began to develop outward-looking policies that stressed exports and the acquisition of foreign technology. This led to a virtuous circle of economic development where the pressure to compete internationally resulted in both an increase in economic efficiency and an investment environment that encouraged the upgrading of labor skills and the acquisition of new technology. Consequently, both saving and investment rates rose, education and skill formation were improved, and there was a rapid shift away from agriculture toward industry. Growth was no longer constrained by how fast the agricultural sector could progress and adopt new technology but was now able to look at a world market for manufactured goods. Much higher growth rates became possible in this environment, particularly when there was a flexible labor market that could adapt quickly to the changing pattern of production, where the labor force was educated, and where macroeconomic policies were generally prudent and consistent. This meant that inflation rates were generally low and fiscal deficits limited, which helped to encourage the rate of growth in domestic investment as well as the inflow of foreign direct investment (FDI).

Each of these four primary areas—openness, macroeconomic stability, labor-market flexibility, and education policy[4]—is discussed and documented in the next four sections. Secondary areas, including industrial- and agricultural-sector policies and initial conditions, are examined next.

---

[4] Quibria (2002) puts education as a secondary category.

These sections on policy are followed by a discussion of the macroeconomic performance of the "miracle" economies during their takeoffs and sustained high growth performance. The next section deals with the policy failures that kept South Asia from achieving higher rates of growth for most of the postwar era. The chapter concludes with a study of the convergence of growth rates.

2.4.1   First Primary Factor: Importance of Outward-Looking Policies and the Emphasis on Exports and Foreign Direct Investment

As with other developing countries, the economies of East and Southeast Asia started the industrialization process by developing import-substituting industries. They included industries that were natural complements to the agricultural base that already existed, such as food processing, textiles and apparel, and footwear. There was also a push toward medium and heavy industries in several countries, including Korea and India. During the 1960s, development economists and policymakers stressed the importance of developing a wide range of domestic industries that could supplant imports. This line of reasoning was termed "bootstrap" development. It was also popularly believed that the developing countries would need large inflows of development assistance to supplement domestic saving in order to accomplish this transformation of the production structure. India took on board these suggestions and began to develop a wide range of domestic industries with the help of the Soviet Union.

Other countries in Asia were more reluctant to follow this model completely. Instead, they turned to Japan as an example of how to industrialize. Japan in the 1960s was building a strong industrial economy based on exports. It had achieved industrial maturity in the 1930s and it returned to this model of development after World War II, with the difference being that it targeted much of its production at foreign markets. Korea, Taiwan, China and later, the major economies of Southeast Asia, followed this model. Soon after developing some industrial capacity in import-substituting industries, they turned their attention to external markets. In Korea, the model was followed most closely as the industrial conglomerates, called *chaebol*, were modeled on the Japanese industrial giant *kareitsu*, such as Mitsubishi and later, Sony and Honda. In Taiwan, the model was adjusted to stress the development of small and medium industries and the network of overseas Chinese in the rest of Southeast Asia, particularly Hong Kong and Singapore, but also in Europe and North America. The emphasis was initially on apparel, which shifted quickly to electronics.

In the Southeast Asian countries of Malaysia, the Philippines, and Thailand, the initial emphasis was on agriculture-based exports such as rubber, sugar, coconut and palm-oil products, and textile fabrics, such as silk. In Malaysia, large rural estates were mobilized to increase production, together with research to increase productivity. Slowly, the emphasis on agriculture-based industry gave way to the development of labor-intensive industries, including apparel and footwear and later, electronics assembly. The emphasis on exports was facilitated by government policies, which varied from country to country.

One of the common threads of these policies was that there was initial protection of these industries through a combination of import restrictions and tariffs so that resources would be allocated to them by the private sector in anticipation of good profit potential. However, these taxes were lower in East and Southeast Asia than they were in South Asia and other developing regions. More importantly, they were reduced over time to minimize the distortions in the allocation of resources that were created (the size of these distortions is discussed in Box 2.1). In South Asia, tariffs were also reduced but it took a longer period of time to do so, resulting in a much slower transition to export promotion from import-substitution, leading to waste and misallocation of resources.

Tax rates and trade distortions are shown in Table 2.3 where two measures of trade taxes are reported. The first, taxes as a percentage of exports and imports, may understate the degree of protection, particularly if taxes are high since there will be less trade in these products. On the other hand, the average tariff rates may overstate the degree of protection for the same reason since most trade occurs in products that

BOX 2.1

Tariffs, Import Licensing, and Import Prohibition

Protection from foreign competition in the form of tariffs, import licensing, or the prohibition of imports can create very high social and economic costs. When tariff rates double, they can increase the inefficiency of resource allocation fourfold. A tariff on imported inputs can also create distortions that are much greater than the tariff alone in the final product price. Moreover, the real protection afforded to an industry can be very different from the nominal rates of protection that would be expected. (This will be further discussed in Chapter 6). In addition, the profit rates of low value-added industries are very sensitive to tariffs on inputs and outputs. As a result, a slight shift in government policy could either result in windfall profits or disaster.

SOURCE: Seiji Naya, *The Asian Development Experience: Overcoming Crises and Adjusting to Change* (Manila: Asian Development Bank, 2002), p. 12.

Table 2.3   Taxes on Trade, 1980–2006

	Taxes as Percent of Exports and Imports			Mean Tariff Rates			
	1980	1990	1999	1980	1990	1999	2006
East Asia							
China	5.7	3.7	1.0	49.5	40.3	17.5	8.9
Hong Kong	0.5	0.4	0.3	0	0	0	0
Japan	0.9	0.9	1.5	9.5	6.9	6.6	n.a.
Korea	4.1	3.4	1.8	20.4	13.3	9.4	9.1
Taiwan	3.6	2.1	1.3	n.a.	9.7	9.7	n.a.
Southeast Asia							
Indonesia	2.9	2.4	0.7	29.0	23.3	11.9	6.0
Malaysia	7.7	3.2	1.6	10.6	13.0	9.1	6.2
Philippines	6.8	6.6	3.6	38.0	24.3	10.2	5.4
Singapore	0.4	0.1	0.1	0.3	0.4	0.4	0
Thailand	6.9	5.4	1.5	32.3	40.8	27.6	10.8
South Asia							
Bangladesh	13.4	12.1	9.5	99.0	102.0	22.1	15.5
India	15.5	21.1	10.8	74.3	79.2	32.9	16.8
Pakistan	15.3	15.2	7.6	77.6	58.8	n.a.	14.8
Sri Lanka	11.7	8.8	3.5	41.3	26.9	20.0	11.0

SOURCES: Seiji Naya, *The Asian Development Experience: Overcoming Crises and Adjusting to Change* (Manila: Asian Development Bank, 2002), pp. 162–163; World Bank, *World Development Indicators 2008*.

are taxed at low rates. Nevertheless, both sets of figures show that there has been a deceleration in the level of taxation, particularly since 1990. Even in South Asia where rates were high in 1980 and 1990, the rates fell in the decade of the 1990s and 2000s. The challenge in South Asia is not only to reduce the rates of taxation, but also to find other revenue sources to replace the tax on trade and also to reduce the level of nontariff barriers, which are not only difficult to measure but also restrict trade. Here we are speaking of bureaucratic procedures and slow processing that increase costs and reduce efficiency.

The transformation to labor-intensive industrialization with an emphasis on exports was supported by the inflow of foreign direct investment, initially in small amounts from Japan and the United States, and later in greater volume, particularly from Japan as it accelerated the movement of its labor-intensive industries offshore when the yen appreciated in value in the second half of the 1980s and early 1990s.

The combination of a shift toward export promotion policies combined with reductions in tariff rates and complemented by the inflow of foreign direct investment and supportive macroeconomic policies (see next section) produced an export boom that lasted more than twenty years, unprecedented in economic history. The ratio of exports to GDP increased by leaps and bounds. The proportion of exports derived from manufacturing also increased dramatically and employment shifted from agriculture to industry, as did value added (see Table 2.4). By 2000, more than 50 percent of GDP was generated by the export sector in all the East and Southeast Asian countries except Korea, Indonesia,

Table 2.4 Export of Manufactured Goods as a Percent of Total Merchandise Exports by Country, 1980–2006

	1980	**1990**	**2000**	**2006**
East Asia				
China	49	72	88	92
Hong Kong	96	95	95	91
Japan	96	96	94	91
Korea	90	94	91	89
Southeast Asia				
Indonesia	2	36	57	45
Malaysia	19	54	80	74
Philippines	21	38	50	87
Singapore	47	72	86	80
Thailand	25	63	76	76
South Asia				
Bangladesh	68	78	91	92[a]
India	59	71	79	70[b]
Pakistan	48	79	85	81
Sri Lanka	19	54	75	70[b]

Latest data is only available from [a]2004 and [b]2005, respectively.

SOURCES: Seiji Naya, *The Asian Development Experience: Overcoming Crises and Adjusting to Change* (Manila: Asian Development Bank, 2002), pp. 168–169; World Bank, *World Development Indicators Online*.

Table 2.5   Exports of Goods and Services as a Percent of GDP, 1970–2007

	1970	1980	1990	2000	2007
East Asia					
China	1.8	7.6	17.5	26.0	40.7
Hong Kong	94.6	89.9	134.3	150.0	207.3
Japan	10.8	13.7	10.7	10.0	17.6
Korea	13.7	34.0	29.1	44.8	45.6
Taiwan	26.1[a]	52.5	46.8	54.4	73.8
Southeast Asia					
Indonesia	13.5	30.5	25.3	38.5	29.4
Malaysia	41.4	57.5	74.5	125.5	110.2
Philippines	21.6	23.6	27.5	56.3	42.6
Singapore	105.6	215.4	202.0	180.0	230.9
Thailand	15.0	24.1	34.1	67.1	73.2
Vietnam	n.a.	n.a.	36.0	54.4	76.8
South Asia					
Bangladesh	6.1	7.2	6.1	14.0	22.0
India	3.5	6.6	7.6	14.0	21.2
Pakistan	7.8	12.6	14.8	16.2	n.a.
Sri Lanka	24.6	31.4	30.5	39.1	29.2

[a]*Taiwan Statistical Data Book.*

SOURCES: Seiji Naya, *The Asian Development Experience: Overcoming Crises and Adjusting to Change* (Manila: Asian Development Bank, 2002), pp. 164–165; *Taiwan Statistical Data Book* (2002); Asian Development Bank, *Key Indicators of Developing Asian and Pacific Countries* (2008).

and the Philippines (see Table 2.5). Hong Kong and Singapore have had the highest GDP percentage share of exports in the region historically and currently; it went up to 207 and 231 percent respectively, in 2007. Indonesia, which was slow to start industrializing because of its earlier dependence on oil, and China, which was also late in starting and is a very large economy with a huge domestic market, were exporting less than 50 percent of GDP.

In South Asia, on the other hand, the rate of export expansion was modest until the 1990s when trade liberalization policies were adopted in several countries. Figures in Table 2.5 show that by 2000, exports of India, Pakistan, and Sri Lanka were generally only one-third (around 15 percent of GDP) of most countries in East and Southeast Asia, except for Sri Lanka which exhibited slightly higher export figures of 40 percent.

In this region, Sri Lanka is an interesting case where agricultural exports, particularly tea, were extremely important in the early years. However, despite more open export policies than its neighbors (mean tariff rates are not significantly higher than those in Thailand or China), Sri Lanka has been unable to develop a strong industrial base because of domestic constraints and a poor climate for foreign investment as a result of civil unrest.

As suggested above, in the minds of many economists, this surge in exports and the income and technological transfers that accompanied it was the main reason that the Asian "miracle" was able to unfold with such vigor and dynamism.

THE ROLE OF TECHNOLOGY   Technology also played a crucial role as the "miracle" economies moved to higher levels of income and development. Growth in income is a function of the growth in inputs and the TFP residual, and this residual is largely a function of improvements in technology. The developing economies in Asia have been able to access new technology in three major ways:

1.   by buying it from foreign companies under license;
2.   by copying it without license; and
3.   by entering into a joint venture and importing the technology through foreign direct investment.

In recent years much of the transfer in technology has been through foreign direct investment.

FOREIGN TECHNOLOGY   Early on, the newly industrialized economies attracted and used foreign technology, but mostly through license. Japan and Korea, in particular, did not encourage foreign direct investment in their economies. Instead, they sent missions overseas to learn about the most up-to-date technology and then copied it. Much was spent on research and development for the adoption of overseas technology in local industries and efficiency improved as a result. Automobiles are a good example. Later, the countries of Southeast Asia bought technology from other countries through the process of foreign direct investment. The amount of investment that flowed into the Asian economies increased rapidly following the Plaza Accord when the industrial countries agreed to enter foreign exchange markets to boost the value of the yen. This caused many industries in Japan to lose competitiveness. As a result, these firms, mostly in labor-intensive manufacturing and electronics, moved offshore to lower-cost locations in Southeast Asia and China. The amount of foreign direct investment increased rapidly as a result (see Table 2.6).

2.4.2   Second Principal Factor: Macroeconomic Policies and the Role of Government

Unlike those countries that followed import-substituting industrial policies, the East and Southeast Asian economies succeeded because their general policy thrust was to clear the way for markets, competition, and contests for resources to play the lead role in the allocation process. Governments supported this market-led development through the pursuit of prudent fiscal and monetary policies, including a low inflation environment, an emphasis on human resource development, the provision of physical and social infrastructure, and the maintenance of a legal framework, essential for a market system to function smoothly. The levels of government financial deficits were generally low and government borrowing was held at prudent levels. In South Asia, budget deficits tended to be higher. Nevertheless, inflation was generally not a problem that had to be addressed on an ongoing basis as it was in Latin America (see Table 2.7).

The governments of the day in the Asian economies were thus also important players in the pursuit of higher rates of growth and development. The success of these economies was not particularly sensitive to the amount of government intervention in the microeconomic aspects of the economy. Government intervention in the industrial and financial sectors was heavy in Japan, Korea, and Singapore, moderate in Malaysia and Taiwan, and relatively weak in Hong Kong and Thailand. Yet all these economics grew rapidly. In the Philippines and Sri Lanka, the policy environments were similar to the more successful economies but growth was slowed by political uncertainty and domestic

Table 2.6   Foreign Direct Investment Inflows by Economy (Annual Average in US$ Millions), 1980–2007

	1980–1985	1986–1990	1991–1995	1996–2000	2001–2007
Bangladesh	–0.1	2	6	160	543
China	718	2,853	22,535	46,846	63,200
Hong Kong	542	1,766	1,671	24,626	31,384
India	62	160	841	2,653	10,202
Indonesia	227	573	2,344	644	2,696
Korea, Republic of	98	676	1,016	5,839	5,062
Malaysia	1,058	1,240	4,530	4,803	4,182
Philippines	35	493	1,016	1,268	1,517
Singapore	1,330	3,443	4,834	8,591	16,732
Sri Lanka	42	37	119	230	302
Taiwan	185	987	1,200	2,438	3,588
Thailand	264	1,175	1,837	3,483	6,590
Vietnam	5	6	776	1,773	2,383
Developing Countries	12,634	26,091	70,232	198,870	296,884
Developed Countries	37,179	123,582	144,303	607,466	658,263
Asia	5,023	14,121	45,288	106,636	185,662
World	49,831	149,702	221,210	827,775	990,201

SOURCE: UNCTAD, *World Investment Report*, various issues.

unrest. In Indonesia, growth was slowed by the early reliance on oil and later by the demise of a single political regime that had been in place for more than thirty years. The effectivity in achieving broad economic stability, export promotion, and tariff reduction and a neutral position toward agriculture combined with outward-looking policies that attracted foreign direct investment and technology transfer were more important than specific industrial, financial and trade policies in stimulating growth.

It is true that some policies, such as financial repression and directed government lending programs, were not particularly beneficial and caused resources to be allocated inefficiently. However, the flow of resources available for investment was quite substantial, but because of the high domestic saving rates and the inflow of foreign capital, these shortcomings were not recognized until the growth bubble of the early and mid-1990s burst in 1997. This episode will be discussed in the next chapter.

What did seem to be important were incentives for the technocrats that ran the government bureaucracy. The experiences of Singapore and Taiwan are notable. In both countries, civil-service wage levels are comparable to those of the private sector so that the most qualified people can be recruited. Promotions are based on merit, not patronage. Finally, there is a strong anti-corruption culture. Conversely in several other countries, salaries for civil servants remain low. Such a system attracts those looking for rent-seeking opportunities and the environment creates a fertile seedbed for corruption and influence

Table 2.7   Average Annual Inflation Rates by Decade as a Percent Change in GDP Deflator, 1961–2007

	1961–1970	1971–1980	1981–1990	1991–2000	2001–2007
East Asia					
Hong Kong	2.5	9.8	8.1	3.7	–1.8
Korea	18.0	21.2	7.6	4.0	1.7
Taiwan[a]	1.5[b]	9.4[c]	3.1	1.9	n.a.
Southeast Asia					
Indonesia	219.8	21.3	8.9	16.3	10.6
Malaysia	–0.6	7.1	2.2	3.8	4.0
Philippines	5.7	13.5	14.8	8.8	5.0
Singapore	1.3	6.3	2.8	1.3	0.9
Thailand	1.5	9.0	4.5	3.9	2.9
South Asia					
India	6.0	9.1	8.4	8.0	4.3
Pakistan	3.1	12.2	7.1	9.7	6.7
Sri Lanka	2.1	12.4	12.6	8.9	10.7

[a]*Taiwan Statistical Data Book.*
[b]Figure computed for the years 1965 and 1970.
[c]Figure computed for the years 1973 to1980.

SOURCES: World Bank, *World Development Indicators 2002*; World Bank, *World Development Indicators Online*; Taiwan Statistical Data Book (2002).

peddling. Even where salaries are high, as in Japan, incentives to perform efficiently are eroded by a system where promotions are made strictly on a seniority basis and rewards are made accordingly. Other aspects of governance are discussed in more detail in Chapter 13.

2.4.3   Third Principal Factor: Education, Labor-Force Growth, and Labor Productivity

Labor productivity in Asia increased rapidly as did total productivity. To a great extent, this was due to the increase in the amount of capital per worker as a result of rapid investment growth and technological transfer. Another significant factor that has influenced increased productivity in the region is the high level of investment given to educating the workforce. Asia has a very literate workforce that makes them highly adaptable to technological changes. In addition, high population growth, particularly in the labor force, was an important source of economic development. Bloom and Williamson (1999) estimate that up to 25 percent of the increase in Asia's growth from the 1960s onwards can be attributed to high rates of expansion in the labor force. The education and training of this rapidly growing workforce was, in turn, crucial to growth in productivity.

Table 2.8 Change in Human Development Index Relative to GDP Growth, 1990–2006

	HDI versus GDP Rankings		
	1990	**2000**	**2006**
East Asia			
China	+44	0	−10
Hong Kong	−3	9	12
Korea	5	−1	−9
Southeast Asia			
Indonesia	13	−1	−12
Malaysia	5	7	5
Philippines	19	−20	19
Singapore	14	4	22
South Asia			
Bangladesh	17	5	−7
India	12	1	6
Pakistan	3	7	9
Sri Lanka	45	−19	−11

Positive (negative) numbers indicate that the HDI is higher (lower) than the GNP rank. If a country moves from a positive to a negative number, it means that the GNP rank has risen, or the HDI has fallen, or both.

SOURCE: United Nations Development Program, *Human Development Report*, various issues.

ROLE OF EDUCATION Historically, the role of capital and saving to facilitate capital equipment purchases has been stressed as the primary engine of economic growth. We see this in the models of Harrod and Domar (1939, 1946) and also in the Solow and Swan (1956) models, even though the latter models emphasize the role of total factor productivity. However, as discussed earlier, a number of economists have recently stressed the importance of education. For example, the Nobel prize winner Robert Lucas (1990) and other proponents of the "new growth theory," including Mankiw and Romer (1991), and Mankiw, Romer, and Weil (1992) suggest that education is even more important than physical capital in raising the rate of growth. Lucas argues that by continuously shifting to products requiring higher skills, the Asian economies were able to raise productivity at a very rapid rate. Countries that remained chained to a set technology, such as some countries in Africa, Latin America, and South Asia, were not able to take advantage of increases in productivity as the NIEs and the Southeast Asian countries did. These countries were very open and subject to the changing forces of comparative advantage. This forced them to continuously adjust their product mix as wages rose and their comparative advantage shifted. The secret was in the shifting mix of production, not in their having a better skill or education mix than other developing countries, although skill development was a necessary condition for this shift to be achieved.

For example, Table 2.8 shows that there has been a gradual increase in the human development index (HDI) of countries in the Asian region, and it had reached a high level by the late 1980s. Even as early as 1980, with the exception of China, the countries of East Asia had high literacy rates for both men and women (see Table 2.9). Literacy rates were somewhat lower in Southeast Asia, although they

Table 2.9   Literacy Rates, 1980–2007

	Men			Women		
	1980	**2000**	**2007**	**1980**	**2000**	**2007**
East Asia						
China	79	92	97	53	76	90
Hong Kong	94	97	n.a.	77	89	n.a.
Korea	98	99	n.a.	90	96	n.a.
Taiwan	86	99	n.a.	66	92	n.a.
Southeast Asia						
Indonesia	78	92	95	58	82	88
Malaysia	80	91	94	60	83	90
Philippines	91	96	93	89	95	94
Singapore	92	96	97	74	88	92
Thailand	92	97	96	84	94	93
South Asia						
Bangladesh	41	52	59	17	30	48
India	55	68	77	25	45	55
Pakistan	38	57	n.a.	15	28	n.a.
Sri Lanka	91	94	93	80	89	90

SOURCE: Asian Development Bank, *Key Indicators of Developing Asian and Pacific Countries*, various issues.

were over 90 percent in Singapore, the Philippines, and Thailand. In South Asia, literacy rates were much lower, with the exception of Sri Lanka. During the next twenty years, there were further improvements in education as enrolment rates in secondary and tertiary education increased. However, by the year 2000, some of the educational advantages over comparable countries at the same level of income had eroded (this is partially reflected in Table 2.8 by the declining HDI values relative to GDP in several Asian countries during the decade). There were two reasons for this. First, the amount of public resources needed to boost the enrolment rates in secondary and tertiary increased rapidly because the cost per student was higher compared with primary education. Secondly, as the incomes of the Asian economies rose, they had to face competition from a set of countries that also had high per-capita incomes and a more educated workforce.[5] The decline in the ranking of the Asian economies in the HDI between the 1990 and 2000 rankings also suggests that the rate of growth in income tended to increase more rapidly for the Asian countries compared with the overall HDI. This is particularly noticeable for China and Indonesia in East and Southeast Asia, and also for Sri Lanka in South Asia, where the decline was quite precipitous (see Table 2.8). In the latter case, the lack of resources devoted to education and other social sectors is understandable, given the civil disorder that occurred for much of the decade.

---

[5] See also Seiji Naya (2002) Table 5, for an illustration of the relative erosion of educational attainments in high-growth Asian economies to other comparable countries over time.

Nevertheless, despite these favorable results, comparisons with other developing countries do not show that the educational attainment in the Asian economies was significantly higher than that of other developing countries. Behrman and Schneider (1994) note that the "miracle" economies had higher primary and secondary school enrolments in 1965 than the international average after controls for per-capita income were imposed. More than two decades later, only Korea and Indonesia had exemplary enrolment rates relative to the international average. They conclude that the "miracle" economies as a group did not have an unusually high schooling attainment despite many years of rapid growth.

This leads to the conclusion that education has to be taken together with labor-market flexibility and the mix of skills developed to deal with a rapidly changing production schedule.

This aspect is illustrated by the case of the Philippines, which had a very high level of human capital development in the 1950s and 1960s. However, because it was unable to put together a matching set of development policies that could take advantage of this highly skilled workforce, it developed slowly and fitfully. Political instability was reflected in the macroeconomic policies that were not conducive to attracting a large inflow of foreign investment, and when they were able to maintain high growth rates for a time in the late 1960s and 1970s, the government introduced a series of controls and agencies that squandered revenues. Furthermore, the Philippines had difficulty overcoming a protectionist lobby that favored local big businesses.

2.4.4   Fourth Principal Factor: Labor-Market Flexibility[6]

The "miracle" economies had very flexible labor markets at the beginning of their growth spurt and this continued throughout the period of rapid growth almost unabated. According to the International Labor Organization (ILO), the "miracle" economies are among the most flexible in the developing world. While there can be disagreements about the desirability and extent of market interventions in the labor market to deal with safety, health, norms for compensation, and child labor, there is little doubt that excessive labor-market regulations have a negative impact on economic development and growth. Regulations raise the cost of labor, diminish employment, and reduce the flexibility of firms to hire and fire. The result is that while those who are employed benefit from the regulations, there are negative impacts on the rest of the labor force, including the poor. The "miracle" economies were able to achieve rapid growth in real wages without protective labor legislation. Korea, for example, which joined the Organization for Economic Cooperation and Development (OECD) in the late 1990s, did not have a minimum wage policy until 1988.

The bundle of these four policies resulted in a number of important macroeconomic developments, including rapid growth and reduction in poverty. These factors, particularly high saving and investment, and increasing productivity, are discussed in the next two sections.

2.4.5   Initial Secondary Factor: Difference in Initial Conditions

Several other factors have been discussed in the literature as possible explanations for the growth of the "miracle" economies and they also deserve mention. They include initial conditions and sector policies.

Initial conditions played an important role in providing a fertile seedbed for development to germinate. The successful East Asian economies differed substantially from other developing economies of Asia in the 1960s in two fundamental respects. First, the subsequently successful countries were by and

---

[6] This section draws heavily on Quibria (2002).

large better endowed than others in Asia in terms of the quality of their human resources. Secondly, income, wealth, and land were also more evenly distributed in these Asian economies in the early 1960s than they were in other Asian countries. In the aftermath of the Korean War and following the migration of large numbers of people fleeing the Chinese mainland, land reforms were undertaken in these two countries that brought about greater equality in the distribution of land and capital resources. At the same time, both of these economies had benefited from strong educational policies in earlier years that resulted in higher levels of human resource development, including nearly 100 percent literacy, a high completion rate in elementary school, and high enrolment rates in secondary school (see Tables 2.9 and 2.12). In China, there was also strong emphasis on education and equality of opportunities so that when the economy opened up to Western ideas in the 1980s, it had a strong and well-educated labor force. In Southeast Asia, the Philippines had been the beneficiary of assistance from the United States that strengthened the education system in the colonial period, and this emphasis on education continued after independence. In Thailand, the monarch controlled some land but there had historically been a policy of relatively even land distribution. As the urban elites made more money in the 1980s and 1990s they bought up land and the distribution of resources became more unequal. This was exacerbated by the lack of secure title and land tenure laws that required tenants of cleared land to work the land or else risk confiscation.

2.4.6 Another Secondary Factor: Importance of Sector Policies

AGRICULTURAL SECTOR POLICIES   In general, as industrialization proceeds, there is a tendency to pursue policies that favor the industrial sector at the expense of agriculture. This is only natural since in the initial stages of industrialization, taxes on agriculture make up the major source of revenue for the government. The risk in following such a policy of taxing agricultural exports and the agricultural sector in general, is that it is not a sustainable long-term strategy because it results in the eventual strangulation of that sector, a reduction in output growth, and stagnation of the rural economy. Because the growth in industrial sector employment is never enough to offset such a loss in income and employment, this type of policy will eventually result in the collapse of aggregate demand and industrial stagnation, even if there is a viable export market. In the case of the Asian economies, there was first a gradual and then more rapid increase in the rate of saving and private investment. This provided resources to fund industrial development and reduced the necessity for taxing the agricultural sector excessively. While an anti-export bias did exist for traditional exports from Malaysia, Thailand, and other East and Southeast Asian economies it was modest. In the case of Thailand, the tax on rice exports created incentives for diversification of the agricultural base to crops with greater profit potential. Furthermore, the Green Revolution was instrumental in raising rural incomes. It was also supported by large amounts of public investment, particularly to extend the amount of irrigated areas.

INDUSTRIAL POLICIES   The term "industrial policy" in the context of the development of the "miracle" economies is taken to mean government policies that were designed to promote particular subsectors, usually capital-intensive industries. These industrial policies included subsidized credit and other policies designed to promote these industries so that they could compete effectively in international markets. These policies became an integral part of the policy apparatus.

Only Korea and Taiwan adopted comprehensive industrial policies. In the other economies, industrial policy was not adopted in a systematic way nor was it particularly important in influencing the evolution of industrial growth and concentration. There was government intervention in most of the other economies but they were sporadic and not well coordinated over time. In Malaysia, there was an effort to support heavy industry in the 1980s and a high-tech push sponsored by the Minister of Industry, Dr. Habibi, in the early 1990s. However, these efforts did not increase international competitiveness and were interpreted by observers as political favors to supporters and, as a result, arbitrary without any well formulated economic objective. In Thailand, Christensen et al. (1997, p. 346) observed that Thai sector policies "were not guided by a strategy of picking winners and have often been marked by patronage and rent-seeking."

The policies in Korea and Taiwan were, on the other hand, systematically thought out. Subsidies were withdrawn if certain performance criteria were not met and there was a vigorous effort to keep the favored industries on track to become competitive in external markets.

Whether these industrial policies in Korea and Taiwan were successful or not has been the subject of considerable research. There is still no uniform agreement on the subject. Little (1996) concluded that it was most plausible that Korea grew despite its industrial policies, while Pack (2000) concluded that industrial policies played a minor role in stimulating growth and should be viewed cautiously, particularly in light of the adverse affects of such policies on the financial sector (see also Chapter 7) and other sectors that had been neglected.

2.5 Aspects of Economic Performance in the "Miracle" Economies

2.5.1 High Growth Rates of Saving and Investment

Rates of saving and investment increased dramatically in many countries in Asia, from paltry levels of 10 percent or less in Korea and Singapore, and somewhat higher levels elsewhere in 1960, to over 30 percent by the 1990s. This achievement is unprecedented in the annals of economic history. To give some idea of the magnitude of this accomplishment, consider the average saving rates for the OECD countries and other developing economies (see Table 2.10). Hong Kong and Malaysia had high saving rates in 1960. Other countries in Asia, for which data are available, recorded saving rates below 20 percent, and often, below 15 percent. By 1970, saving rates had risen but were still below 20 percent in all but six developing economies shown in Table 2.10. By 1990, all economies in East and Southeast Asia had saving rates of over 30 percent except Taiwan and the Philippines. In South Asia, the record was less spectacular but still impressive. Bangladesh, India, and Nepal all raised their saving rates over the period of four decades. By contrast, the saving rate in the United States was never more than 20 percent and was on a declining trend throughout the period, while Japan's saving rate was relatively stable, although it also began to fall in the 1990s.

Apart from the issue of efficiency, the rapidly growing rate of saving was instrumental in providing the resources for the high growth rates achieved in the Asian region in the past few decades. As investment rates were also high, the resource gap among the Asian countries was insignificant. In East Asia, China, Hong Kong, and Taiwan have had an excess of saving over investment since 1980 (see Table 2.11), with the exception of Korea whose saving-investment gap moved from a deficit to a surplus by 2000. In Southeast Asia, Singapore and Thailand moved to a surplus in 2000, while Indonesia and Malaysia had surpluses for all the available years displayed in Table 2.11. The Philippines had deficits in 1980, 1990, and 2000. In South Asia, India has moved between small surpluses and deficits while Bangladesh, Pakistan, and Sri Lanka had substantial deficits in 2007.

2.5.2 Increased Productivity

Beyond the increases in saving and investment, it is likely that improvements in the efficiency with which these resources were used also contributed significantly to the growth in the Asian nations. For comparison purposes, we will first examine estimates of total factor production (TFP) for the

Table 2.10   Gross Domestic Saving Rates as Percent of GDP, 1960–2007

	1960	1970	1980	1990	2000	2007
East Asia						
China	n.a.	29.0	34.1	38.7	38.9	53.8[b]
Hong Kong	18.0	28.2	33.5	35.8	32.3	35.2
Korea	1.9	15.1	23.8	37.2	32.6	30.0
Taiwan	17.8[a]	25.6[a]	32.6	28.1	25.2	28.7
Southeast Asia						
Indonesia	12.4	14.3	29.2	32.3	25.7	26.1
Malaysia	27.4	26.4	32.9	34.4	46.7	36.2
Philippines	16.2	21.9	26.6	18.7	16.5	29.5
Singapore	8.8	18.4	38.8	43.4	49.6	51.4
Thailand	14.1	21.2	22.3	34.0	32.3	32.0
South Asia						
Bangladesh	8.6	10.5	2.2	12.9	17.9	35.1
India	13.6	16.4	18.2	26.8	21.0	37.2
Nepal	n.a.	2.6	11.1	7.9	14.7	9.7
Pakistan	n.a.	8.9	7.8	13.5	14.0	23.9
Sri Lanka	n.a.	15.8	12.0	13.2	17.3	25.1
Industrialized economies						
Japan	33.3	40.3	31.3	33.0	28.0	27.0[c]
United Kingdom	17.8	21.2	19.8	17.6	16.0	14.4[b]
United States	19.3	18.3	19.6	16.4	17.0	12.5[c]

[a]Gross national saving as a percent of GNP, from *Taiwan Statistical Data Book*.
[b]Latest data available from 2006.
[c]Latest data available from 2005.

SOURCES: Seiji Naya, *The Asian Development Experience: Overcoming Crises and Adjusting to Change* (Manila: Asian Development Bank, 2002), pp. 174–175; World Bank, *World Development Indicators Online*; *Taiwan Statistical Data Book* (2002); Asian Development Bank, *Key Indicators of Developing Asian and Pacific Countries* (2008).

industrialized nations. We begin with a caveat that the estimates are sensitive to the accuracy of the variable inputs measured. If the contributions of labor and capital to the growth process are underestimated, then the value of TFP will be overestimated.

The initial estimates of TFP made by Solow and others for the industrial countries were very large, (that is, the inputs of labor, capital, and land, measured in a simple fashion, grew much more slowly than output). The TFP component accounted for as much as 60 percent of total output growth. Conventional factors of production accounted for the remaining 40 percent.

Initial work on TFP in the late 1980s led to tension between the World Bank's view and that of the wider academic community, as represented by Alwyn Young (1992, 1995), Lawrence Lau (1996),

Table 2.11   Saving–Investment Gap as Percent of GDP, 1960–2007

	1960	1970	1980	1990	2000	2007
East Asia						
China	n.a.	n.a.	5.0	13.2	2.4	4.4
Hong Kong	n.a.	8.4	0.7	9.4	6.1	10.9
Korea	–9.4	–10.2	–8.3	–0.1	4.2	1.4
Taiwan	–2.4[a]	0[a]	2.0	5.6	1.7	7.5
Southeast Asia						
Indonesia	n.a.	n.a.	8.3	3.9	1.4	3.3
Malaysia	15.5	8.2	1.8	1.4	21.2	20.3
Philippines	2.7	3.8	–0.6	–4.4	–1.6	5.7
Singapore	n.a.	–14.2	–1.9	10.9	20.0	28.8
Thailand	0.2	–2.6	–5.5	–6.3	10.2	7.1
South Asia						
Bangladesh	n.a.	n.a.	–9.1	–4.2	–5.1	–3.9
India	0.7	1.8	–1.1	3.6	–0.9	–1.1[a]
Pakistan	n.a.	–5.4	–9.8	–3.8	0	–8.3
Sri Lanka	n.a.	n.a.	–20.5	–7.1	–10.7	–10.3

[a]Data from *Taiwan Statistical Data Book.*
[b]Data for 2006 only.

SOURCES: Seiji Naya, *The Asian Development Experience: Overcoming Crises and Adjusting to Change* (Manila: Asian Development Bank, 2002), pp. 180–181; *Taiwan Statistical Data Book* (2002); Asian Development Bank, *Key Indicators of Developing Asian and Pacific Countries* (2008).

and others. The World Bank made a case for a high level of TFP in Asia. Young and Lau disagreed with this, saying that growth in Asia was primarily due to the rapid accumulation of physical capital and labor.

Recent research suggests that many of the differences in opinion can be reconciled by looking at assumptions about the shares of capital and labor in income. Lower assumptions of capital shares result in higher estimates of TFP. Moreover, estimates of TFP have been rising over time as the region opened its borders to foreign investors and the rate of technological transfer increased. This has been reinforced by the rapid growth of the region between 1985 and 1997. This period, the beginning of which coincided with the Plaza Accord, where the Group of Seven (G7) industrial countries agreed to support a yen appreciation, also corresponded to a period of rapid inflow of foreign direct investment and rates of technological transfer. Sarel (1997) shows that the average rate of productivity growth in the late 1980s and early 1990s was 3.2 percent for the NIEs. This is considerably higher than the rate of just over 2 percent for the period 1970–1985. Similar results were recorded by Bosworth and Collins (1996), who found a "U shaped" pattern of productivity growth for the three periods 1960–1973, 1973–1984, and 1984–1994. In the last period, TFP contributed a substantial fraction of total output growth in all the Asian economies. While not as high as the TFP figures obtained for the industrial countries, they are still quite high when compared with the estimates reported by Young (1992, 1995), and Kim and Lau (1994). They are in excess of 45 percent of the overall growth in output per worker in Taiwan, Singapore, and Thailand, and between 30 and 45 percent in Malaysia and Korea. This will be discussed in greater detail in Chapter 5, Section 5.8.

2.6   THE POLICY MATRIX AND ECONOMIC PERFORMANCE IN SOUTH ASIA

Growth in South Asia was considerably slower than in the "miracle" economies during the postwar period. There are a number of reasons for this and we can only speculate what might have happened if they had adopted open and outward-looking policies at an early stage in their development. In terms of the bundle of four primary policies that were responsible for the rapid growth of the miracle economies, there are obvious differences between these policies and those pursued in South Asia.

The South Asian economies were generally not open to trade and to the inflow of foreign direct investment. Sachs and Warner (1995) developed an openness index based on four aspects of trade policy, classifying an economy as open if it had import duties that were less than 40 percent, quotas covering less than 40 percent of imports, a black market exchange premium of less than 20 percent, and an absence of a state monopoly for major exports. They also defined an open economy as one without a socialist government. According to this categorization, none of the South Asian economies was open during the postwar period apart from Sri Lanka and Nepal in 1992. Conversely, all the "miracle" economies were open throughout the period between 1950 and the early 1990s, when Sachs and Warner ended their data series. Because the South Asian countries were not open to trade, there were also very limited inflows of foreign direct investment until very recently.

South Asia had generally inflexible labor markets even though there were high levels of unemployment. This was particularly true in the formal sector. For example, according to the *Global Competitiveness Report* of 1998, although India ranked high in terms of the quality of its labor force as reflected by the number of engineers, scientists, and others with technological backgrounds, it ranked near the bottom in terms of labor-market flexibility. Labor unions were strong and job security was high, particularly given the level of economic development. This situation was generally true in the other countries in South Asia too. As a result, they were not able to respond quickly to shifts in demand according to the change in skill mix required when demand shifted to higher-skilled occupations.

The educational attainment of the workforce in South Asia was, until recently, much lower than in the "miracle" economies (such as Hong Kong and Singapore). This is evident from comparisons of literacy and school enrolment rates in the two economies (see Table 2.12). In South Asia, there has been some improvement in recent years, particularly in the 1990s. Nevertheless, these countries generally lag behind the "miracle" economies and East and Southeast Asia in both educational attainment at the secondary and tertiary levels, and in labor-market skills and rates of literacy. See also Chapter 10, Section 10.3, for a greater understanding of education in Asia.

Macroeconomic policies in South Asia were generally stable—inflation rates were not high and variable and government deficits were not excessive. There were exceptions, including the fiscal crisis in India in the early 1990s. but the record was generally good and certainly better than in other developing regions such as Latin America, where high rates of inflation and macroeconomic instability have been endemic.

Industrial policies were adopted that gave subsidies to several industries but these policies were generally unsuccessful in promoting rapid growth, neither in exports nor in achieving economic

Table 2.12   Educational Attainment in Asia, 1970–2006

	Adult Illiteracy Rate (Percent of People Aged 15 and Above)		Gross Primary Enrolment			Gross Secondary Enrolment			Gross Tertiary Enrolment		
	1970	2000	1970	2000	2006	1970	2000	2006	1970	2000	2006
East Asia											
China	47	15	91	106[d]	111	24	63[d]	76	0	7[d]	22
Hong Kong	21	6	116	94[a]	95	36	72[a]	85	7	27[b]	33
Korea	13	2	103	101	105	42	94	96	7	78	91
Southeast Asia											
Indonesia	44	13	80	110	114	16	57	64	3	15	17
Malaysia	42	13	89	99	100[e]	34	70	69	n.a.	28	29
Philippines	16	5	108	113	110	46	77	83	17	31	28
Singapore	27	8	105	94[a]	n.a.	46	74[a]	n.a.	6	44[b]	n.a.
Thailand	20	5	81	95	108	17	82	78	3	35	46
South Asia											
Bangladesh	76	59	54	100	n.a.	n.a.	46	n.a.	2	7	6[e]
India	67	43	78	102[d]	115[e]	24	49[d]	54	5	10[d]	11
Nepal	84	58	26	118	126	9	51	43	n.a.	5	n.a.
Pakistan	79	57	36	74	84	12	24	30	2	4[b]	5
Sri Lanka	20	8	99	106[c]	108[e]	47	72[c]	n.a.	1	5[b]	n.a.

Figure for the years [a]1996, [b]1997, [c]1998, [d]1999, and [e]2005 each, respectively.

SOURCE: World Bank, *World Development Indicators Online*.

efficiency. This was because the subsidized industries did not have to meet the market test of competing in international markets. Furthermore, they were not sanctioned if they did not meet production and efficiency targets. As a result, a large but relatively inefficient industry sector developed. In addition, the mix of subsidies and directed credit in South Asia also weakened the competitiveness and allocative efficiency of the financial system.

2.7 CONVERGENCE OF INCOME

We conclude this section on the Asian growth experience with a discussion of convergence of income. Whether countries from the lower end of the development spectrum will ever catch up with the development levels of the more advanced and more industrialized economies at the high end of the spectrum is often a question of interest to both theoretical and applied economists. The answer to this question holds the key to determining which economic development and growth strategies are most appropriate at particular points in time. From the review of the Asian "miracle" in the previous section, it seems that the prospects for convergence within this group of countries are good. However, for other regions this may not be the case.

In order to understand the issue of convergence better, we shall discuss some basic concepts relating to the convergence of income.

2.7.1 Absolute Convergence

The hypothesis that poor countries tend to grow faster per capita than rich countries—without conditioning on any other characteristic of the economies—is referred to as absolute convergence. The Solow model says that all economies will converge to the same level of per-capita capital and per-capita income irrespective of where they started out. This would be true even with technical progress, since the technical progress coefficient π is assumed to be constant across all countries.

Is this realistic? Has there been this kind of convergence either within countries or across countries. Let us look at the evidence.

First, if this kind of convergence is to take place, then the poorer countries with lower levels of capital per capita will grow faster. They are closer to the origin of the phase diagram in Figure 2.4.

Using this inference from the Solow model, we can test whether such a relationship exists, that is, is there a relationship between per-capita income in an initial period and growth over an extended period from that initial date. Most studies have worked with logarithmic functions. This is done so that a linear relationship between levels and growth rates can be established and tested through regression analysis. A typical equation might look like Equation 2.29 for thirty years, beginning in 1960.

$$Log\,[Y(1990) - Y(1960)] = a + b\,Log\,Y(1960), \qquad (2.29)$$

where Y is per-capita income and the left side of the equation is the growth rate of income. The growth rate of income is regressed on the initial level of per-capita income. If the theory is correct, we would expect a negative sign on b, that is, when the right-side variable is low, the left-side variable is high. Countries with low income in 1960 would tend to grow faster from 1960 to 1990 than countries with a high income in 1960.

This hypothesis or proposition, however, finds little support when tested with data from various countries. In Figure 2.5, for instance, the average annual growth rate of per-capita GDP between 1975 and 2000 is plotted against the log of per-capita GDP at the start of the period, 1975, for the Asian developing countries. The scatter plot shows that the rate of growth does not seem to depend at all on the initial condition of the economy, measured by per-capita GDP in 1975. From this evidence, there is no reason to believe that these countries' incomes will converge at some point in the future. The absolute convergence hypothesis fails to be supported by the data. Casual observation seems to bear out this conclusion that absolute convergence does not hold.

However, the convergence hypothesis does seem to hold if a more homogenous set of countries is considered.[7] In the OECD after 1950, the poorer countries (those in the bottom half of the distribution in 1950) grew by over 1 percent faster than the rich countries in the top half. Those in the bottom quarter grew more than 2 percent faster than those in the top quarter. The dispersion of income fell

---

[7] According to information reported in UNCTAD (1997), Chapter II.

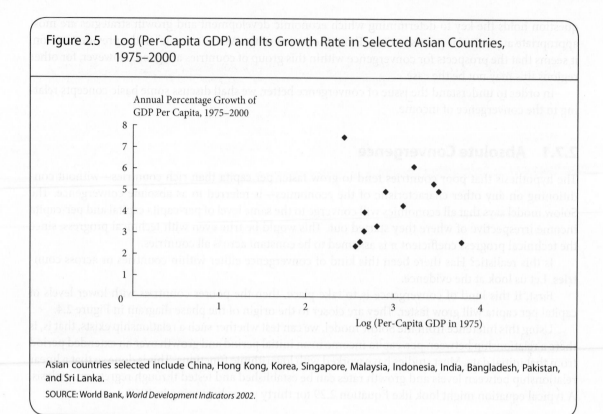

Figure 2.5 Log (Per-Capita GDP) and Its Growth Rate in Selected Asian Countries, 1975–2000

Asian countries selected include China, Hong Kong, Korea, Singapore, Malaysia, Indonesia, India, Bangladesh, Pakistan, and Sri Lanka.

SOURCE: World Bank, *World Development Indicators 2002*.

dramatically. Japan is the best example of rapid catch up, starting way behind the United States in terms of per-capita income and nearly catching up by the 1990s.

In some other cases, using different data sets, the rates of convergence seem very slow. In the United States, for example, the South is still poorer, both in terms of per-capita income and per-capita capital, than other regions, even though slavery ended nearly 150 years ago.

In the case of East and Southeast Asia, we can also see cases of rapid convergence toward the incomes of the industrial countries. Between 1960 and 1990, the NIEs all grew by more than 3 percent faster than the OECD average, while Malaysia and Thailand grew by between 1 and 3 percent faster than the OECD countries over a similar period (see Table 2.13). Hong Kong, Singapore, and Taiwan are already considered rich countries if income per capita is used as a measure of "richness." South Korea recently joined the OECD. Thus, East and Southeast Asia share many characteristics of the regional and dynamic convergence pattern of the OECD countries.

On the other hand, the other developing regions, such as Latin America, Africa, and the Middle East show no such tendency to convergence, as demonstrated by both Tables 2.13 and 2.14. None of the countries in Africa or Latin America—with the exception of Botswana, Lesotho, Morocco, and Tunisia—were able to exceed the growth rates of the OECD. Hence, per-capita income in Africa, for example, may be even lower than it was decades ago since it is diverging further from both the industrial countries and other developing countries and regions.

If the coefficient of variation in per-capita income is used for the three developing regions, income convergence has not happened either. This coefficient increased during the 1960–1990 period in all three regions, most rapidly in Asia as the divergence between South Asia and East and Southeast Asia

Table 2.13   Relative Growth Rates of Developing Countries *vis-à-vis* the OECD, 1960–1990

GDP Growth Differential with OECD	Developing Countries
> 3 percent	Korea, Singapore, Hong Kong, Taiwan
1–3 percent	Botswana, Malaysia, Thailand
0–1 percent	Indonesia, Barbados, Lesotho, Morocco, Tunisia, Seychelles
Average growth of real GDP in OECD	3.2 percent

SOURCE: UNCTAD, *Trade and Development Report* (New York: United Nations, 1997), p. 80.

Table 2.14   Income Convergence Among Developing Regions, Coefficient of Variation in Per-Capita Income, 1960–1990

	1960	1990
Africa	0.49	0.68
Asia	0.46	0.81
Latin America	0.51	0.53
All developing economies	0.62	0.87
Developed economies	0.51	0.34

SOURCE: UNCTAD, *Trade and Development Report* (New York: United Nations, 1997), p. 86.

increased (see Table 2.14). The trend for all developing countries is also toward divergence while for the OECD countries, it is toward convergence.

2.7.2   Conditional Convergence

A more general approach than absolute convergence is called conditional convergence. In conditional convergence, various parameters are allowed to change between different countries or groups of countries. If saving rates, depreciation rates, and population growth rates differ among countries, the levels of income may differ, although the Solow theory would still predict that there would be a convergence in growth rates of income. Nevertheless, the steady state levels of income would differ.

This can be verified by examining Equation 2.10 or 2.13, and Figure 2.3.

There have been many studies on conditional convergence but we will not go into them in detail here. Suffice it to say that they cannot completely explain the differences in growth rates among a wide set of countries. One difficulty is that heterogeneity in the data set would require the use of different regression models for different subsamples (see Ardic, 2002). On the plus side, variations in the saving and population growth rates can explain more than half of the variations in per-capita income across countries. However, the magnitude of the coefficients on these variables is too large to be consistent with the Solow model. This result implies that the effect of diminishing returns is very small. It takes many decades for the effect of diminishing returns to set in.

For all intents and purposes, the Harrod–Domar (1939, 1946) model seems to be a better predictor of the actual evolution of income growth. Yet we know that the Harrod–Domar model is much too simple. What is more likely is that several countervailing factors are working simultaneously to make it appear as if the saving rate and the capital–output ratio alone determine income. There may be a steady state but it is continually being shocked by changes in some of the variables. One thing that could be happening is that shifts in technology have the effect of boosting returns to scale, offsetting the tendency for diminishing returns to set in. Furthermore, if technical progress does not spread uniformly across countries, then the rich countries will continue to have an ever widening edge over the not so rich. A branch of the new growth theory explores these issues in more depth.

In this spirit, the book by Easterly (2001) carefully reviews and examines the empirical research of the past two decades on the topic of economic growth, starting with the Solow model. He looks at the new growth theories that stress the importance of technology and increasing returns to scale. He also reviews a series of studies that examine geographic and institutional factors, such as isolation from or proximity to markets, the role of economic policy, and the extent of corruption. He reviews the cross-country evidence to determine the factors which most influence the growth of income.

The story is quite complicated and there are often no clear answers as research results are often conflicting. Nevertheless, a picture emerges that indicates that the Solow model can be augmented not only by educational and technological variables but also by variables that reflect the openness and competitiveness of the economies, as well as the effectiveness of governance and the extent of corrupt practices. This research, to a significant extent, is consistent with and supportive of the material presented in the previous section with regard to the economic growth experience of the countries in the Asian region. Openness and support of competition, as well as sound and pragmatic macroeconomic policies, worked to support a private sector where saving and investment were high, and where the growth in the labor force was rapid. On the latter point, the importance of the structure of the labor force relative to the size of the nonworking population was also critical during the growth spurt of the 1960s, 1970s, 1980s, and early 1990s (see Chapter 8). Countries and regions within countries that were geographically more isolated (such as Nepal, and the northeast of Thailand) had a more difficult time in sustaining high rates of economic growth.

The topic of convergence of income will be discussed again in Chapter 11, and also in the policy sections of Chapter 5.

2.8   SUMMARY AND CONCLUSIONS

In this chapter, several theories have been advanced to explain economic growth. Components of these theories have been used to explain particular aspects of the rapid growth of the East Asian economies. We then look at the growth experience of the Asian region, drawing on selected aspects of the theories to determine what factors have been most influential in driving regional growth. It was observed that the rate of saving and investment are important factors in growth. A shift in resources away from agriculture and toward industry was another powerful factor stimulating growth. Furthermore, when those industrial resources were harnessed and directed toward external markets, there was an additional contribution to the growth momentum. Several variables that are not explicitly recognized in the general growth theories were also important in determining the growth experience of these Asian "miracle" economies, including the role of government and the attitude toward entering global markets. We have also generally observed that economies that follow prudent macroeconomic policies, adopt an open-trading environment, promote competition, foster economic efficiency, and invest in its people and in new technology have a good chance of growing rapidly, raising living standards, and significantly reducing the level of poverty. On the other hand, economies that follow more restrictive external policies are less likely to use prudent fiscal and monetary policies, and tend to uphold the interests of a privileged few. They are also reluctant to expose producers to competition, new ideas and methods of production, and are less likely to achieve satisfactory growth and prosperity.

In the next chapter, we turn to the various aspects of Asia's recent experience of an economic and financial crisis. In doing this, we will explore another aspect of the growth process that was almost completely ignored in the analysis of the Asian "miracle" that we have just undertaken, namely, the financial sector and its role in economic growth and resource allocation.

REVIEW QUESTIONS

1. The Harrod–Domar growth model is based on the fundamental Keynesian relationship between consumption and income. How does that relationship fit into the Harrod–Domar model?
2. If the marginal propensity to consume in the Keynesian model increases (b in the equation $C = a + bY$), what happens to the saving rate? What does this say about countries that save a large proportion of income relative to those that save less in terms of growth in the Harrod–Domar model?
3. Suppose the efficiency of the economy improves in the sense that more output is generated with the same capital stock. What will this do to the growth rate in the Harrod–Domar model?
4. What does the population growth adjustment to the Harrod–Domar model do to the growth path of income?
5. How would the growth of Europe following the bubonic plague episodes in the thirteenth to seventeenth centuries have been affected if Europe had been following the growth path described by the Harrod–Domar model. Do you think this actually happened? If not, why not?
6. What are the main differences between the Solow and the Harrod–Domar models? Is the Solow model more realistic? How does it introduce more realism into its assumptions?
7. What is the steady state in the Solow model? Describe in words why the economy tends toward the steady state?
8. What are the variables that the Solow and the Harrod–Domar models share in common?
9. Explain how per-capita income in the steady state can increase in the Solow model.
10. Explain intuitively what the new growth theories add in terms of realism to the Solow model.
11. Are structuralist approaches to economic growth consistent with the Harrod–Domar theories of growth? How do they differ in emphasis?
12. List the important variables that economists have identified that contributed to the rapid growth of the Asian economies in the decades of the 1960s to the mid-1990s. How do these variables relate to the variables discussed in the three growth models (Harrod–Domar, Solow, and new growth)?
13. Other developing regions of the world have not been as successful in raising their standards of living in this period. Can you identify several factors that might have been responsible for these poorer results?
14. What evidence is there that there has been a convergence in incomes among the countries and regions of the world, according to Robert Barro? How do his results compare with those we would expect from the Solow model?
15. What is the difference between conditional convergence and absolute convergence? What do you think would be the result if we tested conditional convergence between South Asia, and Southeast Asia, and East Asia?
16. What measures can the poorer countries take to accelerate their growth to bring their standards of living more in line with the rest of the world?

17. What does the term Asian "miracle" mean? Discuss the key aspects of this "miracle" as it evolved during the decades prior to the Asian financial crisis. Be specific, using country examples. Which of these factors do you believe to be the key ingredients to rapid growth?

18. How do the factors that you have identified reflect on the proposition that the Asian "miracle" was a result of "perspiration," and not "inspiration?"

Notes on References and Suggestions for Further Reading

This chapter contains material on the theory of economic growth, as well as the growth experience of the Asian developing economies from the 1960s until the financial crisis of 1997. These topics have been combined to show the relationship between growth theories and the direct growth experience of the region. The key readings on the development of economic theory are listed first, followed by key references for the region. The growth references are listed historically, from the first important growth theories developed following the publication of Keynes' (1936) *The General Theory of Employment, Interest, and Money*, until the most recent contributions. The materials on the Asian development experience are listed by topic.

ECONOMIC GROWTH   References to the original models of Roy F. Harrod (1939) and Evsey D. Domar (1946) are mentioned at the beginning.

The two articles by Robert Solow (1956, 1957) define the neoclassical growth model and served as the foundation of this model for several decades until the 1990s.

Trevor Swan (1956) also developed a similar model about the same time, and this neoclassical model is sometimes referred to as the Solow–Swan model.

Following the neoclassical tradition and expanding upon its assumptions, the next important contributions were made by Gregory Mankiw, David Romer, and David Weil (1992). There was also an important contribution by Robert Lucas, Jr. (1990) at about the same time. Each of the articles introduces the possibility of increasing returns to scale as a result of external factors arising from the contribution of education and innovation to the production process.

Following these two articles, a number of papers were published on the topic of economic growth. They introduced variables in econometric models to test the significance of additional variables in the determination of the growth process. Often, these models were based on cross-sectional evidence collected over time for a number of countries. The issue of convergence was often a main focus of these articles in addition to the exploration of new variables designed to explain differences in growth, such as political institutions, geographical factors, and good governance. Two references are useful in summarizing and extending this work. The book by Robert Barro and Xavier Sala-i-Martin (1995) offers a good summary of the developments of the theory of economic growth, as well as present a wide-ranging and thorough analysis of the empirical evidence. The paper by Jeffrey Sachs and Andrew Warner (1995) also provides a useful review of the issues of growth and global integration, focusing more on political reform and geographical variables.

Outside the neoclassical tradition, other economists were investigating the process of economic growth from the point of view of sectoral interaction. Here, the main contributions are by Hollis Chenery, Sherman Robinson, and Moshe Syrquin (1986) (CRS), and W. Arthur Lewis (1954), and Gustav Ranis and John Fei (1961, 1864) (LRF). Both approaches focus on the shifting importance of different sectors in the process of economic development. CRS focuses on the importance of industrialization and the shifts in production and economic productivity as industrialization takes place. LRF focuses more on the shifts that take place between the rural and urban sectors.

Extensions of these structural approaches focusing on the transfer of resources and production technology across international borders through the process of international trade are also part of the economic growth literature. However, a detailed discussion of these approaches will be taken up in Chapter 5.

ECONOMIC DEVELOPMENT OF ASIA There are a number of articles and books focusing on the economic development of the Asian region from the 1960s until the mid-1990s. We have noted below some of the most interesting and comprehensive references.

On the growth experience itself, the World Bank's (1993) study received much attention when it was first published. It covers the development of the region, with particular reference to East and Southeast Asia, in a comprehensive yet somewhat controversial way. It espouses the view that the development of the region was based on free-market principles, yet its approach and even some of its examples show that other factors were also at work, including a large amount of state intervention and direction, particularly in Korea and Taiwan. It is, nevertheless, essential reading for an appraisal of the important factors that determined the growth experience of these countries.

On the importance, relevance, and contribution of industrial policies, two authors have made particularly important contributions: Howard Pack (2000) and Alice Amsden (1989). One article from each are included to give a flavor of their point of view, which is that industrial policy was widely used as a tool in the development of East Asia.

The importance of technological change in Asia became a contentious issue with the publication of Paul Krugman's (1994) article in the journal *Foreign Affairs* in the early 1990s. Following its publication, a number of articles were published investigating the role of technology and total factor productivity in the Asian experience. The key early articles by Alwyn Young (1992) show that the contribution of TFP was small in Asia in the 1970s and early 1980s. Subsequent articles by Michael Sarel (1997), Barry Bosworth and Susan Collins (1996), and Arnold Harberger (1996) explore more recent data sets and different assumptions about the relative shares of labor and capital. This book's co-author (Dowling) and Peter Summers (1998) explore the possibility of a structural shift in the production function after the Plaza Pccord in 1985 brought about an appreciation of the Japanese yen and more FDI into Asia. The result of all of these researches suggests that TFP has increased in the last twenty years to the point where it is now making a substantial contribution to the growth of the countries of East and Southeast Asia.

Other useful summaries and investigations of the Asian growth miracle written from a current perspective are contained in the monographs by Seiji Naya (2002) and M. G. Quibria (2002).

The Asian Crisis and Recent Developments

3.1 INTRODUCTION

The steady growth of the Asian economies was abruptly interrupted by the financial crisis that beset the region in 1997. In July that year, the Thai baht was attacked, primarily by currency hedge funds. These funds became active in four Southeast Asian currency markets in June–September 1997, setting off a chain of competing devaluations that blew up into a regional financial crisis. A feature of these competing devaluations was the sequencing of the devaluations; the Thai baht first began to decline in June 1997, and was followed by the Malaysian ringgit, the Indonesian rupiah, and the Philippine peso in July.

The devaluations subsequently spread to the Australian dollar and the Korean won in October. The Hong Kong dollar was also attacked in October and while the currency parity with the U.S. dollar was maintained, the stock market fell by about 30 percent of its value in a week. The depreciation of equity indices denominated in U.S. currency, shown in Table 3.1, reflects the changes in exchange rates. From January 1, 2007, until mid-November that year, the depreciation in equity indices denominated in U.S. currency was more than 30 percent, in one case around 25 percent, and around 10–12 percent for the rest of the countries outside Japan. These currency devaluations were substantial, particularly when it is recognized that the bulk of the devaluations took place from July. The implications for the financial and stock markets, and on the components of aggregate demand and international trade, are discussed in subsequent sections.

Equity prices thus fell rather dramatically, as shown in Table 3.1. In large part, the declines in stock market values were triggered by volatility in the foreign exchange markets. However, in the cases of Thailand, Malaysia, and the Philippines, these stock market declines had begun months earlier. For example, between January and May 1997, Malaysian and Philippine stocks had fallen by more than 12 percent and 18 percent, respectively. Between June and November that year, the declines in stock prices, especially for those denominated in U.S. currency, were even steeper—between 40 and 50 percent in Indonesia, Malaysia, Korea, the Philippines, and Thailand, and between 20 and 30 percent in Hong Kong and Singapore. The pegging of exchange rates to the U.S. dollar and the defense of currencies by

Table 3.1   Change of Asset Prices, 1997

Equity Index	January to Mid-November		January to May		June to Mid-November	
	Local Currency	U.S. Currency	Local Currency	U.S. Currency	Local Currency	U.S. Currency
Asian Economies						
Trigger economies:						
Indonesia	−21.8	−48.7	−0.8	−3.6	−26.3	−50.3
Malaysia	−46.6	−59.7	−11.9	−11.4	−40.5	−55.4
Philippines	−43.4	−58.0	−14.7	−14.9	−36.2	−52.4
Thailand	−44.8	−65.5	−18.1	−19.6	−19.9	−51.3
Other Asian economies:						
Hong Kong	−25.4	−25.3	−8.1	−8.3	−27.7	−27.6
Korea	−27.7	−36.7	5.6	0.1	−36.5	−41.3
Singapore	−23.1	−31.6	−9.0	−12.0	−19.6	−27.0
Taiwan	1.9	−9.4	17.2	16.5	−10.0	−18.9
Industrialized Countries						
Australia	−1.8	−12.8	1.8	0.2	−7.5	−14.4
Japan	−11.1	−14.2	−0.3	−8.8	−12.5	−15.2
New Zealand	2.6	−9.4	−5.3	−7.1	1.6	−8.2

SOURCE: Morgan Stanley Capital International (MSCI) equity indices, obtained from Datastream.

central banks resulted in sharp increases in interest rates that helped to turn off portfolio investors. In Hong Kong, where the pegging of the Hong Kong dollar initiated a jump in yields, there was a commensurate sharp decline in equity prices.

Restrictions imposed on the equities markets exaggerated the price declines. In Thailand and Korea, restrictions on foreign investment induced portfolio formation whereby individual stock selection was limited. When markets declined, there was a tendency to reduce the entire country's portfolio weighting to zero, rather than follow a selective approach. Malaysia exacerbated its equity market's decline by imposing price limits on the run.

The lack of hedging facilities in many Asian countries meant that investors had no alternative but to reduce their country portfolio weighting to zero. While the withdrawal of foreigners from these markets may have played a key role, it is important to remember that these stock market declines were primarily due to a herd instinct. In most of these countries, the stock market ownership is largely local (over 75 percent in Malaysia, South Korea, Taiwan, and Thailand). Only in Indonesia and the Philippines, where local ownership is less than 50 percent, are the stock markets dominated by foreign holdings. The ramifications of these dramatic declines in equity prices will be further explored in Section 3.2.1, both in terms of their effects on consumption and investment components of aggregate demand, but also in terms of their effects on the balance sheets of business firms and the financial sector.

3.2 WHY DID IT HAPPEN?

There are several explanations for the financial crisis but none of them is completely satisfactory. A worrying aspect of the crisis is that no one anticipated its extent nor its prolonged nature. However, if we look at history, this has always been the case. The great stock market crash of 1929 was not anticipated by many, nor was the 1987 Wall Street collapse. There were signs of a disequilibrium buildup in all the Asian economies, particularly Thailand, which had been warned by the International Monetary Fund (IMF) to take control of its ballooning external debt. However, the fury of the currency speculation and the widespread collapse of financial markets took everyone by surprise.

In this section, three alternative and even complementary explanations for the crisis are reviewed. The first is the stock market, real estate, and bank credit bubble that had developed in the first half of the 1990s. These developments, combined with a reliance on short-term external borrowing and a belief that the U.S. dollar to local currency parity would be maintained, resulted in a highly leveraged and vulnerable financial sector that caved in once currencies came under attack and confidence waned. The second is a series of developments in the external sector that led to a rapid increase in the current-account deficit, a real exchange-rate overvaluation, and a consequent decline in export competitiveness and earnings. The third is the spillover or contagion effect whereby pressure on the currency and financial markets spread from country to country, exacerbating the crisis and weaknesses in the financial sectors of the various economies.

3.2.1 The Bubble Economy

All the countries in Southeast Asia (including the Philippines which started from a low base) grew very rapidly during 1994 and 1995. Export performance in 1995 was spectacular and economic growth was generally higher than expected. The huge inflow of foreign capital was channeled into both fixed investment and equity portfolios. The current-account deficits widened and stock markets boomed. Stock market exposure is relatively hard to document but it was high, particularly in Malaysia and Korea where, as in Japan, shares were widely held by business enterprises. This left them vulnerable to a shift in investor sentiment and in a tenuous position if stock prices fell.

Under the fixed exchange-rate regimes followed by all these countries, the inflow of foreign capital was generally translated into an expansion in money supply and lending growth. Bank credit to the private sector, particularly in relation to gross domestic product (GDP) growth, rose dramatically in most of these economies, with the exception of Korea (see Table 3.2).

Inflation also began to rise but because these economies were relatively open, price increases were much more apparent in nontraded goods. Real-estate prices rose dramatically alongside similar increases in equity prices. Wages also began to rise in the formal sector, accelerating further as these economies (Thailand and Malaysia in particular) reached full employment.

There was also a buildup of short-term debt denominated in foreign currency. While the extent of this debt was not exceedingly large as a proportion of GDP, it created potential liquidity problems because it was denominated in foreign currency and it was short term. For example, when the Bank of Thailand spent most of its reserves defending the baht, there was little left to pay off short-term debts that were not being rolled over.

The buildup in foreign debt, bank lending, and asset prices occurred against a backdrop of financial sector weakness. The financial sector played a complementary role in the bull market bubble that developed in Southeast Asia in 1995 and 1996. Factors in the financial sector which contributed to the severity of the Asian crisis include the following:

Table 3.2   Growth of Bank Credit to the Private Sector Relative to GDP Growth

	Average Annual Percent Change			Bank Credit to Private Sector (Percent of GDP)	
	1990–1994	1995	1996[a]	1980	1995
Asian Economies					
Trigger economies:					
Indonesia	10.4%	4.4%	5.7%	8.1%	49.1%
Malaysia	3.1	10.5	13.1	33.1	76.9
Philippines	10.7	27.4	31.5	37.9	39.3
Thailand	10.0	11.0	5.8	27.5	88.7
Other Asian economies:					
China[b]	3.8	–0.5	3.8	47.5	83.9
Hong Kong[c]	8.8	8.9	–6.1	71.7	321.4
Korea	2.6	2.2	–0.6	36.2	55.7
Singapore	0.8	7.8	5.7	62.9	84.9
Taiwan	9.2	1.1	–3.9	49.2	143.1
Industrialized Countries					
Germany	2.5	0.8	4.6	74.2	96.1
Japan	0.3	0.5	–1.9	81.0	115.1
United Kingdom	1.3	2.3	3.3	39.9	99.7
United States	–3.5	4.2	–0.6	62.1	63.3
Other G-10 Europe	2.0	–2.6	–0.8	61.0	76.2

[a]Preliminary.
[b]Credit other than to central government.
[c]Total credit. Licensed banks only.

SOURCE: Data from Bank for International Settlements (1997), p. 108.

INADEQUATE FUND MANAGEMENT SYSTEM   The financial sectors in these countries were unable to efficiently handle and disburse the massive inflows of foreign funds, which allowed them to invest as much as 40–50 percent of GDP when economic growth was in excess of 8 percent per annum. More than US$400 billion was invested from overseas sources during the first half of the 1990s. Stock market values also rose rapidly, and a property boom ensued. This was unsustainable and inconsistent with efficient resource allocation.

INEFFECTIVE STERILIZATION OF CAPITAL INFLOWS   The sterilization mechanism that could have been used to choke off some of the excess demand generated by the influx of capital was constrained by thin markets for government securities and a fixed exchange rate. In such a situation, the greater the level of sterilization undertaken, the greater the tendency for the spread between domestic and offshore interest rates to increase. This simply provided an even larger inducement for capital inflows.

RESTRICTIONS ON FOREIGN BANKS' ENTRY   Another factor that aggravated these problems was the restriction on the entry of foreign banks and financial institutions. Apart from Hong Kong and, to a lesser extent, Singapore, East Asian countries do not encourage the entry of foreign firms providing financial services, compared with other countries at similar levels of development. They are also more highly regulated. Consequently, the financial sectors were less "internationalized" in terms of competition from financial service providers based in other countries. In this respect, the financial sectors in these countries were in marked contrast to the traded goods sector and capital movements that are highly internationalized in all the East Asian countries. This segmentation lowered the diversification of financial institutions in these countries, and thereby increased the risk of bank failure. At the same time, internal liberalization allowed domestic banks to enter new markets where returns were higher but where risks were also higher. Offshore banking was one area where lending boomed in 1995 and 1996, particularly in Thailand. The returns on borrowing overseas at low interest rates and relending to local businesses at much higher rates was lucrative, but tended to ignore the exchange-rate risk. Furthermore, there might have been an implicit understanding that a bankrupt bank would be bailed out by the government. This created a moral hazard problem and contributed to an even higher level of risk taking. (See Box 3.1 for a further discussion on moral hazard.)

NONPERFORMING LOANS   As the economies overheated in 1995 and 1996, banks made many risky loans. Supervision and regulation of the financial systems in these countries were inadequate. Unsound projects were approved, uncollateralized loans were made, offshore dollar borrowing, which were unhedged, ballooned—taking advantage of low interest rates in the United States. Loans were made to friends, other corporate managers, and relatives. Evaluation of the credentials of borrowers became slack, and banks controlled or owned by the government often provided loans to ailing or targeted industries. There was a failure of fiduciary responsibility and a breakdown in responsibility to show a profit to stockholders. Lending criteria and capital backing were inadequate and prudential supervision did not contain the spread of risky loans. In Malaysia, the Philippines, Singapore, and Thailand, commercial banks could engage in underwriting stockbroking and fund management. In all the East Asian

 BOX 3.1

Moral Hazard

Moral hazard occurs when agents take more risk because they are insured against the negative consequences of such actions. For example, those with fire insurance may be less vigilant in taking fire prevention measures. Car owners may not take as much care driving or keeping their car secure if they have theft and collision insurance. Banks may lend to riskier borrowers at higher interest rates because they think they will be bailed out by the government if they got into trouble. Aspects of moral hazard were at work in the 1997 Asian financial crisis and the 2007/2008 global mortgage and economic crisis. Believing that the government would ensure against currency depreciation, financial institutions in Asia took unnecessary risks, by borrowing in U.S. dollars without

hedging and then lending in local currency. In the 2007 and 2008 global mortgage and economic crisis, subprime loans were packaged with other loans into mortgage-backed securities, which covered up the full extent of the risk. When similar risky bets by Long-Term Capital Management hedge fund in interest rate derivatives failed following Russia's financial crisis in 1998, the fund was bailed out with the help of the Federal Reserve Bank of New York. Bear Sterns, Merrill Lynch, and Lehman Brothers were among the major creditors of the hedge fund, and went on to become the major players in the 2007/2008 global mortgage and economic crisis. While there are other contributing factors underlying the subprime mortgage crisis and the ensuing global recession, including poor oversight on the part of several government agencies, moral hazard played a major role.

countries except Indonesia and Korea, banks are allowed to hold equity in non-financial and financial institutions, subject to some percentage limitations.

Despite the pervasive problems in the region, the weaknesses in the financial systems of most of these countries were, however, not particularly glaring even up to the end of 1996. The Bank for International Settlements' figures (Table 3.3) show that although high in comparison with the industrial countries, the share of nonperforming loans (NPLs) in the Asian countries was relatively lower in 1995 and 1996 when compared with the crisis years of the 1980s. While many risky loans were extended, it was the currency devaluations that exposed these weak balance sheets. The problems had more to do with the structure of dollar-denominated debts and the devaluation that, combined with poor project selection, created the large numbers of bankruptcies. This was because many customers of banks and other financial institutions used stocks as collateral to borrow offshore at cheap rates. These customers were unable to repay loans when both markets collapsed. Furthermore, the number of bad loans increased as export growth slowed and as the pyramid of credit to fund real estate and stock market speculation collapsed.

Fifty-eight financial institutions were closed in Thailand. Sixteen banks were closed in Indonesia and depositors withdrew about US$4 billion, according to newspaper reports. The health of the financial systems in the other Asian countries has also been questioned. In Malaysia and the Philippines, no bankruptcies were reported, but the strain of the currency devaluation and falling stock prices resulted in slower growth. In Korea, the financial crisis was reflected in the bankruptcy of a number of large conglomerates (*chaebols*), while in Japan, a large, top-twenty bank, a smaller bank, and two stockbrokers were declared bankrupt. The International Monetary Fund (IMF) extended bailout packages to Korea, Thailand, and Indonesia. The Asian countries also developed a scheme to pool assets to help countries in need through the IMF.

Table 3.3   Nonperforming Loans as Percent of Total Loans

	1980s	1994	1995	1996
Asian Economies				
Trigger economies:				
Indonesia	n.a.	12.0%	10.4%	8.8%
Malaysia	30.5	8.1	5.5	3.9
Thailand	15.0	7.5	7.7	n.a.
Other Asian economies:				
Hong Kong	n.a.	3.4	2.8	2.7
Korea	6.7	1.0	0.9	0.8
Taiwan	5.5	2.0	3.1	3.8
Industrialized Countries				
Japan	n.a.	3.3	3.3	3.4
United States	4.1	1.9	1.3	1.1

SOURCE: Data from Bank for International Settlements (1997), p. 107.

HIGH COSTS OF FINANCIAL SERVICES   Cross-country empirical evidence compiled by the World Bank suggests that the limited internationalization of the financial sector also led to higher costs of financial services (higher interest margins and lending rates) to borrowers and slower institutional development. Nevertheless, it was the combination of devaluation and stock market collapse that exposed the financial sector to severe balance sheet problems. This was because many firms had made unhedged borrowing from the cheaper offshore dollar market (see above). Furthermore, loans were often made with shares as collateral.

BALANCE SHEETS   The extent of balance-sheet troubles is difficult to measure without careful country-by-country analysis. As the crisis and post-crisis period evolved, the evidence suggests that balance sheets have been helped considerably by the recovery in demand and the resumption of economic growth in 1999, 2000, and 2001.

3.2.2   External Sector Difficulties

A snapshot of external sector developments in the years preceding the crisis can be seen in Table 3.4. External sector difficulties in the Asian countries were said to have been behind the outbreak of the financial crisis in 1997. They include the following:

RAPID GROWTH IN CURRENT-ACCOUNT DEFICITS   As the boom of the early 1990s progressed, current-account deficits also grew as offshore borrowing increased. While exports were growing rapidly,

Table 3.4   Exchange-Rate Depreciation, Current-Account Balance, and Merchandise Export Growth in Selected Asian Countries (Percent)

	Exchange-Rate[a] Overvaluation	Current-Account Balance (of GDP)		Merchandise Exports (of Growth)	
	June 1997	**1995**	**1996**	**1995**	**1996**
Trigger economies:					
Indonesia	4.2%	–3.3%	–3.3%	13.4%	9.7%
Malaysia	9.3	–10.0	–4.9	20.3	6.5
Philippines	11.9	–4.4	–4.7	28.7	18.7
Thailand	6.7	–7.9	–7.9	23.1	0.5
Other Asian economies:					
Hong Kong	22.0	–3.9	–1.3	14.8	4.0
Korea	–7.6	–2.0	–4.9	30.3	3.7
Singapore	13.5	16.8	15.7	13.7	5.3
Taiwan	–5.5	2.1	4.0	20.0	3.8

[a]The exchange rate is calculated as the real effective exchange rate in June 1997, relative to the average real effective exchange rate prevailing during the June 1987 to May 1997 period in percentage terms.

SOURCE: Morris Goldstein, *The Asian Financial Crisis: Causes, Cures, and Systematic Implications* (Washington, D.C.: Institute for International Economics, 1998), p. 15.

these current-account deficits were viewed as a positive sign that growth-enhancing and capacity-expanding investments were taking place. During this phase of rapid growth, current-account deficits of up to 5 percent of GDP were thought to be easily sustainable, according to conventional wisdom. Even the more conservative IMF and the World Bank did not have any qualms about deficits of 3 percent of GDP. By 1995 and 1996, only the current account of Thailand was in the dangerous zone of nearly 8 percent of GDP (see Table 3.4). However, Malaysia, the Philippines, and Korea were all flirting with a 5 percent current-account deficit by 1996, and this loomed large as merchandise export growth started to soften. On the other hand, Singapore and Taiwan had very large current surpluses and seemed immune from any financial turbulence that might arise in other economies in the region.

OVERVALUED EXCHANGE RATES   Prior to the crisis, the exchange rates for most Asian currencies were loosely tied to the U.S. dollar. Although ostensibly tied to a basket of currencies, the Thai baht was pegged to an exchange rate of 25 baht per U.S. dollar and varied within a very narrow range. The Philippine peso moved more but not beyond a band of 25–27 pesos per U.S. dollar. The Indonesian rupiah, on the other hand, devalued very slowly and deliberately against the U.S. dollar over time. This devaluation was so steady and predictable that it was, in effect, a moving peg against the U.S. dollar. The Malaysian ringgit fluctuated somewhat more than the other three currencies, appreciating against the U.S. dollar during part of the period, as did the Singapore dollar, but more strongly. The Korean won and New Taiwan dollar were tied to the U.S. dollar but they also appreciated somewhat during 1995 and 1996, while the Hong Kong dollar was tightly pegged to the U.S. dollar.

Since most currencies were tied loosely to the U.S. dollar, they followed it down in the first half of the 1990s and then rose with it in the following three years. The first column in Table 3.4 shows the real effective exchange-rate overvaluation in June 1997 (when Thailand devalued) to the average exchange rate for the decade between June 1987 and May 1997. The overvaluations varied from 4.2 percent for Indonesia to 22 percent for Hong Kong, which remained on a fixed parity with the U.S. dollar. In Korea and Taiwan, there was some undervaluation.

These calculations are meant to be suggestive. Other estimation methods may yield different results, depending on the base period and the estimation methodology. Nevertheless, the evidence does suggest that there was some overvaluation of the currencies in the region at the time of the crisis, compared with historical averages. Furthermore, early warning estimates using historical data for Asia and other regions suggest that the real effective exchange rate is one of the best indicators of an impending currency devaluation. (See Dowling and Zhuang, 2002; Athukorala and Warr, 2002; and Goldstein, 1998.)

THE COLLAPSE IN EXPORTS   In 1996, export-growth performance fell substantially, particularly from 1995 when exports had been performing spectacularly (see the last two columns in Table 3.4). It has been widely speculated that China played an important role in this. China had devalued its currency by about 25 percent a year or so earlier and had become quite competitive in a number of markets where the Southeast Asian economies had a strong presence. However, this devaluation was the result of a consolidation of the dual exchange-rate system, and most trade had been taking place at a lower rate for several years. Thus, the Chinese currency devaluation was probably not such an important factor in explaining the export slowdown in 1996. This inference is supported by the work of Fernald, Edison, and Loungani (1999).

Rising wages have been suggested as another possible cause of the export collapse and it is true that wage increases were eroding some of the competitiveness in labor-intensive manufacturing industries in Thailand and Malaysia. Another and possibly stronger factor was the decline of activity in the computer-chip market. The bottom had fallen out of the computer-chip and computer-peripheral markets in the industrial countries. These markets were very important for Malaysia and to a lesser extent, for Thailand and the Philippines. Finally, the exchange-rate appreciation also contributed to a loss in export competitiveness. In any event, as is evident from Table 3.4, the decline in export growth from 1995 appeared to have been quite dramatic.

How bad was the export collapse? If we were looking at another group of developing countries' exports without reference to their 1995 performance, the export performance of 1996 was probably not that bad. Exports from Indonesia and the Philippines grew at nearly 10 percent and more than 18 percent respectively. In the newly industrialized economies (NIEs) and Malaysia, export growth was down to single digits (4 to 8 percent). Only in Thailand was export growth stagnant. Considering that world-trade growth in a good year averages 4 to 6 percent, these export figures are not surprisingly low if compared with other developing countries. Furthermore, the 1996 collapse in exports was still very mild in comparison with previous low export-growth performances. In 1985, for example, export growth was negative in all the major countries of the Association of Southeast Asian Nations (ASEAN), and less than 1 percent in Taiwan.[1] On the other hand, the perception that export growth had collapsed was an important factor in coloring perceptions about the strength of the Asian economies and their abilities to repay their external debts.

In summary, a combination of external factors and a domestic economic boom that had gotten out of control set the stage for the attack on the Thai baht in June 1997. Taken alone, any one of these factors would not have been too worrisome. Taken together, they set the stage for a nascent crisis. The size and extent of the crisis as it evolved took nearly everyone by surprise. This was because of the strength of the contagion effects, which will be discussed in the following section.

3.2.3 Contagion, Globalization, and Financial Integration

To get some idea of what happened during the Asian financial crisis, consider the reversal of capital inflows and bank credit between 1996 and 1997. There was an enormous reversal of net private capital flows to the five crisis economies of Indonesia, Malaysia, Korea, the Philippines, and Thailand between 1996 and 1997, from a US$97 billion inflow in 1996 to a US$12 billion outflow in 1997. This US$109 billion reversal was about 10 percent of the pre-shock GDP of these five economies. On the other hand, the reversal in bank credit was from an increase of US$56 billion in 1995 to a decrease of US$27 billion in 1996. Together, these two shifts in liquidity accounted for nearly 20 percent of GDP (Shirazi, 1998). It was no wonder that these economies suffered a severe economic slowdown.

Several other factors have been suggested, including a slowdown in growth in Europe and a currency appreciation when the U.S. dollar strengthened. Neither of these was particularly critical, however. The developing Asian countries' trade with Europe was limited and this downward trend was more than offset by a strong growth in trade with the United States.

Nevertheless, there were certainly other critical world trends that influenced events as the crisis unfolded. They were mainly related to the interaction between two relatively new phenomena: globalization and international capital mobility. Globalization linked the East Asian markets for goods and assets much more closely to the markets of other countries. This linkage resulted from the liberalization of trade in goods and capital in the East Asian countries, which increased the size of the tradable goods sector as measured by the trade ratio, and the ratio of exports plus imports of goods to GDP. These changes also increased the exposure of the economies of the region to shocks originating in international trade (refer to Chapter 11 for greater details on globalization and its implications on the Asian region).

---

[1] Figures are calculated from various country tables in Asian Development Bank's *Key Indicators of Developing Asian and Pacific Countries* (1999).

The liberalization of trade in capital similarly increased the stock of foreign-owned capital, and of foreign debt, such as corporate bonds denominated in foreign currencies. This increased the exposure of corporations in these economies to shocks in capital markets. However, the financial markets of these Asian countries were less well integrated into the world economy because of restrictions on foreign entry to the financial sector and the lack of development of the futures and derivatives markets. This contributed to the crises and reduced the capacity of the financial sector in these countries to deal with these shocks.

ROLE OF INSTITUTIONAL INVESTORS   The other variable in this international equation is the large investment funds that played a key role in the crisis. A more closely integrated world economy enable institutional investors to have much more knowledge about other parts of the world economy and to act quickly based on this knowledge. They have control over vast amounts of financial resources which, when moved *en masse*, can introduce volatility into the developing economies where markets are thin and underdeveloped. Fund managers tend to act together to pull out of individual markets, either because of a herd instinct leading to a contagion effect, or because these markets do not offer the flexibility of a more structured withdrawal. Combined, globalization and free capital movements have introduced a new equation to the internationalization of the world economy that involves volatility across markets never experienced in the past.

HOW STRONG WAS THIS CONTAGION EFFECT?   One view of the contagion effect is that Thailand served as a "wake-up call" to investors in the Asian region. No one saw it coming since there were no warnings from Moody's, Standard & Poor's, or the IMF, and there were no changes in spreads reflecting increased risks in the run up to the crisis. However, once it happened, there are two possible competing explanations for the spread to other countries. The first is the herd instinct or contagion effect as investors bailed out of all countries without discrimination. This put pressure on the exchange rate and subsequently on the external balance and interest rates. This then led to bankruptcies in the vulnerable banking and corporate sectors, and a severe economic slowdown.

The other explanation offers a more rational reason for the pressure that was put on the other economies, arguing that other countries were forced to undertake competitive devaluation to keep pace with Thailand as markets recognized the need to remain competitive. Does this mean that the other countries would not have suffered at all if the Thai baht had not devalued? This counterfactual is hard to evaluate. However, evidence from research on the early warning systems suggest that most of the other countries were ripe for some currency adjustment since their currencies were overvalued, they had large current-account deficits, experienced low export growth, and made many suspect loans in the bubble economy that had evolved. The possible exceptions were Singapore and Taiwan, both of whom did not have any external financial distress and had had much more modest domestic booms. They were caught in the middle, so to speak, and consequently suffered pressure on their currencies and subsequently, a slowdown in economic activity. Singapore, in particular, with its strong trading linkages to the rest of the region, was adversely affected by the slowdown in the rest of the region. Taiwan was also affected, particularly by the collapse of Hong Kong, but was also buoyed up somewhat by the continued strength in China and in foreign markets. As a result, its GDP growth was not affected as much as the rest of the region.

3.3   POST-CRISIS EXPERIENCE

3.3.1   The World Economy

Commentators from international institutions were initially quick to discount the impact of the current crisis on the world economy. However, weaknesses in Korea and Japan surfaced toward the end of

1997 and these tended to have wider implications. However, when all was said and done, the Organization for Economic Cooperation and Development (OECD) countries, with the exception of Japan and Korea, were not appreciably affected by the crisis. World output growth in 1998 did fall, but this was primarily the result of a slowdown in the growth of the U.S. economy. Asia as a whole, including India and China, which both grew rapidly, registered growth of between 1 and 2 percent (Asian Development Bank, 2002b). This was much lower than the 1997 figure, but it did not drag world growth down too much. More importantly, it did not precipitate into a worldwide recession. In 2001, the U.S. economy suffered a short and shallow recession from which it recovered only slowly in 2002. This reduced the demand for U.S. imports and probably also slowed the growth of the Asian economies as they continued to recover from the 1997 financial crisis. However, as the United States and other industrial countries recovered, there was a salutary impact on growth in the Asian economies.

3.3.2   Economic Growth

The overall economic growth in the Asian economies did not immediately reflect events in the financial sector and in foreign exchange markets. However, 1998 was a bad year for most countries in the Asian region. Growth was negative in all the five crisis countries, as well as Hong Kong. Singapore grew by only 0.1 percent, compared with 8.5 percent growth in 1997. There was, however, a strong recovery in 1999, which strengthened in 2000, particularly in East Asia and Malaysia (see Table 3.5). The recovery of Korea was particularly significant. Nevertheless, the slowdown in growth in the United States and other industrial countries had a negative impact on economic growth in East and Southeast Asia in 2002. The effect of this slowdown in the industrial countries was particularly severe in those countries that had strong trade linkages with the United States, and where international trade in electronics was high. This group of countries included Malaysia, Singapore, and Taiwan, among others.

During the following five years, the global economy recovered and so did the Asian economies. Between 2002 and 2007, economic growth in the Asian region accelerated, led by India and China. Living standards rose and poverty fell (see Table 3.5). Domestic demand and foreign trade were both important factors in the resumption of growth.

Table 3.5   Growth Rates of GDP in Asia, 1997–2007

	1997	1998	1999	2000	2001	2002	2003	2004	2005	2006	2007
China	8.8%	7.8%	7.1%	8.0%	8.3%	9.1%	10.0%	10.1%	10.4%	11.7%	11.9%
Hong Kong	5.1	−5.0	3.4	10.2	0.6	1.8	3.2	8.6	7.1	7.0	6.4
Indonesia	4.7	−13.1	0.8	4.8	3.8	4.3	5.0	4.9	5.7	5.5	6.3
Korea	5.0	−6.7	10.9	9.3	3.8	7.0	3.1	4.6	4.2	5.1	5.0
Malaysia	7.3	−7.4	6.1	8.3	0.3	4.4	5.4	7.1	5.3	5.8	6.3
Philippines	5.2	−0.6	3.4	4.4	1.8	4.4	4.5	6.0	5.0	5.4	7.2
Singapore	8.5	−0.1	6.4	9.4	−2.3	4.0	2.9	8.7	7.3	8.2	7.7
Taiwan	6.7	4.6	5.4	5.9	−2.2	4.2	3.4	6.1	4.2	4.9	5.7
Thailand	−1.4	−10.5	4.4	4.6	2.2	5.3	7.0	6.2	4.5	5.1	4.8

SOURCES: Asian Development Bank, *Asian Development Outlook 2003; Asian Development Outlook 2008.*

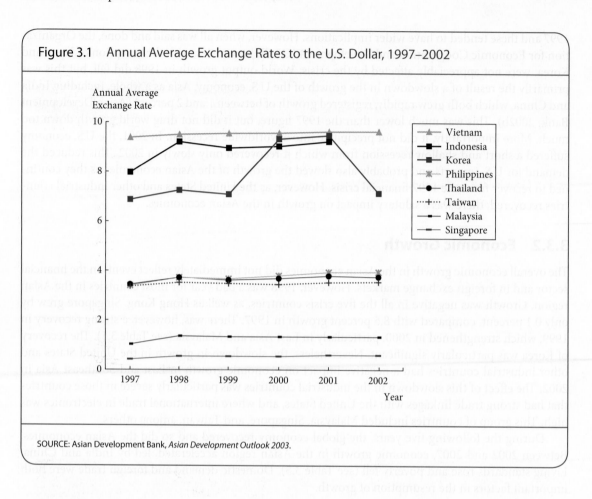

Figure 3.1   Annual Average Exchange Rates to the U.S. Dollar, 1997–2002

SOURCE: Asian Development Bank, *Asian Development Outlook 2003*.

EXCHANGE RATES   Exchange rates have strengthened from their lows in the first part of 1998 (see Figure 3.1). This extends to all currencies, even the Indonesian rupiah, the most adversely affected currency. Depreciation *vis-à-vis* pre-crisis levels was between 15 and 30 percent as of July 2002. In subsequent years, between 2003 and 2007, there was an appreciation of some Asian currencies, particularly in 2006 and 2007—about 6 percent for China relative to 2005, 9 percent for Korea, 12 percent for Thailand, and 16 percent for the Philippines. Other currencies depreciated slightly.

EQUITY PRICES   Stock prices also rebounded. In Korea, they had risen above pre-crisis levels by the middle of 1999. Stock markets elsewhere in Asia also rebounded as funds from the rest of the world started to return. This served to reinforce the optimistic feeling that was spreading throughout the region (see Table 3.6).

From 2002 to 2007, stock markets in Asia generally increased, often dramatically. The Bombay stock market in India increased ninefold, the Jakarta index around sixfold, Korea fourfold, the Shanghai and Hong Kong indices tripled, and the Taiwan stock market index more than doubled. Since the beginning of 2008, however, growth in the industrial countries has faltered, and all the Asian markets have weakened. The extent of this weakness is displayed in Table 3.7. The fall in stock market values since the beginning of 2008 is largely due to weakness in the global markets, particularly for Asian exports as a result of a recession in the industrialized countries. Consequently, this is expected to result in much slower growth throughout the Asian region in 2009.

Table 3.6   Stock Market Recovery[a]

	Dec 1998–Dec 1999		Dec 1999–Dec 2000		Dec 2000–Dec 2001	
	Local Currency	U.S. Dollars	Local Currency	U.S. Dollars	Local Currency	U.S. Dollars
China	21.7	21.6	49.4	49.4	−19.9	−19.9
Hong Kong	61.7	61.2	−10.5	−10.8	−23.9	−23.9
Indonesia	65.0	84.9	−38.1	−52.9	−10.0	−14.3
Korea	70.5	80.7	−48.4	−51.6	27.6	25.4
Malaysia	35.0	35.0	−12.5	−12.5	−2.3	−2.3
Philippines	3.4	−0.8	−34.0	−47.0	−24.8	−27.0
Singapore	69.6	67.6	−20.9	−24.1	−17.8	−22.4
Taiwan	23.6	26.0	−40.3	−43.4	12.3	7.2
Thailand	25.0	19.7	−43.7	−50.8	8.8	7.7

[a]Percent change in stock market prices

SOURCE: *The Economist*, various issues.

Table 3.7   Stock Market Indices, Beginning of 2008 and November 21, 2008

	Stock Market Average		
	January 2008	November 2008	Percentage Decline
China	5,500	1,969	64%
Hong Kong	27,000	12,659	53
India	20,000	8,915	55
Indonesia	2,700	1,146	57
Korea	1,900	1,003	47
Malaysia	1,500	866	42
Singapore	3,500	1,662	52
Taiwan	8,200	4,171	49

SOURCE: Interpolated from chart in http://finance.yahoo.com, January 2008.

RESTRUCTURING   Many weaker firms throughout the region went out of business during the Asian financial crisis. Those that survived were operating more efficiently. Banks started to become more stringent about lending and took greater care to evaluate borrowers. Thailand is a case in point. There was also more transparency and ongoing attempts to deal with corruption and shady business practices. Even as the Asian economies recovered, they put in more efforts to avoid the potential bubble that had resulted in the previous crisis.

3.3.3 Economic Recovery

As we have seen above, the downturn in most economies was not caused by a dramatic fall in exports. Rather, it was a result of a combination of the withdrawal of funds by short-term lenders, a collapse in currency exchange rates, and bankruptcies caused by the burden of unhedged foreign debt.

> Indeed evidence suggests that currency depreciation inflicted much less damage on firms than the rise in interest rates and cut-backs in domestic credit lines because many firms with large foreign indebtedness were export-oriented. If credit lines had been maintained greater competitiveness and growing export revenues would have provided a cushion against rising liabilities in domestic currency as a result of depreciation. . . . In a sense, orthodox policies succeeded in stabilizing exchange rates not by restoring confidence through high interest rates as intended but by creating a deep recession. . . . (UNCTAD, 2000, p. 53).

The report goes on to say that the recession may have been avoided if a temporary debt standstill (their words for moratorium) had been put into effect and borrowers and lenders brought together to reschedule short-term debt. This would have avoided high interest rates and the subsequent reduction in domestic lending and the contraction in aggregate demand. Furthermore, the Malaysian and Chinese experience of fixing the nominal exchange rate did not necessarily lead to currency appreciation since there were effective controls over capital flows.

Recovery came through a revival of domestic demand supported by exports and a restoration of investor confidence. Softer budget deficits and lower interest rates also underpinned the recovery. The slowdown in the growth of the industrial countries in 2001 initially served to moderate the recovery in Asia. However, sustained growth in these countries later helped to reinforce the subsequent recovery of Asia in 2002 until 2007. In addition, as noted below, there was a very strong turnaround in the current-account balances (see Table 3.7). Export performance also recovered significantly.

A dramatic turnaround in the external balance was experienced by many countries, especially the trigger economies (see Table 3.8), which saw huge surpluses, compared with the large deficits in 1996, as can be seen in Table 3.4. These surpluses have grown even more in the past five years, particularly in Malaysia, China, Hong Kong, and Singapore. The primary reason for the quick turnaround in the external balance lies in the collapse in imports in the early years of the recovery, while exports remained relatively strong. This turnaround in the net export balance had a significant stimulating effect on overall GDP and GDP growth (with net exports increasing from a large negative to a large positive figure.) This reinforces the conclusion drawn earlier that the recession in Asia was primarily a failure of domestic demand. The collapse of domestic income resulted in a commensurate fall in imports, which was compounded by the rise in the cost of imports following the currency devaluation. In countries that were less affected by the recession (China, Taiwan, and Singapore to some extent), the change in the current account was much less dramatic, although there were subsequent further improvements in the current account and trade balance in all the countries in the region.

All the crisis economies have made a recovery, although there are still difficulties in resolving nonperforming loans and weaknesses in the financial sectors of several crisis economies, particularly Thailand and Indonesia, which retarded further recovery in 2003 and 2004. However, by 2007, all the trigger economies were in good financial shape.

Countries suffering from a high level of nonperforming loans followed different strategies. These strategies and the structure of banking in Asia are discussed more extensively in Chapter 7. However, it can be said briefly here that in Thailand, where a market-based approach to bad loans was adopted initially, recovery rates were slow and progress limited. Thailand subsequently adopted a government-led approach, as did the other crisis countries—Indonesia, Korea, and Malaysia, which saw more satisfactory recovery rates. The Philippines felt there was no need for a restructuring agency. In Korea, the

Table 3.8   Current-Account Balance for Asian Economies as Percent of GDP, 1997–2007

	1997	1998	1999	2000	2001	2002	2005	2006	2007
China	4.1%	3.1%	1.6%	1.5%	1.2%	1.9%	7.2%	9.4%	11.3%
Hong Kong	–3.1	2.7	7.5	5.5	7.5	10.7	11.4	12.1	13.5
Indonesia	0.7	–0.3	–1.7	–4.6	–5.0	4.1	0.1	2.9	2.4
Korea	–1.7	12.7	6.0	2.4	1.9	1.3	1.9	0.6	0.6
Malaysia	–5.9	13.1	15.9	8.8	5.5	7.6	14.5	16.3	15.5
Philippines	–5.3	2.4	9.4	11.5	8.0	1.6	2.0	4.5	4.4
Singapore	19.0	24.8	25.9	23.6	24.0	21.5	18.6	21.8	24.3
Taiwan	2.4	1.3	2.9	2.4	2.5	9.2	4.9	7.2	8.6
Thailand	–2.1	12.7	10.2	8.2	6.5	6.0	–4.3	1.1	6.1

SOURCES: Asian Development Bank, *Asian Development Outlook 2003; Asian Development Outlook 2008.*

government has been quite proactive in supplying fresh capital and nationalizing banks in difficulty. This initiative proved quite successful and Korea has now recovered substantial strength in its financial sector.

3.3.4   Emerging Development Divide in Asia?

An analysis of the performance of the countries in Southeast and East Asia since the crisis suggests that a development divide may be emerging between these two regions.[2] Putting China together with Taiwan, Korea, and Hong Kong as East Asia, and grouping the five major Southeast Asian countries together (excluding the Mekong countries) reveals several interesting features. Between 1996 and 2002, real GDP growth in U.S. dollars at 1996 prices increased by only 13.3 percent in the ASEAN-5, whereas it increased by 40.7 percent in the East Asian-4 (see Table 3.9). Similarly, stock market and export performance, and the ability to attract foreign investment have been extremely anemic in Southeast Asia but more vibrant in East Asia (see Tables 3.10, 3.11, and 3.12).

To see if this trend continued after the region recovered from the Asian financial crisis, we made a similar comparison of GDP growth between 2001 and 2007 for similar groupings of countries. The results are displayed in Table 3.13.

When China was included, the East Asia-4 grew more rapidly. When China was excluded, the ASEAN-5 grew faster. Based on these growth figures, it is doubtful that the difference in growth performance of the two regions was significant enough to qualify it as a *development divide* in the early years of the twenty-first century.

While the strength in East Asia is largely the result of the rapid growth in China, it is also reflective of the relative speed of liberalization in Korea and Taiwan and their abilities to attract foreign investment and continue to undertake necessary policy adjustments and restructuring. In Southeast Asia, on the

---

[2] This observation was originally made by Ou Chun Hua in a research paper written for a course in the economic development of Asia at the Singapore Management University in 2003.

Table 3.9   Real and Nominal GDP, 1996–2002 (Billions US$)

	Real GDP[a]			Nominal GDP		
	1996	**2002[b]**	**Percent Change**	**1996**	**2002[b]**	**Percent Change**
ASEAN-5	$ 684	$ 775	13.3%	$ 684	$ 549	−19.7%
Indonesia	227	234	3.1	227	177	−22.0
Malaysia	101	120	18.8	101	89	−11.9
Philippines	83	101	21.7	83	75	−9.6
Singapore	91	132	45.1	91	87	−4.4
Thailand	182	188	3.3	182	121	−33.5
East Asia-4	1,782	2,507	40.7	1,782	2,221	24.6
China	825	1,298	57.3	825	1,315	59.4
Hong Kong	157	183	16.6	157	160	1.9
Korea	520	673	29.4	520	464	−10.8
Taiwan	280	353	26.1	280	282	0.7
Japan	4,711	4,910	4.2	4,711	3,991	−15.3

[a]At 1996 prices.
[b]Figures are estimated.

SOURCE: Economic Intelligence Unit (EIU), EIU CountryData (online database).

Table 3.10   Stock Market Index, 1996–2001

	1996	**2001**	**Percent Change**
ASEAN-5			
Indonesia	637.43	392.04	−38.5%
Malaysia	1,237.96	696.90	−43.7
Philippines	3,170.60	1,168.08	−63.2
Singapore	2,216.79	1,623.60	−26.8
Thailand	831.57	303.85	−63.5
East Asia-4			
China	n.a.	1,712.54	n.a.
Hong Kong	13,451.45	11,397.20	−15.3
Korea	832.33	757.52	−9.0
Taiwan	6,933.94	5,551.24	−19.9
Japan	19,361.35	10,542.62	−45.5

SOURCE: Economic Intelligence Unit (EIU), EIU CountryData (online database).

Table 3.11   Market Capitalization of All Listed Companies, 1996 and 2001 (Billions US$)

	1996	2001	Percent Change
ASEAN-5	$ 728.9	$ 316.7	–56.6%
Indonesia	91.0	23.0	–74.7
Malaysia	307.2	119.0	–61.3
Philippines	80.7	21.3	–73.6
Singapore	150.2	117.1	–22.1
Thailand	99.8	36.3	–63.6
East Asia-4	975.7	1,406.1	44.1
China	113.8	524.0	360.6
Hong Kong	449.4	506.1	12.6
Korea	138.8	232.1	67.2
Taiwan	273.7	376.0	37.4
Japan	3,088.9	3,910.0	26.6

SOURCE: World Bank, *World Development Indicators Online.*

Table 3.12   Export Volumes, 1996–2002 (Billions US$)

	1996	1997	1998	1999	2000	2001	2002
ASEAN-5	$329	$340	$315	$344	$406	$363	$378
Indonesia	50	53	49	49	61	56	57
Malaysia	78	79	73	85	98	88	92
Philippines	20	25	29	37	40	32	35
Singapore	125	125	110	115	138	122	125
Thailand	56	58	54	58	69	65	69
East Asia-4	578	629	601	635	771	730	796
China	151	183	184	195	249	267	294
Hong Kong	116	122	111	122	148	123	131
Korea	130	136	132	144	172	150	161
Taiwan	181	188	174	174	202	190	210
Japan	411	421	388	419	479	403	415

SOURCE: Economic Intelligence Unit (EIU), EIU CountryData (online database).

Table 3.13   GDP Growth for ASEAN-5 and East Asia-4, 2001 and 2007

	Average Yearly Growth
ASEAN-5	
Indonesia	5.1%
Malaysia	4.4
Philippines	4.4
Singapore	5.2
Thailand	5.0
Average for ASEAN-5	4.8
East Asia-4	
China	10.2
Hong Kong	4.9
Korea	4.7
Taiwan	3.8
Average for East Asia-4	5.9
Average without China	4.4

SOURCE: Asian Development Bank, *Asian Development Outlook*, various issues.

other hand, reforms have been less dramatic, particularly in Indonesia and the Philippines. The ongoing ability of East Asia to continue to integrate into the new knowledge economy has also increased at a rapid pace (see Chapter 11). Nevertheless, since 2001, ASEAN has managed to maintain an average growth on par with the East Asia-4 even when the extremely rapid growth in China is excluded.

3.3.5   Social Impact of the Economic Crisis[3]

The crisis put extreme pressure on many sectors of the economies of the five crisis countries. The credit crunch made banks reluctant to lend and firms were starved of working capital; currency depreciation made it difficult for firms to service external debt; inflation accelerated and purchasing power fell as the price of imports increased and government revenues came under strain when the tax base contracted and incomes fell. The price of providing public services also increased, while the ability to undertake compensatory spending was constrained by the crisis itself. As a result, there was a fall in output, an increase in unemployment, and the incidence of poverty.

As the crisis deepened and economic conditions worsened, there was an increase in reverse migration as urban residents moved back to the province. Fortunately, the agricultural sectors of the affected countries were not as hard hit as the urban sectors, and the rural areas were able to absorb these

---

[3] See Chu and Hill (2001) for further details.

Table 3.14   Unemployment Rates, 1997–1998

	1997	1998
Indonesia	4.7%	21.3%
Korea, Rep. of	2.6	7.7
Malaysia	2.7	6.4
Thailand	1.9	4.4

SOURCE: Economic and Social Commission for Asia and the Pacific (ESCAP), *Economic and Social Survey of Asia and the Pacific* (Bangkok: United Nations, 1999), p. 119.

returning workers without much trouble. At least, they could provide subsistence levels of food and housing.

The formal rate of unemployment increased dramatically in all four of the crisis countries (excluding the Philippines), as reflected in the estimates made by ESCAP, shown in Table 3.14.

These figures do not tell the entire story as the unemployment rate is compiled mostly from urban employment figures, which exclude the large rural sector where the impact of the crisis was less dramatic. Moreover, self-employment opportunities sometimes provided work for those laid off. However, wages also fell for those already employed.

Estimates of poverty reported by ESCAP show increases from 6.8 percent to 8 percent in Malaysia between 1997 and 1998, while in Thailand, the rate rose from 11.4 percent in 1997 to 15.3 percent in 1998. The estimate of poverty increasing from 11 percent to 40 percent in Indonesia seems improbable.

Budget cuts and reduced incomes had an adverse effect on expenditures on health and education during the crisis. Health budgets were cut by more than 5 percent in Thailand and 4 percent in Indonesia, and consumers also shifted away from expensive health care services to lower quality and cheaper services. The impact on infant mortality and malnutrition has not been estimated but was probably quite substantial.

There was also a higher incidence of mental health problems as unemployment grew, and tighter household budgets increased mental stress, family violence, and the crime rate.

The rates of school dropouts rose as many families found it difficult to afford even the minimal costs of sending their children to school. Instead, they were either put to work in the informal sector or forced to stay at home. In Indonesia, as many as 25 percent of children dropped out of school, the highest rate being for high school students whose school fees were more unaffordable (Knowles, Pernia, and Racelis, 1999). There was greater discrimination against girls, who were often forced to stay at home while limited resources were used to educate the boys in the family.

A detailed and in-depth study of the impact of the crisis by the Asian Development Bank (Knowles, Pernia, and Racelis, 1999) suggests that the impact of the crisis varied significantly from economy to economy and one should be careful about making blanket judgments. For example, they found no consistent evidence that children had been taken out of schools in large numbers as a result of the crisis, nor was there any evidence of significant adverse health effects on children. At the same time, there was a sharp decline in real per-capita income between 1997 and 1998—20 percent in Korea, 12 percent in the Philippines, and by about 24 percent in Indonesia.

They found that households used a number of coping mechanisms to deal with the crisis. Some of them helped to smooth consumption and made adjustments to minimize the impact by working longer hours, delaying purchases of durable goods, and substituting cheaper foods. Others involved postponing or shifting the impact of the crisis to the future, by borrowing or taking children out of school. Since the income constraint was more binding on the poor and institutionalized populations, such as the disabled, the elderly and children in orphanages, these methods were used more often and imply intergenerational loss of welfare as a result of lost schooling. Their study concluded that certain disadvantaged groups, such as the poor, women, children, and the elderly were particularly hard hit by the crisis.

Their study also suggests that better targeting mechanisms have to be developed together with better social safety nets. Monitoring systems also need to be set up to keep track of target populations in situations of crisis. This includes poverty monitoring together with the delivery of public services.

As the Asian economies recovered from the crisis, the unemployment rate fell and growth accelerated. Significant progress was also made in reducing poverty further. Between 1998 and 2002, the percentage of people below the poverty line fell from 13.3 percent to 11.5 percent in the Philippines, from 5.2 percent to 2.4 percent in Thailand, and from 15.4 percent to 12.7 percent in China (Dowling, 2007). Poverty rates also fell in other Asian economies (Dowling, 2008).

3.4 LESSONS AND PROSPECTS FOR THE FUTURE

3.4.1 An Agenda for Reform

Based on the reform agenda prescribed by international banks and aid agencies after the crisis, we list the following items that could be helpful in speeding up reform in the crisis-affected countries of Asia. This list makes much sense and can be easily extended, with some modifications, to global structural reform.

DEBT RESTRUCTURING   Great emphasis is placed on an orderly restructuring of debt. This will be more difficult than in the Latin American case because there are more lenders and borrowers, and the private sector is heavily involved. However, the process has already started and will be made easier as balance sheets improve in 2000 and beyond.

PRIVATE-SECTOR CREDIT LINES   Given the limited resources of the IMF and the conceptual difficulties with the notion of an international lender of last resort, it may be useful for governments to establish credit lines with the private sector. Argentina entered into such arrangements with foreign banks before the Mexican crisis, and they did supply credit to the country. These facilities could be strengthened by multilateral guarantees from the World Bank or the IMF.

REFORM EXCHANGE-RATE REGIMES   Many of the problems faced by developing countries in Asia were the result of "hot" money outflows during the crisis that resulted in abrupt currency devaluations. Many businesses and banks borrowed in foreign currencies and held large unhedged positions. As currencies devalued, they had great difficulty in meeting their foreign obligations. Some went bankrupt. Governments also lost substantial reserves in trying to defend fixed exchange rates.

A pure, flexible floating exchange rate allows continuous adjustment to accommodate changes in relative price movements or commodity markets. Those who advocate such a system argue that a flexible exchange rate provides a clear signal of the effects of government policies. In any event, whether a peg against a basket or a free float is adopted, the new exchange-rate regimes in this region will have much greater flexibility than they had before and this will help to prevent repeat episodes of macroeconomic disequilibrium. By moving to a flexible exchange-rate regime, the chances of such defaults occurring would be minimized since the costs of not hedging would be more apparent. Furthermore, the exchange rate would automatically move in response to capital inflows and outflows, thus reducing the chances of an inflationary bubble arising.

CAPITAL ACCOUNT REFORM The regulation of short-term capital movements, such as through the imposition of taxes, can be considered. The experience of Chile is useful to study in this regard. It is also important to carefully consider further capital market deregulation. This is particularly true when domestic capital markets are underdeveloped or where it is difficult to control excessive risk-taking by domestic banks and businesses.

INTERNATIONAL PORTFOLIO CONTROLS UNCTAD also suggests in its report that controls on international portfolio investment at the source of the lending should be explored. This would be in addition to measures taken by developing country governments to impose capital controls. These controls would involve monitoring and supervision of international financial firms (banks, insurance companies, pension funds, financial conglomerates). Another proposal is to focus on international bank-lending practices by putting a ceiling on lending which would be insured through a new sister institution to the IMF, called the International Credit Insurance Corporation (ICIC).

ESTABLISH MINIMUM INTERNATIONAL STANDARDS OF FINANCIAL PRACTICE Auditing and accounting practices still vary considerably across countries. This makes it difficult for lenders to gauge the financial conditions of borrowing banks and business firms. Differences in corporate governance practices, investor protection, and insider trading also reduce transparency and increase risk. The establishment of minimum international standards would create a floor of credibility which would also help to prevent national problems from spilling over into international markets.

INFORMATION AND TRANSPARENCY The Asian crisis has reinforced the need to pay greater attention to constructing uniform standards for accounting and financial reporting. UNCTAD does not believe that the lack of more general macroeconomic information, such as that supplied through the IMF's Special Data Dissemination Standard (SDDS) system, contributed to the crisis.

GLOBAL SURVEILLANCE How can the existing surveillance mechanism be improved to reduce the probability of future crises? In the Asian crisis and also in the Mexican crisis, the IMF warned Mexico and Thailand regarding its external debt policies. Yet the advice went unheeded both by Thailand and the international financial community. UNCTAD suggests that the emphasis of IMF policies must shift from domestic policies to the possible impact of external policies of the major industrial countries on developing countries and on the surveillance mechanisms that address these issues. They also ask whether the IMF surveillance should be extended to financial regulation and standards for financial reporting (see below for more on this.)

REFORM OF FINANCIAL MARKETS Another set of necessary reforms comes under the heading of financial market regulation. The details will depend upon the existing system of regulations in individual countries.

GREATER COMPETITION Subsequent to the crisis in Latin America, foreign banks flocked to the region, lured by bank privatization and the relaxation of ownership rules. They brought fresh capital and state-of-the-art technology. More than a fifth of Mexico's banking system is now in foreign hands. Asia could learn from this experience. It is still highly protected and restrictions have inhibited the development of new services and narrowed the scope for diversification (only Malaysia has greater than 7 percent of total assets owned by foreign banks). The arguments in favor of foreign participation in this sector are essentially the same as those that have proved very successful in opening up the goods sectors in these countries to international trade and greater competition. However, in arguing for greater competition, we must remember that each of the crises that we have looked at came after the liberalization of banking regulations, which resulted in a move into more risky assets. Competition has to be tempered with strengthened prudential regulations.

CONSOLIDATION   In Latin America, governments moved quickly to close the worst-performing banks. At the beginning of the crisis, the Asian governments were loath to close banks for good, and the number of mergers were also small.

SUPERVISION AND REGULATION   New regulations should follow principles, such as those laid down by the Basle Committee on Banking Supervision (1997). Countries can also benefit from studying new developments in other developing countries, such as Argentina and Chile. In Chile, the central bank regularly visits banks and classifies them based on the quality of their loan portfolios and then publishes the results. In Argentina, regulation is shared between the state and the market. Banks are required to issue bonds linked to the value of their deposits. The price of the bonds indicates the strength of the bank in the eyes of the market. While new methods of regulation such as these would have to be reviewed, a different pattern of regulation with tighter controls in some areas and weaker controls in others is required, rather than a blanket deregulation.

ACCOUNTING AND DISCLOSURE   Tougher accounting and disclosure rules will help to expose weaknesses before they can fester. Greater transparency and higher standards are needed, particularly where the rules are woefully deficient. In Korea, for example, banks do not have to disclose, let alone make provision for all of their suspect loans.

STOCK MARKETS   A major reform would be the introduction and development of the derivatives market, particularly in Thailand, Malaysia, and Indonesia, especially those permitting better hedging of equities exposures. Access by foreign investors should be significantly liberalized (elimination of B shares where they still exist) and the imposition of price limits to trade, such as those adopted by the New York Stock Exchange, should be reviewed.

TRADE POLICIES   Further reforms of trade policies are desirable. However, Thailand and Malaysia have raised tariff rates after the crisis and this could be harmful and unnecessary, particularly given the large exchange-rate devaluations. Countries in Asia have an exceptional record of unilateral reductions in tariff and other border restrictions on trade in goods. Trade liberalization should be continued. In the case of Indonesia, the IMF package requires them to remove the international trading monopolies for some commodities, but others remain. These are particularly objectionable because they combine the monopoly powers of single traders (as with the statutory monopolies in Australia) with the transfer of these valuable implicit property rights to the individuals who were granted the monopolies. These countries have been much less active in reducing restrictions on service trade in general. The current WTO negotiations on an Agreement on Financial Services provide an opportunity for the developing countries to join the industrialized countries in liberalizing trade in these services.

FOREIGN DIRECT INVESTMENT   Another critical area is FDI incentives. These incentives were a factor in the rapid expansion of FDI and capital formation, as a result of which the East Asian countries have been among the most vigorous in the world in offering incentives to attract FDI. The levels of foreign direct investment have risen relative to capital formation in these economies. In 1994, China, Singapore, and Malaysia had inward inflows of FDI that were equal to 25, 24, and 16 percent of gross capital formation, respectively (UNCTAD, 1996, Annex Table 5) and would probably have risen further in recent years. Like border interventions in trade policy, these incentives misrepresent the pattern of FDI flows among countries and, because they are not uniformly available to all sectors, distort the patterns within the host economies. Some economists and other groups, such as UNCTAD (see UNCTAD, 1996, Chapter VI), have sought ways of limiting these incentives, but it is difficult to persuade countries to agree individually to limit their policies for fear that FDI will be diverted to other countries which continue to offer incentives. This suggests that multilateral action may succeed better than unilateral moves. This matter is under discussion in the Asia-Pacific Economic Cooperation (APEC) draft on Non-Binding Investment Principles, and the OECD's Multilateral Investment Agreement, but the developing Asian countries have opposed limitations on incentives in these fora. There needs to be an appreciation in East Asia of the distorting and collectively self-defeating nature of these incentives.

HUMAN CAPITAL   Finally, more long-term measures need to be taken to address the shortage of human capital required to upgrade the productivity capacity in skilled and knowledge-intensive industries. The pattern of international trade is shifting more and more toward these areas. Nearly all of the industries that have increased their share of international trade in the past two decades have been in these industries, particularly computers and electronics. The countries in East Asia have generally taken advantage of this trend and have increased their share of manufactured exports in these industries. However, additional efforts will have to be made to continue the process of technological transfer into these industries and to deepen the product mix of exports. Thailand and Indonesia are particularly at risk if they fail to address these issues, since they have noticeable deficiencies in knowledge and technology-intensive industries.

BETTER UNDERSTANDING OF THE CRISIS PROCESS   The Asian crisis, as many crises before, was unanticipated. This is how a crisis situation is explained. Rapid revisions of expectations and herd mentality are essential components of the anatomy of a crisis. Each crisis is unique, yet we can learn from an in-depth analysis of each individual crisis. The Asian crisis had many of the attributes of a domestic bank run. Careful analysis by many economists suggests that there were no dramatic signs that the crisis was imminent. There is also evidence that the IMF misunderstood the nature of the crisis and was slow to respond to the requirement for a different set of policies.

NEW DATA   Is there new information that should be monitored in order to anticipate another crisis of this type? Furman and Stiglitz (1998) have suggested the ratio of short-term debt to reserves as a possible additional indication of potential financial crisis. They found that the IMF-assisted countries of Korea, Indonesia, and Thailand all had a ratio greater than one. They argue that a high ratio shows a lack of liquidity, and hence, a higher probability of a bank run. They also suggest that it signals poor macroeconomic policies in other areas too. However, some countries do not fit the mould. Singapore was one of the countries with a high ratio, higher than any of the IMF-assisted countries, and Malaysia, another problem country, had a very low ratio.

NEW ANALYSIS   None of the models that had been previously devised by economists to predict potential crisis were able to do so. Furman and Stiglitz (1998) suggest that we need to deepen our understanding of the relationship between financial and real variables in a globally integrated world.

In particular, they stress the importance of understanding the interrelationships within the financial sector as well as how it interacts with the real sector.

By 2008, many of the suggested policy initiatives outlined above had already been adopted. Growth rates have accelerated, exchange-rate regimes have become more flexible, international reserves have increased, and current-account balances have improved dramatically. In fact, two countries in each region (ASEAN-5 and East Asia-4) had double-digit current-account surpluses (see Table 3.15), and the remaining countries also had current-account surpluses.

Table 3.15   Economic Growth, International Reserves, and Government Deficits for Selected Asian Economies, 2003–2007

	International Reserves, 2007 (Millions US$)	Central Government's Budget Balance as Percent of GDP, 2007 (in 2003)	Average GDP Growth (Percent)		Current-Account Surplus/Deficit as Percent of GDP, 2007
			2003–2004	2006–2007	
ASEAN-5					
Malaysia	101,300	−2.8 (−5.0)	6.2%	6.1%	15.5%
Thailand	87,455	−1.7 (0.4)	6.6	5.0	6.1
Indonesia	56,920	−1.2 (−1.7)	4.9	5.9	2.4
Philippines	33,754	−0.2 (−4.6)	5.6	6.3	4.4
Singapore	162,957	12.2 (7.4)	5.8	7.9	24.3
East Asia-4					
China	1,540,000	0.7 (−2.2)	10.0	11.8	11.3
Korea	262,150	−2.3 (−1.8)	3.9	5.1	0.6
Taiwan	270,311	−0.2 (−2.7)	4.8	5.3	8.6
Hong Kong	152,702	7.2 (−3.2)	5.9	6.7	13.5
Other Countries					
India	306,488	−5.5 (−8.5)	8.0	9.2	−1.5
Bangladesh	5,077	−3.2 (−3.4)	5.8	6.6	1.4
Nepal	2,401	−2.0 (−1.4)	4.1	2.7	−0.1
Pakistan	13,345	−5.8 (−3.6)	6.1	6.8	−4.8
Sri Lanka	3,100	−7.7 (−7.8)	5.6	7.2	−4.2
Cambodia	1,621	−3.2 (−6.7)	9.2	10.2	−7.8
Laos	530	−3.1 (−7.9)	6.3	8.1	−18.6
Vietnam	19,931	−4.9 (−4.8)	7.5	8.3	−8.0

SOURCE: Asian Development Bank (2008).

Export performance has underpinned much of the turnaround in the current-account balance. Between 2003 and 2007, exports grew at an average of 14.2 percent in East Asia, excluding China, and more than 17 percent including China. South Asian exports also grew rapidly, at more than 15 percent, while Southeast Asian exports grew even more rapidly, at 17.5 percent. For many of the poorer countries, garments and textiles were the leading exports. In the Lao PDR, the recent discovery and exploitation of copper and gold deposits resulted in an export growth of more than 50 percent in 2005 and 2007. In the more industrialized economies of East Asia, electronics continue to be the strongest foreign exchange earner.

3.4.2   Some Policy Implications

How could the Asian economies have protected themselves against the possible repetition of the Mexican financial crisis and the earlier Latin American crisis? They had several options. These are reviewed below. Their problems stemmed primarily from rapid growth that was destabilizing. What could they have done?

1. They could have cut back on growth. This would have reduced the rapid buildup in investment and foreign direct investment, and helped to moderate inflation and to improve competitiveness, assuming that they remained wedded to the U.S. dollar. To do this, they would initially have had to exercise additional fiscal tightening since under the existing circumstances, monetary policy would not have been very effective and, in fact, could have been counterproductive if the exchange rate had remained fixed.
2. They could also have loosened the attachment of their currency to the U.S. dollar. This would have helped to stem the inflow of short-term capital that hampered efforts to control the money supply and inflation. It would also have reduced the speculative component of the external finance needed to close the gap between investment and saving. Furthermore, it would have reduced the speculative bubble which had begun to build up, and which resulted in much land speculation and unproductive investments of a similar nature.
3. They could have put a tax on short-term capital inflows if there was a reluctance to loosen the exchange-rate peg. James Tobin (1978) proposed this many years ago and there has been revived interest in it.

3.5   Summary and Developments in the New Millennium

Can the region ever return to the golden age of growth of the early 1990s? Apart from the two giant economies of China and India, the answer is probably not. The stronger economies such as Korea, Taiwan, Singapore, and Hong Kong (and to a lesser extent, Thailand, Malaysia, and the Philippines) have already recovered, but they will probably grow more slowly in the long run for two reasons. First, it will be more difficult to maintain rapid growth as incomes continue to approach the levels of the OECD countries; and secondly, the rapid growth of the early 1990s reflected overheating to some extent. In some respects, these economies will be even stronger than in the past as new reforms are implemented and the weaker industries are culled. While the weaker economies, like Indonesia, have taken longer to recover, they are now on a stronger growth trajectory. Indonesia has averaged GDP growth of more than 5 percent since 2002.

Both Hong Kong and China are suffering from a reduction in export competitiveness *vis-à-vis* the rest of Asia because of exchange-rate realignment. Growth in China has remained strong, partly as a result of a very strong expansionary fiscal and monetary policy in the last part of 1998 and in 1999. Nevertheless, problems of NPLs in the state-enterprise sector persist (see Chapter 7 for details).

Hong Kong has suffered a loss because its currency is still pegged to the U.S. dollar. It has also suffered because China's export sector has begun to feel the pinch of relative currency appreciation. Furthermore, China adopted a more flexible exchange-rate regime in 2007 and there has been a modest appreciation of the yuan against the U.S. dollar since then. Despite this, China continues to grow rapidly. In addition, the flow of FDI and other investments into Asia increased as the region became more attractive to investors seeking higher returns in an environment where rates of return to investors in Europe, Japan, and the United States are lower.

Broadening the perspective somewhat to include South Asia, it is clear that growth has also accelerated in this region in the past decade or so. This is demonstrated by the growth rates for the three regional subgroups during the decade, displayed in Table 2.2.

Policy changes in the South Asian economies of India and Bangladesh have contributed to an acceleration in growth in the 1990s and in the new millennium. There has been less progress in Pakistan and Sri Lanka, partly as a result of political unrest and social tension. Pakistan continues to be affected by the situation in Afghanistan and its ongoing dispute with India over Kashmir, while an uneasy truce continues in Sri Lanka. However, by 2007, the South Asian economies were growing nearly as fast as the countries of East Asia (9.6 percent in East Asia versus 8.6 percent in South Asia), and faster than the Southeast Asian region (6.5 percent), as reported in *Asian Development Outlook 2008*, Statistical Appendix Table A1.

From the experience of the rapid growth economies in the East Asian region and the recent successes in South Asia, it seems that a country that embraces prudent macroeconomic policies, promotes competition, and is predisposed to invest in its people and welcome the technology and ideas embodied in new goods and equipment is likely to prosper.

The Asian crisis that began in Thailand in the middle of 1997 took its biggest bite in 1998 when all the major economies in East Asia, except China and Taiwan, registered negative growth (refer to Table 3.5). Since then, growth has resumed, but not as fast as the boom years of the early 1990s and late 1980s. Growth has also been more sporadic. The years 1999 and 2000 saw solid recovery in East and Southeast Asia as China, Korea, Singapore, and Malaysia registered average growth rates of more than 7 percent. In the rest of the crisis-affected countries, growth was more modest, but a significant improvement over the negative growth rate was recorded in 1998. These developments were supported by strong efforts to deal with the financial disruptions and bad loans that had emerged as a result of the crisis.

In the early part of 2001, the U.S. economy began to slow down, entering a recession in the spring. This had repercussions on the economies of East and Southeast Asia, which were dependent on growth in U.S. import demand to help fuel its recovery. Consequently, growth slowed again in the latter part of 2001, and in 2002, especially the heavily trade-oriented economies of Hong Kong, China, Korea, Singapore, Malaysia, and Thailand, whose growth fell by several percentage points. Other economies were also affected, though not as severely, partly because they had not experienced such rapid growth in the previous two years. In 2002, as the U.S. economy began to recover and macroeconomic policies in the region began to focus more on domestic demand and countercyclical action, economic growth recovered somewhat.

The weakness in the region during 2001 and 2002 was partially reinforced by a slowdown in the global electronics cycle, after a rebound in 1999 and 2000 (see Table 3.16). However, by the end of 2002, the Semiconductor Industry Association (SIA) was predicting a strong growth of electronics demand in 2003 and 2004 of 19.8 percent and 21.7 percent respectively, on a year-on-year basis.

Concerns about deflation became more widespread in the early part of the new millennium. This partly reflects the low levels of inflation that have prevailed in most of the industrial economies since the beginning of 2000 and even earlier, and partly the fact that some major economies such as Japan, China, and Hong Kong have been experiencing a fall in prices. In most developing countries in Asia, domestic demand is recovering but external demand is still a key to more rapid growth. China is playing

Table 3.16   Global Semiconductor Downturns in the Last Fifteen Years, 1998–2001

	Slump 1 (1988–1992)	Slump 2 (1995–1998)	Slump 3 (2000–2001)
Recovery	"W" shaped downturn extended by the Gulf war, the oil price shock, the U.S. recession, and the burst of the Japanese growth bubble.	"W" shaped downturn extended by the Asian financial crisis and Japan's economic problems.	Elongated "V" shaped downturn as a result of the U.S. recession, the surge in oil prices, Japan's economic problems, and Iraq concerns.
U.S. rate hikes precede peak in semiconductor cycle	393.7 basis points in 28 months as federal funds rate rose to 9.812 from 5.875, between January 1987 and May 1989.	300 basis points in 12 months as federal funds rate rose from 3 percent to 6 percent, between February 1994 and February 1995.	175 basis points in 11 months as federal funds rate rose from 4.75 percent to 6.5 percent, between June 1999 and May 2000.
U.S. rate cuts precede bottom in semiconductor cycle	681.2 basis points in 39 months as federal funds rate falls from 9.812 percent in June 1989 to 3 percent in September 1992.	75 basis point in 7 months as the federal funds rate falls from 6 percent in July 1995 to 5 percent in January 1996.	525 basis points in 23 months as federal funds rate falls from 6.25 percent in January 2001 to 1.25 percent in November 2002.

SOURCES: Development Bank of Singapore (2001); data from Semiconductor Industry Association (November 2002), Web site at http://www.sia-online.org.

an important role in this continued search for export markets. Its exports to Europe and the United States increased by more than 30 percent in August 2002, compared with the previous year (Brooks and Quising, 2002). Because of the growing influence of China in world trade and the downward pressure that it is exerting on prices, there is some concern that there will be further downward pressure on prices. The problems of coping with deflation are highlighted by the collapse of the Japanese bubble economy in the late 1980s, and the subsequent difficulties that have arisen in that economy, including slow growth, financial sector weakness, and stock market declines.

To deal with deflation, the standard remedy is to increase the money supply and to lower interest rates. However, in cases where the interest rates are already very low, as is currently the case in Japan and the United States, the term structure of interest rates can still be affected by the central bank's purchase of securities to inject more liquidity into the banking system. In the case of the threat of global deflation, such efforts could be coordinated by several countries. Devaluation would also raise the cost of living and imports. It would also stimulate exports but this would not work if deflation is widespread, as it seems to be the case at present. Fiscal stimulus is also possible, but less of a policy option in the Asian economies that are already running large fiscal surpluses, such as China. As events unfolded from 2004 to 2007, the threat of devaluation abated as prices for Chinese exports stabilized and inflation accelerated somewhat in China and Southeast Asia, particularly in Indonesia and Thailand.

At the end of 2002 and in the first months of 2003, the international community was challenged by the rapid spread of a new and highly infectious virus dubbed SARS (severe acute respiratory syndrome.) Attacking the lungs, this virus was fatal in a significant number of cases (between 5 and

15 percent of those contracting the virus, depending on age and physical condition). The virus originated in China and spread quickly to neighboring countries, particularly Hong Kong and Taiwan. From a macroeconomic point of view, its impact on international trade, tourism, and other services had an adverse effect on these economies and on the region generally.

As noted above and explained in further detail in Chapter 11, the share of China in Asia's trade had increased dramatically in recent years. Any reduction in its rate of growth as a result of the SARS epidemic would have secondary effects on the rest of the region through the trade channel. Within China itself, the major impact was on the domestic service sector. Internal travel fell and the virus reduced the inclination of residents to gather in large groups. As a result, retail trade, entertainment, and food services were negatively affected. Exports in the first half of 2003 were not significantly affected although small and medium-sized exporters, who depended on trade fairs and sales calls, had difficulties. Enterprises that had workers with SARS symptoms were subject to quarantine, as well as all other workers with whom they had close contact with. They were also excused from work for ten days. FDI was not likely to have been diverted away from China by the SARS epidemic as it was brought gradually under control. The evidence available at the beginning of the third quarter suggests that this was the most likely scenario.

For the region as a whole, there was a negative impact on growth for the first half of 2003. Estimates made by Merrill Lynch and the Asian Development Bank suggested that growth would be up to 1.5 percentage points slower in several countries (see Table 3.17). These projections assumed that the epidemic would be brought under control within a few months of the time the estimates were made, roughly by the beginning or end of the second quarter of 2003.

Table 3.17   Estimated Impact of SARS on Economic Growth for Selected Asian Economies

	2002 Growth[a,b]	2003 Forecast Growth[a]	2003 Forecast Growth[b]	Estimated Impact of SARS on 2003 Growth[a]
China	8.0%	8.0%	7.3%	−0.5%
Hong Kong	2.3	3.1	2.0	−1.5
India	5.6[c]	4.8	4.4	−0.1
Indonesia	3.7	3.6	3.4	−0.2
Korea	6.3	3.5	4.0	−0.1
Malaysia	4.2	3.7	4.3	−0.5
Philippines	4.6	3.9	4.0	−0.2
Singapore	2.2	1.5	2.3	−0.9
Taiwan	3.5	3.2	3.7	−0.2
Thailand	5.2	3.6	5.0	−0.5

[a]Merrill Lynch data.
[b]ADB data.
[c]India's growth for the fiscal year July 2001 to July 2002 is denoted as 2002.

SOURCES: Merrill Lynch, *The Asian Equity Economist*, April 29, 2003, p. 6; Asian Development Bank, *Asian Development Outlook 2003*.

As events unfolded during the remainder of 2003 and in 2004, the SARS epidemic was brought under control and the region resumed rapid growth until 2008. The timely action of health officials around the region was responsible for the quick containment of the epidemic. An analysis of the growth trajectory of the region showed virtually no long-term effect of the epidemic, as seen from the growth profile presented in Table 3.5 and discussed earlier.

3.5.1   Global Recession in 2008 and 2009, and Developments in Asia

The rapid deterioration in economic growth in the industrialized countries that began in late 2007 and continued and intensified in 2008 has created additional challenges for the developing economies of Asia. Slower growth in Asia in 2009, and perhaps 2010, is anticipated as a result of a slowdown in export demand from Europe, Japan, and the United States. It is difficult to predict how long this recession will last, when it will bottom out, and when industrial economies will return to full employment of labor and capital resources. See Figure 3.2 for a comparison of the extent of job losses in the current and four previous recessions in the United States.

However, Asia is in good shape to offset these anticipated weaknesses in the foreign sector with monetary and fiscal stimulus (see Table 3.15). Most countries have cut interest rates in the last four months of 2008 and early 2009, and falling energy and food prices that have resulted from the slowdown should ameliorate any tendencies toward inflation. Furthermore, most countries have already or will soon put into motion some fiscal stimulus, the most notable being China's projected US$850 billion additional spending on infrastructure over the next few years. East and Southeast Asia have current-account surpluses and all countries in the region have ample foreign exchange reserves.

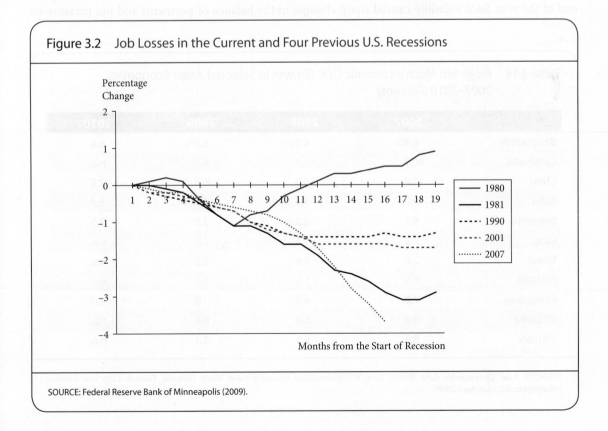

Figure 3.2   Job Losses in the Current and Four Previous U.S. Recessions

SOURCE: Federal Reserve Bank of Minneapolis (2009).

This is in sharp contrast to the macroeconomic picture that faced policymakers at the beginning of the 1997 financial crisis when budgets were in deficit, and foreign exchange reserves depleted as a result of efforts to maintain or prop up exchange rates. India could have a more difficult time than the rest of the region. Although less exposed to foreign trade (its exports are a much smaller component of GDP than in East or Southeast Asia), it has a large fiscal deficit. Other weaknesses include difficulty in financing its investments because of unstable equity markets locally and the lack of foreign investment. Its already high fiscal deficit constrains its ability to provide strong macroeconomic stimulus.

Apart from Singapore and Hong Kong where exports and imports are both in excess of 100 percent of GDP, Malaysia is the most exposed to foreign trade. Its exports are also in excess of GDP, whereas the rest of the Southeast Asian economies have a smaller export share (from about 30 percent for Indonesia to over 40 percent for Thailand). Thailand's prospects will also be adversely affected by political uncertainty while Taiwan will have to fight its way through a recession that has already begun. Korea, on the other hand, has high household debt which could slow the economy further if not for a large fiscal stimulus and currency depreciation of around 30 percent in 2008, which should boost exports.

3.5.2 Volatility in Commodity Markets, Global Recession, and Asian Growth

As the global financial and economic crisis deepened in the last quarter of 2008, the run up in commodity prices that had caused concern about inflation earlier in the year began to diminish. World food prices that had more or less doubled between January 2006 and May 2008 began to moderate as the recession deepened. (See Chapter 4 for further background on the reasons for commodity price volatility.) The price of oil, which peaked at US$140 a barrel in mid-2008 fell to US$40 a barrel by the end of the year. Such volatility caused sharp changes in the balance of payments and put pressure on

Table 3.18   Projected Macroeconomic GDP Growth in Selected Asian Economies, 2007–2010 (Percent)

	2007	2008	2009	2010
Bangladesh	6.4%	6.2%	6.5%	n.a.
Cambodia	10.2	6.5	6.0	n.a.
China	11.9	10.0	6.5	7.9
India	9.0	7.4	4.5	5.6
Indonesia	6.3	6.2	2.5	3.5
Laos	7.9	7.5	7.6	n.a.
Nepal	2.6	5.6	5.0	n.a.
Pakistan	6.8	5.8	4.5	n.a.
Philippines	7.2	4.5	0	1.0
Sri Lanka	6.8	6.0	6.0	n.a.
Vietnam	8.5	6.5	3.3	n.a.

SOURCES: Asian Development Bank (2008), Table A1; International Monetary Fund, *World Economic Outlook: Crisis and Recovery* (Washington, D.C.: IMF, April 2009).

governments to adjust their budgets to reflect these dramatic shifts. This has also generated uncertainty in the business community and a dampening impact on investment. As the global recession deepened at the end of 2008, this volatility, together with its psychological impact on consumers, created the potential for a deep global recession that is unprecedented. Comparisons with the Great Depression of the 1930s seemed more likely every day. However, by early June 2009, it appeared that the low point of the recession had been reached in many developed and developing countries, and the way had been paved for a slow recovery in the remainder of 2009 and 2010.

REVIEW QUESTIONS

1. The Asian financial crisis was a surprise to most economists, even those that specialized on economic developments in the region. Why do you think this happened?
2. Can you generalize the results of your analysis in answering question 1 to the question of predicting an economic shock?
3. Can you think of a few other instances of economic crises that came as a surprise to government, business, financial, and academic observers? What do they have in common with the Asian financial crisis? What are the dissimilarities?
4. Explain how the institutional and cultural setting of financial institutions in Asia contributed to the crisis?
5. Have these institutions changed since the crisis? If so, in what ways?
6. Knowing what we know now about the crisis, do you think governments are better able to predict the onset of another crisis? What kind of measures would you put in place to monitor economic and financial activity as an early warning system?
7. How did SARS and the Iraqi war affect the Asian region? Were these impacts similar to those of the Asian crisis? How were they different?
8. Some observers have suggested controls to cut down on the volatility of capital movements. What are the advantages and disadvantages of such proposals?
9. Governments have built up significant levels of foreign reserves since the financial crisis. Discuss the policy issues relating to such a policy. What would you say to the statement: "You can never have too much foreign reserve cushion."
10. The Asian financial crisis has been characterized as a crisis of the private sector in contrast to previous crises in Latin America that originated in the public sector. Comment on this characterization using concrete examples from the Asian crisis countries. Discuss the progress that has been made in dealing with the aftermath of the Asian crisis in at least two countries. Be specific about the measures undertaken.
11. The recent financial crisis in the industrial countries is not expected to have as big an impact on the Asian economies as the financial crisis of 1997. Explain why this is so.

Notes on References and Suggestions for Further Reading

Accounts of the Asian economic and financial crisis have been summarized and discussed by a number of different authors. There are also a number of Web sites that list references and discuss the causes of the crisis. The main facts of the crisis and its transmission from country to country are generally agreed upon by most economists who have studied the phenomenon. However, the strength of the various factors seems to differ. There are two basic schools of thought—those who believe that "weak fundamentals" reflecting underlying structural weaknesses and speculative bubble aspects were the cause of the crisis, and those who believe that "international contagion effects" were the most important. Morris Goldstein (1998), in a volume published by the Institute of International Economics, presents a balanced account of the crisis and its causes.

N. Roubini has taken a lively interest in the crisis and his Web site offers many references organized according to different aspects of the crisis. To start, you might consult "The Asian Currency Crisis of 1997," at http://www.stern.nyu/~nroubini.

Developments after the crisis are detailed in a number of publications, including those of the Asian Development Bank (2002), the ESCAP (1999), and UNCTAD (1996).

In addition, Shahid Yusuf and Simon J. Evenett (2002) analyze recent developments in the Asian region from the point of view of industrial development, innovation, and globalization.

Two interesting papers written during the time of the crisis and presenting the perspective of the World Bank and the IMF are the short papers by Javad Shirazi (1998) and the International Monetary Fund (1997).

For an analysis of the social implications of the financial crisis, see the 1999 ESCAP survey and the article by C. Knowles, Ernesto Pernia, and Mary Racelis (1999).

John Malcolm Dowling and J. Zhuang (2002) present an interesting analysis of early warning indicators of financial crisis and offer some insights on whether the crisis was caused by weak fundamentals or contagion, while Douglas H. Brooks and Pilipinas F. Quising (2002) summarize some of the discussions on the danger of deflation.

A paper by John G. Fernald, H. J. Edison, and Parkash Loungani (1999) presents an interesting account of the interaction between China and the rest of the region, while two recent monographs from the World Bank discuss prospects for the region and the challenge to innovate. John Malcolm Dowling (2007) presents an interesting account of growth, structural change and technology in the Asian region, including a forward-looking perspective and prospects for the Asian region. These volumes are also of interest for Chapters 5 and 6.

Agriculture

4.1 INTRODUCTION

Economic development has often been equated with the change in the economy where the importance of agriculture is increasingly diminished in favor of manufacturing and service industries. Yet, agriculture is widely acknowledged as a crucial element in the process of structural transformation.

In this chapter, we will discuss the important role that agriculture has played and continues to play in the process of economic development. Particular experiences of transformation in the countries of Asia will be highlighted and what unique factors have helped these economies to achieve a smooth transition.

4.2 AGRICULTURE AND ECONOMIC GROWTH

Agriculture plays a key role in the process of economic development. Most developing countries must rely on their agricultural sector to produce the food necessary to feed their people. The exceptions to this case are those few countries with large natural resource-based exports (such as oil for Saudi Arabia), which provide them with the foreign exchange necessary to import much of their food needs. In the initial phase of industrialization, farmers must produce food not only to feed themselves, but also to feed a growing urban population.

The agricultural sector is a rich source of factor inputs to feed the growing industrial and other modern sectors of the economy. One such factor is labor. With 70 percent or more of the workforce in agriculture-based employment in poor and medium-income economies, the agricultural sector is virtually the only source of increased labor power for the urban sector. Importation of labor resources is another option, but it can hardly be sufficient as a short-term solution.

Another factor input is capital. Agriculture can also be a major source of capital for modern economic growth. Capital comes from invested savings and savings from income. In the early stages of development, capital may build up to support the start of industries, but the rate of capital accumulation from this source may be very slow. It is common for developing countries to import capital in the form of aid or private investment to speed up the rate of capital accumulation, and hence the growth of the economy. South Korea is a case in point, where foreign aid was drawn upon to provide capital. In later years, the burgeoning industrial sector assumed the dominant role as a source of capital for the economy.

A third factor is foreign exchange. In the early stages of growth, agricultural products serve as the principal source of foreign exchange. As such, the agricultural sector's ability to supply foreign exchange enables the economy to import capital equipment and intermediate goods necessary for its continued growth. The availability of foreign exchange also facilitates the inflow of technology and industrial management expertise.

Finally, the agricultural sector is also important in that it provides a rich market for the output of the modern urban sector. The extent to which the rural population depends on products from the industrial sector is directly linked to the type of income distribution current in the economy. If income distribution is highly uneven, the large majority of the rural population will be poor. Their expenditure basket will necessarily be limited to food and other basic necessities, and their demand for industrial products will therefore be low or even close to zero. However, if there is a greater degree of equality in the distribution of income, the living standards of rural families will be higher and this can increase demand for products from the modern sector. If a large rural market exists, local industries can continue to grow after the urban sector market has been saturated, until such time that the industries are better able to compete in foreign markets.

An economic growth model that captures the transition of an economy from being mainly agricultural to becoming mainly industrial-based is the Lewis–Ranis–Fei (LFR) economic model of structural change. In this model, there are essentially two main sectors of an economy—a modern sector and a traditional sector, where the former is primarily based in cities and the latter in the countryside. There are elements of this model which are very important in understanding the pattern of development in many countries. A full discussion of this model is however postponed to the next chapter, when we will see how the process of industrialization takes place and how inefficiencies can arise. For this chapter, only aspects of this model that are relevant to agriculture will be discussed.

One aspect of agricultural development is the seeming paradox that characterizes agriculture as it relates to growth. The experience of a broad range of countries indicates that the relative importance of the agricultural sector to the economy diminishes with growth over time. In particular, the share of agriculture value-added in gross domestic product (GDP) and as a source of employment consistently declines over time, as income increases. Furthermore, the rate of decline is more or less directly proportional to the rate of growth in total output of the economy. Countries that grow very rapidly show a sharper decline in agriculture value-added and employment than do countries that have grown more slowly.

Yet, at the same time that the share of agriculture declines, there is pervasive evidence that a dynamic and vibrant agricultural sector plays a key role in providing a surplus to the rest of the economy. This is particularly true for the industrial sector in the early stages of rapid economic growth. Arthur Lewis puts it quite strongly: "Industrial revolutions and agrarian revolutions always go together . . . economies in which agriculture is stagnant do not show industrial development." (Lewis, 1954, p. 433).

The reason for this seeming paradox is that rapid agricultural transformation and productivity gains are needed in order for a sustainable surplus to be generated for investment in the industrial sector. Trying to squeeze a surplus from an agricultural sector that is stagnant will be unsustainable and result in further stagnation and decay of the economy.

Viewed in this light, there is no contradiction between the need for rapid agricultural growth and the decline in importance of agriculture over time. However, this seeming paradox can be easily misconstrued to imply that agricultural development and the implementation of proper policies in the sector is less important than attention to other sectors, such as industry. Nothing could be further from the truth. As we shall see, one of the features of the successful development of the newly industrialized economies (NIEs) and the Southeast Asian economies has been the strength and dynamism of agriculture.

4.3 AGRICULTURAL TRANSFORMATION IN ASIA

In Asia, the strong relationship between sectoral and overall growth is borne out by evidence from the postwar period. At the beginning of the postwar era, all the economies in Asia were primarily dependent on agriculture. Typically, between 70 and 80 percent of the labor force was employed in agriculture and more than half of value-added was created by the sector. Table 4.1 shows the employment share of the major sectors from 1955 to 1998 for Taiwan. As can be seen, agriculture absorbed the majority of the Taiwanese workforce in the early years. This share gradually diminished over time to as low as less than 10 percent in recent times. In the meantime, the employment share of industry and services sectors gradually assumed a dominant status in the forty-three-year period.

The sectoral share of employment in other selected Asian economies is presented in Figure 4.1, which shows a similar pattern of structural change (see also Table 2.1 in Chapter 2). Furthermore, Southeast and East Asia had both high rates of economic growth and agricultural growth in the last three decades, while the countries in South Asia had lower rates of growth both in agriculture and in GDP. Part of this rapid growth in both agriculture and the overall economy has to do with the initial conditions that prevailed in these countries in the 1970s. In this period, when many of the Asian economies were in the early stages of industrialization, they were fortunate enough to have had high growth rates in both agriculture and GDP. All the future "miracle" economies were in the high growth and high agricultural growth group of countries compiled by the World Bank in 1982. This table is partially reproduced as Table 4.2. It also shows that most of the countries in South Asia were in a lower group for both categories.

There are, however, a few exceptions to these generalizations. Some countries, such as Indonesia and Malaysia, did not have to rely exclusively on primary products as they had large mineral exports. In addition, Korea was able to augment local saving with large amounts of foreign borrowing. Singapore and Hong Kong, being city-states, did not have any agricultural sectors to speak of. Their growth was spurred by the entrepôt function as trading centers and by labor-intensive manufacturing in Hong Kong, and a combination of labor-intensive manufacturing and minerals processing in Singapore.

Nevertheless, apart from these exceptions, none of the Asian countries would have been able to sustain rapid growth for very long without a vibrant agricultural sector. Furthermore, as the

Table 4.1 Sectoral Distribution of GDP Employment as Percent of Labor Force, Taiwan, 1955–1998

	1955	1960	1965	1970	1975	1980	1985	1990	1995	1998
Agriculture	53.6	50.2	46.5	36.7	30.4	19.5	17.5	12.8	10.5	8.8
Industry	18.0	20.5	22.3	28.0	34.9	42.5	41.6	40.8	38.7	37.9
Services	28.4	29.3	31.2	35.3	34.7	38.0	41.0	46.3	50.7	53.2

SOURCE: *Taiwan Statistical Data Book*, various years.

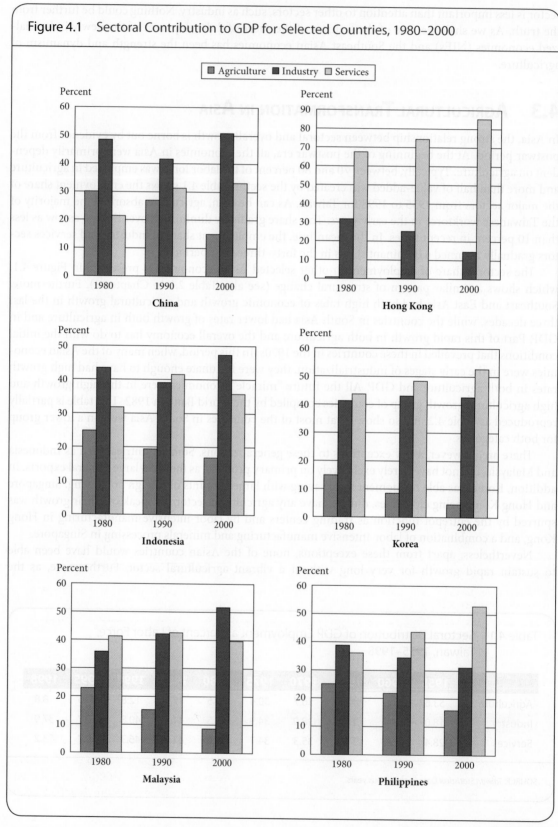

Figure 4.1   Sectoral Contribution to GDP for Selected Countries, 1980–2000

(*continued*)

Figure 4.1 (*continued*)

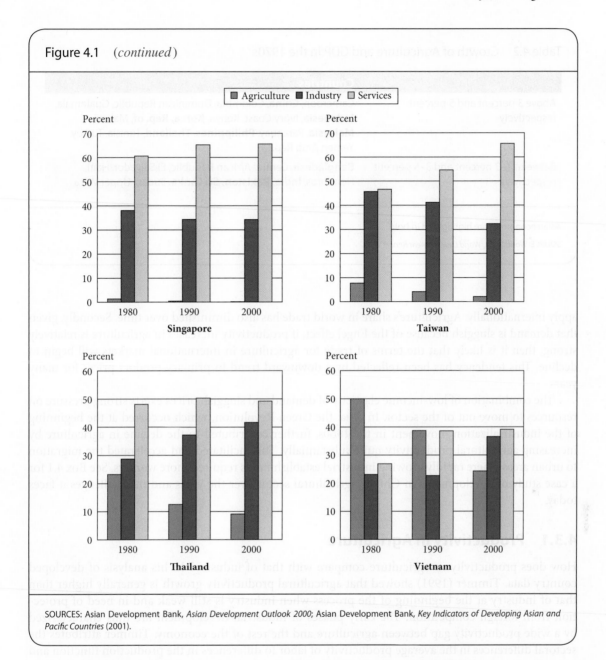

SOURCES: Asian Development Bank, *Asian Development Outlook 2000*; Asian Development Bank, *Key Indicators of Developing Asian and Pacific Countries* (2001).

industrialization drive began to accelerate further, a viable and prosperous rural sector served as a market for industrial goods that augmented urban and overseas demand. As a result, industries continued to prosper during the import-substitution phase until they were more mature and ready to compete in external markets (see Timmer, 1991; and Tomich et al., 1995).

The tendency for agriculture's share of income to fall can also be explained by two additional and powerful effects. First, there is a low-income elasticity of demand for agricultural products, often called *Engel's law*. As income increases, a smaller proportion of this increase in income is spent on agricultural products. Since demand grows slowly, the sector lags behind the rest of the economy. This decreasing domestic demand is unlikely to be made up by foreign trade growth because the Engel effect also

Table 4.2   Growth of Agriculture and GDP in the 1970s

	Countries
Above 3 percent and 5 percent respectively	Cameroon, **China**, Colombia, Dominican Republic, Guatamala, **Indonesia**, Ivory Coast, Kenya, **Korea, Rep. of**, Malawi, **Malaysia**, Paraguay, **Philippines**, **Thailand**, Tunisia, Turkey, Yemen Arab Rep.
Between 1–3 percent and 3–5 percent respectively	**Bangladesh**, Central African Republic, El Salvador, Haiti, Hondorus, **India, Pakistan, Sri Lanka**, Sudan, Upper Volta

Asian economies are highlighted in bold.

SOURCE: World Bank, *World Development Report 1982*.

apply internationally. Agriculture's share in world trade has also diminished over time. Secondly, given that demand is sluggish because of the Engel effect, if productivity increases in agriculture is relatively strong, then it is likely that the terms of trade for agriculture in international markets will begin to decline. This tendency has been reflected by a downward trend in primary product prices for many years.

The combination of low-income elasticity of demand and sluggish prices exerts strong pressure on resources to move out of the sector. In Asia, the Green Revolution, which occurred at the beginning of the industrialization movement in the 1960s, further contributed to the decline in agriculture by increasing agricultural productivity quite substantially. This facilitated and accelerated the migration to urban areas where rapidly growing industrial establishments required more workers. See Box 4.1 for a case study of developments in China's agricultural sector over the years and the challenges it faces today.

4.3.1   Productivity in Agriculture

How does productivity in agriculture compare with that of industry? In his analysis of developed country data, Timmer (1991) showed that agricultural productivity growth is generally higher than that of industry at the beginning of the process when industry is still weak and in need of protection from foreign competition. The early phases of industrial development are thus characterized by a wide productivity gap between agriculture and the rest of the economy. Timmer attributes the sectoral differences in the average productivity of labor to differences in the production function and technological change. More importantly, however, he points out that such differences may also arise from the low mobility of resources, a condition that underlies the persistence of a disequilibrium state, such as surplus labor in agriculture and other low productivity activities, including handicrafts and services. It is the surplus from this increase in profitability of agriculture that serves to fuel the beginning of the industrialization process. Often, in countries where there are wealthy landlords, such as in the Philippines, this agricultural surplus is also the source of a burgeoning industrial empire, as entrepreneurs make the switch from agricultural processing to manufacturing. However, because of the rapid growth and dynamism of the industrial sectors, this was not necessarily true in Asia in the 1960s and 1970s (see Table 4.3). In all cases but India, the rate of productivity gain in agriculture was still extremely high.

BOX 4.1

Agricultural Transformation in China

The agricultural sector in China is significant because it currently employs around 60 percent[1] of the domestic workforce and feeds 25 percent of the world population. Growth in the agricultural sector in China started to speed up with the implementation of various agricultural reforms in the late 1970s. This was done in a bid to improve the standards of living in China, where 60 percent of its citizens, especially those in the rural areas, were living below the poverty line then. The higher prices for government purchases of agricultural products led to an exacerbation of agricultural production and incomes. Further relaxation of government regulations on permitted food production (previously farmers had to concentrate on grain production) allowed farmers to diversify into the production of other food crops, such as sugarcane, vegetables and fruits, and this greatly enhanced the overall efficiency of food production in China, especially in regions which did not favor grain production. The rise in productivity and incomes in the agricultural sector subsequently served as a catalyst to accelerate domestic demand, thereby further stimulating production in the manufacturing and service sectors, and improving overall GDP and standards of living. Recent estimates of the population living below the poverty level show a drop to 10 percent (Central Intelligence Agency, 2002).

However, owing to rising industrialization, agriculture's share of GDP shrank to 15 percent in 2000 from 30 percent in 1980 (see Figure 4.1). Structural changes in agrarian production have also taken place: production of livestock and forestry has doubled, and fishery has increased fivefold, whereas production of crops has fallen from 82 percent to 56 percent (see Box Table 4.1). Increasing emphasis has been placed on the production of labor-intensive commodities, such as livestock, coffee, tea, and dairy products rather than land-intensive commodities. Thus, it is highly likely that China enjoys a comparative advantage in the former since it has a large source of labor but significantly less arable land.

Challenges arising from China's entry into the World Trade Organization (WTO) in 2001 include how to increase productivity and remain competitive in the face of rising competition from foreign agricultural producers,

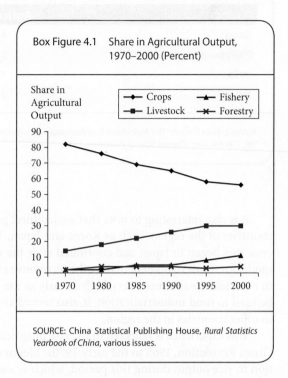

Box Figure 4.1   Share in Agricultural Output, 1970–2000 (Percent)

SOURCE: China Statistical Publishing House, *Rural Statistics Yearbook of China*, various issues.

both in the domestic and international arena, as well as higher than world-averages in domestic production costs and retail prices (see Chapter 11, section 11.3.3 for greater details on how China has dealt with globalization). The stipulated lowering of agricultural tariffs to 17 percent by 2004 also significantly reduced the degree of protection for China's less comparatively advantaged agricultural commodities, for example, soybean. Previously, soybeans had been protected by import licenses and a 114 percent import tariff rate (in 2000). Rising unemployment from foreign competition and sector unemployment is another issue to be dealt with.

Hence, measures undertaken by China's agricultural sector include greater development and adoption of high-technology techniques—particularly through biotechnology development and genetically modified (GM) crops—and implementation of farm product processing to slash costs and increase productivity.

SOURCES: Energy Information Administration (2002); Food and Agriculture Organization (2002).

---

[1] The figure includes the forestry sector.

Table 4.3   Annual Labor Productivity Growth Rates, 1960–1980

	Agriculture	Manufacturing
Korea	4.0%	7.5%
Philippines	3.2	3.5
India	1.3	2.1
Japan	5.3	5.7

SOURCE: Peter Timmer, "The Agricultural Transformation," in Hollis Chenery and T. N. Srinivasan, eds., *Handbook of Development Economics*, Vol. 1 (Amsterdam: Elsevier Science Publishers, 1988).

It is also interesting to note that agricultural productivity growth was also very high in the richer countries of the region, such as Korea and Japan. This is one reason that the industrialization experience that began in Japan and continued after the war in East Asia, in Korea and Taiwan, served as a model for the development of the other economies in the region. Agricultural productivity, particularly in rice yields, was already very high as early as the 1950s and this helped to create a surplus that could be used to fund industrialization. It also served as a yardstick to judge the performance of agriculture in other countries in the region.

This experience is reflected in the rise in agricultural productivity in the region at the height of the Green Revolution, 1965 to the early 1970s. Mellor and Mudahar have calculated the relative contribution to rice output during this period, which is summarized in Table 4.4. It shows that for the period from 1965 to the early 1970s (a somewhat earlier period for Sri Lanka), annual growth in rice production was extremely high. Production growth rates reached 3.2 percent and 3.4 percent, respectively, in India and the Philippines, and went as high as 4.8 percent in both Indonesia and Sri Lanka. In Thailand, where new rice technology was not extensively adopted, production increases were primarily the result of additional sown area. Most of this increase in output was the result of increased yields from higher-yielding varieties and the application of additional fertilizers.[2]

This buoyancy in agriculture had a mutually reinforcing effect on industry in Asia, a synergy unique to Asia. It did not occur in other developing regions and is a key factor in explaining the rapid take-off and sustained growth of industry in the 1970s and 1980s. Strong industrialization strategies were implemented in the late 1960s and 1970s in many countries, financed in many cases by internal savings generated primarily from agriculture. The experience of Taiwan is a case in point. In other cases, such as Korea, overseas borrowing augmented these savings from agriculture.

In any case, there was a mutual reinforcing interaction between agriculture and manufacturing in Asia. Even though farm sizes in Asia were relatively small and population growth was high, agricultural productivity per hectare increased rapidly. As discussed above, this was the result of a combination of the technology associated with the Green Revolution raising output and the rapid rate of rural to urban migration that reduced population pressure in the countryside but also raised demand for agricultural products as living standards improved in the cities.

This pattern of productivity growth in agriculture is significantly different from that observed in Latin America and Africa. In both these cases, land productivity was significantly lower and, in the

---

[2] Because higher-yielding varieties require more fertilizer, it is difficult to separate the two effects.

Table 4.4 Estimated Relative Contributions to Growth in Rice Production in Selected Asian Countries at the Height of the Green Revolution, 1965–1973

| | Year[a] | Annual Growth | Percentage of Total Increased Production | | | | | |
| | | | Attributed to Land Area | | | Attributed to Yield | | |
			Irrigated Land	Rain-Fed and Upland	Total	Fertilizer[b]	Others[c]	Total
India	1965–70	3.2	19.2	5.8	25.0	47.3	27.7	75.0
Indonesia	1965–72	4.8	46.4	–6.8	39.6	25.2	35.2	60.4
Myanmar	1965–73	0.8%	35.8	–23.3	12.5	47.8	39.7	87.5
Philippines	1965–73	3.4	33.1	–7.7	25.4	44.5	30.1	74.6
Sri Lanka	1960–68	4.8	34.7	11.1	45.8	31.9	22.3	54.2
Thailand	1965–72	2.1	10.8	82.2	93.0	13.6	–6.6	7.0

[a] Five-year average centered on the years sown.
[b] One additional kilogram of nutrients (N + P_2O_5 + K_2O) is assumed to produce ten kilograms of paddy.
[c] Includes increased factor productivity resulting from new technology.

SOURCE: John W. Mellor and Mohinder S. Mudahar, "Agriculture in Economic Development: Theories, Findings and Challenges in an Asian Context," in R. Martin Lee, ed., *A Survey of Agricultural Economics Literature: Agriculture in Economic Development*, Vol. 4 (Minneapolis: University of Minnesota Press, 1992).

case of Africa, labor productivity actually fell during the 1970s and early 1980s. The regional trends in agricultural productivity can be seen by comparing the indices of per-capita food production over time between the developing regions (see Figure 4.2). The growth in per-capita food production in Latin America and in the Near East fluctuated within the 10 percent range. The African experience, meanwhile, shows that per-capita food production steadily declined in the last twenty years. This sharp decline suggests that the region as a whole was becoming more underdeveloped. Factors that were seen to contribute to this decline in per-capita food production include insufficient and inappropriate innovation, cultivation of marginal and sensitive lands, severe environmental degradation, sporadic civil wars, and misguided (incentive-reducing) pricing and marketing policies. All these were exacerbated by the highest rate of population growth in the world!

In contrast, the growth of per-capita food production in Asia shows a steady increase over time, by nearly 40 percent by the end of the period. The largest increments were achieved in the late 1980s and early 1990s. Clearly, this difference in the performance of agriculture is a key link in the chain of developments that resulted in the astounding economic success of the Asian region.

4.3.2 Agricultural Development in Monsoon Asia

The nature of the weather cycle in Asian agriculture requires some adjustments to the model of interaction between agriculture and industry as proposed under the LFR model. As to be discussed in Chapter 5, the LFR model suggests that the opportunity cost of labor shifting from agriculture to industry was zero. This did not necessarily hold true for Asia. Let us see why.

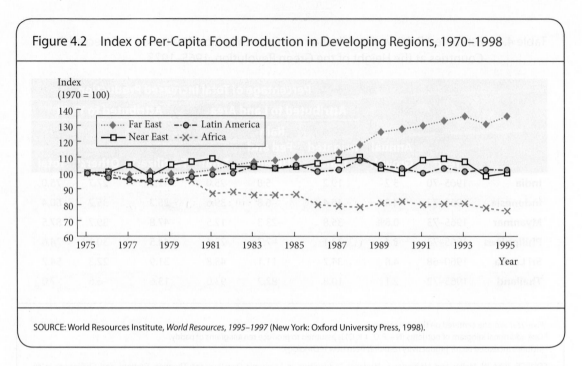

Figure 4.2   Index of Per-Capita Food Production in Developing Regions, 1970–1998

SOURCE: World Resources Institute, *World Resources, 1995–1997* (New York: Oxford University Press, 1998).

Asia receives much more rain on average than other regions of the world and also much greater yearly variation in the level of rainfall. In much of Asia, the monsoon nature of the weather cycle led to reliance on rice production, which is well adapted to growing where there are large amounts of rainfall and flooding. Rice yields per hectare are much higher than for other grains, and it requires more intensive use of manpower. This is the major reason that population densities are much higher in many parts of Asia. At the beginning of the postwar period, traditional farming methods were generally employed to cultivate local long-stalk varieties. Farms were small and planting and harvesting highly labor-intensive, but only during certain months of the year. Rain-fed conditions were the norm. Plantation agriculture was practiced in parts of Indonesia, Thailand, the Philippines, and more heavily in Malaysia. Coconut was the main tree crop in the Philippines while rubber plantations spread in Malaysia, Thailand, and Indonesia. Oil palms were also grown in plantations in Malaysia, beginning in the 1970s. There was also some cultivation of secondary food crops and horticulture. Yet, rice was the staple food crop and much of the land and labor were devoted to its cultivation in most of Southeast Asia.

Because of the seasonal nature of the demand for labor, peasants looked for off-farm employment during the dry or slack season and also during the growing season between planting and harvesting. There were few opportunities to supplement their incomes by growing secondary crops, and multiple cropping was limited because of the lack of irrigation. As a result of the intermittent nature of workforce availability, the industries that developed in the rural areas were also small and labor-intensive. Asian villages were densely populated and surrounded by many small family farms. These farms were complemented by small and flexible labor-intensive workshops and factories, often employing women as well as men.

This was the typical situation in peasant agriculture at the beginning of the postwar era. Farms were small, population densities high, and labor requirements in agriculture were extremely heavy during the planting and harvesting seasons. There was literally no scope for increasing agricultural productivity within the limitations of traditional farming technology. The intermittent nature of the demand for labor in rice planting and harvesting meant that there was no easy way that the industrial sector could grow by attracting full-time surplus labor from the farm. The opportunity cost of this labor was high, particularly during the planting and harvesting season. The opportunity cost was not zero as is suggested by the LFR model.

How then did the shift from agriculture to industry take place in Asia? The two keys were irrigation and higher-yielding varieties. More extensive irrigation helped to regulate the level of water in the fields and also allowed farmers to plant two or three crops with a concomitant increase in income with the same number of workers. The higher-yielding rice varieties were designed for a more stable water level, having a shorter stem and more fruit per plant, and were therefore more suitable for irrigated land. These two developments resulted in a dramatic increase in agricultural productivity in the 1960s and 1970s.

The agricultural surplus was important for two reasons. It gave farmers more income to buy consumer goods and it permitted some workers to migrate to the cities to work in newly established industries without diminishing overall agricultural output. The added income also allowed for the adoption of more labor-saving harvesting and cultivation techniques apart from the improved harvests resulting from a lower level of water in the fields and a less fragile fruit (see Oshima, 1995).

4.3.3   The Efficiency of Traditional Agriculture

The techniques used in traditional agriculture go back hundreds, sometimes thousands of years. In India, for example, peasant farmers have adapted and refined their methods of cultivation, crop rotation, water use, and the use of farm animals to take into account differences in soil fertility, variations in weather factors, and the availability and quality of traditional seeds and other varieties. Given this long history of trial and error, it would appear, *a priori*, that many improvements in economic efficiency made recently in traditional agriculture could not have occurred without some change in technology or improvement in irrigation.

Does the evidence support this view? To a considerable extent it does. Similar conclusions have been reached by a number of studies using data collected from individual farms. Three different techniques have been used in the studies. One group of studies first fitted a Cobb–Douglas production function and then compared the marginal value of products using different factors. If these marginal products were close to equal, then resources were allocated efficiently.

The results of these studies, primarily based on Indian data, suggest that variable factors of production are allocated efficiently, but that the fixed factor, work animals—water buffaloes or bullocks—were not. This is essentially because of the lack of economies of scale. Greater efficiency could be attained if bullocks were shared among farmers, or if the farm size was large enough to effectively utilize these work animals. There are, however, practical difficulties with implementing this sort of arrangement. First, if work animals were "shared," there is a tendency to overwork them—with the cost borne by the owner. Secondly, the need to use work animals tends to coincide across farms—making sharing a difficult matter to put into practice.

A second set of econometric studies concluded that all resources were allocated efficiently, while a third set of studies based on a linear programming model for the state of Maharastra in India concluded that there were inefficiencies since potential output (as calculated from the model) was higher than actual output. The inference from this set of studies was that inefficiencies could be removed by improving cropping patterns.

The tentative conclusion that can be drawn from this review is that traditional agriculture is reasonably efficient, although some minor improvements could be made (see Mellor and Mudahar, 1992). However, it must be recognized that most of these studies were conducted based on data from farms in India. Furthermore, the results are sensitive to the method used for measuring economic efficiency.

Nevertheless, despite the potential for improving traditional agriculture, the thrust of development and the gains in productivity in the years since World War II have been in adopting modern farm technology. In the next section, we explore these developments more carefully.

4.3.4   Why Do Peasant Farmers Resist Innovation and Modernization?

An increase in the production capacities and output levels of farmers bring about improved income levels and higher standards of living. Studies have shown that various innovative approaches to farming and great improvements in technology are the key elements to these increases in productivity.

There is one major obstacle that constantly faces those who introduce new farming techniques and modern technology into a traditional agrarian society and that is the apparent resistance to employ new production methods by most peasant farmers. Economic analysts find this behavior perplexing and many even label it as "irrational." Rational behavior is not consistent with these farmers' response to technology because basic economic analysis says that producers will choose the production method that will increase output for a given cost, or lower cost for a given level of output. Surely, it is said, this "conservative" and "backward" attitude throws away an "obvious" economic opportunity to improve living standards.

There are, however, perfectly justifiable explanations for this seeming irrationality. First, we note that subsistence farming is the main economic activity for about 80 percent of the rural sector in developing countries. Traditional farming systems in many societies define the role of individuals in the family. The fathers and eldest sons prepare the field for planting; the mothers and eldest daughters prepare food each day and take them to the field where the male family members are working. The women help in planting the rice seedlings, other family members tend smaller plots for vegetables, and still others are tasked to tend the animals. All family members interact and socialize in the process. In such a scenario, the adoption of new technology or new varieties of seeds would not just increase yield. It could also be seen as a mechanism for altering the way of life for many rural families. The pattern and timing of the usual tasks would change, as well as individual roles and ways of relating to other family members and the community.

A second important factor for the resistance by peasant farmers to innovation in farming is the fact that change may be accompanied by uncertainty. Even if farmers have been assured of a strong probability of achieving higher yields, they will continue to ask: "What if it fails?" This question assumes greater importance to subsistence farmers (compared with those that are relatively better off) because failure of the new technique or new seed variety can have disastrous consequences. It can mean having two instead of three meals a day; it can mean pulling a child out of school to "serve" in the landlord's house as a servant; it can mean that the farmer may not have access to seeds for the next season's round of crops. Subsistence agriculture is thus a highly risky and uncertain venture because human lives and people's futures are at stake. In such circumstances where threats of starvation are real, the main objective of the farmer is not to maximize income, but to maximize his family's chances of survival. Accordingly, when risk and uncertainty are high, a small farmer may be very reluctant to shift from traditional technology and crop pattern that has served him well over the years, that he has come to know and understand, to a new one that promises higher yields but may entail greater risks of crop failure. Given these circumstances, farmers will consider carefully the move to a better and higher-yielding technology only after seeing whether it has worked for other farms in the same vicinity, and after he is convinced that the risk is worth the change.

An associated issue in this regard is the inadequate insurance and credit markets which could serve as fall-back institutions or mechanisms in the event of crop failure. Any program to raise agricultural productivity among small farmers must incorporate a risk minimization objective through the institution of such commercial markets that can be easily accessed by these farmers.

Moreover, in many parts of Asia and Latin America, the structure of the agrarian sector (including the distribution of land, ownership systems, and so forth) has contributed to the overall low productivity of agriculture. A survey of farmers revealed that disincentives to increasing productivity by adopting new varieties included such reasons as: (1) the landlord secured all the gain, (2) the money lender captured all the profits, (3) the government guaranteed "price" was never paid, or (4) complementary inputs (fertilizers, pesticides, assured supply of water, adequate non-usurious credit, and others) was never made available.

4.4 THE MICROECONOMICS OF AGRICULTURE IN ASIA

Looking at the decision-making process at the farm level, the aim is to translate the inputs of land, labor, fertilizer, pesticides, irrigation, and mechanization into higher levels of output. This process will depend upon the size of the holding and the fertility of the soil, weather conditions, susceptibility to flooding and/or drought, potential for natural disasters, land tenure arrangements, availability of storage and marketing, transfer of technology through an agricultural extension system, and so on. The list is not endless, but very long.

What can we make of all this in terms of generalizing the performance of agriculture in Asia? This is not a book about agriculture and so we must be brief. By focusing on what worked to raise yields in Asian agriculture, we can shorten the list considerably. These developments were achieved either by taking advances in agriculture that had been developed in the industrial countries during their agricultural transition (cropping patterns, water use/irrigation, fertilizers, and pesticides) or applying the fruits of agricultural research and development to the Asian region. For simplicity, this array of possible measures comes under two broad groups: what worked and what did not.

4.4.1 What Worked?

In this section, we look at three aspects of modern agriculture that have served to increase agricultural productivity, both in output per unit of land area and per worker. These are, firstly, the use of improved varieties (Green Revolution), secondly, the extension of irrigation and the resulting double-cropping that took place, and finally, the use of fertilizers, pesticides, and herbicides.

GREEN REVOLUTION   In Asia, the Green Revolution, as it has come to be called, was the phenomena created by the development of new higher-yielding varieties of rice at the International Rice Research Institute, located in Los Banos, near Manila, in the Philippines. These new rice varieties were mimicked by the development of high-yielding varieties at a similar research laboratory in Mexico. The advances made in wheat cultivation were adapted to a lesser extent, because wheat is heavily grown only in the more temperate areas of Asia. The results of the Green Revolution on rice production are evident from the research conducted by Mellor and Mudahar (see Table 4.4). This study broke down rice production growth into several components, including area effects from greater irrigation, and yield effects from fertilizer and new technology. Yields accounted for the lion's share of increased productivity—88 percent in Myanmar, 75 percent in India and the Philippines, and more than 50 percent in Sri Lanka and Indonesia. Only in Thailand, where most of the increase came from an extension in planted area resulting from the clearing of the rainforest, did area planted dominate output gains. This method of increasing output was not sustainable in the long run.

These results of this research have been supported by a number of other studies, which also pointed to the importance of education in implementing the new technology. Education, even at the primary level, was important if these new developments were to be adopted, since they were somewhat more complex than farming with traditional varieties. The proper application of fertilizers, pesticides, and water/irrigation were critical in order to obtain improved yields.

Some observers have argued that the Green Revolution helped rich farmers with extensive land holdings more than small farmers. Hayami and Ruttan (1985, p. 337) argue that this is not true. They cite a number of studies that indicate that there is no evidence that farm size or farm tenure proved a serious constraint to the adoption of high-yielding varieties. They also show that large farmers did not necessarily make more efficient use of these modern varieties. Furthermore, the use of modern varieties did not promote mechanization or reduce employment and earnings. Instead, earnings and employment increased. In addition, for developing countries with large and growing labor forces, small farms were generally more efficient than large farms because the opportunity cost of labor was so low.

APPLICATION OF FERTILIZERS, PESTICIDES, AND HERBICIDES   Table 4.4 demonstrates the complementary importance of fertilizers as they were used in combination with the introduction of new varieties. Fertilizers were most profitable when used with new varieties and appropriate levels of irrigation. Mellor and Mudahar (1992, p. 354) state that the:

> increased use of fertilizer has been the single most important indicator of technological change in agriculture. It reflects increases in irrigation and the development of new crop varieties, since they raise the productivity and profitability of greater quantities of fertilizer.

Although very powerful in many instances, the yield effect of fertilizers was by no means uniform. With rice, for example, it appears to be more effective in the dry season because of greater solar exposure and less damage from weather and pests. Furthermore, field research and evidence gathered on the price elasticity of demand for fertilizers suggests that many farmers use less than the optimal amount. This could arise for a number of reasons, including lack of understanding of the relationship between fertilizer application and yield, supply bottlenecks because of breakdowns in the marketing and distribution channels, lack of proper application of the appropriate combination of fertilizer ingredients, or simply because farmers lacked the money to buy enough fertilizers during the growing season.

Studies of relative yields on small versus large holdings suggest that the income constraint was probably the most binding on small farmers. They also show that fertilizer application was lower than optimal on small plots where farmers were likely to have lower incomes and were unable to buy enough fertilizer to make the optimal application. See also Section 4.6.2 for a further discussion of the income distribution implications of fertilizer use.

IRRIGATION   Assessing the importance of irrigation is complicated by a number of factors. It is true that better irrigation and water management have contributed significantly to agricultural development in Asia by allowing farmers to increase productivity through regulating the flow of water and reducing the risk of flooding. It also introduces flexibility into the cropping system by facilitating the application of fertilizers, allowing farmers to introduce multiple cropping and higher-profit cash crops. From Table 4.4, we observe that in three of the six countries surveyed, irrigation contributed more than 30 percent to increased production. There is also evidence that the spread of irrigation has been reasonably neutral with respect to farm size. However, there are diminishing returns to large-scale irrigation, particularly when the main large-scale schemes have been completed. There is also a growing awareness of environmental and resettlement problems associated with large projects, such as the Three Gorges Project in China (see, for example, *The Economist*, November 1999).

Over the years, the scope for developing large irrigation projects has narrowed. In addition, an analysis of environmental issues and the resettlement of those displaced by these projects suggest that the costs may have been underestimated. As a result, current thinking among resource economists is that future irrigation efforts may best be applied to increasing productivity in rain-fed areas, small and tube-well irrigation, and the rehabilitation and upgrading of infrastructure. A related issue is water pricing. There is growing evidence in Pakistan and parts of India that underpriced water has resulted in growing soil salinity and water logging. This has reduced yields and required additional expenditures to provide drainage to avoid these problems in future.

4.4.2   What Factors Have Not Helped Much?

FARM SIZE   In traditional agriculture, it has been widely observed that there is an inverse relationship between farm size and overall farm productivity. However, does this mean that land reform, which has been recommended on equity grounds, will also result in greater economic efficiency by raising productivity? Studies that have accounted for other factors, such as farming intensity, land quality, and the use of irrigation, suggest that this inverse effect disappears when other factors are held constant. Small farms tend to be cropped more intensely with higher levels of irrigation.

The inverse relationship between farm size and productivity also tends to break down when modern technologies are introduced. The requirement for supplementary inputs such as fertilizer, pest control, and irrigation are much more important when modern technologies are used. Since small farmers tend to have more binding budget constraints than large farmers, they are unable to fully utilize these supplementary inputs to increase productivity.

It is also more difficult to substitute labor for other inputs in a modern technology setting—and more intensive use of the land is one of the strong reasons why an inverse relationship between farm size and productivity can exist.

Taking all these factors into account, we can conclude that as incomes increase it is less likely that small farms will maintain their efficiency advantage over large farms.

CHANGES IN LAND TENURE   There are a number of issues relating to *land tenure*. Let us consider the major forms of land tenure and land use in agriculture. First, there are owner-operated farms. These farms can vary dramatically in size and in the use of technology. Large farms in Asia typically grow plantation crops such as coconuts, rubber, oil palm, tea, and sometimes sugar. Large farms cultivate using hired labor, whereas smaller "family" farms are mainly or solely dependent on family labor. Secondly, farms can be operated under tenancy arrangements. There are two kinds of tenancy arrangements: (1) the tenant gives a proportion of the output to the landlord and, (2) land is rented to the tenant for a fixed fee.

In countries where land distribution is highly unequal, it is often argued that land redistribution should be carried out on equity grounds. In Asia, the distribution of land varies widely. In East Asia, land distribution is fairly even while in South Asia, much of the land is still held by a small proportion of the population.

The historical experience of land redistribution schemes in Asia subsequent to the general redistribution of land in Japan, Korea, and Taiwan in the 1940s and early 1950s, is limited. Programs in the Philippines, for example, had limited success and very few land redistribution schemes have been tried in other countries.

Therefore, research and policy regarding land tenure have focused on the redistribution of land to tenants and/or the establishment of firmer legal grounds for tenancy, including the sale of rights and the passing of tenancy rights to future generations. There are two parts to the argument for strengthening tenancy or converting tenancy to ownership. The latter argument is made on equity grounds, while the former has to do with efficiency.

With regard to efficiency, we first have to study the evidence on the efficiency of owner occupancy versus tenancy arrangements. A number of studies conducted have shown strong evidence that share tenancy is more typical in traditional agriculture, where production is highly labor-intensive and tenancy is a way to keep a store of labor on hand, and also to share the risk. With modernization and the introduction of farm machinery, landowners may begin to cultivate the entire area themselves. At the end of the day, the evidence for the relative efficiency of tenancy or ownership occupancy is mixed. For example, after an extensive review of these studies, Mellor and Mudahar (1992, p. 367) conclude that "The empirical evidence on the efficiency of share tenancy remains inconclusive."

Strengthening tenancy rights, including the sale of these rights, is also an option to be considered. In locations where out-migration to urban areas is high, establishing tenancy rights for squatters and generally strengthening land-use rights serve as an incentive to take marginal lands out of production when job opportunities open up in the urban areas. This helps to improve land use, although it may reduce total agricultural output.

Apart from some legislation that has improved tenure rights and hence land use, the overall conclusion drawn from the above discussion is that land reform has made a minor contribution to the increase in agricultural productivity in the postwar era in Asia.

4.5 MACROECONOMIC ASPECTS OF AGRICULTURAL DEVELOPMENT

The exact nature of the process of rising productivity in agriculture has many facets and varies from country to country. However, several features are common to most countries. In this section, we focus on these macroeconomic policies.

The first thing to recognize when considering macroeconomic policies is that agriculture in Asia is primarily intensive rather than extensive. Therefore, it is important to employ appropriate labor-intensive technology. As labor moves from the rural areas to the cities and incomes grow, the introduction of more extensive capital-intensive technologies could be introduced. Nevertheless, throughout most of the postwar period and particularly at the beginning phases of industrialization, it was important to keep the currency exchange rate at an appropriate level to discourage inappropriate use of capital for technology.

A bonus from exchange rate regimes that tended to undervalue the currency was that the terms of trade for agriculture (with industry) also improved. This was because agricultural products were, in a very real sense, more tradable than industrial goods, which were often more protected than agriculture in the early stages of development.

Thus, the benefits of having an undervalued (as opposed to an overvalued) exchange rate were twofold. It helped agriculture to maintain appropriate terms of trade with industry so that it was not discriminated against, and to promote appropriate labor-intensive production technology.

However, in the beginning of the postwar era this kind of exchange rate policy was not in vogue. Exchange rates were overvalued to keep down the cost of capital imports required for industrial development. This turned out to be counterproductive for a number of reasons. It reinforced import-substitution strategies rather than export promotion. It also created a bias toward capital-intensive industrial development that was not in line with the comparative advantage of the developing countries.

In Asia, import-substitution policies were abandoned quite early and stress was put on export promotion and developing competitiveness in exports. This led to the adoption of exchange rate regimes that were at the same time beneficial to exports and to the continued viability of the rural sector through the terms of trade effect.

Another sometimes forgotten aspect of macroeconomic policy is that interventions designed to protect an industry or a sector or a factor of production usually have unintended and often adverse impacts. Thus, a more general equilibrium approach is often needed to assess the overall impact of macroeconomic or sectoral policies. This is mentioned here because agriculture has often been the victim of such policies. (See Box 4.2 on the Philippine experience.)

BOX 4.2

Philippines' Agricultural Growth and Sector Policies

During the 1970s, agricultural output rose rapidly in the Philippines. Exports grew rapidly following the liberalization of exports and subsequent price increases. Both acreage and yields grew, particularly for rice. Investment in irrigation resulted in a significant increase in double cropping and the development of modern varieties, which thus led to higher yields for rice. During this period, government intervention in commodity markets intensified. The sugar trade was nationalized and a coconut fund was established to promote new investment and stabilize prices. They did not succeed as the funds were diverted from the farmers to the managers of these funds, thus widening the spread between farm gate and world prices.

Subsequently, growth in agricultural output slowed as farm gate prices languished, worsened by the sharp decline in commodity prices following the first oil shock and then the second oil shock a few years later. To make matters worse, export taxes were imposed in 1973 and 1975, ostensibly to stabilize prices but they succeeded only in depressing the income of the sector further. By the late 1970s, the Philippine economy was facing a serious crisis as there was inadequate growth in the industrial sector, forcing new entrants into the labor force to seek employment in the rural sector where productivity was not increasing. As a result, unemployment escalated, putting additional downward pressure on wages. Poverty increased. This crisis induced the government to make changes in the early 1980s but the damage to agriculture had already been done.

SOURCE: Yujiro Hayami and Vernon W. Ruttan, *Agricultural Development: An International Perspective* (Baltimore: John Hopkins University Press, 1985), pp. 381–382.

4.6 MODERNIZING AGRICULTURE AND RURAL WELFARE: LESSONS AND POLICY ISSUES

4.6.1 Mechanization and the Demand for Labor

Demand for labor is an area that has been discussed in several parts of this book. In the agricultural sector, the main concern is when and where mechanization should be introduced. As noted earlier, in most of the developing Asian countries, agriculture is highly labor-intensive. Rice is the staple crop and it requires a significantly higher labor input than wheat, other grains, and most secondary food crops. Several studies have shown that a shift to modern varieties has increased the amount of labor input per hectare but probably decreased the amount of labor per ton of production because of yield increases. A number of studies have also focused on the impact of mechanization on labor demand, productivity, and profitability. From these studies, it can be seen that local conditions play a major role in the decision whether to mechanize or not. This decision should probably be left to market forces as long as there are no subsidies, such as the extension of credit for buying tractors, that can tilt the playing field. This conclusion also assumes that macroeconomic policy follows a neutral exchange rate policy that does not either overvalue or undervalue the exchange rate (see the following section).

4.6.2 Technological Transfer, Growth, and Equity

The introduction of new technology, be it higher-yielding varieties or new methods of crop rotation and cropping systems, or improved irrigation and fertilization, has been the major factor contributing to increased productivity in agriculture in Asia during the past fifty years. For example, the use of high-yielding varieties developed thirty years has ago brought about substantial increases in productivity for rice and wheat. This process of technological transfer must be continued if agriculture is to remain viable and dynamic.

How has this new technology affected income growth and distribution in Asia? Although modern technology has certainly increased the average per-capita income, it may have had an adverse impact on income distribution because there are several forces at work. First, studies in India, Indonesia, and Pakistan suggest that larger farmers consistently used higher levels of fertilizer and obtained higher yields. To the extent that farm size and income are highly correlated, these results suggest a negative impact of the Green Revolution on income distribution in these three countries. Other researchers have investigated the change in the production function as a result of the introduction of new varieties. They have found that most of the higher farm income derived has gone to factors of production other than labor. In another study on wheat production in the Uttar Pradesh region of India, Dixit and Singh (1970) found that only 10 percent of the increased income went to labor. It was even less in some other regions of India.

It has also been argued that after the Green Revolution, rice producers and workers involved in rice harvesting were worse off because of "immiserizing growth," that is, the Green Revolution has increased production beyond demand, thus depressing prices and reducing incomes.

This downward trend in grain prices is generally true and has led many policy advisors to suggest that resources be transferred out of grain production to other food crops, horticulture, tree crops, and aquaculture. For example, there has been a rapid growth of aquaculture production in the Philippines and Thailand in the past decade, and the share of rice in total farm output has diminished rapidly throughout the region.

It is unlikely that the growth in agriculture induced by the Green Revolution will continue in the future without changes being made to the production system and further advances in technology. Growing water shortages throughout Asia will constrain further extension of irrigation networks, as well as present challenges for maintaining or increasing agricultural productivity. Water available for irrigation and for household use has declined and is expected to drop further. Water tables have fallen as aquifers are being pumped faster than they are being recharged. This will limit its future use for irrigation and extension of double cropping, as well as put pressure on water availability, particularly during periods of drought. Urban development has also taken farmland out of production as cities continue to expand, particularly in China (see Chapter 6 for details). This combination of less water and arable land will change the balance of factors responsible for growth in yields and production. Greater reliance will have to be put on new technology and imaginative ways to price and conserve groundwater as well as make use of rainwater. Furthermore, innovative changes in tilling methods to raise production and economic efficiency will also have to be made (see Section 4.6.3).

4.6.3 Genetic Engineering

Another issue is the impact of genetic engineering. Rice still remains the most important food crop, and the sector employs the major part of the agricultural population. In recent years, rice productivity growth has declined. It is now necessary to implement ongoing technological developments that have taken place in rice and in other food crops, horticulture, and livestock. For example, in China a method of planting different rice varieties together has cut the incidence of loss from pests and increased yields dramatically (see Box 4.3). There are also more recent developments in genetic engineering that can be considered—even as there are many associated issues with its implementation. Genetically modified organisms (GMOs) are produced by transferring a gene or set of genes conveying specific desirable traits within or across species. These GMOs are controversial and have been banned in some European countries. However, this method has been widely used in Asia. Approximately 9 million smallholder farmers, mainly in China and India, have adopted an insect-resistant type of cotton (Bt) which has reduced yield losses from insects, saved on pesticides, and increased farmers' incomes. Other genetic biotechnologies based on the selection of improved charactistics

BOX 4.3

Multiple Cropping in China

It has been estimated that multiple cropping is used on one-third of cultivated arable land in China and accounted for half of the total grain yields. Besides intercropping with rice varieties, intercropping between different grain varieties have grown in popularity over the years. Instances include intercropping with wheat and maize, as well as with wheat and soybean. For instance, the former has been practiced by farmers in China's Gansu province, along the Huanghe river in Ningxia and the Inner Mongolia autonomous regions where yields can average more than 12,000 kilograms per hectare. It alone accounted for

more than 43 percent of grain yields in Ningxia in 1995. Hence, such intercropping between different crop grains has led to a favorable increase in yield.

Besides increasing crop production, intercropping is also said to be beneficial for enhancing the nutrients of the crops. For instance, iron deficiency in peanut crops, a major oilseed crop in China, which frequently occurs on calcareous soils particularly in northern China, is supposedly lessened by intercropping peanut with maize. The argument has to do with the release of phytosiderphore from maize roots, which enhances the production of iron nutrients in the peanut crops; however, direct evidence of such a phenomenon has yet to be supported.

SOURCE: Zhang Fusuo and Li Long, "Using Competitive and Facilitative Interactions in Intercropping Systems Enhances Crop Productivity and Nutrient-Use Efficiency," *Plant and Soil* 248 (2003), pp. 305–312.

through more conventional selective breeding have also resulted in better yields for millet, sweet potatoes, rice, and cattle breeding.

4.6.4 Zero Tillage

As its name suggests, zero tillage minimizes or eliminates tilling of the land and retains crop residues as ground cover. Zero tillage saves on labor and energy required to overturn the soil, conserves soil fertility, increases tolerance to drought, and reduces greenhouse gas emissions. However, it requires more weeding and the occasional use of pesticides. Zero tillage has recently been adopted in South Asia in the Indo-Gangetic plain, which stretches from northern Pakistan across India to Bangladesh, and which is fed by several rivers with headwaters in the Himalayas. It is applied in this region in a rice-and-wheat combination. Wheat is planted immediately after rice, without tillage, and the wheat seedlings germinate without irrigation, using the residual moisture from the previous rice crop. The system saves water, and reduces production costs and the incidence of weeds and pests. Rates of return are reported to be very high—as much as 50 percent or more (see World Bank, 2008, Chapter 7).

RESEARCH AND DEVELOPMENT   It has been widely documented that agricultural research and development (R&D) yields high returns in the developing countries (see World Bank, 2008, Chapter 7; and Alston, Chan-Kang, Marra, Pardey, and Wyatt, 2000). The International Food Policy Research Institute (IFPRI) in Washington, D.C., estimates that investment returns in Asia are about 50 percent but the rates of return in other regions are also high. These high payoffs suggest that agricultural research is grossly underfunded. The most important reason is that private investment in agricultural R&D is limited because the benefits cannot always be realized by those who develop them. Seeds can be reused and/or shared with others, but few technologies can be protected by intellectual property rights. Furthermore, most of the agricultural research is carried out in the industrial countries where there is little interest in developing new varieties that only the poor will pay for and benefit from. As a result, most agricultural R&D is carried out by government agencies or institutes funded by consortiums in the industrial countries, such as the Consultative Group on International Agricultural Research (CGIAR).

Recent initiatives by private–public partnerships and the work of philanthropists, including the Bill & Melinda Gates Foundation and others, have increased the amount of research funding and improved the access to research results. In addition, the use of communications technology can help to spread the results of new technology to more farmers by augmenting traditional service delivery with modern information technology, including the cell phones and the Internet.

In India, farmers get information from a variety of sources, including other farmers, input dealers, and the media (see Birner and Anderson, 2007). As the use of cell phones and the Internet spread, innovative ways to connect the rural villages to a variety of information and other useful services are being developed, including linkages by satellite. Decentralization can also help in setting up agenda network where farmers can extend appropriate assistance to one another, and for which they can relate and benefit from. For example, in India, the Agricultural Technology Management Agencies (ATMA) have set up stakeholder information networks at the district and village levels to plan and set priorities for such services. The ATMA at the district level have increasingly taken on the responsibility for the technology dissemination activities at the district level, as well as developing linkages with all line departments, research organizations, and non-governmental organizations. The World Bank estimates that farmers' incomes have increased by about 25 percent in districts where the ATMA are active (see World Bank, 2008, Chapter 7; and http://www.manage.gov.in/natp/atma.htm).

In general, markets for agricultural products function fairly well. These markets are competitive, products are relatively homogenous, and research has shown that farmers in Asia respond to changes in relative product prices by adjusting the area planted accordingly. There is often a lag in this process, however, with best-practice farmers making the quickest adjustment. An improved farm extension network is a key factor for reducing this lag. Better dissemination of new developments in seeds, crop rotation, new varieties, and so forth, can be spread easily through the extension system. Malaysia has a well-developed network of research and extension and has been very successful in developing the capacity to spread the use of new varieties and in cloning in the tree crop sector. Several agricultural research institutes in this country have developed faster growing oil palm and higher-yielding rubber trees in the past three decades. In other countries, this extension network and research need to be improved, and the delivery of needed information widened to the more backward regions of the country.

4.6.5 Food Prices and the Linkages to Energy

In the past few years, there has been increasing volatility in the prices of primary products and energy. Between 2000 and 2007, international prices of wheat more than tripled and rice nearly doubled as the price of oil skyrocketed. High demand in China and India, as well as the industrialized countries was responsible for the price acceleration in food grains, while oil demand increased in the industrial and developing countries alike. With the onset of volatility in the financial markets and the global recession in late 2007 and 2008, prices made an about turn. By the end of 2008, oil prices had fallen back to 2004 levels, and higher levels of production, together with slower demand growth, have resulted in price declines for commodities. Food prices did not fall as far although they declined by about 30 percent from their peak in the summer of 2008. This price roller-coaster aggravates uncertainty in the agricultural sector and creates a climate of increased risk aversion. Fearful of renewed increases in fuel costs and wary of further declines in commodity prices, farmers are likely to maintain the status quo, producing what they are used to and reducing investment in new technology, cropping techniques, or new varieties. This will not be good for the continued growth and vitality of the agricultural sector. Hopefully farmers will see a more stable environment once the global recession comes to an end.

4.6.6 International Trade and Resource Transfer

The relationship between the agricultural sector and international trade in agricultural products will be discussed in more detail in Chapter 6. However, a few details are relevant here. The role of agricultural exports in earning foreign exchange was very important at the beginning of the growth phase for these countries in the 1950s and 1960s. All the Asian countries were primary product exporters, including Korea and Taiwan, both of which exported rice. As development progressed, agricultural exports diminished in importance as Asia became more specialized in industrial exports. Nevertheless, Asia still accounts for a significant share of world trade in agricultural commodities. While the economies of East Asia are net food importers, Southeast and South Asia are still net food exporters.

The structure of tariffs and the level of protection of agriculture from international competition tend to vary inversely with the level of income. Japan, the European countries, and the United States have relatively high levels of protection of agricultural products compared with the developing countries. Put another way, the demand for agricultural protection increases as the share of agriculture in GDP declines and per-capita incomes increase. Such protection policies discourage structural transformation and impose large costs on consumers and taxpayers in the industrial countries through subsidies and higher prices for agricultural products. These high tariffs also harm the developing countries in that they would be able to produce and export more products if the tariffs were lower. Although the successive rounds of the General Agreement on Tariffs and Trade (GATT) and the WTO have lowered tariffs on a wide array of products, agricultural tariffs in the industrial countries remain high. To redress these imbalances, the developing countries must lobby for these tariffs to be lowered in stages. This would open the markets to more products from the developing world. The Doha Round of trade negotiations has ground to a standstill partly as a result of the failure to agree on agricultural tariffs and subsidies.

4.6.7 Shifts Out of Primary Grain Production

There has been a gradual shift in the mix of agricultural goods produced in Asia from primary food grains, such as rice, wheat, and sorghum to secondary food crops, such as livestock, tree crops, horticulture, and fishing. These shifts have occurred in line with changes in comparative advantage, relative prices, and profitability, which have encouraged the diversification of agriculture. As incomes have grown, consumers have demanded more protein and greater choice by incorporating meat, fish, and fowl in their diets. The range of agricultural products has also expanded as incomes increase and tastes become more diverse. Higher productivity in secondary food crops, aquaculture, livestock nutrition, and horticulture together with higher tree crop yields has been made possible by a combination of better technology and advances in cross breeding, scientific advances, and genetic engineering. Mixed farming where livestock and agriculture are combined is also playing a more important role (see Haan, Steinfeld, and Blackburn, 1996). The study was commissioned by the Food and Agriculture Organization of the United Nations, the U.S. Agency for International Development, and the World Bank. Climate changes that are taking place have also required adjustment in the variety of agricultural crops produced.

4.7 Summary and Conclusions

In this chapter, we learned of the important role of agriculture in economic development and how it supported industrialization, particularly in the early phases. Agriculture today continues to impact the lives of millions. Understanding the issues affecting the agricultural sector is crucial to finding ways to improve the lives of the people in the rural areas. Several points may be made with regard to population growth, migration, and the impact of new technology on productivity in the rural and agricultural sectors generally.

First, in order to raise the incomes of poor farmers, an increase in productivity is required. This is a challenge as it must be recognized that labor-intensive technological change would most benefit small farmers and landless laborers. Secondly, it is important to realize that rapid population growth and the lack of opportunities for migration and/or off-farm employment are deterrents to poverty reduction. However, if the multiplier effects of new technology on non-farm employment are strong, a major reduction in poverty can occur. Thirdly, the provision of education and the possible redistribution of assets is also important. This is discussed in more detail in Chapter 9. Finally, research and development, together with the implementation and dissemination of ways to increase agricultural yields and productivity, become more pressing as the extension of irrigation and cultivated area becomes more limited in Asia. To highlight the importance of implementing such a program of research and development, a group of IFPRI economists has mapped out several scenarios which make different assumptions about the extent of commitment to a program. In their scenarios, investment in agricultural research and knowledge play a key role. In a high investment scenario, more aggressive investments in and better management of agricultural research and knowledge would lead to significant improvements in food security and result in higher productivity and lower food prices. When combined with complementary investments in irrigation, water access, efficient water usage, better rural roads, and education for girls, even greater increases in crop yields and livestock can be achieved. Without such changes, food prices will continue to rise and agricultural productivity will stagnate (see Rosegrant et al., 2008).

REVIEW QUESTIONS

1. What are the major factors that contributed to productivity gains in agriculture in Asia in the past twenty-five years? Is the rate of growth of the agricultural sector likely to slow down or accelerate? Reflect on how these factors are likely to change in the future.

2. There has been considerable discussion of the role of mechanization in creating employment and raising labor productivity. Are there any general guidelines to follow in suggesting a mechanization policy for the Asian developing countries?

3. Consider two countries, one that subsidizes agriculture, and another that subsidizes industry. They are identical in all other respects. Which country has a better chance of achieving rapid growth with poverty reduction?

4. Why are the terms of trade between agriculture and industry so important in determining the rate of growth of an economy in the transition from focusing on agriculture to manufactured products?

5. Genetically modified crops (corn, for example) have been developed in the United States and are being exported around the world. There is, however, resistance to these exports in many countries. Why do you suppose this is so?

6. Africa seems to be locked in a cycle of producing agricultural products for export. The terms of trade for these goods continue to deteriorate, creating a downward cycle of slow or negative growth. How has Asia avoided such a cycle? What are the major factors involved?

7. You are having a discussion with another student who says that agricultural growth is not important when it comes to understanding the experience of economic development in Asia. How would you respond to this statement? What kind of evidence is there to either support or refute the student's statement? Use specific country or regional examples where possible.

8. What changes have been occurring in the structure of agriculture in Asia in the past two decades? How are these changes likely to affect the behavior of farmers?

9. Explain why research and development are much more important now than they were a few decades ago.

Notes on References and Suggestions for Further Reading

There are a few important references on the economic development of agriculture. First, the articles by Peter Timmer (1988) and the volume by Hayami and Ruttan (1985) set the stage for further discussion on the agricultural sector in Asia. Although slightly dated, the *World Development Report* of 1980 also has a good summary of the challenges facing agricultural development.

For Asian agriculture, the book by Oshima (1995) and the article by Mellor and Mudahar (1992) are essential references. The issues of the sector are well laid out, and Oshima discusses with precision and clarity the foundations of monsoon agriculture that pervades much of Southeast Asia. The *World Development Report 2008* is a useful review of global developments in agriculture.

Industrialization and Structural Change

5.1 INTRODUCTION: INDUSTRY AS A LEADING SECTOR

The main structural development that separates a modern high-income economy from a traditional low-income economy is the rapid development of the industrial sector. Broadly speaking, in the early stages of development, the industrial sector comprises anything that is not agricultural in nature. It includes all non-agricultural products. This process of industrialization has been very dramatic in many developing countries and accounts for much of the dynamism of the East Asian "miracle" countries and selected rapidly growing economies in Latin America. As a matter of interest, large countries are likely to have a larger share of income generated by the industrial sector because of economies of scale. Furthermore, higher income per capita is closely associated with a higher level of industrialization if we look at a broad range of developed and developing countries. There are exceptions, such as Australia and New Zealand, which developed specialization in minerals and agricultural products respectively. There is also the case of India, which has a large industrial sector but which is still quite poor.

5.2 A MODEL OF STRUCTURAL CHANGE

The Jamaican economist and Nobel Prize winner, W. Arthur Lewis (1954) developed the first two-sector model which attempted to capture the interaction between a traditional agricultural sector and a modern industrial sector for a developing economy. John Fei and Gustav Ranis (1964) built upon his work a decade later. The model they developed is therefore often called the Lewis–Fei–Ranis (LFR) model. This model has two sectors which can be defined as traditional and modern, agricultural and industrial, or rural and urban. These are rather fuzzy definitions and we can expect overlaps between different definitions. For example, there may be traditional characteristics in the informal sector of the urban economy. Or there may be modern agricultural processing industries in the countryside. The essence of the model is to contrast traditional agricultural methods and rural social organization, which revolves around family enterprises, with the modern industrial sector where workers earn wages and industrial goods are produced.

5.2.1   What are the Features of this Model?

First of all, capital accumulation fuels the development of the industrial sector. It grows faster as capital accumulates. There is assumed to be surplus labor in the rural/agriculture sector. The supply of this labor is virtually unlimited. Its opportunity cost is virtually zero. When it is removed from the rural sector, the output of the sector does not change at all, or very little. This would occur when there is high population density in the rural areas and when family farming is widespread. Family farms do not hire labor (and pay them the value of their marginal product). They operate on different principles. Everyone shares in the output, so that workers are essentially paid the value of their average product.

By removing excess labor from the traditional sector and moving it to the industrial sector, the productivity of labor increases. Furthermore, the productivity of those remaining in the rural sector also improves since there are fewer workers—the surplus workers have been removed.

The LFR model assumes a particular kind of social organization in the agricultural sector, which is traditional in nature, and also that the marginal product of the last workers is zero. There are a few ways we can test this theory. We can look at the evidence. There have been sustained movements from the rural to the urban economy in most developing countries. The productivity in agriculture has increased in these cases. It could be because of technology; certainly *prima facia* evidence suggests that there is some validity. The mere fact that lots of workers did migrate and continue to migrate is also evidence in support of the theory. This partly reflects the higher productivity of workers using more capital and therefore a higher wage in the city, but it also reflects the lower average wage in agriculture when the land is flooded with labor.

In the LFR (1954, 1964) model, the surplus labor movement into industry provides a net gain to the society. If the total output of the agricultural sector does not fall, then food production is unchanged and the transferred workers will be fed by the agricultural sector (without trade), which will also be adding to output in the industrial sector.

Once the stock of surplus labor is exhausted, the process of industrial development becomes an interplay between the two sectors as the wage rate is driven up in both sectors. Historical experience tells us that it is important to keep the terms of trade between these two sectors on an even keel. What do I mean by this? If the terms of trade move too strongly against the agricultural sector, they will not be able to buy enough equipment to fuel technological developments in the sector. By starving agriculture, industrialists will choke themselves to death in the long run. If the terms of trade turn against industry, then industrial investments will not be profitable and investment will slow.

5.2.2   Introduction of Trade into the LFR Model

When we introduce the possibilities of trade, the model becomes more complex but the basic features remain. For sustained growth to continue once the surplus labor phase has ended, the balanced treatment by the government in terms of taxes and subsidies has to be maintained in order for growth to be rapid. The surpluses from agriculture have to be mobilized to create investment for the industrial sector. At the same time, these taxes cannot be so high that they strangle the rural sector. One thing we do know is that export taxes, or an artificially low exchange rate, are not good ways to extract the agricultural surplus as these could have detrimental effects on long-term export-led growth. A food self-sufficiency policy is often followed when a more satisfactory outcome can be achieved by trading. Nevertheless, many countries still follow food self-sufficiency policies for political reasons. Farmers can form a powerful lobby and have been able to persuade legislators to enact legislation that restricts trade and provides large subsidies to farmers who are inefficient on the world market. In Asia, Korea and Japan heavily subsidize rice farmers, while the European Community (EC) and the United States also have large farm subsidy programs.

5.3 BACKWARD AND FORWARD LINKAGES

The interaction between the industrial and rural sectors can be studied using the concept of backward and forward linkages. If direct backward linkages are strong, when an industry grows its suppliers also grow. The extent of this linkage can be measured by subtracting the purchases from abroad and its own costs from the value-added generated by the industry itself.

5.3.1 Indirect Backward Linkages

Indirect backward linkages are the secondary effects which growth in an industry has on its suppliers. Industries that have strong backward linkages have low value-added and a large input from local suppliers. General industries with strong backward linkages include leather, clothing, textiles, food and beverages, and paper. The lowest backward linkages are in agriculture, public utilities, mining, and services. Labor-intensive manufacturing industries have the highest linkages, while primary industries have the lowest.

5.3.2 Forward Linkages

Forward linkages tell us how a product is related as an input into the production of a product at the next stage—textiles into apparel, for example, or petroleum into plastics. Forward linkages are a good indication of the extent to which an economy can upgrade its industrial base by using its existing expertise and resource base.

Both backward and forward linkages are determined from coefficients in input–output tables for individual economies. They do not tell us much about the dynamics of the process of industrialization in terms of causation, but they are useful to better understand the interrelationships that exist within an economy, and can serve as a beginning point for analyzing changes in industrial structure. Analysis of changes in these linkages can also be helpful in assessing the progress of an economy in its efforts to industrialize.

The Asian newly industrialized economies (NIEs) and the countries of Southeast Asia began their industrialization process with import-substituting industries but later began to focus on exports in labor-intensive industries, such as leather, clothing, and textiles. Because of the strong backward linkages these industries had on agriculture, there was a mutually reinforcing cycle of growth. At a later stage, these countries moved into more skill- and capital-intensive industries. (See Section 5.8 for further details.)

5.4 ASPECTS OF INDUSTRIAL DEVELOPMENT

5.4.1 Choice of Technology

As part of the process of industrialization, there will be a change in the production process as relative prices of factors change. In the early stages of industrialization, countries have limited capital and plentiful labor. Using simple production theory, factor proportions are determined by the relative cost of capital and labor. Labor-intensive technologies may be appropriate in a poor country with plenty of low-skilled and cheap labor but because of factor market distortions (such as those created by tax breaks for capital equipment), the choice of technology may be more capital-intensive.

5.4.2   Economies of Scale

Economies of scale come into play when a country is exporting, or when production is taking place on a large scale for the domestic market. This enables companies to operate at the low point on their cost curves. In very small countries, it may be difficult to reach a competitive plant size if production is intended for the domestic market alone. Similarly, even in larger countries, some industries may be inefficient—such as the automobiles industry in most Asian countries and Australia.

The standard for measuring the efficiency of an industry is to use the price of imports. Sometimes a protective tariff is imposed to keep out cheaper foreign products through infant industry protection.

5.5   Efficiency Issues

5.5.1   Economic Efficiency and Scale of Production

Which firms are more efficient? Does firm size have a systematic impact on costs? Given economies of scale, we might think that the larger the firm, the more efficient it would be. This is not necessarily the case as size can introduce inefficiencies. Efficiency depends upon a number of special factors. It may be that all firms can be efficient if they have reached a viable size of production that takes full advantage of economies of scale. It is true that there are more small firms in poorer countries but that could just be because of a lack of capital, or the fact that the market size is limited. Better transport and communication also make it possible to have a nationwide production, marketing and distribution strategy where goods are produced in the cheapest locations and then shipped all over the country. In recent years, with the development of information and computer technology, this strategy has been extended internationally through the development of networks for subcontracting and outsourcing.

5.5.2   Do Protected Industries Become Efficient Over Time?

Evidence suggests that there are numerous pitfalls to a strategy of protecting infant industries. These industries and firms will eventually be forced to compete in external markets. In order to be competitive, they should be in an industry where the country has a comparative advantage or else they will be inefficient. A comparison of India with Korea throws up some interesting facts. India protected many of its domestic industries for a long time, for example, automobiles, iron and steel, and others. These industries did not become competitive internationally and have been a drain on the public purse for many years. They were inefficient and not competitive. Only in the 1990s, when regulations on the inflow of foreign capital were relaxed, was India able to produce a range of automobiles at reasonable prices through the use of modern technology. In Korea, subsidies were also given, but these subsidies were performance related—that is, they were withdrawn if the industry did not emerge with strong export products after the initial years of protection. While Korea made many mistakes in promoting heavy and chemical industries in the 1980s, the country also became one of the fastest growing countries in the world during the early 1970s until the early 1990s. It joined the Organization for Economic Cooperation and Development (OECD) in 1996. A similar story can be told for Taiwan, although the emphasis there was on the development of small-and medium-scale industries. These cases and those of the other NIEs and the economies of Southeast Asia are explored further in the following section on the Asian experience.

5.5.3 Are There Advantages to Small-Scale Industrial Development?

Small-scale enterprises (or small and medium enterprises—SMEs) are generally more labor-intensive. Start-up costs are small and entry and exit is easy because of the small amount of capital needed. They tend to fail more frequently. Small-scale firms can be very successful when they concentrate in particular locations where they can share a skilled labor force base and where they can produce differentiated products of high quality. Industries which require craft occupational skills, such as particular kinds of textiles and apparel (batik, silk, specialized cottons), and footwear as well as textiles, are among these. Small-scale firms depend more on economies of agglomeration, which are generated by proximity to firms engaged in similar sectors or in complementary production. Most small producers need access to intermediate material inputs and thus prefer to be close to ports or other transportation facilities. The case of Taiwan is very interesting. The economy has grown very rapidly for several decades and it was not affected much by the Asian financial crisis. Small and medium-sized firms dominate its industrial structure.

5.6 FOREIGN TRADE

Exports are critical in explaining productivity gains in the Asian economies. Internal competition does not seem to be sufficient to bring about high rates of productivity increase. For example, in large countries with low industrial concentration ratios, efficiency rates are still low. The textile sectors in India and the Philippines are good examples. Why? Perhaps it is for licensing arrangements, or a lack of technological transfer as a result of taxes on imports. There is evidence that better internal allocation of resources can add greatly to economic efficiency. Firms financed by foreign direct investment (FDI) are, other things being equal, more efficient than their domestic counterparts. There may be many reasons for this but probably the most important is the need to be competitive internationally.

Strategies for international trade are important for studying the growth experience of developing countries. We will only touch on them now, but will discuss them in more details later.

5.7 OTHER TRANSITION ISSUES

Indonesia has not been able to make the transition to higher value-added products that are in demand in the OECD countries as quickly and as effectively as its neighbors in Southeast Asia. There are several reasons for this. First, Indonesia still has a large oil and natural gas sector and some of its resources are devoted to maintaining and expanding this sector. Secondly, it had a late start in the industrialization process in the early 1980s, and Malaysia, Thailand, and the Philippines had more than a decade's lead in industrializing. Thirdly, it has a labor force that lacks education and training to implement technology in these new industries on a wide scale. Fourthly, even after it began industrializing engineers, who thought they could leapfrog to higher levels of technology, dominated much of its development thinking. Such a strategy was not successful and it further held back the transition to labor-intensive industries that are the country's comparative advantage.

To some extent, Thailand also suffers from a lack of skilled manpower. The educational system is particularly weak in providing technicians with strong secondary school training. The other countries of Southeast Asia, such as the Philippines and Malaysia, are better positioned to take advantage of the opportunities for upgrading their industrial capacity. Their labor forces are better trained and are more familiar with English.

5.8 THE ASIAN EXPERIENCE WITH INDUSTRIALIZATION

The first thing to note about the Asian industrialization and growth experience is that it was unprecedented in economic history. From the mid-1960s to the late 1990s, the growth rate of the East Asian economies of Hong Kong, Korea, and Taiwan, together with Singapore in Southeast Asia—sometimes called the Asian "tigers," or the newly industrialized economies (NIEs)—grew at a faster rate than any other economy or group of economies had in history (World Bank, 1993; and Quibria, 2002). Per-capita incomes increased by about 7 percent per year, so that income doubled every ten years. At the end of thirty years, incomes per capita had increased fourfold.

Furthermore, during the same period the industrial sector's share of gross domestic product (GDP) in these countries also increased sharply (refer to Table 2.1 in Chapter 2). In the case of Korea, the share went from about 24 percent of GDP in 1970 to nearly 38 percent in 1980, and even higher in 1990. This implies an even more spectacular growth rate for the industrial sector than for the overall economy. In Taiwan, Singapore, and Hong Kong, the increase in the share of industry was more modest but it also saw a more rapid growth in the industrial sector than in the economy as a whole.

How were these economies able to sustain such a breakneck pace of growth of industry for such a prolonged period? Economic historians point to a period of growth in the Japanese economy from the Meiji Restoration to the middle of the twentieth century as a comparable period of rapid growth. In fact, it was only about half as fast as the growth of the Asian "tigers."

5.8.1 A Further Look at Total Factor Productivity (TFP)

If we go back to the discussion in Chapter 2, Section 2.2.2, we can begin to see how this was possible. However, we need more than the raw numbers of the Krugman–Lau–Young (KLY) analysis (Krugman, 1994; Lau, 1996; and Young, 1992, 1995). In their views, the reason for the rapid growth was brute force application of a simple Harrod–Domar growth model augmented by the growth of the population. They argue that both the capital stock and the labor force grew rapidly. Combined with good government policies, this was enough to ensure the Asian "miracle."

The question can be raised: "Didn't other countries have a combination of high investment, rapid population growth, and good policies?" There were some but the list of countries is small. Russia and some of its satellites in Eastern Europe had high saving rates and moderately high population growth. However, most economists would agree that they had bad policies until the fall of the Iron Curtain. Spain started from a low base and had high saving rates, moderate population growth and reasonable macroeconomic policies, yet its growth experience was not as rapid as the "tigers." This leads us to believe that there may have been more to the Asian "miracle" than brute force.

How does the evidence of the KLY studies compare with the results of studies using a growth accounting methodology?

We learned in Chapter 2 that the evidence is more favorable to a greater contribution of TFP using the usual growth accounting framework or production function estimation, if we look at more data (Dowling and Summers, 1998; Chen, 1997; Bosworth and Collins, 1996; and Harberger, 1996). See also Table 5.1, which summarizes several estimates, not including Harberger's. Notice that while the absolute numbers are in the range of 1–2 percent, this is still a significant contribution to TFP, considering that the TFP contribution for the industrial countries was in this range during the postwar period, as reflected by Sarel's (1997) estimate[1] for the United States. Aswicahyono and Hill (2002) have assembled evidence of TFP contribution to economic growth for the Southeast Asian countries and

---

[1] Notice that the contribution of TFP to growth is even higher for some countries when the 1991–1996 period is isolated.

Table 5.1   Total Factor Productivity Growth: Results of Selected Studies, 1960–2000

Author	Year	Period	GDP Growth	TFP Growth	TFP Contribution to Total Growth
China					
Bosworth and Collins[a]	1996	1960–1994	4.5%	2.6%	57.8%
Hong Kong					
Young	1994, 1995	1966–1991	7.3	2.3	31.5
Young adj[b]	1994, 1995	1966–1991	7.3	2.4	32.9
Korea					
Young	1994, 1995	1966–1990	10.3	1.7	16.5
Young (adj)[b]	1994, 1995	1966–1990	10.3	1.3	12.6
Bosworth and Collins[a]	1996	1960–1994	5.7	1.5	26.3
Singapore					
Young	1994, 1995	1966–1990	8.7	0.2	2.3
Young (adj)[b]	1994, 1995	1966–1990	8.7	1.0	11.5
Bosworth and Collins[a]	1996	1960–1994	5.4	1.5	27.8
Sarel	1997	1978–1996	5.0	2.2	44.0
Singapore MTI	2001	1985–2000	4.1	1.7	41.5
Taiwan					
Young[c]	1994, 1995	1966–1990	11.8	2.6	22.0
Young (adj)[b,c]	1994, 1995	1966–1990	11.8	1.9	16.1
Bosworth and Collins[a]	1996	1960–1994	5.8	2.0	34.5
Indonesia					
World Bank	1993	1960–1989	6.3	1.3	19.9
Kawai	1994	1970–1990	6.2	1.5	23.8
Nehru and Dhareshwar	1994	1960–1990	6.3	0.2	3.0
Bosworth, et al.	1995	1960–1994	3.4	0.8	23.5
Drysdale and Huang	1995	1962–1990	6.7	2.1	31.3
Bosworth and Collins[a]	1996	1960–1994	3.4	0.8	23.5
Sarel	1997	1978–1996	4.7	1.2	24.5
Malaysia					
World Bank	1993	1960–1989	7.0	1.1	15.4
Kawai	1994	1970–1990	6.7	1.6	23.8
Nehru and Dhareshwar	1994	1960–1990	7.0	−0.2	−2.6
Bosworth, et al.	1995	1960–1994	3.8	0.9	23.7
Drysdale and Huang	1995	1950–1990	6.0	−0.5	−0.8
Bosworth and Collins[a]	1996	1960–1994	3.8	0.9	23.7
Sarel	1997	1978–1996	4.5	2.0	44.1

(*continued*)

Table 5.1   (*continued*)

Author	Year	Period	GDP Growth	TFP Growth	TFP Contribution to Total Growth
Philippines					
Kawai	1994	1970–1990	3.6	−0.7	−19.6
Nehru and Dhareshwar	1994	1960–1990	3.9	−0.8	−21.3
Bosworth, et al.	1995	1960–1994	1.2	−0.4	−33.3
Drysdale and Huang	1995	1950–1990	4.9	0.2	4.1
Bosworth and Collins[a]	1996	1960–1994	1.3	−0.4	−30.8
Sarel	1997	1978–1996	0.2	−0.8	−4.1
Thailand					
World Bank	1993	1960–1989	7.1	2.5	35.2
Kawai	1994	1970–1990	7.0	1.9	27.1
Nehru and Dhareshwar	1994	1960–1990	7.1	0.1	1.3
Bosworth, et al.	1995	1960–1994	5.0	1.8	36.0
Drysdale and Huang	1995	1950–1990	5.8	1.7	29.3
Bosworth and Collins[a]	1996	1960–1994	5.0	1.8	36.0
Sarel	1997	1978–1996	5.2	2.0	38.7
United States					
Sarel	1997	1978–1996	1.1	0.3	27.0

[a]Figures calculated is for per worker.
[b]Young adjusted raises the capital share from 0.3 to 0.35.
[c]Figures are for the economy, excluding agriculture.

SOURCES: Aswicahyono and Hill (2002), Singapore Ministry of Trade and Industry (2001), Crafts (1998), Drysdale and Huang (1997), Sarel (1997), Bosworth and Collins (1996), Bosworth et al. (1995), Young (1994, 1995), Kawai (1994), Nehru and Dhareshwar (1994), and World Bank (1993).

these are reported in Table 5.1. These results support the contention that TFP contribution to overall growth was substantial in Indonesia, Malaysia, and Thailand, particularly shown by the Sarel estimates for the 1978–1996 period and comparing them with estimates for earlier periods. (For further discussion, see Dowling and Summers, 1998; Sarel, 1997; Bosworth and Collins, 1996; Chen, 1997; and Harberger, 1996.)

Part of this can be explained by the growth of the information technology (IT) revolution. Generally, however, there may be even more to it than that. A group of economists have argued that conventional estimation of production functions or the use of growth accounting formulas is flawed. They contend that subtracting the contribution of labor and capital to find the residual contribution to innovation (TFP) misses the boat. They argue that this is because the process of innovation and the growth of labor and capital are interdependent. If this is true, conventional methods of estimating TFP would be misleading. They attribute more explanatory power to the amounts of labor and capital, and discount the contribution to total factor productivity of innovation, learning, and education.

The argument is presented by Alice Amsden (2001) for Korea, Hobday (1995) for the NIEs and other countries, and summarized neatly by Nelson and Pack (1998).

The argument goes something like this. In order to sustain a rapidly growing industrial sector in a quickly evolving global environment, much more is required than just a high rate of investment and appropriate pricing of inputs and incentives for export. It requires a continuous process of learning, innovation, experimentation, and continuing structural change. Firms come and go, and the proof of the efficiency and competitiveness of those who are successful is their ability to adapt new technology to changing domestic and international circumstances.

5.8.2   Historical Transformation of the Industrial Sector

To give you an idea of how the structure of industries within these economies has changed over time, consider a snapshot of their industrial sectors in the early 1960s, 1975, and 1990 (see Table 5.2). In 1960, primary commodities accounted for a large share of total output and exports in Asia while manufactured commodities generally played a supporting role. The percentage of primary commodities as a share of total exports[2] was more than 90 percent for the Southeast Asian countries then—98 percent for Thailand, 97 percent for Indonesia, and 94 percent for Malaysia, to be specific. The NIEs had a lower share of primary commodities but they still ranged from 40 to 62 percent, with the sole exception of Hong Kong with less than 10 percent. The structure of manufacturing was slanted toward labor-intensive products and geared for the domestic market. Manufacturing itself was a small portion of total output.

By 1975, there was a dramatic shift in both the composition of industrials and the share of manufacturing in total output (see Table 5.2). In Korea, for example, the share of manufacturing output grew from 9 to 27 percent of GDP and the machinery and chemical sectors' share rose dramatically to nearly 37 percent of manufacturing from only 12 percent in 1963.[3] A nearly identical shift occurred in Taiwan. In Thailand, Malaysia, and Indonesia, the shift was less dramatic although the share of textiles and chemicals also rose quickly. In Indonesia, the higher production of oil accounted for much of the shift in chemicals even though manufacturing output as a share of income did not increase much.

Nevertheless, in both Thailand and Malaysia, manufacturing reached 18 percent of GDP. By 1990, there were further increases in manufacturing as a percentage of total output and the machinery industry had grown in importance in all the Asian countries, with the exception of Indonesia and Thailand. In the latter case, textiles continued to increase as a share of GDP, while in Indonesia, chemicals continued to be strong. However, exports had jumped to 20 percent of GDP, from 9 percent in 1975.

During this period of rapid industrialization, there were concerted efforts by the United States to protect its domestic industry against imports from Asia. These included barriers against textile exports as the United States joined the Multifiber Agreement. There were also tariffs placed on manufactured goods. At the same time, U.S. subsidiaries were developing manufacturing facilities in East Asia. In the 1970s, they began developing plants for integrated circuits in Singapore, which were for the final assembly of products sent by the United States as exports to Europe and Japan.

---

[2] Figures quoted from United Nations Conference on Trade and Development, *Trade and Development Report* (New York: United Nations, 1996), Chapter II, Tables 33 and 34.

[3] Rodrik (1995) argues that industrial policy in Korea was instrumental in assisting the private sector in making the shift toward export promotion and attracting investment to the export sector, which was very small at the beginning of the period. Investment subsidies to the private sector, support to government-sponsored industries, together with administrative guidance helped to remove the coordination failure that had previously blocked economic takeoff. This facilitation by the government had positive external effects through the transfer of technology and innovation across industries in a non-competitive way.

Table 5.2 Percentage Composition of Manufacturing Output by Industrial Category for Selected Years

Category	1963	1975	1990
Indonesia			
Food	38.0	33.4	20.1
Textiles	8.0	13.7	13.7
Wood	2.0	3.1	10.2
Paper	1.0	2.9	3.4
Chemicals	12.0	30.8	28.3
Non-mineral	4.0	4.3	2.6
Metals	11.0	3.8	11.7
Machinery	n.a.	7.9	9.4
Others	24.0	0.2	0.5
Manufacturing output/GDP	8	9	20
Korea			
Food	21.0	17.8	11.3
Textiles	29.2	22.6	13.2
Wood	5.0	2.7	1.6
Paper	7.2	4.0	4.6
Chemicals	11.9	22.3	17.6
Non-mineral	8.9	5.7	4.6
Metals	14.7	8.9	12.8
Machinery	n.a.	14.2	32.2
Others	2.2	1.9	2.1
Manufacturing output/GDP	9	27	31
Malaysia			
Food	36.6	27.0	15.6
Textiles	n.a.	7.2	6.3
Wood	17.8	11.1	6.8
Paper	8.2	5.3	4.7
Chemicals	14.4	21.0	23.5
Non-mineral	6.3	4.2	6.4
Metals	4.5	6.7	7.6
Machinery	6.9	16.9	28.1
Others	5.2	0.6	1.0
Manufacturing output/GDP	9	18	24

(continued)

Table 5.2   (*continued*)

Category	1963	1975	1990
Taiwan			
Food	41.8	22.1	11.4
Textiles	16.3	17.4	12.5
Wood	4.1	2.5	1.6
Paper	5.6	2.8	5.1
Chemicals	12.7	18.7	21.7
Non-mineral	5.9	5.5	3.9
Metals	12.2	10.2	11.8
Machinery	n.a.	18.2	22.5
Others	1.3	2.8	9.6
Manufacturing output/GDP	14	20	36
Thailand			
Food	53.9	41.0	31.3
Textiles	9.5	15.4	25.5
Wood	8.1	4.4	2.9
Paper	3.0	3.0	2.2
Chemicals	5.6	14.4	10.5
Non-mineral	7.1	2.9	4.2
Metals	5.4	5.7	4.3
Machinery	6.2	9.6	11.8
Others	1.3	3.6	7.3
Manufacturing output/GDP	12	18	26
India			
Food	19.7	10.8	11.5
Textiles	36.3	19.5	12.3
Wood	0.6	0.7	0.4
Paper	3.8	4.9	3.3
Chemicals	12.6	20.2	26.8
Non-mineral	3.5	3.9	4.7
Metals	16.5	16.3	13.1
Machinery	n.a.	23.3	27.3
Others	7.0	0.5	0.6
Manufacturing output/GDP	12	16	19

SOURCE: Alice H. Amsden, *The Rise of "the Rest": Challenges to the West from Late-Industrializing Economies* (New York: Oxford University Press, 2001), pp. 113–115.

Table 5.3 Share of Exports of Primary, Light, and Heavy Industries for Selected NIEs, 1955–1973

	Year	Primary Industry	Light Industry	Heavy Industry
Korea	1955	23.8	17.2	2.4
	1963	20.2	34.2	14.3
	1970	8.7	58.0	14.5
	1973	3.8	48.5	31.0
Taiwan	1956	6.6	18.8	9.4
	1961	7.1	66.0	10.0
	1966	9.1	49.4	20.0
	1971	4.9	48.6	34.0

SOURCE: Hollis B. Chenery, Sherman Robinson, and Moshe Syrquin, *Industrialization and Growth: A Comparative Study* (New York: Oxford University Press for the World Bank, 1986), pp. 158–159.

Despite these difficulties, the production and export of manufactured goods in the NIEs rose as the composition of exports shifted from primary products to light and then heavy industry (see Table 5.3).

It is evident from this table that even in the 1960s, there was a rapid shift out of primary products into manufacturing in both Korea and Taiwan. Much of this transition was into export-oriented industries. Calculations by Chenery et al. (1986, pp. 158–159) show that during the period 1955–1973, 35 percent of the increase in income was generated by export industries in Korea, while in Taiwan, the contribution was 43 percent from 1956 to 1971. Between 1955 and 1963, textiles and chemicals, along with machinery, paper, wood, and petroleum were the major import-substituting sources of growth in the manufacturing sector. However, this changed dramatically during the next decade to 1973 when it saw export expansion across the range of all manufactured product categories (Chenery et al., 1986, p. 184). In Taiwan, the pattern was similar although the shift to export expansion was not as dramatic.

Another way to view the transition in manufacturing that took place is to consider the shift in terms of different levels of technology. S. Lall (1998) has broken down manufacturing into five components:

1. Resource-based industries that include aluminum, food, and oil refining as examples.
2. Labor-intensive industries, including garments, footwear, and toys.
3. Scale-intensive industries, including steel, automobiles, paper, and chemicals.
4. Differential industrial products, including TVs, power equipment, and advanced machinery.
5. Science-based industries, including electronics, pharmaceuticals, and biotechnology.

During the 1980–1995 period, the world growth rate in the science-based industries was much faster than in the other sectors—about 13 percent compared with 8.5 percent for different products, about 8 percent for labor-intensive products, and less for other categories. Lall (1998) has also shown that the share of output in science-based industries increased quite dramatically between 1985 and 1992 in the Asian countries—from 4 to 16 percent in Taiwan, 5 to 31 percent in Singapore, 4 to 42 percent in Malaysia, and 0 to 20 percent in Thailand. In Indonesia, Hong Kong, India, and Pakistan, the increases were minimal. In Korea, the increase was only from 3 to 6 percent. However, there was a large increase in differentiated products, which reflected the push that Korea was making toward heavy manufacturing.

This evidence reflects a growing trend toward the manufacture of skill and research-intensive goods in the NIEs and Southeast Asia, goods that were also increasing as a share of manufactured output generally in the world economy. We will come back to this structural shift in the next section after discussing the electronics sector.

5.8.3 The Electronics Sector

In order to examine the structural transformation in the industrial sectors of the NIEs and to look more closely at the role of technology, it is useful to focus on the electronics industry. This broad industrial category had become the most important export of the NIEs, as well as the countries of Southeast Asia by the end of the 1990s. Hobday (1995) suggests that the changes in the electronics industry can be described by a stylized S curve representing the size of exports, as well as the technological frontier and research and development (R&D) expenditures. In the 1950s and 1960s, the industry grew slowly as firms became familiar with elementary technology, including simple assembly and the assessment and selection of production techniques. In the 1970s, the rate of export growth accelerated and the inflow of technology from foreign firms also increased. Reverse engineering was undertaken and the adaptation of technology was further enhanced. Eventually the industry moved toward indigenous design for manufacturing and applied R&D in the 1990s.

5.8.4 Different Patterns of Technological Transfer

The methods varied from economy to economy. Singapore and Hong Kong were open to foreign direct investment and worked hard to attract it by offering full ownership, low taxes, and access to modern infrastructure and a well-educated workforce. Singapore adopted a hands-on industrial policy and while it did not necessarily try to influence which industries located in Singapore, it played a strong role in helping to train the workforce and to provide industrial infrastructure. Hong Kong took a more hands-off attitude, though it did have a very liberal and open economy. Most of the investment that came into these two countries was via the foreign investment of transnational enterprises (TNCs).

Korea and Taiwan were less open in the manner in which they obtained foreign technology. They did not encourage foreign firms to set up operations. Rather, they adopted arrangements where local subsidiaries produced for the foreign companies, either to their exact specifications (original equipment manufacturing—OEM) or according to their own designs or a combination of foreign and local designs (own design manufacturing—ODM). They did not generally form joint ventures although they sometimes used licensing arrangements. Later in the industrialization process, they also made some overseas acquisitions and formed strategic partnerships with overseas companies to acquire technology.

Even though there were distinct differences in the degree of government intervention and openness to foreign ownership, the NIEs all benefited from the same principles that resulted in success (see the schematic in Figure 5.1). There were four basic factors underpinning their success:

1. Firms benefited from low rates of interest, low inflation, and high rates of saving within the economies.
2. They all responded to the open and outward-looking export-led strategies that were generally followed.
3. All the NIEs developed an appropriate human resource development strategy that complemented and provided trained workers for the growing industrial sector. This included engineering, technical, and vocational schools.
4. Government intervention was undertaken whenever it was needed. At the outset, this included the attraction of foreign industries by Singapore because it felt that the local economy was too

Figure 5.1   Government Intervention and Degree of Openness

Government Intervention	Low FDI openness/ Relatively closed economy	High FDI openness/ Relatively open economy
High	*Korea:* large firms that are locally owned	*Singapore:* large firms that are foreign-owned
Low	*Taiwan:* small local firms and some large foreign firms	*Hong Kong:* small local firms and large foreign firms

weak to do it by itself. In Korea, the government stimulated and supported the formation of large conglomerates following the Japanese model (*chaebol*, following the *kareitsu*). In Taiwan, it involved the setting up of state-owned firms to industrialize, although not in electronics. In Hong Kong, it involved the development of infrastructure and the enhancement of relations with China and Taiwan.

5.8.5   Country Experiences

Hence, over the years, the Asian countries have actively developed their electronics sector although there are differences in their field of specialization owing to differences in the labor force and technological advances. For instance, South Korea and Taiwan have well developed semiconductor industries, while Hong Kong and Singapore dominate the disk-drive and motherboard markets. Table 5.4 provides a ranking of the major exporters of electronics in Asia since 1997. As can be seen, Korea, Taiwan, and China appear to be gaining the lead as major exporters, whereas Singapore and the Philippines have slipped to ninth and twentieth positions in 2000 from fourth and sixth places, respectively, in 1997. Before we discuss comparative advantage in the next section, we will first look at various case studies in Asia to see how their electronics sectors have evolved and developed over the years.

SINGAPORE   Singapore followed a model of attracting foreign enterprises (transnational corporations or TNCs) to set up operations in Singapore. These TNCs were initially attracted by low labor costs, political stability, good infrastructure, and an attractive environment provided by the government which allowed foreign control and ownership of these subsidiaries. Foreign direct investment was attracted initially to the Jurong Industrial Park, including enterprises such as Texas Instruments, General Electric, and Hewlitt Packard from the United States, Fujitsu from Japan, and SGS from Italy. There were also various attempts by the government to promote advances in higher-end technology over the years but these were frustrated by the economic downturns in 1974–1975 and 1985–1986. Nevertheless, upgrading of facilities and technologies was a general practice as the TNCs had to remain competitive in international markets.

In addition to physical infrastructure and favorable government policies that supported the TNCs, the development of telecommunications and transport infrastructure made it an attractive corporate

Table 5.4   Ranking of Major Electronic Exporters in Asia, 1997–2000

	Billions US$				Global Ranking			
	1997	1998	1999	2000	1997	1998	1999	2000
World Market	$644.1	$649.0	$728.0	$876.8	n.a.	n.a.	n.a.	n.a.
Korea	33.9	31.8	42.9	58.7	7	8	6	3
Taiwan	38.6	37.5	44.3	57.8	5	4	4	4
Malaysia	36.3	34.6	44.3	52.4	6	7	5	5
China	21.5	25.3	30.1	43.5	11	11	10	8
Singapore	41.6	36.7	38.6	41.6	4	5	7	9
Thailand	14.1	14.3	15.2	21.6	15	15	14	14
Philippines	14.2	18.6	9.0	9.7	14	13	19	20
Indonesia	2.9	2.4	3.0	7.3	25	28	26	21
Hong Kong	5.2	4.3	3.6	4.0	21	22	24	25

SOURCE: Singapore Ministry of Trade and Industry, "Declining Global Market Shares of Singapore's Electronic Products. Is It a Concern?" Occasional paper, February 28, 2002.

headquarters site. By the early 1990s, there were more than 300 TNCs located in Singapore from North America, Europe, and Japan.

To provide a skilled labor force, the Economic Development Board (EDB) supported technical training, including engineering and technical schools to ensure the growth of the industrial sector. The National University of Singapore and Nanyang Technological University were able to supply a very large number of engineers and other technical graduates and craftsmen, and this availability of low-cost and highly skilled engineers and other workers has been cited as one of the primary reasons for TNCs to locate in Singapore.

By the early 1990s, more than a third of value-added in manufacturing was coming from the electronics industry. Disk drives, integrated circuits (chips), and printed boards were the most important exports, totaling about US$7 billion, US$4.5 billion, and US$3 billion, respectively. The three largest chip firms were Texas Instruments, SGS-Thomson of Italy, and NEC. These firms and others upgraded their production and technology over time.

Electronics production in Singapore is not the leading edge but it has been upgraded continuously over time so that new advances from the parent company have been incorporated. Some backward linkages have also been forged with local suppliers, and forward linkages developed with Hewlett Packard and Canon.

Singapore was the world's largest producer of disk drives in 1991 and this leadership extended into the 1990s. The producing firms included Seagate and Canon Peripherals. Plants graduated from production learning to investment-led innovative learning. Consumer electronics included products from Philips and AT&T. In the case of AT&T, it took less than eight years to develop a high quality of production with advanced technology, taking advantage of the infrastructure that had been put in place. The role of Singapore as a high-technology testing ground for hard-disk drives (HDD) is discussed further in Chapter 6.

Owing to the emergence of China as a relatively low-cost manufacturing base and the fast developing technological capabilities of neighboring Taiwan and Korea, competition in the international arena has intensified and Singapore's attractiveness as an electronics manufacturing base has slipped in recent years (see Table 5.4). This has been exacerbated by the slowdown of the U.S. economy, Singapore's major trading partner, leading to a subsequent decline in export demand and overall economic growth.

In order to remain competitive, Singapore has undertaken various measures to move up the technology value chain. They include the shift of the manufacturing focus from low-end products, such as desktop computers, television sets (TVs) and audio parts, towards high-end electronic components, such as integrated circuits (ICs), transmitter receivers, and optical disk drives. The Ministry of Trade and Industry (MTI) has reported that exports of transmitter receivers grew the fastest at more than 70 percent while certain low-end electronic exports, such as personal computers, declined by 20 percent between 1996 and 2000 (Ministry of Trade and Industry, 2002). Singapore has also encouraged the development of stronger linkages between local suppliers and the multinational corporations (MNCs). Additional measures include the promotion of other high-technology industries in ICs and semiconductors, as well as the establishment of closer ties with other Asian countries through the signing of regional and free trade agreements. The role of the latter is to open up new markets and promote Singapore's new role and capabilities as a producer of high-end components and finished products.

KOREA   Korea became a leader in the chip industry and developed the capability to produce household appliances (TVs and cassettes), as well as small computers and peripherals. Most of the Korean production was not at the technological frontier and took place under OEM, and subcontracting and licensing. TNCs were not welcomed. By the end of the 1990s, Korea had become one of the leaders in chip production worldwide, holding a substantial share of the DRAM (dynamic random access memory) market. They moved slowly from OEM in the 1980s to ODM in the 1990s, and there was a substantial increase in R&D investment as the industrialization process continued. The large *chaebols*, including Samsung, Lucky Goldstar (LG), and Daewoo, were the centers of electronics production as Korea followed the example of Japan in developing large conglomerates. In selected product lines, such as DRAM production, they have developed to a point where they are challenging the Japanese companies. They also face the same problems of management and coordination.

TAIWAN   Taiwan developed its electronics and other industries using the same approach as Korea, in the sense that it discouraged TNCs and instead set up domestic firms using subcontracting, licensing, and OEM/ODM. However, instead of building large conglomerates as in Korea, they relied on small and medium-sized industries which were fast, skillful, and agile in developing new products and adjusting to the intense competition in international markets. These small and medium-sized industries were supported in their development by government policies and the availability of skilled technicians and managers supplied by the educational system. Taiwan became a specialist in the production of desktop and lap-top computers, terminals, monitors, disk drives, peripherals, and other computer components. Eventually, some of the small and medium-sized firms became larger—Acer, for example—as they moved toward OBM (own brand manufacturing) from OEM and ODM. Because of the focus on small and medium-sized operations, it was important for Taiwanese businesses to develop networks of subcontracters and forward linkages with buyers in other countries. They also established linkages with China, Hong Kong, Malaysia, and other countries. They have become quite expert in this kind of networking and now many of the components for their computers are made in other countries, with assembly either in Taiwan, China, or some other location.

COUNTRIES IN SOUTHEAST ASIA   The evolution of industry in Malaysia and Thailand has followed a pattern similar to that of Singapore. In Malaysia, electronics made a substantial contribution to economic growth during the 1980s and 1990s. By the end of the decade, electronics accounted for the major part of total exports and of manufacturing output. The electronics industry began in the 1960s when Matsushita of Japan and other TNCs began assembling radios, TVs, and electrical appliances. In the 1970s, an export promotion policy was adopted and the semiconductor industry took off as Intel and Motorola began chip assembly. By the late 1980s, electronics became Malaysia's largest export sector. The production of consumer goods increased in the 1990s, and there was further diversification of production into disk drives, computers, and color TVs, mainly from Japanese investors. Despite such rapid progress, Malaysia's R&D remains weak and the electronics industry is sensitive to global swings in demand and also to the vicissitudes of foreign investment inflows. However, the active direction of foreign investment inflows into various high-technology and capital-intensive projects by the government has served to enhance and upgrade the strength of its existing electronic capabilities and to further improve Malaysia's attractiveness to MNCs. The government has invested in effective infrastructures to heighten its conduciveness to future investments. This includes, for example, the expansion of Penang Port's capacity to handle one million twenty-foot-equivalent unit containers by 2004.

In Thailand and the Philippines, the emphasis has been on lower-level and simple electronics. In the Philippines, the emphasis was on chip manufacture while Thailand focused on computers, particularly hard-disk drives. Both countries have followed the Singaporean and Malaysian models of relying on TNCs for technology transfer and production know-how. There has been less development of local expertise and backward and forward linkages.

5.9 Comparative Advantage and Asian Industrialization

In this section, we will explore briefly another aspect of the rapid growth of Asian industry as it relates to foreign trade. We will revisit this topic again in the next chapter. However, it is useful to introduce some aspects of this topic now while studying the industrialization experience.

In studying how industrialization evolved in the NIEs and Southeast Asia, we have to assess the efficiency of the process. Here, the notion of comparative advantage comes into play. It is impossible to know what the actual comparative advantage is because this would require knowing all the potential costs for the entire mix of industries in a country. However, there are indirect methods of measuring comparative advantage.

The notion of revealed comparative advantage was first suggested by Balassa (1965). According to this line of reasoning, products that are being exported more intensively are those that a country has comparative advantage in producing and exporting. Unfortunately, this is only an indirect way of measuring comparative advantage. Nevertheless, it does show how competition weeds out the less competitive and rewards those that are efficient by exporting more.

Another way of demonstrating comparative advantage has been suggested by Amsden (2001), who recommends that the mix of industries in Japan and the United States be taken as a benchmark for comparative advantage. Other countries can be measured against these two countries. She suggests that to calculate whether a country would have a dynamic comparative advantage for a product in a sector, the share of output in that sector should be compared with those of the United States and Japan. If it begins to catch up with those of the United States and Japan, then it has attained a (dynamic) comparative advantage in that product. On the other hand, if it starts out at a level above the United States and Japan ratios and gets larger, then it has a (static) comparative advantage.

By looking at the developing countries of Asia, she determines that the NIEs have a dynamic comparative advantage in electrical and non-electrical equipment, as well as transport equipment. This is consistent with the conclusion of an analysis of revealed comparative advantage that shows strong growth in the same industries.

Table 5.5   Share of Asian Manufacturing Exports in Sectors Where the Share of OECD Imports Increased, 1970–1995

	Indonesia	Malaysia	Thailand	China	Singapore	Taiwan	Korea	Hong Kong	World
1970	3.0	5.9	4.2	19.4	22.6	34.5	29.8	45.6	43.2
1975	10.3	17.8	8.9	20.8	29.2	38.3	31.1	36.8	41.9
1980	7.0	26.9	18.6	22.0	33.4	47.0	40.2	48.2	45.7
1985	9.3	36.2	23.4	23.9	40.5	50.6	44.7	48.7	50.6
1990	17.9	55.1	41.8	41.0	57.6	59.0	55.0	49.0	51.7
1995	34.2	66.2	53.9	49.8	74.5	67.8	62.5	49.2	57.5

The products were computers, electronics, pharmaceuticals, instruments, motor vehicles, chemicals, electrical machinery, and other manufacturing and fabricated metals.

SOURCE: Malcolm Dowling and David Ray, "The Structure and Composition of International Trade in Asia: Historical Trends and Future Prospects," *Journal of Asian Economics* 11 (December 2000), Table 8, pp. 301–318.

Another approach is to see if the NIEs and Southeast Asian countries followed a strategy of developing exports in sectors where the United States and other industrial countries' import demand was growing rapidly. The question could also be asked "Did they have a comparative advantage in these product lines?"

Dowling and Ray (2000) have constructed an index of export growth for the Asian economies that is, by design, heavily influenced by the changing structure of exports. If a country changes its export structure in favor of products for which import growth from the rest of the world is growing rapidly, then this index will be larger than when a country's exports are not responding to this shift in world import demand.

What has happened in Asia is that almost all countries have moved swiftly to take advantage of markets that are growing rapidly, such as in electronics, computers, and pharmaceuticals. These three industries rank as the top-three when the average annual growth of world exports is calculated for the 1980–1995 period (Dowling and Ray, 2000, p. 311). Table 5.5 shows the increasing emphasis on manufactured exports such as electronics, computers, and pharmaceutical products in Asia over the years.

A comparison of the Amsden (2001) and Dowling and Ray (2000) analyses shows a significant overlap in the industries that are growing rapidly in Asia and those that have an Amsden-type of comparative advantage.

There are several inferences that we can draw from this evidence on the industrialization experience of the Asian economies:

1.   First, a very dramatic shift took place in the structure of industry and of exports in Asia during the thirty to forty years from the 1960s to the end of the century. The share of manufactured goods in total industrial production increased; at the same time, there was a shift toward manufactured goods as a share of total exports of goods and services (see Table 5.6). This shift took place in Southeast and East Asia primarily, but there was also an upward trend in the share of manufactured goods in South Asia, particularly in India, although the trend was not so rapid.

2.   The shift in production of manufactured goods within Asia corresponded closely to a similar pattern of production that was taking place in the world economy.

Table 5.6 Share of World Exports of Manufactured Goods for Selected Periods

	United States	Japan	NIEs
1965–1969	19.1%	8.5%	2.0%
1975–1979	14.4	11.1	4.8
1986–1990	11.9	13.3	8.6
1991–1993	13.0	12.9	9.0

SOURCE: UNCTAD, *Trade and Development Report* (New York: United Nations, 1996), p. 93.

3. The shift toward manufactured goods production and exports within Asia began with labor-intensive products and moved toward high-intensity technological and science-based exports, especially electronics, in several countries. The shift was particularly strong in Taiwan, Singapore, Malaysia, and Thailand. In Korea, there was an additional emphasis on heavy industry. In Hong Kong, the shift was less dramatic, since there had been a strong emphasis on manufacturing from the early 1970s and Hong Kong did not move as rapidly into the electronics field as did other economies. This reflected the growing entrepôt function that Hong Kong was beginning to play with regard to China, and its continued emphasis on finance and labor-intensive manufacturing. Indonesia, Pakistan, and India did not move as rapidly into science-based fields of manufacturing, partly because of trade restrictions and the inward orientation in the latter two countries, and because of the resource-based nature of exports and production in Indonesia until the latter part of the period.

5.10 THE ROLE OF INNOVATION

Some mention should be made about the importance of innovation in the industrialization process. We have already noted that education together with the expansion of the labor force played key roles in achieving economic growth in the countries of East and Southeast Asia in the decades of the 1970s, 1980s, and 1990s. Growth in the labor force alone contributed about 20 percent of total growth in income (see Bloom and Williamson, 1999). In addition, Temple (2001) suggests that education may account for one-fifth or more of growth in gross output in the OECD countries.

Much of the remaining growth in income resulted from new innovations and the adaptation of innovation from other countries. Innovation requires a creative process of abandoning old ways of doing things and the adoption of new methods and processes. To do this effectively and dynamically requires the ability of the economic system to facilitate the exit of inefficient companies and the entry of new and more productive ones. In East and Southeast Asia, the barriers to entry include not only the need to have sufficient capital, but also to satisfy the government requirements in terms of registration, labor, and other regulations, including environmental and industrial codes. Entry costs are low for small and medium-sized firms and exit is also generally easy by declaring bankruptcy. For larger firms, rules and regulations vary widely. In Hong Kong and Singapore, costs are low while those in South Asia, Indonesia, and Vietnam are high (Djankov et al., 2002). Exit is particularly difficult where large firms have a hold on government agencies or where the fear of adverse employment effects is great. For this reason, many inefficient state-owned enterprises (SOEs) are kept in business in large economies, such as China, India, Vietnam, and Indonesia.

One method for facilitating entry is to set up special economic zones (SEZs) within an economy where sites and services are provided and regulatory and licensing requirements are minimized. Such SEZs have been set up in many countries in the Asian region, including Malaysia, Philippines, Singapore, Indonesia, Southern China, and Thailand. These, and other arrangements involving cooperation between countries, are discussed further in Chapter 6. They include the growth triangle involving Singapore, Johor in Malaysia, and Riau Island in Indonesia, as well as the growth triangle comprising southern China, Hong Kong, and Taiwan. Other initiatives in Southeast Asia, such as the Mekong development and associations among Malaysia, Indonesia, the Philippines, and Thailand, are also discussed.

The concept of SEZs can be extended to the notion of an industrial cluster. Some of these clusters have emerged naturally, with few explicit government incentives, such as the Silicon Valley in California, the northern Italian industrial complex, and the development of the southern China provinces adjacent to Hong Kong. Yusuf and Evenett (2002) examine in detail the concept of clustering. The main kinds of clusters are:

1. large metropolitan agglomerations that contain a mix of different industries;
2. small groups of networked firms with similar but not identical interests, such as in northern Italy, Brazil, and India;
3. clusters which have a few main producers and their suppliers, such as MNC plants with their component suppliers, like those existing in Penang, Malaysia, and in Baatan and the region south of Manila in the Philippines. In the United States, Korea, and China, there are clusters anchored by a major enterprise, such as automobile or steel plants, and their affiliates.

Innovation in Southeast Asia has primarily been the result of spending by MNCs. In East Asia, innovation has been developed through licensing arrangements rather than MNC participation (see Chapter 6; and Hobday, 1995). Recently, the flow of innovative investment began to respond to growing human capital in East Asia, as Korea and Taiwan started to build up strategic alliances with other firms in the industrialized countries using information communication technology (ICT) as a base. Thus, East Asian firms often conduct research jointly with other firms in Europe or the United States. For example, Hsinchu Park (outside Taipei) and Silicon Valley have developed multiple inter-firm associations, according to Yusuf and Evenett (2002). The overseas Chinese network also continues to build, shifting from low- to higher-technology industries. It has worked to supplement and augment formal legal systems within individual countries and to discourage opportunistic behavior. This network also serves to informally enforce standards and to generate information exchange, thus enhancing networking capabilities and developing better marketing skills.

Innovation and technology transfer have taken place most often when capital equipment and components are imported by export-oriented manufacturing firms (see Gill and Kharas, 2007, Chapter 3). This is true for both low- and middle-income countries in Southeast Asia and some countries in East Asia. These kinds of technology transfer require a high level of external financing as well as some local funding, highlighting the importance of financial sector development as an enabler of innovative change (see Chapter 7 for more on this). The business sector plays a key role in both funding R&D and implementing research innovation in new and improved products. A large part of R&D comes from the private sector in Southeast and East Asia, including China (see Gill and Kharas, 2007). State-owned enterprises are notoriously slow to innovate while some innovation comes either from other governmental agencies or institutions of higher education. While most innovation and knowledge still flow from the industrial countries either through joint ventures or foreign direct investment (FDI), some NIEs are producing new knowledge that is on a par with those at the frontiers in the industrial countries. These breakthroughs are being shared among their neighbors in the Asian region. This is reflected in the focus of FDI in East Asia compared with other developing regions. More than 60 percent of FDI in East Asia is in the manufacturing sector as opposed to primary production or services. This is much higher than the proportions of FDI spent on manufacturing in the industrial countries (about 25 percent) and in developing countries as a whole (about 38 percent). Total factor productivity is also higher in firms which receive FDI, and there is some evidence of spillovers to local firms through greater competition, skill acquisition, or imitating the production and management style of the foreign-invested firms (see World Bank, 2005).

Innovation has also taken place in marketing and distribution as ICT and transportation efficiencies have cut costs. Still, freight costs in Asia are double those in Europe and the United States—8 percent of total value versus 4 percent on average (Pedersen, 2001).

5.11   Innovation, Education, and Growth Convergence

We noted in Chapter 2 that the rapid growth in income in Southeast and East Asia resulted in a strong convergence in growth between these economies and the industrial countries. An important component of this growth experience has been the dynamism of the industrial sector and the key role that technology transfer has played. Without the mutual synergies created by technology, education, openness, and competitiveness, such rapid growth would not have been possible. An important additional lesson is that the process of industrialization and innovation is not necessarily linear and those countries that get left behind have to employ a different strategy to catch up with those who have moved forward and acquired a leading edge in new developments. Nelson and Phelps (1966) have argued that learning takes place only when technology is changing. However, if technology changes too fast then those who fall behind can get lost, as noted by Findlay (1978). Leung (2003) has pointed out that appropriate technology as opposed to state of the art technology is the way for these countries to move forward, and a way to access this technology is through FDI. Gill and Kharas (2007, Figure 3.7) also pointed out that R&D not only increases with per-capita income but also accelerates at an increasing pace.

We will discuss these aspects of the industrialization process more thoroughly in Chapter 6. What is important to emphasize here is the need to develop an industrial growth philosophy and policy framework that puts the various components of industrialization in proper perspective. Countries beginning industrialization need an entirely different set of policies for education and technology transfer compared with those economies at a more advanced level. However, to become equipped they will still need some of the modern tools of technology, including computers and information technology, which will be discussed further in Chapter 11.

Furthermore, even when the initial conditions in terms of infrastructure and education are in place, the adoption of new innovations can often be torturous. Hobday (1995) and ADB (2003) have emphasized that the subsidiaries of MNCs and local firms that assemble goods according to standard processes often had difficulty in becoming competitive and maintaining it. The process began in the 1960s and 1970s with OEM and then moved to ODM in the 1980s, and finally to some OBM in the 1990s, particularly in Korea and Taiwan, but also in Malaysia.

5.12   Employment Growth and Industrialization

How does employment grow in a country that is industrializing rapidly? It will depend upon the rate of capital accumulation and technical progress. When technical progress is labor-intensive, it will help employment, and when it is capital-intensive, it will retard the growth in employment. This is a simple yet powerful concept. It is also important that wages be flexible, otherwise labor can be priced out of the market and capital used instead.

This is the risk that faces labor unions and other institutional factors that limit labor mobility. Employment growth is directly related to output growth as well. Using the case of Asia, we observe that no rapidly growing Asian economy has had an employment problem in the long term, at least until the Asian crisis. This is partly because growth was so rapid that it was easy to absorb the labor generated by rapid population growth. However, it was also the result of selected production methods that was first labor-absorbing at a low level of technology (that is, labor-intensive industries like apparel, footwear, and leather products) and later, partly labor-absorbing at a higher level of technology (such as electronic assembly, data inputting, and software development).

All the NIEs and Malaysia and Thailand were running a fully employed economy. Indonesia and Vietnam also improved and the Philippines showed signs of growth that eventually helped the employment situation. In South Asia, which grew more slowly, there was still a lot of underemployment.

5.13 A Model of Rural–Urban Migration

To provide labor for a growing industrial sector, there has been significant migration from the rural to the urban areas where industries are located. The basic building blocks for a model of urban–rural migration are already in place. Productivity in the rural sector is low. It is higher in the urban sector. Therefore, migration will take place. If markets are complete and competitive, this migration will continue until the marginal products in the two sectors are equalized, since workers are paid the value of their marginal products. The surplus labor will be absorbed slowly or quickly, depending on the pace of capital formation in the urban/industrial sector.

There will be modifications of this model, depending upon institutional restrictions, such as wage rigidity and/or market inflexibilities. Several propositions have been put forward. The most convincing is the Harris–Todaro (1970) model, which argues that migration will take place when the expected future income stream in the city (minus relocation costs) exceeds the expected income stream in the rural areas. Such a model implies that a significant amount of unemployment or underemployment can be experienced as long as the stream of income expected in the long run is large.

The Harris–Todaro model implies the existence of continued immigration into the city and rising unemployment, even though wages in the informal sector in the city are very low. This phenomenon has been observed in many places. This results from the fact that there is a segmented labor market in the city. Formal sector wages are kept high in the city and entry is restricted. Workers from the rural areas see both labor markets as potential. They will migrate when the expected wage exceeds the existing rural wage. If the probability of getting a good job in the city is the ratio of employment in the high wage manufacturing sector (l_m) to the total urban labor force (l_u), then the agricultural wage floor (w_f), at which workers would be content to remain in the rural areas, is simply this ratio multiplied by the wage in the manufacturing sector (w_m):

$$(w_f) = \{(l_m)/(l_u)\}\,(w_m)$$

5.13.1 Are Expectations Unbiased?

Whether migrants' expectations are unbiased is another question. There may be wishful thinking that introduces an upward bias. Furthermore, the experiences of friends who had previously migrated could also give a biased picture to potential migrants. Given the skills and background of the migrant, the agricultural wage floor could be considerably lower as the probability of getting a job in the formal urban sector declines. Nevertheless, the feedback from these distortions in terms of reverse migration is likely to be limited since the costs of relocating back to the rural areas will also be very high, and the social stigma of coming home without being a "success" often holds migrants in the urban sector.

5.13.2 Other Evidence

Other evidence on migration suggests that underemployment in the informal sector of the urban areas is not unproductive but rather reflects the limited opportunities in the rural economy. The evidence from Asia, in particular, suggests that job creation in the urban sector eventually results in the reduction in unemployment and underemployment. Therefore, strategies for rapid industrialization should continue, balanced by a greater stress on employment creation in the rural areas, particularly when overall economic growth is not strong.

Although labor markets probably work in a competitive way in both the rural and urban areas, the combination of high expectations and low education generally among the migrants from the rural areas puts a premium on skill and raises the return on higher and secondary education. This is not necessarily an indication of strong market segmentation but a failure of the educational system to keep up with shifting demand. This is particularly true when there is a shortage of private educational facilities for vocational and technical training.

This is evident in the area of computer literacy, programming, and other computer skills. In the Philippines, where there are many private schools and vocational centers, the number of programmers and other computer experts has risen dramatically, and the country now exports different software products around the world. Much of it is low technology but the supply response is very strong, particularly when compared with more centrally controlled countries where private-sector education is limited. Among the countries where English is widely spoken, only Singapore and India are competing with the Philippines in this subsector.

If the urban wage in the formal sector is much higher than the informal wage in the rural sector, but perhaps comparable with the wage in the urban informal sector, then agricultural workers will still migrate, even though the probability of getting a job in the formal sector is low. The number of migrants will continue until agricultural wages equal the weighted average of the wages in these two occupations.

In fact, it is probably unlikely that a worker from the province with little education will make these sorts of calculations. What is more likely is that the lure of the city is enough to attract workers from the rural areas, often in response to letters from friends and relatives who had previously migrated. In Asian cities, migrants from different parts of the country tend to migrate and cluster in different occupations. The tricycle drivers of Jakarta, for example, come predominantly from one part of Java, and workers in other occupations follow similar geographical patterns. This is also true in the case of international migration as recruiters often visit particular villages to recruit workers.

5.13.3 Other Factors Affecting the Migration Decision

Migrants from urban to rural areas have to make the choice of whether to migrate based on incomplete information and a certain amount of risk. In most cases, they are moving from a safe job on a family farm to the insecurity of the city. If individuals are risk averse, that is, they value highly the security of their current job, they will require a greater incentive to move than someone who is risk neutral or a risk taker. This is why many migrants move to places where they have friends or relatives. The risk taker who moves first exerts a pull effect on his mates in the village.

The rural setting also provides a social capital in the form of insurance (loans and other support) from relatives and friends in bad times. This insurance depends on whether the society is highly interconnected so that legitimate insurance claims can be separated from poor judgment or laziness, in which case the insurance system would break down because of moral hazard. (Of course, when it involves the family, there is likely to be insurance even in such cases—for altruistic reasons). Implicit in all of this is the idea of reciprocity in a static and traditional society: "You rub my back and I will rub yours." This is also the basis for the patron–serf relationship in traditional societies generally. It is also fertile ground for discussing the principal–agent relationship which plays a prominent role in much of the recent work on contracts in developing countries.

5.14   Intraregional and International Labor Migration within Asia

International labor migration is often a neglected and sometimes misunderstood subject. This is partly because there is much less freedom in people movement than there is in the movement of capital and goods and services. The restrictions on movements in labor are unlikely to be relaxed, as they present difficult social issues that are not encountered in the movement of other factors of production or international trade. Given these impediments, it is quite surprising that so much international migration has taken place.

Patterns of labor migration are most easily understood by looking at the cycle of economic growth and unemployment. A typical developing country starts with a low level of employment and much surplus labor. As it progresses, its poverty level declines as employment increases along with wage levels when workers' productivity increases. Eventually, it reaches nearly full employment. As it continues to grow, it experiences labor shortages. Depending on the pattern of growth, these shortages could appear in skilled occupations, but more often in unskilled occupations. Of course. there will be in- and out-migration at the same time. There will also be a brain drain in some skilled occupations in the poor countries and some of the poorer sections of the economy may also migrate even when incomes are generally high.

5.14.1   Causes of Labor Migration

Generally, the economic factors for migration are very strong. Low domestic earnings and underemployment will offer a large incentive to migrate. Combined with employment opportunities abroad, this will be enough to stimulate migration, even when there are uncertainties and substantial costs. In Asia, much of the migration is of a temporary nature, particularly when unskilled or semi-skilled workers are involved. Migrants will move without their families for a specific period of time and then return home with a nest egg. Migration of professionals would be on a more permanent basis. Given this, the individual migration experience will often depend upon some special knowledge that a worker obtains about a possible immigration destination from relatives or friends in an informal network, or through recruiters who serve as middlemen.

As economic development accelerates, the attractiveness of out-migration is reduced as labor shortages arise and wages increase. The migration transition occurs when the level of full employment is reached—when out-migration begins to dominate. In Asia, Japan, Korea, and Taiwan have already reached this stage of migration transition. The Philippines, Vietnam, China, and countries in South Asia have still not reached this turning point. These countries supply most of the immigrants to other Asian countries as well as to the industrial countries.

Workers also migrate in order to provide remittance income for their families at home. Besides building a nest egg, migrants regularly send remittances to support their family and relatives. These remittance flows are substantial for the Philippines where it is estimated that remittance incomes form as much as 10 percent of its GDP each year. Bangladeshi, Indian, Pakistani, and Chinese migrants also remit substantial amounts to their home countries. During the financial crisis of 2008–2009 remittance income is expected to fall along with global economic activity. However, international migrants from the developing countries supply a cheap source of unskilled labor, and this demand is unlikely to abate. Nevertheless, any slowdown in remittance inflows to the developing countries in Asia will have an adverse impact on the poor since a large part of these remittances go to this segment of society.

5.14.2 Labor Migration and Public Policy

Immigration in all the high-income countries in the Asian region has been strictly controlled and very selective. The basic immigration policy for all of these countries is very similar and follows what has been dubbed the three S policy—skilled workers are sought for short-term employment in specific sectors. However, the demand for workers has exceeded these narrow requirements and as a result, there is a large excess demand for immigrants and a large flow of illegal workers. Most of these workers are unskilled and they take low-paying jobs in occupations which locals are unwilling to work. Most of these migrant workers are from other countries in the region, primarily Southeast Asia. For example, there are large numbers of Indonesians working in Malaysia, where the language, religion, and ethnic background are similar. There are also large numbers of workers from Mindanao in the southern Philippines working in Sabah and Sarawak in eastern Malaysia. These two states are very close and have cultural and religious ties. In the past, there was a large number of Chinese workers in Hong Kong but this has abated as the Hong Kong manufacturers moved their base to China. There is also an increasing flow of migrants from Myanmar to Thailand, and a smaller influx from Laos and Cambodia.

To analyze the economic impact of this migration, the effects on both the source and destination country need to be considered. First, migration will result in a decrease in the real output of the source country and an increase in the real output of the host country. Since productivity is higher in the host country, migration will raise real world output. There will also be a redistribution of income in keeping with marginal productivity as the increase in labor in the host country will raise the productivity of capital and lower that of labor, assuming that diminishing returns to factors prevail.

HOW ARE INTERNATIONAL LABOR MOVEMENTS RELATED TO MOVEMENTS IN CAPITAL AND CHANGES IN THE PATTERN OF INTERNATIONAL TRADE? Some labor movements will complement the flows of capital, such as FDI. This would be true for managerial and other highly skilled workers who accompany the FDI and who could help to develop the production apparatus and train domestic workers. On the other hand, unskilled labor could contribute to trade substitution if they are employed in import-substituting industries at the low end of the skill chain. This is one reason why these immigrants have been heavily controlled, in addition to the possible perception that they are not "desirable" for raising the economic welfare of the host country.

In some countries, such as the Philippines and China, the governments have followed a conscious policy of exporting labor with a view to raising foreign exchange earnings through remittances. Most of these immigrants are temporary workers and have low skills, but this is changing as the governments try to improve the skills level and therefore the wages earned by immigrants. Some estimates show that as much as 15 percent of the Philippine labor force is now working overseas.

Despite controls on immigration, there has been a rapid increase in temporary, often illegal, migration from labor surplus to labor scarce economies in Asia during the past two decades. This has raised income generally, as migration has raised the productivity of the migrant worker and also contributed to raising wages in the source country by reducing the supply of labor. This movement has increased the flexibility of labor markets, thereby contributing to the ability of countries in the region to respond quickly and effectively to the changing pattern of external and domestic demand.

5.15 THE ROLE OF THE GOVERNMENT

Generally speaking, government policy in the industrial sector has adopted a hands-off attitude in terms of providing direct incentives for individual industries. This is particularly true in the case of Taiwan, where there are no specific industries supported by the government. In the case of Korea, strong industrial policies were advocated and the emphasis has shifted over time. Nevertheless, a bias toward particular large industries has been maintained. In Southeast Asia, a more balanced attitude has prevailed, with few subsidies or promotional advantages offered. Nevertheless, the industry has been nurtured in a number of ways.

5.15.1 Nurturing Growth in the Industrial Sector

Industrial sector growth was nurtured in many ways through the indirect effects of government policy. Exchange rates were maintained in such a way that the industrial sector was not penalized. Educational opportunities were enhanced through a continual buildup of technological capacity, particularly in Korea and Taiwan (see Chapter 10). Furthermore, infrastructure spending was maintained so that transport, communications, and information technology could be used to enhance innovation and productivity. Where policies allowed for the free entry and exit of business firms, a flexible environment conducive to rapid change and adaptation to new techniques and ideas flourished and economic growth accelerated. Finally, labor market policies, even when unions started to grow in the past decade, were flexible enough to allow firms to adapt to changes in demand.

In cases where such industrial policies were not followed, industrial growth has been slower and less flexible. This has been particularly true in those economies where SOEs have established a strong foothold, such as in India and other South Asian countries, and also in Vietnam and parts of the Chinese economy.

5.15.2 Efficiency and Welfare

When markets work well, resources are allocated in an efficient manner. We have seen that this has generally been the case in the evolution of rapid industrial growth in East and Southeast Asia. There have been, however, cases when there was market failure. We saw how the bubble preceding the financial crisis led to a misallocation of resources in several economies in the Asian region. Markets may also fail to allocate resources effectively in cases where there may be elements of a natural monopoly, although recent developments in public utility economics suggest that these elements are less widespread than previously believed. There are also considerations of welfare that have to be taken into account that go beyond the operation of simple market principles. The provision of unemployment and retirement benefits is part of the fabric of industrial policy in the industrial countries. Yet, these are only now being developed in the Asian economies. This area requires a growing share of resources as populations begin to age. Japan is now grappling with these issues, particulary since its population is aging faster than other industrial countries.

To some extent there is a trade-off between efficiency and welfare. We will not dwell on this, but need to recognize the necessity of planning for retirement and that a social safety net should be provided for workers that are retrenched in periods of slack demand. In the past when the region was experiencing unparalleled growth, these considerations were less important. Now that growth has slowed and unemployment has increased, these isses have become more pressing.

5.16 Summary and Conclusions

In this chapter, we have reviewed the process of industrialization generally and in the Asian economies, in particular. Growth in the sector has been characterized by rapid structural change and dynamism, particularly in East and Southeast Asia. The movement from primary products to labor-intensive manufacturing, and then to skill- and capital-intensive manufacturing and services, has been rapid. The role of technology and innovation, including the role of TNCs, was discussed and the experiences of the different countries reviewed. Although East and Southeast Asia chose different paths to attract foreign technology, both regions were successful in developing a vibrant industrial sector and a highly successful export strategy. The chapter also looked at the shift in population from rural to urban areas that accompanied this industrialization process. Issues of labor market flexibility and the role of government policies were also considered.

For the future, it is important to recognize that industrial and employment policies will be critical in helping the private sector to continue to adapt to a changing external environment while incorporating new technology and responding to the challenge of globalization. Flexibility and transparency will both be important as the region continues to move forward and become further integrated into the global production network and the world economy.

Review Questions

1. Assess the strengths and weaknesses of the Lewis–Fei–Ranis model of economic growth and structural transformation. Can you think of ways to improve the model?

2. There are two strands of thought regarding industrialization. The first says that it is important to have a large market in order to take advantage of scale economies and to produce efficiently at low cost. The second says that small-scale industries have been very successful because they have been able to take advantage of shifts in demand, innovation, and fashion because of their size. How do you reconcile these two ideas?

3. Does the answer to Question 2 have anything to do with changes in technology over the past several decades?

4. The debate is over whether the rapid growth in Asia was a result of "inspiration" or "perspiration." What exactly does this phrase mean? Explain the arguments for both sides. Has there been a shift in the evidence over time? If there has, what do you think are the reasons for this shift?

5. Alice Amsden and Michael Hobday, among others, argue that the total factor productivity debate misses the point. What exactly are they talking about?

6. Some writers argue that the development of the electronics industry has been a "doubled-edged sword." Explain how this reasoning goes. What are the trends for the next few years and how will this affect the relative costs and benefits of further intensification of production in electronics?

7. Discuss the interrelationship between education and the shifts that have taken place in industrial production in Asia over the past two or three decades. How does comparative advantage fit into this paradigm?

8. How can state-owned enterprises (SOEs) stifle innovation? In a country with a large SOE sector like the China or Vietnam, has it still been possible to grow rapidly and to stimulate innovation? How has this happened?

9. Is the motivation to migrate from the rural areas to the city generally the same as the motivation to work overseas? Discuss some of the possible differences in the variables that explain migration in these two cases.

10. Hobday, Amsden and others with similar views have written about the industrialization experience of countries in East Asia. What is the basic thrust of their argument? How does their analysis impact on the current debate about the role of China in the future growth and development trajectory of the Asian region?

11. Discuss the total factor productivity question with respect to the Asian developing economies. In the discussion, review the Krugman–Young evidence with respect to the impact of total factor productivity on growth and then examine other evidence that has been presented since their articles were written. If there are differences between Krugman–Young and more recent evidence, explain why and how these differences may have arisen.

Notes on References and Suggestions for Further Reading

The process of industrialization is not discussed explicitly in the models of economic growth. One has to refer to sectoral theories and to the analysis of microeconomics to gather insights into the industrialization process. The work of H. Chenery, Sherman Robinson, and Moshe Syrquin (1986), discussed in Chapter 2, gives a guide to the process.

In addition, this chapter focuses on the shift of resources that takes place between rural and urban sectors as the process of industrialization unfolds. In this regard, the articles and book by John Fei and Gustav Ranis (1961, 1964) and William A. Lewis (1954) are key sources.

The movement and dynamic shifts of comparative advantage are an important ingredient of the process of industrialization and the key article is on the theory of revealed comparative advantage by B. Balassa (1965).

How important was technological transfer to the process of industrialization in Asia? This subject has been investigated by a number of writers in the past decade or so, beginning with Paul Krugman's (1994) article in *Foreign Affairs*, citing the work of Alwyn Young that stirred up the hornets' nest. Other useful contributors to this literature, most of whom have different views from Krugman, and state that TFP was important as an input into the Asian "miracle" growth process are Barry Bosworth and Susan Collins (1996), Nicholas Crafts (1998), Malcolm Dowling and Peter M. Summers (1998), Arnold C. Harberger (1996), and Michael Sarel (1997).

From a different vantage point, Alice H. Amsden (1989), Michael Hobday (1995), R. R. Nelson and Howard Pack (1998), and Linsu Kim and R. R. Nelson (2000) argue that any attempt to attribute the fruits of innovation to a separate variable called total factor productivity misses the boat, because the process of innovation involves changes in the inputs—labor, capital, and technology are interdependent.

Alice H. Amsden (2001), and Malcolm Dowling and David Ray (2000) also investigate the changing pattern of industrial production and relate it to the demand for exports from industrialized countries. This analysis explains why the Asian economies were able to experience such rapid and pronounced industrial and export growth for more than twenty-five years.

See I. Gill and H. Kharas (2006) for a good discussion of technology transfer and the role of foreign direct investment and foreign enterprises in industry.

International Trade and Investment

6.1 INTRODUCTION

With advances in technology, the cost of transportation and communication has fallen so that opportunities for travel, trade, and investments are now greater than ever. Accompanied by more liberal trade regimes than in the past, the amount of trade within and between economies has soared. However, long before people had access to trade via the Internet, telephone, by mail order or through department stores and markets, people had already engaged in trade, through bartering. Although bartering still exists, it is money, credit and debit cards that have facilitated trade.

This chapter looks at the changing pattern and growth of international trade. First, some of the most common theories dealing with the gains from trade will be illustrated. This will be followed by a discussion of trade policies, particularly barriers to trade and arguments against free trade. East Asia's experience will highlight the effectiveness of two of the most commonly cited trade regimes: import-substitution and export-promotion. Finally, the patterns of trade in East Asia will be compared with those of Latin America to show how dramatically trade has changed over the years.

6.2 THEORIES OF INTERNATIONAL TRADE

6.2.1 Gains from Trade

An introduction to international trade usually begins with an autarkic economy. Such an economy can consume only as much as it can produce. Thus, it would be motivated to produce only what it can consume and cannot exploit any economies of scales that may exist. When trade is introduced, the economy can gain through two main avenues: consumption and production.

CONSUMPTION GAINS   With trade, it is possible to reach higher indifference curves through gains realized by consumers. The gains from trade are illustrated in Figure 6.1.

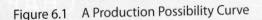

Figure 6.1   A Production Possibility Curve

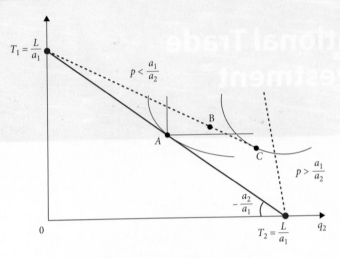

a_1 : quantity of labor required to produce first good, q_1
a_2 : quantity of labor required to produce second good, q_2
p : price of second good in terms of the first, i.e., $p = p_2 / p_1$

SOURCE: Harry P. Bowen, Abraham Hollander, and Jean-Marie Viaene, *Applied International Trade Analysis* (Basingstoke, UK: University of Michigan Press, 1998), Figure 3.1, p. 81.

PRODUCTION GAINS   Trade enables the production and reallocation of gains by allowing countries to specialize in the production of commodities at a relatively lower cost either because of absolute advantage or comparative advantage. The production gains from trade also arises because of expanded production, through utilizing economies of scale resulting from larger markets, or technology transfers which help to expand the production possibility frontier. Trade also enables a country to purchase raw material and intermediate products not available locally. The major difference between absolute advantage and comparative advantage is that in the former case, the country can produce the commodity more efficiently (in absolute terms). To have comparative advantage means that the commodity can be produced relatively more efficiently.

The gains from trade can be broken down into gains from exchange and gains from specialization.

In this model based on Ricardo (1817), for the sake of simplicity, it is assumed that there are only two countries and two final products. A production possibility curve (a straight line in Figure 6.1) shows the production combinations of the two goods in a single country. The goods are produced using labor input L, which is assumed to be homogeneous and supply inelastic, perfectly mobile domestically but internationally immobile. Labor requirements per unit of output are fixed and do not vary with the scale of production. Technologies differ between the two countries and there are no trade barriers or transportation costs. There is competition in both factor and product markets.

Without trade (autarky), it will be optimal for a country to consume the two final goods produced at point A, where the indifference curve intersects the production possibility curve. With trade, the

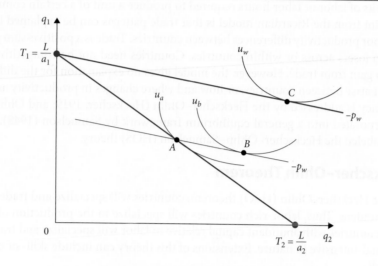

Figure 6.2   Decomposition of Gains from Trade

a_1 : quantity of labor required to produce first good, q_1
a_2 : quantity of labor required to produce second good, q_2
p : price of second good in terms of the first, i.e., $p = p_2 / p_1$

SOURCE: Harry P. Bowen, Abraham Hollander, and Jean-Marie Viaene, *Applied International Trade Analysis* (Basingstoke, UK: University of Michigan Press, 1998), Figure 3.4, p. 87.

country will be able to specialize in the production of a final good where it has a comparative advantage, and the production possibility curve would pivot outwards from point T_1. The optimal point would be to the right of A, at the intersection of the new production possibility curve and a higher indifference curve. Hence, it can be seen that trade allows a country to enjoy greater consumption of goods.

Another production possibility curve that intersects A is constructed in Figure 6.2 so as to demonstrate the effects of a change in the relative prices of the two goods as a result of trade. Production remains unchanged. When the second good is cheaper, more of it will be consumed. The shift in consumption from point A to B displays the gain in utility from the increased consumption of the second good because of the change in relative prices. The subsequent move from B to C represents the increased specialization in production. These two effects are the same as those found when we look at the income and substitution effects of a change in the price of a good in conventional demand analysis. The move from A to B is the substitution effect (no change in income but only in relative prices) and from B to C, the income effect.

Gains from trade can be derived analytically. The main finding according to the Ricardian model is that countries will benefit from trade in proportion to the degree to which their labor productivity is different. In addition, trade will be beneficial if there are favorable terms of trade to the home country. This is in keeping with intuition.

6.2.2 Ricardian Theory of Trade

The Ricardian theory says that differences in technology determine comparative advantage. The theory considers the units of labor or labor hours required to produce a unit of a certain commodity.

A major point from the Ricardian model is that trade patterns can be explained by technological differences or labor productivity differences between countries. Trade is a positive-sum game and therefore there are no losers across or within countries. Countries need not be competitive relative to the other country to gain from trade. However, the model gives no explanation for the differences in labor productivity that arise between countries, or how and where changes in productivity arise and occurs.

This deficiency is addressed by the Heckscher–Ohlin (Heckscher, 1919; and Ohlin, 1933) theory, which was incorporated into a general equilibrium framework by Samuelson (1948). The theory has therefore been labeled the Heckscher–Ohlin–Samuelson (HOS) theory.

6.2.3 Heckscher–Ohlin Theorem

According to the Hecksher–Ohlin (H–O) theorem, countries will specialize and trade in goods which are relatively abundant. Thus, labor-rich countries will specialize in the production of labor-intensive products while countries with abundant capital relative to labor will specialize and trade in commodities that are capital-intensive in nature. Extensions of this theory can include skill- or education-intensive goods as well.

As a result, it is expected that poorer countries will export labor-intensive products while the rich countries will export capital- or skill-intensive products.

The basis of the model is that countries differ from one another according to the factors of production they possess, and that goods differ from one another according to the factors of production. Thus, a labor-abundant country will have a comparative advantage in a good that uses labor relatively intensively (for example, sweaters require machine and yarns, while bread depends on agriculture and farming).

According to the Heckscher–Ohlin theorem:

- trade should be greater between countries that have the greatest differences in economic structures. If there were no differences in the HOS model, there would be no trade whatsoever.
- factor prices will tend to level out as trade continues. This is called the factor price equalization theorem. In a country that has a comparative advantage in labor-intensive products, its wage rate will be low relative to a country that has a comparative advantage in capital-intensive products. As trade takes place, the country producing labor-intensive products will experience an increase in labor relative to capital and thus, the demand for labor will rise relative to the demand for capital and so will the wage rate relative to the cost of capital. Similarly, in a country producing capital-intensive goods, the return to capital will rise relative to the wage rate.

The Rybczynski theorem (Rybczynski, 1955) says that if capital-labor ratios differ between industries then, at constant commodity prices, an increase in the supply of one factor alone will cause the expansion of the good intensively using that factor and a decline in the supply of the other good. The Stolper–Samuelson theorem (Stolper and Samuelson, 1941) says that an increase in the price of any good raises the nominal, relative, and real return to the factor in the production of that good and lowers the nominal, relative, and real return to the other factor.

6.2.4 Imperfect Competition

Both the Ricardian and the HOS models establish a linkage between economic efficiency, factor endowments, and the direction of international trade. They make many simplifying assumptions, including the existence of perfect competition in commodity, factor markets, and the homogeneity of production factors. They also assume that factors are immobile between countries, consumer preferences and production functions are identical, and consumers have identical preferences. They also assume that there are no taxes, costs of transport, or other barriers to trade.

When these assumptions are relaxed, there is a probability that the conclusions of the models may not hold. In particular, there are two aspects of international trade in which these models are deficient when confronted with the actual flow of international trade. First, the model suggests that there should only be a small amount of trade between countries with the same factor endowments. In fact, most of the world trade that takes place between rich countries have very similar factor endowments. Secondly, neither theory considers intra-industry trade, which has shown a significant increase.

To address these aspects, the theory of imperfect competition (oligopoly and monopoly) is applied to international trade. In this framework, the direction of intra-industry trade is determined in large part by differences in relative factor endowments while production differentiation and relative market size determine the volume and composition of international trade.

In models of trade with imperfect competition, greater trade between countries with similar factor endowments arises because of product differentiation and differences in consumer preferences. However, because of the existence of monopolies and the introduction of scale economies, the gains and direction of trade are complex and difficult to analyze.

If trade results in a decrease in market power and the distortions that come with it, then there could be welfare gains from trade as well as from scale economies. However, if the gains from trade are realized in sectors where there is monopoly power, then trade would result in a decrease in competition and an increase in monopoly elements. This could lead to a decline in welfare. In summary, the direction of trade will depend upon the comparative advantage gained from trade, as well as the relationship between the size of the country and its imperfectly competitive industries.

With regard to intra-industry trade, the theory states that the more alike countries are in terms of relative factor endowments, the larger the share of intra-industry to total trade.

Much of the empirical work that has been carried out as well as casual observation seem to confirm the theoretical implications of the monopolistic competitive model. Trade between countries with similar factor endowments has grown as a proportion of total trade. Furthermore, the ability of large oligopolies within a country to distort prices and reduce the supply of goods may have been hampered by the requirement to be competitive internationally. However, there may be cases where this pressure is lessened by the introduction of tariffs to protect domestic markets. The case of Japan comes to mind.

As far as empirical evidence for the validity of the theoretical inferences of models with monopolistic markets is concerned, there is some positive support. The gravity model of international trade, which asserts that the distance between countries and their relative physical sizes are the main determinants of trade, has received wide confirmation in many empirical tests. Correlations have also been found between the extent of intra-industry trade among country pairs and per-capita income, and also between intra-industry trade and measures of cross-country differences in per-capita income. In the latter case, the correlations are negative as expected.

The positive relationship between intra-industry trade and per-capita income is explained by similarities in tastes being correlated with per-capita income. Countries that are more alike, as measured by per-capita income, would have a greater tendency to trade with each other in products in the same industry. Automobiles and other consumer durables are good examples.

In the next section, we explore some of these theoretical and empirical issues in the Asian context.

6.3 TRADE EXPERIENCE OF EAST ASIA

6.3.1 Pattern of Growth in International Trade: Some Facts

International trade volume has grown faster than income in the past thirty years for the world as a whole and also for Asia. The share of East and Southeast Asia in world exports is now more than 20 percent compared with 12 percent in 1990. It is nearly twice as much as the export share of North America and is greater than the total exports of Latin America, South Asia, Eastern Europe, the former Soviet Union, the Middle East, and North Africa and Africa combined. The role that primary products play in trade has declined owing to the relative decline of the agricultural sector over the years (see Table 5.3 in Chapter 5). Conversely, trade in manufactured goods has risen dramatically. This is because of the Engle curve effects. Income elasticity of demand for primary products has been low and falling over time. Prices for primary products have also been on a downward trend for the last century. Lower prices for exports of primary products contrast with stable or rising prices for manufactured goods. This means that the terms of trade for primary products have deteriorated quite dramatically. (The terms of trade is an index based on the value of goods exported divided by the value of goods imported.)

In the face of this trend and as a natural consequence of economic development and growth, the developing countries in general have reduced primary exports and built up manufactured exports. This is true of Asia and, to a lesser extent, Latin America but not Africa (see Table 2.4 in Chapter 2). The underlying inability of Africa to develop a viable manufacturing sector is one of the main reasons that Africa has been slow to develop. In the last forty-odd years, the volume of international trade has risen faster than the growth of income for most countries in Asia (see Table 6.1), and exports have increased as a share of GDP (see Table 2.5 in Chapter 2).

The share of exports in GDP has continued to rise as the region became more industrialized. A greater reliance on exports has helped the region to sustain rapid rates of growth, but at the same time it has made the region more dependent upon import demand from the rest of the world, particularly the industrial countries.

6.3.2 Actual Evolution of Trade

- *It is often thought that trade should be greatest between countries that have the greatest differences in economic structures.* In reality, the major part of trade takes place between rich countries that have similar factor endowments and relative prices (see Table 6.2). This is consistent with the monopolistic competition model described in Section 6.2.4, and this has led to the rapid rise in trade in similar products between the industrial countries, which dominate the trade scene although their share has declined in the past thirty years, partly as a result of the rise in importance of the Asian "miracle" economies.

  Many developing countries are large suppliers of raw primary products and minerals, some of which are capital-intensive in production. This can be explained by supply factors—minerals are found in the developing countries and are exploited by multinationals that use the same technology no matter where they are operating.

- *The factor price equalization theorem states that factor prices will tend to be more equal as trade takes place.* In reality, the factor price equalization theorem does not seem to hold. Wage differentials between developing and developed countries are still large, as are returns on capital. The factor price equalization theorem also does not seem to apply in developed countries' labor markets, as regional wage differentials have been sustained over time.

Table 6.1   Growth in Income and International Trade (Decade Averages of Yearly Rates), 1961–2007

Economy	Decade Growth Rates of Income and Exports[a]									
	1961–1970		1971–1980		1981–1990		1991–2000		2001–2007	
East Asia										
China		3.7	5.4	**12.5**	9.3	**9.8**	10.2	**16.3**	9.4	**25.8**
Hong Kong	9.9	**11.2**	9.2	**9.8**	6.6	**13.6**	4.4	**8.0**	4.6	**8.1**
Korea	8.3	**29.1**	7.8	**21.6**	8.7	**10.9**	6.3	**15.8**	4.6	**12.4**
Taiwan	11.3[b,c]		9.0[b,d]		8.0	**10.8**	6.4	**9.2**	3.4	**7.5**
Southeast Asia										
Indonesia	4.2	**4.4**	7.9	**9.3**	6.3	**2.6**	4.4	**7.1**	5.9	**9.2**
Malaysia	6.5	**5.9**	7.9	**18.5**	6.1	**10.7**	7.2	**12.6**	4.8	**9.1**
Philippines	4.9	**5.5**	6.0	**10.4**	1.8	**4.0**	2.9	**8.2**	4.5	**4.4**
Singapore	10.0		9.1		7.4		7.8		4.3	**10.8**
Thailand	8.2	**10.5**	6.9	**10.0**	7.9	**14.2**	4.6	**10.7**	5.1	**12.5**
South Asia										
Bangladesh	4.1	**3.4**	1.6	**7.3**	3.9	**10.4**	4.8	**11.7**	5.6	**18.4**
India	3.9		3.1	**6.4**	5.9	**6.1**	5.3	**10.6**	7.0	**11.7**
Pakistan	7.3	**9.0**	4.6	**1.8**	6.2	**8.8**	4.0	**5.2**	5.5	**18.5**
Sri Lanka	4.6	**1.6**	4.6	**1.5**	4.3	**6.1**	5.2	**9.0**	4.3	**11.5**
North Asia										
Japan	10.5	**16.1**	4.5	**9.7**	4.0	**5.4**	1.4	**3.9**	2.4	**5.3**

[a] Figures in bold denote exports.
[b] From *Taiwan Statistical Data Book*.
[c] Figure calculated for the year 1965 and 1970.
[d] Figure calculated for 1973 to 1980.

SOURCES: Seiji F. Naya, *The Asian Development Experience: Overcoming Crises and Adjusting to Change* (Manila: Asian Development Bank, 2002); *Taiwan Statistical Data Book* (2008); World Bank, *World Development Indicators Online*; Asian Development Bank, *Asian Development Outlook 2004, 2009*; John Malcolm Dowling, *Future Perspectives on the Economic Development of Asia* (Singapore: World Scientific Publishing, 2008).

The entire complex legal system of controls, taxes, restrictions, and other regulations constitutes a country's international trade regime. To simplify discussion, we will try to organize the analysis by introducing two stereotypical regimes: import substitution and export promotion. While any individual country will have elements of both and some of free trade as well, what we are concerned with here is the main thrust of its international trade policy.

6.3.3   Import-Substitution Trade Regimes

In an import-substitution regime, a country tries to stimulate the production of a different array of domestic goods by levying taxes, licensing, putting quotas on or banning imports. Through this web

Table 6.2 Share of Exports of Industrial and Developing Countries in Selected Years (Billions US$)

Country Grouping	1971	2000	2004
Industrial countries	248.9 (73.8%)	3,984.7 (63.1%)	5,477.8 (59.9%)
Developing economies	89.5 (26.3%)	2,325.4 (36.9%)	3,667.2 (40.1%)
World	338.4	6,310.1	9,145.0

Percentage share is in parentheses.

SOURCES: International Monetary Fund, *International Financial Statistics* (Washington, D.C.: IMF, 2001); *World Development Indicators Online*.

of restrictions on imports, their competitiveness in the domestic market is reduced, leaving space for domestic production. The effect of these restrictions on the society can be evaluated using standard static welfare analysis. The government gets revenue that it spends. Take the case of a tax on a particular product. The consumer pays higher prices for the imported good and so he loses consumer surplus, and domestic (inefficient) production is subsidized. There are also dynamic factors involved in evaluating an import-substitution policy regime. The infant industry and learning-by-doing arguments suggest that with time and some degree of initial protection, domestic industries will eventually become efficient producers on the world market. The Asian "miracle" countries and Japan are good examples. India's car manufacturing industry, on the other hand, is a bad example. The Asian success stories are many—automobiles, cameras, electronics, and almost any other capital-intensive manufactured good you can think of, besides aircraft.

Import-substitution is critically important during the early stages of development and industrialization. During this process, the new industries will have to be subsidized. Through the protection of infant industries, an industrial base is gradually built up. This happened in almost all the developing countries. In the developed countries, the industrialization process took place at about the same time so that there was no need to protect against products from more advanced countries, although tariff barriers were imposed on manufactured goods in many countries until recently. Import-substitution can only take a country so far—particularly a small country. Export promotion strategies also have the advantage of bringing more competitive forces into play because external markets are very competitive.

6.3.4 Outward-Oriented Trade Regimes

Export promotion in Asia and in the newly industrialized economies (NIEs) of Latin America started with labor-intensive products that had strong backward linkages, and then moved into more skill and capital-intensive industries. These were product categories where the income elasticity of demand in the industrial countries had been high since 1980. These included computers, electronics, and pharmaceuticals, as well as electrical machinery. The labor-intensive industries where they started out were at the low end of the growth scale—textiles and apparel, furniture, paper and printing, and processed foods. Those countries in which export promotion has not been successful are either stuck in labor-intensive products or are still in the primary export phase. Indonesia is an example of a country in Asia that has been slow to "graduate" to the rapid growth industries of the countries of the Organization for Economic Cooperation and Development (OECD).

Once the infant industry has matured, the barriers to foreign competition can be dropped and imports allowed in once more. As import barriers are lowered, the trade regime becomes neutral, favoring neither imports nor exports. However, it is possible to develop an export strategy too. Such a strategy subsidizes exports while keeping a low tax on imported inputs that will be used as the components of exports. This strategy can be adopted even as the country is starting an industrial push forward if the country is very small. In this case, production is undertaken primarily for export. This was the strategy of the Asian countries almost from the beginning. They were not concerned about the domestic market. In fact even today, prices in the domestic market in Japan are significantly higher than they are overseas. Dual pricing and collusion among producers work together to keep domestic prices and profits high while maintaining competitiveness in the international markets. Export subsidies are a good example of how exports can be promoted. Tax breaks, better credit terms, and greater availability of loanable funds are also helpful. At the same time, regimes that followed successful export promotion strategies were constantly monitoring the performance of exporters. Those that performed well got more subsidies. Those that did not compete successfully could see their access to cheap credit drying up, their subsidies reduced, and the taxman appearing to audit their books more often.

6.3.5 The "Flying Geese" Development Paradigm

Kaname Akamatsu (1961) proposed the "Flying Geese" Development Paradigm[1] as a general principle for development. It describes the industrialization process of trading nations. The "Flying Geese" model bears a resemblance to the Product Cycle theory[2] that has a more domestic market orientation. The model illustrates how less developed countries can catch up with the developed countries by adopting the industries of the latter. More recent development theories allow foreign direct investment (FDI) to become a channel for the developed countries to recycle their comparative advantage to less developed countries.

The life cycle of a typical industry can be summarized in five stages.[3]

Stage 1
- Product is introduced via imports from an industrialized country.
- Consumers are responsive and raise demand, which induces domestic production.

---

[1] Kaname Akamatsu started to develop the theory in the early 1930s and continued to refine it into the 1960s. He used the lyrical name, *gankoo keitai*, to describe the shape of import, production, and export-growth curves displayed by the few modern industries in Japan before World War II. See Korhonen (1994) for a detailed discussion of Akamatsu and his theory. Dowling and Cheang (2000) explore the empirical implications of the "Flying Geese" model and shifting comparative advantage using recent data for Asia.

[2] The Product Cycle theory is developed by Vernon R. (1966). The key difference between the two theories is the perspective taken. As the Product Cycle theory was developed to explain the characteristics of shifts in comparative advantage of American industries, it takes the perspective of the developed countries. It describes how a new product is invented and developed from its infant stage to the exporting stage, and finally to its declining stage. On the other hand, the "Flying Geese" model was developed to explain the characteristics of shifts in comparative advantage of Japanese industries when Japan was still a developing country; it takes the perspective of the less developed countries. It describes how a new product is introduced to the less developed countries via imports (this stage should correspond to the exporting stage of the Product Cycle theory) and how the less developed countries acquire the necessary production technique to become exporters (this stage should correspond to the declining stage of the Product Cycle theory).

[3] In Akamatsu (1961, 1962), the development of a typical industry ends at the exporting stage. However, here it is necessary to consider the declining stage and the relocation of the industry to other developing countries. Hence, the five-stage version of the theory presented in Yamazawa (1990) is adopted.

Stage 2
- Import-substitution policies are imposed.
- Small foreign direct investment interest.

Stage 3
- Growth of domestic demand slows and imports diminish in absolute terms.
- Production remains high as exports begin.
- FDI increases.
- Developed country loses comparative advantage in this particular product.

Stage 4
- On maturity, production slows down.
- Exports growth slows or even declines.
- FDI declines.

Stage 5
- Government reduces protection.
- Declining industry must relocate in order to survive.

In the first stage, domestic imitations cannot compete with foreign imports because of their inferior quality and high production cost. Imports therefore remain high and a run on the country's foreign exchange may occur. Nevertheless, the important role of the government in this early stage is to provide market conditions conducive for domestic entrepreneurs to begin production. Thus, the government needs to draw up reliable commercial and legal frameworks, and protective polices to support domestic production. The protective policies are necessary to help correct the current-account deficit. These policies should also facilitate the acquisition of necessary technology and know-how and capital goods to improve the quality of the product and reduce costs. As a result, domestic demand will grow and this will allow the industry to engage in more efficient large-scale production. When product quality improves, price becomes competitive, and domestic products will gradually replace foreign imports. At this stage, there is little interest expressed by foreign investors. Investments are small because the domestic market is relatively small, or there is an inappropriate legal framework or inadequate commercial infrastructure, such as transport and communication facilities.

In stage 3, exports continue to grow and enable the import of capital goods for the continued expansion of production. FDI increases as the economy develops better education and improvements in the commercial and legal framework, and when the developed country loses its comparative advantage.

At later stages of the life cycle, the government needs to ensure that its policies enable the industry to gain access to global markets for the products. However, as the industry faces maturity, production will slow down in the face of increasing costs and intensified competition from late-starting countries. To ensure competitiveness, the government needs to reduce protection. Eventually, exports will decrease whilst domestic demand declines. FDI will fall, as investors are attracted to late-starting countries. At this stage, wages and other costs of production also become so high that even the best-practice domestic firm loses comparative edge, and the industry must relocate in order to survive.

Using Asia as an example of a region where the "Flying Geese" theory can work, we divide the entire region into three groups of countries. These groups are arranged according to their relative state of economic development. Japan is the lead country, followed by the NIEs as the newly rising countries, and lastly, the ASEAN-4 (Malaysia, Indonesia, Thailand, and the Philippines) as the follower countries. This regional hierarchy allows development to trickle down from Japan, first to the NIEs and then to the ASEAN-4. These countries trade and interact with each other, having a common goal in mind: to advance to higher technological sophistication, as happened in the ASEAN-4 in the 1970s. The advantageous position of having an established, and often protected, domestic market, coupled with the acquisition of standardized production technology, makes large-scale production possible.

In Akamatsu's original thesis, the process of structural change is by no means easy and conflict-free, especially for the less developed countries. With the inflow of cheap foreign products, industries in traditional handicrafts will collapse. The cheap imports benefit consumers but harm domestic producers. Eventually, however, the cheap imports will force domestic production to shape up and introduce the economy into the global community. Yet, in recent accounts of the theory, especially in terms of East Asian development, a harmonious picture seems to have emerged. The restructuring of an economy is relatively cost-free and transition is smooth.

Domestic investment merely withdraws from the declining industries and flows into the sunrise and exporting industries. There is no trade-off between aggregate domestic investment and FDI. In addition, unemployment is not an issue. This harmonious version of the paradigm may be accurate as far as the interests of the Japanese multinational corporations coincide with those of the NIEs and the ASEAN-4. Besides, Japan is able to maintain its technological lead over the NIEs and the ASEAN-4 and will probably remain cost-competitive in human- and technology-intensive products for years to come. Thus, the countries in the Asian region seem to be progressing in an orderly manner.

The paradigm predicts regional integration and interdependence among the economies. The countries in the region will depend on each other for markets for their imports and exports. The advanced countries will need the less developed countries for reverse imports of products that they can no longer produce cost-effectively. On the other hand, the less developed countries will depend on the advanced countries for capital goods and technology know-how to develop their industries. FDI is also mutually beneficial as it acts as a channel for the advanced countries to recycle comparative advantage and the developing countries to attain technology transfer, managerial, and other production skills.

The pattern of trade evolving from the "Flying Geese" paradigm stresses inter-industry trade. This pattern of trade is in line with the argument that the countries are interdependent as they are at different stages of development and thus produce complementary products. The less developed countries will specialize in labor-intensive production whilst the advanced countries will specialize in capital-intensive production. As a result, intraregional division of labor according to the individual country's comparative advantage develops. However, as the region becomes more and more integrated, inter-industry trade is likely to be replaced by intra-industry trade. This is because as an economy develops, its production structure and trade pattern become more complex. Intermediate products can be produced and exported. Moreover, FDI is likely to be placed in industries that complement the developed countries' exporting industries. Thus, regional trade gradually takes on an intra-industry character.

Finally, there is the danger of "hollowing out" in the advanced countries, as experienced by Japan in the late 1980s and early 1990s. As a country climbs up the scale of economic development, its manufacturing sector is likely to become cost inefficient unless there are constant technological breakthroughs to keep the industries cost-competitive. Although this may not be explicitly implied by the theory, Japan has demonstrated this when its currency appreciated sharply after the 1985 Plaza Agreement. This phenomenon shows the impact of exchange rate on a country's comparative advantage. Japanese enterprises find it almost impossible to stay cost-competitive without moving offshore as the appreciation of the yen accelerates. At the same time, the strong yen makes imports from and investment in the NIEs and ASEAN-4 cheap and attractive.

6.4 ISSUES/CONSIDERATIONS IN TRADE

Within a physically large country like Australia or the United States that is composed of a number of different administrative areas, there is essentially free trade of goods and services across these provincial or state borders. Within the European Union, there is now virtually free trade among the member countries of the Union. In other regions of the world, there are fewer examples of free trade although the North American Free Trade Area (NAFTA) and the MERCOSUR Free Trade Area in Latin America are committed to gradually establishing free trade within their respective areas

More typically, there are restrictions on trade between countries. Various taxes (duties) are imposed on imports or exports. These can be in lump-sum form or *ad valorem*. Sometimes licenses are granted to export or import particular goods. Alternatively, the law may ban some exports or imports. All of these different taxes or regulations distort the workings of the free market and nullifies the law of comparative advantage.

6.4.1   Effective Rates of Protection in Developing Asia

The effective rate of protection is the percentage by which the value-added of a product at a particular stage of processing in a domestic industry can exceed what it would have been without protection. In other words, by what percentage would the sum of wages, interest, profits, and depreciation allowances payable by local firms, as a result of protection, exceed the sum that would have been incurred if these same firms had to face unrestricted competition, that is, no tariff protection from foreign producers. It is the difference between the value-added in domestic prices and that of world prices, expressed as a percentage of the latter.

The effective rate of protection is higher than the nominal rate, which is the rate of tax levied on the final product. This is because the effective rate is computed on a lower base as the value-added is less than the total price.

What are the effective rates of protection in Asia? First, countries in the region uniformly began their industrialization with tariffs that protected a wide range of domestic industries. This was true for Japan, Korea, Taiwan, and later on, the other Southeast Asian countries. Only Hong Kong and Singapore were basically free traders from the outset.

Japan briefly protected a number of industries in the early stages, but it removed these barriers gradually as its export competitiveness improved. Even as late as the 1970s, however, the rates of protection were still high in textiles and non-ferrous metals. In Korea, although protection was slowly reduced, by 1983 most sectors were still being protected by some combination of tariffs and nontariff barriers. While exporters faced competition from international prices, there was considerable protection for goods sold on the domestic market, and the same can be said for Japan, but to a lesser extent. Taiwan's experience is similar to that of Korea, and as late as in 1980, more than 40 percent of imports still received nominal protection in excess of 31 percent. In Southeast Asia, there has been a reduction in tariffs in recent years, but a relatively high rate of protection still exists for manufactured products, resulting in higher prices domestically, although the dualism between the external and internal markets is much less than it is in Japan and the NIEs. In Chapter 2, we noted that the mean tariff rates and trade taxes decreased between 1980 and 1999 (see Table 2.3). However, the mean tariff rate remains fairly high in Southeast Asia, and even higher in South Asia.

6.4.2   How Do Manufactured Exports Increase Productivity?

The relationship between exports and productivity arises from the role that exports play in helping economies adopt international best-practice technologies. In the NIEs, a higher level of labor and cognitive skills permitted more firms to quickly adopt new technology and also to adapt existing technology to local conditions. Even if exports began on the basis of productivity change due to domestic efforts such as plant reorganization, the cumulative magnitude of productivity growth over many years is most unlikely to have been the result of domestic efforts alone. Clearly, an important benefit of export orientation has been an increased ability to tap into the best-practice of world technology and business practices, as well as the business network.

Statistical analyses by the World Bank (1993), Jeffrey Sachs and Andrew Warner (1995), and others show that outward-oriented trade policies are very important variables in explaining growth in a cross-section of developing countries. The World Bank study also shows that human capital and exports are important determinants of total factor productivity. A high level of total factor productivity is found in the high growth Asian economies. In particular, the studies have found that manufactured exports and the share of manufactured exports in total trade are particularly important in explaining growth. This is probably because of the crucial role of manufactured exports in technology transfer and innovation and the move toward best-practice methods, as explained above, combined with better education.

6.4.3   Fallacy of Composition

Are there fallacies of composition in the export push strategy? Can latecomers succeed? The argument here is that if all developing countries adopted an export-growth strategy, then there would be a flood of products into developed country markets and this would give rise to protectionist pressures. This is the thrust of an article by William Cline (1982) some years ago. He developed a simulation model where he assumed that all developing countries follow the example of the NIEs. With this model, he then derived the export penetration of developing countries in industrial country markets. He argued that the simulations suggest an intolerably high level of penetration in developed country markets that would only lead to further protection by the developed countries.

The paper was written more than two decades ago and since then, the developing countries' share of world exports has continued to increase. The Uruguay Round has also been successfully completed, the WTO is functioning well, and the volume of world trade is increasing more rapidly than ever. Yet this kind of argument is still popular in some development circles. What it fails to recognize is the dynamic nature of comparative advantage, the growth of new products, and the influence of new technology on the product mix. It also fails to recognize that the trade component of North America, Europe, and Japan as a share of total output is still small, despite the rapid growth in trade. Therefore, the impact on domestic output and employment is relatively insignificant even if the share in total trade of the developing countries increases. It seems that the power of protective sentiment is still prevalent as the breakdown of the Doha round of trade negotiations in July 2008 demonstrates (see Chapter 11 for further discussion.)

6.4.4   Adopting and Accessing Technology

Despite the protectionist nature of the trade regime in the early years, the Asian "miracle" economies were the most open to foreign technology among the world's economies, according to a study by David Dollar (1990) (see Figure 6.3). Thus, the protection of the domestic economy did not extend to the importation of new technology. This is because all the economies exempted imports used for processing exports from their tariff schemes through a system of duty drawbacks or exemptions. This is one important difference from other countries that began industrialization on the basis of import-substitution.

In addition, export orientation facilitates the move toward international best-practice. As we saw in the Chapter 5, the importation of technology, either through the FDI of transnational corporations (TNCs), or through subcontracting arrangements with foreign firms, forces exporters to continually upgrade and improve their productive facilities if they want to compete in export markets. As a secondary effect, this international competitiveness indirectly forces domestic firms to become more

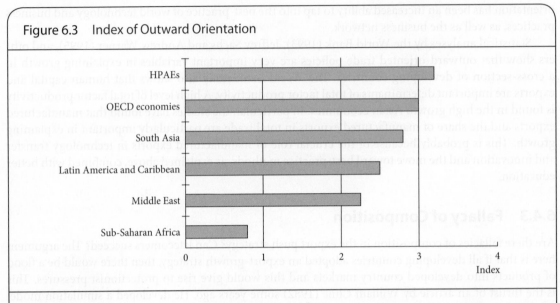

Figure 6.3   Index of Outward Orientation

High-performing Asian economies (HPAEs) refer to Japan, Hong Kong, Korea, Singapore, Taiwan, China, Indonesia, Malaysia, and Thailand.

SOURCE: David Dollar, *Outward-Oriented and Growth: An Empirical Study Using a Price-Based Measure of Openness* (Washington, D.C.: World Bank, East Asia and Pacific Region, Country Department 1, 1990). Adopted from World Bank, *The East Asian Miracle: Economic Growth and Public Policy* (New York: Oxford University Press, 1993).

competitive as trade barriers are reduced and foreign competition is reflected by pressure on local producers. Research has shown that subsidiaries of TNCs are more productive than domestic firms, and FDI does result in a more effective use of resources. However, the evidence of several plant-level studies does not show that there are positive spillovers from TNCs to their direct domestic competitors, although these spillovers could have also been vertical in nature rather than horizontal (Saggi, 2002).

Knowledge of new technology becomes available even if markets are imperfect, if regimes are open and exports are encouraged. Markets may be subject to problems of imperfect and asymmetric information and moral hazard, resulting in the reluctance of the holder of the technology to share it for fear that licensing will leak the information to competitors or that there will be a violation of patent laws. Nevertheless, an emphasis on exports allows this information asymmetry to be overcome through several channels. The purchase of new equipment required to maintain competitiveness of exports is encouraged by an open trade regime. Furthermore, foreign direct investment is encouraged in a high-export environment.

Having a foreign partner who has invested directly allows a domestic firm to have access to know-how on marketing, industrial organization, new technology, and so forth. The foreign partner can also bring with it technological licensing, which is particularly important for new products. The support of exports by domestic firms, with or without a partnership with foreign firms, allows the transfer of non-proprietary technology. This is crucial at the low end of the technological scale. For example, the technology for the production of footwear and textiles/apparel can be purchased on the market without license restriction.

Information from customers can be helpful in designing new products that are more reliable, have better quality, and are more acceptable to consumers in overseas markets. Knowledge from returning nationals can also be utilized, particularly when they have been trained in best-practices overseas. As a result, domestic research and development can be enhanced. Thus, a focus on foreign markets and partners, as well as technology, is particularly relevant to the NIEs as they reach the higher stages of development.

6.4.5 Pattern of FDI Inflows

The pattern of foreign direct investment in Asia demonstrates how this relationship has evolved over time. Table 6.3 shows the stock of foreign direct investment in the Asian economies during the past twenty-seven years. In 1980, only Hong Kong had a large stock of FDI, amounting to nearly 80 percent of all the FDI in the region, according to the UNCTAD estimates shown. However, over the next two decades, other countries, particularly China and Singapore, were able to attract large inflows of FDI. In 2001, these three countries accounted for about 70 percent of all FDI in Asia. Other countries in the region, including Malaysia, Indonesia, Korea, Taiwan, and Thailand, were also able to attract FDI. While much of the investment in Indonesia was in the petroleum sector, the other countries were able to attract inflows into the electronics and the information and communication technology (ICT) sectors. The annual rate of increase in this foreign-controlled capital stock was also quite rapid in the decade of the 1990s. There was a thirteenfold increase in India (from a very low base) between 1990 and 2001, and a ninefold increase in China, an eightfold increase in Korea, a fivefold increase in Malaysia, and three- to fourfold increases in the Philippines, Singapore, Taiwan, and Thailand.

Table 6.3   Stock of Foreign Direct Investment in Asia for Selected Years (Billions US$)

	1980	1990	2001	2007
Asia	$160.0	$315.4	$1,325.7	$2,709.6
China	6.2	24.8	203.1	327.0
Hong Kong	124.2	148.2	451.9	1,184.5
India	1.2	1.7	22.3	76.2
Indonesia	10.3	38.9	57.4	59.0
Korea	1.3	5.9	47.2	119.6
Malaysia	5.2	10.3	53.3	76.7
Philippines	1.3	3.3	14.2	19.0
Singapore	6.2	28.6	104.3	249.7
Taiwan	2.4	9.7	32.0	48.6
Thailand	1.0	8.2	28.2	85.7
Vietnam	n.a.	0.3	15.9	40.2

Data displayed are different from Table 2.6 (Chapter 2) since data for FDI stocks measure the accumulated values of historical FDI at a certain point in time, whereas FDI flows measure only current additions to stock over a period of time. The former is preferred here as it allows a clearer view of the overall level of FDI inflows into these countries as it has less year-on-year volatility.

SOURCES: UNCTAD, *World Investment Report* (2002); UNCTAD, *World Investment Report* (2008).

Table 6.4 Matrix of Inflows of FDI and Potential for Selected Countries, 2006

	High FDI Performance	Low FDI Performance
High FDI Potential	*Front-runners* Brunei, Hong Kong, Malaysia, Singapore, Thailand, United Kingdom	*Below Potential* China, Japan, Korea, Taiwan, United States
Low FDI Potential	*Above Potential* Vietnam	*Under-performers* Philippines, India, Indonesia, Myanmar, Nepal, Philippines, Sri Lanka

SOURCE: UNCTAD, *World Investment Report* (2008).

There are several reasons why capital flows to Asia increased in the 1980s and 1990s. Liberalization of trade and current accounts continued and this served to attract both FDI and portfolio inflows. There was also a partial or complete opening of capital accounts in several countries which facilitated both the movement of portfolio investment and the easy repatriation of funds for multinational corporations (MNCs) wishing to change strategy and repatriate rather than reinvest within the country. Furthermore, the 1990s was a period of rapid and vibrant growth in Asia compared with the low profitability and slow growth in the industrial countries. Finally, rules governing the holding of domestic assets, including stocks and bonds by foreigners, were relaxed and there was a perception that the supervision and regulation of equity markets in Asia was improving. See Table 6.4 for UNCTAD's ranking of countries according to the FDI performance and potential indices in 2006.

6.4.6 Employment, Migration, and Skills Issues

Education and timing had a lot to do with the difference in how technology was adopted in different parts of Asia. East Asia had an already highly educated labor force, and thus was able to adopt overseas technology either by licensing or purchasing directly (or in some cases pirating). These countries, especially Japan and Taiwan, also had high saving rates or they borrowed heavily from overseas to augment their saving (Korea). As a result, they had very small amounts of foreign direct investment, with the exception of Japanese investments in Korea.

The countries in Southeast Asia started to industrialize later. They had a less well-trained labor force and thus relied on primary exports for foreign exchange revenue to a greater extent than did the NIEs. Although they had a rapid buildup in saving when the growth period began, they also relied on foreign funding to a larger extent than did Japan or Taiwan. Thus, their paths to development were somewhat different. For the Southeast Asian countries, the Plaza Accord brought a strong inflow of FDI from the neighboring countries which were ready to move offshore with some of their more elementary technology and forge industrial alliances. The same options were not available to the NIEs as Japan was the only developed country in the region when they were in the market for FDI. Of course, the United States was a factor, but as the region developed, the regional alliances became more important, particularly the Asian alliances. Still, Japan had to overcome the stigma of its war role in many of these countries.

6.5 Institutional Frameworks that Facilitate Trade

6.5.1 Currency Exchange Rate

The currency exchange rate is by far the most important factor in deciding trade policy. Since the exchange rate determines the international value of the domestic currency, it directly affects the profitability of firms producing for the international market, or firms facing foreign competition. Economists use the concept of an equilibrium exchange rate to determine whether a currency is overvalued or undervalued. There are many ways to measure this. One way is to base it on the market. If the market for foreign exchange is free, it will determine the equilibrium rate.

Suppose there is a free trade regime and an equilibrium exchange rate during this regime. An across-the-board tax on all imports is levied. What happens? The demand for imports declines as domestic prices are raised to reflect the tax. As the demand falls so also does the demand for foreign currency to pay for these imports. What then happens to the exchange rate? In a supply–demand framework, the demand for the foreign currency has fallen and so will its price. Thus, the domestic currency will increase in value *vis-à-vis* the foreign currency. If there is an export subsidy or tax break, what happens? The currency tends to depreciate. Other things being equal, import-substitution will result in a currency appreciation, and export promotion will result in a currency depreciation. As this process takes effect on the exchange rate, it reinforces the particular policy followed. A depreciation in the exchange rate brings greater international competitiveness to the country, while a currency appreciation makes exporting more expensive and domestic production more attractive.

6.5.2 Capital Movements

International capital markets became more competitive and open during the 1980s and 1990s. Funds could move freely into the developing countries. In the 1970s, most of the international capital movements were in the form of loans from Western banks—primarily those from the United States—into Latin America. There was not much equity investment and the private sector was not involved to a great extent (such as bank lending to firms in Latin America). In the 1980s and particularly in the 1990s, markets in Asia opened up. This time there was a significant increase in portfolio investment and short-term bank lending to the private sector.

6.5.3 Other Factors

While many developing countries would have given their right arm to be in the same situation as the NIEs and the economies of Southeast Asia during this period, these economies also went off the rails following the Thai baht devaluation in mid-1996. The rapid buildup of foreign inflows had implications for a number of stabilization issues. The most critical was the current-account deficit.

THE CURRENT-ACCOUNT DEFICIT   How large can or should the current-account deficit get? The economics profession has not reached a consensus on this. From the point of view of a developing country with good investment potential, the current-account deficit can be at any level, as long as the investment which it finances is more productive than in alternative uses elsewhere. The point here is that the developing countries are usually capital scarce and labor rich at the beginning of their development. Thus, the returns to this scarce capital are high and remain high for some time. However, there are constraints.

ABSORPTIVE CAPACITY   High investment rates of 40 percent of GDP (Shirazi, 1998, p. 4) require complementary inputs of labor and some of this investment must be in infrastructure to support investment in machinery and new plants. Thus, there is a supply side constraint which puts a ceiling on the amount of investment that can be absorbed without introducing a troublesome loss of efficiency and costly bottlenecks.

PRICE STABILITY AND COMPETITIVENESS   The second constraint is price stability and international competitiveness. Most of the economies in question have maintained a close relationship between their currencies and the U.S. dollar. During the decade following the Plaza Accord, the dollar depreciated against many other currencies, including the yen, and those economies that stuck with the dollar benefited internationally. Those countries that maintained stable price regimes benefited the most, since their domestic inflation rates were as low as or lower than their trading partners. When inflation rates crept up as a result of continued rapid growth and capacity constraints and the U.S. dollar strengthened against the yen, several of these countries began to lose their competitiveness, reflected in the lower export earnings during the first half of 1996.

In these circumstances, the risks of maintaining a large current-account deficit multiply. A "Catch 22" situation could arise if these countries have to devalue their currencies to maintain their export competitiveness. When they do, foreign investors that enter these markets with the expectation that the currencies would remain fixed against the dollar, will exit and the value of the currency will plummet even further, with possible disastrous domestic consequences, such as inflation and unemployment. This was the dilemma that the Asian countries faced during the crisis period. At one point, the rupiah was devalued by as much as 80 percent.

6.6   The Asian Experience in Intra-Industry and Intraregional Trade

With regard to the composition of international trade, as the level of development increases, the thrust of trade is toward exporting more manufactured goods. The structure of imports remains relatively unchanged, although there will be a shift from finished manufactured goods imports to capital goods and raw materials, as well as semi-finished or unfinished inputs.

6.6.1   Intraregional Trade

We have already discussed in some detail the importance of international trade and the role of exports in raising incomes and stimulating the economies of the region. Let us now look at the role of intraregional trade, immigration, and capital movements and how they have affected the growth and development process in the region. We begin by noting that the share of Asian (including Japanese) trade in total exports and imports of the Asian countries has increased greatly in the last two decades. We can then pose the following question.

6.6.2   Why Has the Share of Intra-Asian Trade in Total Asian Trade Increased So Much Over Time?

There are four basic reasons why this has occurred. First, the growth in income and the geographic proximity within the region have stimulated trade. This is to be expected, as there is considerable evidence that, other things being equal, trade is more likely to take place between countries which are close to each other.

Secondly, there has been rapid growth in different kinds of regional cooperation arrangements that have facilitated trade. Thirdly, other factors such as fluctuating exchange rates, technological

BOX 6.1

Role of Singapore in the Development of Hard-Disk Drives (HDD)

The development of the hard-disk-drive industry demonstrates how supply linkages enabled Singapore to maintain a crucial role in this industry despite higher costs. Competition in the HDD industry has been intense for many years, with suppliers from many countries driving profits down by competing on price and delivery time. Personal computer manufacturers were a big factor in driving the market for HDDs. Singapore was a recipient of FDI from the United States and even though its wages were higher than its neighbors, it was able to gain market share by maintaining technological superiority.

"No other location possessed the depth of engineering resources to make them (HDD). Singapore also assumed a more explicit role in developing and managing the regional production network, functioning as a transfer station for the introduction of new products. Finally, the country began to diversify into new niches, including media, drive design and other branches of data storage" (Yusuf and Evenett, 2000, p. 152).

As a result, Singapore became the focal point for the initial testing of new HDD and other related products in Asia. Subsequently, after approval, these products were then sent to other locations in Southeast Asia for bulk production. Some high-end products were still produced in Singapore, particularly if they did not require large production runs.

SOURCE: Shahid Yusuf and Simon J. Evenett, *Can East Asia Compete? Innovations for Global Markets* (Washington, D.C.: World Bank, 2002).

developments in telecommunications, and lower transportation costs have helped to stimulate trade within the region (see Box 6.1 for the role of Singapore in the production of hard-disk drives in the electronics industry.). Finally, as incomes have grown and developing Asia has begun to produce more manufactured goods, their trading pattern has begun to resemble that of the OECD countries. They are beginning to trade more in industrial products where there is a higher degree of product differentiation.

The example of Singapore in the production of hard-disk drives also points to the importance of developing a skilled and flexible labor force and the maintenance of an open trading environment that is able to attract significant inflows of FDI.

6.6.3   Rapid Economic Growth and Geographical Proximity

Other things being equal, we would expect to see more rapid growth in trade between countries that are growing rapidly than between countries which are growing slowly. If the elasticities of import demand are the same between a slow growing and a rapidly growing country, then the latter will have a faster increase in imports than the former. Since Asia is generally a rapidly growing region, the share in trade of these countries in the overall trade of an individual country would increase. The close proximity of these countries in Asia compounds this trend. Research has shown that the shorter the distance, the more trade will take place. This is because of lower transportation costs but also the better knowledge about and familiarity with the nearby countries. As more complicated production and supply chains are developed, as seen in the example of Singapore, air-freight services become more important for maintaining and extending the production networks and supply chains. According to Yusuf and Evenett (2002, p. 153):

> . . . for an East Asian economy to protect its national carrier from competition in its domestic market is highly disadvantageous. Protection lessens the airline's motivation to improve its reliability and reduce transit and transhipment times. Development of ICT has made processing orders and scheduling pickups and deliveries more efficient, as demonstrated by Federal Express's operations throughout East Asia.

6.6.4   Shifts in the Direction of Trade

Intraregional trade in East Asia has expanded at a more rapid pace than trade with the rest of the world. It now accounts for more than half of the trade volume in the region (including Southeast Asia). This is the result of the continuing division of labor combined with the growth of manufactured goods in total trade, and is characteristic of all countries in the region (see Table 6.5). This expansion in intraregional trade is not because there has been a shift away from trade with the rest of the world. Rather, it has resulted from the development of a *triangular* pattern of exports (see Gill and Kharas, 2006) whereby the East Asian NIEs and Japan ship parts to China and ASEAN where processing is completed and then shipped to markets outside Asia, such as the European Union, the United States, and Canada. This new pattern of trade has been particularly strong for products such as electrical appliances, office equipment, telecommunications equipment, and textiles and apparel.

6.6.5   Shifts in Commodity Composition of Trade

There has also been a shift in the commodity composition of international trade where exports have moved from light manufacturing, including textiles, wood and paper products, and furniture, to machinery, particularly electronics and telecommunications equipment. This shift was particularly rapid among the ASEAN countries (except Indonesia). The triangular pattern of trade noted in Section 6.6.4 has been particularly strong in electronics where 80 percent of electrical appliance exports are parts and only 20 percent are finished goods.

This new pattern of trade and production networks is an extension and deepening of outsourcing that originated in Japan after the Plaza Accord of 1985, which is discussed further in Section 6.6.9. The

Table 6.5   Intraregional Exports: Share of Exports to Trading Partner in Total Exports (Percent)

	East Asia		China		Japan	
	1990–1994	2000–2004	1990–1994	2000–2004	1990–1994	2000–2004
East Asia	n.a.	n.a.	6.4%	11.1%	8.6%	8.2%
China	60.5	45.3	n.a.	n.a.	15.8	14.3
Indonesia	62.0	56.9	3.6	5.4	32.9	21.0
Hong Kong	47.0	55.5	29.9	39.3	5.4	5.4
Japan	34.6	43.1	3.7	10.0	n.a.	n.a.
Korea	40.8	46.6	4.2	15.6	15.7	9.8
Malaysia	54.7	54.2	2.5	5.3	13.6	11.5
Philippines	36.1	53.7	1.2	4.2	17.4	16.4
Singapore	48.2	56.4	2.0	6.1	7.8	7.0
Taiwan	42.7	55.2	0	10.3	11.3	9.2
Thailand	41.7	48.3	1.5	5.3	17.3	14.7
Vietnam	n.a.	49.0	n.a.	9.6	n.a.	15.7

SOURCE: Indermit Gill and Homi Kharas, *An East Asian Renaissance: Ideas for Economic Growth* (Washington, D.C.: World Bank, 2006).

main reason was to reduce costs by locating the production process near sources of consumer demand and to centralize production to take advantage of agglomeration economies, as well as to facilitate and disseminate new technologies. It should be noted that the pattern of trade is vertical rather than horizontal in nature. Vertical trade is characterized by products of different quality and price, such as for standard-color and hi-definition televisions, whereas horizontal trade involves products that are similar in function, price, and quality. These horizontally traded products differ only by design or other minor characteristics. Most trade in East Asia is vertical and commonly includes goods such as footwear, garments, and electronics, as well as in components of these products. This means that several different countries can participate in different stages of a single production chain. A personal computer, for example, may have its keyboard, central processing unit, screen, and other components made in different countries but assembled together at the final location.

6.6.6 Responding to China

The rapid rise of China both in terms of income and international trade has dramatically changed the landscape of Asia. China is now the fifth-largest economy in the world and the third-largest in trade behind the United States and Germany. Its exports have grown at more than 20 percent per year and its income at about 10 percent in the last decade or so. Between 1990 and 2002, its share of world trade more than tripled. Its trade with Japan rose from 5 percent to 18 percent, with the United States from 3 percent to 11 percent, and with the European Union from 2 percent to 7 percent (see Gill and Kharas, 2006). The composition of Chinese exports has also changed—from clothing, footwear, and light manufacturing to office machinery, telecommunications equipment, furniture, and electronic products. In the process, it has moved beyond the production of specialized exports suggested by simple comparative advantage. It has an export mix that is more characteristic of a country with three times more income per capita. Now China competes with other countries in Asia in several different dimensions. While there are many ramifications to the Chinese trade growth paradigm, several results can be highlighted. First, for those products in which Chinese exports are growing fastest, competitors in Asia are refining their own products and moving to higher value-added and more sophisticated products rather than competing head-on against China. Secondly, the market for finished machinery products is more competitive and other East Asian exporters have had to lower their costs to compete. By and large, this has been successful although there have been shifts in comparative advantage, and China has gained in some markets at the expense of other countries. Thirdly, the triangular pattern of trade discussed in Sections 6.6.4 and 6.6.5 is typical of what is happening in the machinery industry and also in electronics. The increase in China's exports of finished machinery has been facilitated by a concomitant rise in Chinese imports of parts and components from other East Asian economies. Fourthly, there is some evidence that Chinese exports to the European Union may be opening up markets for other East Asian economies (see Gill and Kharas, 2006).

6.6.7 Economic Growth, Exports, and Product Variation[4]

The complex system of production networks described in Sections 6.6.4 to 6.6.6 has also provided a stimulus to economic growth by increasing efficiency, innovation, and productivity. Intense competition for export markets within Asia has resulted in specialization in high-technology exports, which has generally raised the level of comparative advantage[5] and economic efficiency. There has also been a commensurate increase in the variety of new products and this has reduced the start-up costs while

---

[4] This section draws heavily on Gill and Kharas (2006).
[5] As measured by revealed comparative advantage.

increasing returns to scale. There is evidence from several sources that changes in product varieties are positively correlated with changes in total factor productivity. In Korea, for example, the growing number of new products being exported is correlated with a strong growth in total factor productivity. In Japan, however, there has not been much growth in new export products recently, and total factor productivity growth has also been slow. One side effect of the triangular trade pattern and the density of the network that connects suppliers and final product exporters is the sensitivity to trade barriers and changes in the structure of protection. For example, Hanson, Mataloni, and Slaughter (2003) have found that a 1 percent fall in trade costs leads to a 2–4 percent increase in the quantity of intermediate inputs imported by affiliates from their U.S. parent companies. These inputs are then processed into finished products.

One danger of the production system that has evolved is the reliance upon foreign firms to drive innovation and research and development. Domestic innovators have been few and far between. However, this is changing in China as foreign firms have started to increase their investment in local research and development.

6.6.8 Regional and Subregional Cooperation

Formal and informal mechanisms for improving relations between neighboring countries within Asia can have a stimulating impact on the growth of trade within the region. Let us focus first on regional cooperation, particularly on the pattern of trade, migration, and capital movements *within the Asian region,* and the institutional mechanisms which have been developed to stimulate and foster such international movements of goods and factors of production.

One good example of subregional cooperation is the development of the Greater Mekong Subregion (GMS), which comprises the southeastern countries of Cambodia, Laos, Myanmar, Thailand, Vietnam, and the Yunnan province of China. Beginning in 1993, the Asian Development Bank (ADB) began assisting these countries in regional cooperation and economic development in the environment, energy, telecommunications, transport, human resource, and tourism sectors. The six countries agreed to foster greater economic integration in trade and investment. As a result of the agreement, trade liberalization has been taking place both unilaterally and collaterally. Nontariff barriers have been eliminated and privatization and deregulation have occurred. These changes in regulations and policies have worked in tandem with the region's investment strategies to attract greater FDI inflows into the region, thereby promoting economic growth and facilitating higher standards of living. An investment regulatory framework conducive to foreign investment has been implemented together with efforts to build adequate supplies of energy resources, telecommunication services, and a transport network to ensure the smooth flow of information, goods, and factors of production.[6]

6.6.9 Bilateral Trade Agreements, APEC, ASEAN, WTO, NAFTA, EU, and SAARC

Within Asia, there have been a number of bilateral trade agreements (FTAs) signed between Asian nations and the industrial countries. These agreements, between two parties, spell out tariff reductions that are mutually agreed upon. These bilateral treaties are outside the realm of the WTO and are more wide ranging. They are not considered as being particularly beneficial for the world trading system since they create an overlapping system of trade preferences and agreements that is difficult to understand, and that could create a new pattern of distortion. Ordinarily, these agreements relate to the trade

---

[6] Refer to the ADB Greater Mekong Subregion website at http://www.adb.org/GMS for more details.

between two countries, with other countries being excluded, unlike the MFN (most-favored nation) agreements where all trading partners benefit. Most FTAs include preferential tariffs for products that are produced in the countries referred to in the FTA that meet country of origin rules. In the case of a recent agreement between Singapore and the United States, however, the bilateral agreement contains a provision that could also benefit Indonesia, Malaysia, and perhaps other trading partners of Singapore. It allows for some components made offshore to be included in the agreement if the company involved is incorporated in Singapore. This effectively means that firms can use Singapore as a base for goods manufactured elsewhere. Currently, this would apply primarily to southern Malaysia and the adjacent Indonesian islands of Batam and Bintan. However, it could extend to other locations too. The agreement is aimed at cutting costs by speeding up customs clearance procedures in the United States and also contains the waiver of a small merchandise-processing fee. The spirit of this agreement can be extended to other bilateral FTAs in the region to enable the economies to take advantage of their extensive offshore production facilities and thereby lower costs by having these goods included under the FTA umbrella (see *Far Eastern Economic Review*, 2002).

LACK OF FORMAL MECHANISMS IN ASIA   When compared with other regions in the world, there are few formal mechanisms within Asia to facilitate regional cooperation. The Americas have established the North America Free Trade Association (NAFTA), and MERCOSUR, a regional trading association in Latin America, while Europe has the European Union (EU), and Africa has a number of formal regional organizations designed to foster greater intraregional trade.

The only viable formal organizations within developing Asia are the Association of Southeast Asian Nations (ASEAN) and the South Asian Association for Regional Cooperation (SAARC). In 1989, APEC (Asia-Pacific Economic Cooperation) was started but so far it has not done much to foster regional cooperation. However, there are a number of study groups within APEC which have been active in exploring areas for potential cooperation. Of course, there is also the Closer Economic Relations (CER) agreement between Australia and New Zealand.

PREFERENTIAL TRADING AREAS OUTSIDE ASIA   Maintaining our focus on developing Asia, we see that contrary to NAFTA and the European Union, neither APEC nor ASEAN has tried to develop a strong preferential trade area. In a customs union, tariffs are lowered among the members and a common tariff wall is erected to outsiders. Rather, the trade regimes in most of the countries in developing Asia have evolved by stressing the lowering of tariff barriers in a unilateral form, that is, tariffs are lowered on a product for all importers without any requirement of reciprocity. This is referred to as the most-favored-nation clause. If one country gets a concession, other countries can get it too if they want it.

OPEN REGIONALISM   APEC has coined the term "open regionalism." This may sound like a contradiction but the term is meant to connote an international arrangement whereby tariffs are lowered among the APEC members but these preferences can also be extended to other trading partners. So far no concrete agreements have been reached to lower tariffs although APEC members have pledged to implement free trade by the year 2020. Skeptics have stressed the difficulties that such a diverse group of countries will have in agreeing to a common agenda for tariff reform. On the other hand, many of the working groups can help to provide a better international environment by facilitating border movements, establishing international criteria for investments, product standards, international property rights, including patents and licenses, and so forth.

SPECIAL FEATURES OF ASEAN   The members of the Association of Southeast Asian Nations include most of the countries located in Southeast Asia: originally, Brunei, Indonesia, Malaysia, Thailand, the

Philippines, Singapore, and later joined by Vietnam, Cambodia, Laos, and Myanmar. The ASEAN Secretariat is located in Jakarta. For many years, ASEAN was relatively inactive. A series of regional projects was suggested in the 1970s so that each country could supply other members with particular products. This proved cumbersome and inefficient and was later dropped. Later, under a regional trading agreement called AFTA (ASEAN Free Trade Area), the ASEAN members agreed to reduce tariffs through a common effective preferential tariff (CEPT) scheme. This scheme aimed at lowering internal tariffs among the ASEAN members in a series of steps by the year 2003. It was originally confined to manufactured goods and processed agricultural products but was later expanded to include other products, particularly agricultural products and some services.

Other agreements within ASEAN seek to explore cooperation on border issues and to facilitate investment flows between the member countries. Up to now, there have not been any substantial reductions in tariffs but the members are very serious about these tariff reductions. They have also not yet formalized any scheme to erect a common tariff barrier against other countries outside ASEAN.

UNILATERAL TRADE LIBERALIZATION   Unilateral trade liberalization is a system favored by most economists. Such a system benefits from the reduction of trade barriers without other new trade barriers being erected. Individual countries lower trade barriers and this applies to all in a MFN context. In this way, there is trade creation without any trade diversion. In contrast, the European Union, by erecting a common external tariff and lowering tariffs internally, has stimulated trade within the Union but this may have diverted trade away from the rest of the world.

SPECIAL ECONOMIC ZONES   Subnational zones are called special economic zones, the most common of which is the export-processing zone. These zones are set up within a country primarily to attract exporters to locate their facilities in these zones. The foreign company, often in partnership with a local firm, is encouraged to locate in the special economic zone to take advantage of preferentially low duties on imports needed for export production, and tax incentives and other special privileges granted by the host country. Bonded warehouses and other methods are used to ensure that these zones are isolated from the rest of the country where duties on the same imported products would be higher.

There are a number of these zones all over Southeast Asia and in China. Much of the growth in manufactured exports from Asia has originated in these zones. Obviously, these subnational zones discriminate between different producers located within the national borders and raise questions about the efficiency of piecemeal reforms. They have helped to reduce trade restrictions and stimulated the flow of capital from multinationals through foreign direct investment.

A closely related form of subnational zone is the financial service zone, such as a financial offshore center. These zones provide preferences for the financial industry in the same way that the export-processing zone provides preferential treatment for manufacturing.

GROWTH TRIANGLES   In addition to subregional special economic zones and formal regional cooperation among countries, there are also cooperative arrangements which involve parts of different economies. For example, there are several cooperative arrangements within ASEAN which seek to jointly develop different regions of separate economies. In the East Asian Growth Area, for example, Indonesia, the Philippines, Malaysia, and Brunei have agreed to develop a small region that includes the island of Borneo (Sabah and Sarawak in East Malaysia, Brunei and Kalimantan in Indonesia), as well as Mindanao in the Philippines and Sulawesi in Indonesia. There is also a cooperative venture involving Thailand, Malaysia, and Indonesia to develop an area surrounding the Malacca Straits, taking advantage of common religious and cultural characteristics of groups in the provinces of northern

Sumatra, southern Thailand, and northern Malaysia. This is called the IMT-GT (Indonesia–Malaysia–Thailand Growth Triangle).

Each of these growth triangles, or growth regions, is to identify joint projects and cooperative schemes that would lift the growth of the region. In addition to providing a growth stimulus to these subregions, such growth triangles are also attempting to address regional poverty issues, since these regions are often generally poorer than the country as a whole.

6.6.10   Other Factors

EXCHANGE RATE ADJUSTMENTS   Following the Plaza Accord in 1985, the realignment of currency exchange rates brought about a shift in comparative advantage and improved the competitiveness of Asian exporters who remained tied to the U.S. dollar. This has been reflected not only in the changing pattern of trade but in a shift in the pattern of production with the transfer of some manufacturing activities from Japan and Taiwan to lower wage countries in Southeast Asia and also to China. The increase in trade in capital and intermediate goods as a result of these transfers of production platforms away from the NIEs and Japan has contributed to the rapid growth in intraregional trade in Asia.

REDUCTION IN TRANSPORT COSTS   Lower costs of transportation and the development of more efficient port facilities in Southeast Asia have also contributed to growing intraregional trade. There is substantial evidence that the costs of transportation have been lowered as a result of better port handling facilities and the development of larger cargo ships. Between 1990 and 2004, freight costs as a percentage of import value fell from about 10 percent to 8 percent, lower than any other developing region but still higher than freight costs for the developed countries. (For further details, see Yusuf and Evenett, 2002; and Gill and Kharas, 2006).

IMPROVED TELECOMMUNICATIONS   New technology in telecommunications, particularly in the use of fax and e-mail, have complemented the decisions by many multinational firms to adopt production platforms in different locations. The desktop computer is a good example, since the components are often produced in several different locations and then shipped for assembly in yet another location.

LIBERALIZATION OF REGULATIONS ON FOREIGN DIRECT INVESTMENT   The liberalization of capital flows has followed, usually with a lag, the liberalization of trade. Liberalization of regulations on FDI has proceeded hand in hand with other factors to facilitate the growth in trade, particularly in intermediate goods.

It should be kept in mind that these factors are not necessarily additive. There are interaction effects that are difficult to capture in a simple statistical analysis. For example, the increase in incomes and lower tariffs have given consumers more options to explore products from neighboring countries, and to trade with those who have a similar cultural heritage.

INTELLECTUAL PROPERTY RIGHTS   Intellectual property rights (IPRs) have become an important factor in determining the flow of FDI in selected industries. Generally, IPRs have been trade-related and applied asymmetrically across countries and this has distorted the pattern of world trade. The structure of IPRs policy can also have a significant impact on FDI, if the products need IPR protection, and the enforcement of such protection is weak in a host country. Furthermore, in order to control and protect their intellectual property, firms may choose FDI rather than licensing (see Saggi, 2002, for further details of research in this area, most of which is theoretical). In terms of its effect on growth, Gould and Gruben (1996) have found that a strengthening of IPR protection is more conducive to growth when it is accompanied by a liberal trading policy. This could be because trade liberalization curtails local monopoly power but enforces IPRs that are truly global in nature.

INDUSTRIAL ESTATES   The setting up of industrial estates is one way that governments give an indirect subsidy to business firms locating in the region. The development of industrial estates has been a major vehicle for the governments of several countries, including China and the countries of Southeast Asia, to promote labor-intensive manufacturing. Tax concessions and duty drawbacks, together with infrastructure, are the main inducements in these schemes.

6.6.11   Industrial Policies and Exports: Some Case Studies from Asia

The interface between industrial and trade policies is very strong, and Japan, Korea, and Taiwan have all used industrial policies to promote different industries with a view to achieving a better export performance. Thus, industrial policies and export policies are closely intertwined. The NIEs and Japan have used government policies to promote different subsectors.

JAPAN   In the early years, Japanese industrial policy aimed to encourage sectors that faced income-elastic demands in the international market and exhibited economies of scale, large fixed costs, and the potential for learning-by-doing. In later years, industrial policy had a narrower technology basis—for example, the promotion of integrated circuits in the electronics industry. Steel automobiles, textiles, shipbuilding, and aluminum smelting were promoted in the early years, followed by electronics and semiconductors later on. The policies followed included the availability of selected credit, protection, and limited/supervised entry into specific sectors by new firms.

KOREA   In Korea, there was an attempt to follow the Japanese model—after all, Japan was the colonial power in Korea for many years before and during the war. They used "contests" in order to determine whether firms deserved continued protection. They also adjusted the trade regime to make inputs available to producers at world market prices. Heavy and chemical industries were promoted as well as iron and steel, metal products, machinery, electronics, and industrial chemicals. These subsidies had not only an export component to them—that is, to facilitate the shift out of labor-intensive products—but also a defense component, since they were in "conflict" with North Korea for the entire postwar era.

TAIWAN   In Taiwan, the government authorities made an intense effort to direct the sectoral evolution of the economy through tariffs, quantitative restrictions, and credit controls. There were, however, no systems of subsidies like those in Japan and Korea, and the extent of the intervention was less pervasive. The industrial structure evolved with a large number of smaller firms rather than the large conglomerates which typified the industrial structure of Korea and Japan. Two large industrial parks have been developed by the government to assist the shift to high tech within Taiwan. The shift offshore and the secular decline in saving and investment are concerns for the country.

MALAYSIA   In the 1980s, Malaysia experimented with the protection of heavy machinery and chemical industries similar to that followed by Korea, but it was dependent on public investment. However, it ran into financial difficulties and the government divested its share to the private sector. The industries were concentrated on steel, automobiles, cement, and paper. The World Bank study on the East Asian "miracle" gives more details of the development scheme and the decreasing role of the government, as well as the subsidies given to these industries (World Bank, 1993, p. 311). The Proton car is one of the well-known heavy industry projects that are still receiving subsidies from the government.

INDONESIA AND THAILAND There was very little intervention in the industrial sector in these two countries, with the exception of the aircraft industry and railway rolling stock in Indonesia associated with Minister Habibi. In Thailand, there is now an Eastern Seaboard Development Authority through which the government supplies the infrastructure but there is little actual government investment in the project, although there is probably a subsidy to firms locating in the industrial estate.

6.7 TRADE IN SERVICES

The share of services in total international movement of goods and services grew to about one-fifth of total trade and services by 2001, reaching about US$1.4 trillion, according to Yusuf and Evenett (2002). Services grew even faster than trade. Financial services comprise the major part of business services which support trade in manufactured goods that has been a critical factor in economic development in Asia. Services trade is also an important component of the balance of payments for developing countries in Asia. By 1997, trade in services made up a substantial share of total exports in several Asian countries, almost reaching the OECD average (see Table 6.6).

Part of the reason for the wide variation in the share of services in international trade has to do with historical traditions. In Japan, there is a lack of emphasis on trade in goods and financial services, one of the major components of services trade. This is also the case for countries that have copied Japan, such as Korea. The Philippines, having followed the U.S. model, has given a greater emphasis

Table 6.6 Trade in Services as a Percent of Total Exports, 1997

	Share of Service as Percent of Exports
Asian Economies	
Hong Kong	58%
Indonesia	11
Korea	16
Malaysia	16
Philippines	37
Singapore	30
Thailand	22
Other Economies	
France	22
Germany	13
Italy	23
Japan	14
United Kingdom	23
United States	25

SOURCE: A. Hardin and L. Holmes, "Service Trade and Direct Foreign Investment," Australian Industry Commission Staff Research Papers, 1997, in *Can East Asia Compete? Innovations for Global Markets*, by Shahid Yusuf and Simon J. Evenett (Washington, D.C.: 2002), p. 90.

on services trade and this has been complemented by a rapid development of software exports and management services to the rest of Asia. Hong Kong, being an entrepôt port that has become a service center for much of the trade from China, also has a large services sector. Singapore too has a highly developed services export industry, although it is smaller than that of Hong Kong, as it has a strong electronics industry that is primarily export-oriented.

The underdevelopment of the financial sector in many Asian countries has also played a role in the slow development of business services. This topic is covered in greater depth in Chapter 7. However, it can be noted here that the lack of a widely diversified and internationally competitive financial apparatus in Asia has meant that many of these services have been supplied by the industrial countries, particularly the United States.

The Yusuf and Evenett (2002) report also points out that this lack of service acumen in the supply of financial services internationally also applies to other business services, including legal and accounting services. The supply of these services is also tied to the location of head offices and regional headquarters for large multinationals. Hong Kong has a strong lead in this area, primarily because of the substantial FDI inflows that it managed to build before 1980.

Typically, high-technology business services in Asia remain underdeveloped compared with manufacturing technology. This can be traced partly to the shortage of personnel, particularly in non-English-speaking countries such as China, Indonesia, and Thailand, and also the result of an industrial strategy that followed the Japanese model to a significant extent, putting more emphasis on hardware than software. Furthermore, in the transition to higher value-added products for export, a similar transition to higher value-added services to complement the manufacturing operations was not carried out.

6.8 Issues in International Trade and the Balance of Payments

6.8.1 Level of International Reserves and the Current-Account Balance

Since the Asian financial crisis there has been a dramatic shift in the current-account balance and the level of reserves of the Asian economies. This reflects the weaknesses of those countries that did not have a strong reserve position and were experiencing significant current account deficits. The economies with large international reserves were able to hold their exchange rates steady (such as Hong Kong and China) or suffered only modest depreciations (such as Singapore and Taiwan) while the other crisis countries suffered extensive currency weaknesses. For a panel of Asian economies, reserves doubled to nearly US$1 trillion in 2002 from just under $500 billion in 1996. By the end of 2008, reserves had risen further to more than US$3.3 trillion. This has been accompanied by a significant turnaround in the balance of payments, as noted in Chapter 3.

Are reserves too high? Using the traditional measure of three months of import cover as a minimum, all the crisis countries, except Korea, had an adequate import cover in 1996, before the crisis. A more demanding standard is the ratio of reserves to short-term external debt, particularly if there is a likelihood that access to foreign borrowing may be cut off. In 1996, three crisis countries did not have sufficient reserves to meet this standard (Malaysia and the Philippines did). However, with the rapid buildup in reserves since the crisis, all the crisis countries and China were able to meet this more stringent requirement by 2008. This suggests that the ability of the Asian crisis countries to face external shocks has greatly improved. In addition, many developing member countries of the Asian Development Bank are projected to continue running significant current-account surpluses and accumulate further reserves over the medium term.

Has the reserve buildup gone too far? To maintain a higher than optimal level of reserves is costly since these reserves earn low rates of interest and they could be used to prepay expensive external debt.

This has happened selectively but the question is whether central banks should be more aggressive in reducing the level of external debt by using their high level of reserves.

6.8.2   Should Capital Flows Be Regulated?

Since the Asian financial crisis, there has been a debate about whether short-term capital inflows should be controlled. Those advocating controls note the destabilizing role that short-term portfolio movements had in creating a speculative bubble in the mid-1990s, and then in destabilizing the economies once the crisis had begun by withdrawing these funds *en masse*. The critics also point out that while short-term trade credit is a critical necessity to finance international trade, portfolio investment and short-term lending do not carry with it the desirable features of bringing innovation and new technology and business practices that come with foreign direct investment. It does, however, provide increased liquidity to the industrial sectors of the recipient countries. Is that enough to justify the possible destabilizing effects of portfolio and other short-term lending and investment?

Joseph Stiglitz (1998) has made some suggestions with regard to this question. He suggests the elimination of tax and regulatory and policy distortions that have stimulated these flows in the past, such as the Thai policy of encouraging short-term external borrowing. He also suggests that banking regulations should be strengthened to limit foreign currency exposure. Should countries go so far as Chile, which taxes short-term loans? This would depend upon individual country circumstances. In addition, Stiglitz suggests that the international community needs to consider the issue of who should bear the costs of risky decisions. Up to now it has been the lender. Stiglitz believes that there should be some sharing of risk and responsibility. If such a scheme were widely adopted, it would serve to reduce the volatility and riskiness of short-term international lending.

The global economic crisis of 2008 and 2009 that originated in the subprime mortgage failure in the United States, which subsequently spread to the rest of the world, has highlighted the importance of developing a stronger regulatory apparatus both domestically and internationally. The sale of so-called toxic mortgage-backed securities to both financial institutions and nonbank financial intermediaries—an area that is currently not well regulated—compounded the crisis and facilitated the spread to the rest of the industrial countries and eventually, to the developing countries as well. The failure of existing regulatory institutions to monitor and control these assets led to a pyramid of risk which was not well understood either by the financial institutions themselves, the regulatory agencies, or the general public. Discussions on appropriate controls are now ongoing in the United States and other OECD countries as well as in international institutions, such as the World Bank, the International Monetary Fund (IMF), the Asian Development Bank, the World Trade Organization, and the United Nations. Although policy efforts are now focused on a recovery from the ongoing global economic crisis, there have also been proposals for modifying the international financial architecture and funding modalities. A proposal to increase the capital of the IMF has widespread support, as do suggestions for strengthening domestic institutions in the OECD countries, as well as international regulatory agencies, such as the Bank for International Settlements.

6.9   SUMMARY AND CONCLUSIONS

This chapter has demonstrated the key role that international trade has played in the growth and development of the Asian economies generally, and in East and Southeast Asia in particular. After discussing the various theories on why international trade can be beneficial to all economies, the chapter went on to study the "Flying Geese" model and the differences between import-substitution and export-promoting types of international trade regimes. The "Flying Geese" model and the Gravity model were used to explain the evolving pattern of international trade in Asia. It became clear that the rapid shift away from primary products toward skill- and capital-intensive exports as well as services was a fundamental reason that the region was able to grow so rapidly while other developing regions did not do nearly as well.

The following sections looked at the shifts in the trade and tariff regime, and the transfer of technology through foreign direct investment. Both were crucial components of the export strategy described above. Lower tariffs and the inflow of technology helped the region to maintain a shifting comparative advantage as it moved toward a higher skill and capital-intensive mix of exports. Finally, the chapter considered the increasing role of intraregional trade and the importance of greater regional integration as global value chains evolve with advances in technology and lowered costs of transportation and communication.

The analysis of convergence in Chapter 2 highlighted the conditional convergence of some Asian economies with the industrial countries. We can see this from the experience of the NIEs, all of which can now be considered industrial countries by any categorization. This process of convergence goes beyond income. There has also been a convergence in international trade as the pattern and mix of trade of the Asian countries has begun to look more like the trade pattern of the industrial countries. It is also likely that the share of total factor productivity has also increased, as noted in Chapter 3 and Sections 6.4.2, 6.6.7, and 6.6.8. As Asian economies become further integrated into the global production network, it is critical that they take advantage of comparative advantage to build a global platform of production and services. Further development of high technology services, including financial and business services, will be critical to the continued development of the international trade capabilities of the Asian economies.

REVIEW QUESTIONS

1. Explain why the assumptions of the Ricardian model of international trade are not particularly realistic. Why do we study this model if the assumptions are not realistic?

2. How does the HOS model modify the Ricardian model? Does this add sufficient realism to the model?

3. Is there any relationship between the Gravity model and the Ricardian and HOS models? Which model is more realistic in your view?

4. How do you explain the fact that the theories of international trade that we have discussed stress that more trade takes place when factor endowments are different with the empirical results that most trade takes place between rich countries with similar factor endowments?

5. Import-substitution policies are very attractive and have been adopted by many developing countries. Explain the advantages of such policies.

6. Eventually import-substitution policies were replaced by other policies. What were these policies and why were they adopted?

7. Explain the rationale for dual pricing. What is the difference between dumping and dual pricing?

8. The "Flying Geese" model is based on shifting comparative advantage. Does this model have its roots in international trade theory or in growth theory? How can growth theories be adjusted to take the "Flying Geese" paradigm into account?

9. Discuss the relative costs of an import tariff versus an import ban. What is the crucial distinction between the two economic effects? Demonstrate graphically.

10. What is the fallacy of composition suggested by William Cline? What are the empirical results regarding this fallacy? Are they different from the theory? Why?

11. Foreign direct investment has helped many countries to develop in Asia. Still, there is some reluctance to accept or attract foreign direct investment in certain countries. Explain their motivation?

Have any countries been successful in growing rapidly without much FDI? If so, how did they do it? Can their experience be replicated?

12. Discuss how the factor price equalization theorem worked in Asia and how did it relate to the "Flying Geese" model?

13. Explain the statement, "The Asian financial crisis was intimately related to foreign trade."

14. Discuss why there has been such a large increase in intraregional trade in the past decade, even while there is so much concern about competition from China.

15. Discuss the relative advantage of bilateral preferential trade agreements and multilateral agreements?

16. How does the discussion regarding trade in services relate to innovation developments in globalization, and in information and computer technology?

17. Explain the meaning of triangular trade. How does this term relate to the trade relationship between China and other Asian economies?

18. Discuss how the rapid growth in China has impacted on the other countries in Asia in terms of the pattern of international trade.

Notes on References and Suggestions for Further Reading

The foundation for the study of specialization and international trade that began with David Ricardo has a long and illustrious history. If we want to delve more deeply into the theory of international trade and investigate the various theorems mentioned in the chapter, such as the Stolper–Samuelson (1941) theorem and the Rybczynski (1986) theorem, we can begin with a text on international trade, such as *Applied International Trade Analysis* by Harry P. Bowen et al. (1998).

The "Flying Geese" theory also has a long and illustrious history in Asia, beginning with the works of Kaname Akamatsu (1961, 1962). Raymond Vernon's (1966) work is in the same vein and puts a somewhat different spin on the product cycle from a domestic perspective. Bela Balassa (1965) gives a thorough introduction to the ideas of revealed comparative advantage that underpin the theory, whereas John Malcolm Dowling and Cheang C. T. (2000) explore the empirical implications of the "Flying Geese" model and shifting comparative advantage using recent data.

There is a large body of evidence that suggests that countries with outward-looking trade policies have been able to grow faster than other countries that have followed more restrictive trade regimes. The papers by David Dollar (1990, 1992), and Jeffrey Sachs and Andrew Warner (1995) are among the most interesting and compelling. See also the work of Sebastian Edwards (1998), who reviews the empirical literature that studies the relationship between trade and growth.

The paradigm of export-led growth has not been accepted by all economists, particularly in the period before it became well established as a set of policies that were followed by countries in other developed regions with some success. The paper by William Cline (1982) is a good example of this point of view.

We have discussed industrial policy in the previous chapter. However, the paper by Howard Pack (2000) is worth repeating. Based on the examination of the experience of many developing countries, it warns against the use of industrial policy to change the export mix. To put the subject of international trade in the perspective of growth in Asia, it is worth returning to the books by Seiji Naya (2002) and the World Bank (1993).

Finally, the publications by Shahid Yusuf and Simon J. Evenett (2002), as well as the Asian Development Bank's special chapter in the *Asian Development Outlook* for 2003 put the challenges for the region in perspective, in terms of international trade, competitiveness, and industrial policy.

Savings and the Financial System

1. Income smoothing is not possible because of borrowing constraints and imperfect capital markets.

2. Income smoothing is not optimal, when many pensioners are matched with the most productive in future.

3. Future incomes are uncertain or it is difficult to plan over a lifetime. This is particularly true when individuals are self-employed or beyond upper agriculture harvests. It has also been shown that the poor usually have a very short time horizon and a high discount rate. This is why it is difficult for them to break out of the cycle of poverty. Thus, in these models people do not spread their potential over their lifetime. Rather consumption is more closely related to current income.

7.1 INTRODUCTION

Saving plays a key role in determining growth, as seen in Chapter 2. It is also important to know how saving behavior is conditioned in order to explore the implications for macroeconomic policy and the impact of changing government policies. Much of the literature on the developing countries deals with how these models can be used and tested. This chapter aims to summarize the impact of different variables on saving behavior for the developing countries, instead of looking deeply into alternative tests for these models. Following a review of saving behavior, the chapter continues with a discussion of banking and credit markets in the developing countries with particular reference to the economies in Asia.

7.2 SOME SAVING MODELS

Total saving is the sum of government, business, and private saving. In developing countries, most saving is accumulated by private households and the unincorporated business sector. Government saving has not grown much in the developing countries and corporate saving is relatively small.

Virtually all research in this area has been devoted to the study of private or household saving. There have been two major developments in the theory of personal consumption and saving since Irving Fisher (1930) and Frank Ramsay (1930) set up saving as a choice between present and future consumption in the 1920s. In the Keynesian (see Keynes, 1936) model, saving is primarily a function of current income, and borrowing to sustain income is not considered. This borrowing constraint is relaxed in income smoothing models.

7.2.1 Keynesian and Income Constrained Models

These models start with the simple observation that consumption may depend upon current income (the centerpiece of the Keynes' [1936] *The General Theory*). In the simple models of consumption behavior presented at the beginning of an economics course, the consumption function is presented as a linear function of income while saving forms the residual: $C = a + bY$ and $Y = C + S$, so $Y - S = a + bY$ and $S = -a + (1 - b)Y$, where S is also a linear function of income.

This model was overtaken by more plausible theories in the 1960s and 1970s that allow for consumption and income smoothing over time—that is, borrowing to smooth consumption so that it does not depend completely on the current level of income. Nevertheless, the simple Keynesian model featuring the importance of present income has made a comeback with the work of Deaton (1989, 1991, 1992) and Hall (1978). Hall argues that expected future income is subject to random changes so that current income is the only reliable predictor of current consumption and saving. Alternatively, income smoothing does not occur or is weak and this vitiates the life cycle model.

There are several possible reasons for this:

1. Income smoothing is not possible because of borrowing constraints and imperfect capital markets.
2. Income smoothing is not applicable since many generations live together, weakening the need for individuals to save.
3. Future incomes are uncertain so it is difficult to plan over a lifetime. This is particularly true when individuals are self-employed or depend upon agriculture harvests. It has also been shown that the poor usually have a very short time horizon and a high discount rate. This is why it is difficult for them to break out of the cycle of poverty. Thus, in these models people do not optimize their potential over their life cycle. Rather, consumption is more closely related to current income.

7.2.2 Income Smoothing Models: The Permanent Income and Life Cycle Hypotheses

These are models that allow for consumption smoothing over some time horizon without constraint. Families can borrow and save at will in order to smooth their consumption patterns to compensate for fluctuations in income. The time horizon in these models can either be a person's lifetime or a longer (sometimes infinite) time horizon. The permanent income hypothesis (PIH) of Friedman (1957) and Hall (1978) assumes an infinite lifetime horizon.

In the Friedman version, consumption is based on permanent income (YP), and all transitory income (YT) is saved: $C = a + b\, YP$. where $YP + YT = Y$.

Permanent income is determined as a declining weighted average of past income, for example, $YP(t) = b\, (Y(t - 1) + b^2\, Y(t - 1) + \ldots\ldots$

In the life cycle hypothesis (LCH), Modigliani (1970) assumes a finite horizon (lifetime). There is a time profile of saving and consumption that leaves the individual either with no saving at death, or a predetermined bequest at death (see his 1970 article, for example). This model is characterized by a hump in the saving function during the maximum earning years.

It is important to know which of these competing theories is most appropriate for the developing countries. Saving is a key variable in determining growth, as we have seen earlier. How saving behavior is conditioned is also significant in order to explore the implications for macroeconomic policy and the impact of changing government policies. Much of the literature on the developing countries deals with how these models can be used and tested. The aim of this chapter, however, is to summarize the impact of different variables on saving behavior for developing countries, rather than delve deeper into alternative tests of these models.

In either income-smoothing models or in income-constrained models, there are several broad categories of variables that can have an impact on savings. Before discussing these results, we will first look at the realism of the unconstrained income-smoothing models, such as the pure LCH or PIH.

Evidence suggests that the LCH/PIH model does not strictly apply to the aggregate of all consumers. Many consumers, even in developed countries, are affected by liquidity constraints. As a result, some consumers will follow LCH/PIH but a large proportion—as much as half, according to Campbell and Mankiw's (1989) estimate for the United States—will consume a constant proportion of income. Thus, it may be useful to enter a variable which serves as a measure of financial constraints on borrowing, or alternatively on financial market liberalization. But this is getting ahead of our story.

7.2.3 Determinants of Savings

In this section, we look at the variables that have been incorporated into regression models of saving behavior. Several saving models in the economic literature are reviewed here to determine which variables are the key influences of saving behavior. It is assumed here that the variables on the right-hand side of these regressions are the causes of changes in saving and not the other way around. If causation runs in the other direction, and indeed it might, and if the lags are long, we do not introduce any bias by testing simple models. However, the fact that saving can cause changes in, say, income and income growth (two explanatory variables used in many papers) may contribute to a virtuous growth cycle, where rapid growth leads to an increase in savings. It would also be worthwhile to look into different statistical techniques for testing models of saving behavior.

REAL INTEREST RATES Higher real interest rates stimulate saving by offering higher financial returns for abstaining from consumption through the substitution effect. On the other hand, higher interest rates result in more income for creditors and this stimulates consumption through the income effect. Furthermore, a negative income effect could manifest as a decline in pension contributions when interest rates rise. Most of the empirical evidence shows a limited interest rate effect. What may be more relevant is the stability and reliability of an interest rate regime. This would be the case if inflation is low and there are no unanticipated increases in prices which could push interest rates down sharply. Such a reliable interest rate environment would provide a positive inducement to savers. Given that financial liberalization may have changed interest rate effects, the lack of an interest rate is not surprising. Financial liberalization can boost saving by providing more institutional opportunities for saving at lower costs. McKinnon (1973) argues this point strongly. Financial liberalization may also remove constraints to saving by allowing for more borrowing opportunities. This would tend to depress saving rates. In cases where financial liberalization has been undertaken, both of these effects have been observed, although the liberalization effects on raising saving is weaker than the evidence that access to credit depresses saving and increases consumption.

ROLE OF THE GOVERNMENT If the government raises taxes (increases government saving), incomes will decline and private saving can also be expected to diminish, other things being equal. Will the off-set be complete? The evidence seems to suggest that it is not (Ricardian equivalence[1] is rejected). Most research on the developing countries (see Masson et al., 1995, 1998; and Westcott, 1995), suggests that

---

[1] Ricardian equivalence suggests that when government saving goes up, private saving will go down by an equal amount. The reasoning is that if government reduces current taxes (current government saving), it will have to increase them some time in the future and rational forward-looking households will anticipate this and increase current saving in order to provide for this future tax liabilities. Ricardian equivalence predicts that the increase (reduction) in private saving will exactly offset any reduction (increase) in government saving.

about half of the change is reflected in a decrease in private saving. The effects on saving will depend upon whether the change in the fiscal deficit occurs through a change in the tax rate or in the rate of government spending. Increased government spending may lower the resources available to the private sector and hence, have a negative effect on private saving independent of its impact on the deficit. There is some evidence that governments in large developing countries, as proxied by the share of government expenditures in gross national product (GNP), may have a negative effect on private saving (see Masson et al., 1995; and Harrigan, 1998). This could result from the crowding out of private investment (and saving) by the public sector. Government policies toward saving can also have an impact on the private saving rate. Public pensions can lower private saving because they may substitute for private pensions. Feldstein (1995) has argued that a public system based on pay-as-you-go instead of on actuarial principles would lower national saving because pensions would be paid for by the still unborn children who could not adjust their saving behavior. There would also not be a full offset from the working population because Ricardian equivalence would not hold (see Harrigan, 1998, for details).

GROWTH IN INCOME   If workers believe that a change in income is permanent, in a LCH/PIH world, consumption would be adjusted upward accordingly and the current saving rate could fall. On the other hand, those who do not earn from current income but from accumulated assets, such as those who are retired, might dissave at a lower rate as a result of the wealth effect of more rapid income growth. The increase in income could also have an impact on the rate of return on capital and hence the real interest rate. Whatever the theoretical significance of growth in income, empirical tests by a number of researchers have found that there is a strong relationship between income growth and saving. This evidence for developing countries is strongly affected by the results for those Asian countries that have had high-income growth and high saving rates. This has important implications for countries like Japan, where the growth rate has fallen significantly. However, saving rates in Japan have not fallen as expected.

POPULATION AGE STRUCTURE   LCH implies that the age structure plays an important role in saving behavior. The saving rate is expected to decline as the population ages. A country with a very low dependency rate (large working population as a ratio of total population) can be expected to have a higher saving rate in an LCH model. The young and the retired are usually dissavers. Several cross-section studies have confirmed this result. See Masson et al. (1995) for reference. However, these macroeconomic results across countries are in conflict with some microeconomic studies which show that age-consumption profiles do not differ enough to explain why aggregate consumption should be affected by demographic factors. The LCH assumption that lifetime income is all "used up" at the moment of death, may also be erroneous. Since the time of death is uncertain, bequests may not be planned. Alternatively, bequests may be part of a bargain with children in exchange for taking care of their parents. An alternate model, called the dynasty model, postulates that individuals build fortunes and save in order to make bequests to family members. There is the, perhaps apocryphal, story that Henry Ford maintained an MPC of 0.5 throughout his lifetime. In a household where there are several generations living together, there is no individual saving structure since assets are held in common. In this setting, the age structure of the population should not have any effect on saving.

LEVEL OF INCOME   If LCH and PIH are correct, then saving should not be related to current income. However, several researchers (inspired by Hall, 1978) have found that current income is an important explanatory variable. These results lend partial support to the idea that there are liquidity constraints and/or that income smoothing may be in response to short-run income fluctuations.

It also suggests that precautionary saving motives are stronger than life-cycle effects in the developing countries.

TERMS OF TRADE   The terms of trade effect works through an unanticipated and transitory increase in income by an improved trade balance. Since changes in the terms of trade are usually viewed as temporary, they would be incorporated into the LCH/PIH framework as transitory, with a strong positive effect on saving. The empirical literature finds this to be generally supported (see Masson et al., 1995; and Ostry and Reinhart, 1992).

An unexpected improvement in the terms of trade can have a positive effect on the saving rate because it represents a windfall gain in income and, according to the life cycle and permanent income models, would be saved (see Obstfeld, 1982). The terms of trade effect can be substantial if the shift is large. For example, the oil shocks of the 1970s represented a sharp shift in the terms of trade in favor of oil exporters and a similar increase in the rate of world saving as these funds could not be spent as fast as they accumulated.

DEGREE OF FINANCIAL LIBERALIZATION AND STABILITY   A general rule of thumb regarding saving would be that financial stability and liberalization are positively related to the rate of private saving, other things being equal. A predictable and stable financial environment that offers a range of financial instruments can be expected to call forth a higher level of saving from the private sector than a volatile and capricious financial and economic environment. However, an alternative view would be that increased volatility could lead to a greater precautionary motive for saving. Theory gives no guidance apart from the recognition that a more liberal environment should lead to higher saving rates.

7.3   DETERMINANTS OF SAVING IN DEVELOPING COUNTRIES AND IN ASIA

Figure 7.1 shows the level of gross domestic saving rates as percentages of GDP in the world. Developing countries, such as those in South Asia and Latin America, generally saved up to approximately 20–25 percent of GDP between the 1960s and 2000s. However, they lagged behind those of East Asia. The level of saving in East Asia has surpassed that of the world since the early 1970s, with a saving rate of about 47 percent of GDP in 2006. Saving rates in South Asia has been rapidly increasing since 2001 and is currently at 35 percent of GDP. However, Higgins (1998) states that after 2010, the greying population in the East Asian countries (such as Singapore and Hong Kong) would have a substantially reduced number of working-age adults in the workforce which would adversely impact upon their level of saving in the future. Hence, he concludes that in the future, higher levels of saving would most likely come from developing countries, such as South Asia and Latin America, where a high proportion of the population would be in the labor force or rapidly approaching working age.

7.3.1   Determinants of Saving in Developing Countries

The Masson et al. (1995) study reports a number of regressions, some of which are shown in Table 7.1. The results show that the rate of growth of GDP, the terms of trade, per-capita income, total wealth, the dependency ratio, and the current-account surplus/GDP are all significant explanatory variables for a large sample of developing countries over a long period. Per-capita income enters in a non-linear fashion, with the square of the variable also being significant. A negative sign indicates a diminishing

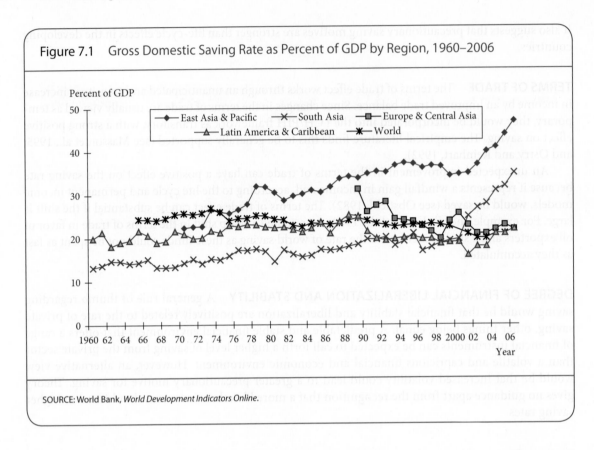

Figure 7.1 Gross Domestic Saving Rate as Percent of GDP by Region, 1960–2006

SOURCE: World Bank, *World Development Indicators Online*.

effect as the saving rate increases. All the variables have the expected signs, as discussed in the previous section. Two variables not discussed above but included in the regression are the current-account surplus/GDP ratio (equal to minus foreign saving) and wealth. The current-account surplus/GDP variable was added to reflect the impact of foreign savings/transfers on domestic saving. The sign is correct and suggests that an increase in foreign saving equal to 1 percent of GDP reduces the national saving rate by about 0.4 percentage points. The sign of the wealth variable is also positive, suggesting that saving rates are higher for the wealthy.

7.3.2 Determinants of Saving in Asia

For Asia, there is evidence imbedded in the study by Masson et al. for high- and medium-income developing countries (reported in Table 7.1) that suggests that the variables explaining saving in these countries are similar to those that explain saving behavior in all developing countries. Apart from Nepal, India, Bangladesh, and Myanmar, all the countries in developing Asia are in the high- and medium-income countries, which had similar patterns of significance for the explanatory variables as the entire group of countries reported above. In addition, scatter plots of bivariate relationships between saving and some of the most important explanatory variables, such as income growth, foreign saving, and the dependency ratio, confirm the importance of these variables in explaining variations in saving in Asia. Furthermore, individual country studies for Korea (Dowling, 1984), the Philippines (Nam, 1989), and Southeast Asia (Harrigan, 1998) give support for the importance of income and demographic variables. A careful review of this and other evidence led Harrigan (1998, p. 42) to conclude that:

Table 7.1 Panel Estimates of Private Saving/GDP Ratios for Forty Developing Countries with Separate Country Constant Terms, 1982–1993

Explanatory Variable	Private Saving/GDP Ratio	
Central government budget surplus/GDP	−0.626	(9.40)[a]
Central government capital expenditure/GDP	−0.233	(2.69)[a]
Central government current expenditure/GDP	0.007	(0.11)
GDP growth rate	0.142	(3.59)[a]
Percent change in terms of trade	0.007	(0.63)
Per-capita income	0.823	(3.65)[a]
Per-capita income squared	−0.008	(2.67)[a]
Private wealth/GDP	0.007	(1.14)
Dependency ratio	−0.198	(6.33)[a]
Inflation	−0.049	(1.60)
Current account surplus/GDP	0.463	(11.19)[a]
Real interest rate	−0.021	(0.63)
Adjusted R²	0.306	3.36
Number of observations	480	

Figures in parenthesis denote absolute *t*-ratios.

[a]denotes significance at the 5-percent level.

SOURCE: Paul R. Masson, Tamim Bayoumi, and Hossein Samiei, "International Evidence on the Determinants of Private Savings," IMF Working Paper WP/95/51 (1995).

A trinity of fast growth, fiscal rectitude and slowing population growth have been associated with high savings in Asia. Where one or more of these ingredients have been missing, savings have suffered.

These conclusions are supported by an econometric study of discretionary private saving behavior in Southeast Asia using an error correction model for the period 1971 to 1991. Harrigan (1998) concludes that GNP growth has a positive effect on saving in both the short and long run. Investigation of the possible simultaneity effect caused by the feedback of saving on investment and income suggests that these effects are weak. The terms of trade effect is positive and this result is consistent with the economic theory discussed earlier, and also with results from other sets of developing and industrial countries. With respect to dependency, young age dependency (the proportion of the population 15 years and under) has a very strong impact on the saving rate, while the proportion over 65 years does not. This asymmetry may be because the burden of the elderly has not changed as much as the sharp decline in the youth dependency in the latter years of the sample period. An interesting facet of the Harrigan model, which has not been explored elsewhere, is that as the share of agriculture to total income contracted, there has been a negative effect on the level of discretionary private saving. This could be because agricultural income has a wider variance than non-farm income and hence a higher precautionary motive to save. It could also be that as agriculture shrinks, the degree of financial liberalization increases along with the availability of consumer credit and debt, thus reducing the propensity to save. An analysis of government saving and expenditure behavior on private discretionary savings strongly suggests a rejection of Ricardian equivalence. While an increase in government saving exerts a short-term depressing effect on saving, there is no impact in the long run. Finally, the results suggest that financial liberalization and stability are positively related to the level of private saving. Inflation has a negative short-run impact and a higher real interest rate is positively related to saving in the long run.

Harrigan (1998) concludes that rapid income growth, selective terms of trade effects (for Malaysia in particular), financial deepening, reduction in young age dependency (particularly in Singapore and to a lesser extent, in Thailand and Indonesia) and a reduction in the size of government (Malaysia and Thailand) has boosted private saving. There was also a significant depressing effect on saving caused by the decline in the agricultural share of income. However, this does not suggest that a return to agriculture would be beneficial to private saving since this structural transformation has been accompanied by a number of other factors, such as more rapid income growth and lower youth dependency, which have had much stronger effects on saving.

7.4   INTRODUCTION TO THE FINANCIAL SYSTEM

The financial system is an integral component of modern economies. In most Asian countries, commercial banks constitute the primary component of the financial system. However, informal financial institutions also play an important role. Furthermore, in the last decade or so, other financial institutions, including insurance companies and pension funds, as well as stock and bond markets, have gained greater importance. Before the Asian financial crisis, a number of weaknesses in the banking system were noted, which eventually, along with other developments in international trade and finance, led to the crisis itself.

The aim of this chapter is threefold. First, the banking systems and credit markets are discussed generally and briefly, along with the topics of financial repression and liberalization. This is followed by a summary of the experience of developing countries in general, and Asia in particular. A section on the Asian financial crisis highlights the shortcomings in the institutional structure of the bank and credit system with reference to this crisis. A number of developments in financial policy and regulation following the financial crisis are discussed in the next section. The chapter concludes with a discussion on informal finance and how it relates to the formal sector and monetary policy.

7.5   BANKING AND THE FINANCIAL SYSTEM

The banking and financial systems in the developing economies in Asia evolved from systems that were in place during the colonial period. In South Asia, Taiwan, Malaysia, Hong Kong, and Singapore, the British system was adopted, while in East Asia, the Japanese model was adopted in Korea. In cases such as Thailand and China, which were not colonized to any significant extent (some coastal cities, such as Hong Kong, did have significant colonial influence), the financial systems were borrowed from the industrial countries.

In most cases, these financial systems were dominated by the banking system and commercial banks. The government in turn controlled the banking systems. By and large, commercial banks were either owned or controlled by the central bank. In South Asia, this was a persistent pattern of ownership and control that has changed only slowly in the past decade or so. In East and Southeast Asia, with the exception of Hong Kong, which has been dominated by private commercial banks from its inception as a trading center by the British in the nineteenth century, there has been a slow devolution of control and ownership by the government.

Nevertheless, by the early 1970s, the region as a whole could be characterized by the widespread presence of financial repression. Financial repression is a situation, first described fully by Shaw (1973) and McKinnon (1973) in the early 1970s, where government taxes and subsidies distort the domestic capital market (compared with a free and competitive system where private banks are supervised by a central bank) by imposing interest rate restrictions and high reserve requirements. At the same time, there are compulsory credit allocations to some sectors and the lack of credit to others. As a result, loans extended by banks were not thoroughly analyzed in terms of risk or project viability. Competition among banks was also limited, particularly as foreign banks were not allowed to enter the market or where their presence was highly regulated. In these cases, there were few incentives for improving bank efficiency. In a study of the Organization for Economic Cooperation and Development (OECD) countries, for example, Terrell (1986) concludes that the exclusion of foreign banks reduces competition, making domestic banks more profitable but less efficient. Since requirements were high already, excess funds were often parked in government securities rather than used to seek out high-yielding, low-risk investments in the private sector. Furthermore, in countries where foreign banks were allowed to compete vigorously, such as Singapore and Hong Kong, there was much greater efficiency and lower profit margins.

This kind of banking system evolved during a time when development thinking believed that the government had to play a strong role in mobilizing and allocating credit to facilitate investment and promote economic development. There was a widespread belief that the private sector was too weak to mobilize sufficient resources and that the banking system was to be used as an instrument by the government to step in. Interest rates had to be controlled and some sectors subsidized further to keep the costs of investments low. Since the private sector's role in saving and investments were minimized, the impact of low (and sometimes negative real) interest rates on savings of the private sector was not systematically considered.

7.5.1 Financial Repression

These various controls and schedules interacted, resulting in a financial system that did not allocate credit to the public in an efficient manner, and the banking sector played a smaller role than it could have in a more competitive and free environment. Such "repressed" financial systems were characterized by low or negative real interest rates and a low and sometimes falling ratio of monetary assets to GDP/GNP. In a repressed system, the government usually plays a dominant role in controlling the banking system by imposing these kinds of controls, using banks to serve as the instruments for allocating credit to key selected sectors. Often, specialized banks were created to address the needs of particular sectors. Rural banks were often created for this purpose in the early stages of development and were complemented by banks focusing on key industries later in the development process.

At the same time, credit to other potential borrowers was lacking. As a result, informal or "kerb" markets developed outside the formal financial system to mobilize and direct credit to those sectors not effectively serviced by the formal financial and banking system. The overall impact of these developments was a fragmented banking system where the organized banking system serviced only a small part of the total capital market while informal finance emerged to serve the needs of other borrowers. Capital was allocated inefficiently within the banking system since potential borrowers were not properly screened, competition within the banking system was limited, and loans were extended based on preferential credit allocations and not on economic feasibility studies or project evaluation. Interest rates did not reflect the interaction of the supply of and demand for funds. Neither did they reflect the riskiness of projects. Instead, interest rates were determined by fiat based on the perceived importance of the sector to which the funds were being allocated—the more important and critical the sector, the lower the rate of interest. Self-finance within enterprises was also impaired when real interest rates were low or negative as it became difficult to save for needed projects. Finally, financial deepening outside the banking system was difficult in the face of financial repression. This was true not only because it was discouraged by the government and the central bank, but also because of the lack of liquidity and the arbitrariness of government policy, and the potential or actual lack of financial stability.

7.5.2   Financial Liberalization

How then were the "miracle" economies of East and Southeast Asia able to develop such dynamic economies? In parts of East Asia, particularly in Hong Kong and to a lesser extent in Singapore, the banking system was not encumbered by too many regulations and restrictions. In Korea and Taiwan, there was clear evidence of financial repression, but the policies of the government did supply cheap finance to support key sectors in the industrialization effort. Thus, in some sense, financial repression was not as great a handicap in East Asia as it was in South Asia, where the other policies of openness, competitiveness in exports, and more liberal industrial policies were not followed. In China, after opening to the rest of the world in the 1980s, financial incentives were used to develop the town and village enterprises as foreign investment from Taiwan and Hong Kong was allowed to enter. However, the continued support of inefficient state-owned enterprises (SOEs) drained resources for many years. Even now, the budget support for these enterprises continues to be a challenge. In Southeast Asia, financial repression was not as extensive as in South Asia, and more private-sector involvement was permitted. As industrialization proceeded, financial liberalization continued and strengthened, although elements of the old system remained, as we shall see when we look into the financial crisis of 1997.

Very simply, financial liberalization is designed to remove all the restrictions that characterize financial repression. These include the lowering of reserve requirements, freeing up interest rates, and allowing them to respond to market forces. Managed credit allocations to key sectors should be reduced or eliminated, and loan officers should be required to evaluate potential borrowers on the merits of the project and not to give loans indiscriminately based on other noneconomic criteria. Competitive forces should be allowed to operate in the banking system to improve economic efficiency through the relaxation of entry requirements, both domestically and for international banks. Together with these measures, price levels should be effectively controlled to keep inflation to a minimum. In this way, positive real interest rates can be easily maintained. Given the strong theoretical backing of Shaw (1973) and McKinnon (1973), many countries undertook financial liberalization.

7.5.3   Asian Experience of Financial Liberalization

In the 1960s and 1970s, the commercial banking system was tightly controlled by the government in almost all the Asian countries. Banks were owned and operated by the government and it was believed that one purpose of the banking system was to help further the government's objectives of making loans to subsidized sectors through a process of direct credits. It was believed that private banks would not make such loans. Furthermore, interest rates were controlled and credit allocation schemes were used. Banks were required to hold government debt that cut the cost of borrowing by the government. Prudential regulations were largely neglected since the government controlled the banking system. Banks and development finance institutions (DFIs) were the main financial intermediaries. DFIs were introduced to further allocate credit to particular sectors, and they were given appropriate names such as Agriculture Development Bank or Industrial Development Bank. Organized markets for private equities and bonds were either nonexistent or very thin, and few licenses were granted for other nonbank financial intermediaries such as insurance companies or pension funds. The quality of loan portfolios was not an important consideration, being outweighed by the need to direct credit to different sectors at subsidized rates. The only exceptions to these generalizations about banking during this period were Hong Kong and (later) Singapore.

In the 1980s and early 1990s, financial liberalization began in the NIEs and in Southeast Asia. More competition was permitted as regulations on private and foreign banking were relaxed. Interest rates were deregulated to a large extent while directed credit and requirements to hold large amounts of government securities were reduced. A modicum of independence was also evident as they became more autonomous and escaped the grip of the Treasury. Some prudential regulations were introduced, including auditing and oversight functions.

In South Asia, the pace of reform, with the possible exception of Sri Lanka, was slower as fewer changes were implemented and the structure of the financial system remained repressed. A country-by-country summary of regulations in the early to mid-1990s is displayed in Table 7.2.

7.5.4 Measures of Financial Repression

Nevertheless, substantial evidence of financial repression remained in several countries. This is shown by some aggregate measures of financial deepening. One such widely used measure of financial repression and financial liberalization is the ratio of money plus quasi money (M2) to GDP/GNP. The ratio rises with liberalization and falls with financial repression. A comparison of these ratios for Asia in the last thirty years shows that this ratio has been increasing rapidly in East and Southeast Asia (see Table 7.3).

The cases of Malaysia and Thailand are particularly noteworthy. From fairly low levels in 1970 (not much higher than ratios in South Asia), the ratio rose to more than 1 by the end of the 1990s. In Thailand, the commercial banking system was predominantly private and extensive liberalization took place in the 1980s. Compulsory credit to priority sectors was reduced and interest rates were largely deregulated in the early 1990s. Exchange controls were also relaxed and the reserve ratio was reduced to 7 percent in 1991. A facility (Bangkok International Banking Facility) was introduced in the mid-1990s to help the domestic and foreign banks to borrow in overseas markets. Later in the decade, these liberalization measures, which were adopted without the accompanying prudential controls and safeguards, helped the financial system to participate in a stock and property market bubble that resulted in a run on the currency and the beginning of the financial crisis.

Hong Kong and Singapore, particularly the former, had high ratios that increased further over the period. Writing in 1988, McKinnon characterized this ratio in the rapidly growing economies of Japan, Germany, Taiwan, and Singapore as having a value of 0.75 (75 percent) or more. By 1999, Malaysia, Thailand, and Singapore had joined Japan, Taiwan (not shown in Table 7.3), and Hong Kong in this club. Taiwan began banking reform in the 1980s as foreign exchange controls were lifted, interest rates decontrolled, and new private banks were authorized to do business. However, tough restrictions were placed on the capital required for these new banks. There were no directed credits either as the government adopted a hands-off policy with regard to bank-lending requirements. Korea (and the United States, which has a ratio unchanged from the 1970s) continues to rely on foreign loans to a greater extent than the other countries and thus, its ratio has not increased as much. Furthermore, until recently it pursued a vigorous policy of directed credit, and consumers and other borrowers not targeted had to rely on the "kerb" market. While this situation has changed in recent years, the financial ratios still reflect these earlier practices.

In South Asia, there has been some progress in financial liberalization in recent years but the M2/GDP ratio has remained lower than in the other countries in the Asian region. This trend is particularly noticeable in Sri Lanka and Pakistan. In the latter economy, the ratio has remained unchanged after thirty years. The banking system remains dominated by government-owned institutions, as private banks control less that 20 percent of all assets. There has been some interest rate deregulation

Table 7.2   Banking Regulations in Asian Developing Countries in the Mid-1990s

	Bank Ownership	Entry Restrictions	Interest Controls and Government Debt Purchase Requirements	Interest Subsidies and Directed Credit
Bangladesh	Mostly government	Limited entry—rapid easing	Interest controls being relaxed—high debt purchase requirements	Both still used but being lowered
India	Mostly government	Limited entry—slow easing	Interest rates controlled—debt purchase required but being relaxed	Both still used extensively
Indonesia	Mostly private	open	Both controlled by government—bond holding an instrument of monetary policy	Both subsidies and directed credit continue to be used
Korea	Mostly private	Restricted to both domestic and foreign firms	Interest rates being relaxed—no bond purchases required	Little directed credit and few subsidies left
Malaysia	Mostly private	Limited entry for both	No interest control—some bond purchases required	Interest subsidies now but directed credit continues to be used
Pakistan	Mostly government	Entry for both	Both interest controls and debt holding requirements being liberalized	Both still used extensively
Philippines	Mostly private	Limited entry—gradual easing	Interest controls relaxed—some bond holdings required	Directed credit still used. Interest subsidies being reduced
Sri Lanka	Mostly government	Easy entry in theory—limited in practice	Some interest controls and large debt holding required	Both recently reduced
Taiwan	Mostly government	Restricted but easing	Interest rates being relaxed—no bond purchases required	Little directed credit and few subsidies left
Thailand	Mostly private	Limited entry—gradual easing	Interest controls relaxed—some bond purchases required	Directed credit used. Interest Subsidies being lowered

SOURCE: Asian Development Bank, *Asian Development Outlook 1997*.

although reserve requirements remain high at around 30 percent, but progress in further deregulation and reduction in the scope of the government in directing credit has been slow.

In India, the M2/GDP ratio has grown more rapidly than in other South Asian countries. However, the financial system still shows signs of financial repression. Banks are publicly controlled and interest rate caps remain in place. Bank licensing was eased in 1992 and some measures have been taken to reduce reserve requirement and the scope of directed credit. However, more needs to be done, including reform of bank supervision and finance institutions that have high levels of nonperforming loans.

Indonesia also exhibits signs of continued financial repression as the M2/GDP ratio increased from a very low level to a more moderate 0.36 by 1999. Nevertheless, these figures belie substantial

Table 7.3 Comparison of the Ratio of Money Supply (M2) to GDP/GNP, 1970 and 1999

	1970	1999
Bangladesh[a]	0.31	0.39
China[b]	0.33	0.26
Hong Kong[c]	1.80	2.20
India	0.23	0.56
Indonesia	0.10	0.36
Korea	0.33	0.68
Malaysia	0.34	1.10
Pakistan	0.43	0.43
Philippines	0.29	0.63
Singapore	0.66	1.20
Sri Lanka	0.23	0.35
Thailand	0.29	1.00
Japan	0.74	1.30
United States	0.63	0.62

Earliest year reported is from [a]1973, [b]1979, [c]1991, respectively.

SOURCE: International Monetary Fund, *International Financial Statistics* (Washington, D.C.: IMF, 2000).

liberalization of the financial system that began in the 1980s with deregulation and the introduction of private banks, lowering of reserve requirements, deregulation of interest rates, and reductions in the scope of directed credit. However, the liberalization measures were not accompanied by tighter prudential controls and many of the practices that existed before liberalization were continued. This led to bad loans and growing weakness of bank portfolios as the bubble of the mid-1990s ballooned.

In the Philippines, banks were also liberalized in the 1980s. As a result, the banking system is basically in the hands of the private sector. There are only two development banks channeling funds to needy enterprises in the rural areas and to some urban industries. Foreign ownership is allowed up to 40 percent, and no branches are allowed to be set up by foreign banks outside of Manila. Interest rates are not regulated and reserve requirements are low. There are some directed credit allocations but they apply mainly to rural banks. As a result of these reforms and the difficulties experienced in the 1970s, the financial sector in the Philippines was not highly leveraged in the early and mid-1990s, and was therefore able to withstand the financial crisis without having to introduce an asset management company to deal with bank loans. Nevertheless, the financial system has been weakened by the lack of a good prudential and regulatory system and the continued presence of corruption and crony capitalism.

In the case of China, where we have data only from 1979, the ratio has fallen slightly over twenty years. There are several factors working here. First, financial repression still exists as state banks dominate and funds are channeled from the banking system to state-owned enterprises. Interest rates remain controlled and there is a lack of competition. Secondly, much of the finance for the vibrant private sector in the southern coastal region has come from foreign sources. Thirdly, the growth of the local stock market, also financed in part by foreign funds inflow, has been responsible for some growth in total liquidity of the financial system.

7.6   FINANCIAL LIBERALIZATION IN THE DEVELOPING COUNTRIES

Until the onset of the financial crisis, the Asian economies seemed to have had reasonable success in implementing financial liberalization. They were able to avoid the problems encountered by Latin America in controlling fiscal spending and inflation. Fry et al. (1996) estimate that about 2 percent of GDP on average is lost by moving a country from financial repression to financial liberalization. If this revenue cannot be made up through fiscal adjustments in taxes or expenditures, then a financial crisis could result when the government turns to the printing press to finance this deficit, resulting in destabilizing inflation. This was what happened in several Latin American countries in the 1980s, leading the well-known Latin American development economist, Carlos Diaz-Alejandro, to write an article entitled "Good-bye financial repression, hello financial crash" in 1985.

Asia managed to avoid this problem of finance, probably because it was growing fast and had a relatively elastic tax base. It had also instituted strong habits of fiscal probity that prevented it from developing the inflationary bias that plagued Latin America for years (see Chapter 3). Asia did develop difficulties in the second half of the 1990s, leading up to the financial crisis of 1997. This resulted from residual effects of the period of financial repression that had been carried over into the liberalization period. Because they were not dealt with as part of the overall process of liberalization, they remained a weakness that became more evident as the economies of the region heated up in the early 1990s. We will return to these weaknesses later.

Meanwhile, in the earlier period the Asian economies had made the transition quite well. The cases of Japan (see McKinnon, 1988, upon which this section is based), Taiwan, Thailand, and Korea are instructive. In Japan, liberalization began in the 1950s and 1960s. Monetary policy was stable as were prices. Thus, nominal and real interest rates were very similar. Secondly, only after substantial deepening of the capital market, such as the development of securities markets and finance and insurance companies, did the central bank loosen its control over commercial banks. Thirdly, there was very little foreign borrowing and so foreign exchange rate risks were minimal.

The key to the success of liberalization in Asia was the maintenance of a high real rate of interest, even when banks were still state-owned (this was also true in Taiwan) or where there were sectors that still received directed credit (such as Thailand). Where there was high level of foreign borrowing and inflation was a problem, the balancing act was trickier. In Korea, between 1979 and 1983, inflation was still high as the aftermath of the second oil shock was still being played out. As inflation fell in late 1982 and 1983 as a result of strong macroeconomic policies, the exchange rate was managed as a crawling downward peg to follow inflation. Interest rates were also scaled downward as inflation slowed. By doing this, the interest rate differential between the United States and Korea was maintained and capital inflows discouraged. As additional support, capital controls were kept in place to prevent a buildup in foreign borrowing during the liberalization process.

There are a number of other risks and considerations that have to be taken into account when we consider the case of small open economies that depend upon international trade and where there is inflation and exchange rate risks. If there is an implicit or explicit (deposit insurance) belief that banks will be bailed out if they fail, the situation is made even more delicate. These were the conditions that faced the Asian crisis economies as the bubble economy of the mid-1990s evolved. Financial liberalization had been in full swing. Interest rates were being liberalized and restrictions on the banks dismantled. The flow of capital into the country was proceeding vigorously as capital controls were being dismantled. Yet the banking and financial system had not adapted well enough from an institutional point of view. Loans were being made without careful analysis; there was a lack of competition as the pace of liberalization was slow in allowing best practice foreign banks to do business with local customers.

The ability of the financial system to cope with the rapid inflow of foreign capital and strong growth in securities and real estate markets was complicated by the growing exposure to exchange rate risk, as well as the risk of inflation building further as growth exceeded sustainable levels. This is where we pick up the story of the Asian financial crisis, as it was described in Chapter 3. The emphasis here is on the financial sector and aspects of financial magnitudes prior to the onset of the crisis. As mentioned earlier, the banking system was the cornerstone of the financial sector throughout Asia. Stock markets were only beginning to develop, and apart from a few countries like Thailand and Japan, had established nonbank financial intermediaries such as finance companies specializing in real estate and insurance companies.

Bond markets, particularly corporate bonds, were also not well developed. Monetary policy did not work through the government bond market as it had done in the industrial countries for many years. Furthermore, gearing ratios were quite high as reflected in high debt to equity ratios. Table 7.4 shows that these ratios were sometimes over 2, a level unheard of in the industrial countries where these ratios were much lower, in the neighborhood of 0.5. Additionally, the ratio of short-term to total corporate debt was also high (see Table 7.5).

Another factor that is often forgotten, and which was mentioned earlier, is that the institutional arrangements and practices that were developed during the period of financial repression did not change much when financial liberalization took place. There was little competition among the banks and efficiency was low. Directed lending, personal contacts, and seat-of-the-pants evaluation of potential borrowers were commonplace, and serious evaluation of risks and potential returns were the exception. Finally, the risk of moral hazard was high in many countries as there was an implicit understanding that bankrupt banks would probably be bailed out. This resulted in riskier portfolio selection by bank managers.

Table 7.4   Debt Equity Ratios for Selected Asian Countries, 1996

	Debt Equity Ratio
Hong Kong	1.56
Indonesia	1.88
Japan	2.21
Korea	3.55
Malaysia	1.18
Philippines	1.29
Singapore	1.05
Taiwan	0.80
Thailand	2.36

SOURCE: Asian Development Bank, *Asian Development Outlook 1999*, p. 27.

Table 7.5   Ratios of Domestic and External Short/Long-Term Debt for Selected Countries, 1996

	To Total External Debt		To Total Domestic Debt	
	Foreign Short-Term	**Foreign Long-Term**	**Domestic Short-Term**	**Domestic Long-Term**
Indonesia	20.5	19.6	31.4	28.5
Korea	29.4	17.0	27.7	25.8
Malaysia	32.1	11.0	35.7	21.2
Philippines	19.7	21.3	25.5	33.5
Taiwan	22.3	19.2	23.9	34.6
Thailand	29.6	12.3	32.0	26.1

SOURCE: Asian Development Bank, *Asian Development Outlook 1999*, p. 29.

7.7   THE FINANCIAL CRISIS OF 1997

As described briefly in Chapter 3, the Asian crisis had three main components. First, because banks believed implicitly or had been assured that they would be bailed out in case of a crisis, a strong moral hazard developed as commercial banks made more and more risky loans and the financial bubble grew bigger. This resulted in both a land and stock market boom as prices were bid up and available supply remained limited. Stock markets crashed in several countries prior to the crisis but this did not arrest the financial bubble. It undermined the economy further when stock prices fell even further after the crisis began. Banks were not only guilty of making imprudent loans; but they were also not used to due diligence in assessing the credit risks of borrowers, and this failure became even more evident as banks made more risky loans.

As the financial crisis unfolded, the weaknesses in the five crisis countries were exacerbated by the currency depreciation and the buildup of nonperforming loans of companies that had large outstanding external liabilities that they were unable to service.

After the crisis, all the affected countries were able to slowly recover and deal with their financial sector weaknesses. Many of the weaknesses identified prior to the crisis that were outlined in the previous section continue and need to be addressed. Briefly, they include the need to:

1. introduce better processes to identify worthy borrowers and make greater use of loan collateral.
2. further deregulate of financial transactions.
3. introduce a greater degree of prudential regulation of banks.
4. introduce more competition and reduce restrictions on licensing and entry.
5. support the development of new markets, particularly for new financial assets that will allow investors to hedge their investments, including forward and futures markets.
6. continue to privatize state banks.
7. improve lender recourse, including the legal seizure of assets.
8. improve accounting and auditing practices.

As part of the restructuring efforts following the financial crisis, insolvent financial institutions have been closed, merged, or recapitalized to varying degrees. Corporate debt problems have also been addressed through corporate and debt restructuring. Individual country experiences are spelled out in more detail in Box 7.1.

BOX 7.1

Financial and Corporate Restructuring in Asian Economies

Financial and corporate restructuring was required after the financial crisis since the level of nonperforming loans (NPLs) had ballooned. This had an adverse impact on the financial stability of the banking system and the corporate sector. It also served to keep the level of new lending to a minimum, further retarding the potential for the corporate sector to recover from the crisis. In all five of the crisis-affected countries (Malaysia, Indonesia, Korea, Philippines, and Thailand), the task was to deal with insolvent financial institutions and the general problem of nonperforming loans. A process of closure and mergers of banks accomplished this through the recapitalization of existing banks and dealing with the debts of the corporate sector. The primary emphasis was on the banking system and devising methods to dispose of nonperforming loans. All the countries established new agencies to deal with NPLs, generically called asset management companies (AMCs). Over the five-year period after the crisis (1997–2002), the level of NPLs was reduced. The most progress was made in Korea and the least in Indonesia and the Philippines (see Box Table 7.1). In Thailand, new NPLs continued to emerge so that the level of NPLs did not fall as significantly as anticipated. Nevertheless, bank lending to businesses and households rose and economic growth resumed. However, these figures were distorted somewhat by the fact that bank balance sheets improved in all the crisis countries but the Philippines. This was accomplished by the formation of AMCs that took many of the NPLs off the hands of the banking system at a discount for possible resale. Korea and Malaysia were the most successful in disposing of these assets—60 percent and 100 percent respectively, by the middle of 2002. In Malaysia, the AMC Danahata was able to able to buy up bad loans and pay the

banks 80 percent of anything it recovered above the price it paid. The key was that Danahata determined the offer price and if the bank refused to take it, it was forced to write the loan's value down to Danahata's offer price anyway. The director of Danahata said that the main reason for success was the strength of the Danahata act.

Less progress was made in corporate restructuring although in Malaysia, the Corporate Debt Restructuring Agency was able to restructure virtually all the corporate debt it handled and it was disbanded in August 2002. In Korea, restructuring of the top *chaebols* moved ahead, aided by strong growth in the economy in the intervening five-year period. Daewoo was sold to General Motors, and Hynix is in the process of being sold to Micron. In Thailand, a special debtor committee was set up to help resolve unpaid loans and more than half of the loans referred to the committee were resolved by 2002. In Indonesia, a similar task force helped to resolve debts. However, there were a few bankruptcies and the resolution of outstanding debts to everyone's satisfaction may take some time.

Bank credit expanded in Korea and Malaysia, the two countries that had the best record in clearing NPLs. In the other crisis countries, credit expansion was slower and was still below pre-crisis levels in all three countries—as much as 40 percent below in Indonesia and 20 percent in the Philippines and Thailand—up to the middle of 2002.

Capital adequacy ratios also improved after the crisis and all crisis countries were above the 8 percent Basle norm, in the 10–15 percent range for all countries but Indonesia, which was just above the Basle floor.

In China, NPLs declined slowly from a peak of nearly 30 percent at the end of 2000 to just over 23 percent by the middle of 2002 (see Box Table 7.1). AMCs sold about 13 percent of the NPLs they acquired from the banking system. However, recent reports in the popular press suggest that the level of NPLs may remain a serious problem.

Box Table 7.1   Nonperforming Loans in the Crisis Economies and China

	NPLs at End of 1998	NPLs in Mid-2002
Indonesia	Nearly 50%	About 18%
Korea	About 8%	Under 2%
Malaysia	About 10 %	About 10%
Philippines	About 12%	About 18%
Thailand	Over 40%	About 10%
China	About 30%	About 23%

SOURCE: Asian Development Bank, *Asian Economic Monitor* (October 2002), Web site at http://aric.adb.org.

SOURCES: Asian Development Bank, *Asian Economic Monitor* (October 2002), Web site at http://aric.adb.org; *International Herald Tribune*, December 16, 2002.

Generally, asset management companies (AMCs) were created to facilitate debt restructuring. These AMCs took the bad debts off the hands of the banks and worked to collect and write down these debts, often with the help of government financial support. By taking these nonperforming loans (NPLs) off the balance sheets of the banking system, the way was cleared for banks to begin to relend after the crisis.

7.8   INFORMAL FINANCE

In many developing countries, there are significant sectors of the population that are unable to obtain credit from institutions in the formal financial sector, such as banks and credit unions. As a result, informal financial institutions have emerged that do not fall under the supervisory umbrella of the central bank or the ministry of finance. These informal institutions have no or very limited linkages with the formal financial sector. Furthermore, efforts to reform the formal sector to incorporate informal finance have not been particularly successful. A credit guarantee scheme is the primary method for addressing the lack of collateral by the banking system. This lack of borrowing capacity has been a major deterrent to lending to the poor over the years in many countries. The problem with these schemes generally is that the commercial banks have not been willing to share the risk of credit guarantees, primarily because it is difficult to measure the risk involved and then to determine the costs of a scheme.

Rather than try out such a system, commercial banks have shied away. On the other hand, if the government were to supply a credit guarantee, it would defeat the purpose of a commercially viable guarantee, since the government will finance the losses and the problem of moral hazard would arise.

Schemes in which the risks are shared by the government and the banks have also not been successful. Therefore, with the exception of a few special banks that we will discuss below, the formal sector and policies and programs suggested by the World Bank and others to involve the formal banking sector have not been successful.

In this section, we first list the reasons why informal finance exists and the different kinds of informal financial mechanisms and institutions, before discussing them in more detail. Then, the size of the informal sector will be examined and some recommendations put forward for further integrating the informal with the formal sector.

7.8.1   A Rationale for Informal Finance and a Simple Taxonomy of Informal Financial Institutions

Informal finance plays an important role in most of the Asian economies. This is because large segments of the population still face major impediments to entry into the formal financial system. Thomas (1993) lists these six reasons:

1. Access to banking facilities is limited for the squatters, slum residents, and in some areas of the rural economy.
2. Banks lend primarily for investment and not for consumption.
3. Transactions and appraisal costs are high as a proportion of the potential loan or other transaction, and this discourages lending.
4. The banks lack information about the credit worthiness of potential borrowers.
5. These borrowers do not have sufficient capital to submit a credit report.
6. Banks believe that the borrowers are too poor to repay at a commercial rate of interest.

To address this gap in borrowing options for the poor, a number of different institutions and schemes have been developed.

7.8.2 Group Finance

There are a number of ways in which individuals can form groups to mobilize resources to lend outside the formal banking system. These groups accumulate the savings within the group and then lend to members of the group exclusively, or to members of the group, as well as outside the group.

Rotating saving and credit associations (Roscas) have a long history in many parts of the world and are found in many countries (see Ghate, 1994, for more details). Members agree to contribute a specified amount each to a general pot, or kitty, at specified intervals for a certain period of time. The sum collected is then allocated to members of the group in rotation until all members have had a chance to take the kitty. The first person to take the kitty has an interest-free loan for the duration that the Rosca is in force. The Rosca can be organized by a group of friends or by an outside manager. The way in which the Rosca is distributed varies depending on the agreement—it could be by lottery, or an agreed order, or bidding by participants. In bidding, the person taking the kitty would offer the largest discount, which serves as a proxy for an interest rate, and also gives some return to other members who take the kitty later on. If there is no bidding, then the first to take the kitty benefits the most while the last only gets back the money he put in.

Suppose the Rosca has ten people who agree to contribute $10 a week for ten weeks. Each week the kitty of $100 is distributed to one of the members. The lucky person who gets the kitty the first week receives $100 and only has to contribute $10 a week for the next nine weeks. The person who gets the $100 the second week also has an interest-free loan for eight weeks. The last person to get the kitty puts in $10 a week and only gets back the same amount he or she puts in at the end of ten weeks, with no interest.

Another way is to develop a bidding system in which those who need the money urgently are willing to pay an implicit interest to those who are willing to wait for the kitty until the later rounds. In this case, the bidder in the first week might be willing to take only $90, thus paying an implicit interest of $10 during the ten-week period. The extra $10 would be added to the kitty in the next week and so on. In this way, the one who bids last will benefit from a higher implicit interest payment together with the agreed contributions.

Roscas help to solve the six problems mentioned earlier by organizing people who have no access to borrowing from the formal system and by keeping transaction costs low since the organization is simple and transparent, and the members know each other. In addition, since the bidding system establishes an interest rate, it acts as a market to determine the value of scarce funds. Default on payment is possible but it is discouraged by the fact that members will exert pressure on one another. This helps to bring together those who want to participate and who know the rules of the game. Most Roscas have traditionally excluded women and that is one reason that the successful non-governmental organizations (NGOs) discussed below have catered to women almost exclusively. Credit unions are larger and more formal versions of Roscas but these have not been popular in Asia, except within the context of the formal financial sector.

7.8.3 Money Lenders, Landlords, and Pawnshops

All three of these forms of informal finance relate one lender to many borrowers. By tying the credit to the farmer, the landlord reduces transaction costs while money lenders depend on their local knowledge of the borrower and also the threat of "physical enforcement" to keep down the rate of default. Interest rates are higher than in the formal markets but there is also evidence of competition that tends to keep rates down. While annualized interest rates may be very high, borrowers who are desperate because of the need to pay doctor's bills or other pressing personal situations, and who can repay the loan quickly, may be willing to pay such high rates. Pawnshops depend on reselling an item that is pawned, often paying deep discounted prices to ensure making some return on the loan, or charging high rates of interest for the redemption of the pawned item.

7.8.4 Non-Governmental Organizations (NGOs)

NGOs can operate outside the formal banking system or become a member of the formal banking community at a later date. The following are examples of NGOs in the Asian region.

GRAMEEN BANK IN BANGLADESH   The Grameen Bank (GB) is the most successful NGO, which has become a rural banking cooperative and copied in many countries. The main feature of the Grameen Bank is that it is owned primarily by its depositors, who are also its primary borrowers. This is why it can also be classified as a cooperative. Initially, the Bangladesh government provided some of the start-up capital but the government's share has gradually been reduced. The GB is able to assess creditworthiness efficiently without any need for collateral. The key is to depend on the borrowers to self-enforce repayment, since the borrowers are also the shareholders. The system works with small units that are supervised externally by the GB and monitored internally. Each member's loan depends upon the repayment record of others in the group. Initially, one member of a group receives a loan and if that is successful, others may then apply for loans. There is both peer pressure and peer support. If a member leaves a group without repaying his/her loan, the debt has to be repaid by the group. When an individual member has trouble repaying the loan, he/she is sometimes assisted by the group. There are weekly repayment meetings by several groups (six groups of five members in the case of Bangladesh) in which all members can participate.

By working in this cooperative type of environment, enforcement and monitoring costs are minimized. The risk of default is shifted from the GB to the borrowers since risk is shared within each of the groups. The borrowers use local knowledge and peer pressure to keep risks low. Potential borrowers know that they will be penalized if they default. Borrowers are charged the prevailing commercial loan rates, and there is neither a tax nor a subsidy. According to J. J. Thomas (1993, p. 244):

> The fact that poor borrowers can pay this rate of interest and still achieve such high rates of repayment confirms the fact that access to credit is more of a problem for the poor than the particular level of interest rates.

See Box 7.2 for information on the origins and operations of the Grameen Bank, as well as details of its advantages and drawbacks.

BANK GADANG BALI IN INDONESIA   The Bank Gadang Bali, which started as a small money-lending business founded by a local shoemaker and his wife and which led to other successful microcredit schemes in Bali, Indonesia, has blossomed into a local bank with many branches in Bali. It specializes in small loans and deposits and sends mobile bank-vans around the countryside every day to collect deposits, loan repayments, and extend new loans.

The success of Bank Gadang Bali is also reflective of a rural setting where many small borrowers and savers come from similar social and economic circumstances, thus cutting down on the cost of credit appraisal. There is also peer pressure to repay loans.

7.8.5 How Large is the Informal Finance Sector in Developing Asia?

Estimates of informal credit are available for a few countries as reported in Ghate (1994) and summarized in Table 7.6. The proportion of outstanding household debt to the informal sector was quite substantial in the early 1980s. Ghate has reported that the proportion has decreased compared with estimates made in the earlier periods, and there is no reason to doubt that this trend has continued as efforts have been made to extend the number of bank branches, consumer lending has increased, and efforts have been made to make funds available to the poor. Informal lending would also have decreased as the extent of poverty has been reduced, the rural sector has shrunk, and the nonpoor have accumulated assets that can be used as collateral.

BOX 7.2

Grameen Bank

According to the brochure circulated by the Grameen Bank (GB), the Grameen Bank Project began in one village in 1976. In 1983, it was transformed into a bank under a law passed for its creation. The poor, most of whom are women, own the bank. It works exclusively for them. The borrowers of the GB are also the majority stockholders; the government holds a small residual. The total number of borrowers is 2.4 million, and 95 percent of them are women. The GB has more than 1,000 branches serving over 40,000 villages, with a total staff of more than 10,000. It has distributed over 150 billion Tk and the repayment rate is around 98 percent. In 2002, loans of more than 14 billion Tk were disbursed. It has financed nearly 90 percent of outstanding loans from its own fund and the savings from its depositors, 83 percent of whom are its own borrowers. The GB has become less reliant on donor assistance and since 2003, it has been able to finance all of its loans from its own resources. The GB did borrow from both the central bank and commercial banks immediately after the devastating flood of 1998, to give fresh loans to the borrowers, most of whom lost their assets. All these post-flood loans have been fully paid off. The GB has made profits in all but three years since it started business.

The GB provides three types of loans: income-generating loans, with the highest rate of interest, and housing and education loans for the children of its borrowers at lower rates. It also offers scholarships to the children of its members, with priority given to females. Students who succeed in reaching the tertiary level of education are given higher education loans, to cover tuition, maintenance, and other school expenses. The GB has also provided loans to borrowers to buy cell phones to enable them to offer telecommunications services to more than 20,000 villages where this service never existed before. This has become a very profitable business for those who own these phones.

The GB also has a life insurance program that provides benefits to its members. Borrowers are not required to pay any premium for this life insurance, since they come under this insurance coverage by being a shareholder of the bank. According to an internal survey, more than 40 percent of the families of Grameen borrowers have moved out of poverty, and incomes of the remaining families are moving steadily upward.

The GB seems to have had a positive effect on reducing poverty. Education and literacy have increased and those who have participated and repaid loans have been integrated into the community as they repaid loans and exercised some control over their lives. The GB type of program has been extended to China under the auspices of the United Nations, and the idea has been copied in several other countries in Asia and Latin America (Pitt and Khandker, 1998). However, it has also been remarked that since the success of the GB is built on a foundation of trust and mutual understanding among small groups of poor women, there exists problems in extending such a scheme to larger and more diverse groups in other countries, as demonstrated by the Oxfam and Indian experiments, summarized in Thomas (1993).

The GB has depended and continues to depend upon donations, and it takes very few deposits. It depends on weekly meetings of its borrowers to put pressure on each other to repay the loans. Although the GB may get its loans repaid, it is still not self-financing but depends on donations for its operatings. It has also been criticized because its women borrowers often serve as a conduit to transfer the loans to their husbands who sometimes use the loans to finance consumption rather than for productive investment. The GB has also been criticized for not putting any emphasis on the development of technology or skills. According to others, its primary advantage is its simple structure and its ability to cut overheads by devolving decision-making down to the village level (see two opposite views of the institution by Neff, 1996; and Sarker, 2001. See also Pitt and Khandker, 1998).

SOURCES: Mark Pitt and S. Khandker, "The Impact of Group-Based Credit Programs on Poor Households in Bangladesh: Does the Gender of the Participants?" *Journal of Political Economy* 106 (October 1998), pp. 958–996; Gina Neff, "Microcredit, Microresults," *Left Business Observer* 74 (1996), Web site at http://www.panix.com; Abu Elias Sarker, "The Secrets of Success: The Grameen Bank Experience in Bangladesh," *Labour and Management in Development Journal* 2 (2001), pp. 1–17, Web site at http://labour-management.anu.edu.au/prt/voltwo/2-1-abusarker.pdf.

Table 7.6 Household Borrowing in the Rural Sector in Seven Asian Countries in the Late 1970s and 1980s

Kind of borrowing	Bangladesh	India	Philippines	Thailand	Korea	Malaysia	Sri Lanka
Proportion of borrowing from the informal sector (by rice farmers)	36	80	70	52	50	70	45
Proportion of outstanding household debt owed to informal sector (rural plus urban)	39	40	23	44	51	62	n.a.

SOURCES: Prabhu Ghate, *Informal Finance: Some Findings for Asia* (Manila: Oxford University Press for Asian Development Bank, 1994); J. J. Thomas, "The Informal Financial Sector: How Does It Operate and Who Are the Customers?" in Sheila Page, ed., *Monetary Policy in Developing Countries* (London and New York: Routledge, 1993).

7.8.6 Establishing Linkages between Informal Finance and the Banking Sector

There are a number of ways that the formal sector can assist informal finance without breaking the existing institutional setup. With NGOs, the linkage can be established by extending lines of credit or other forms of lending from the banks to the NGOs. In the case of the Grameen Bank, it was established initially with the help of formal bank participation. In cases where the NGOs receive support from external sources on a concessional basis, this would complicate this form of cooperation. Nevertheless, given the limited scope of activity of most NGOs, governments and the banking system can offer a supportive environment for their further expansion. In the case of the Roscas (1994, p. 188), Ghate reports on a proposal for Nepal where the Roscas would act

> both as a continuing source of funds flowing to the banks, and as a conduit for lending of bank funds to Roscas members. . . . the amount offered by the winning bidder as the discount in each round, instead of being distributed to the other members, be deposited in a bank account where it will accumulate to serve as collateral for lending by the bank to the Rosca on the basis of joint and several liability. The Rosca will onlend to its members.

Another way that the banking system can interface with informal markets is to provide similar kinds of services. This means being able to charge higher rates when administrative costs are high, and being able to make loans without much risk to borrowers who have no collateral. In the Philippines, a "moneyshop" experiment was carried out by the Philippine Commercial and Industrial Bank (PCIB) in the early 1970s. The PCIB set up small branches in markets and made small loans at higher than market rates to borrowers who brought their goods to the market. Payments were made on a daily installment basis to collectors stationed in the market. They also accepted deposits, and these deposits grew as a result of the experiment. Interest rates in the informal market also fell as a result. This kind of lending by banks was expanded further when interest rates were deregulated in the early 1980s, although the size of loans became larger and riskier, and smaller borrowers were dropped.

7.8.7 Informal Finance and Monetary Policy

The main effect of monetary policy on informal finance, and on the poor generally, is through the inflation tax that results from increasing prices. Because those involved in informal finance are generally poor and unable to accumulate much in the way of saving, their assets are primarily in goods and cash. As a result, they are more adversely affected by inflation than the richer segments of society that can accumulate interest-earning assets. On the other hand, the availability and the cost of informal finance is unlikely to be as affected by changes in monetary policy compared with the formal sector. Therefore, to help the poor to continue to make strides in raising their standards of living, monetary policy should focus on maintaining a stable price level as its primary objective.

7.9 GLOBAL FINANCIAL CRISIS OF 2008/2009 AND ITS IMPACT ON ASIAN FINANCIAL MARKETS

Chapter 3 examined the impact of the global financial crisis on income and employment in the Asian economies. The real impact of lower export demand and the outflow of financial capital from the Asian region were explored. In this section, we look a little more closely at the implications of the global financial crisis on the Asian financial markets. As Chapter 3 indicated, the Asian financial markets were relatively stable when the global financial crisis began in 2008. Many reforms that had been suggested following the 1997 Asian financial crisis had been adopted and bank balance sheets were in better shape. The size and incidence of NPLs had also been reduced. The practice of short-term overseas borrowing to refinance longer-term local projects at higher interest rates was also curtailed. Exchange rates, while still loosely tied to the U.S. dollar, were also more flexible than they were before the 1997 financial crisis. Banks and other financial institutions were well aware of the risks of assuming a secure dollar link when making overseas borrowing commitments.

Despite these changes in regulations and banking practices, the global economic crisis that began in late 2008 and continued through the early months of 2009 has created additional financial stress on Asian financial systems. Stock markets have weakened considerably as the industrial sectors have suffered from lower levels of production and manufactured exports. Tables 3.24 and 3.25 in Chapter 3 show the sharp decline in exports and this has been mirrored by the decline in stock market prices throughout the region. These are displayed in Table 7.7. The outflow of portfolio investment is reflected by the fall in stock prices. Foreign direct investment has been less volatile than short-term capital movements and is not expected to fall dramatically in 2009. Furthermore, government stimulus packages are expected to help shore up private investment. For example, Singapore has announced a US$13.5 billion stimulus package designed to preserve jobs, stimulate bank lending, and enhance international competitiveness through tax relief and grants to businesses. Another US$1.7 billion has been allocated to the upgrading of infrastructure and health and educational facilities. China also has recently taken steps to shore up its economy by announcing a US$586 billion infrastructure investment program to be implemented over 2009 and 2010 (amounting to about 6 percent of GDP). The projects will include low-income housing, electricity, water, rural infrastructure, environmental protection,

Table 7.7   Stock Market Indices, End February 2008 and 2009

	End February 2008	End February 2009	Percent Decline
China (SHSZ300)	4,500.00	2,200.00	51.0%
Hong Kong (HS)	25,000.00	12,894.00	48.4
Korea (KOSPI)	212.04	136.98	35.3
Malaysia	1,376.62	896.51	34.9
Singapore (STI)	3,094.00	1,614.00	47.8
Thailand	804.15	434.24	46.0
MCSI[a]	29.73	16.63	44.0

[a]This is an index of Asian stocks.

SOURCE: Various Web sites.

and technological innovation. This package is intended to boost consumer confidence, as well as to provide jobs and additional spending to offset the anticipated slowdown in exports. Other countries in the region are also implementing stimulus measures. For these reasons, while there are reports of increases in NPLs in a few countries (such as Korea and Vietnam), it is unlikely that the region will suffer from the same financial sector difficulties that it experienced during the Asian financial crisis a decade ago.

7.10   SUMMARY AND CONCLUSIONS

This chapter has dealt with the broad topic of saving. It has included a discussion of motives for saving and the role of the banking system as a financial intermediary in mobilizing saving and translating it into productive investments. The chapter stressed the critical role that saving has played in the economic development of Asia and its interaction with other variables that has led to changes and modifications in saving behavior. Institutional features of the banking system have been highlighted, including the tendency of the financial system to serve as a financier for the government to fund projects favored by it. It was emphasized that financial liberalization within Asia has proceeded rapidly but sometimes without due care to revamp and modify the institutional structure and regulations governing the financial system. This contributed to the financial bubble that preceded the Asian financial crisis. Despite these difficulties and challenges, the continued mobilization of saving is a key ingredient to the health and ongoing growth of the economies in developing Asia.

REVIEW QUESTIONS

1. The importance of income in determining savings has persisted since the time of Keynes. Why have other theories failed to displace income as the most critical variable in saving theory?
2. What is Ricardian equivalence and what does it have to do with the level of saving?
3. Demographic factors seem to have a powerful influence on saving in Asia. Why should it be so in this developing region and not in others?

4. Why do you think that Harrigan found that the share of agriculture in GDP had a significant positive effect on saving?

5. The evidence on Asian banking systems shows that there was a significant amount of financial repression throughout the region. Yet the region grew rapidly in spite of it. Does this mean that financial repression does not have a negative effect on economic growth and the allocation of resources?

6. What is a "kerb" market? How do you think it got its name? Why did these markets spring up and thrive in Asia during the period of rapid growth in the 1960s, 1970s, and 1980s?

7. Contrast the financial liberalization experience of Hong Kong and Singapore with that of India and the other countries of South Asia.

8. Explain why certain variables, such as the ratio of money supply to GDP, are used to measure the degree of financial repression. When liberalization takes place, what should happen to these variables? Why?

9. Explain why financial liberalization may not necessarily result in an acceleration of economic growth and increase economic efficiency.

10. What went wrong with the financial liberalization measures taken in Southeast and East Asia? Refer to particular country examples.

11. Explain what the terms "adverse selection," "moral hazard," and "free rider" mean when speaking of the Asian financial crisis?

12. Which AMCs in the crisis-affected countries were most effective, and why?

13. Why is there so much informal finance in the Asian countries but not in the industrial countries?

14. Explain how a Rosca works using a simple example with money values.

15. What is likely to happen to the demand for informal finance when an economy takes a downturn, or falls into recession, and unemployment increases?

16. In question 15, what will happen to the spread between interest rates in the formal sector and the "kerb" market rate of interest?

17. Why are the Asian economies in a better position to deal with the global financial crisis of 2008 and 2009 than they were in the 1997 Asian crisis?

18. Why aren't there more banks like the Grameen Bank and Bank Gadang Bali serving the residents of the countries in the Asian region?

Notes on References and Suggestions for Further Reading

This chapter has two distinct sections. The first section on savings has its traditions in the macroeconomic literature of consumption. This literature is vast. To get a flavor of it, there are a few articles that should get you started. Articles on the determinants of saving and consumption include the classics by Milton Friedman (1957) and Franco Modigliani (1970), as well as the more current paper by Robert Hall (1978), stressing the importance of current income as a determinant of saving.

Other determinants of saving and consumption apart from income have been suggested and are reviewed concisely by Masson et al. (1995, 1998) and Robert Wescott (1995). The work by Masson et al. suggests that savings and economic growth are intertwined so that growth can lead to savings in many instances. The work by Wescott takes a more conventional view.

For Asia, the best article is that of F. R. Harrigan (1998), although it is a little difficult to follow for those without a statistical background. He explores the various determinants of saving within an Asian context for time series data over the last few decades.

Turning to finance, the classic references are the two books by Edward S. Shaw (1973) and Ronald McKinnon (1973) dealing with financial liberalization. These references are quite old now but are still classics to be read at your leisure. For a more recent treatment, Ronald McKinon's (1988) later article, Maxwell J. Fry's (1988) book, and the edited volume by Sheila Page (1993) are good references. For financial sector reform in small open economies, see Maxwell Fry's *Sequencing Financial Sector Reform and Development in Small Economies* (1994).

With respect to Asia, there are two sets of readings. The first deals with the situation existing in Asia before the financial crisis in terms of the degree and extent of financial liberalization that had taken place. Here, the work of the Asian Development Bank, edited by Shahid N. Zahid (1995), together with the review of the region by the Asian Development Bank (1996, 1997) just prior to the crisis is quite interesting and useful.

For recent developments in financial policy, the fallout from the Asian financial crisis, and recent developments in connection with the global financial crisis of 2008, see Gerard Caprio, Jr., et al. (1998), John Malcolm Dowling (2009), and William E. James et al. (2008).

See also the Web site of the Regional Economic Monitoring Unit of the Asian Development Bank. The report for June 2002 gives a retrospective of the five years since the crisis, and more recent issues give an update of recent developments. For informal finance, the key Asian reference is by P. Ghate (1994), although it is a little dated.

Population

8.1 INTRODUCTION

World population has followed an S-shaped pattern of growth over time. In antiquity, the rate of population growth was very slow. Birth and death rates were both very high. As death rates fell with the development of modern medicine, population growth accelerated in the eighteenth and nineteenth centuries and continued into the twentieth and now, the twenty-first century. Asia's population grew very slowly in the nineteenth century—less than 0.5 percent—but began to accelerate in the twentieth century—to 1 percent per year between 1900 and 1950, and 2 percent during the second half of the twentieth century (Asian Development Bank, 2002). The rate of population growth in developed countries fell from 1.3 percent per year in early 1960 to about 0.7 percent per annum by 2000,[1] while that for the developing countries decreased slightly, from 2.3 percent to about 1.8 percent over a similar period.[2] This suggests that, compared with the immediate post-World War II period, developed countries now contribute very little to population growth.

In Asia, on the other hand, population growth rates were among the highest in the world during the period since World War II. Between 1950 and 1990, the total population of Asia (18 countries) increased by 125 percent, compared with only 112 percent growth for the world population (Sanderson and Tan, 1995, p. 4).

Population is always a subject of interest to analysts of economic growth. In the early days, many economists, led by Thomas Malthus (1798), warned of the gloomy consequences of an ever-increasing population. These included hunger, famine, and poverty as population growth consumed any addition in income and wealth. This kept income and standards of living at subsistence levels and in a low-level poverty trap.

---

[1] *World Development Indicators Online* data for high-income countries.
[2] *World Development Indicators Online* data for low-income countries.

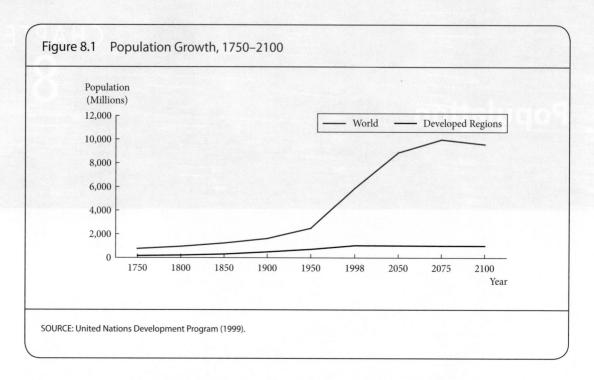

Figure 8.1   Population Growth, 1750–2100

SOURCE: United Nations Development Program (1999).

Much of this Mathusian way of thinking has changed, as economies managed to increase (food) production through better and better technology (see Figure 8.2). Many have even proposed that population growth is essential to economic growth. To this day, the question of whether rapid population growth is desirable for economies remains unsettled, although most economists and demographers would argue that the negative aspects of population growth more than offset the positive aspects of further population growth. Nevertheless, population growth is a serious concern for economists and policymakers alike as it has important policy implications, particularly for developing countries.

In this chapter, we examine the manner in which population affects and is affected by the development process, as well as the microeconomic issues dealing with economic determinants of fertility. We will then look into particular country experiences, including population issues and policies.

8.2   SOME BASIC CONCEPTS

To be able to embark on a meaningful discussion of population and its role in economic development, it is necessary to understand a number of basic concepts and terms. The concepts discussed here are common tools to help us undertake useful analysis of population issues.

8.2.1   Birth and Death Rates

Birth and death rates are two fundamental concepts necessary to understand population issues. Birth rates refer to the number of births per thousand people, while death rates represent the number of deaths per thousand people. A birth rate of 26 for Bangladesh in 2005 means that there were 26 newborn babies per thousand people during that year. In the same way, a death rate of 8 implies that an average of 8 deaths occurred per thousand people in Bangladesh for that year.

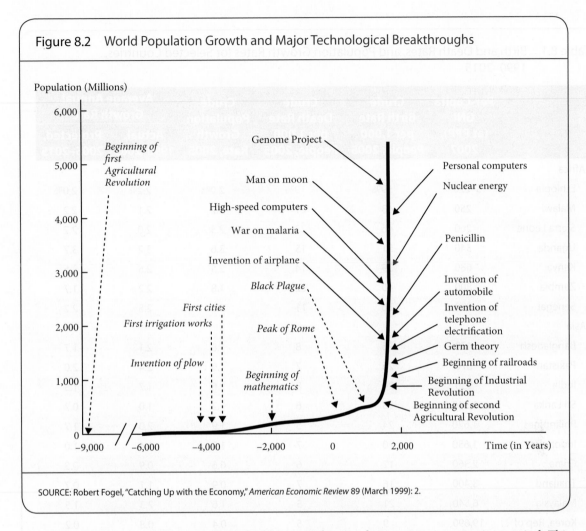

Figure 8.2   World Population Growth and Major Technological Breakthroughs

SOURCE: Robert Fogel, "Catching Up with the Economy," *American Economic Review* 89 (March 1999): 2.

The population growth rate is the net addition to the population over a certain time period. This measure is likewise expressed as the number of additional individuals per thousand people and can be derived simply as the birth rate minus the death rate. In our example, the population growth rate is therefore 18 per thousand people. It is, however, customary to give this statistic in percentage, and thus the population growth rate for Bangladesh is often presented as 1.8 percent.

Table 8.1 shows birth, death and population growth rates for a diverse set of countries. It presents this information alongside the per-capita gross national income (GNI) and the countries are grouped according to their regional location. It is immediately obvious that poorer countries tend to have higher population growth rates. In the case of the African countries, all have relatively high birth and death rates. The highest population growth rate is registered for Uganda, and this is because it has the highest birth rate in the group while its death rate is relatively lower than those of the other countries in the region. Zambia, on the other hand, registered the lowest population growth rate in the set because its birth rate is on the low end of the scale, while its death rate is the second-highest in the group.[3] It is thus clear that both birth and death rates jointly determine the growth rate of the population.

---

[3] To a large extent, the high death rate is a function of the low-grade or inadequate state of medical facilities in the country at that particular point in time.

Table 8.1   Birth and Death Rates, and Population Growth Rates for Selected Countries, 1990–2015

| | Per-Capita GNI (at PPP), 2007 | Crude Birth Rate per 1,000 People, 2005 | Crude Death Rate per 1,000 People, 2005 | Crude Population Growth Rate, 2005 | Average Annual Growth Rate | |
					Actual, 1990–2005	Projected, 2005–2015
Africa						
Ethiopia	$ 220	39%	19%	2.0%	2.2%	2.0%
Malawi	250	43	21	2.2	2.1	2.2
Sierra Leone	260	46	23	2.3	2.0	2.2
Uganda	340	51	15	3.6	3.2	3.7
Kenya	680	39	14	2.5	2.5	2.5
Zambia	800	40	22	1.8	2.2	1.7
Senegal	820	36	11	2.5	2.5	2.2
Asia						
Bangladesh	470	26	8	1.8	2.1	1.7
Pakistan	870	26	7	1.9	2.4	2.0
India	950	24	8	1.6	1.7	1.3
Sri Lanka	1,540	18	6	1.2	1.0	0.7
Philippines	1,620	24	5	1.9	2.0	1.7
Indonesia	1,650	20	7	1.3	1.4	1.0
China	2,360	12	6	0.6	0.9	0.5
Thailand	3,400	16	7	0.9	1.1	0.7
Malaysia	6,540	21	5	1.6	2.3	1.5
Korea, Rep of	19,690	9	5	0.4	0.8	0.2
Hong Kong	31,610	8	6	0.2	1.3	0.9
Singapore	32,470	10	4	0.6	2.4	1.1
Japan	37,670	8	9	−0.1	0.2	−0.2
Latin America						
Honduras	1,600	28	6	2.2	2.6	2.0
Paraguay	1,670	29	5	2.4	2.2	1.8
Ecuador	3,080	22	5	1.7	1.7	1.3
Peru	3,450	22	6	1.6	1.7	1.4
Jamaica	3,710	16	6	1.0	0.7	0.3
Panama	5,510	22	5	1.7	2.0	1.5
Brazil	5,910	20	7	1.3	1.5	1.1
Argentina	6,050	18	8	1.0	1.2	0.9
Uruguay	6,380	15	9	0.6	0.7	0.5

(*continued*)

Table 8.1 *(continued)*

	Per-Capita GNI (at PPP), 2007	Crude Birth Rate per 1,000 People, 2005	Crude Death Rate per 1,000 People, 2005	Crude Population Growth Rate, 2005	Average Annual Growth Rate	
					Actual, 1990–2005	Projected, 2005–2015
Venezuela	7,320	22	5	1.7	2.0	1.6
Mexico	8,340	18	4	1.4	1.4	1.0
Europe and North America						
New Zealand	28,780	14	7	0.7	1.2	0.6
Italy	33,540	10	10	0	0.2	–0.1
Australia	35,960	13	6	0.7	1.2	0.9
France	38,500	13	9	0.4	0.5	0.2
Germany	38,860	8	10	–0.2	0.3	–0.1
Canada	39,420	11	7	0.4	1.0	0.8
United Kingdom	42,740	12	10	0.2	0.3	0.2
Netherlands	45,820	12	8	0.4	0.6	0.3
United States	46,040	14	8	0.6	1.1	0.8
Sweden	46,060	10	10	0	0.4	0.3
Switzerland	59,880	10	8	0.2	0.7	0

SOURCE: Data from World Bank, *World Development Indicators Online* (2008).

Countries in Asia appear to have made big strides in their population-control efforts in the last two decades. The birth rates for 2005 were significantly lower than those for Africa, while death rates compared favorably with those of the advanced economies in Europe and North America. Within the region, Pakistan and the Philippines rank the highest in terms of population growth rates, while Bangladesh follows as a close third. The fact that Pakistan and Bangladesh feature the high birth rate characteristics usually associated with poorer economies is not surprising. The high birth rate in the Philippines, however, strongly reflects the low success rate of birth-control programs administered to a Roman Catholic-orientated population.

Sri Lanka, in particular, lowered its birth rate to 12 babies per thousand people by 2005, and by this measure, has performed very well compared with other higher income countries in the Asian region. Among the middle-income Asian economies, Malaysia ranks next to the Philippines, with the highest population growth rate, both resulting from high birth rates. On the other hand, Indonesia and Thailand have achieved population growth rates that are lower than higher income Malaysia, and comparable with those of Singapore and Korea.

The population growth story among the Latin American countries is mixed. At one extreme are countries such as Honduras and Paraguay whose population growth rates continue to be high because of difficulties in pushing the birth rates downwards. At the other end of the scale are countries such as Jamaica which, in spite of its relatively low income levels, appear to have had success in keeping low birth and death rates.

For the richer economies in Europe and North America, as shown in the table, it is notable that the population growth rates are very low, less than 1 percent, with many very close to 0. In this group, the populations of Australia, New Zealand, and the United States have grown the fastest, followed by France, Canada, and the Netherlands. The increase in population in these countries is mostly due to in-migration. In 2001, the growth rates for Italy and Germany were –0.1; four years later in 2005, Italy appeared to have slowly turned that around, while Germany's population continued to shrink.

The projected ten-year population growth rates are shown in the last column of Table 8.1. We see from here that Uganda will lead Africa and the rest of the world in population growth, with an expected average yearly growth rate of 3.7 percent. In Asia, Bangladesh and the Philippines will lead the population growth with each country having a projected annual growth rate of 1.7 percent. Similarly, in Latin America, Honduras and Paraguay will spearhead growth in the region with projected annual growth rates of 2 percent and 1.8 percent respectively, for the period 2005–2015. In contrast, the table also shows that the more advanced economies will experience significant declines in their population growth rates in that same ten-year period.

8.2.2 Population Age Distribution

Singular measures of population change, such as birth and death rates, mask a lot of other useful information that are of significant interest and relevance to those who study population dynamics. To make meaningful analysis, it is also important to know the age distribution of the population. This is provided when the population shares of each age group is given. Such information can help us distinguish between two countries with high population growth rates, but where one is a young population that has a large proportion of their members in the childbearing ages and thus has a high birth rate, while the other is a very mature population where high death rates are registered for the older age groups.

The age distribution of the population in the various regions of the world is given in Table 8.2. We can see from here that about 2 in every 5 persons in Africa are under 15 years old, while only 6 in every 100 persons there are aged 60 or over. In Europe, meanwhile, there are less than 2 children for

Table 8.2 Distribution of World Population by Age and Region, 2005 to Mid-2007

	Percentage Distribution, 2005			Population, Mid-2007		Density per Km²
	<15	**15–59**	**60+**	**Millions**	**Percent**	
Africa	41%	53%	6%	944	14.0%	31
Asia	28	63	10	4,010	60.5	126
Europe	16	64	24	733	11.3	32
Latin America and the Caribbean	30	61	10	569	8.6	28
North America	21	63	20	335	5.1	15
Oceania	25	61	17	35	0.5	4
World Total	28	61	12	6,626	100.0	49
More developed regions	17	63	24	1,221	18.4	27
Less developed regions	31	61	9	5,405	81.6	65

SOURCE: United Nations Population Reference Bureau, *World Population Data Sheet* (2007).

every 10 people, while 1 in every 4 persons is aged 60 or older. The proportions in North America are a little less extreme than those in Europe, but the pattern is clear. More developed economies tend to have both a lower proportion of the population under 15 years old, and a greater proportion of those in the 60 and older age group. Less developed economies, on the other hand, tend to have significantly younger populations and thus higher dependency ratios. The young populations in Africa, Asia, and Latin America will push population growth rates further up in the near future when this generation of kids reaches childbearing age, and this can be a problem. A low dependency ratio is perceived as more desirable for economic growth. Having a larger proportion of workers in the population implies greater ability to support those not working (children in particular) and therefore less drag on the economy. Additionally, national investments in education and health can have greater impact per person if the dependent population is relatively small.

As it happens, the working-age population moves into retirement over time and eventually puts an additional burden on the rest of society. The size of this burden will depend to a large extent on whether they have saved enough during their working years to support themselves, or whether the state will have to provide a subsidy. Aging populations are receiving greater attention in policy forums in Japan and generally, within the Organization for Economic Cooperation and Development (OECD). The challenge is reinforced by continued declines in birth rates and extension of life expectancy in these developed countries.

On a more micro scale, the age structure within populations also provide important insights into growth, employment, and other welfare issues affecting particular economies. Table 8.3 presents an international comparison of individual country population distribution broken down by age. Differences in the age structure have mixed effects on the percentage of the labor force to be employed. Growth in an economy would be more likely to occur if a vast majority of the population are in the working-age group (15–64 years old) and are actually employed. This means that the dependency ratio is low, and that a significant proportion of the population is contributing to economic production. In this case, national income can be used more effectively to support children in education and health until they get to working age; dependent retirees can also be provided with more generous pensions and other allowances as they advance in age.

A rapidly growing population is normally characterized by having a high proportion of persons under 15 years old. In the table, this is exemplified by India, Pakistan, and the Philippines—countries where those aged under 15 years take up more than a third of the population share. This youth effect, as it is normally called, creates a large supply of people too young to work and is typical of developing economies. On the other hand, a slowly growing population is characterized by a large proportion of people who have reached retirement (usually 65 years old). This retirement effect is typical of developed countries where there are high life expectancy rates. In the table, this effect is largest in Germany, Italy, and Japan, with more than 25 percent of their populations aged 60 or older. It is nonetheless possible for countries to experience both youth and retirement effects simultaneously as better public-health policies reduce death rates while birth rates remain high. Which effect dominates?

Rapid population growth also affects the percentage available to be employed through the female availability effect. With a slower growth rate and fewer children to care for, more women are available to join the labor force. Both the dominance of the youth effect (over the retirement effect) and the female availability effect suggest that rapid population growth reduces the percentage of the population in the labor force which, in turn, has a depressing effect on economic growth per capita.

8.2.3 Other Demographic Measures

The total fertility rate (TFR) is the total number of children a woman is expected to have over her lifetime if she bears children at the current age-specific birth rates. It is calculated from the age-specific fertility rate, which is the average number of children per year born to women of a particular age group

Table 8.3   Age Distribution in Selected Countries, 2005 and 2050

	2005				2050			
	<15	15–59	60+	80+	<15	15–59	60+	80+
Asian Countries								
Bangladesh	35.2%	59.1%	5.7%	0.4%	20.8%	62.2%	17.0%	1.9%
China	21.6	67.4	11.0	1.2	15.3	53.6	31.1	7.3
Hong Kong	15.1	69.5	15.4	2.8	11.2	49.4	39.4	13.5
India	33.0	59.6	7.5	0.7	18.2	61.6	20.2	3.1
Indonesia	28.4	63.3	8.3	0.6	17.5	57.7	24.8	4.0
Korea, Rep of	24.2	62.5	13.3	0.9	16.6	58.8	24.6	4.1
Malaysia	31.4	61.9	6.7	0.6	18.3	59.5	22.2	4.0
Pakistan	37.2	56.9	5.9	0.5	21.8	61.7	16.5	2.0
Philippines	36.2	57.9	6.0	0.5	19.7	62.2	18.2	2.6
Singapore	19.5	68.2	12.3	1.5	11.1	49.0	39.8	14.8
Sri Lanka	24.2	66.1	9.7	1.1	16.7	54.3	29.0	6.0
Thailand	21.7	67.0	11.3	1.3	15.8	54.4	29.8	7.0
Industrialized Countries								
Australia	19.5	62.7	17.8	3.5	16.3	53.5	30.2	9.3
Canada	17.6	64.5	17.8	3.5	15.6	52.5	31.9	10.0
Germany	14.4	60.6	25.1	4.4	13.7	49.4	37.0	13.1
Italy	14.0	60.7	25.3	5.1	13.3	48.1	38.6	13.3
Japan	13.9	59.7	26.4	4.8	11.3	44.8	44.0	15.5
United Kingdom	18.0	60.8	21.2	4.5	16.2	53.6	30.1	9.2
United States	20.8	62.6	16.6	3.5	17.3	56.0	26.8	7.6

SOURCE: United Nations Population Reference Bureau, *World Population Data Sheet* (2007).

in a particular country. Life expectancy rate is another useful measure to characterize a population. It refers to the average number of years a person is expected to live. Life expectancy rates are generally lower in less developed economies as a result of high infant mortality rates (IMR). These indicators more or less reflect the state of the medical facilities in an economy. Low life expectancies and high IMRs tend to be the same in economies with low access to medicines, medical facilities, or assistance (refer to Tables 9.4 and 10.12 in Chapters 9 and 10).

In Table 8.4, we can see that the total fertility rate in Africa is a high 5.0, a rate that is about twice that of any other region in the world. Africa also has the lowest life expectancy rate at 53, while people tend to live longest in North America, Europe, and Oceania (mostly Australia and New Zealand). Furthermore, we see that the survival rates of newborn babies and young children are very low in the poorer regions of the world—as can be seen by the very high infant mortality rates.

Table 8.4   Other Demographic Measures, 2007

	Total Fertility Rate	Life Expectancy at Birth (Years)	Infant Mortality Rate (IMR) Per 1,000 Births
Africa	5.0	53	86
Asia	2.4	68	48
Europe	1.5	75	6
Latin America and the Caribbean	2.5	73	24
North America	2.0	78	6
Oceania	2.1	75	27
World Total	2.7	68	52
Developed regions	1.6	77	6
Developing regions	2.9	66	57

SOURCE: United Nations Population Division, *World Population Prospects: The 2006 Revision, Highlights* (New York: United Nations, 2007).

Life expectancy in developing countries has risen rapidly as a result of improvements in public health. For example, 25 percent of the mortality decrease in postwar Sri Lanka was due to the eradication of malaria (Birdsall, 1988, p. 481). Generally, these advances in the area of public health have been more important than rising incomes in increasing life expectancy. These increases in life expectancy were more rapid than those achieved by the industrial countries when they were at the same level of development in the nineteenth century. On the other hand, fertility has declined faster than it did in Europe in the nineteenth century. This is because of better education, growth in income, and the rapid movement of the population from rural to urban areas, as well as the availability of contraception. Furthermore, fertility declines started at lower levels of per-capita income although from higher initial levels.

Fertility and income levels are inversely related, although the relationship is loose. Figure 8.3 shows the decline in the fertility rates of selected Asian countries from the 1970s onwards as their income per capita rose. The Asian experience relating to falling fertility rates and population growth is discussed in Section 8.5.2.

8.3   THE THEORY OF DEMOGRAPHIC TRANSITION

Most of the industrialized countries have passed through three stages of population growth. The conceptual framework that summarizes this evidence is called the demographic transition (see Figure 8.4). In the first stage, when the economy is primarily agrarian, birth and death rates are both high, with birth rates slightly higher than death rates to ensure that the population is growing over time. In the second stage, which commences when the economy begins to industrialize, advances in medical technology causes a dramatic drop in death rates. However, birth rates continue to be high. In the third stage, when the economy is fully industrialized, birth rates begin to fall and catch up with the declining death rate.

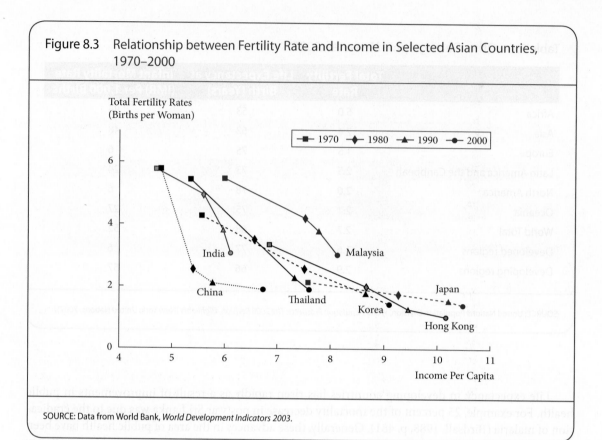

Figure 8.3   Relationship between Fertility Rate and Income in Selected Asian Countries, 1970–2000

SOURCE: Data from World Bank, *World Development Indicators 2003*.

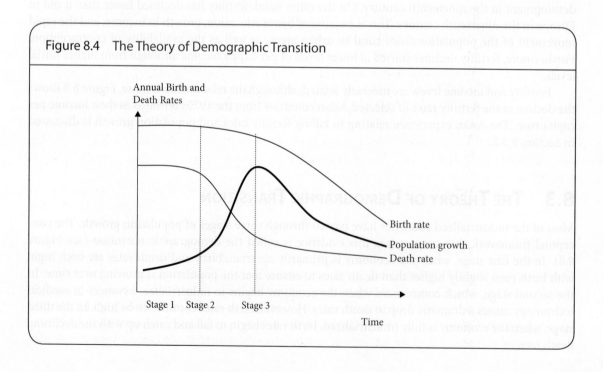

Figure 8.4   The Theory of Demographic Transition

The experience of the now industrialized economies of the world suggests that the various phases of demographic transition took place over a long period, with noticeable changes occurring over hundreds of years or so. Stages 1 and 3 imply a very slow growth of the population, while Stage 2 implies a relatively rapid rise in population numbers. This creates a bulge in the age distribution of the population that can continue for many years. When the population group within the bulge reaches working age, and until they hit retirement, the dependency rate—the ratio of those not working to those working—falls to a lower level. Before and after the bulge, the dependency ratio is much higher.

This depiction of demographic transition is supported by evidence from a wide variety of economies. However, the relationship is more dramatic when time series for individual countries is analyzed compared to a simple evaluation of cross-section data for a panel of countries. This is because demographic transition takes place at different times for different countries and the slope of the curves may be slightly different. Nevertheless, both time-series and cross-section studies generally support the demographic transition paradigm.

8.3.1 Demographic Transition in Europe

Demographic transition can take many years, even centuries, to occur. Hence, its economic impact can only be felt over a long period of time. Stage 1 characterized all human populations until the late eighteenth century when the balance between birth and death rates was broken in Western Europe. Stage 2, the stage when the population exploded as a result of declining death rates, began in the late eighteenth century in northwestern Europe and spread over the next one hundred years to the south and east. Reductions in the death rate resulted from a lower incidence of malnutrition and starvation owing to improved food supply from the more productive agricultural sector. The introduction of new food crops (mainly potatoes and maize from America) also increased the quantity of foodstuff in the European diet during this period. Equally significant to the decline in death rates in Europe was the growing scientific knowledge about causes of disease. This series of medical discoveries, embodied in the germ theory of disease, resulted in significant improvements in the water supply, sewage, and other public-health systems, as well as improvements in food-handling practices and general personal hygiene.

The transition of the European population was nonetheless slow. Agricultural productivity in the early eighteenth century proceeded very slowly and there were random shocks as a result of bad weather throughout history. There were also the random effects of epidemics in Europe, such as the plague. Estimates by demographers suggest that it took about 35,000 years for the population to double from the appearance of man until the Middle Ages. Around the time of Christ, there were an estimated 250 million people in the world. By the early 1800s, there were about one billion, and now there are over 6 billion. Thus, the doubling time is now about forty years (or a growth of 2 percent per year).

Given the above, why did birth rates not fall quickly to match the decline in death rates? The main reasons given to explain this include the age structure of the population, the long time lags between adjustments to the overall birth rate and the fertility behavior of particular groups. If the population distribution favors younger people (a triangular or pyramid-shaped population distribution) then, even if fertility declines for some age groups, it will take some time for the overall birth rate to fall. Compounding this effect is the fact that the response of family size to reductions in infant mortality is quite sluggish. Sometimes, the average number of children in the family does not fall significantly for decades or even generations. In Section 8.4, we discuss a general theory of household formation involving a number of variables that help to determine the overall pattern of fertility of a family. If there are lags in adjustment to changes in these parameters, then there can be long lags between a decline in the death rate and the subsequent fall in birth rates. Often it takes at least a generation for the change to be noticeable. Surveys of "modern" families in developing countries suggest that small families of two or three children are the norm. However, the parents of these "modern" families often had many children.

A third factor could be the influence of social norms in countries where agriculture is still the main source of income and employment. These norms are established and maintained within the context of traditional societies, and by definition, only change slowly. In particular, in traditional societies, it may take a generation or more for the nuclear family to be more desirable than a large extended family. A survey of students in a management course in Iran during the early 1970s showed an average of over six children ever born to the students' own parents while they themselves had or planned to have an average of 2.3 children only. This is a significant change of thinking that took only one generation to occur; it also showed the importance of education in the family formation process.

The general decline in birth rates that moves the population into Stage 3 did not begin in Europe until the late nineteenth century. Factors that have contributed to this include urbanization, increased female literacy and employment, and advances in birth control, although the last did not come into play until the second half of the twentieth century. The natural increase in the population in Europe was also slowed by the custom of marrying relatively later in life. Early marriage was not the custom in Europe that it now is in so many developing countries.

8.3.2   Demographic Transition in Developing Countries

In developing countries, the demographic transition is seen to occur more rapidly. The developing countries of today remained largely agrarian long after Europe and America had, and this delayed entry into Stage 2 enabled them to take advantage of modern medical technology which facilitated the rapid decline in the death rates. Interestingly, the largest improvements in child mortality rates occurred in countries where female literacy had increased the most. At the same time, birth rates have remained high in these countries even to this day, the main reason being that the social and behavioral changes necessary to effect a fertility change often run in conflict with traditional and religious values. Associating large numbers of children with higher status, or strong preference for sons over daughters, continue to drive birth rates up in many such economies. In addition, the use of artificial birth control was, and still is, met with strong resistance in many rural areas.

This is particularly instructive in the case of Taiwan (see Figure 8.5). The change in the age distribution of the population between 1960 and 1998 was quite dramatic. From a pyramid structure dominated by the young in 1960 it moved to a more rectangular structure where each age cohort up to about 50 years had a relatively equal share of the population. The position of the aged and the young is reversed in the interim.

In terms of economic efficiency, countries that are currently in Stage 2 of the demographic transition may have an advantage in that they can draw on the experiences of their more advanced neighbors (such as policy infrastructure) and thus achieve better outcomes for themselves This group includes Southeast Asia and some countries in the Middle East, Latin America, and Africa.[4] Some demographers believe that this is an important factor in explaining the rapid growth of the Asian region, where a large and growing workforce is at hand to meet the production and consumption needs of a growing economy.

---

[4] The newly industrialized countries of South Korea, Taiwan, Singapore, and Hong Kong are not included in this list, since they joined Japan, North America, and Europe in the low birth, low death category years ago.

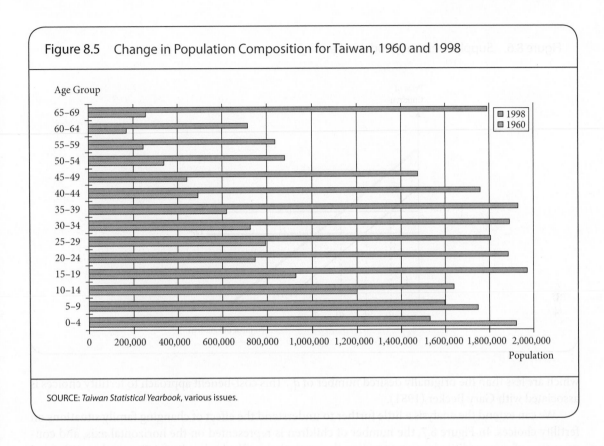

Figure 8.5   Change in Population Composition for Taiwan, 1960 and 1998

SOURCE: *Taiwan Statistical Yearbook*, various issues.

8.4   Determinants of Fertility and Birth Rates

There are two approaches to the discussion of fertility and birth rates. The first is an economic approach that analyses these issues within a demand-and-supply framework. The second approach is more eclectic and brings other factors into the fertility equation.

8.4.1   The Economics of Fertility

The economic approach attempts to explain determinants of childbearing using what is called the microeconomic theory of fertility. In this theory, children are treated just like any other consumer good for which there are costs and benefits to their "consumption." Accordingly, the childbearing decision of a household can be represented within a traditional demand-and-supply framework (see Figure 8.6).

The demand curve for children is assumed to be downward sloping, implying that the more expensive children are, the less of them will be demanded. This is captured by the line D_1. For simplicity, we assume a uniform marginal cost curve MC though there is no reason why this curve cannot be downward sloping as well because of the economies of scale associated with increasing numbers. Given the D_1 and MC_1 lines, the desired number of children is determined by the point where $D_1 = MC$ which corresponds to the point q_1. In this framework, the desired number of children can be reduced by an inward shift in the D_1 line and/or an upward shift of the MC curve. The new equilibrium points associated with the new demand and marginal cost curves result in having either q_2, q_3, or q_4 children, all of

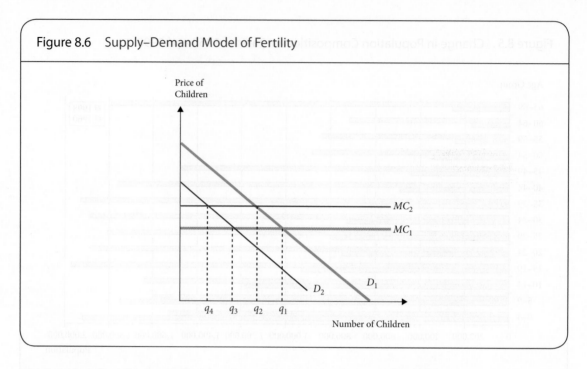

Figure 8.6   Supply–Demand Model of Fertility

which are less than the originally desired number of q_1. This cost-benefit approach to fertility choices is associated with Gary Becker (1981).

We can extend the analysis a little further to understand the effect of changing family situations on fertility choices. In Figure 8.7, the number of children is represented on the horizontal axis, and consumption of commodities is represented on the vertical axis. The budget line $A'B'$ says that with fixed income, parents have to choose between having more children, or consuming more of other goods. More children imply having less material goods to enjoy, and having less children enables one to devote more resources to material goods. The steeper the budget line, the higher is the price of children, relative to goods. The slope of this budget line is therefore a measure of the cost of having children. An increase in income implies a parallel outward shift of the budget line AB to the line $A'B'$. Reduced income moves this line below AB and closer to the origin. There are three indifference curves in the diagram showing three levels of satisfaction that may be derived for all the possible combinations of goods and children that the parents could choose from. According to the demand-based theory of fertility, the household chooses the combination of goods and children which maximizes family satisfaction on the basis of its subjectively determined preferences. In the diagram, this is represented by the point e, corresponding to c_1 (children) and g_1 (goods).

If family income increases, the household's budget line would shift upward to line $A'B'$. As a result, the family would adjust its satisfaction levels accordingly and hence choose c_2 (children) and g_2 (goods).

An increase in the value or "price" of raising children can come not just through the increase in the price of direct "children" expenditures. Sending women to college and increasing women's wage incomes increase the opportunity costs of raising children as well. Such implied or indirect costs that may be incurred if good job opportunities or more wage income has to be given up to have the mother stay home to care for children instead. An increase in the price of children relative to other goods can cause households to substitute commodities for children. In this case, the budget line will pivot towards the origin around the point A', to the line $A'B'$ and cause the household maximizing utility consumption combination to occur at a lower indifference curve, at point f.

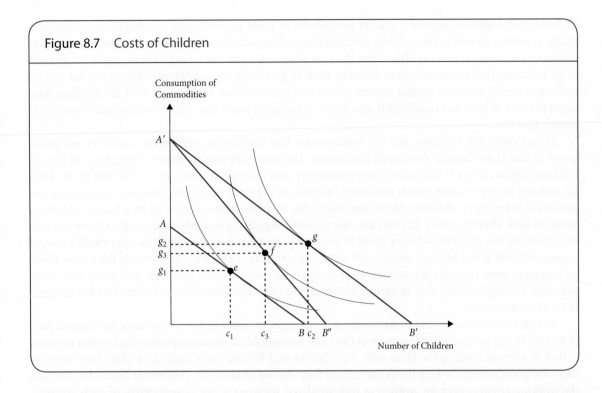

Figure 8.7   Costs of Children

In summary, Becker's (1981) model of household fertility says that the demand for children is positively related to the household's income and wealth and negatively related to the price of children (including the opportunity costs involved). Furthermore, the demand for children is also influenced by the price of substitutes (negatively related), complements (positively related), and parents' taste for other goods *vis-à-vis* children (negatively related if taste for other goods changes positively). Evidence suggests that the theory, as far as it goes, is reasonably accurate.

The Becker model can be modified by introducing the quality of children as an additional variable and also by making the quality and quantity of children jointly determined. If we do this, we find that one of the interesting results is that since quality and quantity are substitutes, an increase in the price of one will cause an increase in the demand for the other. Therefore, if this kind of substitution takes place, an increase in the cost of schooling (measure of quality) will lead to an increase in the number of children demanded. Conversely, a fall in school tuition fees will lead to a fall in the number of children demanded. That is, fewer "quality" children will be substituted for more children of lower "quality."

8.4.2   The Demand for Children in Developing Countries

Why is there a high demand for children in the developing countries? To answer this question, we first look at the costs and then the benefits associated with children, as well as the factors that influence the fertility choices of parents in developing countries.

THE COSTS   There are at least two kinds of costs associated with children. One is the direct costs—children have to be fed, clothed, kept healthy, and schooled. Direct expenditures on children vary widely across the spectrum of economic development. More importantly, the composition of the expenditure basket of households with children varies markedly from country to country. Households in the developing countries devote almost all costs for child maintenance on food and other necessities, while those in developed countries expend a greater proportion of child expenditures on education, sports, and music activities, as well as other forms of human capital investments. In agrarian societies, there is less emphasis on formal schooling. Therefore, the cost of raising a child in an agrarian society is lower than in an industrialized economy where children need to go to school and parents have to pay for school uniforms, shoes, bus fares, pocket money, sports and music tuition fees, as well as child-minding fees. Since the cost of land and buildings is also lower in the rural areas, the cost of housing additional children is also less.

Direct costs are, however, not the main reason that families in developing countries are much larger in size than those in developed economies. The more important element impacting on household fertility decisions is the indirect or opportunity cost associated with having children in the family. Indirect or opportunity cost is measured in terms of the time, effort and resources foregone in the process of bringing up children. Most commonly, this includes income given up by a parent who stays home to look after the child. In this case, the opportunity cost is roughly equivalent to the wage rate multiplied by the number of hours spent in parenting. In rural communities, the opportunity cost of raising children is low because women have few opportunities to earn money outside the home. Once employment opportunities for women start to open up (with industrialization and more education perhaps), the opportunity cost of raising children will rise, thus dampening the demand for children in these communities.

In this connection, having more children in agrarian societies is not a hindrance to women's participation in the production of services in the rural household. A common picture that comes to mind is that of women tending the farm with their babies tied behind their backs in a cloth bag. Besides, there are grandparents to help them out in case they choose to leave the children at home. In contrast, the working environment for women in industrialized societies is not as supportive of such arrangements—normally, women cannot bring their children to work and have to pay for child-minding services to enable them to work. In addition, as mentioned above, housing costs may be higher in an urban setting. Clearly, the opportunity cost of having children is higher in more advanced societies simply because of the logistics.

THE BENEFITS   Apart from the joys and pleasures of being a parent, children do bring in a number of economic benefits to the household, and these tend to increase demand. In developing countries, children begin to assist in a range of farm and household production activities at a very early age. Children in the rural economies are often given such responsibilities as feeding the pigs, cows, and chicken, cleaning the animal houses, selling home-grown vegetables in the nearby market, and looking after their younger siblings while their parents work in the farm—all of which add up to the economic production of the household. Children thus have a very high economic value to the agrarian household. In an urban setting, in contrast, such roles for children are limited as they do not just go to school, but also stay in school for many more years than children in the rural areas. This raises the costs of bringing up children in cities and other urban areas.

Another important reason for the high demand for children in developing countries is that they are considered the principal providers of old-age security for the parents. Why is this so? Unlike the situation in developed countries where social security institutions for the elderly are well established, in many developing countries, retirement funds, pension and such other systems to support the elderly outside the family are not well developed, if at all. Children fill this role. One result is the common family arrangement of having parents live with their children in their old age. Contrast this with the abundance of retirement villages in more advanced societies. Will this role differ between rural and urban sectors? Perhaps only when the chance of getting a government pension is higher in an urban setting.

Ray (1998) presents a simple model to capture the insurance motive for having children in developing countries. Accordingly, the number of children born is determined so that $1-(1-p)^n>q$, where n is the number of children, p is the overall probability that a child will grow up and take care them in old age, and q is the probability that at least one child will take care of them in old age. It is argued that q is likely to be large, particularly for risk-averse people. If p increases dramatically, then this threshold will fall. However, for most people in traditional societies, revisions of these probabilities may take a generation or more. If a family is risk averse or prefers a son to take care of them in old age, then the threshold will be very high. As an example, suppose $p = \frac{1}{2}$ and $q = 0.90$. We can then work out a formula where n has to be at least 4. If p increases to 0.8, a very dramatic change indeed, then n falls to 2. If q is very high, say 0.975, then even if p is 0.8, the number of children goes to 3. The reduction in mortality (after age one) is a factor that is closely related to the insurance motive but its effect is complex. A reduction in mortality has a strong effect on fertility because it results in a family shifting from what Ray calls a hoarding strategy to a targeting strategy. If a family knows that when a child survives past infancy, the chances are high that he will survive for a long time, then the family does not have to "hoard" or have many children to cover the possibility that some will die before the parents reach old age.

8.4.3 Other Factors

In addition to the standard microeconomic approach of Becker, there are several other factors that have either direct or indirect effects on the family's fertility decision. These effects require a more general equilibrium approach which provides underlying reasons why some of the standard variables might change. In this sense, they are included as second stage variables that have behavioral ramifications for fertility.

Better education for women lowers fertility rates and this important factor works through a number of different channels. Higher education enhances job opportunities that raise the opportunity cost of having children. For educated women, the opportunity to have higher income, to pursue a career, and/or enjoy a certain lifestyle is weighed heavily against having children. If they have a different preference function for children than their partners or husbands, educated women are better able to assert themselves and have greater input in the decision to have children—when and how many. More educated women have greater bargaining power at home. Furthermore, the higher levels of self-awareness that educated women have give them greater control over their destiny and their bodies. Educated women also tend to marry later.

The intergenerational impact of education on fertility levels needs emphasizing too. Empirical evidence shows a ripple effect. Better-educated mothers have better-educated children—particularly better-educated daughters—and this has important implications for the fertility decisions of the next generation of mothers.

The trade-off between the quality and quantity of children, as noted earlier, is another important consideration in having children. In an expanded version of the Becker model, these two variables are determined together as the household undertakes its utility maximization decision. As incomes rise, there is a substitution effect of quality for quantity that works to lower fertility. This impact on fertility becomes stronger when compounded by the effect of having more educated women in the household, which leads to having more educated daughters, which in turn can lead to further substitution of quality for quantity in the next generation.

Some analysts believe that lower infant mortality rates serve to lower fertility levels. Olsen (1983) argues this particularly for the case of developing economies where the old-age insurance system is not well developed. Ray (1998) provides a simple model linking the demand for children, old-age insurance motive, and infant mortality rates. His model neatly associates low infant mortality rates with low fertility rates, though this is still a strong point of contention in the literature. Whether this is true or not depends upon the price elasticity of demand for the surviving children. If the demand is inelastic, then mortality declines should reduce fertility. The empirical evidence suggests that families do not completely replace a lost child. More than likely, cultural and other factors compound the true association of infant mortality on fertility level. In some societies, for example, the status of the father or mother is associated with the number of children—that is, the more children (sometimes, the more male children) one has, the more prestige and respect one gets from the villagers or community. Such cultural factors will tend to influence family decisions to "replace" or not replace an infant who died. The widespread desire of traditional families to have sons is continuing to make an impact on fertility levels in developing countries. In addition, if this preference remains strong, as it still is in China, India, and Korea, social norms and expectations can raise the probability of having another child to "replace" a lost son, more than a lost daughter.

8.5 POPULATION GROWTH AND ECONOMIC DEVELOPMENT

Does population enhance or inhibit economic development? How? Consider the following definition of output:

$$O = L \cdot X \tag{8.1}$$

where O is the output level, X is the output per worker, and L is the number of workers. In per capita terms, this is equivalent to

$$\frac{O}{P} = \frac{L}{P} \cdot X \tag{8.2}$$

This equation states that output per worker is a product of two factors: the share of the population that is in the labor force and the output per worker (productivity). Each of these factors provides a channel through which population growth affects economic growth. In this section, we address one specific question of this population growth puzzle and then look at the population growth experience of countries in Asia. Here, we draw on both economic theory and empirical evidence to come to a clearer understanding of this issue.

8.5.1 Is Rapid Population Growth Undesirable?

If markets work and individuals are making informed choices in the society, then it could be that rapid population growth is socially optimal. The right answer, however, is not so easily obtained, if at all.

What do growth models predict? The growth models studied in Chapter 2 clearly showed the impact of population growth on income. In the Solow (1956) model, there are constant returns to scale and this ensures that a faster rate of population growth and the labor force will reduce the capital-to-labor ratio, and therefore, the productivity of labor. Equation 2.20 in Chapter 2 shows explicitly that when the population growth rate goes up, the equilibrium level of income per capita falls. Furthermore, in the Lewis–Fei–Ranis (1954, 1964) model introduced in Chapter 2, labor is absorbed into the manufacturing sector only insofar as the manufacturing sector is able to absorb it as a result of technical progress or capital accumulation. Other things being equal, population growth will lower the wage rate and the level of income. Coale and Hoover (1958) also suggest that a higher population growth rate will reduce income growth because children consume and do not produce. Overall, these theories conclude that rapid population growth is indeed undesirable.

On the other end of the scale is another group of economic and political analysts who argue that a rapid rate of population growth brings many benefits for the economy and society as a whole. Under this viewpoint, a rapidly growing population increases consumer demand, which allows the manufacturing sector and infrastructure to take advantage of economies of scale in production, to lower costs, and provide a sufficient and low-cost labor supply necessary to achieve higher levels of output. A large growing population also provides a rich source of labor resources, particularly for labor-intensive agricultural activities.

There are, therefore, many opposing views to this question. In this book, no single answer will exists. If we take a closer look at the inner workings of developing and relatively poorer countries, we will realize that there are external diseconomies that result from having young, highly dependent populations. The following sections will discuss each in turn.

POPULATION GROWTH AND NATURAL RESOURCES   Rapid population growth exerts greater dependence on land, forest, and water resources for consumption and subsistence. For non-renewable resources, population growth reduces the time horizon of usage but not necessarily the per-capita consumption since the price of the resources will rise to reflect growing scarcity. For renewable resources, on the other hand, common property resources may be overused and could even result in the extinction of species. The argument here is that better property rights are needed to define and circumscribe the use of these resources rather than to arbitrarily reduce the rate of population growth. Furthermore, the burden on the environment must be factored in as one of the costs of more rapid population growth because the larger the population, the greater the adverse environmental impact on the economy as a whole. In other words, the larger the population, the larger are the negative externalities. (This will be fully discussed in Chapter 12.)

POPULATION GROWTH AND ADDITIONS TO HUMAN CAPITAL   At the family level, large families tend to spend less on health and education per family member than smaller families. However, there are risks to controlling fertility to address this issue. It could reduce overall welfare if parents are altruistic and include children in their utility functions. It is probably true that elimination of unwanted births would raise average education levels, and this may be the way to address this issue (see below). Large family size reduces the educational opportunities for the children of such families, and also the rate of saving by raising the dependency rate.

High fertility harms the health of both mother and children. While this may be recognized and accounted for by many families in decision making, it is highly unlikely in families where women have little or no bargaining power, as may be the case in rural villages, or where the literacy rate is low. Family members in large families are likely to go hungry more than small families. Again, this may be in the utility function of the family but there may be a case of moral hazard, particularly if there are some feeding programs in place.

POPULATION GROWTH AND INEQUALITY   In developing countries, large families tend to cluster among the poor. This perpetuates poverty and exacerbates inequality by lowering the rate of return to labor and increasing the returns to capital. In addition, if the poor have more children, they will be worse off because per-capita income within the family will be lowered. Large families are also most likely to spend less on health and education per capita and this will tend to have a negative impact on income distribution. If society does not want this to happen for social reasons, then it is an external diseconomy and justifies market intervention.

8.5.2   Patterns of Population Growth in Asia

Historical estimates of world populations indicated a slowly growing population for Asia until the early 1900s. There was a steady balance of birth and death rates for the economies in the region, most of which were primarily agricultural and very traditional in nature, akin to Stage 1 of the demographic

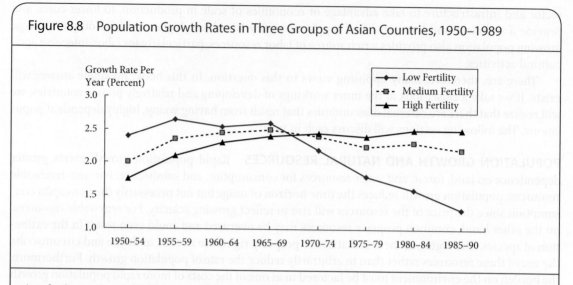

Figure 8.8   Population Growth Rates in Three Groups of Asian Countries, 1950–1989

Low fertility group includes China, Republic of Korea, Democratic Republic of Korea, Sri Lanka, and Thailand; medium fertility group includes India, Indonesia, Malaysia, Myanmar, Philippines, and Vietnam; and high fertility group includes Bangladesh, Cambodia, Laos, Nepal, and Papua New Guinea.

SOURCE: J. Warne Sanderson and Tan Jee-Peng, *Population in Asia* (Washington, D.C.: World Bank Regional and Sector Study, 1995), p. 29.

transition phase. Population levels began to boom only in the mid-1900s when medical technologies from overseas started to be used locally, leading to significant success in pushing death rates down. Birth rates nonetheless remained high.

In the 1950s, population growth trends began to differ across the countries in the region. Earlier in the postwar era, population growth in the NIEs of Taiwan, Singapore, South Korea, and Hong Kong, as well as China had been generally much higher than those in South Asia. Figure 8.8 shows that at its peak, the average rate of population growth in the NIEs was much faster than that of South Asia today.

In the mid-1960s, the population growth rates of the NIEs started to fall dramatically as economic growth and industrialization began to accelerate. By the mid-1970s, these were below those of the other countries in the region, and by the 1990s, they were even lower (see Figure 8.8 and Table 8.5). The difference in the experience of these two groups of countries (the NIEs and China versus South and Southeast Asia) reflects the dramatic decline in fertility in the former. Earlier, the death rate had also been falling, more so than in the poorer countries, and this accounted for its faster growth in population. In South Asia, with the exception of Sri Lanka, however, neither the birth nor the death rates changed much until the 1980s when birth rates began to decline.

By the 1990s, many countries in Asia had begun or nearly completed the demographic transition. As can be seen in Table 8.1, China, the NIEs, Sri Lanka, and Thailand had relatively low rates of increase in population (less than 1.5 percent) while the other countries in South Asia and the Philippines still had relatively high rates of increase in population (1.5–3.0 percent).

Since population growth is determined by an interaction of total fertility and infant mortality, it is useful to compare them for different countries (see Table 8.6). Countries with low fertility (under 2.1 percent) will eventually reach zero population growth. In countries with somewhat higher fertility

Table 8.5 Population Growth in Individual Asian Countries, 2005–2010 (Percent)

	Annual Rate of Population Growth, 1965–1990	**Population Growth Rate, 2005–2010**
China	2.35	0.58
NIEs		
Hong Kong	2.18	1.00
Singapore	2.46	1.19
Korea, Rep. of	2.01	0.33
Taiwan	2.45	0.36
South Asia		
Bangladesh	3.52	1.67
India	2.97	1.46
Pakistan	4.21	1.84
Sri Lanka	1.91	0.47
Southeast Asia		
Indonesia	2.82	1.16
Malaysia	3.66	1.69
Philippines	3.74	1.72
Thailand	3.26	0.66

Figures are based on estimates.

SOURCE: United Nations Population Division, *World Population Prospects: The 2006 Revision, Highlights* (New York: United Nations, 2007).

(between 2.1 and 4 percent), population growth rate will continue at a modest rate. For countries with TFR over 4 percent, population growth will be more rapid.

Similarly, the infant mortality rates (IMR) of countries can be put into three separate categories—below 20 deaths per thousand, between 20 and 50 deaths per thousand, and over 50 deaths per thousand. The high-income countries are concentrated in the cell with low TFR and low IMR. For Asia, this includes the NIEs and Sri Lanka. Countries with higher TFR and IMR are displayed moving up the table toward the northeast corner where most of the South Asian countries are located.

While lower birth and death rates often seem to be a by-product of economic development, some countries and regions of other countries that still have relatively low levels of per-capita income have made significant progress in lowering population growth. In Asia, this includes, for example, Sri Lanka, Indonesia, China, Thailand, and some states of India. In all these cases, there have been substantial efforts on the part of the governments to lower fertility and infant mortality rates. These efforts have borne fruit and are discussed further in the next section.

8.5.3 Policies to Reduce Population Growth in Asia

Apart from rapid economic growth as an explanation for the demographic transition, it is possible that the same institutional developments in health and education that allowed these countries to reduce

Table 8.6   Classification of Asian Economies by TRF and IMR[a]

Infant Mortality Rate (IMR)	Total Fertility Rate (TRF)		
	Less Than 2.1	**Between 2.1 and 3.9**	**4 or More**
100 or more			Afghanistan
50–99	Azerbaijan, Kazakhstan	Bangladesh, India, Mongolia, Myanmar, and several Central Asian republics	Bhutan, Cambodia, Lao, Nepal, Pakistan, Papua New Guinea
20–49	China, Thailand	Indonesia, Philippines, Vietnam	Most Pacific islands
Less than 20	Hong Kong, Korea, Singapore, Sri Lanka, Taiwan	Fiji, Malaysia, Tonga	

[a]Most recent year for which figures are available.

SOURCE: Asian Development Bank, *Key Indicators 2002: Population and Human Resource Trends and Challenges* (Manila: ADB, 2002).

mortality rates after World War II were also brought to bear on fertility and family planning (Sanderson and Tan, 1995).

FAMILY PLANNING AND CONTRACEPTIVE USE   The relationship between contraceptive use and fertility rates needs to be negative for any family planning program to be successful. Various forms of such programs have been implemented in many developing countries around the world, but the strength of that relationship remains unclear in practice. The wide range of outcomes observed in Southeast Asia during the 1980s has largely been inconclusive, particularly when comparing the experiences of Malaysia, Thailand, and the Philippines.[5] There has been very little achievement in the Philippines while significant success has been noted in the use of contraceptives in Thailand and Malaysia. In the Philippines, for example, contraceptive use was reported to be 44 percent; yet total fertility rate was 4.3 births per woman. This compares with 3.5 births per woman in Malaysia, which reported a similar rate of contraceptive use. Most likely, there are other factors besides contraceptive use to explain these differences in fertility outcomes (see below).

In India, the network of family planning and contraceptive facilities, such as buildings and equipment, is quite extensive, with about 1,100 married women of reproductive age per fixed facility. This is a much lower ratio compared with all other countries except Thailand, where the ratio was 990. However, progress in fertility reduction does not seem to be commensurate with the provision of facilities. Perhaps other supply factors, such as the availability of trained personnel and birth-control materials, such as condoms and IUDs (intrauterine devices, are also important. Furthermore, the demand factors, including women's education, may also account for the slow reduction in fertility in India.

In the Philippines, on the other hand, the important role of the Catholic Church and the extremely low budget for resources devoted to population control are believed to be largely responsible for the lag in response to fertility rate declines during the past several decades. Compared with its neighbors

---

[5]   Primarily based on information and figures cited in Sanderson and Tan (1995).

at similar levels of development, fertility rates in the Philippines are much higher (4.3 versus 2.6 and 3.3 births per woman in Thailand and Indonesia, respectively, in the late 1980s[6]). Domestic spending was estimated to be 0.02 percent of GDP in 1988, much lower than other countries. Furthermore, programs for fertility control have been primarily the result of foreign-funded assistance. The government itself does not have a well-funded comprehensive program for population control, perhaps because of pressure from the Catholic Church hierarchy.

Comparisons between Indonesia and India are also instructive. Of the four major components of family planning—contraceptive supplies; training of staff; information, education and communication (IEC); and incentive payments, particularly sterilization—Indonesia allocated nothing for incentive payments while India allocated 60 percent of its budget. On the other hand, Indonesia allocated more than 60 percent of its budget to contraceptive supplies while India gave less than 30 percent. India spent only 12 percent on IEC while Indonesia spent 38 percent of its budget on items in this category. Was India's program misdirected? Many observers think so.

In the late 1980s, Thailand, Malaysia, and Sri Lanka devoted nearly 80 percent of their budgets to contraceptive supply. This may have been appropriate in these countries because the infrastructure for education and sites had already been developed. Nevertheless, there were significant differences in the success of these programs, with Thailand and Sri Lanka being more successful.

Compared with an average usage of less than 45 percent during the mid-1980s (Sanderson and Tan, 1995, p. 21), contraceptive prevalence rates had risen by 2000, with the highest usage coming from East Asia (more than 70 percent), followed by Southeast (58 percent) and South Asia (48 percent) (see ESCAP, 2002). With the greater usage of contraceptive methods within the individual Asian countries, a tendency toward a greater decline in fertility rates was observed. ESCAP (2002) figures show that contraceptive usage in Malaysia and the Philippines fell below the Southeast Asian average, and its incidence of modern contraceptive methods usage were the lowest within the region—less than two-thirds of all methods. This might have contributed, among other factors, to the high fertility rates of 3 children per woman experienced in these two countries.

In general, the linkage between family planning and the use of contraceptives is loose since there are numerous other methods for controlling family size. At the same time, there have been many studies on the effect of contraceptives on fertility in developing countries, yielding a range of conclusions.[7] What can be safely concluded from all these is that government initiatives are well in place in many economies, yet their net effect on family formation continue to be small.

IMPROVEMENT IN WOMEN'S EDUCATION   Experience has shown that in many developing countries, women's education has been instrumental in changing the perception of family size. This operates through a number of channels, all of which tend to raise the opportunity cost of having children, substitute quality of children for quantity, and provide greater opportunity to women in determining the size of the family. Improvement in women's education has also had a beneficial effect on other variables, such as overall family health and decline in infant mortality.

ECONOMIC INCENTIVES AND DISINCENTIVES   In the late 1970s, when population growth was seen as very high in Singapore, the government imposed tax penalties and social pressure on those families that had more than two children. Health and education subsidies for the first two children were generous but the same were severely reduced for subsequent children. Housing entitlements, in

---

[6] *World Development Indicators Online.*
[7] The availability of abortion appears as a significant factor in many of these studies.

government housing estates openly favored smaller families. This two-child policy proved so highly successful in pushing birth rates down in just a few years that the problem has now been reversed. More recently, the Singapore government resorted to the same economic incentive and disincentive schemes, but this time to encourage couples to have more children. Tax benefits increased with larger family size. In addition, health, education, and housing benefits to families increased with more children in the family.

Similarly, in an effort to increase the natural growth rate of its population, the Australian government provides a one-off payment of A\$5,000 to families with the birth of every child. This was started in 2005 solely for the purpose of increasing fertility rates and works alongside other cash allowances and family benefits already in place for many years. Generally, a progressive tax system and reorientation of the subsidy system could be introduced if a strong population policy is deemed desirable. Surprisingly, very few countries in Asia have used this approach.

COERCION AND QUOTAS   In India, there was a time under Indira Gandhi when sterilization for men was encouraged. Sometimes coercion was even used. In China, the government instituted a one-child policy in 1982 to curb the growth of its already large population (see Box 8.1 for greater details of population policies in China since the 1950s). This approach put a clear break on the nation's accelerating fertility rates, but it also brought with it a number of unintended consequences. The policy appears to have resulted in more rampant corruption in certain localities, as well as a significant increase in infanticide, particularly of baby girls, since many families preferred having sons to daughters. The one-child policy in China has thus had its share of harsh critics from around the world. More generally, such coercive policies do not leave the fertility decision to the individuals themselves. They effectively impose a relatively more severe welfare burden on poorer and rural-based households, as they would be the ones who would prefer and benefit from having more children in the family.

 BOX 8.1

China's Population Policy Experiment

China's population was recorded at 1,271 million in 2001 (ADB, 2002), making up one-fifth of the world's population. Being the most populous country in the world, it is not surprising that its demographic makeup would eventually be of political interest. Throughout history, various population control campaigns have taken place. These policies have ranged from being suggestive to radical, with varying degrees of effectiveness.

Prior to the 1950s, population growth was not of much concern. The government of the day believed that "... even if China's population multiplied many times, it [China] would find a solution." This opinion rapidly changed in the early 1950s when China's population ballooned to more than half-a-billion! This provided the impetus for a comprehensive population-control program to be put in place. Contraceptive manufacturing thus began in the mid-1950s and the first family-planning program was

thus implemented. Although the campaign was stopped because efforts were directed to the Great Leap Forward and communization movements, it did pave the way for future birth-control programs.

The second birth-control campaign began in 1962 and provided a guide to the ideal number of children, with slogans such as "Two children is just right, three is too many, and four is a mistake." The campaign was complemented by an incentive program that rewarded families with a small number of children (through income, grain and housing subsidies, and even free land). These benefits were withdrawn once a family exceeded a threshold number of children. The Cultural Revolution also assisted the campaign.

Family planning was promoted in earnest from 1971. Adjusting childbearing norms was the focus of this policy which was reasonably effective: "Wan, Xi, and Shao," which meant later marriages, longer birth intervals (4 years), and fewer children (2) were the encouraged

Box Figure 8.1 Population Age and Sex Structure for China, 2000

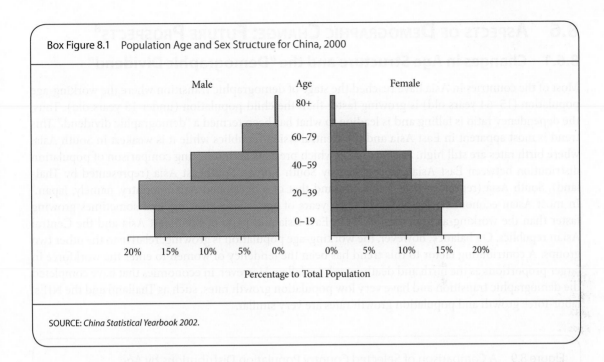

SOURCE: *China Statistical Yearbook 2002.*

norms. By the end of 1978, the birth rate had been halved to 12 per thousand in just a matter of eight years. Despite such reductions in population growth, political leaders were concerned about the cohorts born in the 1950s and 1960s reaching childbearing age in the 1980s. It was inevitable that population growth would soar. In response to their concerns, a policy far more ambitious than any other before, was put in place. The "one child per family" policy was announced by the government at the end of 1978. By September 1980, the campaign was carried out vigorously.

The policy provided financial and housing incentives to families who held one-child certificates. Families who had more than one child faced penalties, including deduction of a fixed percentage of salary and loss of preferences for government subsidies. Some special considerations were given to minority Chinese under exceptional circumstances. Despite being so ambitious, the policy did not halt population growth as effectively as the "Wan, Xi, and Shao" campaign.

The radical policy also raised a number of ethical questions. Firstly, policy ineffectiveness arose because policy can influence demographic changes only to a certain extent. The previously suggested policies had already adjusted the norms and in the rural areas, legislation had been met with resistance. The ethical concern was the family's preference for boys. This culturally instilled preference has led to reports of infanticide, selective abortion of female babies, and higher rate of girls being put up for adoption. The male to female ratio by 2000 is 117 boys to 100 girls. Ethics aside, it is predicted that in the future many eligible bachelors will find it difficult to find a wife, due to the scarcity of women.

Thus, since the late 1990s, China has started reconsidering its one-child family-planning program, in view of external pressure exerted by human rights groups and the United States. By early 2000, the government had further relaxed its policy and permitted two "only child" couples who marry to have two children. In the meantime, there have been changes in the desirable number of children in Chinese households arising from economic progress and rising costs of living. The desired number of children in the rural areas has shrunk to two and the figure is even lower in urban households. The New Population Law passed in 2002 takes a far gentler approach than that of the 1980s. The government emphasizes the importance of informed choices, preferring to influence the masses through family education, reproductive care, and proper contraception methods, leaving them to voluntarily decide upon family size but with due adherence paid to the relevant policies and regulations. Furthermore, in order to protect the rights of civilians, government officials who use coercion to implement the family planning program will now be subjected to criminal laws.

SOURCES: Joan Kaufman, "China's Population Policy: Recent Developments and Prospects for Change," *China in Transition: A Look Behind the Scenes.* Presentation for the National Committee on U.S.-China Relations/Center for Strategic and International Studies, September 25, 2002, available at http://www.csis.org/china/020925kaufman.pdf; China Internet Information Center, available at http://www.china.org.cn.

8.6   Aspects of Demographic Change: Future Prospects[8]

8.6.1   Changes in Age Structure and the "Demographic Dividend"

Most of the countries in Asia have reached the stage of demographic transition where the working-age population (15–64 years old) is growing faster than the child population (under 15 years old). Thus, the dependency ratio is falling and is leading to what has been termed a "demographic dividend." This trend is most apparent in East Asia and the Central Asian republics while it is weakest in South Asia, where birth rates are still high. See Figure 8.9 which presents an interesting comparison of population distribution between East Asia (represented by South Korea), Southeast Asia (represented by Thailand), South Asia (represented by Pakistan), and that of a developed Asian country, namely, Japan.[9] In most Asian economies, the group over 65 years of age is also growing, and sometimes growing faster than the working-age population, as in East Asia and parts of Southeast Asia and the Central Asian republics. On balance, however, the working-age population is growing, relative to the other two groups. A contributing factor to this trend has been the tendency of women to enter the workforce in larger proportions as the birth and death rates have fallen. However, in economies that have completed the demographic transition and have very low population growth rates, such as Thailand and the NIEs, labor-force growth and population growth rates are very similar.

Figure 8.9   A Comparison of Selected Country Population Distributions by Age and Sex Within Asia, 2000

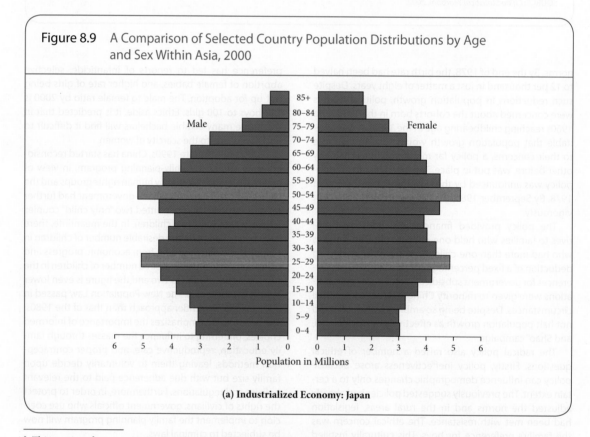

(a) Industrialized Economy: Japan

---

[8] This section draws on Asian Development Bank (2002), *Key Indicators of Developing Asian and Pacific Countries* (theme chapter).

[9] Note that the figure is by no means representative of all the countries within the Asian region, but it would adequately serve to paint for the reader a general picture of population composition within Asia.

Figure 8.9 (*continued*)

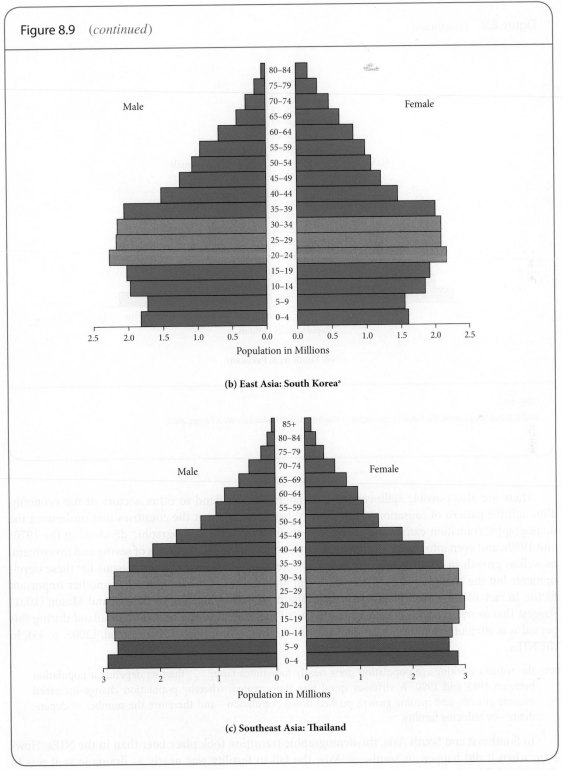

(b) East Asia: South Korea[a]

(c) Southeast Asia: Thailand

(*continued*)

Figure 8.9   *(continued)*

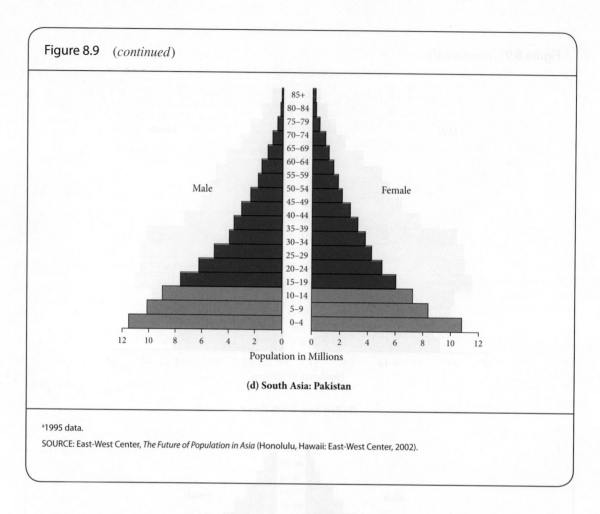

(d) **South Asia: Pakistan**

[a]1995 data.

SOURCE: East-West Center, *The Future of Population in Asia* (Honolulu, Hawaii: East-West Center, 2002).

There are also possible spillovers of a demographic dividend to other sectors of the economy, although the pattern of causation is not clear. What is clear is that the countries that underwent the demographic transition earlier and therefore benefited from the demographic dividend in the 1970s and 1980s, and even into the 1990s in the case of China, also had higher rates of saving and investment, as well as growth in GDP. As seen in earlier chapters, there are many other reasons for these developments but the changing pattern of population growth cannot be discounted as another important factor. In fact, Bloom and Williamson (1998); Bloom, Canning, and Sevilla (2003); and Mason (2001) suggest that as much as one-fourth to two-fifths of the growth in the NIEs and Thailand during this period was attributable to favorable demographic trends. According to Bloom et al. (2003, p. 45), in the NIEs,

> the region's working age population grew nearly four times faster . . . than its dependent population between 1965 and 1990. A virtuous spiral was thus created, whereby population change increased income growth, and income growth pushed down population—and therefore the number of dependents—by reducing fertility.

In Southeast and South Asia, the demographic transition took place later than in the NIEs. However, when it did happen in Southeast Asia, the fall in fertility was nearly as dramatic as it was in the NIEs, followed closely by South Asia. However, the demographic divide was far less pronounced (see Table 8.7).

Table 8.7   Annual Population Growth in Asia

Region	1965–1990			1990–2015[a]		
	Total	Working Age	Non-Working Age	Total	Working Age	Non-Working Age
East Asia	1.75	2.43	0.66	0.74	0.94	0.32
South Asia	2.28	2.49	2.02	1.69	2.17	0.94
Southeast Asia	2.26	2.66	1.74	1.43	2.00	0.43

Definitions are somewhat different from their conventional use in this book.

[a]Projected rates.

SOURCE: David E. Bloom, David Canning, and Jaypee Sevilla, *The Demographic Dividend: A New Perspective on the Economic Consequences of Population Change* (Santa Monica, CA: RAND Corporation, 2003), p. 54.

8.6.2   When Will the Demographic Dividend Disappear?

As populations age and the demographic dividend dissipates, more and more countries will be experiencing low population growth together with lower death and birth rates. This points to an aging population, the age structure of which begins to look more like a rectangle and then a "reverse" triangle or pyramid. This means that the working population as a percentage of the elderly population will decline dramatically. Projections by the United Nations Population Division show that by 2050, the ratio of the working-age population (15–64 years) to the population over 65 years will have declined from 12 to 1.7 percent in Japan between 1950 and 2050 (*International Herald Tribune*, 2002). The changes are less dramatic for other countries but the trend is noticeable, particularly where the demographic transition has been in place for some time. In Asia, this is most noticeable in Korea and Taiwan.

How long will that take to happen? The answer is: not for some time. Nevertheless, advance planning is needed. Now populations are still very young, compared with those in the Organization for Economic Cooperation and Development (OECD) countries (see Table 8.8), where the 60+ category is more than 16 percent (23.3 percent in Japan). The countries that will have a substantial increase in the proportion of the population over 60 years have already achieved high levels of income with well-organized social security systems, such as Taiwan and Singapore. However, because the demographic transition for many other Asian countries took place at relatively low levels of per capita income, they will face an aging problem at a much lower level of per-capita income than did the OECD countries. Simulations by the United Nations suggest that dependency ratios were even greater than the OECD countries in 2000 (for example, Sri Lanka, China, and Thailand, in Table 8.8). Therefore, these economies must make provisions for their aging populations now. It is uncertain whether the historical solution of having aging parents live with their children will continue as a long-run solution. There is evidence that this pattern is beginning to break down in Taiwan and other East Asian countries.

A complicating factor is the retirement age. Earlier retirement had been closely related to per-capita income in the past. Will this trend continue into the future, particularly as life expectancy increases further? Currently, the statutory retirement age is lower in most developing Asian countries than it is in the OECD countries (55 or 60 years compared with 65 years in Japan, the United Kingdom, and Australia; there is no age limit in the United States). Refer to Box 8.2 for a further discussion of aging and its policy implications in Asia.

Table 8.8   Aging Measures: Percentage of Population Aged Above 60

	2000	2005	2050
China	10.1%	12.2%	38.4%
Hong Kong	14.4	18.2	52.9
Korea, Rep. of	11.0	14.2	28.7
Singapore	10.5	13.8	54.6
Sri Lanka	9.8	10.8	35.0
Thailand	8.4	12.6	36.8
Indonesia	7.6	8.9	28.8
India	7.5	8.2	23.3
Vietnam	7.5	8.6	30.9
Malaysia	6.5	7.3	26.2
Nepal	5.8	6.2	15.4
Philippines	5.5	6.5	20.8
Bangladesh	5.0	6.1	18.9
Pakistan	3.7	6.4	18.5
OECD Countries			
Japan	23.3	31.2	59.5
Canada	16.7	21.3	41.9
United Kingdom	20.7	25.7	39.3
United States	16.1	20.1	34.4

SOURCE: United Nations Population Division (2002, 2006).

 BOX 8.2

Aging and Its Policy Implications in Asia

Rapid aging in the Asian region, especially for the more economically advanced countries, will have important implications on future resource allocation and government policies, particularly in terms of health care for the elderly (see Chapter 10 on health patterns and trends in Asia).

However, health care for the elderly is generally not regarded as a high priority within most developing Asian countries since they are more concerned about meeting health care demand for basic preventive, curative, as well as reproductive services. For instance, India, Indonesia, and the Philippines concentrate on the provision of maternal and child health and reproductive health services. The mode of health care financing, be it paid out-of-pocket by the individual or by the government, or by a combination of both, and the form of provision (public versus private sector) for elderly health care provision are also issues that need to be settled.

Other areas of concern include the level of savings and public pensions schemes needed to guarantee a certain standard of living for the elderly. However, coverage of public pension schemes tends to be rather limited in most Asian countries, except for Japan and Singapore (see Box Table 8.2).

Box Table 8.2   Coverage of Pension Schemes in Selected Asian Countries, 1992

Country	Percentage of Workforce Covered
Japan	100
Singapore	100
Malaysia	96
Philippines	53
South Korea	26
China	21
Indonesia	7
India	1
Bangladesh	0

SOURCE: East-West Center, *The Future of Population in Asia* (Honolulu, Hawaii: East-West Center, 2002).

How these issues influence the future resource allocation patterns and government budget spending in Asia will largely depend on priorities set by the government in the individual countries. For instance, if the government decides to place more emphasis on providing for the elderly, this will reduce the availability of funds needed for other essential purposes and might impact upon future economic growth prospects. On the other hand, if the government decides in favor of spending for the young and economically active group, with less resource allocated to the care of the elderly, this will eventually affect the overall quality of living in the country in the long run. Hence, it will be up to the individual countries to determine their optimal balance of resource allocation needed so as to achieve economic growth without compromising on the needs and standard of living of the elderly—often a tricky and difficult process. It will also depend on the willingness of the taxpayers to support the public programs for the elderly.

SOURCE: East-West Center, *The Future of Population in Asia* (Honolulu, Hawaii: East-West Center, 2002).

8.7   SUMMARY AND CONCLUSIONS

In this chapter, we discussed the way in which population growth has adjusted to economic development. We also discussed the mutually reinforcing interplay between population growth and economic development, the way that changes in the dependency ratio affect growth, and how the population movement from rural areas to the cities has worked to reduce the rate of fertility. The chapter also pointed out the important relationship between population growth, fertility, and education, particularly women's education. In the final sections, methods to control population growth were discussed alongside various aspects of the "demographic divide." It was noted that public policy to control population growth and to plan for the changes in population structure is still evolving. From a public policy point of view, it is important to focus on these issues since they will have an increasingly important role to play in the future of the Asian region. The richer economies that underwent the demographic transition ahead of many Asian economies are now experiencing an increase in the dependency ratios through their aging populations. If this is the future of many Asian populations, governments will have to carefully plan and implement policies to ensure that a shift in budget allocations toward the care of these aging groups is not made at the expense of the welfare of other age groups in the economy.

How then should population programs be developed and evaluated? Which programs are most effective? Should ethical considerations be involved? These are clearly difficult questions to resolve, and are made more complex by the fact that we do not know enough about the costs and benefits of the different programs of population control. Furthermore, there are some revisionist population theorists that argue that the effects of population growth can be beneficial as well as detrimental. They also argue that since these decisions are made within a family, they are personal choices that tend to optimize welfare. If changes are to be made, they should be made in the external macroeconomic environment that these families face. Nevertheless, where social costs of high fertility exceed private costs—as they do in places like Bangladesh and parts of Africa—the rationale for stronger public policy measures is quite strong.

In an extensive review of the literature for the *Handbook of Development Economics*, Nancy Birdsall (1988), one of the best-known economists in this field and a former vice-president of the World Bank, says virtually nothing about public policy. Likewise, there appears to be very little information on the relative effectiveness of different public policies. Thus, there is much work yet to be done. We do know that education for women yields very high returns. We also know that birth-control measures have been effective in several countries. The benefits of other, more specialized, packages of population control are less well understood. Questions such as "How budgets should be spent?" and "What are the costs and benefits to each kind of intervention?" need to be addressed in greater depth.

REVIEW QUESTIONS

1. What were some of the factors that led to a rapid increase in population in the sixteenth and seventeenth centuries?
2. What accounts for the continued growth of the world population subsequent to this acceleration of growth in the sixteenth and seventeenth centuries?
3. Explain how rapid population growth can contribute to rapid economic growth even when the Solow and other growth models all show that population growth reduces the level of income in the steady stage.
4. Explain how demographic transition contributes to rapid population growth.
5. Do you think that countries that are poor now will experience a demographic transition similar to the countries of East Asia in the last few decades? Why?
6. What are the factors that slow down the demographic transition? Can they be speeded up? How?
7. The theory of population growth at the family level has been explained by Becker and others by treating children as commodities. Do you agree with this approach? Is something missing?
8. What aspects of having children in developing countries are not captured by Becker's model? How are these aspects different and/or similar to those in more advanced economies?
9. Do you think that the role of women in economic development is critical? Why?
10. In your own experience and those of your friends and family, do you think that the model of trade-offs between child quality and quantity is consistent with experience? Explain.
11. The explanation for the fall in population growth in Asia suggests that accelerating growth was instrumental in the rate of decline. Is it not logical then that all we have to do is concentrate on economic growth and population growth will take care of itself?
12. Why do you think that effective methods of birth control for men, apart from condoms and sterilization, have not been developed?
13. Does Asia have special population issues that are not present in other developing countries? If so, what are they?

14. How can the demographic divide be narrowed in South and Southeast Asia? Is this an important policy issue? Why?
15. It has been noted that there is very little discussion in the literature about the relative effectiveness of different kinds of population policy. Why has there not been more research on this topic?

Notes on References and Suggestions for Further Reading

There is very good documentation on trends in population growth for both the industrial and developing countries available from various international organizations. They include:

Population Division of the Department of Economic and Social Affairs of the United Nations Secretariat (http://www.un.org/esa/population/)
Population Reference Bureau (http://www.prb.org)
United Nations Population Information Network (http://www.un.org/popin/data.htm)
World Bank (http://www1.worldbank.org/hnp/)
World Development Indicators (http://www.worldbank.org/data)

Based on this information and other historical sources, several informative and interesting articles have been published in recent years. Three are strongly recommended. Angus Maddison (1995) talks about economic growth, as well as population growth, while Michael Kremer (1993) focuses on technology, and Livi-Bacci Massimo (1997) on population growth. The Kremer paper also contains an interesting model of long-run growth which highlights the interrelationship between population growth and technological change.

The *World Development Report* of the World Bank (various years) is a rich source of interesting review articles on population trends and issues. The economic historian Robert Fogel (1999) has written an interesting article both from the point of view of population growth and technology. Figure 8.2 is from page 2 of his article.

Nancy Birdsall (1988) and David Bloom and others (2003) have written interesting articles on the subject of population from an economic perspective. David Bloom and his colleagues focus on the demographic transition while Birdsall's review article touches on a wide range of population topics.

Turning to Asia, there are a number of interesting articles. The article by Andy Mason (2002) deals with recent trends and projections of population growth in Asia. There is a very interesting section on HIV/AIDS which dovetails nicely with material covered in the next chapter.

David Bloom and Jeffrey Williamson (1998) and J. Warne Sanderson and Tan Jee-Peng (1995) have written two interesting articles about the Asian experience. Bloom and Williamson discuss the role that population growth and demographic transition have played in stimulating growth in the Asian "miracle" economies. Sanderson and Tan, on the other hand, explore a number of facets of population growth. One particularly fascinating development is the speed of the demographic transition in East Asia, compared with the transition in the European countries two centuries ago. Another worthwhile reading is the East-West Center (2002) publication on the population in Asia, which provides a comprehensive study of all aspects, from family planning and fertility, gender, changing youth population and aging, to its implications on economic development.

Poverty and Income Distribution

9.1 INTRODUCTION

Despite sustained economic growth in many developing countries, poverty remains widespread. In 2005, 25 percent, or about 1.4 billion people around the world lived in poverty. Asia is host to a vast majority of the world's poor—there are 207 million in China and 455 million in India. Overall, Asia is home to more than 911 million people who struggle to meet basic food, clothing, and housing needs—that is, 66 percent of the world's poor are found in Asia (World Bank, 2008).

Equally disturbing is the fact that the gap between the rich and the poor has grown, rather than diminished, with the sustained growth in income. In 1960, the richest twenty economies in the world had per-capita incomes that were about eighteen times greater than the poorest twenty economies. After thirty-five years of record growth in total world income, this income differential has more than doubled (World Bank, 2001). Within countries, similar trends can also be observed, that is, that the fruits of economic gains over the years have accrued only to a select few.

9.1.1 The Vicious Circle of Poverty and Inequality

The alleviation of poverty and minimization of economic inequality is at the core of all development policies. This is rightfully so because children who are born into poor households will have lesser opportunities than those in richer ones. The impact of such differences is more marked in developing countries where the government faces greater constraints in its ability to provide much needed assistance to improve the lot of their poor citizens.

It is not hard to imagine how life evolves for children living in an urban slum area of Mumbai, Manila, or Beijing. Very young children are sent out to earn money by doing menial jobs such as peddling cigarettes on the streets. The children earn (little) money at the expense of attending school. Parents who are uneducated tend not to value education highly, and even if there were some incentives to educate their children, the opportunities to send their children to a good school are limited.

Furthermore, the sacrifice required to send a child to school is substantial, even if tuition charges are low. The cost of clothing/uniforms, transportation, and books are quite high relative to the income levels of the poor.

Children raised in poverty have no peer groups or role models to instill in them the virtues of education and human capital acquisition. Since everyone around them is poor, there are no opportunities for building up either human or physical capital. In many cases, drugs and crime (and perhaps sport) are the only ways out of this low-level trap. When they are old enough, they begin to have children and the cycle of poverty is repeated.

Unless this cycle is broken for many families, the result is the perpetuation of poverty to successive generations. In addition, the gap between the rich and poor in the society will be perpetuated and perhaps get worse.

9.1.2   Is Climate a Factor?

In the past, some economists have talked about a climate theory of development. Specifically, it was propositioned that a temperate climate provides a more conducive environment for economic growth. Statistics show that this theory is not without basis. Almost all successful and modern industrial economies are situated in the temperate zone, or the colder places of the world. In contrast, almost all developing economies are situated in tropical or subtropical climatic zones. Extreme heat and humidity does affect conditions of production—as heat causes a more rapid rate of soil deterioration—as well as causes the rapid deterioration of other natural resources. The health of the workforce in warmer countries is also more adversely affected as there is greater frequency of air- and water-borne infections, and diseases spread more rapidly. In addition, working in a warmer climate is more taxing on the physical body, and hence, labor productivity tends to be lower.

While the climate theory of development has long been debunked in favor of other theories, a recent study by Gallup, Sachs, and Mellinger (1999) provides fresh evidence for this theory. Mapping out the latest data on gross domestic product (GDP) per capita, they observe that countries in the geographical tropics are nearly all poor[1] and that almost all high-income countries are in the mid and higher latitudes (see Figure 9.1). Their comprehensive analysis of the complex relationship between geography and growth reveals that tropical regions are indeed hindered in development relative to the temperate regions, and attribute this to the higher disease burden and limitations on agricultural productivity in the tropics. Their study demonstrates that climate, and geography in general, continues to matter greatly for economic development, alongside the importance of economic and political institutions. From an analytical point of view, they strongly recommend the reintroduction of geographical considerations into the econometric and theoretical studies of cross-country economic growth.

9.2   MEASURING POVERTY AND INEQUALITY

Poverty, in its broadest sense, means the inability to access for a minimal or acceptable standard of living. This loose definition, however, contains subjective notions, reflecting the fact that what one needs or finds "acceptable" or "minimal" is a very relative matter. Poverty standards and definitions thus vary across different countries.

---

[1] The geographical tropics refer to the areas between the Tropic of Cancer and the Tropic of Capricorn. This is a band on the globe in which the sun is directly overhead at some point during the year.

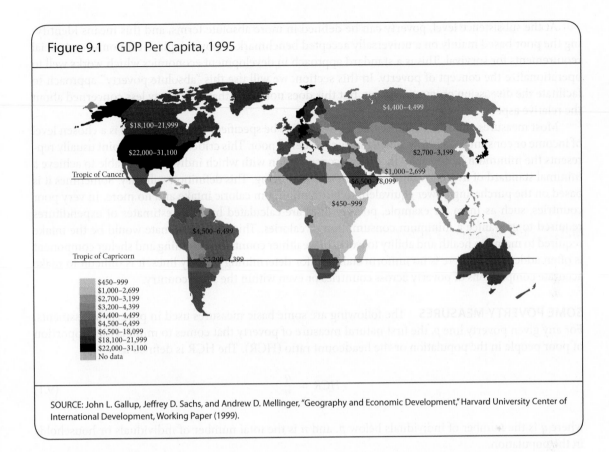

Figure 9.1   GDP Per Capita, 1995

$18,100–21,999

$22,000–31,100

Tropic of Cancer

$4,400–4,499

$2,700–3,199

$1,000–2,699

$6,500–18,099

$450–999

$4,500–6,499

Tropic of Capricorn

$3,200–4,399

$450–999
$1,000–2,699
$2,700–3,199
$3,200–4,399
$4,400–4,499
$4,500–6,499
$6,500–18,099
$18,100–21,999
$22,000–31,100
No data

SOURCE: John L. Gallup, Jeffrey D. Sachs, and Andrew D. Mellinger, "Geography and Economic Development," Harvard University Center of International Development, Working Paper (1999).

The concept of inequality can be more easily defined but is no less contentious. Economic inequality refers to the uneven distribution of income or expenditure[2] across population groups. According to some, these income gaps are inevitable consequences of growth and development and will correct itself in due course. Others, however, believe that observed gaps can be avoided or at least minimized through government intervention. This implies policy interventions aimed at assisting disadvantaged groups to improve their situation.

Clearly, these two concepts of poverty and inequality are complex and very much interrelated. In this section, we define some objective measures first and then return to these and other related issues.

9.2.1   Measurement of Poverty

In development economics, poverty is generally defined as the inability to access resources to enjoy a minimal or acceptable standard of living. This definition is simple, intuitive, and easy to understand. However, minimum needs or acceptable standards of living vary from country to country, from individual to individual, in accordance with one's cultural, economic, and social norms and expectations. Hence, this broad definition is not very useful when measuring poverty, and even less so when making cross-country comparisons.

---

[2] The economic literature on inequality strongly indicates that consumption or expenditure inequality is a better measure of welfare compared with the more traditional income inequality. To facilitate discussion in this section, we use the term "income inequality" to refer to the general notion of unequal distribution of income or expenditures in a population.

At the subsistence level, poverty can be defined in more absolute terms, and this means identifying the poor based mainly on a universally accepted benchmark of physiological, economic and social requirements for survival. This is a standard approach in development economics which works well to operationalize the concept of poverty. In this section, we will use this "absolute poverty" approach to facilitate the discussion on measurement, but this does not imply that we are any less concerned about the relative aspects of the poverty issue.

Most measures of poverty require that a poverty line be specified. The poverty line is a chosen level of income or consumption below which one is considered poor. This critical threshold point usually represents the minimum "acceptable" income or consumption with which individuals are able to achieve a minimal standard of living to maintain health and well-being. This definition will vary. Sometimes it is based on the purchasing power equivalent to buy a minimum caloric intake and no more. In very poor countries, such as India for example, poverty lines are calculated by using estimates of expenditures required to guarantee a minimum consumption of calories. This caloric estimate would be the intake required to maintain health and ability to work. In wealthier countries, a clothing and shelter component is often added. Since there is no uniform standard for determining poverty lines, it is difficult to make accurate comparisons of poverty across countries or even within the same country.

SOME POVERTY MEASURES   The following are some basic measures used in poverty assessments. For any given poverty line p, the first natural measure of poverty that comes to mind is the proportion of poor people in the population or the headcount ratio (HCR). The HCR is defined as

$$HCR = \frac{q}{n},\tag{9.1}$$

where q is the number of individuals below p, and n is the total number of individuals or households in the population.

Poverty analysts rarely rely on the headcount ratio alone as, like many aggregate measures, it fails to capture and differentiate the various "states" of poorness. In other words, the depth or severity of poverty is not reflected at all in the HCR. To see how HCR alone can give a misleading impression of poverty, consider two countries, A and B, with the same headcount ratio. In country A, all households in poverty are very close to the poverty line. With a small subsidy from the government, citizens in A could all be lifted out of poverty, in the sense that they would be on or just above the poverty line after the subsidy. In country B, on the other hand, incomes of poor households fall significantly short of the poverty line—starvation is widespread and there is very deep poverty for a large proportion of the poor. Intuitively, country B is in a much worse shape than country A, yet the poverty estimates using the headcount ratio are identical.

What is needed is a poverty measure that considers the depth of poverty. To achieve this, we take each poor person's income y and note its distance from the poverty line p, that is, take $(p - y)$ for all $y_i < p$. We then add all these differences and obtain the total income required to raise everyone's income to the poverty line, $\Sigma(p - y)$ for all $y_i < p$. This is the total income required to eliminate poverty.

This leads to two common and more informative measures of poverty. The poverty gap ratio (PGR) is defined as

$$PGR = \frac{\sum_{y_i<p}(p-y)}{nm},\tag{9.2}$$

where n is the total population, and m is the mean income. The denominator nm in this measure is the total income in the economy. A closely related measure, called the income-gap ratio (IGR), is also commonly used and is defined as

$$IGR = \frac{\sum_{y_i < p} (p - y)}{p \cdot q}, \tag{9.3}$$

where p is the poverty line and q is the total number of people in poverty as previously defined. The denominator, $p \cdot q$, is therefore the total income of the poor if they were all to have incomes at the poverty line.

As can be seen, the PGR gives the ratio of total income transfer necessary to eliminate poverty to gross national income or GNI. The IGR, on the other hand, tells us the total income needed to remove poverty relative to the total income of all poor if they are all raised to the point where they escape poverty. The IGR will be much larger than the PGR. The choice between the PGR and the IGR depends on the context of the problem that they are being applied to. By dividing the total income shortfall gap by the total income in the economy, the poverty measure may appear to be small and may indicate that the severity of poverty in a highly unequal but wealthy society is not a major concern. PGR can thus understate inequality. On the other hand, if we divide the income shortfall by the total amount of resources needed to lift everyone's income up to the poverty line as in IGR, we may be overstating the degree of poverty in the economy.

ISSUES ON POVERTY MEASUREMENT   From the working definition of the poverty line given above, a number of conceptual and measurement issues stand out. Given that we agree to a universal norm for nutrition, housing, and clothing requirements, there still remains a wide degree of variation in what individuals find "acceptable" and "minimal," as needs vary between households in different regions within a country, between countries, and between the broad regions of the world. For example, the families in some rural areas may not see the need for post-secondary education for their children, while city families may believe this is essential. Another example: one may feel poor in Australia if one does not own a car or a color TV, but in the Philippines, having neither of these conveniences is not necessarily a hindrance to a good life. As we can see, these "components" of the poverty line are evaluated *relative* to the prevailing socioeconomic standards. As such, they are important in the determination of a national poverty line.

There is also the issue of whether we measure poverty on a household or the individual level. The standard practice is to treat a household as poor when its total income or consumption level is below a chosen poverty line. Many transfer and benefit schemes and public policies are thus directed toward the upliftment of the whole household. The basic assumption under this approach is that each member of the household—the father, the mother, and each of the children in the family—are equally well-off. In practice, however, this is not always true, particularly when traditional norms are allowed to play a big role in the distribution of resources within the household. In many traditional households, boys are often favored over girls when parents have to make a choice on who goes to school and who does not. In times of a crunch in resources, such as during the Asian financial crisis, the mother may give up some of her share of food for others in the family at the expense of her health and long-term well-being.

Even without the presumed inequities in the distribution of household resources, an issue of differences in the needs of individual household members also arises. On average, children require less to sustain them than adults, and thus household incomes or expenditures need to be adjusted for such demographic differences so that figures across households are comparable. Adult-equivalent scales, which are weights applied to household members to represent relative needs, are often used to address this problem.

9.2.2 Measurement of Inequality

When an economy achieves economic growth and development, the benefits are ideally filtered down to each one (individual or household) in the society. Unfortunately, this does not necessarily happen. It is more common for the so-called "fruits of development" to accrue to some members of the society more than others. In other words, the rich gets richer and the poor gets poorer. If this is indeed true, then it is certainly a matter of ethical concern: is this right? If not, what is the ideal distribution? What is fair? But does it really matter? After all, "a rising tide lifts all boats" is often the counter argument used by people who say that we should not worry about it. Some also say that a small amount of inequality in the distribution of income is necessary so that the economy will continue to grow and develop.

This is clearly a complex issue. Before we delve into it, let us first get acquainted with a number of basic tools and measures that should be useful along the way. In the following sections, we look at common measures of inequality and a framework for analyzing inequality and economic growth/development. We also look at trends of income distribution across selected countries.

BASIC PROPERTIES OF INEQUALITY MEASURES   Conflicting results displayed by conventional inequality measures have been a major source of dissatisfaction among practitioners in the field of income distribution analysis. The overwhelming conclusion, after several years of debate and discussion, is that there is no single best measure of economic inequality mainly because the concept is essentially a normative one. Researchers today are more confident in using different measures. The choice of a measure is highly dependent on the particular aspect of inequality in question. There are, however, three basic properties that inequality measures must satisfy, and they are as follows:

1. *Mean or scale independence.* This property holds if, when all income levels are increased (or decreased) by the same proportion, the inequality measure remains unchanged. In other words, the measure must be independent of the scale of which income is measured.
2. *Population-size independence.* This property holds if an equal increase or decrease in population across all income levels does not result in a change in the inequality measure. Inequality should remain unaffected if a proportionate number of persons are added at all income levels. We should then be able to compare the inequality level in the small state of Singapore and the large country of India or China.
3. *Pigou–Dalton transfer sensitivity.* This property holds if an income transfer from a wealthier person to a poorer person that does not make the latter wealthier than the former brings about a decrease in the inequality measure. This property requires that the inequality measure be sensitive to transfers at all income levels.

In many studies analyzing income distribution, a fourth property called decomposability is added. An inequality measure has this property if it can be broken into several components—either by income source or by population. This is a useful property for identifying sources of inequality in populations.

SOME INEQUALITY MEASURES   Some of the most common measures of inequality are presented below. The notation used is as follows: Let x_i denote the income of any individual i, in a population consisting of n individuals. It is often useful to arrange incomes from lowest to highest, that is,

$$x_1 < x_2 < \ldots < x_n.$$

The sum of all incomes in the population is denoted by $\sum_{i=1}^{n} x_i$ and the average or mean income μ is defined by $\mu = \dfrac{1}{n}\left(\sum_{i=1}^{n} x_i\right)$. Note that the total income of all individuals in the economy can also be given as μn.

The first measure is the range, simply defined as the difference between the highest and lowest income, that is,

$$R = x_{max} - x_{min},$$

where x_{max} and x_{min} refer to the highest and lowest levels of income in the population, respectively. This measure will give an idea of the spread of incomes but is often limited because it ignores the distribution between the two extreme points.

The mean absolute deviation is a better measure of inequality than the range in the sense that it takes advantage of the information on each income in the entire distribution of incomes. This measure adds up all the (absolute) differences of each income x_i from the mean, and the total is then taken as a proportion of the total income in the population. Thus, we have

$$M = \frac{1}{\mu n} \sum_{i=1}^{n} |x_i - \mu|.$$

The mean absolute deviation does account for the overall income distribution but still remains unsatisfactory because it violates the property no. 3 above—the sensitivity of transfers between individuals in the middle points.

The coefficient of variation, CV, is a popular inequality measure which avoids this particular weakness of insensitivity to transfers by attaching greater weight to incomes which are further from the mean. In this measure, squaring the differences of each income from the mean does this. This measure is thus defined as

$$CV = \sqrt{\frac{Var(x)}{\mu^2}}, \text{ where } Var(x) = \frac{1}{n} \sum_{i=1}^{n} (x_i - \mu)^2.$$

This measure has many desirable properties. It satisfies both the mean independence and population size (or scale) independence properties. More importantly, it always satisfies the Pigou–Dalton property of transfer sensitivity.

Sometimes, researchers find it more appropriate to make conclusions about inequality issues through analysis of the logarithm of incomes. In this case, the measure of inequality used is the variance of the logarithm of income defined by

$$Var(\log x) = \frac{1}{n} \sum_{i=1}^{n} \left(\log x_i - \log \bar{\mu}_i \right)^2,$$

where $\bar{\mu}_i$ is the geometric mean of the distribution. Like the CV above, this measure satisfies both the mean independence and population size independence properties although it is not totally sensitive to transfers for the whole range of incomes. This is, nonetheless, often desirable because it is decomposable by income source.

The Kuznets income ratio is another popular way to analyze inequality in income distributions. This approach considers the income shares of different income groups in the population. Specifically, individuals are grouped into income quintiles and no inequality occurs when each quintile group has an equivalent 20 percent share of the nation's total income. The top and bottom ends of the distribution are of particular interest. Some inequality occurs if income accruing to the poorest 20 percent of the population is less than 20 percent of national total income. By the same token, inequality results when the richest 20 percent of the population has more than a 20 percent share of the total income. This information was first used by Simon Kuznets (1955) to come up with a simple measure of inequality. The Kuznets income quintile ratio is the ratio of the income earned by the top 20 percent of the population to that received by the lowest 20 percent. A ratio of 1.0 indicates perfect equality, and the greater the value of the ratio over 1.0, the more unequal is the distribution of income in an economy.

In general, this ratio can be obtained for any given proportion of the population, such as the top and bottom 10 percent, or deciles. Such ratios are useful for initial assessments of the inequality.

THE GINI COEFFICIENT AND THE LORENZ CURVE   Of all the inequality measures, the Gini coefficient is the most widely used. Using the same notation above, the Gini coefficient is defined as

$$G = \frac{1}{2n^2\mu} \sum_{i=1}^{n} \sum_{k=1}^{n} |x_i - x_k|,$$

which effectively sums up all possible pairs of incomes in the distribution, normalized by n^2 representing the number of all possible pairings multiplied by the mean income μ of the distribution $(x_1, x_2, ..., x_n)$. Note that the income pairings are counted twice, hence the sum of all differences is further divided by 2.

The value of the Gini index ranges from 0 to 1. A value of 0 implies that all incomes are shared equally among each unit (individual or household) in the population (perfect equality), while a value of 1 means that all incomes accrue to only one person or household in the entire distribution (imperfect inequality). Low inequality populations have Gini ratios of 0.4 or less for their distribution, while high inequality populations have Gini ratios greater than 0.4. Note that the Gini coefficient is sometimes expressed in percentage form, as is the practice by the World Bank. In this case, we simply multiply the obtained Gini by 100.

The Gini coefficient appears in various forms and one conventional formula that is computationally convenient is written as

$$G = \sum_{t=1}^{n-1} \eta_{t+1}\pi_t - \sum_{t=1}^{n-1} \eta_t\pi_{t+1},$$

where η_t refers to the cumulative share of income, and π_t is the cumulative share of population. One appeal of the Gini coefficient is that it is a very direct approach to inequality measurement, taking note of the difference between every pair of incomes. It is, by far, the most popular measure of economic inequality.

The Gini coefficient is often viewed in relation to the Lorenz curve, which is a graphical representation of the relationship between the cumulative shares of income and the cumulative shares of the population. In fact, the observed pairs $(\eta_1\pi_1), (\eta_2\pi_2), ... (\eta_n\pi_n)$ used in the computation of the Gini coefficient are used to construct a Lorenz curve. This is done by plotting the pairs of (cumulative) income and population shares in a unit box, as in Figure 9.2.

The diagonal line AC represents zero inequality while the curve tracing the points ABC is the Lorenz curve. If total income is equally distributed among members of the population, the Lorenz curve will be the diagonal line AC, which runs from the lower left corner to the upper right-hand corner of the unit square in Figure 9.2. In this case, any given proportion of the entire population enjoys the same proportion of total income. Hence, this line is referred to as the egalitarian line. In the case where total income is not equally distributed, the lower income groups usually have a smaller share of total income in the economy. In such a distribution pattern, all pairs of income and population shares will form a line similar to ABC, which is the Lorenz curve for that population. The distance of the Lorenz curve to the diagonal line indicates the extent of inequality: the further the curve is away from the diagonal line, the greater the degree of inequality.

Figure 9.2   The Lorenz Curve

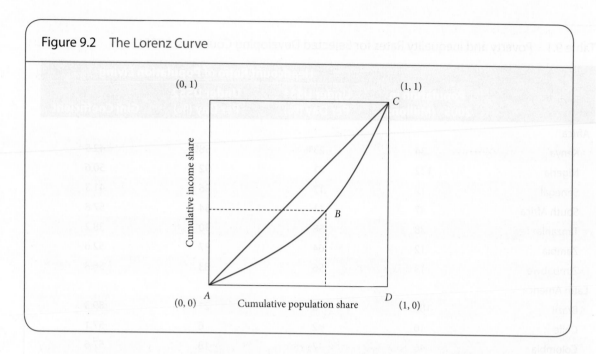

The Gini coefficient G is easily derived from a Lorenz curve by noting that it is the ratio of the area bounded by the diagonal and the Lorenz curve to the total area in the (lower) triangle. That is

$$G = \frac{Area\ between\ AC\ and\ ABC}{Total\ area\ in\ ACD}$$

9.3   TRENDS IN POVERTY AND INEQUALITY

Until recently, data on poverty and inequality have been scarce. Poverty and inequality estimates in the past had been based on group data and a long-term analysis of trends was almost impossible. Today, studies on these two important issues abound as dramatic improvements have been made in data availability and reliability in the last fifteen years or so. The most recent studies use household level data.

9.3.1   Poverty and Inequality in the World

Over the years, the World Bank has managed to conduct surveys across countries so that international comparisons of poverty can be made. Table 9.1 presents some poverty incidence rates for selected countries using the conventional international poverty lines of US$1 and US$2 per day.[3] Poverty lines for the world's regions are then presented in Table 9.2. The choice of an international poverty line is highly arbitrary and the World Bank's US$1-a-day benchmark has recently been changed to US$1.25 in light of new data (Chen and Ravallion, 2008). More recent studies present results using alternative poverty lines (see, for example, Sala-i-Martin, 2006).

---

[3] The World Bank uses PPP-adjusted GDP per capita.

Table 9.1 Poverty and Inequality Rates for Selected Developing Countries, 2005[a]

	Population in 2005* (Millions)	Headcount Ratio of Population Living		Gini Coefficient
		Under US$1 Per Day (%)	Under US$2 Per Day (%)	
Africa				
Kenya	34	23%	58%	42.5
Nigeria	132	71	92	50.6
Senegal	12	17	56	41.3
South Africa	47	11	34	57.8
Tanzania	38	58	90	38.2
Zambia	12	64	87	52.6
Zimbabwe	13	56	83	56.8
Latin America				
Brazil	186	8	21	89.3
Chile	16	<2	6	57.1
Colombia	46	7	18	57.6
Ecuador	13	18	41	43.7
Guatemala	13	14	32	59.9
Honduras	7	15	36	55.0
Jamaica	3	<3	14	37.9
Mexico	103	3	12	54.6
Panama	3	7	18	56.4
Venezuela	27	19	40	49.1
Asia				
Bangladesh	142	41	84	31.8
China	1,305	10	35	44.7
India	1,095	34	80	32.5
Indonesia	221	8	12	34.3
Laos	6	27	74	37.0
Nepal	27	24	69	36.7
Pakistan	156	17	74	33.0
Sri Lanka	20	6	42	33.2
Thailand	64	<1	25	43.2

[a]Poverty line expressed in World Bank standard PPP-adjusted dollars per capita. The data were obtained using the latest survey year between 2000 and 2005.

SOURCE: World Bank, *World Development Indicators Online* (2008).

Table 9.2   Poverty by Region, 1970–2000[a]

	2000 Population	Poverty Rates (Percent)							Change			
		1970	1975	1980	1985	1990	1995	2000	1970–2000	1970s	1980s	1990s
World	5,660,040	0.202	0.185	0.159	0.121	0.100	0.080	0.070	-0.132	-0.043	-0.059	-0.030
East Asia	1,704,242	0.327	0.278	0.217	0.130	0.102	0.038	0.024	-0.303	-0.110	-0.115	-0.078
South Asia	1,327,455	0.303	0.297	0.267	0.178	0.103	0.057	0.025	-0.277	-0.036	-0.164	-0.078
Africa	608,221	0.351	0.360	0.372	0.426	0.437	0.505	0.488	0.137	0.020	0.065	0.051
Latin America	499,716	0.103	0.056	0.030	0.036	0.041	0.038	0.042	-0.061	-0.074	0.012	0.001
Eastern Europe	436,373	0.013	0.005	0.004	0.001	0.004	0.010	0.010	-0.003	-0.009	0.001	0.006
Middle East & North Africa	220,026	0.107	0.092	0.036	0.016	0.012	0.007	0.006	-0.102	-0.071	-0.025	-0.006
Poverty Headcounts												
World		699,896	708,825	665,781	548,533	495,221	424,626	398,403	-301,493	-34,115	-170,560	-96,818
East Asia		350,263	334,266	281,914	182,205	154,973	61,625	41,071	-309,192	-68,349	-126,941	-113,902
South Asia		211,364	234,070	236,366	176,536	113,661	69,582	33,438	-177,926	25,002	-122,705	-80,223
Africa		93,528	109,491	129,890	172,175	204,364	269,733	296,733	203,205	36,361	74,474	92,369
Latin America		27,897	17,014	10,195	13,836	17,406	17,379	21,012	-6,885	-17,702	7,211	3,606
Eastern Europe		4,590	1,991	1,418	369	1,906	4,238	4,402	-188	-3,172	488	2,496
MENA		11,250	10,954	4,991	2,507	2,101	1,466	1,264	-9,986	-6,259	-2,890	-837
Fraction of World's Poor in Each Region												
World	100.0%	100.0%	100.0%	100.0%	100.0%	100.0%	100.0%	100.0%				
East Asia	30.1	50.0	47.2	42.3	33.2	31.3	14.5	10.3	-39.7%	-7.7%	-11.0%	-21.0%
South Asia	23.5	30.2	33.0	35.5	32.2	23.0	16.4	8.4	-21.8	5.3	-12.6	-14.6
Africa	10.7	13.4	15.4	19.5	31.4	41.3	63.5	74.5	61.1	6.1	21.8	33.2
Latin America	8.8	4.0	2.4	1.5	2.5	3.5	4.1	5.3	1.3	-2.5	2.0	1.8
Eastern Europe	7.7	0.7	0.3	0.2	0.1	0.4	1.0	1.1	0.4	-0.4	0.2	0.7
MENA	3.9	1.6	1.5	0.7	0.5	0.4	0.3	0.3	-1.3	-0.9	-0.3	-0.1

[a]World Bank poverty line was originally US$1.50 per day or US$570 per year.

SOURCE: Xavier Sala-i-Martin, "The World Distribution of Income: Falling Poverty and ... Convergence, Period" Quarterly Journal of Economics 121 (May 2006), pp. 351–397.

The sample of countries for Africa in Table 9.1 indicates that, by and large, poverty pervades all economies in the region. On average, these countries have about 43 percent of their population surviving on less than US$1 a day, and 72 percent on less than US$2 per day! South Africa fares the best, while the heavily-populated petroleum-based economy of Nigeria fared the worst. Poverty rates in the countries of Latin America and Asia are considerably lower, though the problem remains insidious. In Latin America, the countries of Ecuador, Venezuela, Honduras, and Guatemala are of most concern, with about 17 percent of their people living under US$1 per day, or 38 percent living below US$2 per day. In Asia, the South Asian economies of Bangladesh and India stand out, with an average of 38 percent and 82 percent incidence of those living under US$1 and US$2, respectively. Viewed another way, Bangladesh has 4 people in every 10 that are considered very poor, while in India 3.5 people in every 10 are considered very poor (using the US$1-per-day poverty line). Because of the enormous size of their populations, the poor in India and China combined make up more than two-thirds of the poor people in the world.

With regard to inequality, we find that the Gini coefficients for countries in Asia are, on average, significantly lower than those in Africa, and Latin America in particular. Of the countries listed under Asia, China registers the highest level of inequality at 44.7, followed closely by Thailand at 43.2. The others in the region have Gini levels that are significantly lower. In Africa, South Africa registers the worst level of inequality, with a Gini coefficient of 57.8, followed by Zimbabwe at 56.8, and then Zambia at 52.6. Interestingly, South Africa is seen to be the highest-earning country in the region in absolute terms (with earnings of US$212 billion in 2006), and second from the top in terms of per-capita income at US$5,390 in 2006.

Meanwhile, inequality in the countries of Latin America appear to be much worse, with many of them having Gini coefficients higher than 50. Of the listed countries, Guatemala's inequality rating is the worst at 59.9, followed by Brazil at 59.3, and then Colombia at 57.6. In fact, Latin American countries register the highest Gini coefficients in the world, and this is mainly attributed to the highly inequitable distribution of agricultural land in the region. According to statistics from the Food and Agricultural Organization (FAO), 1.3 percent of landowners in Latin America hold 71.6 percent of the land under cultivation. This impacts greatly on the degree of income distribution across the population.

Table 9.2 decomposes world poverty by region, using US$1.50 per day as the international poverty line. More significantly, it presents the poverty rates in five-year intervals from 1970, and thus makes it possible to evaluate changes across a thirty-year span. Poverty rates in Asia were close to one-third in 1970, but by 2000, they had declined to 2.4 percent. Poverty rates in East Asia were thus reduced by a factor of over 10! A more detailed analysis by Sala-i-Martin (2006) show that all countries in this region experienced a steady decline in poverty rates over time, with Papua New Guinea as the only exception. The South Asian region, likewise, exhibits an equally dramatic decline in poverty rates over the thirty-year period, with significant breakthroughs occurring primarily in the 1980s and 1990s. The success of the post-1980 Indian economy has been identified as a major contributor to this positive outcome.

In contrast, a worsening of poverty rates over time is evident in the African region. Country-to-country analysis reveals that most countries in the region had dismal growth performances over time, and hence poverty increased all over the continent. As seen in the table, the region's overall poverty rate in 1970 was at 35 percent—a rate that is only slightly higher than those of South and East Asia at that time. By 2000, poverty rates in Africa had reached almost 50 percent. This disappointing outcome of poverty rates in Africa, combined with the great success in reducing poverty in the other two poor regions of the world (South and East Asia) means that the majority of the world's poor now live in Africa. Indeed, Africa accounted for only 14.5 percent of the world's poor in 1970. In 2000, despite the fact that it accounts for only 10 percent of the world population, Africa accounted for 67.8 percent of the world's poor (see bottom pane of Table 9.2).

Figure 9.3   Regional Poverty Rates (US$1.50-a-day Poverty Line)

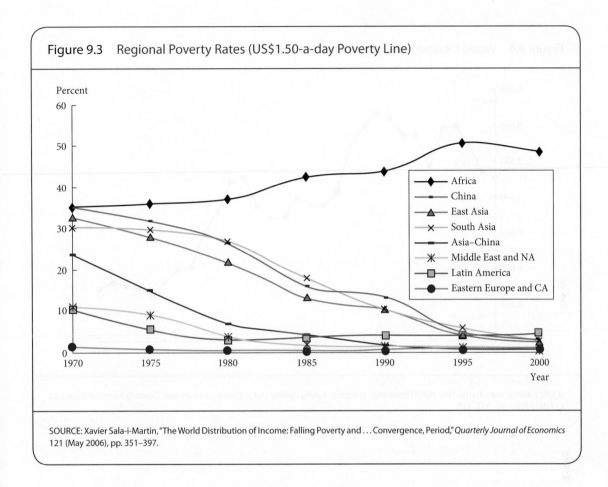

SOURCE: Xavier Sala-i-Martin, "The World Distribution of Income: Falling Poverty and . . . Convergence, Period," *Quarterly Journal of Economics* 121 (May 2006), pp. 351–397.

Past estimates of income inequality indicated that world inequality had worsened over time (Bourguignon and Morrison, 2002). More recent statistics, however, show that this is no longer true. Indeed, the gap between the rich and poor around the world declined between 1970 and 2000. Figure 9.4 shows that world income inequality, as measured by the Gini index, peaked in the late 1970s, and has been declining since then. This favorable decline in the world's inequality index reflects the rapid growth rates of some of the largest yet poorest countries, such as China and India. Also contributing to the decline were the rapid growth rates concurrently experienced by the newly industrializing countries of Taiwan, Hong Kong, South Korea, and Singapore.

Sala-i-Martin (2006) has calculated the world distribution of income for selected years using the World Bank database and the work of Deininger and Squire (1996). He simulated estimates of five income shares for 138 countries, from 1970 to 2000, and then estimated the distribution of income for each country and each year. The results were then integrated to give an estimate of the world distribution of income. They are shown in Figure 9.5 with US$1- and US$2-per-day[4] poverty lines superimposed. This chart reveals several interesting conclusions. First, comparing the 1970 and 2000 figures, the world distribution of income (WDI) seems to have changed over that period and shifted to the right. In 2000, the WDI curve depicted a normal distribution that was slightly skewed to the right, with a peak of just under US$2 per day, or about US$750 per-capita income. The country income distributions in

---

[4]   Sala-i-Martin (2006) uses PPP-adjusted GDP per capita.

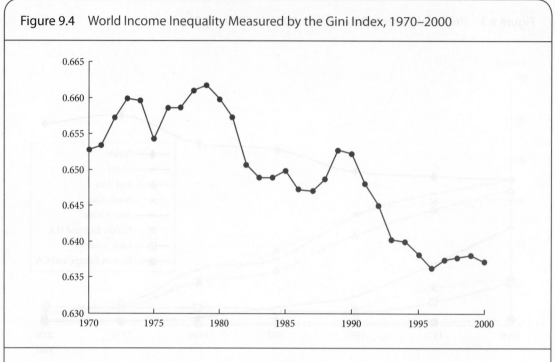

Figure 9.4   World Income Inequality Measured by the Gini Index, 1970–2000

SOURCE: Xavier Sala-i-Martin, "The World Distribution of Income: Falling Poverty and . . . Convergence, Period," *Quarterly Journal of Economics* 121 (May 2006), pp. 351–397.

the chart show that this was mainly due to the success of Chinese and Indian households in increasing their incomes. The curve flattened out from the US$6,000 per-capita income level onwards, where the thick tail represents the concentration of people in this income band in the USSR, Japan, and the United States. By the end of the century, the WDI curve was centered around the US$2,000 per-capita income level, supported by the Indian peak in this income region. In the meantime, China's income distribution curve had flattened significantly relative to India's, and caused the WDI to flatten more gradually from the US$6,000 income level.

9.3.2   Poverty and Inequality in Asia

The poverty measures for the Asian countries for 1990 and 2007 (or the latest year between 2002 and 2007 for which data were available) are shown in Table 9.3. In the first two columns, it is seen that the East and Southeast Asian economies have been very successful in lifting their citizens out of poverty between 1990 and 2007, as the proportions of people living under the US$1-a-day (PPP) poverty line had halved in most economies. In contrast, countries in South Asia had been struggling. The headcount ratio in Bangladesh and Sri Lanka increased by 2 and 1 percent, respectively, while India had managed to push its ratio down by almost 10 percent. The best performer in the group was Nepal, which reduced its headcount ratio from a high of 45.7 percent in 1990 to a low of 24.7 percent in just fifteen years.

In the next two columns, poverty ratios based on national poverty lines are presented. National poverty lines are income levels that are chosen by the countries themselves to measure poverty based on self-assessed local economic and social conditions. They are therefore not internationally comparable

Figure 9.5 The World Distribution of Income and Individual Country Distributions, 1970 and 2000

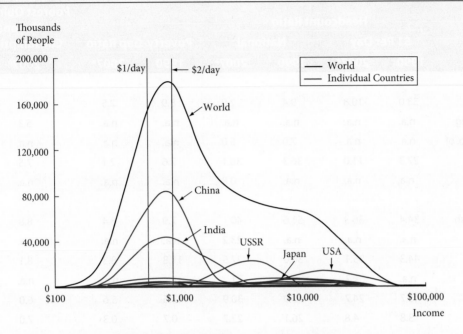

(a) The WDI and Individual Country Distributions in 1970

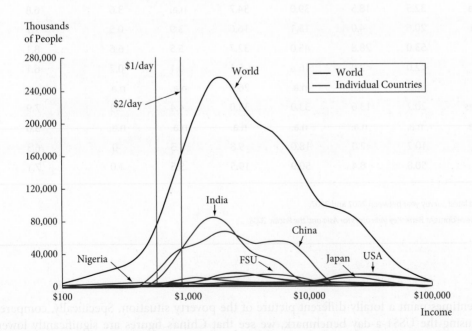

(b) The WDI and Individual Country Distributions in 2000

SOURCE: Xavier Sala-i-Martin, "The World Distribution of Income: Falling Poverty and . . . Convergence, Period," *Quarterly Journal of Economics* 121 (May 2006), pp. 351–397.

Table 9.3   Poverty Measures for Asian Economies, 1990–2007

	Headcount Ratio				Poverty-Gap Ratio		Share of Poorest Quintile in National Consumption
	$1 Per Day		National				
	1990	2007[a]	1990	2007[a]	1990	2007[a]	2007[a]
East Asia							
China	33.0	10.8	9.4	2.0	8.9	2.5	4.3
Hong Kong	n.a.	n.a.	n.a.	n.a.	n.a.	n.a.	5.3
Korea, Rep. of	n.a.	n.a.	7.0	5.0	n.a.	n.a.	n.a.
Mongolia	27.3	11.0	36.3	36.1	7.6	2.1	7.5
Taiwan	n.a.	n.a.	n.a.	0.8	n.a.	n.a.	n.a.
South Asia							
Bangladesh	34.4	36.3	51.6	40	7.9	8.4	8.8
Bhutan	n.a.	n.a.	n.a.	23.2	n.a.	n.a.	n.a.
India	44.3	35.1	36.0	27.5	11.8	8.3	8.1
Maldives	n.a.	<2	n.a.	21	n.a.	n.a.	n.a.
Nepal	45.7	24.7	42.0	30.9	13.6	5.6	6.0
Sri Lanka	3.8	4.8	26.1	22.7	0.7	0.3	7.0
Southeast Asia							
Cambodia	32.5	18.5	39.0	34.7	n.a.	3.6	6.8
Indonesia	20.6	4.0	15.1	16.6	3.9	0.5	7.1
Lao PDR	53.0	28.8	45.0	32.7	5.5	6.6	8.1
Malaysia	<2.0	<2.0	16.5	5.1	0.1	0.7	6.1
Myanmar	n.a.	n.a.	n.a.	26.6	n.a.	n.a.	n.a.
Philippines	20.2	13.6	33.0	33.0	4.4	2.3	7.9
Singapore	n.a.	n.a.	n.a.	n.a.	n.a.	n.a.	5.0
Thailand	10.2	<2.0	18.0	9.8	1.3	0	6.3
Vietnam	50.8	8.4	50.9	19.5	5.5	1.0	7.1

[a]This refers to the latest survey year between 2002 and 2007.

SOURCE: Asian Development Bank, *Key Indicators for Asia and the Pacific 2008*.

and oftentimes paint a totally different picture of the poverty situation. Specifically, compared with results using the US$1-a-day benchmark, we see that China's figures are significantly lower, even indicating large gains in poverty alleviation. All the countries in South Asia registered improvements throughout. Significant improvements were also seen in Cambodia, Malaysia, Lao PDR, Thailand, and Vietnam. There was no change for the Philippines and poverty appears to have worsened in Indonesia.

BOX 9.1

Chronic Poverty in Asia

If a family lives below the poverty line for a sustained period of time, say a few years or longer, then we can say that the family is chronically poor. If a family comes in and out of poverty depending on circumstances that are temporal in nature, such as temporary illness or unemployment, then the family is characterized as being temporarily poor. Families can experience several periods of poverty and still not be classified as chronically poor.

Chronic poverty can be mild or severe, depending on how far the family is below the poverty line. Generally, all chronically poor have had incomes below the poverty line for an extended period of time. Recently, the Chronic Poverty Research Centre (2008) estimated the extent of chronic poverty for countries around the world and these are reported in Box Table 9.1.

Who are the chronic poor in Asia? According to Adams and Jane (1995), chronic poverty is indicated if the family is in the poorest quintile of the income

distribution for three successive years. Other studies, such as by McCulloch and Baulch (1999), put chronic poverty down to being poor for five years. It is not easy to identify chronic poverty at a point in time as poverty trends can mask poverty dynamics. Some households could have moved out of poverty while others moved into poverty and are struggling to escape. Once they have fallen into poverty, intergenerational transmission of poverty is likely to occur unless they have access to education and social capital.

According to the estimates from Chronic Poverty Research Center (2008, p. 9), the likelihood of households in South Asia suffering from chronic poverty is quite substantial. Estimates range between 126 and 176 million. South Asia alone accounts for close to 40 percent of the chronic poor in the world. The incidence of chronic poverty in East and Southeast Asia is much lower, mostly in Indonesia, the Philippines, and Vietnam.

Box Table 9.1   The Poor and the Chronically Poor in East and South Asia, 2008

	Proportion of Poor Who are Chronically Poor Over Five Years		Proportion of Poor with US$1.25 Per Day	Number of Poor with US$1 Per Day (in Millions)[a]
	Low Estimate	High Estimate		
East Asia				
China	.15	.25	.25	200
Indonesia	.15	.25	.25	27
Philippines	.30	.40	.22	19
Vietnam	.35	.45	.20	19
South Asia				
Bangladesh	.20	.30	.50	75
India	.25	.35	.44	342
Nepal	.50	.60	.55	15
Pakistan	.25	.35	.22	35

[a]Figures have been rounded to millions.

SOURCE: Chronic Poverty Research Centre (CPRC), *The Chronic Poverty Report 2008–09*, Annex E (Manchester: CPRC, University of Manchester, 2008); Asian Development Bank, *Asian Development Outlook 2008*.

SOURCES: Chronic Poverty Research Centre (CPRC), *The Chronic Poverty Report 2008–09* (Manchester: CPRC, University of Manchester, 2008); Asian Development Bank, *Asian Development Outlook 2008*; Neil McCulloch and Bob Baulch, "Distinguishing the Chronically from the Transitorily Poor: Evidence from Rural Pakistan," Institute of Development Studies Working Paper 97 (1999); John Malcolm Dowling and Yap Chin-Fang, *Chronic Poverty in Asia: Causes, Consequences and Policies* (Singapore: World Scientific Publishing, 2009).

The poverty gap ratio (PGR) represents the proportion of national income required to eliminate poverty, that is, to raise each poor man's income to the poverty line so that he/she is no longer poor. In this sense, this shows poverty relative to the total resources of an economy. The table shows the figures for 1990 and 2007, and indicates that PGRs have been reduced over time. The highest PGRs are those of Bangladesh and Bhutan, at around 8 percent. This means that alleviating poverty in Bangladesh and Bhutan will require much more domestic resources compared with their Asian neighbors. It also implies that growth will be relatively harder to achieve since assisting the poor directly means having less resources to devote to production and investment.

The last column shows the consumption share of the bottom 20 percent of the population. The estimates are derived from household expenditure surveys and are a broad measure of inequality in the economy. Figures close to 20 percent are desirable as they indicate low inequality, while very low figures (less than 10 percent) indicate high inequality. Thus, the poorest 20 percent of the population in all the Asian countries covered have consumption shares between 4.3 and 8.8. This is strongly indicative of highly unequal income distribution.

Poverty indicators and their trend over the years are usually accompanied by changes in other social indicators in the economy. Thus, overall gains in poverty alleviation in Asia are both a cause and a reflection of changes in health, education, and other social indicators. From Table 9.4, we see three key social indicators for selected countries in the region. The East Asian "tigers" (Hong Kong, Korea, Singapore, and Taiwan) are in a league of their own. Their statistics register the most dramatic improvements over time, particularly South Korea, which was clearly poor in the 1960s and was the poorest of the four "tigers" in 1967. By 2005, life expectancy, infant mortality rates, and adult illiteracy rates for these countries had become comparable to the most advanced countries in the world. Consistent with the poverty measures, the table also shows that improvements in the social indicators were more significant in Southeast Asia than in South Asia. Of particular interest is the Philippines, where illiteracy had been reduced to low levels by 1995, in spite of the fact that the country was unable to make as much progress in other social areas and in achieving economic growth.

9.3.3   Income Inequality Comparison

The Gini indices for many countries have been tabulated and compiled by Deininger and Squires (1996). In general, they find that income inequalities, as measured by the Gini index, are lower in Asia than other parts of the world. For example, Gini indices of 0.5 or more are most commonly found in Latin America and in a few multiracial African countries, such as South Africa and Kenya. In contrast, the Gini indices for many developing countries in Asia lie in the range 0.3 to 0.4 and have tended to be fairly stable or even declining over time.

The details of their calculations along with other figures compiled by Quibria (2002) are shown in Table 9.5 which shows the minimum, maximum, and average Gini coefficients, as well as the average ratio of the top quintile to the lowest quintile. Generally, the table shows that income distribution in Asia is more equitable than in Latin America and that there has been a downward trend in inequality in several countries over the sample period. Thailand and Hong Kong are the exceptions.

Figure 9.6 shows the shares in the national income of the lowest and highest quintile groups in selected Southeast Asian countries and Australia. There are great disparities in income shares between these two groups in the 2002–2005 period. The ratio is highest in Malaysia, followed by Vietnam, China, the Philippines, and Thailand, all of whom register income shares for the top-income quintile at 42 percent or more. These income shares have actually improved compared with those of the 1990s, when income shares of the top quintile were all above the 40 percent mark, and those in the bottom quintile had income shares below 10 percent. Such inequalities are not quickly corrected, although the trend does seem to be downward for most countries. This is because income inequality

Table 9.4   Social Indicators in Asia

	Life Expectancy at Birth (Years)			Infant Mortality Rate Per Thousand Live Births			Adult Illiteracy Rates Above 15 Years (Percent)		
	1967	1997	2005[a]	1967	1997	2005[a]	1970	1995	2005[a]
East Asia									
Hong Kong	68	79	82	23%	5%	4%	22%	8%	9%
Korea	58	72	77	58	9	5	13	3	5
Singapore	67	76	79	26	4	3	27	9	1
Taiwan	64	75	80	24	6	8	46	6	8
Southeast Asia									
Indonesia	46	65	69	124	47	34	44	16	10
Malaysia	59	72	73	50	11	10	42	16	11
Philippines	56	68	70	72	33	28	16	6	7
Thailand	57	69	69	84	33	12	20	6	7
South Asia									
Bangladesh	43	58	62	140	75	61	76	62	53
India	48	63	63	145	71	63	67	47	39
Nepal	41	57	61	175	79	65	84	64	51
Pakistan	48	62	64	145	95	75	79	59	50
Sri Lanka	64	73	71	61	17	12	20	10	9

[a]Figures pertain to available statistics from the latest year of survey, between 2000 and 2005.

SOURCE: United Nations, "World Population Prospects: The 2006 Revision, Highlights," UNPD Working Paper No. ESA/P/WP 202, 2007.

tends to be closely associated with disparities in other social dimensions, such as in educational, health, and employment opportunities. It also includes the complex issue of gender bias in the provision of social services.

9.4   SELECTED ECONOMIC ISSUES ON POVERTY

9.4.1   Elasticity of Poverty to Changes in Income and the Distribution of Income

If we have time series information on changes in income, poverty, and income distribution, we can calculate a series of elasticity measures that give us a better insight into the relationship between income growth, changes in the distribution, and the extent of poverty reduction. Consider first the elasticity of poverty with respect to a change in income, and call it E_p.

$$E_p = \frac{Rate\ of\ change\ in\ poverty}{Rate\ of\ change\ in\ income}$$

Table 9.5   Gini Coefficients for Asian Economies, Latin America, and the United States

	Number of Observations	Gini			Standard Deviation	First Year	Last Year	Ratio of Top to Bottom Quintile	Trend
		Average	Minimum	Maximum					
China	12	32.7	25.7	37.8	3.8	1980	1992	5.2	n. a.
Hong Kong	7	41.6	37.3	45.2	2.8	1971	1991	9.5	Up
Indonesia	11	33.5	30.7	38.6	2.2	1964	1993	5.2	Level with peak in late 1970s
Korea	14	34.2	29.8	39.1	2.6	1953	1988	6.3	Up until late 1970s, then down
Malaysia	6	50.4	48.0	53.0	2.0	1970	1989	14.2	Level
Taiwan	26	29.6	27.7	33.6	1.5	1964	1993	4.7	Down to late 1970s, then up
Philippines	7	47.6	45.0	51.3	2.5	1957	1991	12.0	Down after 1965
Singapore	6	40.1	37.0	42.0	1.8	1973	1989	6.7	Level
Thailand	8	45.5	41.3	51.5	3.8	1962	1992	11.6	Strongly up
Bangladesh	10	34.5	28.3	39.0	3.5	1963	1992	5.7	Down after 1980
India	31	32.5	29.2	37.1	2.1	1951	1992	5.0	Down
Pakistan	9	31.5	29.9	32.4	.9	1969	1991	4.7	Down after 1985
Sri Lanka	9	41.7	30.1	47.8	6.1	1953	1990	8.0	Down
United States	45	35.3	33.5	38.2	1.3	1947	1991	8.5	n. a.
Japan	23	34.8	32.5	37.6	1.4	1962	1990	7.1	n. a.
Latin America	100	50.1	37.9	61.9	6.1	1950	1994	16.0	n. a.
East Asia and the Pacific	123	36.2	25.7	53.0	6.5	1953	1993	7.2	n. a.
South Asia	60	34.1	28.3	47.8	4.5	1951	1992	5.5	n. a.

SOURCES: Klaus Deininger and Lyn Squire, "A New Data Set Measuring Income Inequality," *World Bank Economic Review* 10 (September 1996), pp. 565–591; M. G. Quibria, "Growth and Poverty: Lessons from the Asian Miracle Revisited," ADB Institute Research Paper 33 (February 2001), pp. 1–123.

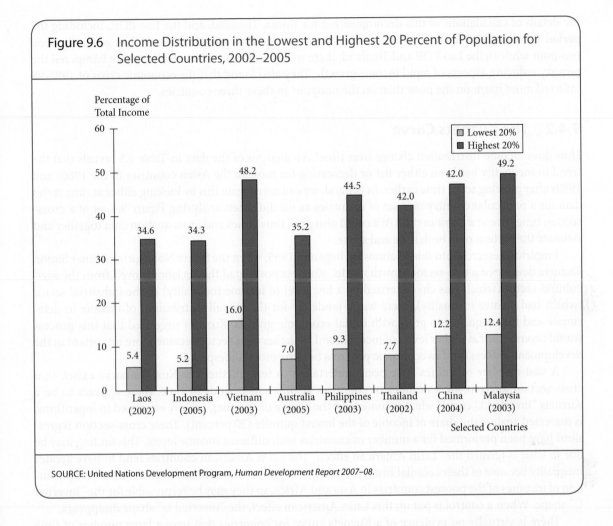

Figure 9.6   Income Distribution in the Lowest and Highest 20 Percent of Population for Selected Countries, 2002–2005

SOURCE: United Nations Development Program, *Human Development Report 2007–08*.

Referring to national poverty lines in Table 9.4, consider the case of Vietnam. Between 1990 and 2007, poverty incidence fell from 50.9 percent to 19.5 percent, about 62 percent in total or roughly 3.4 percent per year. If the growth of income in the country during that period was 6.2 percent per annum, then by dividing 3.4 percent by 6.2 percent, we get a poverty elasticity of about 55 percent. In the case of Korea, during the same period, income growth was about 8.2 percent a year, while the rate of poverty ratio fell from 7 percent to 5 percent over the eighteen-year period. This is equivalent to a 1.5 percent decrease in the poverty rate per year. The poverty elasticity in Korea thus works out to be about 12 percent. Similar calculations can be made for the other countries in the Asian region.

In addition, the poverty elasticity E_p can be divided into two parts, called the pure growth effect and the income inequality effect (see Kakwani and Pernia, 2000; and Datt and Ravallion, 1992). The first component is the percentage change in poverty when the income distribution does not change, and the second is the change in poverty if inequality changes and income does not. In the case of most Asian countries, both of these effects have been pro-poor—that is, the income distribution has become more equal over time. The income effect will always be positive. In the case of Thailand, however, a deteriorating income distribution has had a negative impact on poverty. Kakwani and Pernia (2000) report the details of calculations of this decomposition for Korea, Thailand, and the Lao PDR, including the period following the Asian financial crisis. They conclude that growth in Korea has generally been pro-poor while in the Lao PDR and Thailand, there were income distribution effects that hampered the poverty reducing aspects of rapid income growth. They also found that the economic crisis of 1997/98 inflicted more harm on the poor than on the nonpoor in these three countries.

9.4.2 The Kuznets Curve

How does income distribution change over time? An analysis of the data in Table 9.5 reveals that the trend in inequality has been either flat or decreasing for most of the Asian countries in the 1980s and 1990s after peaking some time earlier. In general, we can investigate this by looking either at time series data for a particular country or a set of countries as we did when analyzing Figure 9.4, or at a cross-section time slice at a point in time. We could also pool time series and cross-section data together and estimate the pattern over both time and space.

Empirical research into this relationship began in 1955, when the future Nobel prize winner Simon Kuznets developed a two-sector growth model. Kuznets postulated that as labor moved from the agricultural sector (which was characterized by a low level of income inequality) to the industrial sector (which had greater inequality), there was a tendency for the overall distribution of income to deteriorate and for inequality to grow with initial economic growth. Kuznets suggested that this process would reverse itself at higher levels of income (and as the services sector became more important in the development process) and as economic progress became more widespread.

A vast number of studies have been undertaken to test whether the Kuznets curve exists. In a cross-section analysis for a number of countries at different periods of time, there appears to be a Kuznets "inverted U curve" when income (and the square of income), usually expressed in logarithms, is regressed against the share of income of the lowest quintile (20 percent). These cross-section regressions have been performed for a number of countries with different income levels. This finding may be due to what is termed the "Latin American effect." The Latin American countries tend to have greater inequality because of their colonial history. Their per-capita incomes lie midway between the distribution of incomes of the poorest countries in Asia and Africa, so they may be responsible for the "inverted U" shape. When a control is put on this Latin American effect, the "inverted U" shape disappears.

There is virtually no evidence of a Kuznets curve for countries that have a large number of time series data, except England, where there was an upsurge of inequality during the Industrial Revolution. Other developed and developing countries do not have data going back that far.

Lindert and Williamson (1985) gathered longitudinal data for analysis and found that inequality declined with increased income. While their results are useful, it would be hard to generalize because the data they used covered only a few countries. For other countries, there is some evidence of an inverse U shape in the postwar period, that is, that inequality worsens as a country gets richer.

When data are pooled and a regression is run, we are implicitly assuming that all countries have the same income-inequality relationship—that is, the curve relating these two variables is the same for all countries. If the structural pattern is different, then a regression of this type will have no meaning. When researchers introduced a dummy variable for Latin America, they were assuming that all the other countries had the same relationship "among themselves," while Latin American countries had a different relationship "among themselves." When more flexibility is introduced to reflect differences in slopes and intercepts for different countries, the Kuznets curve disappears.

When we studied the process of economic growth earlier, we reviewed the work of Barro (1997) and others. In its simplest form, these economists regressed economic growth on the level of per-capita income in the base period. Then they added variables, such as education and other measures of initial human capital endowments. They found some tendency for income growth to be higher when human capital endowments were higher. In the same spirit, Alesina and Rodrik (1994), and Deininger and Squire (1998) augmented Barros' variables with initial inequality of income and inequality of land. They found that both inequality distribution variables entered the equation significantly and in such a way that lower inequality of land and income, particularly land, was positively related to economic growth. A dummy variable for democracy was insignificant.

These two studies provide some support for the argument that land redistribution is a good way to increase growth. Remember, however, that these studies are subject to the same caveats as the studies on the Kuznets curve. They were conducted on a cross-section of countries over time, with no slope dummy variables to account for different structures in different countries or country groups. What if we have a dummy for East Asia in such regression? Would it have the same consequence as the Latin American effect in the Kuznets regressions? This remains to be investigated.

9.4.3 Is Inequality a Necessary Condition for Growth?

The validity of the Kuznets inequality curve hypothesis remains unresolved. The conflicting results from empirical studies have fuelled debates about the effect of growth on inequality levels (and vice versa) and what this implies for national development. On the one hand, many economists say that inequality is unavoidable in the process of growth and that, in fact, it is necessary so that growth can be sustained. The main argument of this group is based on the belief that high personal and corporate incomes generate savings and investments, which is an important element of growth. In this sense, some people need to be rich to be able to perform this role in the economy. Accordingly, higher inequality is equated with higher growth and any attempts at redistribution (of income or assets) will only lead to lower growth. Such redistribution attempts are thus seen as defeating the purpose of development as it can only lead to longer periods of inequality.

There are many counter arguments to this line of thinking. While many development economists agree that savings and investments are important ingredients for growth, the rich in developing countries are not known to have frugal lifestyles, focusing mainly on saving and investing. In fact, many rich families in developing countries are known to splurge on luxuries. In particular, their excessive expenditures on international travel and overseas shopping sprees, jewelery, and acquiring properties in other countries do not really help domestic demand!

It was also been pointed out that low incomes and low living standards can only lead to lower growth because it limits the ability of individuals to reach their full potential. We know that people with higher educational levels work better, more efficiently and thus have higher productivity. It is the same with healthier individuals.

Another important argument why inequality should be addressed via higher incomes is that an economy made up of households and individuals with higher incomes and living standards demand more consumer goods. Attempts to equalize incomes in such an economy are thus helpful in stimulating domestic demand—and therefore assist economic growth in this way.

It has also been pointed out in the literature that when people are able to share in the so-called fruits of development—by experiencing higher standards of living as the economy progresses—they are more encouraged to actively participate in the development process. This has an important psychological effect that is greatly beneficial to national development goals.

Finally, it is important to recognize that of the two ways of raising incomes, by reducing inequality or by raising the growth rate in per-capita living standards, the latter is by far the more important approach. It would require an enormous adjustment in the distribution of income to achieve the same addition to living standards for the poor as an additional percentage point of sustained growth. Furthermore, as we have seen by looking at the data for Asia, this kind of remarkable shift in income distribution has not occurred and is not likely to happen in the future.

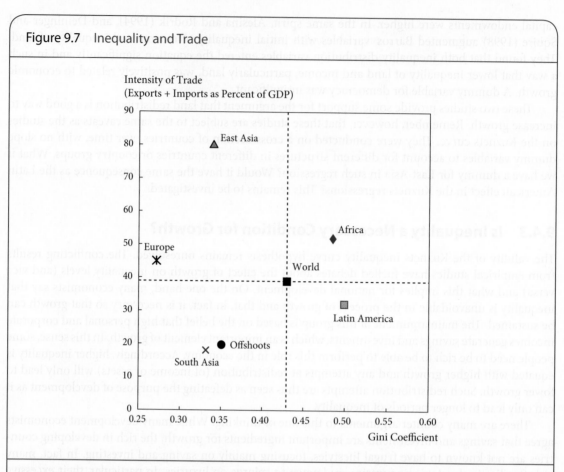

Figure 9.7   Inequality and Trade

Data refers to the mid-1990s. Offshoots refer to land-rich countries such as Australia, Canada, and the United States.

SOURCE: Juan-Luis Londono, "Comment on 'Globalization and Inequality: Historical Trends,' by Kevin H. O'Rourke, and 'Fear of Globalization: The Human Capital Nexus,' by Daniel Cohen," in Boris Pleskovic et al., eds., *Annual World Bank Conference on Development Economics 2001/2002* (Washington, D.C.: World Bank, 2002), pp. 94–102.

9.4.4   How Does Inequality Relate to Openness?

Is there a relationship between openness and income inequality in a country? This question is relevant if we want to evaluate the trend in globalization, which will be mentioned again in Chapter 11. We discuss it here because it is an important and interesting relationship that bears on our study of poverty and income distribution. Juan-Luis Londono (2002) presents a fascinating figure that shows the relationship between the Gini coefficient and the intensity of trade (exports plus imports divided by GNP) for the various regions of the world in the mid-1990s. Figure 9.7 shows that East Asia has a much higher rate of openness and a low Gini coefficient, as low as any other region besides Europe and almost as low as the United States, Australia, Canada, and South Asia. Africa and Latin America have much higher levels of income inequality, while their exposure to trade is also smaller.

An important point to note here is that East Asia has been able to minimize significant increases in inequality as it promoted a trade-based growth strategy. This has been made possible by an emphasis on trade, without a natural resource base (see Figure 9.8 comparing human capital and

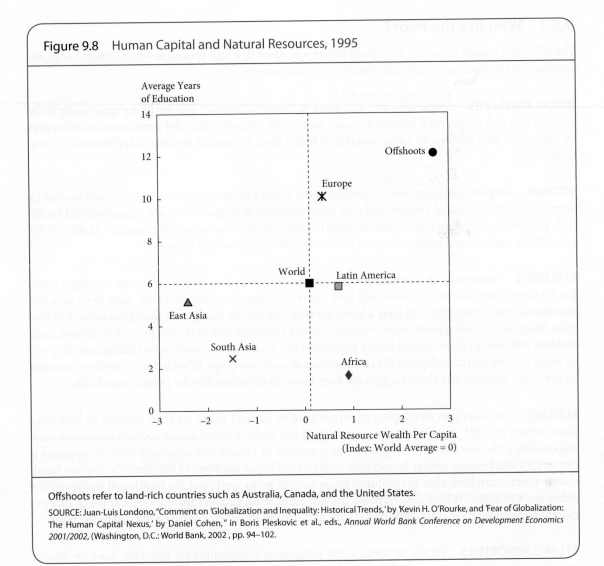

Figure 9.8   Human Capital and Natural Resources, 1995

Offshoots refer to land-rich countries such as Australia, Canada, and the United States.

SOURCE: Juan-Luis Londono, "Comment on 'Globalization and Inequality: Historical Trends,' by 'Kevin H. O'Rourke, and 'Fear of Globalization: The Human Capital Nexus,' by Daniel Cohen," in Boris Pleskovic et al., eds., *Annual World Bank Conference on Development Economics 2001/2002,* (Washington, D.C.: World Bank, 2002 , pp. 94–102.

natural resources for 1995). Latin America and Africa, on the other hand, have substantial natural resources but have not been able to convert these assets into rapid growth or trade. Educational levels have not been an obvious advantage or disadvantage in this regard. The average level of schooling in Latin America and East Asia is about the same.

9.5   The Unequal Burden of Poverty

Poverty, as experienced by countries, households, and the people within them, is rarely experienced evenly. Some countries are poorer than others, some households are poorer than others, and some individuals can experience poverty more acutely than other members of the same household. In this section, we break down poverty within a country by identifying the vulnerable groups and providing analysis on why or what made them so. Doing so provides a clearer insight into the issue and will also lay the ground for the policy discussions that follows.

9.5.1   Who Are the Poor?

The following groups of people have been repeatedly identified and proven to be the most vulnerable members of the national community because of their poverty.

RURAL DWELLERS   People who live and work in the rural areas of the world are more likely to be poor. In Asia and Africa, rural poverty accounts for over 60 percent of the total population and often over 80 percent of total poverty. In Latin America, it is less than 50 percent because of higher urbanization levels.

WOMEN   Women constitute over 70 percent of the world's poor—particularly households headed by women. A combination of current and past discrimination is responsible—low education and health indicators are the primary reasons for women's poverty. Recent studies indicate a greater likelihood for households headed by women to be poor compared with those headed by men.

CHILDREN   On average, children are poorer because the poorer households tend to be the bigger families. Children born into poor families will have lesser opportunities compared with those born in richer households. For a start, they will have a lower survival rate during infancy. As they grow older, it is also more likely that crucial opportunities in health care and education will be denied to them by default. Such children will have to share limited family resources (e.g., food, clothes) with more siblings and they will be asked to work and contribute to the family coffers at a very early age. In societies where there tradition values males above female children, girls are even more disadvantaged in the poorer households.

ELDERLY   The elderly in developing countries tend to depend solely on their families to look after them in their twilight years. While this is traditional and most children would not turn away from such responsibility, the burden of looking after aging parents in households with very limited resources is not an easy one because poorer households tend to have larger numbers of children. On the one hand, elderly parents can look after the children while parents go to work, but the health and welfare of the elders tend to suffer. Where governments provide little, if no support for the medical needs of their elderly population, medicines, health checkups and trips to the doctor can be a burden to the poor.

ETHNIC MINORITIES   Ethnic minorities and indigenous populations are generally poor for similar reasons such as discrimination and because they are rural-based—American Indians, Indians in South America, aboriginal people in Australia, Kurds in Iraq and Turkey, Tamils in Sri Lanka, Tibetans in China, hill tribes in Thailand, and the Philippines. In the United States and Australia, the human welfare indicators—life expectancy, infant mortality, nutrition and education—for indigenous populations are much lower than for the rest of the population.

9.5.2   Why Are Some People Poor?

There are three fundamental reasons why people are poor.

1. They have a very low stock of human capital, such as education, training, or skill development. In India, over 70 percent of heads of poor households are illiterate compared with about 30 percent in the general population and much less for those above the poverty line.
2. They have a very small amount of physical capital, such as land or machinery. Those lacking education, minority groups, children, and the elderly are generally poorer. This is because there is limited access to land and irrigation facilities. Those without access to land have a

much higher incidence of poverty. Much of the evidence shows that tenants do as well as owners, other things equal, and contrary to some popular beliefs, are also no slower than owner-operators in implementing new technology.

3. Even if they have physical and some human capital, their employment opportunities may be blocked because of discrimination—for example those living in backward or bypassed areas, such as the northeast of Thailand which gets little water, the dry areas of Baluchistan in Pakistan, and the outer islands of Indonesia.

Within the household, the burden of being poor rests unequally among the members. Inequalities among household members—that is, who gets the more favorable treatment for resources such as education and health, etc.—tend to be highly correlated to the member's (potential) capacity to earn income. Those who are denied opportunities tend to be females, both adult and children, and the elderly. This happens as a decision not of individuals but as a family or a household—a decision that is manifested in the actions of each family member—including those who are denied the opportunities themselves. How this decision is reached is beyond the scope of this chapter. However, it is worthwhile to note that an increase in the level of women's education has been shown to bring with it greater bargaining power in the household, and more resources to the children (especially female children) and better care for the elderly.

9.5.3   Rural versus Urban Poverty

Within a single country, the poor exists in both rural and urban areas (see Table 9.6). Particular aspects of poverty in these two regions can, however, differ significantly. For example, the incidence of poverty in the urban areas is commonly known to be lower than in the rural areas and that the illiterate, women and children bear the brunt of poverty in urban areas. The situation is changing rapidly as industrializing cities attract inward migration from the countryside. That said, the advent of rural migrants have caused poverty incidence rates to increase in the urban areas, particularly in cities where there are no government assistance programs available to ease the transition pains for such new city dwellers.

ASPECTS OF RURAL POVERTY   Poverty is usually associated with the lack of ownership of productive assets. In rural areas, the majority of the poor are found among the landless tenants or those who own very small parcels of land. The poor participate in all forms of rural non-farm employment, largely cottage and traditional industries, but in general, households with a significant proportion of income from agricultural labor tend to be poorer. In Indonesia, this group accounts for the highest incidence of poverty at 38 percent, followed by self-employed households which have agriculture as their main source of income. In the Philippines, roughly two-thirds of the rural poor are engaged in farming (including fishing). The poor there experience greater unemployment and inadequate access to modern agricultural machinery, mainly because they lack access to credit facilities.

As noted above, education is another productive asset that the poor generally lack. In Indonesia, poor households in which the parents have low education levels have a greater tendency to keep their children from attending school. These children are instead asked to help out on the farm, do housework, or look after their younger siblings. Hence, net school enrolments are lower among the rural poor compared with the nonpoor in all age groups, with the difference widening with the increase in the age of the child. Therefore, there are high illiteracy rates for poor rural households. For those who are not illiterate, there is little evidence of schooling beyond the primary level.

Because of their limited access to productive assets, the rural poor have limited capacity to improve their productivity. If some own a small parcel of land, there are limited economies of scale to be gained from improving land productivity. Additionally, because they generally have only a few years

Table 9.6   Urban and Rural Poverty in Selected Countries

	GNI PPP Per Capita, 2006 (US$)	Population Below National Poverty Line (Percent)		
		Survey Year	Rural	Urban	National
Africa	$2,550				
Sierra Leone	850	2003–2004	79%	56%	70%
Yemen, Rep. of	920	1998	45	31	42
Zambia	1,000	2004	78	53	68
Nigeria	1,050	1992–1993	36	30	34
Kenya	1,300	1997	53	49	52
Ghana	2,640	2005–2006	39	11	29
Lesotho	4,340	1999	n.a.	n.a.	68
Tunisia	2,160	1995	14	4	8
Latin America and Caribbean	8,630				
Honduras	3,540	2004	70	30	51
Ecuador	4,400	2001	n.a.	n.a.	45
Peru	6,070	2004	72	43	53
El Salvador	5,340	2002	50	29	37
Paraguay	5,070	n.a.	n.a.	n.a.	n.a.
Dominican Rep.	8,290	2004	56	35	42
Colombia	7,620	1999	79	55	64
Brazil	8,800	2002–2003	41	18	22
Nicaragua	4,010	2001	64	29	46
Asia	6,630				
Nepal	1,630	2003–2004	35	10	31
Bangladesh	2,340	2000	53	37	50
Mongolia	2,280	2002	43	30	36
Pakistan	2,500	1998–99	36	24	33
Vietnam	3,300	2002	36	7	29
India	3,800	1999–2000	30	25	29
Sri Lanka	5,000	2002	8	25	23
China	7,730	2004	n.a.	n.a.	3
Philippines	5,980	1997	37	12	25
Thailand	9,140	1998	n.a.	n.a.	14

GNI PPP per capita is gross national income in purchasing power parity (PPP) divided by the mid-year population.

SOURCE: World Bank, *World Development Indicators Online* (2008).

of education, poor farmers also tend to be ill-equipped to absorb new knowledge on how to increase farm yield through new technology. The spillover effects of technology transfer will also be limited. The poor generally have a very short planning horizon. They tend to favor solutions to problems that take effect immediately rather than concern themselves with long-term strategies. Physically, the incidence of sickness may be higher and illnesses may last longer and be more debilitating since the poor have limited access to medicines and medical facilities, and are more likely to be exposed to unclean water and poor sanitation.

ASPECTS OF URBAN POVERTY   Unemployment in rural areas drives people to migrate to urban areas—and migrants form the majority of the urban poor. Since most new migrants will not have much financial and physical capital to begin with, they will have to rely on the educational or vocational training they have had prior to the migration. Lack of such training and/or skills reduces their chances for employment and this has been identified as a major factor for poverty in urban areas. A vicious cycle of poverty perpetuates. Poverty results in high dependency rates, low education of children, and low wages, as well as significant periods of underemployment.

Unemployment rates are not a good index of employment for urban areas. These measured rates are low, but underemployment is very high in many cities. Unemployment is low simply because someone in the family must earn money or the family will starve—there is no social security system in these countries. Where do the urban poor work? The urban poor are predominantly self-employed or engaged in small-scale enterprises. They rely heavily on work in small-scale enterprises. In Asia, they operate small shops and service establishments, sell food and cigarettes, hawk lottery tickets and newspapers, repair cars and bicycles, transport passengers in pedicabs and motorized tricycles, collect and reprocess trash and scavenge in garbage dumps. In all the major Asian cities, there are many families who eke out a living by gathering and selling items collected from huge garbage dumps.

9.5.4   Poverty Affects All Markets

CREDIT MARKETS   The poor cannot borrow from formal credit markets because of the lack of collateral. Therefore, in case of an emergency or to smooth incomes, they have to go to informal markets which charge higher rates of interest.

GOODS MARKETS   Since the poor have very low incomes and cannot afford the cost of storage, they cannot buy in bulk. Thus, the cost of goods per unit is higher, often much higher than when purchased in bulk and stored.

LABOR MARKETS   In urban areas, the poor tend to find themselves living in poor communities called ghettos, in the fringe of cities. Employment opportunities in ghettos are limited and it is necessary for them to find employment far from their place of residence. Therefore, transportation expenses as a proportion of income incurred by the poor may be much higher than for other income groups. Poor nutrition contributes to low income by reducing energy levels, increasing the incidence of sickness and disease, and making the poor a bad employment risk.

9.5.5   Aspects of Labor Absorption and Unemployment

Poverty and unemployment are closely related economic phenomena. More specifically, there is usually a high unemployment rate in areas where there is widespread poverty. This is because for most households, labor is normally the only productive asset that people can depend on for their daily existence, particularly in developing countries. If there are not enough opportunities to work, it usually results in the impoverishment of the household and all its members.

More often than not, analysts need to look beyond the picture that official unemployment rates paint regarding employment conditions in the economy. A more accurate representation of the employment situation can be drawn from the underemployment rate—that is, the ratio of employed workers looking for more work to the total number of workers—which is usually much higher than the official unemployment rates.

Labor market dualism is prevalent in poor countries. This means that wages are much higher in the formal sector than in the informal sector. Unions and other restrictive practices help to retard the growth of the formal sector and perpetuate dualism. Even without strong unions, there has been a trend toward wage-setting in the formal sector, resulting in rising unemployment in Africa and Latin America.

Industrialization cannot be relied on to solve the unemployment problem in many developing countries. Industrial growth cannot supply enough jobs to absorb the underemployed and unemployed. The elimination of factor price distortions can help to improve labor absorption, but this is limited by the small size of the formal sector in some countries.

Labor market discrimination against minorities and women and children occurs in two ways—low pay for equal work and occupational discrimination. There are some occupations that are dominated by certain racial, ethnic, or social groups. Nurses and doctors are good examples of past sex discrimination. How many male nurses and female doctors are there?

9.6 POLICY: WHAT CAN BE DONE?

Rapid economic growth, more than any other factor, reduces poverty even if income distribution worsens. Unless there is rapid growth, strategies that stress social spending on the poor may work for a time but will eventually collapse under the burden of high spending. The experience of Sri Lanka is a case in point. In the mid-1980s, the Sri Lankan government embarked on an ambitious social assistance program which was helpful in alleviating the plight of many poor people in the economy. The program, however, did not coincide with a significant growth of the economy and could only be financed by larger and larger budget deficits. In the end, these programs had to be cut back. They were not sustainable because economic growth was too slow to sustain them.

There are other factors that complement growth strategies to address poverty concerns. Agricultural extension to small farmers can be very helpful when properly packaged with local support and input. Spending on rural infrastructure, particularly roads and sewage, can raise the standards of living in bypassed areas by opening up markets for agricultural products and permitting capital to flow into the region more freely. This spending is more effective when channeled to local authorities rather than undertaken by the federal government. Subsidized credit is usually ineffective in helping the poor since it is co-opted by other groups. Group lending, cooperatives, and rural development banks following the Grameen Bank (Bangladesh) model have been moderately successful.

Experience has also shown that appropriate currency exchange rates and open trade regimes can help to absorb labor and reduce poverty. Schemes to redistribute physical assets and land generally do not work in alleviating poverty. Land reform has been successful in a few cases but it is generally a failure. Establishing secure tenancy rights, with inheritance, have been more successful.

Longer-term strategies must always include the provision of education and health programs to all citizens. Experience has shown that the rates of return to education are very high. Health programs have also proven to be very helpful in the long term.

9.6.1   Some General Policy Prescriptions

Many policy options have been suggested for poverty reduction. Some of these policies have been successfully implemented in a number of countries but that does not guarantee that a particular measure will work in all countries. This is because many of these measures are difficult to implement. There is also usually some pervasive discrimination against the poor throughout the entire economic system.

Some measures that have been effective include:

1. Removal of distortions that stimulate capital-intensive production technologies—such as exchange rates, subsidies and tax breaks, and preferential tariffs.
2. Redistribution of assets in the form of land and physical capital.
3. Development of a human capital base for those who are poor in terms of better access to education, on the job training, and other programs to develop skills.
4. Implementation of a progressive tax system and imposition of high taxes on transfers of wealth within a family. Such a policy will help the government to implement its social objectives and prevent families from developing wealth dynasties.
5. A program to increase subsidies and direct transfers to the poor. Case studies of Sri Lanka and Tanzania are instructive. These two countries managed to raise life expectancy, lower infant mortality rates and improve educational levels through programs targeted at the poor. As a result, social indicators such as life expectancy, literacy, and infant mortality have improved greatly compared with other countries with similar levels of per-capita income. They succeeded very well for a time but the program became difficult to sustain when economic growth faltered.

9.6.2   Some Policies for Addressing Rural Poverty

UPLIFT THE STATUS OF WOMEN   In landless households, women experience a number of problems and challenges, particularly in South Asia, during the slack period in the agricultural season. Because of high infant mortality rates and poverty, landless families generally have relatively small families. Where some land is available, family sizes tend to be larger as children can do some chores. They can also diversify into truck gardens, raising livestock, and so forth. Thus, there is a need to provide more land, or some land, to landless women and also some employment during the slack season. For these families and the women in particular, work opportunities should form the most important thrust of public policy. For families with some land, improving agricultural efficiency can increase household incomes. Greater emphasis on truck gardening and improvement on animal husbandry would help. Greater emphasis could also be given to health and sanitation which would help women to save time and energy in doing their household chores.

RELAX TENANCY REGULATIONS   With respect to land reform, governments should relax tenancy regulations rather than try to undertake further land reforms. Furthermore, the evidence is not strong that land reform has served the purpose of reducing poverty. It is also very difficult to enact, particularly in countries where the entrenched interests are strong. Land reform in Latin America is a good example.

CHECK RURAL CREDIT SCHEMES   In the field of rural credit, there are stereotypes of the unscrupulous, gouging penny-pinching money lender who charges high interest rates to the unsuspecting poor. A benevolent government, by providing agricultural credit can do much to lift the poor onto a higher income plateau. Evidence suggests that the benefits from rural credit are minimal in most situations, and informal credit markets are often competitive and charge high rates to compensate for the high risks of lending to poor marginal farmers. Therefore, it is important to carefully evaluate government programs to assess whether they actually improve economic efficiency in a situation where the availability of financial resources to rural households is constrained.

ENCOURAGE LABOR MIGRATION   Seasonal and long-run labor migration will help to reduce poverty in the rural areas, which is usually much higher than in the urban areas. This would be of particular benefit to landless peasants. Since urban areas are also growing relatively faster than rural areas, particularly where openness and industrialization have promoted rapid growth, policies to facilitate such movements would yield high returns. Information networks subsidized by the government could also help to facilitate rural to urban migration. The elimination of bureaucratic restrictions on migration would also help. The case of China is a good example. There has been a massive internal migration from the central and western provinces to the eastern and coastal provinces, particularly to the Pearl River delta area and to the export processing zones, as well as Shanghai and the Pudong area. Initially, the government discouraged such migration and refused to provide any support to the migrants. Now migrants can avail themselves of some subsidized food although they are still illegal in the sense that they do not have residence permits.

PROVIDE RURAL INFRASTRUCTURE   Provision of rural infrastructure, particularly in the poorer areas, can improve the integration of bypassed and backward regions into the mainstream of economic activity and increase the poor's access to markets. This is particularly true of roads and access to electricity. Studies of rural road networks show high returns to secondary roads, particularly where they are linked to growing urban markets for rural produce. These road networks also permit easier access of migrant labor to the cities. Generally, greater integration of the rural areas with the rest of the economy is desirable, although there are some risks, since there will be a reduction in self-sufficiency. Many studies on the rates of return to various rural projects show that road construction and improvement is one of the most effective ways to increase incomes in rural areas.

APPROPRIATE CURRENCY EXCHANGE RATES   When exchange rates are overvalued, it taxes exports and subsidizes imports. Both of these actions hurt the farmers. By modifying the currency exchange rate regime, the terms of trade for the agricultural sector are improved and rural incomes will rise. Other policies that promote rapid growth are also useful since they create employment opportunities and induce the marginal farmers and the landless to move into industrial sector employment. This process has resulted in virtually full employment in Korea, Taiwan, and Malaysia, and to a lesser extent, Thailand.

ESTABLISH PROPERTY RIGHTS   It is important to establish property rights. If this is not workable, then security of tenure and the ability to sell the ownership rights should be established. In Thailand, for example, forests have been converted (illegally) to farming. Yet, even though the land has been farmed for many years, the tenants have little incentive to undertake improvements that would raise productivity because without the proper ownership documents, there will always be the possibility of poaching or that the government will confiscate their land. There are also adverse environmental effects to these policies. Secure tenancy brings with it the possibility of using the land as security to borrow funds, to undertake improvements, and to adopt better and more efficient technology. In Thailand, for example, more secure tenure would allow farmers to take up part-time employment in the urban areas during slack seasons without the risk of losing their land to other poachers because they have no security of tenure.

9.6.3 Some Policies for Addressing Urban Poverty

ACCELERATE ECONOMIC GROWTH Since there is no land to redistribute and the provision of infrastructure is not so much of an issue, the major "poverty alleviation" policies required in urban areas have to be geared toward increasing the rate of income growth. Local business and domestic production need to be encouraged and promoted. The entire set of policies discussed in Section 9.6.1 and the particular exchange rate argument made with respect to rural poverty in Section 9.6.2 are relevant here. An appropriate currency exchange rate is important in urban areas because an overvalued exchange rate makes capital-intensive imports cheaper and impedes the development of labor-intensive manufacturing activities. In other words, an overvalued exchange rate would stifle the economy's ability to support small local businesses and also penalize those which manufacture for export. On the other hand, a market-determined exchange rate would be more stimulating to the local economy. The increased production activities will generate more employment and be much more effective in raising the living standards of the poor.

PROVISION OF SOCIAL SERVICES Provision of social services such as education and health also plays an important role in reducing urban poverty. In fact, Sri Lanka achieved very high levels of life expectancy and low infant mortality rates by making social services available to both urban and rural residents. The Indian state of Kerala has an exemplary record of providing social services. However, as the experience of both Kerala and Sri Lanka demonstrate, such programs cannot be sustained without rapid economic growth. The government budget will not be able to provide the resources because tax revenues will not rise. Thus, the targeting needs to be done very carefully.

DEALING WITH SQUATTERS One-third of urban residents in Asia (Deolalikar et al., 2002, p. 27)—perhaps higher in Africa and lower in Latin America—live in substandard slums and squatter settlements. This means households with ten or more people to a room, with no permanent roof or walls, unsecure tenancy, and little or no access to safe water and sanitation facilities. Many governments have addressed the squatter problem by building heavily-subsidized housing for the poor. While this solution was popular with policymakers, the desired social outcome—improved living standards and poverty reduction in the urban areas—did not materialize. The poor reacted differently from what was generally expected. First, most of the poor could not afford to maintain the property. Instead, these properties were rented out to the nonpoor who had enough resources to rent and maintain it. The experience in Manila, Jakarta, Bangkok, and other Asian cities suggests that it is better to provide sites and services, good drainage, some water and sewage facilities, and security of tenure. The poor will then build their own homes, usually slightly better than those they had occupied in the squatter settlement. Finance for house construction could also be provided but so far there has been little success, mainly because the poor are so poor that they cannot afford to pay any rental or mortgage. This is the reason that they are living where they do—paying no rent.

LAND USE More rational land-use schemes need to be developed. In general, rent controls do not allocate resources effectively and often result in the deteriorating stock of housing because of poor maintenance of rent-controlled properties. More competitive markets that reflect land values for urban land need to be established. Squatter settlements are often in prime real-estate locations, yet resettlement is difficult because urban infrastructure is often not available to transport them into the city if they are resettled. The cases of Bombay and New York are instructive. In Bombay, a few people control much of the urban land and as a result, little land is available for accommodating the influx of immigrants from the countryside. Thus, slums grow rapidly. In addition, the cost of land has escalated and prices for all housing have risen. In New York, rent controls resulted in many landlords abandoning apartment buildings—it was not economically viable to maintain them. As a result, many blocks of flats in Manhattan and other boroughs were left empty. And the land is valuable! Because of poor land-use policy, the land in both cities has been inefficiently distributed and priced. To complicate matters further in other cities in Asia, the military has control over large sections of the urban landscape. The Philippines and Thailand are good examples. These two cities have terrible traffic congestion that could be partially relieved if these large holdings were converted to private use. Such a program has recently been started in the Philippines.

9.7   CONCLUSION

The Asian developing countries have generally been extremely successful in reducing poverty during the past several decades. This success has mainly been the result of rapid economic growth. Selectively, other factors have also been important in helping reduce poverty, particularly among disadvantaged groups that have benefited from specific policies designed to target them, such as asset redistribution, land reforms, and some subsidy programs. Generally, however, these policies have not played a major role in poverty reduction. Many policy changes and outcomes in the education and health sectors have been supportive of poverty reduction and have contributed to more rapid growth. These include a massive education program that has virtually eliminated illiteracy in several countries, and public-health programs that have reduced infant mortality rates and increased life expectancy. It is hard, however, to identify the extent to which these programs have, in and of themselves alone, contributed to a reduction in poverty.

To take advantage of the potential benefits that can be gained from globalization and the commensurate spread of technology and increases in productivity, the poorer countries in Asia will have to further develop their economies and their policy frameworks to benefit from this enhanced flow of resources. This will require developments in the labor markets, especially human resource development, as well as macroeconomic and sector policies that enhance competition and increase economic efficiency, while at the same time opening up opportunities for the poor.

Notes on References and Suggestions for Further Reading

The topic of poverty and income distribution has perhaps drawn more interest than any other single topic in economic development. Reducing poverty is the avowed objective of the World Bank, the Asian Development Bank, and other regional development agencies, including the Inter-American Development Bank and the African Development Bank. Economists in the developing countries, particularly India, have also been drawn to the topic, and hundreds of articles are written each year on the subject. The field is so vast that it is difficult to pick only a few key articles. Nevertheless, some do stand out. First, for the data on poverty, the World Bank is an important resource. The data set assembled by Klaus Deninger and Lyn Squire (1996) has enabled many other economists to discuss and test numerous theories of poverty and income distribution. Building on this data set, Xavier Sali-i-Martin (2006) has developed a series of income distribution statistics for a number of countries that is quite fascinating. Many new studies on this topic that also use World Bank data sets have been published. That of Chen Shaohua and Martin Ravallion (2008) is particularly significant because they redefine international poverty lines that deviate from the World Bank's standard measure of US$1 a day to US$1.25 a day standard in light of new data.

There are a number of ways to measure poverty and income distribution. Several good references are available, although the discussions can sometimes be very technical. A. B. Atkinson (1975) is the primary source for income distribution, while Amartya K. Sen's (1976) article reviews different measures of poverty.

Simon Kuznets (1955) first studied the relationship between income distribution and the level of income, and his research spawned a voluminous series of articles on this subject. Deininger and Squires' work (mentioned above) shows that the Gini coefficient does not change much over time. Their work is a good example of the application of Kuznets' analysis using an up-to-date sample showing that the Kuznets' curve does not find much support using this data set.

An interesting recent article by Kristin J. Forbes (2000) analyzes the relationship between growth and income distribution and finds that countries grow faster at the outset if income distribution is more equitable, but over time, when income distribution improves, growth tends to slow down.

For the Asian economies, the recent work of the Asian Development Bank (2008) stands out. For a comprehensive analysis of urban and rural poverty in the 1970s and 1980s, see the books edited by M. G. Quibria (1994, 1996) and Ernesto M. Pernia (1994), and journal articles by Francois Bourguignon and Christian Morrison (2002).

References for Box 9.1 on chronic poverty include that by the Chronic Poverty Research Centre (2008), the Asian Development Bank (2008), the article by Neil McCulloch and Bob Baulch (1999), and the book by John Malcolm Dowling and Yap Chin Fang (2009).

Simon Kuznets (1955) first studied the relationship between income distribution and the level of income, and his research spawned a voluminous series of articles on this subject. Deininger and Squires' work (mentioned above) shows that the Gini coefficient does not change much over time. Their work is a good example of the application of Kuznets analysis using an up-to-date sample showing that the Kuznets curve does not find much support using this data set.

An interesting recent article by Kristin J. Forbes (2000) analyzes the relationship between growth and income distribution and finds that countries grow faster at the onset if income distribution is more equitable, but over time, when income distribution improves, growth tends to slow down.

For the Asian economies, the recent work of the Asian Development Bank (2008) stands out. For a comprehensive analysis of urban and rural poverty in the 1970s and 1980s, see the books edited by M. G. Quibria (1993, 1996) and Ernesto M. Pernia (1994), and journal articles by Francois Bourguignon and Christian Morrison (2002).

References for Box 9.1 on chronic poverty include that by the Chronic Poverty Research Centre (2008), the Asian Development Bank (2008), the article by Neil McCulloch and Bob Baulch (1999), and the book by John Malcolm Dowling and Yap Chin Fang (2009).

Human Resource Development: A Focus on Education and Health

10.1 INTRODUCTION

In recent years, development economists have begun focusing on human resources as a vital component in stimulating rapid economic growth. While physical capital and natural endowments of land and resources are also important, human resources play a critical role in bringing about the structural and technological transformations that are required to industrialize and raise per-capita incomes rapidly. People, not machines, make the crucial decisions that result in improved allocation of resources and the implementation of new technology. They save and invest in new technology and infrastructure, and also decide how resources are to be used and mobilized. It is therefore critical that these human resources be developed and nurtured to ensure that they are capable of making these important decisions.

Human capital is defined as human capacities that raise productivity. Labor productivity increases in particular are essential for sustained growth in the economy. The improvement of human capital has therefore become a prime objective in economic development in many countries, including those in Asia. The main channels of intervention are through the provision of education and better health and nutrition. A well-educated, highly-skilled and healthy citizenry makes for a highly productive workforce. Investments in human capital accumulation can only lead to increased income and improved standards of living.

Hence, the policy imperative for Asia is one of pursuing economic growth and development alongside continued investment in its people through the provision of education and better health. Human capital investments in health and education are an effective mechanism for bringing marginalized groups into the mainstream. Such human capital investment not only provides people with better skills to participate in the economy, but also gives them greater capacity to deal with external shocks and to pursue choices that are welfare enhancing for themselves and those around them. There is widespread evidence that education is one of the most prominent determinants of movements out of chronic poverty. Health-related shocks, on the other hand, push people into poverty. The growth elasticity of poverty is another important consideration in terms of the impact of growth. Empirical evidence suggests that the impact of economic growth on poverty is greater with higher levels of human capital. For example, evidence from Indian state-level data indicates that, although growth was associated with poverty reduction, the extent to which poverty declined varied substantially between states. The higher the level of public expenditure on development and basic education and health, the greater the responsiveness of poverty to growth (Ravallion, 2001, 2004).

This chapter focuses on how the Asian economies have been able to undertake such investments and how resources have been devoted to the task of raising educational attainment and improving health to complement the growth of physical capital and adapt to a dynamic economic environment, both domestically and internationally. We will also discuss some of the issues and challenges faced by these Asian economies in their efforts to provide health and education services for their populations.

10.2   THE ECONOMICS OF EDUCATION

Education can be defined broadly as any or all forms of human learning. It can be formal, involving a schooling system with a structured program, using textbooks and having lessons within the confines of a classroom. It can also be informal, where knowledge is acquired in a very unstructured way, as children learn from their parents and relatives, or through apprenticeship schemes that teach a trade. Children learn planting techniques and other skills in the fields as they watch their elders, and eventually become part of the agricultural community as a result of this kind of informal training. In this chapter, however, we focus on formal education, which has been the principal mechanism for developing human skills and knowledge over the past few centuries. This is what we refer to as education in this chapter. It includes primary, secondary, and tertiary education.

A rapid expansion of the public educational system occurred worldwide from the 1960s onwards, as governments in both developed and developing countries became convinced that the provision of educational opportunities to the largest possible section of the population was a critical component for national development. Many countries in the developing world made a commitment to provide universal primary education and also to make a sustained effort to spread education more widely at the secondary level.

Several factors led to this approach. First, there was mounting empirical evidence that educational attainment and economic growth and development were closely related. On a microeconomic level, this was reflected by the high correlation between educational attainment and earnings for a whole range of occupations in many countries (see, for example, Psacharopoulos, 1994). It is no wonder then that governments have been willing to spend a significant proportion of their national incomes on public education. In the same way, it is also not surprising that parents became more willing to devote a larger part of their disposable income to the education of their children. At the macroeconomic level, it was reflected by a significant relationship between increases in expenditure on education and the level of educational attainment and rates of growth in income in several countries. Furthermore, the developing countries were able to observe that educational levels were much higher in the industrial countries and that this was one reason why they were able to continue to develop new technologies and increase productivity.

10.2.1   Factors Affecting Spending on Education

Growth in demand for public education is partly a result of growth in real income per capita. The income elasticity of public expenditures on primary and secondary education has been estimated to be around 1.5, suggesting that when incomes double, spending on education will rise by 150 percent (Schultz, 1988, p. 546). The education process is labor-intensive by nature, but studies have consistently shown that productivity has not increased much in this sector. Additionally, there has been a decline in teacher salaries relative to average incomes in many countries. The low remuneration has clearly helped to keep the cost of education at the primary and secondary levels affordable, but if the trend continues, the teaching profession may in the long run find it difficult to attract enough highly motivated and capable individuals. Certainly, keeping the balance between the quality of teachers and the cost of providing education is a huge challenge for policymakers.

In the developing countries, the rapid growth of the population has resulted in a substantial increase in the number of school-age children. This has placed a heavier burden on the carrying capacity of school systems, which has resulted in split shifts, a reduction in the expenditures per student, larger classes, and shared text materials in some cases. Given the limited resources and the large demand for public educational services in the developing countries, many conclude that the quality of public schooling has deteriorated in many of these countries in the past few decades.

In some developing countries, the shortfall in the supply of educational services relative to demand has led to the growth of privately funded schools. Some policymakers favor such developments not only because it takes the pressure off the public purse, but also because many economists and policymakers believe that a privately run school system is more responsive to shifts in demand and other economic forces than a public education system.

There is a risk, however, that a private school system may perpetuate the maintenance of social elites as the rich would send their children to better private schools and the poor would have to be satisfied with an inferior public school system. As a result, in many developing countries where private education has been allowed to flourish, this twin system of providing educational services to the population has led to inequalities in "quality," a dichotomy that continues into the provision of tertiary level education. It also affects employment outcomes as employers in such developing countries tend to favor graduates of private schools over their public school counterparts.

10.2.2 Rates of Return to Education

EVIDENCE FROM MICROECONOMIC STUDIES   Evidence from microeconomic studies suggests that there are high rates of return to investment in education for the individual. Nevertheless, since education is considered to be a merit good, there is a rationale for government subsidies. Society benefits from the positive externalities that arise from the provision of education, particularly at the primary and early secondary levels. For example, it is generally agreed that educated people are more law-abiding and hence, make better citizens. They can make more informed decisions in voting and be more responsible citizens. They may also contribute "social" goods such as music, art, literature, science, and so forth, which have value to the society beyond the return to the individual.

The problem in assessing whether there is a divergence between social and private returns is how to evaluate the returns to the individual as opposed to the returns to society. Theoretically, private returns to education can be calculated as the internal rate of return to the individual that equalizes the present discounted private opportunity cost and direct cost of schooling with the discounted value of the after-tax gain from schooling. Social returns to education add in subsidies to the costs and on the returns side, add net benefits to society and taxes paid by the individual (see Figure 10.1). The major reason that education is subsidized is that the external benefits are thought to be very high (including the positive effects of income redistribution that education also addresses).

What are the rates of return for different levels of education? Are social returns higher than private returns as we expect them to be? Microeconomic analysis on returns to education have been carried out in many countries (see Psacharopolous, 1994). The studies generally suggest that scarce resources are best spent on primary education, where both social and private returns are highest, with successively smaller shares of "public" resources devoted to secondary and tertiary education. There

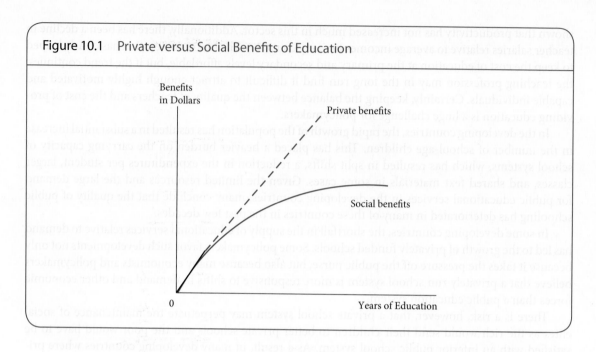

Figure 10.1   Private versus Social Benefits of Education

are two reasons for this conclusion. First, the cost of primary education is much lower (per capita), and the social returns are perceived to be very high. Furthermore, both social and private returns decline with higher levels of education, particularly beyond the secondary level. The additional burden on public resources is also substantially higher per pupil at the tertiary level. Psacharopoulos summarizes a number of studies that show that the returns to primary education can be more than 25 percent, but falling to around 15 percent for secondary education, and slightly lower for tertiary education.

In Figure 10.2a, the stylized graph shows that expected private returns always exceed private costs regardless of the number of schooling years. It further shows that private returns to education rise at an increasing rate while costs expand at a slower rate. Thus, private returns to tertiary education may be even higher than those for secondary education, despite the possibility of diminishing returns setting in. In Figure 10.2b, the social returns and costs to education are presented. Social returns far outweigh social costs at all levels of education, with most gain accruing at the primary and secondary levels. The earlier years of schooling show the highest net social gain because the receipt of a basic education enables people to be better citizens through their literacy and numeracy. The gains then taper off at the higher levels. In the graph, this net social gain is calculated as the vertical distance between the social returns and social costs curves. Maximum gains will be at that point where the slope of the two curves equal each other. In the graph, this is around the fifth year of schooling.

There is a further difficulty with subsidized public education at the tertiary level, apart from the fact that social costs exceed social returns. The public education system is generally criticized for being less responsive to changes in demand than a private system. From this point of view, a dramatic shift in demand for job skills in the labor market would be better addressed by an educational system which has a larger private component and which is, therefore, better able to respond to changing relative wages. As an example, notice that private schools specializing in computer technology and languages have mushroomed all over developing Asia in the past few decades in response to a growing demand. The private sector is leading the response of the educational system in providing facilities for learning these languages and technical skills.

Figure 10.2   Private versus Social Benefits and Costs of Education

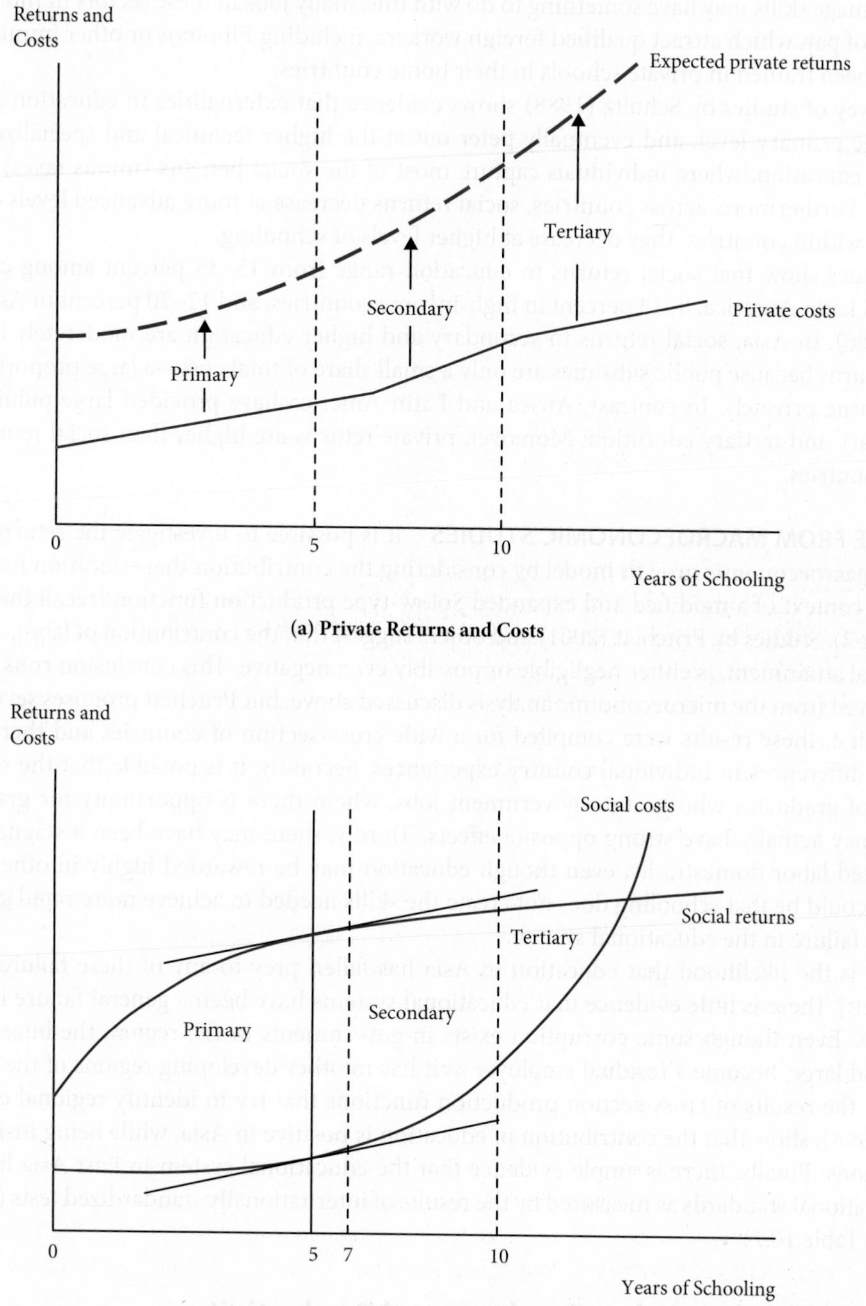

(a) Private Returns and Costs

(b) Social Returns and Costs

Where the school system has not been able to accommodate the growth of private schools as rapidly, it has a tendency to fall behind. In Indonesia, for example, the predominantly public educational system has been unable to generate a supply of highly trained financial and managerial professionals. While language skills may have something to do with this, many jobs in these sectors in Indonesia offer high rates of pay, which attract qualified foreign workers, including Filipinos or other immigrants who may have been trained in private schools in their home countries.

A survey of studies by Schultz (1988) shows evidence that externalities in education are greatest at the basic primary level, and eventually peter out at the higher technical and specialized levels of university education, where individuals capture most of the social benefits (minus taxes) from their education. Furthermore, across countries, social returns decrease at more advanced levels of development and, within countries, they decrease at higher levels of schooling.

Estimates show that social returns to education range from 15–35 percent among countries in Africa and Latin America, 8–13 percent in high-income countries, and 12–20 percent in Asia (Schultz, 1988, p. 586). In Asia, social returns to secondary and higher education are moderately higher than private returns because public subsidies are only a small share of total cost—a large proportion of total costs is borne privately. In contrast, Africa and Latin America have provided large public subsidies to secondary and tertiary education. Moreover, private returns are higher than social returns in low-income countries.

EVIDENCE FROM MACROECONOMIC STUDIES It is possible to investigate the returns to education in a macroeconomic growth model by considering the contribution that education makes to output in the context of a modified and expanded Solow-type production function (recall the discussion in Chapter 2). Studies by Pritchett (2001) and others suggest that the contribution of labor, adjusted for educational attainment, is either negligible or possibly even negative. This conclusion runs contrary to those derived from the microeconomic analysis discussed above, but Pritchett proposes several reasons for this. First, these results were compiled for a wide cross-section of countries and therefore, there would be differences in individual country experiences. Secondly, it is possible that the rent-seeking behavior of graduates who go into government jobs, where there is opportunity for graft and corruption, may actually have strong opposite effects. Thirdly, there may have been a stagnant demand for educated labor domestically, even though education may be rewarded highly in other countries. Finally, it could be that schooling does not create the skills needed to achieve more rapid growth. This suggests a failure in the educational system.

What is the likelihood that education in Asia has fallen prey to any of these failures suggested by Pritchett? There is little evidence that educational systems have been a general failure in the Asian economies. Even though some corruption exists in governments in the region, the bureaucracy has not, by and large, become a residual employer as it has in other developing regions of the world. Furthermore, the results of cross-section production functions that try to identify regional effects, done by Lau (1996), show that the contribution of education is positive in Asia, while being insignificant in other regions. Finally, there is ample evidence that the educational system in East Asia has achieved high educational standards as measured by the results of internationally standardized tests (see Mingat, 1995; and Table 10.7)

10.2.3 Education, Labor Earnings, and Productivity

EDUCATION INCREASES LABOR MARKET EARNINGS There is considerable evidence that education and experience explain a large proportion of the variation in labor market earnings. This is true for many different countries and is a powerful reinforcement on the importance of education as a tool for lifting incomes, alleviating poverty, and improving income distribution.

EDUCATION AND PRODUCTIVITY   How does education enhance productivity? This subject has been studied most often for the case of farmers—a workforce group for which researchers have a long tradition of econometric production and management studies. Based on this body of studies, there are three main channels through which education can affect productivity.

1. Education might enhance the productivity of measured inputs, including that of an hour of labor.
2. Education reduces the cost of adjusting to changes in the mix of inputs and outputs to production. For example, more educated workers are able learn the use of new machinery at a shorter time than uneducated workers. A more educated workforce implies less cost in the search for the most efficient combination of inputs to production.
3. Education increases the ability of workers to adapt to new technology and their willingness to change the traditional ways of doing things.

The studies also show significant differences in the adaptive response of more educated workers. In the case of farmers, the studies have found that those who had more years of schooling were more flexible and adaptable in the sense that they were able to find off-farm employment during the slack periods.

10.2.4   Education and Women: The Virtuous Cycle of Education

Women's education has many direct and indirect benefits in the development process. Improving women's education has the beneficial external effect of decreasing fertility and infant mortality rates, and of increasing the "quality" of surviving children, who tend to be better educated and healthier. In this "virtuous cycle," educated women feel greater empowerment within the home, take better care of themselves and their offspring physically, and feel a greater responsibility to have fewer children. How this process takes place is still not well understood. One possible approach is to look at the household as a production unit and to model how greater schooling allows the household to better purchase health inputs, given the greater earning power of the woman outside the home, the increased productivity of the working mother at home, and her efficiency in using health inputs.

BARGAINING MODELS   Alternatively, the household can be viewed as a bargaining situation between husband and wife. Having a higher education raises the opportunity cost of having children and increases the bargaining power of the mother within the home, allowing her to obtain more resources within the family for herself and her children. Both models are difficult to estimate, given the scarcity of data, and are complicated by the fact that often the husband's education tends to be highly correlated with his wife's. This is particularly true in highly educated families. Therefore, it is difficult to separate the individual influence of either of the two bargaining agents. Nevertheless, there is some evidence that women's participation in the labor force is suppressed in societies where the social norms are traditional, and where women are discouraged from entering the workforce and urged to stay at home. In these cases, there may be beneficial effects on infant mortality and general child health without a commensurate increase in labor-force participation on the part of women.

Cameron, Dowling, and Worswick (2001) generally confirm this conclusion in a recent study. As part of a broader study of the determinants of labor-force participation rate (LFPR) in Korea, Sri Lanka, Thailand, the Philippines, and Indonesia, they examine the role of women's education. They found that tertiary education had a significant impact in raising women's participation in the labor force in four of the five countries (Korea was the exception). By contrast, primary and intermediate education had a limited impact on LFPRs, with the exception of Indonesia. They conclude that it is important to consider the cultural context and that in countries with traditionally-defined gender roles, such as in Sri Lanka and Korea, increases in labor-force participation is less likely to raise LFPRs than in economies where gender roles are less rigidly defined, such as the Philippines and Thailand.

10.3   EDUCATION IN ASIA

In most nations in the Asian region, the rapid expansion of educational opportunities is seen as a key strategy toward sustained growth and long-term national development. Resources have, therefore, been and continue to be expended so that enrolment rates are continuously improved and literacy rates increased, in line with the general commitment of providing universal education in the shortest possible time. The country's income per capita and its dependency ratio are the two important variables that play central roles here. Per-capita income and dependency ratio jointly determine the educational attainment of the population at any point in time. In other words, these variables are the critical determinants of the economy's ability to lift the average educational attainment of its population.

10.3.1   The Population Factor

Economic growth and changes in fertility have been dramatic in Asia in the past fifty years as we have seen in previous chapters. An interesting aspect of this dynamism has been the changing relationship between the number of dependent or non-working members of the population (those aged under 15 and over 65 years), and the number of people in the labor force (those aged between 15 and 65 years). In the 1970s, the dependency ratio in Asia averaged about 51 (ranging between 46 and 56; see Table 10.1), that is, there are about 51 dependents for every 100 workers. This is a high ratio which is reflective of the young and rapidly growing populations in these Asian nations. These ratios in Asia are also high compared with those found in the more advanced economies of Europe and North America. Dependency ratios have gradually decreased since then, owing to dramatic falls in population growth rates occurring over time. The decline has been highest in the relatively richer Asian countries, such as Korea and Singapore, as is evident in Table 10.1.

10.3.2   Educational Spending

Spending on education absorbs a much larger proportion of government budgets than most other expenditures. It is thus important that we study the allocation of resources to this sector. The budget share of educational expenses to GDP has steadily increased for most countries in Asia over time. In the 1960s, the share of education in GDP ranged from less than 1 percent in Nepal and Bangladesh to as much as 3.09 percent and 3.74 percent in Singapore and Sri Lanka, respectively. By the mid-1990s, the education sector's share in GDP averaged about 3.2 percent, with Thailand and Malaysia standing out as having the largest shares of more than 4.6 percent of GDP, and very comparable with those seen in Australia, Japan, and the United Kingdom. In the 2002–2005 period, this share of education continued to rise for many countries, led by South Korea (its share increased to 4.6 percent from 4.07 percent seven years earlier), and Malaysia (its share increased to 6.2 percent from 4.62 percent over the same period). The share of education in Malaysia's budget is now above those of the major industrialized countries, except for New Zealand, which had 6.5 percent share during 2002–2005 (see Table 10.2). There appears to be a weak correlation between an increase in per-capita income and a nation's share of the budget for education.

Table 10.1   Dependency Ratios for Selected Asian Economies[a]

	1970	1980	2002	2007	Percent Decline (1970–2007)
South Korea	52	37	24	18	65%
Singapore	48	30	20	18	63
Thailand	56	47	29	22	61
Malaysia	56	44	33	32	43
China	44	44	26	19	57
Sri Lanka	49	42	31	27	45
Philippines	53	48	37	35	34
Indonesia	50	48	35	29	42
India	49	45	35	32	35
Bangladesh	55	46	42	34	38
Nepal	46	49	51	37	20

[a]Dependency ratios used here are defined as the percentage share of the population under 15 years to those between 15 and 65 years.

SOURCES: 1970, 1980, and 2002 figures from Alain Mingat and Tan Jee-Peng, *Education in Asia: A Comparative Study of Cost and Financing* (Washington, D.C.: World Bank, 1992); 2007 figures from the United Nations Population Reference Bureau (UNPRB), *World Population Data Sheet* (2007).

DISTRIBUTION OF PUBLIC EXPENDITURES BY LEVEL OF EDUCATION   There is a pronounced shift in the proportion of public expenditures on education by the level of schooling (primary, secondary, and tertiary) as income per capita in a country increases. Mingat and Tan (1992, pp. 114–116) has shown that in lower income countries, the 10 percent best-educated cohort tends to receive more than half of the total amount of public spending. This figure falls to only 13 percent in higher income economies (10 percent would be perfect equality). This is in line with the earlier observation that the economies in South Asia spend a large proportion of their budgets on subsidizing the rich who are going to college.

We noted in Chapter 2 that education was one of the most important ingredients for maintaining rapid rates of growth for the "miracle" economies of Asia. This conclusion is borne out by the foregoing analysis, although the experience of the Philippines shows that continued improvements in educational attainment is a necessary but not a sufficient condition for rapid economic growth.

EDUCATION EXPENDITURE AND LEVEL OF INCOME   If we consider the costs of public education calculated as a percentage of per-capita GDP, as reported in Table 10.3, it is striking that countries with low per-capita incomes spend the least on primary education. This includes the countries in South Asia and the Philippines.

Further to this, the proportion of gross national product (GNP) devoted to tertiary education is as much as forty times devoted to primary education, particularly for several countries in South Asia. In contrast, countries such as Indonesia, Korea, and Malaysia devoted more resources to both primary- and

Table 10.2   Public Spending on Education as Percent of GDP, 1960–2005

	1960	1970	1980	1990	1996–1998	2002–2005
Asian Countries						
Bangladesh	0.46%	n.a.	1.10%	1.49%	2.35%	2.5%
Brunei	n.a.	n.a.	1.23	3.89	4.39	n.a.
China	n.a.	1.25	2.51	2.34	2.29	1.9
Hong Kong	1.63	2.43	2.43	2.84	2.92	4.2
India	1.94	2.44	2.82	3.65	2.95	3.8
Indonesia	n.a.	2.62	1.65	0.99	1.43	0.9
Korea, Rep. of	n.a.	3.51	3.64	3.44	4.07	4.6
Malaysia	n.a.	3.98	5.72	5.07	4.62	6.2
Nepal	0.37	0.59	1.84	2.01	2.51	3.4
Pakistan	1.09	1.65	1.97	2.60	2.70	2.3
Philippines	2.25	2.74	1.72	2.88	3.20	2.7
Singapore	3.09	3.18	2.74	3.09	3.07	3.1
Sri Lanka	3.74	3.98	2.70	2.68	3.39	n.a.
Thailand	n.a.	3.21	3.39	3.55	4.70	4.2
Industrialized Countries						
Australia	2.60	3.82	5.24	4.88	4.77	4.7
Japan	3.91	3.89	5.72	n.a.	3.48	3.6
New Zealand	3.38	4.67	5.66	6.16	7.17	6.5
United Kingdom	n.a.	5.33	5.58	4.80	4.71	5.4
United States	4.59	7.39	6.60	5.09	5.01	5.9

SOURCES: United Nations Development Program, *Human Development Report 2007/2008*; World Bank, *World Development Indicators 2002*.

secondary-level education, and relatively less on tertiary education. As an economic strategy, the former is seen as more effective in laying the foundation for higher growth rates in the future—that is, compared with the resource bias of South Asian countries toward tertiary education. It is, thus, probably no accident that the South Asian countries grew more slowly than the NIEs and the economies of Southeast Asia.

One reason why the Philippines, Korea, and Indonesia spend relatively less on tertiary education is that this sector is supported by the private sector to a significant extent (see Table 10.4). In the case of Thailand, the figures show a relative neglect of secondary and tertiary education.

There is, however, very little correlation between the share of the private sector in higher education and the level of per-capita income, although none of the poorer countries have a significant share of private-sector involvement. This suggests that there is some scope for implementing a system of fees for higher education and shifting some of these resources of the public sector to primary and secondary education.

Table 10.3   Operating Costs of Education as Percent of Per-Capita GNP during the Mid-1980s

	Primary	Secondary	Tertiary
Bangladesh	6	30	285
China	7	23	199
India	6	17	231
Indonesia	13	23	91
Korea	17	23	71
Malaysia	14	21	190
Nepal	9	14	249
Philippines	6	9	50
Sri Lanka	6	9	83
Thailand	16	15	40
Average	**10**	**19**	**149**

Figures are rounded up to the nearest unit.

SOURCE: Alain Mingat and Tan Jee-Peng, *Education in Asia: A Comparative Study of Cost and Financing* (Washington, D.C.: World Bank, 1992), p. 29.

Table 10.4   Tertiary Education Financed by the Private Sector in the Late 1980s (Percent)

Country	Percentage	Country	Percentage	Country	Percentage
Bangladesh	16%	Indonesia	48%	Philippines	85%
China	0	Korea	60	Sri Lanka	20
India	7	Malaysia	15	Thailand	26

SOURCE: Alain Mingat, "Toward Improving our Understanding of the Strategy of High Performing Asian Economies in the Education Sector," Paper presented at the Asian Development Bank International Conference on Financing Human Resource Development in Advanced Asian Economies, Manila, Philippines, November 17–18, 1995, p. 21.

10.3.3   Trends in Enrolment Ratios

Looking at enrolment rates over the past fifty years, a number of developments are evident (see Table 10.5). Firstly, primary education has become quite universal in most countries. However, the quality of this education can vary substantially and the figures in some instances seem high, since by walking around in any of the major cities in South Asia, it is obvious that the 100 percent figure is an overstatement. Furthermore, overaged students and repeaters tend to distort the enrolment numbers at the primary level (see Table 10.6 for actual educational survival rates from grade four to grade five). These survival rates in education are closely related to levels of per-capita income, suggesting that the efficiency of education is highly correlated with income per capita (see Figure 10.3).

The data in Table 10.5 also show that the NIEs started in 1950 with a very strong primary education base, but so did a few other countries, such as Sri Lanka and the Philippines, which now have much

Table 10.5 Gross Enrolment Rates by Level of Schooling (Percent)

	Primary		Secondary		Tertiary	
	1950	2000[a]	1950	2000	1950	2000
Bangladesh	n.a.	100	n.a.	46	n.a.	7
China	21	106	5	63	<1	7
Hong Kong	50	94	13	72	1	27
India	26	102	4	49	1	10
Indonesia	41	110	2	57	<1	15
Korea	88	101	16	94	1	78
Malaysia	57	99	5	70	<1	28
Pakistan	24	74	10	24	1	4
Philippines	93	113	23	77	10	31
Singapore	77	94	7	74	2	44
Sri Lanka	80	106	20	72	1	5
Thailand	73	95	6	82	2	35

[a]Most figures pertain to 2000, but some can be for any year between 1996 and 1999.

SOURCES: Alain Mingat, "Toward Improving our Understanding of the Strategy of High Performing Asian Economies in the Education Sector," Paper presented at the Asian Development Bank International Conference on Financing Human Resource Development in Advanced Asian Economies, Manila, Philippines, November 17–18, 1995, p. 9; World Bank, *World Development Indicators Online* (2003).

lower per-capita incomes. We have noted this in earlier chapters and speculated on the reasons that they were not able to capitalize on a strong primary education base, as did the NIEs. Bangladesh and Pakistan, on the other hand, stand out as countries that have made little progress in education generally. Note that right after World War II, there was much less disparity in per-capita incomes, but the gap has increased over time. Could the divergence in income in subsequent decades be partially the result of a stronger commitment to education by the NIEs?

In the NIEs, the mean number of years of schooling (see Psacharopoulos and Arriagada, 1986, Table 3.2.) for the workforce was more than eight in Hong Kong, Korea, and Taiwan by 1980, and increased further in the 1980s and 1990s. By 2000, the gross enrolment rates for secondary education in Singapore, Hong Kong, and Korea were over 70 percent. The tertiary education level had also increased to over 20 percent in all the countries, with Korea having a high 78 percent for tertiary education! Singapore had lower educational attainment levels, and the Philippines had a higher average level of educational attainment than Singapore in 1950. In fact, the Philippines started out with the highest level of primary, secondary, and tertiary education in all of Asia in 1950. While progress in education was slower in the Philippines than in some other countries, it remained the third-highest ranking in secondary education in 2000, surpassed only by Korea and Singapore. It took fourth place for tertiary education.

In Southeast Asia, the mean number of years of school for the workforce in the Philippines and Malaysia in 1980 was close to the average of the NIEs, but much lower in Thailand and Indonesia. By 2000, secondary-school enrolment rates had generally increased to be almost on par with the NIEs, but

Table 10.6   Survival Rates in Primary School (Percent)

	Through Grade Four, 1990	Through to Grade Five, 2005
South Korea	100	99
Singapore	100	100
Taiwan	100	100
Hong Kong	100	100
Malaysia	98	98
Thailand	91	93
Philippines	79	75
China	89	n.a.
Sri Lanka	99	n.a.
India	68	79
Pakistan	52	68
Bangladesh	51	65

SOURCES: Alain Mingat, "Toward Improving our Understanding of the Strategy of High Performing Asian Economies in the Education Sector," Paper presented at the Asian Development Bank International Conference on Financing Human Resource Development in Advanced Asian Economies, Manila, Philippines, November 17–18, 1995, p. 11; UNESCO, *Education for All Global Monitoring Report* (2008).

Figure 10.3   Relationship between Survival Rates in Primary Education and Per-Capita GDP for Selected Asian Countries, around 1985

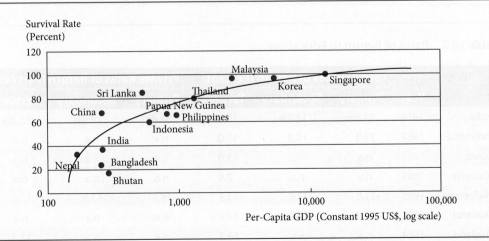

SOURCES: Alain Mingat, "Toward Improving our Understanding of the Strategy of High Performing Asian Economies in the Education Sector," Paper presented at the Asian Development Bank International Conference on Financing Human Resource Development in Advanced Asian Economies, Manila, Philippines, November 17–18, 1995, p. 55; World Bank, *World Development Indicators 2002.*

Indonesia's was still below this and its tertiary enrolment rates were half the rate in the NIEs. However, the Philippines could well be put in the high-level category since its mean years of schooling was quite high by 1980 and continued to improve in the 1980s and 1990s, but more slowly than its neighbors in Southeast Asia. Even now, Filipinos fill many of the skilled service jobs in finance and the tourist industry in Indonesia. In South Asia, the mean number of school years completed was very low even in 1980, with the sole exception of Sri Lanka, which could well be put in the moderate or even the high category.

Hence, gains in tertiary education were most pronounced in East Asia and in Singapore, where enrolment rates went from single digits in 1970 to 27 percent in Hong Kong, 49 percent in Singapore, and 78 percent in Korea, by 2000 (see Table 10.5). The last is particularly noteworthy as many of the tertiary graduates were engineers, scientists, and managers. This was a major factor in Korea's rapid growth in the higher technology and capital-intensive industries in the 1980s and 1990s. In Southeast Asia, the most impressive gains were made in secondary education where enrolment rates doubled and tripled from the 1970s onwards. In South Asia, the increases in enrolment were less spectacular. In tertiary education, enrolment rates remained low in 2000, having increased only slightly over the sample period.

Additional insights into the pattern of educational attainment in Asia can be gleaned by examining Table 2.12 in Chapter 2, which shows the illiteracy rate (the converse of the literacy rate reported in Table 2.9), as well as the school enrolment rate for primary, secondary, and tertiary education in East, Southeast, and South Asia from the 1970s onwards.

10.3.4   Rates of Return to Education

Table 10.7 shows the rates of return to education in Asia culled from a number of separate studies, as reported by Mingat and Tan (1992). As expected, the returns are higher for primary education and lower for higher levels of education. However, these results do not show the intrinsic value or merit good of education that would be reflected by higher social rates of return *vis-à-vis* private rates of return. Perhaps this is because the countries examined for which both rates of return were calculated

Table 10.7   Rates of Return to Education

	Year	Social Rates of Return (Percent)			Private Rates of Return (Percent)		
		Primary	Secondary	Tertiary	Primary	Secondary	Tertiary
India	1978	29.3%	13.7%	10.8%	33.4%	19.8%	13.2%
Indonesia	1982	18.0	15.0	10.0	n.a.	n.a.	n.a.
Korea	1982	n.a.	10.9	13.0	n.a.	n.a.	n.a.
Malaysia	1983	n.a.	n.a.	7.6	n.a.	n.a.	n.a.
Philippines	1985	11.9	12.9	13.3	18.2	13.8	14.0
Thailand	1975	12.0	24.0	12.9	n.a.	n.a.	n.a.
Thailand	1984	n.a.	n.a.	13.3	n.a.	n.a.	17.4

SOURCE: Alain Mingat and Tan Jee-Peng, *Education in Asia: A Comparative Study of Cost and Financing* (Washington, D.C.: World Bank, 1992), p. 48.

Table 10.8   Girls-to-Boys Ratio by Level of Schooling, 2000

	Primary	**Secondary**	**Tertiary**
Pakistan	0.55	0.63	n.a.
India[a]	0.77	0.66	0.61
Nepal	0.79	0.69	0.25
China[a]	0.92	0.83	n.a.
Thailand	0.94	0.94	0.82
Indonesia	0.95	0.95	0.75
Malaysia	0.95	1.05	1.04
Bangladesh	0.96	0.99	0.51
Philippines	0.96	1.05	1.06

[a]Figures are for 1999.

SOURCE: United Nations, Statistics Division, *Millennium Indicators*, available at http://www.unstats.un.org/unsd/.

are at the poorer end of the income scale. It may also be that tertiary education is not considered a merit good.

Another recent study by Cohen (2002) compares the rates of return to education together with experience. The approach follows that originally developed by Mincer (1974). The rates of return to education in Asia are nearly identical to those in the United States for the period of the 1980s and 1990s, at just under 10 percent. The returns for the first year of experience are somewhat higher in Asia—about 4 percent versus 3 percent in the United States. This study also concludes that the rates of return in poor countries have risen in the past few decades, contradicting the conventional wisdom that poor countries would experience a decline in returns to education as globalization raises the demand for low-skilled workers in these countries. Rather, the openness to globalization raises the returns to education in the poor countries since the flow of technology enables many of them to begin manufacturing skill- and capital-intensive products that require more highly skilled and educated labor.

10.3.5   Gender Disparities in Educational Attainment

Gender disparities exist at all levels of education for most countries, but they tend to fall as incomes rise, as do literacy differentials. Refer to Table 2.9 in Chapter 2. Only the results for South Asia (such as Bangladesh, India, and Pakistan) show a highly skewed pattern of discrimination against women. A similar skewness is observed in the girls-to-boys enrolment ratio, by the level of schooling, as shown in Table 10.8, although in several Southeast Asian countries, such as Malaysia and the Philippines, the enrolment rate for tertiary education has been higher for females than for males.

10.4   GENERAL ISSUES IN EDUCATION POLICY

There is no doubt that education plays a very important role in the economic development of nations. We have outlined above some of the important aspects of education provision, but there remains much more to say. In this section, we discuss a few other important issues that are directly relevant for policymakers.

10.4.1   Greater Privatization of the School System

An argument can be made for greater privatization of the school system by allowing private schools to coexist with public schools. This gives students greater choice and also helps to promote competition between public and private schools. A study of the Philippines by Jimenez (1987) shows that administrators in private schools who are financed by local funds have greater incentive to minimize costs while maintaining quality. The provision of a private-school alternative also helps to reduce the budget burden on the public purse as a result of these competitive factors. For example, in Asia as a whole, the index of private-school financing and the index of costs per capita for higher education are inversely related (see Figure 10.4). However, the curve flattens out at about 40 percent financing. Perhaps there is a range of funding for tertiary education by the private sector of around 50 percent. At higher rates of private financing of higher education, the social selectivity of a totally privately funded higher education system will work to exclude the poorer segments of society. Studies in the Philippines and China also show that the unit cost of education tends to fall with the size of enrolment in the school. This is true for both secondary and tertiary education.

The proliferation of private schools, however, may exacerbate existing income and wealth inequities within an economy. Poorer families tend to send their children to public schools, while more affluent

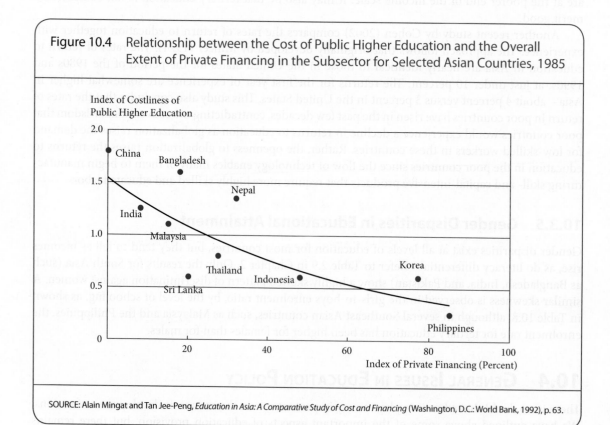

Figure 10.4   Relationship between the Cost of Public Higher Education and the Overall Extent of Private Financing in the Subsector for Selected Asian Countries, 1985

SOURCE: Alain Mingat and Tan Jee-Peng, *Education in Asia: A Comparative Study of Cost and Financing* (Washington, D.C.: World Bank, 1992), p. 63.

families send their children to private schools. While there are economically justifiable reasons for allowing private education systems to flourish, this dichotomy drives a wedge between graduates of "public" and "private" education systems, and does affect labor market outcomes as employers tend to favor graduates of private schools more than their public-school counterparts.

10.4.2   Teacher's Pay, Class Size, and Educational Efficiency

There is also evidence that efficiency improves as the student-to-teacher ratio increases up to a point. A study by Leroy (1995) shows that the pupil–teacher ratio does not have much effect on educational outcomes when the range is 25 to 50 pupils per teacher. At the same time, the pupil–teacher ratio tends to decline with higher income. Therefore, it may be a good strategy for poorer countries to increase class size while improving teacher quality. As incomes and education budgets increase, they can gradually reduce class size.

Surprisingly, teachers' wages are not highly correlated with the level of economic development. However, the NIEs have paid, relative to the level of wages in manufacturing, more than other countries—1.91 versus 1.41, according to Mingat (1995, p. 46).

The NIEs have also performed very well in internationally standardized tests administered in a number of industrial and developing countries (see Tables 10.9 and 10.10).

A tentative conclusion that can be drawn from the above results is that the strategy followed by the NIEs to pay higher wages to teachers and to have larger class sizes led to more efficient education. Higher test scores in Korea and Singapore reflect this. Whether such a strategy would benefit other countries would have to be studied carefully because of the differences in local conditions. However, *prima facie*, it seems to be a good starting point for reform. In Indonesia, Thailand, and the Philippines, the results of internationally administered tests were less satisfactory, providing further evidence that the approach followed in East Asia has been more efficient and productive.

10.4.3   Quality versus Quantity of Education

The rapid increase in demand for educational services has been based on the notion that having more years of schooling is more likely to boost one's earnings in the labor market. Furthermore, there is some evidence that past a certain threshold of income, there is bound to be greater substitution between the quantity

Table 10.9   Scores on Internationally Administered Competence Tests

Economy	3rd Grade	4th Grade	5th Grade	8th Grade
Korea	422	471	577	643
Singapore	414	484	601	607
Hong Kong	387	447	564	588
Thailand	309	354	494	522
International average	334	391	493	520

Korea and Singapore finished first or second worldwide in all four grades.

SOURCE: Don Adams and David Chapman, *The Quality of Education: Dimensions and Strategy*, Vol. 5 (Manila: Asian Development Bank, 2002).

Table 10.10   Science and Mathematics Average Scores at Age 14

	Mathematics		Science
Singapore	604	Taiwan	569
Korea	587	Singapore	568
Taiwan	585	Korea	549
United States	502	United States	515
Thailand	467	Thailand	482
Indonesia	403	Philippines	345
Philippines	345	Japan	550
International average	487	*International average*	488

SOURCE: Shahid Yusuf and Simon J. Evenett, *Can East Asia Compete? Innovations for Global Markets* (Washington, D.C.: World Bank, 2002), p. 42.

and quality of education obtained. How much of the variation in earnings is a result of quality differences? A related point is the family background of the student. It is important to recognize that all three of these variables are probably highly correlated in most samples—that is, higher quality, higher quantity, and "good" family background tend to go together. Thus, the returns to education have to be interpreted carefully. Simply offering to extend the same quality of education to a wider cohort will probably give a lower rate of return than estimates based on data where all three variables are changing over time. This is because some of the increase in wages/earnings will be attributed to the increase in quantity of education, whereas the quality of education and the background of the student will also be important determinants of earnings on their own account. Moreover, studies conducted with panel data suggest that a pupil's home environment and social status are much less important in developing countries than it is in developed countries. These studies also show that the variation in academic achievement attributable to factors internal to the school system, such as the physical infrastructure and facilities, the quality of the teachers, and the availability of books, and other teaching materials and facilities, play a much more important role in the developing world than it does in developed countries. Despite these caveats, there is still a strong economic and social incentive to invest in education. These findings also reinforce the conclusion that greater emphasis should be put on providing good facilities and teachers.

10.4.4   Tertiary Subsidies and the Brain Drain Problem

Tertiary education tends to be much more costly relative to primary education in developing countries than it is in developed countries. For example, tertiary education per pupil in India costs 50–100 times more than that for primary education (Mingat and Tan, 1992, Table 3.2.). The wage differentials between the tertiary graduate and those who obtained less years of schooling tend to be higher in developing *vis-à-vis* developed countries. It was also pointed out earlier that the external benefits of education diminishes with more years of schooling—that at higher levels of education, greater benefits accrue to the individual more than to the society. This reality must be recognized by policymakers in developing countries where large subsidies are often given to higher education, which tend to have a regressive effect on the taxation system. An associated problem is the phenomenon called "brain drain" (see Box 10.1). When higher education is subsidized and there is international labor mobility, there is likely to be a larger "brain drain" problem. This wastes public resources and indirectly provides a subsidy to the richer country, which does not have to spend on training for the immigrant. The solution is to reduce the subsidy to higher education dramatically.

MORE ON THE "BRAIN DRAIN"   It is generally observed that the better educated are the most likely to migrate. In the early stages of development, rural to urban migration is more attractive to the more educated agricultural workers. This is because real wages are generally higher in the urban areas.

This increased tendency to migrate occurs not only within national boundaries, but also internationally. This is exacerbated by a situation where there are too many highly educated citizens who cannot find employment locally that is commensurate with their qualifications. These issues are discussed further in Box 10.1.

10.4.5   Inequality Effects and Missing Credit Market

The educational levels and quality of education in Asia vary widely among countries. The policies that an individual country follows at a particular time will depend upon the status of the existing system. In many instances, the existing system tends to perpetuate the education of the ruling class and

 BOX 10.1

Educated to Emigrate

It is undeniable that human resource development is one of the primary ways that an economy can raise incomes and bring about technological transfer. As shown above, the gains from education to the individual are substantial. Primary education alone can increase productivity whilst secondary and tertiary education can enable better adoption and development of technology, as well as bring about greater understanding of the requirements for raising living standards further.

Unfortunately, a phenomenon known as the "brain drain" is often witnessed in developing countries. "Brain drain" concerns the emigration of skilled or highly educated people, such as accountants, doctors, nurses, engineers, business managers, and university teachers, from developing to developed countries. For example, between 1985 and 1990, Sudan lost 17 percent of its doctors and dentists, 20 percent of its university teachers, and 30 percent of its engineers. The Philippines, during that time, lost more than 12 percent of professional workers to the United States. In 1989, more than 40,000 people emigrated from Hong Kong, of which over 25 percent were highly skilled professionals. At any one time, more than 40,000 Hong Kong residents hold student visas in developed countries,

and it is anticipated that a large percentage of these students will eventually emigrate permanently.

The problem of "brain drain" is exacerbated when the skill is acquired at considerable social cost to the government of the home country, for example, when the emigrating student's studies have been funded by the government through a scholarship.

Labor migration enables resources to be allocated where productivity is highest and thus, from the point of view of overall labor productivity and economic efficiency, the free flow of labor resources across national boundaries should be encouraged. The "brain drain" is really an issue about the distribution of the gains from the productivity of skilled professionals who have emigrated.

Some academics have suggested a tax on emigrants who have received free education at home before emigrating in order to allow the home country to recapture the costs of education. Questions arise, however, about how such a system would be enforced and administered. Another alternative that has been used by several countries is to require students who have had government scholarships to sign a bond. Such a bond would require that they pay for the cost of their education if they emigrate, or else work for the government for several years to pay off the bond.

SOURCE: United Nations Development Program, *Human Development Report 1992*.

discriminate against the education of "gifted" poor children, particularly in rural areas where facilities for primary education may be weak.

A balance needs to be struck between the different objectives of a subsidized education. If there is great inequality in the redistribution of income, more generous subsidies may be given to gifted students, even at the tertiary level. In a comparative study of Kenya and Tanzania, Armitage and Sabot (1986) found that higher school fees in Kenya resulted in a higher secondary enrolment. This could have helped Kenya to achieve more rapid development than Tanzania, which followed a policy of keeping secondary education free but reduced enrolment by test screening. To understand how these policy issues apply in particular countries, we have to understand the existing educational system in these countries and assess the quality of the education provided.

One way to address the inequalities raised above is through the development of a well-functioning credit market. Low levels of wealth hinder or even bar productive educational choices because of the failure of credit markets. For the poor, educational loans are difficult to obtain because of a lack of collateral. In India and Thailand, there seems to be a working credit market for education—but it may still be inaccessible to the poorest income groups.

10.4.6 Implications for Policy

Based on the above analysis, we can draw five tentative policy conclusions:

1. Curbing population growth means lower dependency rates and increases the ability of the society to educate its population with the same resource base.
2. It pays to educate teachers more intensively and to pay them well, even at the expense of having slightly larger classes.
3. It is advantageous to spend on education for girls and primary education in general. Investment in these areas shows high payoffs, both in social and private returns.
4. It pays to encourage private providers of tertiary-level education and possibly at the secondary level as well if they do not already exist.
5. Experiments with higher pupil–teacher ratios and decentralization of authority over school management, the curriculum, and the budget, may also be advantageous.

10.5 HEALTH AND ECONOMIC DEVELOPMENT

Health is a very important component of development. Ensuring the general health of the people around the world is the overriding concern of international agencies such as the World Health Organization (WHO). Understandably, there are personal gains from having good health but organizations such as the WHO and national governments also recognize that the general health of the citizenry is an important element in national development.

In this book, we define health as the overall well-being of an individual. This definition covers the physical, mental, and social state of the person and is essentially the definition used by the WHO and other international agencies. In simple terms, health means the absence of illness and infirmity. That said, there will be instances when we use "health" to refer to the general well-being of the population. In this context, we talk about morbidity and mortality rates, which refer to the chances of a person becoming sick or dying (presumably due to illness), respectively. The former is a difficult statistic to measure, as trips to the doctor are the only available information that can be used to estimate this probability for the population. However, not everyone sees a doctor when they fall ill. In the developing countries, this problem is worse since access to medical services can be remote. The measurement of morbidity may also be complicated by the gravity or seriousness of the illness being reported. In contrast, mortality rates can be and are more closely monitored. In most countries, the national statistical agencies maintain databases of births and deaths in the economy, and their regular publications contain these statistics for the year. Statistics on the causes of death also provide important clues to the general well-being of the population and, as such, can be used to form another set of health measures. Unfortunately, these sets of information are not always available or reliable.

Other statistics are also commonly used, such as infant mortality, life expectancy at birth (number of years a person is expected to live), crude birth rates and, of course, crude death rates.

A healthy population is an important ingredient for economic growth and development. Good health increases the worker's strength and stamina and enables him/her to work longer hours and concentrate more effectively. There is little argument that a healthy and fit workforce is better able to increase national productivity. Good health is also known to improve the performance of children in school. When children are well fed, they tend to have a longer concentration span, absorb what is taught more effectively, and are generally able to participate better in class activities.

Besides increasing the quantity and improving the quality of human resources, health expenditures can also extend the availability or productivity of non-human resources. The clearest example is the large tracts of land rendered inhabitable or unusable by endemic diseases. Malaria and typhoid fever blocked access to many parts of Latin America, Africa, and Asia before these diseases were brought under control in the twentieth century. Even today, schistosomiasis makes it unsafe for people to enter lakes and streams in sections of Africa, and trypanosomiasis (an African sleeping sickness) restricts the range of the livestock industry. So far, no chemical means of control have been discovered for either of these diseases. China, however, has made progress against schistosomiasis through mass campaigns aimed at ridding lakes and streams of the snails that transmit the parasite. The success of such efforts can substantially enhance productivity and increase the amount of arable and habitable land.

10.5.1 Health Patterns and Trends in Developing Countries

Health conditions have been improving gradually over the years. Table 10.11 shows that life expectancy rates—that is, the number of years a person is expected to live—have increased between 1960 and 2005. In general, life expectancy is higher in developed countries than in developing countries, but this gap has narrowed in the last forty years. This is due to the availability of safe water, sanitary facilities, immunization, and access to health services in most countries, Asia and other parts of the world, as shown in Table 10.12 (p. 285).

Income has long been accepted as the major force driving improvements in health for many countries. The experience of many countries has shown that a dramatic decline in death rates occurs when countries become industrialized and living standards and incomes rise. As a result of lower mortality rates, life expectancy rates have risen substantially in recent years.

Advances in medical technology have benefited both rich and poor countries. Figure 10.5 (p. 286) shows that while, in general, people in richer countries have lived longer in both the 1930s and 1960s, life expectancy rates in poorer countries have caught up rapidly in the later period. This is shown by the steeper 1960s curve for the lower income range. This phenomenon is also suggested by the point where life expectancy curves begin to flatten out. This point occurs at much lower income levels for the 1960s curve than for the 1930s curve—at about US$600 per-capita income versus about US$1,000 in the 1930s curve. All in all, this shows that increasingly, income has become less important as a determinant of mortality.

We have known for a long time that poor health and poverty go together. Recent research carried out by the World Bank provides empirical evidence showing that the poor health of a population is a detrimental factor for economic growth. Furthermore, the WHO Commission on Macroeconomics and Health has released its assessment of health and economic development (WHO, 2001). This

Table 10.11   Total Life Expectancy Rates at Birth, 1960–2005

	1960	1970	1980	1990	2000	2005
Australia	70.7	71.4	74.4	77.0	78.9	80.4
Bangladesh	39.8	44.2	48.6	54.8	61.2	62.0
Brunei	62.4	67.0	71.0	74.2	76.2	76.3
Cambodia	42.6	42.4	39.5	50.3	53.8	56.8
China	36.3	61.7	66.8	68.9	70.3	72.0
Hong Kong	66.0	70.0	74.1	77.6	79.8	81.5
India	44.3	49.4	54.2	59.1	62.8	62.9
Indonesia	41.5	47.9	54.8	61.7	66.0	68.6
Japan	67.7	72.0	76.1	78.8	80.7	81.9
Korea, Rep. of	54.2	59.9	66.8	70.3	73.2	66.7
Lao PDR	40.4	40.4	44.8	49.7	53.7	61.9
Macao, China	59.3	65.8	72.1	76.9	78.9	80.0
Malaysia	54.3	61.6	66.9	70.5	72.5	73.0
Mongolia	47.0	52.7	57.7	62.7	67.0	65.0
Myanmar	43.8	48.4	51.5	54.7	56.1	59.9
Nepal	38.5	42.4	48.0	53.6	58.9	61.3
New Zealand	70.9	71.5	73.2	75.3	78.2	79.2
Pakistan	43.9	49.4	55.1	59.1	63.0	63.6
Philippines	53.4	57.4	61.3	65.6	69.3	70.3
Singapore	63.7	67.7	71.5	74.3	77.7	78.8
Thailand	52.6	58.4	63.6	68.5	68.8	68.6
United Kingdom	70.8	71.7	73.8	75.6	77.3	78.5
United States	69.8	70.8	73.7	75.2	77.1	77.4

SOURCES: World Bank, *World Development Indicators 2002*; United Nations Population Division, *World Population Prospects: 2008 Revision Highlight*, Working Paper ESA/P/WP 210, 2009.

assessment also finds a close relationship between health and the level of income per capita. This relationship between growth and health happens through the production function, as poor health reduces labor productivity and the ability to absorb new technical change (see also Section 10.9).

The strength of the relationship between the levels of GDP per capita and mortality for the Asian developing countries is depicted in Table 10.13 (p. 287). It demonstrates, among other things, the extremely strong relationship between declining infant mortality and GDP per capita.

10.5.2   Aspects of Health in Developing Countries

While the good health status of the population is essential for economic growth and development, the pursuit of good health for every citizen is an important goal in its own right. It must be recognized that

Table 10.12   Selected Health Indicators

		Health Care—Health Expenditure			Safe Water		Sanitation		Fully Immunized One-Year-Olds	
		Public (Percent of GDP)	Private (Percent of GDP)	Per Capita (PPP US$)	Population Using Improved Sanitation (Percent)		Population Using An Improved Water Source (Percent)		Against Tuberculosis (Percent)	Against Measles (Percent)
	Rank	2004	2004	2004	1990	2004	1990	2004	2005	2005
South Asia										
India	128	0.9%	4.1%	$ 91	14%	33%	70%	86%	75%	58%
Nepal	142	1.5	4.1	71	11	35	70	90	87	74
Pakistan	136	0.4	1.8	48	37	59	83	91	82	78
Sri Lanka	99	2.0	2.3	163	69	91	68	79	99	99
East Asia										
China	81	1.8	2.9	277	23	44	70	77	86	86
Hong Kong	21	n.a.	n.a.	n.a.	n.a.	n.a.	n.a.	n.a.	n.a.	n.a.
Indonesia	107	1.0	1.8	118	46	55	72	77	82	72
Japan	8	6.3	1.5	2,293	100	100	100	100	n.a.	99
Korea, Rep. of	26	2.9	2.7	1,135	n.a.	n.a.	92	97	99
Lao PDR	130	0.8	3.1	74	30	30	n.a.	51	65	41
Malaysia	63	2.2	1.6	402	94	94	98	99	99	90
Myanmar	132	0.3	1.9	38	24	77	57	78	76	72
Philippines	90	1.4	2.0	203	57	72	87	85	91	80
Singapore	25	1.3	2.4	1,118	100	100	100	100	98	96
Thailand	78	2.3	1.2	293	80	99	95	99	99	96
Vietnam	105	1.5	4.0	184	36	61	65	85	95	95

SOURCE: United Nations Development Program (2007/2008), Web site at http://hdr.undp.org.

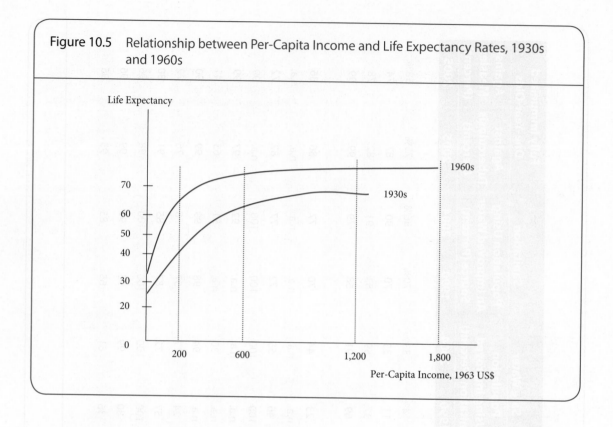

Figure 10.5   Relationship between Per-Capita Income and Life Expectancy Rates, 1930s and 1960s

decisions to invest in health should not primarily depend on whether it has high rates of economic return. Good health increases the human potential in all areas and is rightly regarded as a basic human need.

In this section, we discuss three main aspects in the context of their implications for policy: (a) environmental health; (b) malnutrition and food consumption; and (c) medical services.

ENVIRONMENTAL HEALTH   One effective approach toward better health outcomes in developing countries is through the improvement of environmental sanitation. In many developing countries, the spread of infectious and parasitic diseases can be effectively controlled by ensuring that people have access to clean water and the provision of an adequate waste disposal system. Experience has shown that such measures have effectively controlled the spread of waterborne diseases, such as typhoid, dysentery, and cholera. Improving housing conditions—with better ventilation and space—can also minimize the spread of tuberculosis. Health risks for these diseases are exacerbated by the presence of urban slums, especially in developing countries. These are pockets within a city that are highly populated by the poor and housing conditions are very cramped.

MALNUTRITION AND FOOD CONSUMPTION   A person suffers from malnutrition if his/her food intake does not meet minimal nutritional requirements for the physical body to function well. In most developing countries, malnutrition simply means not having enough food to eat. It is a major cause of ill health and premature death. Having the right amount and kind of food for the young is very important as they are still growing. Inadequacies in their diets affect their physical and mental development—and this will affect the quality of the adult population in the future.

Table 10.13 Income and Mortality Measures for the Asian Economies

	GDP Per Capita (PPP US$)	Population (Millions)	Life Expectancy at Birth (Years)	Infant Mortality Rate (Per Thousand Live Births)	Under 5 Mortality Rate (Per Thousand Live Births)
	2005	Mid-2007	2005	Mid-2007	2005
World	$9,543	6,625	68.1	52%	76%
More developed	5,282	1,221	77.0	6	11
Less developed	1,499	5,404	66.1	57	83
Less developed (excl. China)	n.a.	4,086	64.0	61	n.a.
Asia	n.a.	4,010	68.0	48	n.a.
Asia (excl. China)	n.a.	2,692	66.0	53	n.a.
East Asia and the Pacific	6,604	1,960.60	71.7	25	31
South Asia	3,416	1,587.40	63.8	60	80
Number of Economies					
9 economies	Under $1,999				
11 economies	$2,000–3,999				
7 economies	$4,000–9,999				
3 economies	$10,000+				

Data have been adjusted based on reviews by UNICEF, WHO and UNFPA to account for well-documented problems of underreporting and misclassifications.

SOURCE: United Nations Development Program (2007), Web site at http://hdr.undp.org.

What causes malnutrition and how can nutritional improvements contribute to economic development? The consumption of food, like any other goods or services, is determined by three elements: income, prices, and tastes.

Income

Engel's law says that poorer households devote a greater proportion of their budget to food and that they have a relatively high income elasticity of demand for food. This means that any additional income will be used to purchase food for the household. At higher income levels, the budget share of food declines in favor of other goods and services. Income, therefore, is an important indicator of food consumption levels, particularly at lower levels of household income. There is, nonetheless, recent research showing that an increase in income is not a guarantee that the general calorific intake of the population will increase because of the substitution effect that occurs—substitution for tastier, better quality, or wider variety of food, rather than on more calories.

Prices

There is a much evidence accumulated from household studies showing that the poor are very sensitive to changes in the prices of a food basket and they tend to make strong substitutions when prices change. How does this relate to the nutrition content of this food basket? If we derive a demand function for nutrition rather than the food bundle itself, a number of unexpected conclusions can be drawn from the literature. This happens because of strong cross-price substitution effects among different foods together with variations in nutrient-to-food conversion ratios. For example, if the price of rice increases, we would expect the nutrition content of the diet of the poor to decrease, other things being equal. However, what happens is that there is a sufficiently large increase in the demand for other relatively nutritious foods to offset the decline in nutrition resulting from the fall in rice consumption.

A related point is the response of the poor versus the rich to price changes. Own price elasticities are much higher for the poor than for the rich (for cereals, close to negative one for the poor, and near zero for the rich, according to one study). Within households, female children are generally made to accept a greater nutritional burden of adjustment when there are unfavorable price movements. The nutrition of others in the family moves much less.

Taste

Cultural beliefs and tastes in the consumption of particular types of food can impede nutritional improvement. Many traditional societies have beliefs about the health effects of various foods that are not supported by modern nutritional science. More often than not, these beliefs can be harmful to the health of certain segments of the population. Soybean products, for example, have been found to be a cheaper source of protein than animal products, yet their potential as a primary provider of this much-needed nutrient in the household diet is yet to be fully exploited in the poor countries of Africa or South Asia, where meat is still preferred.

10.5.3   Medical Facilities and Services

Medical facilities and services in the developing countries are very inadequate in providing for the health needs of the growing populations. Table 10.14 shows indicators of health care facilities for selected countries in the Asian region (also refer to column 2 in Table 10.12 for percentages of populations with access to health care). For a start, public expenditure on health in developing countries has always lagged behind those for education, defense, etc. Furthermore, compared to developed countries, these health expenditures are very low, even as a percentage of GDP (see Table 10.15). This has resulted in a stock of medical resources—facilities and personnel—that are far from adequate for the needs of the population. There are usually long queues in the few established health centers, insufficient medicine supplies, and a lack of trained health personnel to support these services. The number of physicians willing to practice in the public sector is also limited because many doctors are lured by the prospect of higher income in private practice.

In addition to inadequate supply, health services in developing countries are also unevenly distributed with large urban–rural differentials in the quality of services provided. On the one hand, there is a strong drive to acquire the latest medical technology to make the domestic capacity comparable to Western economies. Thus, much is spent on medical machines that support, for example, open-heart surgery. This usually happens in the cities, where the interests of the urban elites are satisfied. On the other hand, rudimentary medical care to sick infants and children is woefully inadequate, particularly in the rural areas of the country.

In addition, the developing countries spend far more resources on curative health care when it is well known that preventative health care is the more sensible approach. Experience has proven

Table 10.14   Health Care Facilities in Selected Asian Countries, 2000 (Per 100,000 Population)

	Health Care Facilities			Health Care Personnel		
	Hospitals	**Hospital Beds**	**Admissions**	**Physician**	**Pharmacists**	**Nursing Personnel**
Brunei	10	260.0	10,828.0	99.3	7.4	253.0
Indonesia	1,145	59.9[a]	2,433.1[a]	12.5[b]	3.4[b]	2,541.0[b]
Japan	9,266	1,312.6[b]	10,182.7[b]	201.5	171.3	122.0
Malaysia	120	147.0[a,b]	6,991.0[a,b]	67.1	10.0	1,000.0
Philippines	1,712	32.6	923.5	124.5	58.1	226.0
Singapore	28	293.7	9,708.2	138.8	27.3	248.0
Thailand	n.a.	219.7[b]	13,004.0[a]	29.4[b]	9.8[b]	618.4[b]
Vietnam	842	233.5	n.a.	1,865.0	7.7	1,708.0

[a]Only government hospitals
[b]Figures are for 1999.

SOURCE: Southeast Asian Medical Information Center and International Medical Foundation of Japan (SEAMIC/IMFJ), *SEAMIC Health Statistics* 2001 (Tokyo: Southeast Asian Medical Information Center, 2001).

that inoculation campaigns, mosquito spraying, and eradication of pests such as rats, have produced dramatic improvements in health conditions in some low-income countries, most notably in China. The main issue for governments is on how to strike a balance between curative and preventive health care.

10.6   PUBLIC-HEALTH POLICIES AND THE ASIAN EXPERIENCE

The World Health Organization's Commission on Macroeconomics and Health released an assessment of the health conditions in developing countries in 2001 (WHO, 2001). Among their findings were that mortality rates for children under 5 years old in the poor economies (under US$1,000 per-capita income) are nearly twenty times higher *vis-à-vis* the rates in the rich economies (over US$20,000 per-capita income). The report provides strong evidence that better health raises the productivity of labor and the level of wages, and that as health improves and wages increase, the health of women also improves, which in turn results in better health and education outcomes for their children. In the end, the report recommends greater investment in the health programs because improved health definitely promotes more rapid growth.

The experience of the developing countries in Asia supports these conclusions. Table 10.16 compares the rates of growth in real per-capita income between 1965 and 1999, with different initial per-capita incomes and initial infant mortality rates (IMRs) for 1965. These comparisons show that much higher rates of growth were achieved by countries with low IMRs in 1965 than by those with high IMRs (5.4 percent versus 1 percent).

Table 10.15   Public Spending on Health as Percent of GDP, 1990–2005

	1990	1995	2000	2005
Australia	5.31%	5.55%	8.3%	8.8%
Bangladesh	0.71	1.14	3.1	2.8
Bhutan	1.71	2.62	5.4	4.0
Brunei	1.60	0.74	2.5	2.0
China	2.15	1.92	4.6	4.7
Korea, Rep. of	1.75	1.70	3.6	3.5
India	0.90	0.80	4.3	5.0
Indonesia	0.57	0.63	1.7	2.1
Japan	4.59	5.47	7.6	8.2
Malaysia	1.49	1.23	3.3	4.2
Myanmar	1.05	0.38	2.1	2.2
Nepal	0.83	0.68	5.4	5.8
Pakistan	1.13	1.02	2.5	2.1
Philippines	1.49	1.36	3.5	3.2
Samoa	2.84	3.07	5.5	4.9
Singapore	0.98	1.24	3.4	3.5
Sri Lanka	1.54	1.64	3.7	4.1
Thailand	0.95	1.26	3.4	3.5
United Kingdom	5.07	5.89	7.2	8.2
United States	4.71	6.03	13.2	15.2
Vietnam	0.88	1.07	5.4	6.0

SOURCES: World Bank, *World Development Indicators Online*; World Health Organization, *World Health Statistics 2008*, available at http://www.who.int/whosis/whostat/2008/en/index.html.

10.6.1   Subsidies and Nutrition

There appears to be a mismatch in the food products that are subsidized and those food products that the poor consume. Studies have shown that meats, poultry, and dairy products have been given some subsidies in several developing countries. However, these products are too costly for the poor to consume. If subsidies are to be given, they should be for grains, such as rice and wheat, which are most heavily consumed by the poor.

10.6.2   Raising Incomes Through Direct Transfers

Raising incomes through direct transfers does not necessarily improve nutrition and health. While this point is still being debated, there is some evidence that the income elasticity of nutrition expenditures may be very small in some countries. In these cases, it may be better to provide direct nutrition through a subsidy to augment programs to raise the incomes of the poorest and most deficient groups.

Table 10.16   Growth Rate in Per-Capita Income between 1965 and 1999 for Different
Income Per Capita in 1965, and Different Infant Mortality Rates in 1965

Income Per Capita In 1965	Infant Mortality Rate in 1965		
	Less than 40	Between 40 and 99	100 or Greater
Less than US$500	n.a.	4.4%	2.2%
More than US$500	5.4	3.6	1.0

SOURCE: Asian Development Bank, *Key Indicators of Developing Asian and Pacific Countries* (2002).

10.6.3   Macroeconomic Effects

It is difficult to assess how macroeconomic adjustment policies have affected nutrition and health outcomes. The evidence for adverse impacts is not strong. However, when economic growth falters for a prolonged period, the health effects can be catastrophic. The experience of Russia in recent years is a case in point. An analysis of the impact of the Asian financial crisis on health may also provide some useful insights as to how public policy can be improved in the areas of health provision and services. Preliminary results suggest that it may have more to do with the failure of the government's health and delivery system to react promptly to the crisis than with specific policies relating to health.

10.6.4   Charging Fees for Health Care

It has been discussed earlier that health care in developing countries is severely under-financed. Prices have generally played a minor role in generating resources for financing health services or in determining those who have access to them (Jimenez, 1987). According to recent estimates, only 7 percent of the cost of publicly provided health services in developing countries is currently recovered through user fees. This has led to proposals to increase the fees charged for health services and to institute charges for those who are provided with free medical care. The revenue generated would be used to expand health services.

Jimenez (1987) recommends that we account for externalities generated by each type of health service. If the externalities are large—that is, when society benefits significantly from the provision of one unit of service to an individual or a household—then this type of health service must be provided below cost. However, if the benefits from a particular health service accrue mainly to the individual—in other words, when the externalities are low—then the cost for this type of service should be borne by the individual. Broadly speaking, one will not want to charge fees for preventative health care services, but one will want to charge a reasonably high price for curative health care. If there is excess demand on these high-priced services, then prices can be further increased. The revenues generated can then be reinvested in expanding services. If there is no excess demand generated, then the effect of a fee increase on revenues and the level of services provided would depend on the elasticity of demand for health services. Available evidence suggests that this demand is highly inelastic, since some people regard some services—particularly curative services in health emergencies—as necessities. Jimenez notes, however, that user fees for the highest cost services can be brought close to the cost of providing them only if medical insurance is widely available, since few of the people unfortunate enough to require such services are able to afford them.

In the context of a developing country where most households and individuals are not able to afford primary health care for themselves and their family members, it is an uncomfortable thought that people will only be provided with medical and health service if they can pay for some, if not all, of the cost of the service. More often than not, those who use public-health services are the poor. Instituting charges for currently free services will not matter much to the rich—they simply do not use them—but it will affect the poor greatly. In terms of policy, governments should devote more resources to preventative care and improving environmental health so that morbidity rates, particularly among the poor can be improved. If and when this happens, demand for preventative health care services can be eased.

10.7   HIV/AIDS in Asia

The widespread prevalence of diseases such as malaria, tuberculosis, and HIV/AIDS pose significant constraints to development in low- and middle-income countries. The impact of HIV/AIDS has been particularly devastating in sub-Saharan Africa where some countries are now seeing declines in life expectancy rates of up to twenty years as a result. According to the World Health Organization (WHO), the Human Immunodeficiency Virus/Acquired Immune Deficiency Syndrome or HIV/AIDS for short, has now become the leading cause of adult mortality at the global level. It was the main cause of some 4.9 million deaths in 2004, and morbidity effects are expected to rise even more substantially in coming years. Latest WHO statistics indicate that as of early 2009, more than 40 million people around the world live with the AIDS virus.

HIV/AIDS reached Asia and the Pacific region in the mid-1980s, with the early impact affecting mainly intravenous drug users (IDUs). As would be expected of communicable diseases, the transmission of the virus eventually gathered pace so that by the early 1990s, other population groups had become substantially impacted as well. National prevalence rates in Asia are still way below those recorded in some sub-Saharan African countries, as can be seen in Table 10.17. That said, the absolute numbers of people having HIV/AIDS in Asia and Africa are quite comparable on account of the fact that Asia includes countries that have some of the largest populations in the world.

10.7.1   Economic Impact on Asia

There are several mechanisms[1] through which HIV/AIDS can affect the workings of economies. First, unlike most other deadly diseases, HIV/AIDS directly affects people of working age. It is a debilitating disease which can directly reduce worker productivity significantly. The general weakness of workers infected with the virus can result in high absenteeism rates; it can also cause lower productivity for workers who end up as carers for the infected family members. AIDS can also cause many firms in the economy to slow down in its operations because of the need to recruit and train new staff to replace employees who become incapacitated by or die of AIDS.

Secondly, the susceptibility of working-age individuals can lead to a potential reduction in saving rates and disposable incomes. Lower disposable incomes can arise because AIDS results in a smaller pool of working-age people able to earn. In addition, the high cost of treatment leads to substantially reduced savings for the affected households.

Thirdly, high rates of AIDS-related deaths reduce the stock of human capital. Increased incidence leads to higher death rates and shorter life expectancies, two effects that can serve as a disincentive for individuals to acquire costly educational capital since benefits are expected to be enjoyed in a shorter period than otherwise. Furthermore, the future stock and quality of educational capital

---

[1] The discussion in this section follows Chapter 3 of ADB, *Asia's Economies and the Challenge of AIDS* (2004).

Table 10.17   HIV/AIDS in Asia and Sub-Saharan Africa for 15–49 Age Group, 2003

	Prevalence Rate (Percent)	Number of People Living with HIV/AIDS (Thousands)
Asia		
Cambodia	2.6%	170
Thailand	1.5	560
Myanmar	1.2	320
India	0.9	5,000
Papua New Guinea	0.6	16
Vietnam	0.4	200
China	0.1	830
Sub-Saharan Africa		
Swaziland	38.8	200
Botswana	37.3	330
Lesotho	28.9	300
Zimbabwe	24.6	1,600
South Africa	21.5	5,100
Eritrea	2.7	55

SOURCE: UNAIDS, *AIDS Epidemic Update 2006*, Web site at http://www.unaids.org.

can be placed at risk if children whose parents die prematurely of AIDS are unable to continue their education.

10.7.2   Vulnerable Groups

Four major groups exhibit a very high-incidence of HIV/AIDS: sex workers (both male and female) and their clients, men who have sex with other men, and intravenous drug users. In many Asian countries, men visit sex workers on an intermittent basis: 5–20 percent according to an ADB study. In some countries, such as China, there is also a risk from infected blood. The rates of infection have been sampled in these groups and found to be quite high—up to 40 percent or higher in several surveys in Asian economies among sex workers and intravenous drug users (ADB, 2002.)

It is also possible to identify high-risk groups through the industry or economic sector they work in. HIV is most likely to infect individuals in sectors that involve mobile and sex-aggregated labor, such as trucking, fishing, and the military; sectors that are involved with sick people, such as health care; and sectors that may be particularly sensitive to the risk of ill health, such as tourism.

10.7.3   Measures to Contain the Spread

To contain HIV/AIDS, it is necessary to control the spread from these highly infected groups as well as foster behavior within these groups that will reduce the threat of transmission of the disease. To further control the disease, it is necessary to take action to prevent it from reading epidemic levels. There are several ways to do this that have proved quite successful in some Asian economies.

1. Promote the use of condoms among sex workers and bisexual men.
2. Publicize the necessity for using measures to protect against AIDS, such as condoms, and highlight the importance of not sharing needles.
3. Make condoms and needles widely available and at reasonable prices, or supplied free in clinics.
4. General promotion of HIV/AIDS awareness through public media and non-governmental organizations (NGOs), as well as newspapers and magazine articles.

These methods have been reasonably effective in the economies where they have been widely adopted, including Thailand and parts of Cambodia (see Box 10.2). They need to be extended to other countries where efforts have been curtailed by social customs, religion (as in Philippines), or the lack of budgetary resources devoted to it.

Systematic analysis of survey data on AIDS and other sexually transmitted diseases reveal some important regularities about the variables involved. First, wealth matters. Wealthier women know about condoms and have access to them. Women from the wealthiest income quintile want to be tested for AIDS and they know where to get a test better than poorer women. Wealthier women are more exposed to the media and are, therefore, more likely to be exposed to the national public-health campaigns. Wealthier women have less need to travel from one place to another. Finally, married women from wealthier households are 50 percent more likely to have spoken to their spouses about avoiding AIDS than their counterparts from the poorer households.

Secondly, education matters too! In similar fashion, educated women have a better understanding of HIV/AIDS as a disease—how it is contracted and what are its consequences. Thus, educated women are more willing to use condoms and engage in less risky sexual behavior.

The implication of these two points is clear: once HIV penetrates society, the poor and the uneducated are likely to be at highest risk. There is, therefore, much to be gained by engaging in highly targeted HIV/AIDS information campaigns that are specifically tailored for the poor and the uneducated. Government initiatives that seek to provide alternative and more sources of income will also be helpful. In addition, government programs aimed at getting more children and young adults to attend school for more years will go a long way in reducing the incidence rate of AIDS and eliminating the social and economic threats brought on by a full-blown epidemic.

Finally, enormous progress has been made in treating HIV/AIDS in industrial countries with a variety of drugs that have been developed in the past decade. These drugs need to be made more readily available to sufferers at reasonable prices. A start has been made in Africa where these drugs are now being supplied at more reasonable prices. However, greater efforts need to be made to extend the regional coverage. Advocates of such programs point out that for a fraction of the defense budgets of the major industrial countries, the coverage could be extended to most of those now infected with HIV/AIDS while providing technical and logistic support to prevent the epidemic from spreading further. These resources have been made available in the United States, and as a result, the spread of the disease has been slowed dramatically.

It is doubtful, however, that such treatment will be widely available in Asia in the near future. Forecasts made by Eberstadt (2002) show that there will be more than 30 million new AIDS cases in India and China between 2000 and 2025, even under the most optimistic assumptions, and over 100 million in the case of a severe epidemic. This would result in around 20 million deaths in India and China in a mild epidemic, and over 50 million in a severe one. In a mild epidemic, there would be as many as 1 million new cases each year in 2015. Life expectancy would be reduced in both countries, and so would the working-age population. More money and larger budgets would have to be allocated for the care of AIDS patients. Estimates of gains in GDP per capita made by Eberstadt, using World Bank data and projections, suggest that both China and India would suffer very substantial declines in income

BOX 10.2

AIDS in Cambodia

HIV was first detected in Cambodia in 1991, and 2.7 percent of Cambodians are now HIV positive, the highest prevalence rate in Asia. The roots of the Cambodian HIV/AIDS epidemic can be found in the country's emergence from the relative isolation of the Vietnamese-backed Heng Samrin government. The transition period entailed the arrival of the United Nations Transitional Authority in Cambodia (UNTAC) whose job was to ensure the smooth implementation of the Agreements on the Comprehensive Political Settlement of the Cambodian Conflict, signed in Paris on October 23, 1991. The U.N. operation involved approximately 22,000 military and civilian observers in March 1992. During this period, large numbers of refugees were resettled, the Cambodian economy experienced a boom, and there were significant (ongoing) IMF-backed market liberalization programs as well. The sex industry also grew explosively, fuelled partly by foreign peacekeepers (a high percentage of whom admitted contact with sex workers), and also newly prosperous Cambodians with money to spend. Economic development was, however, highly uneven, with uneducated rural women benefiting the least. As a result, a plentiful source of supply was created to meet the growing demand for commercial sex.

The Cambodian HIV epidemic is fuelled mainly by heterosexual sex. In 2001, there were 74,000 adult women and 86,000 adult men living with HIV, with prevalence rates among different groups showing wide variation: 31.1 percent of those who worked in brothels, 16.1 percent of indirect sex workers (those who had other jobs but also sold sex), and 3.1 percent of police officers.

However, prevalence rates are currently falling as a result of the country's well-orchestrated prevention campaign. This is most likely the result of information campaigns on the danger of AIDS and the growing use of condoms. Cambodian authorities followed in the footsteps of Thailand and launched the "100% Condom Use" campaign in 2004, which aims to ensure that condom use is universal in brothels. As in Thailand, this drove down the prevalence rates in both the direct and indirect commercial sex industries. Cambodia has shown what can be done to combat AIDS, even in a country faced with a soaring epidemic and with very little money or resources to spend on health.

SOURCE: David E. Bloom, Ajay Mahal, Larry Rosenberg, Jaypee Sevilla, David Steven, and Mark Weston, *Asia's Economies and the Challenge of AIDS* (Manila: Asian Development Bank, 2004).

growth per capita—by about a third by the year 2015 under the mild epidemic assumption in both countries, compared with a baseline solution of no new AIDS cases between 2002 and 2015.

It is also interesting to note that there has been a dramatic shift in the causes of death from infectious diseases worldwide and that this trend is projected to continue. According to the UNAIDS (2006), the percentage of death from infectious diseases as a result of AIDS in the 15–59 age group in the developing countries will increase from less than 9 percent of total deaths to more than 37 percent by 2020. Surprisingly, this proportion will be nearly 74 percent in Latin America and the Caribbean, and in the 30–40 percent range in sub-Saharan Africa and Asia. This is because Latin America and the Caribbean countries are projected to make the most progress in reducing other infectious diseases, while HIV infection is predicted to continue to rise.

Another factor to consider is that among European and North American populations, a mutant gene—CCR5-delta 32—is present in a small proportion of the population. This mutant gene, which was discovered by geneticists studying the spread of the plague in England in the seventeenth century, seems to provide immunity from AIDS if the person has two of these mutant genes, and lessens the probability of contracting AIDS for those who come into contact with the AIDS virus (see Dean and O'Brien, 1997). This mutant gene is not present in Asian or African populations. The impact that the presence of this gene has on the spread of AIDS has not been thoroughly investigated and it may be small, even though more than 10 percent of those sampled in many European countries have this mutant gene. One theory is that the gene developed two hundred thousand years ago and spread slowly from the north to the south of Europe. Another theory is that it developed in response to the plague in Europe, since it also provides immunity from this disease. Whatever the genesis of this mutant gene, it may provide scope for genetic engineering as a way to end the scourge of the AIDS epidemic.

10.8   Summary and Conclusions

In this chapter, we have reviewed various aspects of education and health, especially with regard to the experience of the Asian economies. The importance of establishing an effective and forward-looking framework for public policy has been emphasized. The differences in approach followed by different countries have also been discussed. We have noted the important roles that education and health have played in the economic development of Asia and highlighted the mutually reinforcing relationship between these two variables. Growing economies can and do devote increasing resources to improve educational, health and nutritional standards. Investment in human capital can also accelerate growth through increased labor productivity, encouraging greater physical investment, and reducing the dependency burden of the population. Once this mutual dependence is recognized, the case for allocating larger resources and more effective and efficient allocation of these resources to education and health becomes an even more pressing and critical policy agenda for developing countries in Asia.

Review Questions

1. In recent years, there has been a significant shift in emphasis away from physical capital and toward human capital or labor as the key input into the production function and as a contributor to growth. Why do you suppose this did not happen earlier?

2. Rates of return to education tend to decline in keeping with the theory of diminishing returns. If this is so, why is it that labor productivity keeps increasing over time?

3. Explain the difference between a merit good and a normal good? Are there other merit goods besides education?

4. What is the justification for subsidizing higher education?

5. Why is the length of time that it takes to become educated such an important issue in dealing with the shifting demand for different kinds of labor inputs into the production process?

6. Consider the production function for education. Has it changed substantially over time? How does it compare with the production function for banking services?

7. It is asserted that there does not seem to be much of a relationship between educational attainment and the pattern of spending on education. Does this seem strange to you? Why do you think that there is so little understanding of how to effectively and efficiently educate people?

8. Because the rates of return to education fall as the level of education increases, one would expect poorer countries to spend the most on primary education? However, this is not the case. Why?

9. The evidence from East Asia suggests that the key to better education is better-qualified teachers, and this can be achieved through higher salaries for teachers, as well as better ongoing training and development activities. Why do you suppose this finding has taken so long to emerge and why have other countries not adopted such an approach?

10. Gender discrimination in education is much higher in South Asia than it is in East and Southeast Asia. How does this relate to the standard of living and economic growth?

11. Despite near equality in educational opportunity for females, job and wage discrimination still exists. Why?

12. Explain why there are still large subsidies for higher education in many countries despite diminishing returns to spending on education and evidence that the gains from higher education accrue more to the person and not to society as the case would be for primary and secondary education.

13. There is a bias away from primary health care and preventive medicine and toward establishing large hospitals in urban areas. Discuss how and why this bias has arisen.

14. The bias in spending toward curative procedures and away from preventative and public health is widespread throughout the developing world. How can this bias be addressed through public policy?

15. Why is it important to recognize that the caloric content of food is not equivalent to a healthy dietary requirement?

16. Why is it important to distinguish the income distribution aspects of public-health policy from the health aspects of such policies? Give an example.

17. Epidemics pose numerous problems for public-health delivery systems and for public-health policy. Discuss some of these issues with respect to HIV/AIDS and SARS.

18. Why is women's education such an important ingredient in economic growth in developing countries in Asia? Be sure to explore all the possible synergies that contribute to the role of education for females in stimulating growth over time. Use specific country examples to illustrate your point.

Notes on References and Suggestions for Further Reading

Education played and continues to play a critical role in the economic development of nations. The key lessons regarding the importance of education in the growth process were first investigated by T. Paul Schultz and his article in the *Handbook of Economic Development* (1998), together with Nancy Birdsall's (1988) article in a later edition of the handbook are useful starting points. See also the early work of Jacob Mincer (1974). The summary by George Psacharopoulos (1994) focusing on returns to education is also worthwhile reading.

For the role of education in the Asian economies, see the general summary by Alain Mingat and Tan Jee-Peng (1992). Strategies for providing education are discussed in volume 5 by Don Adams and David Chapman (2002), and Mark Bray (2002). Also listed is the more recent publication by Asian Development Bank (2008).

The paper by Lisa A. Cameron, J. Malcolm Dowling, and Christopher Worswick (2001) demonstrates the importance of women's education in raising women's labor-force participation rates. The World Bank study by Shahid Yusuf and Simon J. Evenett (2002) is wide-ranging in scope. It has a good discussion on education in the context of technology transfer and innovation.

Two papers by Alain Mingat (1995) and Alain Mingat and Tan Jee-Peng (1998) investigate the relative strategies for providing education in terms of rates of return to the various inputs, such as teaching skill, class size, and institutional setting. Information on education in developing countries can be found in the UNESCO *Statistical Yearbook* and the UNESCO Web site at http://www.unesco.org. Additional information on education can be obtained from the World Bank Education home page at http://www1.worldbank.org/education/.

Turning to health, the World Bank's *World Development Report* for 1998 contains a review of health issues on a global level. For Asia, the Asian Development Bank's *Key Indicators* has a good review of health in the region.

The subject of AIDS/HIV has attracted attention recently and those interested can refer to the Asian Development Bank's *Key Indicators* (2002), and the publications by David Bloom et al. (2004), Nicholas Eberstadt (2002), Ajay Taydon (2005), and the Web sites of UNAIDS (http://www.unaids.org) and WHO (http://www.who.int).

Globalization and the New Economy

11.1 INTRODUCTION

Globalization refers to the ongoing economic, social and political integration of economies around the world that has taken place since World War I. As a result, international flows of capital and labor have risen over the decades. Trade in goods and services, and capital flows through foreign direct investment (FDI) and financial investment in equity and debt have been accelerating rapidly between countries. Labor flows, such as migration and tourism, have also become a global phenomenon. Consequently, international frameworks have been set up to deal with global issues such as the safeguarding of international financial transactions and intellectual property rights.

- There has been a growing trend toward greater political, economic and social integration of countries within continents and also among continents. The Association of Southeast Asian Nations (ASEAN), the Asia-Pacific Economic Cooperation (APEC) forum, and the European Union (EU) are evidence of this trend.
- In particular, there has been an increase in the international trade of goods and services that has been facilitated by lower tariffs and the removal of nontariff barriers.
- There has been an increase in the flow of portfolio investments in stocks and bonds across national borders as investors have become aware of profit-making opportunities in other countries, and the flow of information regarding these alternatives has increased and become more reliable.
- There has been an acceleration in the flow of FDIs from traditional investors and a spread in FDI as an investment vehicle for many new countries.
- The formation of strategic alliances between companies in different countries for production, marketing, and distribution of products has increased dramatically. There has also been rapid growth in the size and reach of transnational corporations which have production, marketing, and distribution platforms in many different countries.

- There has been an increase in the scope of the terms of international agencies dealing with global issues, including the United Nations, the International Monetary Fund (IMF), and the World Bank.
- There has been an increase in the flow of both temporary and permanent migrants, as well as in the number of applicants for migration around the world. This includes migrants within industrial countries, particularly within Europe, as well as migrants from the developing countries.
- Tourism has become more and more internationalized as visa requirements have been relaxed. Information about alternative foreign tourist destinations has been widely disseminated through improvements in telecommunications, and travel to foreign locations has become easier and less costly, as airlines have become more efficient and their routes and destinations have expanded.

Globalization has brought with it an increasing concern about the impact of greater interrelationships on the health and stability of the world economy. Globalization and the ever-increasing usage of information communication technology (ICT) have caused changes to the traditional methods of production and operations, and have created what is termed as the "new economy," which is relatively more knowledge- and technology-based. The "new economy" will be explored in greater detail in Section 11.4 after first understanding the impact that globalization has upon the world in general, and on Asia in particular.

11.2   WORLD TRENDS IN GLOBALIZATION

The extent to which the world economy has become more globalized can be further appreciated by analyzing a few trends.

11.2.1   International Trade

The volume of world trade has been increasing more rapidly than world income for many years. This means that total trade as a proportion of income has risen dramatically. The impact has been greater for countries that traded extensively in the initial period following World War II, but it has also been substantial for large land-based economies where trade has traditionally been a smaller percentage of gross domestic product (GDP). Some of these trends are shown in Table 11.1. World trade in exports increased more than 20 percent in the past decade, compared with the 1980s—from 18.2 percent of world income in the 1980s to 22 percent in the 1990s, according to the IMF. This is because world trade grew nearly twice as fast as world income in the 1980s and the 1990s, on average. Current IMF figures show that the amount of world trade in exports has escalated to 28 percent of world income in the 2000s.

11.2.2   Financial Flows[1]

Financial inflows that fall under the description of short-term capital/financial flows include short-term bank loans, short-term portfolio investment, such as equities, and government securities and (non-inter) bank deposits. There has been enormous volatility in most of these components. Consider, for example, the two components of short-term credit (including trade credit) and portfolio equity

---

[1] World Bank, *World Development Finance* (1999); and discussion in Chapter V of UNCTAD, *Trade and Development Report: Capital Flows to Developing Countries* (1999a), p. 99.

Table 11.1 World Trade and World Output Averages for 1982–1991, 1992–2001, and 2002–2007 (Billions US$)

	World Trade Average			World Output Average			World Trade as a Share of World Output by Decade		
	1982–91 (1)	1992–2001 (2)	2002–07 (3)	1982–91 (4)	1992–2001 (5)	2002–07 (6)	(1) / (4)	(2) / (5)	(3) / (6)
At market exchange rates	3,063	6,377	12,183	16,855	29,835	43,160	18.17	22.03	28.2
At purchasing power parity for output	3,063	6,377	12,183	21,436	37,102	54,364	14.3	17.4	22.4

SOURCES: International Monetary Fund, *World Economic Outlook 2000* (Washington, D.C.: IMF, 2000); International Monetary Fund, *World Economic Outlook 2008* (Washington, D.C.: IMF, 2008).

investment. In the past thirty years, there have been two surges in these investments in the developing countries.

The first cycle started in the second half of the 1970s and was the result of a surge in short-term bank lending. There was virtually no portfolio investment in the developing countries at that time. This cycle lasted until the second oil shock and the ensuing debt crisis in Latin America. The lending cycle, based largely on lending to Latin America, coincided with the wave of financial liberalization that occurred in the region, particularly in the Southern Cone countries. At its peak, fund flows totaled between US$20 and US$30 billion per year in the late 1970s and early 1980s.

The second boom began in the late 1980s and lasted until the Asian financial crisis in 1997. This boom resulted from an increase in both portfolio investment and short-term credit. It was geographically more broadly based than the earlier boom, extending beyond Latin America to include most of the Asian developing countries. This boom was strongly influenced by the liberalization of capital accounts in many countries, combined with the dismantling of exchange controls. With rapid growth in the equity markets and better information about companies listed on these markets, there was a strong inflow of portfolio investment that complemented bank lending. A low interest rate environment in the developed countries also made the high return investments in these developing countries more attractive. Portfolio equity and short-term loans reached almost US$100 million by the mid-1990s. This was more than 30 percent of total net capital inflows, and almost 40 percent of capital inflows.

Both short-term loans and portfolio equity investments fell rapidly in the second half of the 1990s, the former as a result of the Mexican crisis of 1995, and the latter following the Asian financial crisis of 1997. By the end of that year, the combined flows had declined by about 85 percent from the peak. There was a rebound in the following years until the global downturn that began in early 2008 and continued into 2009, when both FDI and portfolio inflows fell drastically. The volatility of portfolio equity investments and short-term bank lending was far greater than the other components of capital flows, such as FDI, which followed a more stable path, as we saw in the previous section.

Capital inflows tell only a part of the story of the flow of funds in and out of a country. To get a full picture, we need to consider outflows as well as inflows. Globalization has affected outflows too. As a result of the liberalization of capital transactions and markets, the outflow of capital by residents has become increasingly important in determining a country's net capital flows.

To get an idea of the situation in the developing countries, UNCTAD has compiled a complete capital account for all developing countries and a somewhat smaller group which it calls emerging market economies. In this group are most of the Asian economies—with the exception of Hong Kong, Singapore, and Taiwan—for which the international financial balance sheet is characterized by out-flows rather than inflows of capital.[2]

The coexistence of capital inflows with outflows has grown as global financial integration increased. It is widespread in the developed countries where the process of integration has been going on for many years. For example, the United States has been a net importer of capital for nearly twenty years but, at the same time, it has been a net exporter of FDI. Lending and investment abroad by U.S. banks and funds are not inconsistent with massive new portfolio inflows into the stock and bond markets.

For the developing counties as a group, net capital inflows and net capital flows (subtracting capital outflows) are recorded for the decade of the 1990s in Table 11.2. The inflow of more than US$200 billion per year was partially offset by outflows of more than US$60 billion per year. When measured as a percentage of GDP, there was a slight downward trend in net capital inflows between 1992 and 1996, followed by the devastating fall as the Asian financial crisis took hold. Capital flows fell from about 3.5 percent of GDP in 1996 to about 1.5 percent of GDP in 1998, as capital outflows increased dramatically.

The third wave of capital flows to and from developing countries started in the early 2000s and is ongoing. According to the recent UNCTAD's *Trade and Development Report* (2008), capital has been flowing "uphill"—from poor to rich countries since the Asian financial crisis in 1997–1998. Contrary to economic theory, developing countries are exporting capital and appear to be growing faster than the countries receiving the capital inflows. This is especially true of the developing countries in Asia, which have accumulated tremendous foreign exchange reserves.

11.2.3 Foreign Direct Investment and Multinational Enterprises (MNEs)

Foreign direct investment goes beyond trade and portfolio flows as a mechanism for linking economies. Wholly-owned foreign firms or domestic firms with foreign partners serve as a continuing linkage between best-practice foreign technology and local firms. This ongoing interface extends the

Table 11.2   Capital Flows in Developing Countries, 1990–1998 (Billions US$)

Net capital inflows	$1,890.6
Net capital flows	$1,313.4

SOURCE: UNCTAD, *Trade and Development Report: Capital Flows to Developing Countries* (New York and Geneva: United Nations, 1999).

---

[2] They include Argentina, Brazil, Chile, Columbia, Egypt, India, Indonesia, Malaysia, Mexico, Pakistan, Peru, Philippines, Republic of Korea, South Africa, Thailand, and Turkey.

globalization of best business practices to firms in developing countries through transfers of various aspects of innovation, accounting, management, inventory management, quality control, marketing and distribution. We studied the various issues surrounding FDI in Chapter 6. In this section, we review the changing pattern and size of FDI to the developing countries as an aspect of globalization.

FDI is closely tied to the fortunes of multinational firms, and both have grown rapidly in the last thirty years. From next to nothing in the 1970s, FDI in both the developed and developing countries has risen at a dramatic rate. By the end of 2000, annual FDI inflows totaled about US$830 billion world-wide, with nearly one quarter going to the developing countries (see the third last column of Chapter 2, Table 2.6). This is only about 2.7 percent of world GDP, yet it represents an enormous transfer of investment funds, given the collective size of the world's developing economies. By 2000, Table 11.3 shows that the FDI inflows account for a smaller percentage share of gross investment in the developing countries compared with that for the developed countries—with the exception of Latin America and the Caribbean which exhibit double-digit figures. This is primarily due to a higher proportion of gross investment in these regions being fuelled by high domestic savings. By 2007, FDI inflows appeared to have slowed, especially in the developed countries such as the United States.

What is even more surprising is that the flow of FDI has not been dramatically affected by any of the shocks to the developing economies over this period, although FDI has fallen since the beginning of the global financial crisis in 2008. It is true that there was a significant surge in FDI to both the developing and developed countries during and just after the second oil shock. In 1983, the recycling of petrodollars to the Middle East coincided with a sag in FDI to the developing countries, and as a result,

Table 11.3   FDI Inflows as a Percentage of Gross Fixed Capital Formation, 1990–2007

	Annual Average FDI Inflows		
	1990–1995	**1996–2000**	**2005–2007**
World	4.1%	12.6%	12.5%
Developed countries	3.6	12.8	12.4
Europe	5.4	21.5	19.7
European Union	5.5	21.8	19.8
Other developed Europe	3.6	16.0	18.0
Japan	0.1	0.6[a]	0.6
United States	4.3	12.4	7.5
Developing countries	5.7	11.7	12.2
Africa	4.9	8.8	19.7
Latin America and the Caribbean	7.4	18.6	16.3
Asia and Oceania	5.3	9.6	10.5
Southeast Europe and CIS[b] (transition economies)	4.8	13.5	18.3

[a]Annual figure computed from 1997 onwards.
[b]Commonwealth of Independent States (CIS).

SOURCES: UNCTAD, *World Investment Report* (2002); UNCTAD, *World Investment Report* (2008).

FDI to the developing countries nearly matched the flows to the developed countries. However, subsequently the flow of FDI increased at a very rapid pace, especially to the developing countries, which grew from US$14.2 billion in 1986 to US$1,237.9 billion in 2000.

Thus, the flow of FDI has increased dramatically over time. The flows to the developing countries are particularly interesting. Using a base of 100 in 1970, these flows increased twenty-five times by the mid-1990s in current dollar terms, and by over five times in constant dollar terms.[3] By the latter half of the 1990s, these flows averaged around US$200 billion per year, or about 2.7 percent of world GDP (Table 2.6).

However, in 2001, there was a dramatic decline in FDI flows—the sharpest reported since 1970—which have been attributed to the slowdown of growth in the developed countries and the sluggish international stock markets. The developing countries have been relatively less affected than the developed countries although they sustained a fall of 14 percent and 59 percent, respectively (UNCTAD, 2002, p. 3). There was also a slowdown in FDI flows in 2008 (UNCTAD, 2008).

Information on foreign direct investment by industry and the transfer of technology embodied in this transfer is more difficult to ascertain. Generally, it would depend upon a host of factors. Some writers would even contend that some FDI is devoid of technological transfer and is detrimental to the national interests of the recipients, who often grant numerous tax concessions and spend money to develop sites and services for potential foreign investors.

Foreign direct investment is undertaken primarily by multinational enterprises (MNEs). These are companies or enterprises operating in several countries. There are various definitions of a multinational corporation. The world's leading authority on MNE, John Dunning (1993, p. 4) says that an MNE has two distinctive features:

> First, it organizes and coordinates multiple value-adding activities across national boundaries and, second, it internalizes the cross-border markets for the intermediate products arising from these activities. No other institution engages in both cross-border production and transaction.

Ideally, any company involved in such cross-border activities would be defined as a MNE. However, the usual definition has a cut-off point of 25 percent or more of its output capacity/sales coming from outside the country of origin. Estimates of the size and the number of MNEs vary, and consistent data is not available, since different countries have different definitions and cross-border ownership is difficult to measure. The UNCTAD's *World Investment Report*, together with the work of Professor Dunning is probably among the best sources of information on FDI and multinational corporations. The *World Investment Report* estimates that about 25 percent of global output is produced by MNEs. One-third of this output is estimated to come from the home country and the rest from overseas affiliates. As the size of FDI has grown during the past decades, so have the power, reach, and influence of MNEs. Foreign-affiliated sales of goods and services in the international and domestic markets in 1998 (US$11 trillion) was considerably larger than the total sum of world exports (US$7 trillion) (UNCTAD, 1999).

Globalization has also resulted in the tremendous rise in cross-border mergers and acquisitions (M&As) since the mid-1990s[4] (see Figure 11.1). Such strategic alliances between companies in different countries could be due to a multitude of reasons, ranging from an increase in efficiency to the sharing of common resources, to capture a larger share of the market or to cut losses through restructuring. No matter what the reason is for the alliances, their general aim is to remain competitive in the international arena.

---

[3] See IMF (2000, p. 101); UNCTAD's *Trade and Development Report* (1999a), part II; and also World Bank, *World Development Finance* (1999) p. 101, chart 5.1.

[4] The dip in the values of cross-border alliances in 2001 was due to the same reason for the fall in FDI discussed earlier. See UNCTAD (2002) for greater details.

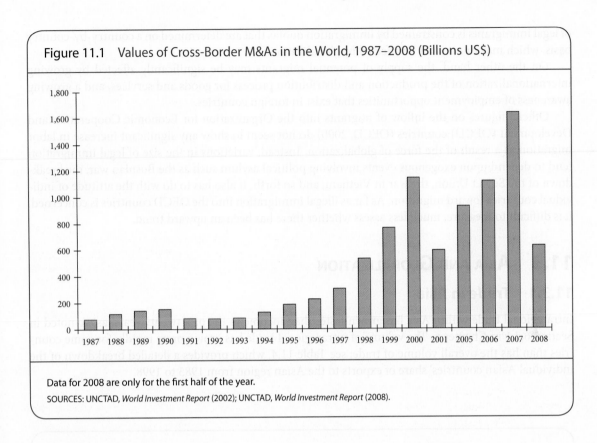

Figure 11.1   Values of Cross-Border M&As in the World, 1987–2008 (Billions US$)

Data for 2008 are only for the first half of the year.

SOURCES: UNCTAD, *World Investment Report* (2002); UNCTAD, *World Investment Report* (2008).

11.2.4   Labor Migration

International migration of labor has been going on for centuries. There was significant migration from Europe to the "new world" between the sixteenth and nineteenth centuries, and there were also waves of immigration to the United States and Latin American from Asia in the nineteenth and twentieth centuries. While there was a special set of factors underlying each wave of migration, there appear to be a few stylized facts that are common to all international migration. Migration can be for any number of reasons: to avoid religious or ethnic persecution, to flee a war zone or natural disaster, or to seek a better life, both economically and socially. Lumped together, these reasons for international migration can be called push factors.

At the other end, there are a series of pull factors. These include the scope for greater economic opportunity, political and religious freedom, ease of migration, relationships with friends or family who had previously migrated, and facility with the language and customs of the country to which potential migrants apply to enter.

Globalization has had the major effect of opening up the awareness of migration opportunities on the pull side, as well as revealing to potential migrants the chance to improve their standards of living, through better and more comprehensive information on the push side. Markets for labor have arisen and been publicized by recruiting agents that advertise positions in the sending countries.

The economics of international migration and the impact that globalization can have on the flow of migrants is complicated by the nature of the flow of human resources, as opposed to the investment of capital. The flow of migrants is much more restricted than the flow of capital. In many ways, the flow of legal immigrants is constrained by immigration quotas that are determined on a country-by-country basis, which may or may not be affected by globalization.

On the other hand, the supply of potential migrants may be significantly affected by growing internationalization of the production and distribution process for goods and services, and a growing awareness of employment opportunities that exist in foreign countries.

Official figures on the inflow of migrants into the Organization for Economic Cooperation and Development (OECD) countries (OECD, 2000) do not seem to show any significant increase in labor migration as a result of the force of globalization. Instead, variations in the size of legal immigration tend to depend upon exogenous events involving political asylum such as the Bosnian war, the breakdown of the Soviet Union, the war in Vietnam, and so forth. It also has to do with the attitude of individual countries toward migration. As far as illegal immigration into the OECD countries is concerned, it is difficult to measure, much less assess whether there has been an upward trend.

11.3   ASIA AND GLOBALIZATION

11.3.1   Trade in Asia

Intraregional trade within Asia has grown faster than income in the past twenty years, as we noted in Section 6.3.1 in Chapter 6. The volume of intraregional trade has grown more rapidly for some countries than has the overall volume of trade; see Table 11.4, which provides a detailed breakdown of the individual Asian countries' share of exports to the Asian region from 1985 to 1998.

Table 11.4   Percentage Share of Total Exports Going to Asian Countries that were Members of the Asian Development Bank (excluding Japan), 1985–1998

	Share of Exports	
	1985	1998
Hong Kong	35.6%	41.6%
Korea	12.9	30.2
Singapore	36.7	41.5
Taiwan	15.6	36.7
China	38.2	31.5
Indonesia	17.2	31.1
Malaysia	38.1	37.4
Philippines	19.5	20.2
Thailand	27.1	27.3
India	8.9	19.5
Pakistan	16.0	18.8
Sri Lanka	11.2	7.6

SOURCE: Asian Development Bank, "Asia's Globalization Challenge," *Asian Development Outlook* [special chapter] (Manila: ADB, 2001).

Surprisingly, the largest shift has been in East Asia. In Hong Kong and Taiwan, a rapid increase in trade with China has resulted in a higher share of Asian exports. In Korea, the export of manufactured goods to the rest of Asia, such as automobiles, has been responsible for the sharp increase in the Asian share. In Singapore, total trade with the rest of the region has increased because of the increased penetration of Singapore's exports to Malaysia and Indonesia, particularly electrical products. For the rest of the region, the share of intra-Asian trade has not changed much apart from Indonesia and India. In the latter case, the opening up of the economy in the 1990s has helped the country to integrate more with its neighbors in Southeast and East Asia. In Indonesia, some of the increase has come from oil exports but also other primary materials and labor-intensive manufactured products. On the other hand, China's relative share of exports to the Asian region has declined as it actively sought out new markets for its labor-intensive manufactured goods in the OECD countries, and thereby increased its penetration of non-Asian export markets.

With only a few exceptions the Asian share of exports to Japan has generally decreased, sometimes quite dramatically (see Table 11.5). This reflects the growing globalization of exports from the developing countries in Asia, as well as the increase in intraregional trade within the region. In the case of Indonesia and Malaysia, this represents a decline in primary exports, such as oil, rubber, and palm oil. In the case of Korea, China, and the Philippines, it probably reflects the fact that during the 1990s, the Japanese economy grew much more slowly than the United States, leading to a generally slower demand for imports.

A broader picture of trade within the Asian region and with the rest of the world can be seen in Table 11.6. In the last decade, trade within Southeast Asia has more than tripled, while that within China and Hong Kong more than doubled, and that between China, Hong Kong, and Southeast Asia

Table 11.5 Percentage Share of Total Exports from Asian Countries that were Members of the Asian Development Bank Going to Japan, 1985–1998

	Share of Exports	
	1985	**1998**
Hong Kong	4.2%	5.3%
Korea	15.0	9.3
Singapore	9.4	6.6
Taiwan	11.3	8.4
China	22.3	16.2
Indonesia	46.2	17.6
Malaysia	24.6	10.5
Philippines	19.0	14.4
Thailand	13.4	13.7
India	11.1	5.1
Pakistan	11.3	3.4
Sri Lanka	5.1	4.7

SOURCE: Asian Development Bank, "Asia's Globalization Challenge," *Asian Development Outlook* [special chapter] (Manila: ADB, 2001).

Table 11.6   Exports as a Percentage of GDP, 1982–2006

	1982	2006
Bangladesh	4.2%	19.0%
China	12.3	40.1
Hong Kong	86.0	205.4
India	6.1	23.0
Indonesia	26.3	30.9
Japan	14.5	14.3
Korea	33.2	43.2
Malaysia	127.1	117.0
Nepal	10.0	13.6
Pakistan	11.9	15.3
Philippines	21.3	46.4
Singapore	n.a.	252.6
Sri Lanka	26.3	31.6
Taiwan	44.8	61.3
Thailand	20.1	73.7
Vietnam	negligible	73.5

SOURCES: World Resources Institute, *Earth Trends: Trend in Goods and Services* (Washington, D.C.: WRI, 2009), Web site at http://earthtrends.wri.org/searchable_db/index.php?theme=5&variable_ID=658&action=select_countries; *Taiwan Statistical Yearbook* (2008).

and between Korea, Mongolia, and Southeast Asia tripled. Trade between Korea, Mongolia, and China has increased more than fivefold. It is evident from these figures that the trade with China has grown very rapidly. Most of this trade has been in manufactured goods. Anecdotal evidence and analysis of overall trade patterns suggest that more finished goods are shipped from China, while parts and semi-finished goods are shipped to the country for further processing into finished goods for export.

As was noted in Chapter 3, the growing interrelationship between the Asian and industrialized countries has heightened the transmission of economic shocks. These economies have been most affected by a decline in demand for its exports as well as the withdrawal of funds from equity markets. Both have created stress throughout the region. To appreciate the extent of this impact on Asia, it is important to recognize that the Asian region is even more closely integrated with the global economy than it was a decade or two ago (see Table 11.6). Many countries now have export to GDP ratios of more than 40 percent (China, Korea, Philippines, Thailand, and Vietnam) and others up to 100 percent (Hong Kong, Malaysia, and Singapore). This increased dependence on exports means that a slowdown in demand from the industrial countries has a strong negative impact on economic growth throughout the Asian region.

In addition, the balance of trade has shifted in favor of Southeast and East Asia. Thus, the growth of China and its neighbors has become more intertwined in terms of international trade connections in the past two decades. This is an important aspect of globalization that should not be forgotten.

Table 11.7 Share of Asian Exports, 2007

	China	Japan	United States	EU-27
China	n.a.	9.9%	22.5%	**23.7%**
India	10.3	2.2	13.8	**21.6**
Indonesia	10.0	**20.7**	10.2	11.3
Japan	**20.7**	n.a.	20.1	14.8
Korea	**27.1**	7.1	12.3	14.8
Malaysia	13.3	9.1	**15.6**	12.9
Philippines	**23.1**	14.3	16.8	16.9
Singapore	**20.1**	4.8	8.8	10.7
Taiwan	**40.7**	6.5	13.0	10.9
Thailand	**15.4**	11.9	12.6	13.9
Vietnam	8.1	12.5	**20.8**	19.7

Exports from countries in the first column to countries in the first row. Figures in bold reflect the largest destinations.

SOURCE: Nomura Securities, *Nomura Economics Asia*, February 2009.

China's and Hong Kong's exports to the rest of the world have grown faster than those of other countries in the region (more than threefolds compared with a doubling of exports from Korea and Mongolia, and a somewhat higher rate for Southeast Asia.). Trade figures between China alone and the rest of the world are expected to be even higher. This is partly due to the fact that China started from a low base but it is also true that the Chinese export engine is running faster than the rest of the region. This Chinese domination is reflected in the share of Asian exports by destination (see Table 11.7). It is clear that China dominates the rest of Asia, as well as the United States and the European Union in terms of share, as shown by the numbers in bold type in Table 11.7.

The bottom line is that there is a legitimate concern that China will dominate the rest of Asia in the acquisition of new technology and exports. However, there is also a good chance that the rest of the region will be buoyed up by the trade with China and China's trade with the rest of the world. Trade between the NIEs and China and between Southeast Asia and China is mainly in manufactured goods and not in raw materials. Trade in manufactured goods, primarily in components and parts, between China and the rest of Asia has grown remarkably in the past two decades. Whether the role of Southeast Asia as a subcontractor for China will continue or not is uncertain. However, it is likely that the amount of trade will continue to grow and it will contribute to the prosperity of all the regions in this part of the world. There are no indications that the growth of China and its interrelationships with the rest of the Asian region will have a detrimental impact on the growth of Southeast Asia and the rest of East Asia. There is, however, a continuing relationship with the industrial countries in Asia (Japan), Europe, and North America. As the global recession spread from the United States to Europe and to Asia, the need to adopt a global strategy for restoring the global economic balance becomes increasingly more evident. This has been discussed already in Chapter 3 but we will touch on it again in the next section where we also consider whether a shift in the pattern of FDI affects the terms of international trade.

11.3.2 The Rapid Rise in Capital Inflows

FOREIGN DIRECT INVESTMENT   The major part of capital inflows into the NIEs and Southeast Asia in recent years have been in the form of foreign direct investment. Focusing on these inflows, several patterns deserve comment. In recent decades, FDI inflows to the Asian economies have soared from US$3.7 billion in 1980 to US$132.5 billion in 2000 (Table 11.8). Considering the total inflows in U.S. dollars, all Asian subregions had higher inflows in 2000 than in 1980. However, the distribution of these inflows has changed dramatically, and the shift away from Southeast and East Asia toward China is quite striking since in the early and mid-1980s, the FDI inflows to China had been negligible.

Between 1980 and 2000, Southeast Asia's share fell from roughly two-thirds of the total to less than one-tenth, while East Asia's share (including China) jumped from 26 percent to 88 percent (see Table 11.9).

Table 11.8   Asian Intraregional Trade in Exports (Billions US$)

Host	China and Hong Kong		Southeast Asia		Korea and Mongolia		Rest of World	
	1990	**2001**	**1990**	**2001**	**1990**	**2001**	**1990**	**2001**
China and Hong Kong	$ 47	$ 117	$ 10	$ 29	$ 2	$ 16	$ 85	$ 294
Southeast Asia	9	39	26	87	5	14	102	250
Korea and Mongolia	4	28	5	16	0	79	59	106
Rest of world	70	213	103	199	52	101	2,801	4,633

Rest of the world includes all economies except Korea, Mongolia, Southeast Asia, China, and Hong Kong.

SOURCE: Asian Development Bank, *Asian Development Outlook 2003*.

Table 11.9   FDI Inflows Within Asia (Millions US$)

	1980	**2000**	**2007**
Hong Kong	$ 710 (19%)	$ 61,938 (46%)	$ 54,343 (20.5%)
China	51 (2%)	40,772 (31%)	83,521 (31.5%)
Southeast Asia	2,435 (65%)	10,455 (8%)	67,850 (26%)
Rest of Asia	495 (14%)	19,343 (15%)	59,092 (22%)
Asia	3,691 (100%)	132,508 (100%)	264,806 (100%)

Figures in parenthesis represent the percentage of total FDI inflows.

SOURCES: Asian Development Bank, *Asian Development Outlook 2003*; Asian Development Bank, *Asian Development Outlook 2008*.

By 2000, FDI inflows into China were substantially higher than in both Southeast Asia and the rest of Asia. The second point is that as a percentage of total investment, FDI plays a still relatively small part in China. Hong Kong's share has more than doubled and is more than China's, reflecting its growing role as an entrepôt gateway for the mainland. Southeast Asia's share has shrunk to less than 10 percent from 65 percent in 1980. These trends suggest that if China maintains its rapid rate of growth and continues to improve its economic efficiency, there is wide scope for increasing the amount of foreign direct investment even further. Surprisingly, despite the doubling of FDI inflows into China, its share has remained fairly constant, at 32 percent of FDI inflows into Asia. Hong Kong's share has declined in recent years while Southeast Asia and the rest of Asia have successfully played catch-up.

It is also interesting to consider what happens when FDI inflows are deflated by the size of the country's share in world trade. This can be done by comparing a country's share of global inward FDI to its share of global GDP.[5] UNCTAD has compiled such an index in its *World Investment Report* and it is displayed in Table 11.10. A country with a value greater than one implies that the country is attracting more FDI than is implied by the size of its economy.

China has moved slightly up in rank from 61 in the world to 47, and its ratio has increased from 0.9 to 1.2 in a decade. What is more dramatic is the fall of Singapore from the top ranking to 18, and its value decline from 13.8 to only 2.2 within the same period, and the fall in ranking of the other Asian economies, with the exception of Vietnam and Hong Kong. By 2007, Singapore had managed to regain 7th position, but China had fallen to 88th position.

Table 11.10   UNCTAD Inward FDI Performance Index, 1988–2007

| | 1988–1990 | | 1998–2000 | | 2007 |
	Value	Ranking	Value	Ranking	Rank
Singapore	13.8	1	2.2	18	7
Hong Kong	5.4	4	5.9	2	1
Malaysia	4.4	8	1.2	44	71
Thailand	2.6	25	1.3	41	64
Myanmar	1.9	36	0.6	82	99
Philippines	1.7	39	0.6	89	96
Vietnam	1.0	53	2.0	20	43
Taiwan	0.9	58	0.3	112	111
China	0.9	61	1.2	47	88
Indonesia	0.8	63	−0.6	138	104
South Korea	0.5	93	0.6	87	130
Japan	0	128	0.1	131	135
Asia	1.07	n.a.	0.85	n.a.	n.a.

SOURCES: UNCTAD, *World Investment Report* (2002); UNCTAD, *World Investment Report* (2008).

---

[5] This was suggested by Lim Tiong Pin in a paper he wrote for a class in "The economic development of Asia" at Singapore Management University in 2003.

How will these developments in the flow of FDI impact on the rest of the Asian region? First, it is important to recognize that the flow of FDI, while an important source of innovation, increased economic efficiency, and new technology remains a small fraction of total investment in the region, even in the NIEs and East Asia, where it has risen to more than 10 percent. (This is not to minimize the importance of FDI in several economies, such as Singapore and Malaysia, where FDI is substantially higher.) Secondly, the growing interrelationship between China and the rest of the region through greater trade will mean that the rapid growth of the former will provide trade opportunities as well. This is evident from an analysis of the shift in trade between 1990 and 2001, shown in Table 11.6.

It is interesting to note that while exports from China to the rest of the world have increased dramatically, so has the trade between the other Asian regions and China. Furthermore, the trade balance has shifted strongly in favor of both East Asia and Southeast Asia, although the latter region still has a deficit with China. This evidence suggests that the growth in China's trade with the rest of the world also pulled along with it the rest of the region through trade linkages. It is also important to note that this growth in trade between China and the rest of the region has been in manufactured goods. While the trade might be easily characterized as the export of parts and components from East and Southeast Asia and the import of finished goods into the countries of these regions, the picture is not so simple. Rather, the growing interrelationship between China and its neighbors can be considered as an extension of the network of interrelationships between suppliers and finished goods exports in a global value chain network that was discussed earlier in Chapter 6.

Going back to the earlier question in Section 11.3, will the shift in the pattern of FDI eventually be felt in terms of international trade, the answer is not clear yet from the figures shown above. However, it has to be recognized that these flows, important though they may be, carrying with them new technology and innovation, are still small compared with the overall level of investment in these countries.

As the global financial crisis of 2008 unfolded, the pattern of capital flows to Asia changed quite dramatically. Results for the first two or three quarters of 2008, as reported in Table 11.11, show that as FDI slowed in Hong Kong, China, Singapore, and Thailand, the net FDI inflows in the first half of 2008 declined noticeably from the trend (see Table 11.11). While FDI in India has not fallen yet, portfolio flows have already reversed and FDI can be expected to follow in about a year's time if history is any guide. A further decline in FDI would have significant repercussions on the Asian countries, since these inflows have been one of the major sources of advanced technology and higher productivity in technology-intensive industries. At the same time, a fall in portfolio investment has had an adverse impact on household wealth, and eventually, on consumption and investment.

CROSS-BORDER MERGERS AND ACQUISITONS Dunning (2001) commented that there appears to have been a rapid increase in cross-border mergers and acquisitions (M&As) in the Asian countries since the 1990s. He classified the Asian developing countries under three separate groups based on differing levels of human development and found that cross-border M&As were more common in the more advanced NIEs and China than in the other Asian countries during the mid-1990s. Table 11.12 gives the accumulated market values of cross-border strategic alliances of selected Asian countries from 1991 to 2001, and the data supports Dunning's findings. Further increases in M&As continued right up to the global financial crisis in 2008/2009.

11.3.3   Labor Migration and Remittances in Asia

In Asia, there has been a trend toward the integration of economies on many levels. In the realm of international trade, we saw in a previous section that the volume of intraregional trade within Asia increased rather dramatically in the past couple of decades, particularly in the NIEs. Migration has also

Table 11.11   Net Capital Inflows in Asia, 2005–2008 (Billions US$)

	PRC		Hong Kong		India		Indonesia		Korea		MA		Philippines		Singapore		Taiwan		Thailand	
	FDI	Port	FDI	Port	FDI	Port	FDI	Port	FDI	Port	FDI	Port	FDI	Port	FDI	Port	FDI	Port	FDI	Port
2005	90.3	−5.9	6.4	−31.5	4.6	12.1	5.3	4.2	2.0	−3.5	1.0	−3.7	1.7	3.5	7.0	−3.3	−4.4	−2.9	7.5	5.5
2006	87.9	−96.8	0.1	−26.7	6.8	9.5	2.2	4.2	−4.5	−23.2	0.04	3.6	2.8	3.0	12.5	−9.0	0.03	−18.9	8.0	3.6
2007	172.3	13.8	6.7	4.7	10.1	34.8	2.1	5.5	−13.7	−24.6	−2.7	5.3	−0.5	4.4	11.7	−17.2	−3.3	−40.1	7.3	−6.9
2008 Q1	n.a.	n.a.	7.2	−24.3	6.4	**−3.7**	**1.1**	1.9	−4.8	−10.0	−0.9	6.6	0.5	0.4	2.5	−3.2	−2.6	2.9	**1.8**	4.2
2008 Q2	n.a.	n.a.	**−10.3**	3.0	10.1	**−4.2**	**1.0**	4.3	−2.9	6.0	0.9	**−7.4**	0.2	**−0.6**	**0.9**	−6.0	−1.5	**−10.8**	**0.3**	**4.2**
2008 Q3	n.a.	n.a.	n.a.	n.a.	n.a.	n.a.	n.a.	n.a.	−2.3	**−12.8**	n.a.	n.a.	n.a.	n.a.	n.a.	n.a.	n.a.	n.a.	n.a.	n.a.

Figures in bold denote a recent deterioration.

SOURCE: William E. James et al., "The US Financial Crisis, Global Financial Turmoil, and Developing Asia: Is the Era of High Growth at an End?" ADB Economics Working Paper Series No. 139, December 2008.

Table 11.12   Values of Cross-border M&As (Millions US$)[a]

	1991–2001 (Accumulated Values)		2007	
	Sales	**Purchases**	**Sales**	**Purchases**
China	$ 13,552	$ 5,166	$ 12,185	$ 4,529
Hong Kong	41,726	35,900	12,991	13,430
India	6,179	4,970	18,830	11,265
Indonesia	8,623	2,275	4,027	1,389
Korea	26,399	9,434	5,041	10,228
Malaysia	6,504	18,106	4,582	5,610
Philippines	13,115	1,138	4,779	763
Singapore	13,184	39,398	10,379	27,436
Taiwan	5726	3,055	5,495	1,525
Thailand	10,482	1,390	3,199	431

[a]Calculations made from figures from *World Investment Report*.

SOURCES: UNCTAD, *World Investment Report* (2002); UNCTAD, *World Investment Report* (2008).

increased but it is more difficult to assess the magnitude of the shifts, primarily because much of the migration has been irregular or illegal. The broad pattern is, however, quite clear.

Richer countries that grew rapidly in the 1980s and 1990s have low levels of unemployment and are, in fact, experiencing a growing need for a variety of skilled workers that are in short supply in the domestic labor force. While the movement of unskilled labor has received wide publicity, there is also a strong flow of immigrants in some skilled and professional occupations. The main recipients of this new wave of migration are Japan, Singapore, and Taiwan, and more recently, Malaysia and Thailand. Japan and Taiwan have attracted labor from all over the Asian region, while Singapore has experienced a large migration from Malaysia, especially from adjacent locations on the Malaysian mainland, either on a daily basis or more permanently.

Some countries have been both significant importers and exporters of labor. For example, a few years before the Asian crisis, Thailand had been importing labor from Myanmar, Vietnam, and to a lesser extent, Laos and Cambodia. Yet it also sent many migrants to the Middle East. Malaysia has been importing labor from Indonesia and sending migrants to Singapore.

The Philippines, Indonesia, and the poorer countries of Indochina—Vietnam, Cambodia, and Laos—have higher levels of unemployment and a somewhat lower standard of living than the rest of the region. Because of these pressures on the labor market and larger income differentials in these countries, they have been the largest suppliers of migrants to the rest of the region. In the case of the Philippines, facility with English has allowed migrants to move to many different countries where English is spoken.

The relaxation of visa and travel restrictions and the growing regional integration within Asia have made it easier for people to move around the region. For example, ASEAN members can travel freely between member countries for short periods of time without a visa.

Remittances are closely related to the flow and pace of international migration. As noted in Chapter 5, these flows are not likely to be seriously disrupted as a result of the global financial crisis, which began in 2008. However, some softness has surfaced and the World Bank recorded a slight fall in remittances as a share of global GDP between 2007 and 2008. Further declines in 2009 are possible.

11.3.4 Role of International Institutions

The role of international institutions in the process of globalization has been multifaceted. At one level, the flow of resources to the developing countries generated by these institutions has fallen quite dramatically in the past three or four decades. Flows of international assistance into the Asian developing countries have been confined primarily to South Asia in recent years, although there is some acceleration in the rate of assistance to the Mekong countries. China also receives assistance but it is small relative to the size of private capital inflows and the domestic economy as well as domestic investment (see Table 11.13).

Table 11.13 Official Development Assistance and Official Aid, 1960–2006 (Current Millions US$)

	1960	1970	1980	1990	2000	2006
East Asia						
China	n.a.	n.a.	$ 66	$ 2,080	$ 1,740.0	$ 1,245
Korea, Rep. of	250	275.0	139	52	−200.0	n.a.
Southeast Asia						
Cambodia	27	19.0	281	42	398.0	529
Indonesia	81	465.0	949	1,740	1,730.0	1,404
Lao PDR	33	69.0	41	150	281.0	364
Malaysia	13	27.0	135	469	45.4	240
Philippines	51	46.0	300	1,280	578.0	562
Thailand	43	74.0	418	797	641.0	−216
Vietnam	191	437.0	229	189	1,700.0	1,846
South Asia						
Bangladesh	n.a.	n.a.	1,280	2,100	1,170.0	1,223
Bhutan	n.a.	0.2	834	47	53.0	94
India	727	825.0	2,190	1,410	1,490.0	1,379
Nepal	8	24.0	163	426	390.0	514
Pakistan	252	421.0	1,180	1,130	703.0	2,147
Sri Lanka	11	49.0	390	730	276.0	796
Total[a]	1,687	2,311.2	8,595	13,053	9,580.4	n.a.

[a]This includes other official development assistance and official aid which were not listed here.

SOURCES: UNCTAD, *World Investment Report* (2002); UNCTAD, *World Investment Report* (2008).

The main role that international institutions can play in the current globalization scenario is to work for further reductions in trade barriers, and to resolve issues regarding trade in services, and intellectual property rights, as well as environmental issues, labor and industrial standards, banking and other financial regulations, and other aspects of trade policy such as dumping. In this connection, the World Trade Organization can play a major role. As the world recession of 2008 and 2009 deepens, the role of international institutions has taken on new dimensions. In particular, it is important for these institutions to guard against the threat of protectionism that has tended to emerge during periods of global recessions, such as the interwar period and the years following the great depression of the 1930s. There is also a concern that the globalization of finance might be at risk since the worldwide recession has spread through the banking and financial systems of the industrialized countries.

11.3.5 How Have the Asian Economies Dealt With the Globalization Issue?[6]

Many of the Asian economies have integrated quickly into the increasingly globalized world economy, as we have seen in previous chapters. However, the two giants in the region, China and India, have been slow in opening up their economic systems. It is worth looking at the policies followed by these two countries.

CHINA   China embarked on a wide-ranging series of economic reforms in the late 1970s which eventually propelled the country from an inwardly focused, highly centralized communist state to center stage as one of the most important trading nations in the world economy. A series of internal steps were critical to that transformation. One of the first steps that the new leader at that time, Deng Xiaoping, did was to tighten control of population growth. This strategy, which culminated in a one-child per family policy, was quite successful in the urban areas but met with resistance in the countryside. Eventually, they were relaxed somewhat. Still this policy was instrumental in reducing the rate of population growth dramatically. While this policy had little effect on the process of globalization, it had a long-term effect on the growth of the labor force, which in later years became critical to the implementation of reforms in the industrial sector.

The second reform took place in agriculture, where the household responsibility system (HRS) replaced the commune system. In this system, the communes leased plots of land to individual households, who delivered a fixed quota of their produce to the commune. The household kept the remainder, either to sell in the private markets that quickly developed, or to consume themselves. These reforms had an enormous stimulating effect on agricultural output. From 1978 to 1986, when the HRS spread to cover nearly all the communes, the value of farm output in current prices almost tripled.

The increased incomes in the countryside contributed to a virtuous cycle of growth. Increased production and procurement prices raised rural incomes and saving rates. Higher incomes, in turn, created demand for consumer goods that were in short supply. To meet this demand, local governments began to direct saving into collectively owned firms, town and village enterprises (TVEs). Increases in farming efficiency created a pool of labor that could work in these TVEs. As a result, industrial production in the countryside accelerated. The TVEs' share of industrial output rose quickly from almost nothing to more than a third of total industrial output. During the 1980s, TVE output grew at an average rate of 30 percent per annum (Kennedy and Vietor, 2001, p. 4).

---

[6] The country experience of China and India draw heavily on the summaries presented by Kennedy and Vietor (2001).

As industrial output rose rapidly, trade and investment reforms also took place that quickly transformed the landscape of a country that had been virtually isolated from the rest of the world. It had no direct foreign investment and a trade ratio to GDP of only 10 percent in the mid-1970s. Three related sets of reforms accomplished this transformation.

The first was trade reform that took place on a piecemeal basis. This continued throughout the 1980s. It involved the licensing of new foreign-trade corporations (FTCs) by local governments in order to bypass the twelve FTCs that were authorized by the central government. By the end of the 1980s, the number of FTCs had mushroomed to more than 5,000, and the number of domestic firms with trading rights increased to more than 10,000. This liberalization of the trading environment at the firm level was accompanied by a slower liberalization of the tariff regime.

The second policy initiative was a liberalization of foreign direct investment. This was much more controversial, but by compromising to hold the liberalization to a few geographical areas in the southern part of the country, China was able to attract enormous inflows of FDI, so that by the mid-1990s, it was the largest destination of FDI among all the developing countries. The four coastal cities designated as special economic zones (SEZs) in the early 1980s grew at double-digit rates for the next two decades.

The third set of reforms involved foreign currency. The currency was depreciated in real terms during the 1980s and early 1990s, and foreign currency transactions were slowly deregulated. The current account was freed up although the capital account was not. Nevertheless, regulations in the SEZs were relaxed enough so that the pace of economic activity could proceed at a rapid pace.

These reforms led to a dramatic transformation of China's links with the outside world. Exports grew at a extremely rapid rate for two decades. Merchandise exports in U.S. dollar terms grew thirteen-fold from 1980 to 2000. Exports rose from less than 11 percent of GDP to 23 percent. The response of FDI was slower, but equally as spectacular by the end of the 1990s. From US$57 million in 1980, FDI grew to more than US$40 billion by the mid-1990s, an increase of 700 percent in less than twenty years. The SEZs were the focal point for both exports and FDI, particularly in the 1990s. By the end of that decade, foreign invested enterprises accounted for more than 40 percent of total exports.

China has been striving hard to reform formerly protected state-owned enterprises (SOEs) which have generally been inefficient and running at a loss over the years. This involves massive restructuring or even closure of the SOEs, and substantial layoffs estimated to affect about 35 million people in the next few years (Smadja, 2001). However, this move is critical if China wants to make a successful transition to a market-oriented economy and to remain competitive. The progress of such reforms has remained extremely unevenly distributed throughout the country and faced strong opposition from the SOE employees, which have led to massive strikes and civil unrest, especially in the countryside. If not handled well, this will have dire consequences on China's future economic growth.

Greater private-sector participation has been encouraged in order to increase the economy's synchrony with market demand forces and efficiency of resource allocation. China has formally recognized private ownership since 1998, but more needs to be done to safeguard the rights of private enterprises—for instance, the establishment of a legal framework (Smadja, 2001). Other reforms in the agricultural[7] and financial sectors, such as the cleaning up of bad bank loans by asset management companies (AMCs), have also been established to improve its competitiveness in the domestic and global arena.

INDIA India followed a policy of government controlled and directed growth for most of its history from 1947 until the beginning of the 1990s. These policies focused on the control of the economy through four complementary policies: extensive regulation of international trade and investment,

---

[7] Refer to Chapter 4, Box 4.1, for a greater understanding of the agricultural sector in China.

control of key sectors of production, central control of domestic investment, and an elaborate system of licensing and regulation.

In pursuit of an import-substitution strategy, regulations were introduced to control foreign exchange transactions and imports, with the former being allocated according to a priority list. Debt repayments received the highest priority, followed by capital goods, raw materials, and lastly consumer goods, which were rarely approved. Policies toward foreign investment depended upon the ability to earn foreign exchange and the government's attitude toward the role that foreign investment could play. Between 1957 and 1970, joint ventures were encouraged but the first oil shock and a balance of payments crisis resulted in a reversal of the policy. Then in the late 1970s, the policy was reversed after the second oil shock. However, by that time, India had become one of the most isolated major countries in the world. Exports plus imports were less than 15 percent of GDP.

To control key sectors, the government nationalized a number of industries, including commercial banks, life insurance, and large firms in processing and manufacturing, such as fertilizer, mining, chemicals, steel, and oil industries. By the 1980s, the government owned nearly half of India's industrial assets. The returns were low and efficiency poor. Despite high rates of investment, India's growth was hampered by poor infrastructure that further reduced industrial productivity and efficiency.

Because the financial sector was owned by the state and foreign capital investment was controlled and during some periods, effectively prohibited, the government had a virtual lock on how investment was allocated in the economy. The Planning Commission established investment policies for state-owned firms, and directed the private sector through its regulation and control of banks' portfolios.

The government bureaucracy controlled all licenses to do business (both entry and exit) as well as many prices and the expansion of industrial capacity. This regulatory control extended to all private firms as well as the public sector. This control of capacity was introduced ostensibly to prevent duplication and reduce "unnecessary competition." In fact, it was used to prevent new and potentially more efficient firms from entering the market while protecting the already established, no matter how inefficient.

Industrial policy throughout this period tended to steer development toward more capital-intensive industries, even though there were many incentives on the books for small businesses.

The end result of this bureaucratic network of controls and regulations, such as subsidies, taxes, prohibitions and controls, was a highly inefficient and cumbersome economic system that grew slowly, without much competition or new technology. It produced the same products year after year at high costs. It did not follow its international comparative advantage in labor-intensive products for export but rather remained isolated from the international community, moving forward at its own slow "Indian rate of growth." By the beginning of the 1990s, it had been left far behind in nearly every aspect by the NIEs and the countries of Southeast Asia.

In the 1990s, the policy stance was radically modified. Considerable progress was made in that decade in overhauling foreign trade and investment regulations, in reducing state control of industry, in liberalizing the financial sector, in freeing up investment decisions, and in eliminating many regulations on capacity creation and import licensing.

This process of reform proceeded in fits and starts, but the Indian economy is now much more open than it was a decade ago. The rupee was devalued to help exporters and made fully convertible on the current account. Most import licenses were eliminated, and tariffs were lowered and simplified. The rules for approving foreign direct investment were revamped and the ceiling on foreign ownership removed. There was also a concerted effort to reduce the role of the public sector in the economy, including the opening up of some sectors to the private sector, the sale of government assets, and the closure of loss-making businesses. Capacity licensing was dramatically reduced and the banking system was opened up to foreign ownership and entry. Interest rates have also been partially deregulated.

There was, and continues to be, opposition to the reform. Begun during a period of turmoil following the assassination of Prime Minister Rajiv Gandhi, it survived the failure of the Congress Party, was reelected, maintained, and extended by the current coalition of ruling parties. Despite these difficulties, the reforms had a powerful effect on those sectors of the economy where openness and competition had been most apparent. Economic growth accelerated, particularly after 1996, to 7 percent by the end of the decade. There was an influx of foreign direct investment, trade as a proportion of GDP increased to nearly 20 percent, the economy became more open, and portfolio investment also increased. The information technology sector became a showpiece for the reform effort as many new companies were listed both at home and on foreign bourses.

There are still many areas where the reforms have been less effective, or not been implemented at all. The insurance industry is still protected. There have also been disputes regarding FDI, including the validity of contracts and property rights. The Enron power project has been particularly contentious and has damaged India's reputation in the eyes of some foreign investors. Privatization has moved slowly as it faces opposition from many groups within the country. Nevertheless, India has made significant strides toward opening up the economy, and is likely to continue to open further in the future.

MALAYSIA Malaysia initially favored the development of import-substitution strategies and heavy industries, such as the manufacture of cars, methanol, pulp and paper, which made use of labor-intensive and assembly-type production techniques, and emphasized domestic demand and self-sufficiency. From the mid-1980s, Malaysia realized the importance of foreign markets in accelerating economic growth through exports and investment, and trade liberalization programs began in earnest.[8] The structure of exports eventually shifted from an agricultural base dominated by food crops, rubber, and palm oil to an industrial-related base with manufactured goods and electronic/IT products. The share of manufactured goods in merchandise exports rose from 19 percent in 1980 to 80 percent in 2000 (refer to Table 2.4 in Chapter 2).

The government has placed a greater emphasis on higher value and high-tech production activities to further improve productivity levels in the export sector. Exports of electronic and related peripherals are expected to become more important as Malaysia proceeds toward its goal of becoming a high-value-added manufacturing center. Malaysia also plans to position its service sector as a regional hub of excellence, in areas such as transportation and education. New growth engines in the agricultural sector, in high-tech industries such as aquaculture, agro-technology, and urban horticulture, have also been developed.

Other reforms, such as the liberalization of foreign investment and privatization, have also been implemented. Administrative rules and regulations have been relaxed to create a more favorable investment climate—for both private and foreign players. Formerly protected industries have had to face up to growing competition from other players in the field, undertake the appropriate measures to increase efficiency, or risk closing down. State-owned corporations, such as the airline and shipping companies, have also been sold off to investors. The influx of foreign investments has also brought with it greater physical capabilities, technology transfer, and economic revenue. Thus, such market-oriented policies have lessened government budgetary pressures and increased overall productivity levels.

With growing competition, especially from China, in the international markets, Malaysia has been keen to adopt information technology and to establish a knowledge-based labor force to upgrade itself

---

[8] Actually, trade liberalization measures had taken place as early as 1968, but were abandoned later when it was noted that there was a lack of linkages between foreign investment and domestic manufacturing (Common, 2003). Thus, on one hand, there was rapid foreign investment and economic growth in free trade zones but, on the other hand, there was little change in domestic production.

in the scale of production. The government recently tried to establish English as the medium of learning nationwide through primary and secondary schools, but has faced opposition from local Chinese business groups. International best practices for firms, such as ISO certifications, have been introduced. The public and private sectors have also collaborated to launch an extremely large-scale project named the Multimedia Super Corridor, reportedly worth US$20 billion, to accelerate growth in the IT industry. Thus, most initiatives to improve international competitiveness appear to be in place, but it remains to be seen whether the degree of implementation is effective and sufficient.

THE PHILIPPINES The Philippines has actively developed an export-oriented sector, mainly agricultural-based, to generate sufficient foreign exchange to repay debts incurred by President Ferdinand Marcos and his cronies in the 1960s up to the mid-1980s. That particular period was characterized by systematic corruption, patronage, misappropriation of public funds, civil unrest, and martial law. Marcos' cronies were rewarded with financial incentives in terms of loans at special rates, together with monopolistic control over state industries. Thus, wealth was amassed by those in power at the expense of the public, leaving behind inadequate infrastructures and other social problems, such as poverty and unemployment.

The Philippines has embarked on government policies such as the liberalization of exports and FDI, deregulation, privatization, and land reforms since the late 1980s to generate economic growth and to enable it to repay accumulated foreign debts. Such debt payments took up a large proportion of the Philippines' government budget, thereby leading to insufficient funds for the provision of social services, such as basic preventive health services like immunization.

Trade reforms were implemented after the fall of Marcos from power but economic development did not really take off until the early 1990s (Henderson, 2002). Trade was liberalized and import tariffs eliminated. Domestic manufacturing was further stimulated with the setting up of export-processing zones. In the early phases of trade liberalization, exports were mainly concentrated in primary commodities, such as food crops, minerals, and timber, of which the Philippines has a natural abundance of supplies and enjoys comparative advantage. However, there has been an increase in the trade in manufactured products, such as electronic manufactures, in recent years.

Furthermore, the establishment of the Foreign Investment Act allowed the entry of foreign investors and attracted substantial capital inflows into the country. Annual average FDI inflows rose by more than 2.5 percent—from US$493 million at the end of 1990 to US$1,268 million by 2000 (see Table 2.6 in Chapter 2). The openness of the economy to global capital flows may also partially explain why the Philippines was hit by the Asian financial crisis in 1997/1998. However, the Philippine government appears to hold the view that greater liberalization of trade and FDI, and global integration was and continues to be essential for its economic development—this was reaffirmed by its aims to fulfill World Trade Organization (WTO) and ASEAN Free Trade Agreement (AFTA) conditions, as stated in *The Medium Term Philippines Development Plan, 1999–2004*.

In addition, the Philippines deregulated the banking sector as well as previously protected state industries, such as telecommunications, airlines and shipping, oil-refining and water supplies, in a move to improve the overall efficiency and growth of the economy. Fourthly, public–private partnerships and the privatization of public utilities were carried out. However, implementation has been slow (Hayllar, 2003).

Finally, land reforms have been implemented with the aim of improving the domestic effectiveness of the agricultural sector, which accounts for two-thirds of the workforce, and to increase its competitiveness in the world since its exports are primarily agricultural products. Land reforms were suggested as early as in 1987 but were delayed by fierce opposition from the elite for almost a decade. About 200,000 landless farmers have now received land parcels (Hayllar, 2003, p. 265).

Over the years, the speed and effectiveness of government reforms were to some degree hindered by a constantly changing political leadership, which created uncertainty and lessened its attractiveness to foreign investors. Indeed, the Philippines has experienced not less than four new political leaders in the past two decades: President Corazon Aquino in 1987, Fidel Ramos in 1992, Joseph Estrada in 1998, and Gloria Arroyo in 2001. Hence, the level of political stability and efficiency of government agencies and their policies have significantly impacted on investors' confidence and subsequent inflows of foreign investment.

Overall, the government reforms appear to have improved the Philippines' level of openness and competitiveness. The existence of a skilled and relatively low-cost base of English-speaking workforce is a plus factor for the Philippines when competing in the global economy. Its low cost makes it particularly attractive for global outsourcing and production strategies by foreign companies. For instance, the local Manila call centers charge only one-sixth of the costs (US$200–300 per month) incurred in southern United States and offer excellent quality service (Henderson, 2002). The Philippines has also been moving up the production scale toward the manufacture of more sophisticated value-added products, such as electronics and other high-tech products from agricultural food processing, hence appearing well-set for competition in the international arena. However, critical issues such as the unequal distribution of income and lack of adequate infrastructure need to be resolved for a more effective usage of all available resources.

11.3.6   Increased Economic Volatility and Economic Cooperation

Globalization made itself evident during the Asian financial crisis of 1997, when the crisis which began in Thailand spilled over into the rest of the region. The crisis demonstrated several characteristics that were further exacerbated by globalization. First, there was a buildup of a sense of euphoria just before the crisis. This led to overinvestment and greater risk-taking. The crisis was triggered by a dramatic shift in expectations and was reinforced by incomplete, missing or misleading information which strengthened the swing in expectations. Secondly, globalization made markets easier to enter and exit but it also facilitated the spread of panic and contagion across markets. While the other countries that were affected may also have had weaknesses in their corporate and financial structures and institutions, there was no doubt that the ability of investors to move money around easily helped to exacerbate the domino effect on the rest of the region. Thirdly, financial liberalization preceded most of the financial crises in the world economy in the last hundred years. Fourthly, fixed exchange rates contributed to the crisis.

In recent years since the crisis, a number of proposals have been made to help reduce the chance of further contagion effects in the future and for improving the flow and accuracy of information, as well as to strengthen the financial systems. Some of these proposals have already been reviewed in Chapters 3 and 7. In this section we will focus on the proposals to provide central banks with swap arrangements, and more broadly, to consider creating a common currency or an optimal currency area.

Following the Asian crisis, there was renewed interest in developing a greater spirit of cooperation among central banks in the Asian region. This culminated in a formal initiative adopted by the ASEAN finance ministers at a meeting in Brunei Darussalam on March 24–25, 2000, to explore ways to expand swap arrangements between central banks in the region. These swaps are designed to support central banks in countries where currencies might come under attack and would need to supplement their foreign exchange reserves. This initiative, dubbed the Chiang Mai Initiative, as it was first discussed in a meeting of ASEAN finance ministers in Chiang Mai, Thailand, was extended in the Brunei meeting to establishing a swap arrangement among all the ASEAN countries and to augment these arrangements with similar agreements between the ASEAN members and China, Japan, and Korea. The ASEAN

Secretariat subsequently developed a series of proposals, and later, a number of swap arrangements were announced on a bilateral basis.

The idea of extending the Chiang Mai Initiative to developing a common currency for the region has also been discussed in academic circles, and informally at the government level. The idea would be to adopt a common currency in the same spirit that the European Union adopted the Euro. Several authors, including Madhur (2002) and Eichengreen and Bayoumi (1999), have discussed the economic arguments for and against having a common currency. The economic fundamentals required for a so-called optimal currency area require a number of conditions. These include trade and economic integration, wage and price flexibility, and the ability to absorb external shocks in similar ways (shock symmetry), as well as labor mobility. Analysis of these conditions for Asia led Eichengreen and Bayoumi to conclude that, from a purely economic perspective, the East Asian/ASEAN region is as suitable for becoming an optimal currency area as Europe was before the Maastricht Treaty.

There are many advantages to having a common currency, including greater opportunities for trade and flexibility in wages and prices, as well as enhanced competition and greater economic efficiency. The risks and volatility of a floating exchange rate for an individual country are also mitigated by a common currency. On the other hand, there are risks and challenges to forming an optimal currency area, including the loss of control over monetary policy as well as some loss of autonomy in fiscal policy. Another possible risk is that a weak banking system could undermine a common currency arrangement. While banking crises have not been as widespread in the Asian developing economies that are involved in such a proposal, forming such an area would entail significant risks particularly when the memory of the financial crisis of 1997 is still fresh in the minds of the ASEAN members.

The conclusion that most economists and others who have studied the possibility for an optimal currency area have reached is that while the economic fundamentals required are not significantly different from Europe before Maastrict, apart from wider differences in the levels of per-capita income, the political climate is not nearly as well developed as Europe was. For this reason, it is unlikely that an optimal currency area will work in the near future, although greater integration is likely to take place through the extension of the Chiang Mai agreement to other countries and wider cooperation between central banks in the region.

11.3.7   Has Globalization Been Good for Developing Countries?

There are now many critics of globalization. This is partly a result of the acceleration in the pace of globalization in the past two or three decades and the information and technological revolutions that have increased efficiency and slashed the costs of transportation and communication. Looking at the longer sweep of history, globalization has been taking place since the first explorers set out to see what was over the horizon.

The focus of the criticism of globalization seems to be primarily on the tendency for the richer industrial countries to continue to exploit the developing countries, despite the growth of the global trading system and the establishment of the WTO. The critique of the industrialized countries has several components.

INDUSTRIAL COUNTRIES DO NOT TRANSFER ENOUGH TECHNOLOGY TO DEVELOPING COUNTRIES   The argument here is that while some technology is transferred, it is almost never at the cutting edge, and there is often very little actual transfer of technology. Korea is a case in point. Much of the technological transfer from its partners in the automobile industry was made only at the urging of the Korea partner. In the case of Daewoo, General Motors helped a textile company to become an international conglomerate not because of its own vision but because of the vision of its Korean partner.

Generally, multinationals are content with getting by with a limited amount of technological transfer. In the case of the North American Free Trade Agreement (NAFTA), the agreement prohibits the transfer of technology to local companies. In Malaysia, the evidence is that local firms have benefited to some extent from the transfer of technology in the computer industry but not nearly as much as the local partners of multinationals. In the Philippines, there has also been very little transfer of technology to local firms.

INTELLECTUAL PROPERTY OF INDUSTRIAL COUNTRIES IS PROTECTED AT THE EXPENSE OF THE DEVELOPING COUNTRIES   The protection of intellectual property is required in order to provide incentives for new research and development. This is why patent laws were developed and enforced. However, the developing countries argue that there should be exceptions in obvious cases where the public good of the world economy would be better served by reducing the reach and application of some of this protection. Maintaining a high price for AIDS medicines that help HIV/AIDS patients live longer has long been the policy of drug companies. Recently, they have acceded to pressure to provide subsidies to poor African countries where the drugs could have a significant impact in alleviating the pain and suffering of large numbers of people with HIV/AIDS. In the view of many trade economists, this is a royalty collection issue and not a trade issue. The World Bank has estimated that enforcement of intellectual-property rules will result in a transfer of US$40 billion from the poor countries to companies in the industrial countries (Rosenberg, 2002). Critics of the WTO and globalization argue that this is unfair.

SUBSIDIES TO FARMERS IN INDUSTRIAL COUNTRIES ARE IN VIOLATION OF FREE TRADE   Food subsidies to farmers in the industrial countries lower prices in the international market, increase the export of farm products from these countries, and reduce the imports from developing countries. European, American, and Japanese farmers receive large subsidies from the government, as much as 35 percent of income in Europe, and 20 percent in the United States (Rosenberg, 2002). This allows them to export farm products at prices below their production cost and undercut prices in other countries where no subsidies are given. Since farmers in the developing countries are often in the poorest income categories, these policies have a strong negative impact on poverty in these countries.

THE STRUCTURE OF AID, TECHNOLOGICAL TRANSFER, AND LOCAL CONTENT REQUIREMENTS MAKE IT DIFFICULT FOR AGRICULTURAL EXPORTERS TO MOVE UP THE LADDER TO EXPORT MANUFACTURED GOODS   This line of reasoning is more relevant in Africa than it is in Asia. Nevertheless, it is important to recognize that the power of moving away from commodities cannot be underestimated. Prices for commodities such as coffee, cocoa, rice, sugar, and tin have dropped dramatically over the last twenty years, and this deterioration in terms of trade is an important reason that living standards in sub-Saharan Africa have fallen so dramatically. Countries in Asia, particularly the Central Asian republics, need to bear these trends in mind.

INTERNATIONAL AGENCIES SUCH AS THE IMF AND THE WORLD BANK HAVE NOT SERVED THE INTERESTS OF THE DEVELOPING COUNTRIES   This blanket criticism has something to do with the frustration that many poor countries feel when they see others move ahead while they are falling further behind. Some of the criticism is well deserved, but these agencies are making efforts to reform themselves and change. One problem in the past was that the IMF had applied the same remedy for all cases of financial and macroeconomic distress. We have reviewed the errors that were made during the Asian financial crisis in Chapter 3. In response to these criticisms, a recent panel report by a group advising the U.S. Congress on international financial institutions suggested that the IMF should

confine itself to short-term crisis assistance. Furthermore, the policies for structural reform that have worked well in Asia seem not to have worked as well in Latin America. Yet they have not grown as rapidly as Asia, with a few exceptions. Many economists argue that this is because of inherent structural problems, such as uneven income distribution and economic control by small elites, which the international agencies are unwilling to address.

IMMIGRATION HAS BEEN RESTRICTED EVEN AS CAPITAL HAS MOVED MORE FREELY As discussed earlier in Chapter 8, immigration laws have not been adjusted as quickly as regulations on the international flow of other resources. One way to address this problem would be to extend schemes for short-term migration that already exists in some areas. For example, short-term immigration of Turkish workers to Germany, workers from Indonesia to Malaysia, as well as from several countries to Singapore, and from the Asian economies to the Middle-East oil producers already exist. By extending these kinds of arrangements in a formal way, there could be greater benefits to other developing countries. Dani Rodrik (2002) estimates that it could generate US$200 billion annually in wages to the poor, as well as additional technological transfer.

Henceforth, globalization is a phenomenon that will have a life of its own, a trend that will affect the lives of millions of people. By harnessing its beneficial aspects and minimizing its detrimental consequences, greater progress can be made in transferring resources and taking advantage of comparative advantage. The point of this section is that there is still a long way to go.

11.4   INFORMATION TECHNOLOGY AND THE "NEW ECONOMY"

In the past twenty years, there has been a rapid transformation of the economies in the industrial countries. There are a number of aspects in this transformation, which are important for the analysis of the developing countries in Asia. In the United States, this process of transformation has been labeled the "new economy," the "information economy," or the "knowledge economy."

There are two widely used definitions of the "new economy." The first definition stresses the development of a knowledge-based economy in a new business environment, the introduction of innovative systems, human resource development (HRD), and the intensive use of information and communication technology (ICT). The second is a narrower definition based on ICT, with increasing and accelerating labor productivity and a restructuring of the economy, together with a significant increase in total factor productivity.

In the following sections, we will discuss several aspects of the "new economy." In Section 11.4.1, we will introduce aspects of the "new economy" as they relate to the industrial countries, with particular reference to the United States, where most of the research and analysis has taken place. These include the trend toward the globalization of business, the growth of information technology and the service economy, and trends in the labor force and competition. In Section 11.4.2, we discuss the impact that these transformations of both the nature of the production function and the structure of goods produced has made on economic growth, inflation and unemployment in the United States and other industrial countries. In Section 11.5, we explore the implications that the "new economy" has for economic development and economic policy in the Asian economies.

We will also look at other factors that may contribute to more rapid growth and increases in productivity such as genetic engineering. At the same time, we ignore the downside risk of further environmental degradation. Instead, we will concentrate on the various aspects of innovation and technology in the knowledge, information, telecommunication, and computer industries. Factors that reinforce the development and dissemination of technologies in these industries, such as globalization and improved governance, are also considered.

11.4.1   The Nature of the "New Economy" in the Industrial Countries

There are two or three fundamental changes that have taken place in the United States and other industrial countries in the past two decades which have led to the characterization of the "new economy." The first of these is the strong trend toward the globalization of business. We have seen in earlier chapters that the trend toward globalization has resulted in a rapid growth in international trade and a reduction in the barriers to trade. It has also resulted in rapid growth in foreign direct investment and portfolio investment. Some economists have estimated that more than half of the world's total output of goods and services is now contestable—which means that not only are exporters jockeying for foreign markets but firms that formerly were protected by trade or other restrictive barriers are also now becoming subject to competition. The share of international trade in total GDP has risen in many countries in the past two decades, even in large and diverse countries like the United States and Australia. Since the collapse of the Soviet Union and with the establishment of the World Trade Organization, the trend toward the wide use of markets has spread to all corners of the globe. The European Union (EU) and the NAFTA, as well as the Asia-Pacific Economic Cooperation (APEC) forum and ASEAN, have also contributed to the spread of trade and free market forces.

The second trend is the revolution in information technology. This is a multifaceted revolution and involves the rapid development of computing equipment, including much faster speed, smaller housings and lower prices. Adding to this is the development of high-speed transmission of information by relay stations, satellite, and fiber optic cables. The result has been an explosion in the use of fax machines, cellular phones, and the Internet. This has combined with the rapid spread of computers to homes and offices to create a service sector specializing in the provision and analysis of information and visual images that is growing much faster than the rest of the economy. They even provide entertainment for the elderly in retirement homes.

Together with computing power has come the digitalization revolution that has permeated all information—not only in words and data, but in pictures and video as well. These two broad trends are reflected in labor-force statistics and value added. In the United States, high-technology share of industrial value-added in manufacturing rose to more than 25 percent in the late 1990s from 18 percent in 1970, and its share of GDP also increased. The service sector has grown at the expense of manufacturing as computer programmers, managers, and office workers have replaced riveters, fork-lift operators, and other manufacturing workers. Managerial and professional jobs have increased as a share of total employment (from 22 percent of the workforce in 1979 to nearly 30 percent by 2000) while occupations requiring less skill have declined. There were less than 5,000 computer programmers in 1960, less than one-tenth of one percent of the workforce. By the year 2000, there were over 1.3 million, or nearly one percent of the labor force.

To serve the wide-ranging uses in all areas of the economy and throughout the world, the computer-chip market has been showing double-digit growth for many years, and its share in GDP has also risen although prices have fallen dramatically. The "new economy" has brought with it a dramatic acceleration in innovation, a telescoping of the time lag for the introduction of new models, an explosion of new products, a shorter product life, and greater competition and improved efficiency. There are more new firms, more new products, and more firms going out of business. Shoppers can now do so electronically, as well as physically visit their favorite store as the information technology revolution has expanded the range of choices exponentially through the Internet.

The growth of information technology, computers, and the Internet has transformed the face of corporate America. Housing and automobiles were the driving force behind growth for many years. Slowly, they are being supplanted by information technology which now accounts for about one-third of total U.S. growth each year. Because of the enormous gains in productivity in computers, the costs of information technology (adjusted for quality) have also fallen dramatically. This has helped to contribute to price stability, despite the economy being in the longest peacetime expansion in history. Some economic historians equate it with the technological breakthroughs that fuelled the nineteenth century development of the railroad, or the automobile in the twentieth century. In that sense, it is a technology that transcends its own particular industry, spilling over into the entire economy, increasing productivity, and changing the way businesses are operated.

Combined with the growth of the Internet, information technology has the potential to reduce costs and increase efficiency to such an extent that the level of sustainable growth may increase substantially. This can and is happening in the United States in two ways. The first is through retailing over the Internet. This has been called B2C or business to consumer. We alluded earlier to Amazon.com, a mammoth online book retailer. There are others too, including eBay, etc. They provide substantial discounts on a wide range of retail products and have attracted a growing list of customers.

However, this kind of business is likely to be dwarfed by business-to-business (B2B) transactions in the future. These transactions will allow firms to search out least-cost suppliers and the highest quality, with substantial reductions in search costs. The increased efficiency and greater competition among suppliers is also likely to have a salutary effect on inflation.

There have been various estimates of the impact of these cost-saving activities. Currently, it is estimated that less than 0.5 percent of all intercompany transactions takes place over the Internet. Even the most optimistic projections show this figure rising to a little over 5 percent within five years. However, the cost savings could be significant, even with such small usage. For example, it has been suggested that Internet use may reduce the costs of producing a car by around 14 percent. This effect includes the computerization of final custom purchases as well as the move to B2B outsourcing.

In general, there are five ways that the Internet can increase company efficiency and/or achieve other cost savings. A company that moves its supply chain management onto the Internet can achieve savings in several ways. First, the cost of processing purchases from suppliers can be reduced. Secondly, it may be able to reduce inventories by adopting efficient and sophisticated just-on-time arrival inventory management. Thirdly, it may be able to purchase inputs at lower prices by streamlining the intermediation process. Fourthly, it may induce more competition among existing suppliers, resulting in lower input costs. Fifthly, suppliers may also be able to increase productivity by using the Internet.

11.4.2   Economic Performance in the "New Economy"

It is difficult to quantify the impact of changes in technology on economic performance, simply because technology is difficult to quantify. Neoclassical growth theory has basically given up trying to estimate the impact of technology. The Solow model says that the impact of technology and other factors that may raise productivity, such as management and industrial organization, are contained in a residual, which is measured as the difference between outgrowth and the contribution of labor and capital to that growth. In the case of the "new economy," measuring the impact of information technology, computers, and the Internet on economic performance is complicated by the fact that they are so closely interrelated to each other that a breakdown of individual components is difficult, and also by the lack of a long-time series to analyze.

Nevertheless, some attempts have been made. In one scenario, the initial impact of the Internet is to lower costs and prices. In the following round, cheaper input prices leads to changes in production plans, including more spending on information processing, and more output. The spending on information is likely to result in greater competition among intermediate suppliers and a profit squeeze as competition increases. The outcome is likely to be a combination of lower prices and higher output. Seeing downward pressure on prices, policymakers are likely to lower interest rates to stimulate demand. This would raise output and lower the non-accelerating inflationary rate of unemployment (NAIRU). The trade-off between inflation and growth would be improved.

Table 11.14　Labor Productivity Growth in Selected OECD Countries, 1989–1999

	Average Annual Rate of Change in Value-Added Per Person Employed	
	1989–1995	**1995–1999**
Canada	1.0%	0.9%
Denmark	2.0	0.9
Finland	3.0	2.7
France	1.4	1.6
Germany	2.3	2.3
Italy	1.9	0.7
Japan	1.2	0.8
Korea	5.0	2.7
Netherlands	1.2	0.7
United Kingdom	2.0	1.2
United States	1.1	1.9

SOURCE: APEC Economic Committee, *The New Economy in APEC: Innovations, Digital Divide, and Policy* (Singapore: APEC, 2002), p. 71.

Another approach is to look at recent trends in productivity in the United States and other OECD countries. Since 1995, there has been a sharp acceleration in the rate of growth in labor productivity in the United States (see Table 11.14). This has not been the case in other OECD countries, however.

Looking back at history, labor productivity has had a cyclical component, falling during a recession and accelerating in the initial stages of recovery. The current surge in productivity is the first time in the postwar period that it has happened during the ongoing stage of the recovery. There has been some analysis of the underlying series that make up these productivity figures. The IMF suggests, for example, that the productivity surge is the result of a rebound from lower productivity earlier in the decade, and that estimates of total factor productivity do not show a significant increase in recent years. They also argue that the improved trade-off between inflation and unemployment may be the result of demographic shifts that have moved more of the workforce into middle age where unemployment rates are low, while the proportion of high unemployed seems to have shrunk.

Other economists have confined their study to the direct impact of computers on output in sectors where they have been heavily utilized, such as information technology, banking, and some sections of manufacturing. While estimates of the impact of computers on productivity in these industries are large, the contribution to total productivity is relatively small, since these sectors, although growing rapidly, are still relatively small.

11.5　ASIA AND THE "NEW ECONOMY"

11.5.1　A Taxonomy of Countries

The post industrialization transition to a "new economy" has been widely discussed in the United States, as we have seen in Section 11.1. As part of that transition, the service sector has become dominant. It employs the major proportion of the labor force and makes the largest contribution to value-added.

In the United States, computers and electronic data processing and interchange have penetrated all levels of the economy, and the use of information technology in the banking and finance sectors and industry is widespread. More recently, the use of the Internet has blossomed and is being used for retail sales (B2C), purchases by businesses (B2B), and for inventory and management purposes. We might identify the United States as category 1A in participating in the new economy.

In Europe, the use of the Internet is not as widespread but it is similarly well developed in the use of IT in banking and finance and for certain accounting and management functions. Let us say, then that the European and other OECD countries are in category 1B.

How do developing countries fare in this identification scheme? Most of them would fall below Europe, and we call it category 2. However, there are exceptions, such as Singapore and Hong Kong, and perhaps Taiwan and Korea. Table 11.15 shows the information society index ranking of fifty-five developed and developing countries. From this, we see that most industrial countries are in the highest level together with Singapore and Hong Kong, at level 1, while Taiwan and Korea are at level 2, and Malaysia is at level 3. Most of the other Asian economies are at level 4.

SINGAPORE   Singapore is at level 1, and it is top in Asia (see Table 11.15). Hong Kong follows closely behind. The progress of the information economy is quite advanced, with B2B electronic commerce worth over US$50 billion in 2000 (EIU, 2003). This is partially due to the strong presence of multinational companies in the country. B2C trails behind B2B, but there has been a rise in online purchases, Internet banking, and share trading in recent years because of its user-friendliness as well as its well-established electronic payment mode. The provision of a multitude of interactive government services, such as payment of utility bills and income taxes, can be found at a single Web site http://www.ecitizen.gov.sg, thereby eradicating unnecessary duplication of services and improving overall efficiency of the government bodies. With regard to consumers, two out of five Internet users in Singapore enjoy broadband services, but a recent report pointed out that the actual number of subscribers is comparatively low, at 300,000 out of 1.2 million users (*The Straits Times*, April 17, 2003). Hence, there appears to be space for the further growth of information service providers (ISPs).

CHINA   China seems to be concentrating on the first stages of the information revolution, or what the author calls electronic data interchange (EDI). This involves simple things like e-mail, electronic bulletin boards, ATMs, and other electronic bank transfers. They have not moved to the next level, which includes inventory management, electronic catalogs, and point-of-sale data gathering. They have also not yet developed B2C and B2B transactions. Thus, China would definitely be classified under level 4.

INDIA   India is also definitely at level 4, although there are sectors of the Indian IT industry that are very highly developed. Generally, however, the information economy is only evident in a few best-practice firms and the financial sector.

THE PHILIPPINES AND MALAYSIA   In Southeast Asia, the Philippines and Malaysia are definitely at levels 3 and 4, respectively. They have electronic banking and stock exchanges, e-mail, and other electronic transfers and management techniques. They are also beginning to use the Internet more effectively in business dealings.

THAILAND   Thailand is at level 4. They have basic EDI, online trading, and some Internet banking. The last is held back by the lack of electronic legislations, particularly the long-awaited passing of the Electronic Transaction Bill which was supposed to be enacted in 2000. Hence, business and banks alike have delayed going online. Only a small fraction of the local business (15 percent) engages in electronic supply chain management (EIU, 2003).

Table 11.15   Information Society Index Ranking

Rank	Country	Score
LEVEL 1		
1	Sweden	6,496
2	Norway	6,112
3	Finland	5,953
4	United States	5,850
5	Denmark	5,837
6	United Kingdom	5,662
7	Switzerland	5,528
8	Australia	5,382
9	Singapore	5,269
10	Netherlands	5,238
11	Japan	5,182
12	Canada	5,126
13	Germany	4,937
14	Austria	4,868
15	Hong Kong	4,745
LEVEL 2		
16	New Zealand	4,483
17	Belgium	4,439
18	Taiwan	4,296
19	Korea	4,283
20	Ireland	4,202
21	France	4,104
22	Israel	4,029
23	Italy	3,844
24	Spain	3,675
25	Portugal	3,262
26	Greece	2,877
27	Czech Republic	2,759

Rank	Country	Score
LEVEL 3		
28	UAE	2,676
29	Hungary	2,573
30	Poland	2,288
31	Argentina	2,252
32	Malaysia	2,220
33	Chile	2,183
34	Bulgaria	2,154
35	Romania	2,094
36	Costa Rica	2,056
37	Panama	2,047
38	South Africa	2,029
39	Venezuela	1,890
40	Russia	1,863
41	Turkey	1,861
42	Mexico	1,785
43	Ecuador	1,738
LEVEL 4		
44	Saudi Arabia	1,689
45	Brazil	1,670
46	Columbia	1,590
47	Thailand	1,563
48	Philippines	1,553
49	Peru	1,367
50	Jordan	1,317
51	Egypt	1,263
52	China	1,198
53	Indonesia	1,172
54	India	1,108
55	Pakistan	955

SOURCE: World Times/IDC, "Information Society Index Ranking," (Boston: World Times, Inc, 2001).

INDONESIA   Indonesia is also at level 4. It has enabled consumer services such Internet and mobile-phone banking, which started taking off in 2000. B2C is the predominant form of e-commerce, and much greater than B2B. Wireless commerce is still in the process of development and its potential seems promising with its large cellular market. The government has also signed an agreement with Malaysia for the electronic exchange of export data in 2000.

VIETNAM   Development of the new economy in Vietnam is still in its infancy, and has been hampered by its lack of developed telecommunication infrastructure and limited penetration of users. Internet usage remains minimal, though the total number of Internet users had risen to 1.5 million by 2002, but it is still less than 2 percent of the total population (International Telecommunications Union, 2003). The risk of cybercrime and piracy is high since regulations for the legislation environment are not quite in place. Thus, it is placed at level 4 in terms of technological sophistication.

11.5.2   The Potential Impact of the "New Economy" on Developing Asian Countries

GROWTH OF TRADE WILL CREATE ADDITIONAL OPPORTUNITIES   The volume of world trade has been growing faster than income for several decades and barriers to trade have been falling rapidly. More openness in trade and also in the flow of capital should facilitate the spread of the "new economy" to the emerging economies, particularly those for which international trade has played a significant role in economic development. Within Asia, there are many countries that fit into this category. All of the NIEs are heavy traders. In Hong Kong and Singapore, the volume of trade is as large, or larger than its GDP. Furthermore, the level and sophistication of telecommunications, information technology, and computers are very high.

KNOWLEDGE INTENSITY AND TELECOMMUNICATIONS/COMPUTERS WILL CREATE OPPORTUNITIES FOR THE EXPORT OF SKILL-INTENSIVE SERVICES   Singapore, India, and the Philippines have already developed substantial software and data entry platforms in the past decade. In the future, this expertise will be extended to help these economies to enter into the knowledge and information aspects of the "new economy" more fully. In the case of India, there is a risk of dualism arising as the modern technology sector outpaces the more traditional sectors of the economy.

GROWTH OF THE INTERNET COULD CREATE A MORE LEVEL PLAYING FIELD   The capacity of poorer countries to market retail products and to bid for subcontracting jobs in the industrial countries could very well be enhanced by the spread of the Internet. However, the extent of this penetration will depend greatly on whether these developing countries can compete in this market by supplying quality products or inputs in a timely manner. The Internet has the capacity to cut the search costs and improve economic efficiency but only if this new technology is embraced by a wide section of the economy. If this proves successful, new Internet companies will be able to take advantage of economies of scale in a truly world market. There are a few success stories in the developing countries that show the potential for the "new economy" to spread quickly.

OPPORTUNITIES FOR ACCESS TO CAPITAL WILL INCREASE AS FDI GROWS AND AS THE WORLD STOCK MARKETS BECOME MORE INTEGRATED   There are a number of instances where new high-tech companies in developing countries have been able to access venture capital funds from the industrial countries. China managed to procure US$1 billion from U.S.-based venture capital fund, IDG, for investment in its Internet businesses in 1999. Hong Kong's Pacific Century CyberWorks and two other U.S. investment funds have also set up a US$1.5 billion venture capital fund to invest in emerging Internet companies. Local venture capital funds, although not as much as those from the developed countries, have been set up, particularly within major business centers of Southeast Asia and Hong Kong. There is anecdotal evidence that some US$5 billion venture capital flowed into the Asian high-tech industry in 1999 (Darrow et al., 2000).

THERE WILL BE GREATER PAYOFFS TO IMPROVING EDUCATION AND COMPUTER SKILLS   There is substantial evidence in the theory of human capital that the returns to education are quite high. The emphasis in the past had been on returns to women's education and the synergies that these investments have with health, fertility, population growth, and infant mortality. In the future, there will also be high returns to investment in vocational and tertiary education, especially in the fields of computer science, software development, and the Internet. Many of the opportunities for training can be developed by the private sector. Already there has been a rapid expansion of training in these occupations in Thailand, the Philippines, India, Singapore, and Malaysia. Most of these facilities have sprung up in the private sector and they should be encouraged. One of the risks of such training is that these IT specialists may be recruited by foreign companies after their training, thus contributing further to the brain drain. This is all the more reason for encouraging the private sector to engage in training, as there will be no wastage of public resources.

MORE OPPORTUNITIES FOR VENTURE CAPITAL, MERGERS AND ACQUISITIONS, AND FOREIGN PARTNERSHIPS AND ALLIANCES WILL ARISE   The emphasis placed on the knowledge sectors in Hong Kong and Singapore is a good example of this trend. They have also formed sizeable government-sponsored venture capital of their own, such as Hong Kong's US$100 million capital pool, and Singapore's US$1 billion Technopreneur fund (Darrow et al., 2000). Moreover, the alliances that have been developed in Taiwan are interesting. Their experience has shown that even small and medium-scale industries can compete internationally. They have been able to develop a global strategy which emphasizes the transfer of production lines that have lost its comparative advantage to other countries, particularly China, where the labor costs are cheaper but where Taiwan can still take advantage of its marketing and distribution networks worldwide. This shows that Taiwan seems to be well adapted to the Internet and the "new economy." Small and medium-sized enterprises (SMEs) in Taiwan have also forged a series of strategic alliances with firms in other countries, particularly in the computer and electronics industries, so that they can cover the globe with their products. This network is strategically placed to take advantage of the growth of the "new economy" and the Internet.

11.5.3   Individual Country Experiences

Various country experiences with the "new economy" will be discussed below. The order of discussion will proceed along the spectrum of ICT development in Asia: from the more technologically advanced NIEs (such as Hong Kong, Singapore, and Taiwan), followed by the Southeast countries, and subsequently to China, India, and lastly, Vietnam.

HONG KONG   The NIEs are already in a good position to take advantage of the efficiency gains that will arise from the "new economy" and high technology. In Hong Kong, the continued relocation of manufacturing industries to China and the slowdown in the major service sectors following the Asian financial crisis prompted the government to take greater initiatives to develop high value-added and high-tech industries. There is a Science Park under construction, as well as a Cyberport and a Silicon Harbour. These are all being developed in cooperation with the private sector. Human resources are also being developed in computer science, science, and other technology areas within higher education. The three universities in Hong Kong are playing a key role in this process and there has also been an acceleration of the flow of students attending foreign institutions of higher learning. In the past, high-tech industries were considered too risky but now they are being promoted vigorously. IT industries complement the traditional areas of strength in Hong Kong, such as finance and trade services. It is also an area of comparative advantage, since Hong Kong has one of the best IT networks in the world. On the finance side, a Global Enterprise Market (GEM) has been started and is currently dominated by small and venture capital companies in the high-tech area. Some big U.S. technology stocks have also been listed on this market.

SINGAPORE   In Singapore, there are initiatives to build on a strong existing base of computer and IT skills. A Ministry of Communication and Information Technology was created, and the National Computer Board and Telecommunications Authority were merged into the Info-Communications and Development Authority (IDA). Furthermore, a master plan for the information and communications industry is being developed. Greater emphasis is being placed on skills upgrading, with funding derived from taxes on employers. Singapore also receives large inflows of foreign direct investment from the United States, which includes state-of-the art telecommunications and information technology. Immigration laws have also been relaxed to allow the influx of foreign talents. Thus, Singapore is well positioned to take advantage of efficiency gains flowing from "new economy" developments.

The Singapore government has also actively sought to establish e-government[9] and encourage e-commerce. Cyber laws passed to ensure their smooth functioning include the Electronics Transaction Act and Evidence Act—they recognize online transactions and electronic evidence in courts, respectively.[10] The Local Industry Upgrading Program has been set up by the Economic Development Board to encourage companies to promote greater participation in info-communications through partnerships with industry players and research institutes. Approximately 105 small and medium enterprises have been fully e-enabled (Asian Development Bank Institute, 2002, p. 7). Deregulation in the telecommunication industry has also served to push forth household and business access to broadband media and applications, extending the outreach to more Internet users, thereby widening the penetration of the domestic market by e-commerce providers.

Although ICT has contributed considerably to the economic growth of Singapore, there is still some way to go to reach its maximum potential. This is because the Asian countries have generally attained high GDP growth rates through ICT exports rather than through productivity increases (Prakash, 2002). The number of patents accruing to local companies is still small compared with the developed countries. Thus, Singapore has felt the need for local technology creation, rather than relying on technology acquisition from abroad. As a result, besides building upon the existing base of ICT, Singapore has sought to develop local technological capabilities. A third Science Park has been established with the participation of worldwide institutes, such as INSEAD and John Hopkins, for this very purpose.

TAIWAN   In Taiwan, the government has traditionally followed a policy of promoting small and medium-scale industries. Many companies in the computer and other IT fields have developed strategic alliances and partnerships with overseas firms.

---

[9] The term "e-government" follows the World Bank's definition and is taken to mean the public-sector equivalent of e-commerce. For more details of e-government in the Asian region, refer to Westcott (2001) who takes a broader view of the term so as to better capture the benefits arising from ICT usage in the public sector and throughout the economy.

[10] In an Accenture report of e-government capabilities in twenty-three countries, Singapore was ranked second, before developed countries, such as the United States, Australia, and the United Kingdom, in terms of e-government maturity level (Nua Internet Surveys, April 9, 2002).

These networks are well placed to take advantage of "new economy" developments. So far the government has not developed any high-level bodies to supervise such activities. Nevertheless, the private sector has been very active in keeping up with recent developments in line with its global strategy of marketing and distribution of IT products.

MALAYSIA AND THE PHILIPPINES   In Southeast Asia, there are fewer opportunities to take advantage of "new economy" developments, particularly in countries where English is not widely spoken, such as Indonesia and Thailand. As a result, Malaysia and the Philippines should lead the push into "new economy" areas.

CHINA   China's IT industry is expected to become a strong growth engine in the next ten years, though its strength lies in manufacturing rather than software development. In order to overcome its relative lack of human expertise in this particular field, since only 3.5 percent of China's population has tertiary education, the government has plans to set up one hundred world-class universities to promote high-technology learning (Lewis, 2001, p. 346). A "Government Online" project to equip government bodies with ICT has been started since 1999. In the same year, a law was passed to legally bind contracts made over the Internet. China is also in the process of formulating legislation to deal with copyright infringements and intellectual property rights issues. One distinct example showing the positive stance of China in upholding intellectual property rights is its award to the Swedish furniture company, IKEA, its Chinese Internet name, which originally belonged to a Chinese cybersquatter[11] (EIU, 2002a).

However, its progress has been hampered by its limited ICT penetration and lack of clear direction in legislation. ICT infrastructures tend to be unevenly distributed in the country and concentrated in the more economically developed eastern coastal cities, such as Guangzhou and Shanghai. In comparison, the percentages of the country's Internet users in western China's Tibet, Qinghai, and Ningxia (0.1, 0.2, and 0.3 percent, respectively) pale in comparison with the figures for Guangzhou and Shanghai, which account for 10.4 percent and 9.2 percent, respectively (Xinhua News Agency, 2002). Furthermore, even though Internet users (59.1 million in 2002) tend to be concentrated in the cities, it only accounts for a mere 4.6 percent of the total population (International Telecommunications Union, 2003). However, it must be noted that, despite its relatively low penetration, its absolute size is not to be taken lightly especially when it is expected to rise by leaps and bounds in the near future with China's rising economic importance.

With regard to legislation, the regulatory control of the ICT environment is not clear-cut. The provision of Internet access and the control of the content of Internet websites are governed by two separate government entities, the Ministry of Information Industry and the State Administration of Radio, Film and Television, respectively; this has led to conflicts in administration. Its attempts at increasing Internet censoring, coupled with its greater proficiency through the acquisition of foreign high-tech expertise, is another worrying trend in ICT adoption in China (EIU, 2003). Another concern is the lack of competition in the telecommunication industry which has resulted in high connection fees demanded by local Internet service providers (ISPs). However, the situation is likely to change in compliance with WTO regulations, which agreed in 2006 to allow for 50 percent foreign investment in the telecommunication industry.

---

[11] Cybersquatters are termed as such because they deliberately set out to acquire ownership rights of domain names similar to well-known foreign companies so as to earn a fee from its relinquishment.

INDIA   On the other hand, unlike China, India's expertise lies in software development and it has already built up a strong base with an English-speaking population and ICT professionals. High-technology learning has ranked high in its priorities since the 1950s. It has since then become the world leader in offshore software development, with more than one-third of *Fortune 500* companies as their clients (Economist Intelligent Unit, 2003). India has also developed an array of Internet services, such as the provision of government services and Internet banking. The iLEAP-ISP scheme providing free multilingual word processor to all Internet users was designed to deal with local language content so as to enhance its accessibility to the public.[12] Cooperation between the public and private sectors to foster ICT development has been encouraged. One such cooperation resulted in the creation of the Simputer to allow illiterate users to access the Internet.

However, the physical ICT infrastructure needed to make use of such services is sorely lacking, not to mention the costly access and limited usage of ICT. Demand for personal computers continues to rank low in consumer priorities despite falling personal computer prices. The number of Internet users per 10,000 inhabitants is only 159, many times less than that of China, which was 460 in 2002 (International Telecommunications Union, 2003). In addition, despite the privatization of the cell phone and long-distance phone markets in the 1990s, India continues to monopolize Internet bandwidth allocation through its state-owned company, Videsh Sanchar Ngiam Limited (VSNL); this has caused inefficient delays, up to hours at times, to go online (Economist Intelligent Unit, 2000).

VIETNAM   Vietnam's ICT development has been lagging behind most countries in the region, with its low Internet penetration and usage, high access costs, and lack of electronic legislation, and consumer protection. Thus, there is a case for greater improvements in the country's state-owned telecommunications industry and the extent of IT infrastructure. Vietnam has signed an agreement with its more ICT-advanced neighbor, Korea, to draw on its expertise in infrastructure development and online resources management. Supporting educational policies have been set up to expand the base of IT personnel needed. Software businesses have been exempted from paying four years' worth of corporate income taxes in order to further accelerate the development of the ICT industry. Vietnam has also come up with an ambitious US$$6.7 million plan to develop the integration of local businesses with e-commerce by 2005 (Economist Intelligent Unit, 2001).

11.5.4   Policies for Promoting the "New Economy" in Asia

Policies for promoting the new economy in Asia include:

DEVELOPING ENTREPRENEURSHIP   It is essential to have a strong entrepreneurial culture that is supported by appropriate government policies in order for innovation and adaptation of new technologies to take place. A wide array of government policies at both the microeconomic and macroeconomic levels, as well as institutional support would enhance the level of entrepreneurship. In Asia, it is not the richest countries that have the best record for developing an attractive environment for entrepreneurs. Rather, a survey conducted by the International Institute of Management (*World Competitiveness Year-book*, 2002) shows that Hong Kong, Taiwan, and Malaysia have the best environment, followed by the Philippines and Korea. Thailand, Singapore, and Indonesia are in a group toward the bottom, while China and Japan are at the bottom of the list. APEC (2002) lists several key factors contributing to a good entrepreneurial environment. These include firstly, a financial market that facilitates access to

---

[12] "Appendix 3, National ICT Approaches: Selected Case Studies, India," *Digital Opportunity Initiative Report* (2003), available at http://www.opit-init.org/framework/pages/appendix3Case4.html.

financing. This would include tax cuts for venture capital firms and access to a second-tier market that handles riskier ventures. NASDAQ is the best-known and widely traded financial market but other markets have also sprung up, such as the KOSDAQ (Korean Association of Securities Dealers Automatic Quotation System) in Korea, the Growth Enterprise Markets (GEM) in Hong Kong, SESDAQ in Singapore, and TIGER in Taiwan. At the same time, it is important to maintain firm prudential and disclosure regulations. Assistance for start-ups from the government can also help to foster entrepreneurship, including help for groups such as women, ethnic groups, SMEs, and other targeted groups. Developing cooperation between universities and the business community, such as those in Silicon Valley between Stanford University and the dotcom companies, is also critical. Such relationships are being developed in Singapore, and Taiwan, in the Hsinchu Science Industrial Park.

CLOSING THE DIGITAL DIVIDE   The digital divide can be defined as the ability to access, exchange, and process information through digital equipment. If firms have to rely on foreign technology and value chain networks established by multinationals, then it will be difficult for domestic firms to capture new export markets and penetrate existing markets. Therefore, the multinational firm can play an even more pivotal role in helping developing countries to cross the digital divide. At the same time, because of growing international competition, it will be difficult to protect economic rents and maintain product niches. There is a growing tendency for products to be concentrated in a few economies led by multinational firms. Large firms will also benefit because they have an advantage in processing information and can benefit from economies of scale in doing so. They also have the capital to undertake changes in products quickly when new technology comes on stream.

Asia now occupies a strong position as the largest exporter of information-intensive products to the United States. In 2000, the share of the Asian economies in total U.S. imports of these products exceeded 75 percent (see Table 11.16). However, apart from Japan and Korea, a large proportion of these products are manufactured by multinationals.

Closing the digital divide requires local manufacturers and businesses, including service providers, to undertake more training and education in ICT. Currently, there are big gaps between the richer countries and the poorer ones in terms of access to information technology (see Table 11.17).

Japan, the United States, Hong Kong, Singapore, and Taiwan have the most intensive use of ICT. The other countries, with the exception of Korea, are far behind. Furthermore, an investigation of the

Table 11.16   Share of Information Products (HS8471 and HS8473) Exported to the United States, 2000 (Percent)

Percent of Information Products by Selected APEC Members to the United States	
China	11.4%
Japan	16.4
Korea	8.8
Taiwan	11.9
ASEAN	27.3
Rest of APEC	75.7

SOURCE: APEC Economic Committee, *The New Economy in APEC: Innovations, Digital Divide, and Policy* (Singapore: APEC, 2002), p. 118.

Table 11.17   Information Technology Indicators, 2002 (Per Thousand People)

	Telephone Mainlines	PCs[a]	Internet Hosts	Internet Users[a]
United States	659	625	373	538
Japan	586[a]	382	56	449
Taiwan	583	396	76	383
Hong Kong	567	387	58	431
Korea	489	556	15	552
Singapore	464	508	48	540
Malaysia	198[a]	126[a]	3	273
China	167	19	0.1	46
Thailand	99	28	1	78
Vietnam	69	10	0.0	18
Philippines	42	22	0.4	26
India	40	6	0.1	16
Indonesia	36	11	0.2	19

[a]Figures are estimated.
[b]Figures are for 2001.

SOURCE: International Telecommunications Union, "ICT free statistics homepage" (2003), Web site at http://www.itu.int/ITU-D/ict/statistics/.

effect that these variables have on labor productivity, conducted by APEC (2002) for a group of nearly one hundred countries, suggests that the impact of these variables on labor productivity is significant and positive. Therefore, increasing the penetration of ICT is a priority for countries that are now lagging behind.

THE ROLE OF GLOBAL PRODUCTION NETWORKS[13]   The importance of information technology in integrating subcontractors into the global production networks cannot be overemphasized. For example, in Taiwan, subcontractors in both original equipment manufacturing (OEM) and own design manufacturing (ODM) (recall the definitions in Chapter 5) had to develop an information network to service brand-name manufacturers. New information technologies have allowed brand-name production and marketing on a global scale, and this has enabled marketing firms to bargain for a better deal from suppliers and contractors. These firms rely on subcontractors such as the OEM/ODM subcontractors to supply goods from production lines, after-sales service, and sometimes even product design. Subcontractors coordinate inventory and shipment schedules with the marketing firm and this requires information technology connections that may be expensive but serves to cement the relationship between the subcontractor and the marketing firm. The development of these global production networks tends to deepen market concentration as brand names dominate the market because of their ability to produce and distribute on a worldwide scale. It also tends to increase the size and concentration of subcontractors.

---

[13] This section draws heavily on Section 3.1.5 of the APEC (2002) report.

Nevertheless, while the integration of subcontractors and marketing activities is taking place worldwide, production is still focused in the least-cost regions. In the case of electronics equipment, the concentration tends to be in China and Southeast Asia. Notice that these are not the most highly sophisticated Internet using economies. The coordination of production and delivery requires an efficient internal communication network, which is easier to establish. However, Internet capability may help some countries, such as Singapore, to develop niche markets for technical support, customer services, and call-center type of activities.

In addition to having a reliable subcontractor, logistics is critical for the smooth operation of global production networks. Transportation and smooth and transparent customs clearance procedures are important, as well as a digital communication network. In most cases, the former factors are much more important to establish at the outset and will have an important influence on the location of the production and distribution sites.

In the case of PC manufacturing, two different systems have been adopted. The first, which we call the "spider" system, organizes the production of components at several different sites. These components are then shipped to a central site where they are assembled and shipped to the final markets. The second is the more traditional "central assembly" system where all components are made, assembled, and shipped from one location. In both systems, there tends to be a concentration of manufacturing in a small region. Even in the "spider" system, the time-to-market logistics suggests that the goods be produced close to one another. In the PC industry, the "spider" system would be confined to production sites in Southeast and East Asia.

Over time, there has been and will continue to be a shift in the production platforms from higher to lower-cost locations. Between 1985 and 2000, the share of computer hardware production shifted from the United States (49 to 26 percent), and Japan (18.9 to 16.3 percent), and Europe (19 to 15 percent) to the developing countries in Asia (3 to 29 percent).

As hardware becomes more and more standardized, firms in the computer industry are stressing on business solutions and more customized products to reach niche markets. This should give a large part of the actual production to subcontractors who have developed a strong digital connection with the global marketing company.

11.6   CONCLUSIONS AND PROSPECTS FOR THE FUTURE

This chapter has included material on two separate but related issues: globalization and the "new economy." These topics are interrelated to the extent that there is a growing tendency for production and international trade to be complimentary. With this trend have come a number of interrelated issues and challenges that must be faced collectively by the world economic community. These issues require attention from not only individual governments but also all governments in the "global village."

There are a number of issues that have arisen as a result of the seemingly breakneck pace of globalization. Many of these issues were mentioned and discussed in Chapter 3. In the context of a reform agenda for Asia in the aftermath of the Asian financial crisis, they include issues such as debt restructuring, establishing credit lines with the private sector by international lenders such as the IMF, reforming currency exchange rate systems, including capital-account reform, international portfolio controls, prudential accounting and other regulations, as well as FDI and trade policies and human development.

These issues are also pertinent to a wider global agenda. They can be extended to include the broader issues of environmental degradation and poverty. Within the context of the major international institutions that deal with global issues, such as the World Bank, the IMF, and the World Trade Organization, some observers believe that these two issues have not been given sufficient attention.

Stiglitz (2002) argues that the IMF has been more responsive to the financial interests of the industrial countries, while the WTO has paid attention to trade interests in these same industrial countries. As a result, the interests of the developing countries have not been given sufficient attention in the policies of either of these institutions. He argues that what is needed is a shift in stance so that the policies of these two institutions are better aligned with those of the developing countries.

There are a number of components of such a policy shift that would put a more humane face on the development agenda of these institutions, and the industrialized countries in general, as they deal with the complex issues of globalization.

Such an agenda would involve the following:

1. A shift in emphasis on the part of the IMF to focus exclusively on the resolution of crises as they arise in the developing countries. In dealing with these crises, it should be recognized that inflation is not the only parameter to be considered. Employment and economic growth are also crucial. Once this new perspective is adopted, greater emphasis would be put on restoring growth and reducing poverty, and less on fiscal austerity.
2. Further reduction in the use of conditionality to achieve compliance with fiscal and monetary performance criteria. This would be replaced by consensus building and dialogue to achieve a stronger policy environment and more stable and higher rates of growth.
3. An increase in transparency of information and decision-making processes within the IMF and the World Bank.
4. Reconsideration of interventions in the capital market and in financial sector bailouts to allow for serious consideration of capital market controls in selected cases as well as financial bailouts, the costs of which would be borne jointly by the creditor and the lender.
5. Greater consideration of environmental and social issues in the lending activities of the World Bank and other multilateral institutions.
6. Wider application of debt relief to a broad cross-section of developing countries beyond the poorest of the poor, which may have had corrupt or ineffective governments in the past.
7. Recognizing the interests of the developing countries more completely in multilateral trade negotiations, such as the Doha Round of the WTO. This would include dealing effectively with farm subsidies in Europe, the United States and Japan, and the liberalization of the services sector where developing countries have a comparative advantage, such as maritime services and computer software. It also includes the intellectual property rights (IPRs) for critical drugs to deal with illnesses such as AIDS. In this regard, it is important that negotiations for the resumption of the Doha Round continue. These negotiations were suspended at the end of July 2008. The talks sought to cut tariffs and subsidies for farm products, as well as liberalize trade in services. While there is a chance that the Doha Round may resume, the differences between the United States and the developing countries are large. The two sides could not agree to bind tariffs near to the prevailing rate, which would have prevented protective tariffs from increasing in response to perceived trade threats. With the failure of the talks, there are fears that the influence of the WTO may be further eroded:

> Development is about transforming societies, improving the lives of the poor, enabling everyone to have a chance at success and access to health care and education. This sort of development won't happen if only a few people dictate the policies that a country must follow. (Stiglitz, 2002, p. 252)

In the political process, the rights of those with the fewest resources, or those sectors in which lobbyists cannot make a living by getting legislation passed, are those that are often bypassed in the legislative process. In the case of globalization, it is the poor and others without a strong interest group lobby and funding, such as environmentalists, whose rights and desires have not been adequately represented in globalization regulations that have been enacted up to now.

To address their concerns, a proactive policy has to be adopted that goes beyond the Washington consensus. The present policy puts a heavy weight on the free market and the allocation of resources and effort, in accordance with the principles of these markets. We know that markets often fail and we also know that there are ways to rectify these market failures. These actions need to be looked at again, particularly with regard to the poor and the environment.

REVIEW QUESTIONS

1. Why has there been acceleration in the growth of trade between China and the rest of the world and a decline in the importance of Japan's trade with the rest of the Asian region?
2. The flow of capital into Asia has increased, yet the flow of labor out of Asia has continued. What are the reasons for the difference in the pattern of movement in these two factors of production?
3. Globalization is reflected in an increase in trade and foreign investment. How have these patterns changed in the past decade or so? What does this say about the possible shift in growth potential within the region in the future?
4. What has been holding back the economies of South Asia from becoming more fully integrated into the world economy through globalization?
5. How does the experience of South Asia compare with that of the Southeast Asian economies?
6. If you were in a debate over the impact of globalization on developing countries in Asia, which side of the debate would you want to be on—the debate team that argues that globalization has been good for the region or the team that says globalization has been a negative influence on the region?
7. There are two widely used definitions of the "new economy." The first definition stresses the development of a knowledge-based economy within a new business environment, the introduction of innovative systems, human resource development, and the intensive use of information and communication technology (ICT). The second is a narrower definition based on ICT and increasing and accelerating labor productivity as well as a restructuring of the economy with a significant increase in total factor productivity. Which of these definitions is most useful in studying the spread of the "new economy" from the industrial countries, particularly the United States to developing countries in Asia?
8. Despite a high concentration of exports in the ICT industry, the Asian economies have relied on multinational enterprises to supply technology. What are these economies doing to increase R&D and entrepreneurship?
9. How can economies that are caught on the wrong side of the digital divide catch up? Is this a lost cause and will the ICT revolution be another way for richer countries to outdistance their poorer neighbors?
10. Discuss the issue of globalization from the point of view of how it affects the more disadvantaged members of society and also from the point of view of whether it has introduced greater volatility into the world economy. After discussing these two issues, suggest a series of concrete measures to be adopted at the international level, and designed to address these two issues.
11. How will the global financial crisis of 2008 and 2009 impact the future of globalization? What measures can international organizations take to address globalization issues in the current economic climate?

Notes on References and Suggestions for Further Reading

In the first part of this chapter, trends in globalization were reviewed. The topics of globalization and international trade are intimately related. However, in this chapter special reference was made to the trends and developments that have taken place in the past two decades, as well as the changing pattern of capital flows and foreign direct investment. Two references are suggested for a review of the topic of globalization generally, the book by Robert Kennedy and Richard Vietor (2001), the special issues on globalization by Dani Rodik, M. Obstfeld, R. C. Freenstra, and John Williamson in the *Journal of Economic Perspectives* (1998), and the two books by Joseph Stiglitz (2003, 2006). See also the article by Tina Rosenberg (2002) for a non-economist's view of globalization.

John H. Dunning's (2001) article gives a brief explanation of globalization and its causes, and discusses the impact of globalization upon FDI in the Asian developing countries. The integration of Asian economies is discussed thoroughly in Asian Development Bank (2001) and Barry Eichengreen (2002).

The second part of this chapter deals with what has been called the "new economy." Various aspects of the information technology revolution, including its impact on Asia and global outsourcing are discussed. The key reference here is the recent World Bank volume by Shahid Yusuf and Simon Evenett (2002) on competition in Asia, and also the theme chapter in Asian Development Bank's *Asian Development Outlook 2003*. See also Brahm Prakash's (2002) paper for a review of the growth and development of ICT in the Asian countries, as well as its potential.

The International Telecommunication Union Web site provides up-to-date statistics on information technological indicators, as well as interesting case studies of its development in the Asian countries. Another informative website on ICT is that of the Economist Intelligent Unit e-business forum, with an international ranking of about sixty countries' extent of e-readiness. Its approach is pragmatic and business-inclined, and provides excellent details on the level of a country's ICT infrastructure, e-commerce and its laws and regulations.

The Environment and Sustainable Development in Asia

12.1 INTRODUCTION

The protection and preservation of the environment has increasingly become a major concern for many economists, managers, and policymakers across the world. More than ever, individuals, communities, governments, and international agencies feel threatened by the dramatic rate of deterioration of such natural treasures as agricultural soil, rainforests, and river systems; there is fear of extinction of fish stocks and exhaustion of mineral or oil resources. The main concern is how to ease environmental pressures and meet current consumption needs at the same time. In developing countries, the latter seem to take precedence over the former.

Environmental degradation detracts economies from the pace of economic development by imposing costs on developing countries through health-related expenses and the reduced productivity of resources. Smoke particles and dust are major causes of respiratory diseases and severe water pollution increases the risk of dysentery and other health hazards. Overall, these negative effects lead to a less healthy and thus less productive workforce. Moreover, these negative health effects demand expenses that can otherwise be used in more productive pursuits.

The role of the environment in the success of development efforts cannot be stated enough, particularly in the case of Asia—home to almost half of the world's population, two-thirds of whom live on income below a dollar a day. The range of environmental problems in the region is huge. Air pollution in Asian cities is among the worst in the world. Rivers here are far more polluted than the rest of the world. There are growing quantities of hazardous toxic waste—and safeguards are absent or largely ineffective. These environmental concerns pose a major challenge to economists, scientists, and policymakers alike. There is considerable debate on how these issues must be approached, but these concerns extend beyond national boundaries. The global implications of national environmental problems are also important for governments and populations everywhere around the world.

In this chapter, the role of natural resources in economic growth and development is examined. We will look at the economic causes and consequences of environmental devastation and explore potential solutions to the cycle of poverty and resource degradation. We will first present a model interrelating the environment with the economy, followed by a brief discussion of basic conceptual and economic tools necessary for the discussion. We then look at traditional economic models of the environment, and see how these apply and are able to explain present-day environmental concerns.

12.2   THE ECONOMICS OF THE ENVIRONMENT

The environment is a unique economic resource. At the most basic level, we human beings cannot be without the land that we walk and live on, without the air that we breathe, and without the water that we drink. Indeed, the environment is a very special resource because, unlike most other resources, it provides a fully integrated life-support mechanism that makes human existence possible. Just like every other resource that we own, we would wish to avoid wasteful use and/or cause wilful damage to our physical environment so that it may continue to provide life-sustaining services. In this section, we examine the nature of the environmental good and provide economic tools of analysis for understanding why the market often fails in its consumption.

12.2.1   The Economic Value of the Environment

The environment does have well-defined economic functions. The natural resources of a country directly provide essential inputs to most production activities. Forests provide timber for the housing and construction industry. Rivers and seas provide rich fish harvests, and natural navigable waterways serve as important channels for the transport of goods. The rich rainforests are an important source of medicinal plants and chemicals.

The environment also acts as a waste receptacle for all wastes generated by the natural system itself, as well as by all production and consumption activities we engage in the economy. When the waste generated is below the environment's assimilative capacity, it is all naturally recycled and goes back into the natural environment as primary inputs to production and consumption. For example, vegetable wastes are naturally recycled into soil on the forest floor, or into nutrients within a river system. Such waste is not considered harmful and no damage to the environment occurs. However, when waste levels exceed the environment's assimilative capacity or tolerance level over extended periods of time, the damage caused is often permanent and irreversible.

Finally, the environment is a direct source of utility through the provision of aesthetic services, such as a beautiful sunrise or sunset, clean rivers for swimming, fishing or recreational boating, and rich mountain forests for bushwalking or hunting. All in all, there are basically four ways in which the environment supports the economy, and Figure 12.1 is a simple model which illustrates these interactions.

12.2.2   The Market for Environmental Goods

Any system of exchange or trade (the market) accords an economic value to any good or service that is bought or sold. If market forces are left to themselves, the exchange results in market-determined prices and output levels that are efficient and maximizes total welfare in the economy. This basic microeconomic principle also applies to the market for environmental goods.

Figure 12.2 shows the market for some environmental resources, where units of consumption are plotted on the horizontal axis, and associated costs and benefits are plotted on the vertical axis. The market demand curve D represents the quantity of an environmental good demanded by consumers, given its price. Viewed alternatively, D incorporates each individual's willingness to pay for an additional unit of consumption of this particular commodity and thus summarizes the private benefits of consumption from the market exchange. D is also otherwise referred to as the marginal benefit (MB)

Figure 12.1   Economic Functions of the Environment

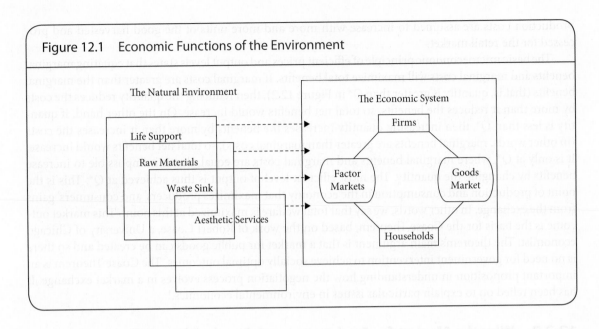

Figure 12.2   The Market of an Environmental Good

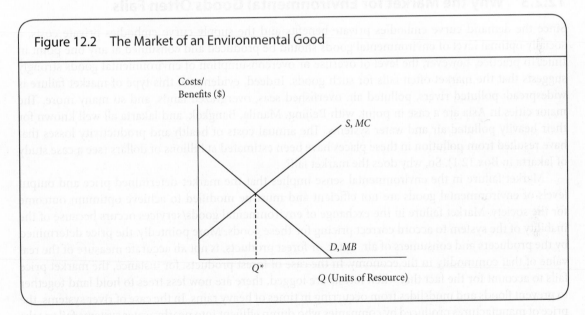

curve because it traces the additional unit of benefit (or utility) gained with the last unit of resource consumed. The curve slopes downwards because consumers derive less and less benefit as more and more units of the goods are consumed, according to the law of diminishing marginal utility.

The supply curve S, on the other hand, reflects the cost of producing the environmental good. This includes the price of the environmental good itself (whether they be trees from a forest area or fish in the rivers or open seas), as well as the cost of harvesting and processing them for distribution in the market. The costs incurred in this production process are considered private costs as they are all borne by the supplier. The supply curve S thus represents the total costs incurred in the production of this commodity, and is also alternatively called the marginal cost (MC) curve. S is upward sloping because production costs are assumed to increase with more and more units of the good harvested and processed for the retail market.

The basic microeconomic principle of efficient prices and output levels states that equating marginal benefits and marginal costs will maximize total benefits. If marginal costs are greater than the marginal benefits (that is, quantity is greater than Q^* in Figure 12.2), then reducing the quantity reduces the costs by more than it reduces the benefits, so total net benefits would increase. On the other hand, if quantity is less than Q^*, then increasing quantity increases the benefits by more than it increases the costs (in other words, marginal benefits are greater than marginal costs), so total net benefits would increase. It is only at Q^*, where marginal benefits and marginal costs are equal, that it is impossible to increase benefits by changing the quantity. The most efficient level of output is thus achieved at Q^*. This is the point of production and consumption in the economy that maximizes producers' and consumers' gains from the exchange. In other words, we say that total welfare is maximized at this point. This market outcome is the basis for the Coase Theorem, based on the work of Robert Coase, a University of Chicago economist. The theorem's main argument is that a market for public goods can be created and so there is no need for government intervention to achieve socially optimal outcomes. The Coase Theorem is an important proposition in understanding how the negotiation process evolves in a market exchange. It has been relied on to explain particular issues in environmental economics.[1]

12.2.3   Why the Market for Environmental Goods Often Fails

Since the demand curve embodies private benefits and the supply curve embodies private costs, a socially optimal level of environmental goods should be produced and consumed at any one point in time. In practice, however, the level of overuse or overconsumption of environmental goods strongly suggests that the market often fails for such goods. Indeed, evidence of this type of market failure is widespread: polluted rivers, polluted air, overfished seas, overgrazed lands, and so many more. The major cities in Asia are a case in point, with Beijing, Manila, Bangkok, and Jakarta all well known for their heavily polluted air and water systems. The annual costs of health and productivity losses that have resulted from pollution in these places have been estimated at billions of dollars (see a case study of Jakarta in Box 12.1). So, why does the market fail?

Market failure in the environmental sense implies that the market-determined price and output levels of environmental goods are not efficient and must be modified to achieve optimum outcome for the society. Market failure in the exchange of environmental goods/services occurs because of the inability of the system to accord correct pricing for these goods. More pointedly, the price determined by the producers and consumers of air, water, or forest products, is not an accurate measure of the real value of that commodity in the economy. In the case of forest products, for instance, the market price fails to account for the fact that when forests are logged, there are now less trees to hold land together to prevent floods and mudslides from occurring in times of heavy rains. In the case of river systems, the price of manufactures produced by companies who dump effluent into nearby water systems fail to take into account the loss of freshwater fish stock downstream. Such incorrect prices lead to the overuse of the resources, with neither the producer nor the consumer bearing the cost of restoring the damage or misuse of natural resources.

Market failure is often seen in the environmental goods market because many natural resources are open-access. Rivers, the sea, the air we breathe, the mountain ranges, the watersheds, and the forests are some familiar examples. Open-access resources are often considered common property, and having no well-defined owners, it is impossible to exclude anyone from using or availing of the resource.

---

[1] For the full exposition on its basic principle, see Coase (1960).

BOX 12.1

Market Failure in Jakarta

Jakarta, Indonesia, embodies many of the contradictory forces at play in rapidly industrializing megacities of the world. These "engines of growth," as they are so commonly called, play a vital role in national economic development. Yet at the same time, worsening environmental problems threaten economic prosperity and human health. In Jakarta, city officials have begun to grapple with these problems and their consequences in earnest.

Jakarta's air pollution is one of the main reasons why there is such a high level of respiratory disease in the city. Respiratory tract infections account for 12.6 percent of mortality in Jakarta—more than twice the national average. Ambient lead levels, which regularly exceed health standards by a factor of 3 or 4, are associated with increased incidence of hypertension, coronary heart disease, and IQ loss in children.

Jakarta's water quality is poor and suffering under the combined strain of domestic and industrial pollution. The poor state of water in the city impacts greatly on both human health and aquatic life. Diarrhea is responsible for 20 percent of deaths for children under the age of five in Jakarta. Organic pollution has also contributed to the decline of coral reefs within Jakarta Bay. In the Angle estuary in Jakarta Bay, the mercury content in commercial fish species far exceeds World Health Organization guidelines for human consumption.

SOURCE: United Nations Environment Program, *World Resources 1996–97: The Urban Environment* (Washington, D.C.: World Resources Institute, UNEP, and the World Bank, 1996).

Anyone can graze, harvest, or fish. If so, the market mechanism will find it difficult to restrict consumption to socially optimal levels.

Figure 12.3 illustrates this effect. On the horizontal axis lies the unit of the resource, as before, and on the vertical axis is the cost and benefit (in dollars) of each unit consumed. The marginal benefit curve D slopes downward and is assumed to be the same for the consumer paying for the good and for the wider society. In other words, the marginal private benefit is equal to the marginal social benefit $(MPB = MSB)$. The upward sloping lines are the marginal social cost lines, and as can be seen, the lines for the individual and the larger society diverge—that is, the marginal private cost curve is not the same as the marginal social cost curve $(MPC \neq MSC)$. Thus, two equilibriums arise, one at the intersection of the marginal benefit curve and the marginal private curve, E_p, and another at the point E_S, where the marginal benefit curve and the marginal social curve intersect. E_p indicates optimal consumption at Q_p units and E_S indicates optimal consumption at Q_S units, $Q_S < Q_p$.

The rest of the diagram is instructive. Note that MPC lies below MSC for all Q. This means that for every unit of Q that is extracted or used, society bears some costs that are not borne by the individual. This leads the individual to consume the resource at a level that is significantly above what is socially optimal. From the diagram, the individual extracts $(Q_p - Q_S)$ units more than what is efficient for society. In practice, this means overharvested forests, overfished seas, and too many graziers on open lands.

Figure 12.3 typifies the case of an industrial producer discharging effluents from a paper mill into a river, which severely pollutes the water system and kills the freshwater fish. Other downstream users of the river, such as recreational swimmers and fishermen, are severely disadvantaged (through diminished utility of the river) and thus bear the "external" costs of the industrialist's production activity. A similar analysis can be applied to the case of severe industrial traffic noise, which forces inner residents to keep their windows closed; and to the case of photochemical smog from car exhausts, which causes asthma in children and other respiratory diseases.

The concept of externalities is another way to view market failures. An externality refers to either a cost incurred or a benefit gained (both in utility terms) by a third party that has directly resulted from the exchange of goods or services between a consumer and a producer in the market. In the example

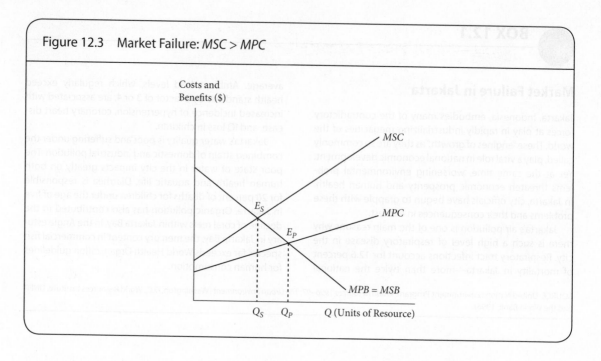

Figure 12.3   Market Failure: *MSC > MPC*

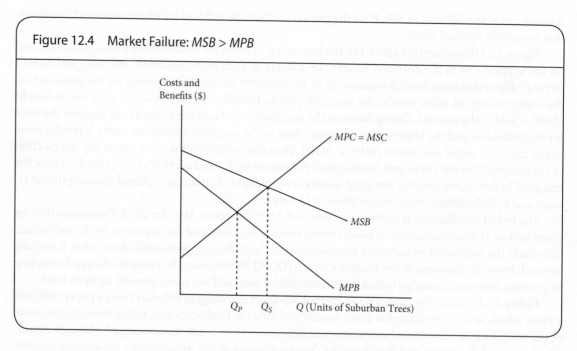

Figure 12.4   Market Failure: *MSB > MPB*

above, the extra cost (in the form of diminished utility from river use) borne by the recreational swimmers and fishermen is thus an externality or an external cost.

Note that the idea of externality applies to both costs and benefits, and thus not all externalities are detrimental. Figure 12.4 demonstrates positive externality for the case of suburban residents who decide to plant trees in their neighborhood to improve the landscape. Since tree-loving residents make tree-planting decisions by equating marginal private costs and marginal private benefits, the market level of suburban trees will be Q_p, where the socially optimal quantity is Q_s. Therefore, $Q_s < Q_p$ because the decision to supply trees also generates wider social benefits such as reducing water run-off and soil erosion, and improving air quality. Left alone, individuals will plant just up to Q_p trees. To reach Q_s level, city governments need to provide some form of subsidy to such community activities to encourage residents to plant more trees.

PROPERTY RIGHTS   Market failure in environmental goods often arises because of improperly designed or inadequate property rights systems governing economic resources. Property rights refer to a bundle of entitlements defining the owner's rights, privileges, and limitations for the use of the resource. Property rights can be vested either with individuals, as in a capitalist economy, or with the state, as in a centrally planned socialist economy. As we will see, existing property rights systems determine how producers and consumers use an environmental resource, and a properly designed property rights system is critical for society's efficient use of its natural resources.

There are four basic characteristics of property rights systems that can produce efficient allocations in a well-functioning market economy. First, all resources are privately owned (universality). Second, the system prevents non-owners from extracting any benefits from any productive use of the property (exclusivity). More generally, we say that the benefits and costs from (private) ownership accrue only to the owner. This includes the costs of maintaining and keeping the property, proceeds of goods sold from any productive use of the property, or proceeds from selling the property, should the owner decide to do so. Third, all property rights are transferable from one owner to another in a voluntary exchange (transferability). Fourth, the property and all benefits derived from there are deemed secure from involuntary seizure or encroachment by others (enforceability). If these features are in place in a property rights system, the owners of resources have all the incentives to ensure that their resources are used efficiently. Farmers who own land, therefore, have an incentive to fertilize and irrigate it because these measures increase land yield, and consequently, their incomes. In the same fashion, they also have an incentive to rotate crops if that raises the productivity of their land.

PROPERTY RIGHTS AND OPEN-ACCESS RESOURCES   For many types of goods and resources, the system of property ownership can be adequately defined, where ownership entitlements and rules are widely recognized and fully supported by formally established laws and enforcement schemes. That is why one person is not able to make his neighbor's front yard a garbage disposal site, or cut the trees in the community park. For many natural resource goods, however, any property rights system can be rendered inadequate. For example, who has the property rights to clean air and clear, unpolluted water systems? Who owns the fish in the river system and the open seas? For such natural resources, defining ownership can be a difficult matter.

The overuse and abuse of open-access resources, such as air, rivers, and seas, result because ill-defined property rights provide insufficient grounds for excluding non-owners from accessing and using the resource. Use of the resource without the accompanying incentive to look after it for the future or for other users (where these responsibilities come from ownership) often lead to destruction and damage. For example, if fishing access is not controlled in the rich natural lakes of the Australian island state of Tasmania, anybody who wants to fish can decide to harvest as much as he can, diminish the lakes' supply of fish in the future, and also increase the cost of harvesting fish. There is also the case of illegal logging activities in Malaysia and Indonesia, which have resulted in soil erosion, flooding, and landslides, as well as the loss of natural habitat for many rare species of animals and plants. Then, still in Asia, open-access sea water around Manila is overfished (see Box 12.2) while air pollution in many large cities in the region has resulted in a sharp increase in respiratory illness. Many of these problems of overuse have been categorized using the term "tragedy of the commons," a reference to overuse of common areas in towns in the United Kingdom in the early twentieth century.

BOX 12.2

Open-Access Fishing

Seafood provides close to 20 percent of the world's total food supply, and the accelerating disappearance rate of the world's marine catch of fish and shellfish has ominous implications for the seafood supply of the nearly 1 billion people who depend largely on the sea for sustenance. In Southeast Asia, the sea provides up to 100 percent of all animal protein in daily diets.

According to Ed Gomez, Director of the Marine Science Institute of the University of the Philippines in Metro Manila, nearly all waters within 15 kilometers of land in

Southeast Asia are considered overfished. Large organized fishing operations, often using trawlers (also known as the strip miners of the sea) precipitate the collapse of fish stocks from years of overharvesting. Trawling is a harmful technique because it does not discriminate between mature, harvestable fish from young schools. However, it is small-scale fishermen and their families who often pay the price of low supply. The cost of harvesting increases as boats have to move further away from the coastline, and they are forced to use illegal and destructive fishing gear, such as poisons, dynamites, and fine mesh nets to put food on the table.

SOURCE: People & the Planet (2000–2009), Web site at http://www.peopleandplanet.net.

PUBLIC GOODS   Externalities in many markets are caused by the indivisibility and non-exclusive nature of some consumption goods. For such goods, the benefits from consumption are indivisible if one person's use or enjoyment of the good is not able to diminish the amount available for others, such as the case of the sunset or the mountain view. The benefits from consumption can also be non-exclusive in the sense that once the good or resource is provided, it is impossible to prevent others from enjoying the benefits provided by that good, even those who fail to pay for them. A well-known example of this is national defense: the provision of security services via a national defense program to one citizen, or group of citizens, automatically enables every other citizen in the country to enjoy it as well. Such is the nature of these kinds of goods, often called public goods.

The indivisible and non-exclusive nature of public goods present large difficulties for their owners or caretakers because it is difficult to assign clear property rights over them and ensure that their use is efficient and sustainable over time. Furthermore, these features result in what is known as free-riding—which is the tendency of public good consumers to derive benefits from the resource without obligation to contribute to its provision. Overconsumption will thus result because each person is able to free-ride on the contribution of others. In the consumption of clean river systems, for instance, those who strongly oppose pollution will be willing to pay large amounts to keep the river system free of chemical effluents and other harmful discharges. The larger majority of people will, however, continue to swim and fish in that river even if they did not make any contribution to keeping it in its pristine state.

Public goods, if supplied exclusively by the private market, would be in short supply because of this "free rider" problem. Since its use cannot be controlled, many people would use the resource without paying for it, and the private sector would have little incentive to supply the good. This, in turn, explains why the government provides many essential public goods such as parks and wildlife areas, national defense, clean air, and clean water.

12.2.4   Dynamic Efficiency, Sustainability, and Discount Rates

The efficient allocation of natural resources needs to be considered in the context of sustainability of use over time as any decision today can influence the quality of the environment and the stock of resources available in the future. For example, the decision to extract oil from the ground today affects the ability to extract in the future. As we will see below, the decision to extract oil today depends on how much people are willing to pay for oil in the future.

Consider the case of an oil producer who faces the problem of how much oil to take out of the ground to sell now and how much to leave for future extraction for selling later. If he intends to maximize his profits, efficiency conditions dictate that he will continue to seek to sell today until the point where his marginal cost is equal to his marginal benefit. In the absence of market failure, this corresponds to extracting q units of oil, which equates marginal social cost to marginal social benefit. Unlike the standard static analysis, the owner needs to incorporate an additional opportunity cost factor in his decision. This is the cost of not having the oil available in the future and is sometimes known as user cost or rent.

The price of oil, at any particular time T, can be represented by

$$P_T = MUC_T + MEC_T \tag{12.1}$$

where MUC_T is the marginal user cost at time T and MEC_T is the marginal extraction cost at time T. Equation 12.1 implies that the price of oil at any time T includes not only the current cost of extracting the last barrel of oil from the ground MEC_T but also the opportunity cost of not having that barrel of oil for future extraction or selling (MUC_T). If the resource is left in the ground, the MUC_T is calculated by using interest or discount rates applied to net future benefits from the resource.

It should be clear by now that the interest rate (and associated discount rates) assumes an important role in this intertemporal decision making. If the producer believes that by extracting all the oil today and putting all proceeds from the sale in the bank, he can avail of a higher rate of return than if he decides to leave the oil in the ground for extraction and selling at a later time, then the decision will be to extract all resources now. However, if the producer anticipates being able to sell oil later at a substantially higher price, then he will tend to leave the oil in the ground until that later time. If interest earnings are considered to be a flow of income over time, the oil producer will make a choice that will maximize the sum of the present values of the earnings potentially received in each period. For the efficient dynamic allocation of the oil resource, the interest rates to be used to discount future net benefits must therefore be such that it makes the producer indifferent to which period he extracts and sells the oil. In other words, the present value of the marginal user cost must be the same in all periods.

As can be seen, the interest rate that is used to discount future incomes plays an important role in the calculation of economic benefits that can be derived from natural resource goods. If resources are to be allocated efficiently over time, firms must use the same rate to discount future net benefits as is appropriate for a large society. If firms were to use a higher rate, they would extract and sell resources faster than would be efficient. Conversely, if they were to use a lower than appropriate discount rate, they would be excessively conservative. This begs the next question: Are private and social rates the same? If not, what causes them to diverge?

To answer these questions, we need to look at Equation 12.1 again. The user cost of capital, as represented by MUC_T, can be further broken down into two components: the risk-free cost of capital and the risk premium. The risk-free cost of capital is the rate of return earned when there is absolutely no reason to believe that actual earnings will be substantially lower (or higher) than the expected return. The risk premium, on the other hand, is an additional cost of capital required to compensate the owners of this capital if there is sufficient reason to believe that expected and actual rates of returns may differ. Therefore, because of the risk premium, the cost of capital is higher in risky industries than in no-risk industries.

That social and private discount rates sometime diverge may arise from the fact that perceptions of risks and risk premiums differ between those that represent society's interests at large (usually the government) and those of private firms or individuals. If the risk of certain private decisions is different from the risks faced by society as a whole, then the social and private risk premium may differ. One obvious example is the risk posed by a change in government legislation. If the firm is threatened by government takeover at some point in the future, it may choose a higher discount rate to make its profits before nationalization occurs. From the point of view of society—as represented by the government—this is not a risk and therefore a lower discount rate applies. When private rates exceed social rates, the market is unable to allocate resources efficiently. There is market failure because current production will tend to be higher than the level that is desirable from society's point of view. Energy production and forestry resources often are subject to this source of inefficiency.

12.3 Addressing Market Failure in Environmental Goods

The presence of market failures in the economy creates an important role for governments to intervene and minimize the adverse impact of production and consumption externalities on the environment. There are three broad approaches that governments have invariably employed to correct market failure affecting environmental resources. These are: (a) engagement in public education on the environment, (b) development and implementation of command and control regulations, and (c) the provision of economic incentives in the market system. In contrast to the command and control approach, which essentially defines behavior as legal or illegal and specifies penalties for engaging in illegal behavior, economic incentives work by making individual self-interest coincide with the interest of the wider society. Examples of market-based economic incentives include pollution taxes, pollution subsidies, marketable permits, deposit-refund system, bonding and liability systems. In this section, we discuss two: taxation and marketable pollution permits.

12.3.1 Provision of Information

Many governments have tried to influence community attitudes and public behavior toward action that are deemed environmentally-friendly by providing critical information about the environment—its value, the social and economic impact of wasteful uses of resources, and the long-term consequences of permanent or irreversible environmental damage. It is believed that people are not well informed of the true benefits of environment preservation and the underlying costs of environmental degradation and this is reflected in their production and consumption behavior. If it is appreciated and understood that the benefits of using water wisely or not littering are substantially greater than the costs, then production and consumption decisions can be altered toward more environmentally-friendly choices. Governments can then design and implement a public education program that emphasize these points.

One approach toward this greater awareness of benefits over costs is to engage in a public information campaign. Some campaigns use prominent figures in the government, in the sports or music industry, or in other circles to "talk" to the public via public forums or media outlets. These "celebrities" are tasked to make public statements that encourage the general public to behave in more environmentally friendly ways. Currently, many levels of government as well as firms and not-for-profit organizations are engaged in such programs aimed, for example, at reducing the volume of waste and increasing recycling.

By and large, this moral suasion approach is ameliorative action, and in many cases it would have been better for society if the environmental damage had been prevented in the first place. Compared to prevention, such public information campaigns can be expensive and often not a very effective way of curbing pollution or environmental damage, particularly where it involves common-access properties. In that case, there would be a greater tendency for people to free ride on the contribution or efforts of other people in maintaining a satisfactory environmental quality. It is thus unlikely that problems such as air pollution, global warming, water pollution, and the depletion of the ozone layer will be effectively addressed by such policies. In spite of this, the governments continue to engage in them because they tend to be high-profile activities that may win votes.

Alternatively, the government can lead or fund activities that contribute directly to improving the environment, and therefore mitigate environmental market failures. Planting of trees, stocking fish, treating sewage, and cleaning up toxic sites are some of the activities that have been undertaken to this effect, which has helped to promote environmental awareness more widely across a range of people, including children. Many such community-based campaigns go a long way in making people aware of the relative benefits and costs of making consumption or production choices that are harmful to the environment.

12.3.2   Regulation

The regulation of pollution markets, through the use of command and control policies, has greater ability to modify environmentally degrading behavior and improve or protect the quality of the environment in an economy. In a regulatory regime, the suite of direct control mechanisms includes specific laws, and strict rules and regulations, and the associated set of penalties that are applicable to those who violate them. Such policies define the boundaries within which individuals, households, or firms (and any other generator of externalities) are allowed to operate. If one's behavior remains within these boundaries, then the household or firm is behaving lawfully. However, if behavior extends beyond these boundaries, then the firm or household is deemed to be behaving illegally and will suffer penalties specified by the rule or law.

Examples of command and control restrictions on inputs would include requiring sulfur-removing scrubbers to be installed on the smokestacks of coal-burning utilities, requiring catalytic converters on automobiles, and banning the use of leaded gasoline. Command and control regulations that take the form of restrictions on outputs include emission limitations on the exhaust of automobiles, prohibitions against the dumping of toxic substances, and against littering.

The regulatory approach to environmental problems requires that the regulatory authority decides on how much pollution or environmental damage is acceptable. The agency then develops standards and enforces them. Such a system can be very effective where the polluter is easily identified and where effective means for correcting pollution are available. Automobile exhaust emission standards are one good example where regulation has been used effectively; banning smoking in public buildings and providing limits to lead content in petrol are other examples. This approach has also been used for many years in the regulation of public utilities. Regulation does not require an elaborate system of calculations of costs and benefits but it does require some kind of scientific basis for determining the acceptable emission levels. In developing countries, the possibility of corruption and bribery to avoid regulation must also be taken into account in deciding how to enforce them.

12.3.3   Taxation

The use of tax in environmental policymaking has proven to be a useful instrument for governments seeking better ways to achieve sustainable levels of environmental resource use. In principle, the government could achieve optimal rates of resource use by imposing taxes that reduce the incentive for producers to enter common access properties or manufacture polluting products. A tax is a way of inducing firms or households to internalize the cost of their harmful production or consumption activities. When imposed on manufactured output, the tax effectively increases the price of the good, which then encourages less consumption in the economy. A 30 percent tax imposed on each liter of leaded petrol consumed will effectively discourage marginal users of motor vehicles from relying on their cars as their main form of transportation. If the tax can be levied on the externality itself, there is an additional incentive to invest in reducing external costs. A tax on the quantity of pollutants, for example, would give petrochemical plants an incentive to abate pollution, because their total tax can be substantially reduced in this way.

Taxes that internalize external costs have two important advantages over regulation. First, they allow the producer to choose the method of reducing access to common resources, so that rents are not dissipated in wasteful expenditures forced by regulators. Taxes can also generate substantial revenues for the government. These revenues can be used to fund environmental programs, or to compensate citizens for the harm caused by pollution and other forms of environmental degradation.

12.3.4 Marketable Permits

An innovative way to address market failure, particularly with regard to open access resources, is to create a property rights system through the use of marketable permits. These permits allow holders to harvest a common resource up to a certain limit, or grant them a license to pollute the environment up to a specified amount. This "right" to pollute is sometimes not an appealing notion, but there are strong indicators that these permits may yet be the most efficient way to reduce pollution and resource overuse.

Figure 12.5 shows how a pollution permit works. A supply schedule S represents the external costs of pollution—manifesting itself through generally poor health of the citizenry (high rates of morbidity), unsightly environment, lower property values, fewer and more expensive recreational possibilities, and reduced productivity and income. That S is upward sloping indicates that when the level of pollution is high, the level of damage costs is also high; and when pollution levels are low, the costs imposed on society by the small amount of pollution is also relatively low. There is also a demand schedule on the part of society that relates the quantity of pollution to the cost of pollution abatement or reduction. This is the downward sloping curve D in the diagram and it indicates that the cost of having very little or zero pollution levels in the economy is very high, while pollution abatement costs are low when high levels of pollution is tolerated. An equilibrium solution is reached where the two curves S and D intersect. The associated point Q^* corresponds to the optimal level of pollution that is

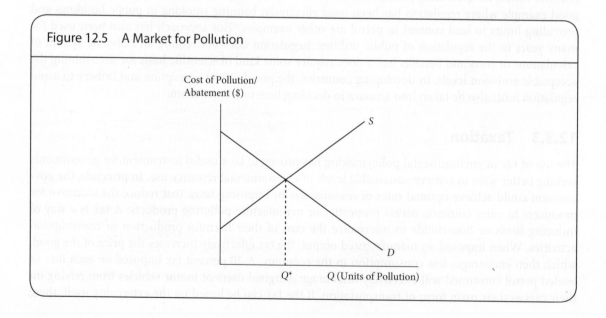

Figure 12.5   A Market for Pollution

automatically generated by the market. If Q^* can be established by the government as the target level of pollution for the economy, it can then decide to distribute permits to firms which allow them to emit pollutants up to some specified limit. Any firm polluting above its limit or without a permit would, if detected, be fined or shut down. The sum of the individual firm's limit to pollute must necessarily be below or, at most, just equal to Q^* so that total emissions can be reduced or maintained at the socially optimal level Q^*.

One major advantage of marketable permits over command and control policies is that once the initial allocation of permits is made, polluters are free to buy and sell their "rights" to pollute. Polluters thus have the choice to buy more "rights" if their circumstances warrant this to be a more cost-effective production strategy. If, for instance, a steel manufacturer finds that his pollution permit allows him less emission than what his current production technology can achieve, he might find it more cost-effective to buy more permits and pollute at a higher level until he is able and ready to upgrade his current production methods. On the other hand, many firms might find it more economical to sell off their "rights" in a bid to minimize their pollution costs. A market for pollution permits is thus established. (See Box 12.3 on the Kyoto Protocol.)

Economic incentives such as taxes and marketable pollution permits appear to be very effective mechanisms for curbing the pollution problem in many economies in the world today. They are generally accepted as being better than command and control policies because they leave the buyer and seller with a choice. Taxes have a disadvantage in that the response of polluters to the taxes may differ

BOX 12.3

Emissions Trading Under the Kyoto Protocol

The marketable permit approach is the basis of Kyoto Protocol's emissions trading program. This treaty was negotiated in December 1997 in the city of Kyoto, Japan, and came into force on February 16, 2005.

"The Kyoto Protocol is an agreement under which industrialized countries will reduce their collective emissions of greenhouse gases by 5.2 percent compared to the year 1990 (but note that, compared to the emissions levels that would be expected by 2010 without the Protocol, this limitation represents a 29 percent cut). The goal is to lower overall emissions of six greenhouse gases—carbon dioxide, methane, nitrous oxide, sulfur hexafluoride, hydrofluorocarbons, and perfluorocarbons—averaged over the period of 2008–2012. National limitations range from 8 percent reductions for the European Union and some others to 7 percent for the United States, 6 percent for Japan, 0 percent for

Russia, and permitted increases of 8 percent for Australia and 10 percent for Iceland."

"Text of the Kyoto Protocol,
United Nations Environment Program"

Emissions trading, as set out in Article 17 of the Kyoto Protocol, allows countries that have emission units to spare—emissions permitted them but not "used"—to sell this excess capacity to countries that are over their targets. Since carbon dioxide is the principal greenhouse gas, people speak simply of trading in carbon. Carbon is now tracked and traded like any other commodity. This is known as the "carbon market."

More than actual emissions units can be traded and sold under the Kyoto Protocol's emissions trading scheme. Transfers and acquisitions of these units are tracked and recorded through registry systems under the Kyoto Protocol. An international transaction log ensures the secure transfer of emission reduction units between countries.

Emissions trading schemes may be established as climate policy instruments at the national and regional levels. Under such schemes, governments set emissions obligations to be reached by the participating entities. The European Union emissions trading scheme is the largest in operation.

SOURCE: United Nations Framework Convention on Climate Change, Web site at http://unfccc.int/kyoto_protocol/mechanisms/emissions_trading/items/2731.php.

substantially from the target level of pollution. The more elastic the damage function *S* is, the more likely it is to be a problem. However, marketable pollution permits do not have this problem and is more effective in combating pollution.

12.4   THE STATE OF THE ENVIRONMENT IN ASIA

Asia is the most economically dynamic region in the world. In the last decade alone, growth in industrial and agricultural production in the region has outstripped global growth rates, and between 1990 and 2004, some 270 million people escaped poverty. However, economic progress has been achieved at a high price, with concerns that pressures exerted by economic growth would continue to degrade the natural environment. The United Nations report shows that the region is already living beyond its environmental carrying capacity. In this section, we take a close look at the natural endowments of Asia, relative to other world regions, and the drivers of environmental change in the region. We then use economic theory, outlined in the first half of this chapter, to summarize, evaluate and understand the policies to promote "green" growth in the region.

12.4.1   Asia's Natural Environment

Asia is richly endowed with abundant natural resources. According to statistics from the World Resources Institute (WRI), the region lays claim to 88 percent of the world's aquaculture harvest, almost half of the world's marine-fish catch, and over one-third of the world's agricultural lands (see Figure 12.6). This is in addition to having the second-largest rainforest complex in the world, more

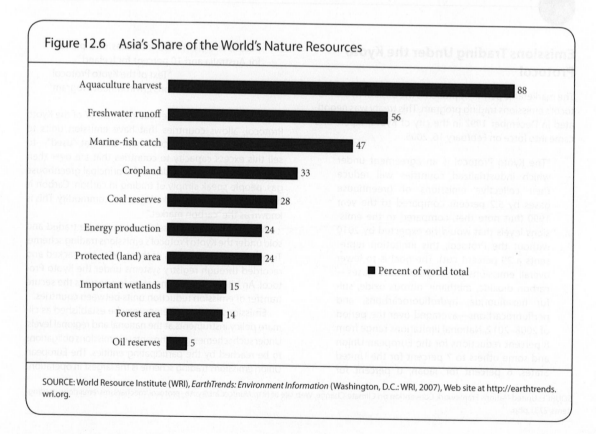

Figure 12.6   Asia's Share of the World's Nature Resources

SOURCE: World Resource Institute (WRI), *EarthTrends: Environment Information* (Washington, D.C.: WRI, 2007), Web site at http://earthtrends.wri.org.

than half of the world's coral reefs, and about 15 percent of the most important wetland areas in the world.

This rich set of natural resources and diverse ecosystem has fuelled the remarkable advances in the economic, technological, and political conditions of the region's member nations. At the same time, the rapid economic expansion of the member states has put the region's natural environment at great risk. Indeed, environmental degradation in the region is pervasive and the accelerating rate of its destruction, if left unchecked, will undoubtedly constitute a substantial constraint on its future economic development and a major obstacle to attaining higher standards of living for the populations.

FRESHWATER RESOURCES   The population explosion and the rapid rates of economic growth that characterized the Asian region in the last three decades has exacted a huge toll on the region's natural resources, with freshwater resources experiencing the largest negative impact. World Resources Institute (WRI) statistics show that freshwater withdrawals increased in Asia more than any other part of the world during the past century. The Asian Development Bank (ADB) further points out that the inadequate supply of clean water is the most severe environmental problem in many parts of the region, impairing people's health conditions and effecting slower growth through lower productivity levels. Accordingly, the region has about 56 percent of global runoff, but has the lowest per-capita availability of freshwater. The problem is most severe in India, Pakistan, and South Korea (see ADB, 1997).

Irrigation in Asia accounts for 80–85 percent of total freshwater withdrawals (WRI, 2007), but water distribution rates are low because of inefficient large-scale irrigation systems which were established in the late 1970s and early 1980s, during the Green Revolution period. The ADB estimates that in some areas, only 40 percent of withdrawn water is actually delivered to crops. Water quality has steadily declined, degraded by sewage, industrial effluent, urban and agricultural runoff, and saline intrusion. Levels of suspended solids in Asia's rivers have almost quadrupled since the late 1970s, typically containing four times the world average and twenty times more than those for the OECD member nations (GEO-3). Access to safe water appears worst in South and Southeast Asia with almost one in every two persons having no access to a safe drinking water source, and/or sanitation services (see Box 12.4 on China's water challenge).

Most of Asia's major rivers are either polluted or running dry. In China, the Yellow River in its most important agricultural region is severely polluted and ran dry (in its lower reaches) 226 days of the year in 1997. In another part of the region, the Amu Darya's and Syr Darya's water flow into the Aral Sea has been reduced by three-quarters, and has caused a catastrophic regression of 53 feet in the sea's water level between 1962 and 1994. The Aral Sea area suffers the highest rate of infant mortality because poor water flow and fertilizer runoff has fouled the seabed. The World Commission on Water for the 21st Century estimates that the fouling of waterways and surrounding river basins contributed to a total of 25 million people who were made refugees as a result of environmental problems in 1999.

AIR QUALITY   Asia ranks among the world's most polluted regions, with levels of ambient smoke particles and dust—major causes of respiratory diseases—generally twice the world average and more than five times as high as in the industrial countries and Latin America. Throughout the region, lead emissions from vehicles far exceed the upper limits set in the industrial countries.

Urban air pollution is the single, most important issue in any discussion on air quality in the developing countries. In Asia, the high rates of economic growth have led to rapid and unplanned urbanization, with a large number of people concentrated in the cities. High levels of urbanization have resulted in increasing urban air pollution as a result of transportation, energy production, and industrial activity all concentrated in densely populated urban areas. Between 2007 and 2008, urban population in Asia is expected to more than double, with an increase of 1.8 billion people. South Central Asia, including India, is projected to increase by nearly three times, while in East Asia, urban population is expected to double (Population Reference Bureau, 2008).

BOX 12.4

China's Water Challenge

The Chinese used to describe their water resources as "inexhaustible." No longer. China has a total surface run-off of 2,700 billion cubic meters a year, ranking fifth in the world after Brazil, Canada, the United States, and Indonesia. "But actually China is a water-deficient country," says Qu Geping, the chairman of the Environmental and Resources Protection Committee of the National People's Congress, China's highest legislature. With its huge population of nearly 1.3 billion, this translates to a little more than 2,000 cubic meters of water to each person per year—which is barely equal to the amount actually consumed by each person annually in the United States. This per-capita water volume is only one-quarter of the world average. Yet China's water supplies are falling behind demand as industry and the cities grow and agriculture struggles to keep pace with a population heading for 1.3 billion.

According to Qu Geping, the ideal population size for China's limited water resources is no more than 650 million people. The country's huge population has long outstripped its water balance. Even though China's per-capita water consumption remains low—averaging only about 100 liters a day—supply still cannot keep pace with growing demand. According to the Ministry of Construction, while China's urban water supply capacity grows 7 percent annually, the demand goes up by 10 percent. In the countryside, more than 20 million hectares of farmland and 93 million hectares of pastures are thirsting for water. It is a situation made worse by the pressure of people on existing and former wetlands.

During the past fifty years, much land was reclaimed from lakes in order to feed an ever-growing population. That cost China 35 billion cubic meters of freshwater resources. Dongting and Boyang Lakes, two of the major basins for floods of the Yangtze, China's longest river, have shrunk by 46 and 40 percent, respectively, in surface area in the past forty years. Meanwhile, their storage capacity has also decreased from more than 30 billion to around 17 billion cubic meters. Hubei in central China was once known as "a province of more than a thousand lakes," but many have shrunk and disappeared. In the late 1950s, it had 1,066 lakes; now it has just 182.

Furthermore, excessive exploitation of groundwater has resulted in land subsidence and falling groundwater levels in many Chinese cities. In Xi'an, capital of Shaanxi Province, the groundwater table has dropped so much that the ground level is sinking five times as fast as in the 1970s. "Some 80 percent of the groundwater resources in North China have been exploited," says Wang Weizhong, an official with the Ministry of Science and Technology. "It no longer pays to develop the remaining ones." He adds that the water problem "has become a major restriction on the development of China's economy."

SOURCE: Xiong Lei, "Water Challenge for China, Country Report 1: China," in *People & the Planet 2000–2003* (2001), Web site at http://www.people andplanet.net.

The environmental impacts are particularly severe in cities of ten million or more inhabitants, especially in Asia where some countries have a combination of intense industrial activity, large population density, and a high rate of motor vehicle use. These cities have become known as "megacities" and in Asia, they include Bangkok, Beijing, Delhi, Manila, Seoul, and Tokyo. United Nations Environment Program (UNEP) statistics further show that in the vast majority of Asian cities, transportation is the major source of pollution, with the number of cars in the region growing exponentially (see Box 12.5). Estimates from the Asian Development Bank, for example, show that in Delhi and Manila, the number of cars has doubled every seven years. Other causes of air pollution are the burning of fossil fuels (coal, oil, and natural gas) in domestic heating, power generation, industrial processes, and motor vehicles.

A heavy dependence on fossil fuels in the region is accompanied by substantial air pollution and escalating greenhouse gas (GHG) emissions. Much of the increase in atmospheric GHG concentrations stems from historic fossil fuel use in the industrial nations. About three-quarters of the anthropogenic emissions of carbon dioxide during the past twenty years are due to fossil fuel burning. The United States is the largest emitter of GHGs in the world, accounting for about 19 percent of total emissions, but Asia plays an important and growing role in climate change. Nations in the region contribute 38 percent

BOX 12.5

Lethal Inhalation in the Philippines

Metro Manila ranks among the top-ten megacities of the world for air pollution, with levels that pose serious health risks to its citizens. The damage bill to the economy in terms of medical expenditures and lost productivity is estimated to be around US$1.5 billion a year. Unless drastic action is put in place to reduce air pollution in Manila to healthy levels, residents there will bear the brunt of air pollution.

Case 1: For more than five years now, Daniel has been driving a jeepney in Pasay City in the Philippines. Recently, he has been coughing hard and is losing weight. In the afternoon, he has mild fever and is sweating at night. One bleak Wednesday, he decided to see a doctor. The diagnosis: he has tuberculosis (TB).

Case 2: Carlos was a healthy baby when he was growing up in a small town in Davao del Sur in the southern part of the Philippines. When his father was promoted as a manager in a company where he is working, the

family moved to Manila. Two years after their arrival in the metropolis, Carlos developed asthma—much to the surprise of his parents.

Studies conducted by the College of Public Health of the University of the Philippines (UP) some years ago showed that jeepney drivers are exposed to pollution for eight to ten hours daily. High levels of carbon monoxide, sulfur dioxide, and other lung irritants are slowly but unknowingly being inhaled by these transport workers. Jeepney drivers are not alone. Traffic policemen and metro aides (street cleaners) are also susceptible to lung infections because of their exposure to smog and fumes. Apart from catching TB, inhaling harmful substances from polluted air can cause blood poisoning, headaches, nausea, and blurred vision.

Children are not spared. The UP study showed that children who were exposed to high levels of fumes experienced hallucination, headache, dullness, restlessness, irritability, loss of memory, and the ability to concentrate. Some of them also developed asthma like Carlos.

SOURCE: Henrylito D. Tacio, "Lethal Inhalation in the Philippines," in *People & the Planet 2000–2003* (2003), Web site at http://www.peopleandplanet.net/doc.php.

of global carbon dioxide emissions from commercial energy use. Asia's heavy dependence on carbon-intensive fuels, such as coal and oil, produced an annual rate of growth in carbon dioxide emissions that was twice the average world rate of 2.6 percent per year from 1975 to 1995. Industrial release of carbon dioxide grew 60 percent faster in Asia than the rest of the world in the last few decades. However, carbon dioxide emissions per capita are low, little more than half the world average, and barely more than 10 percent of the level in North America in 1995.

Asia is also known to be the biggest consumer of wood fuels, accounting for nearly 44 percent of global consumption. In the rural areas, the big problem is indoor air pollution from the combustion of biofuels for heating and cooking. Old, inefficient cookstoves exacerbate the problem, with women and children bearing the heaviest health costs. Indoor pollutants, such as sulphur and nitric oxides, and arsenic compounds, result from open fires which burn biomass (stubble, dung, and other residues), coal, or wood. According to the World Health Organization, these pollutants are a special threat to the 1 billion women and children who spend more time indoors.

LAND AND FORESTS   Asia was once home to many of the world's richest, most diverse forest. Virgin forest cover in Asia totaled more than 15 million square kilometers, nearly one-quarter of the world's total, but 72 percent of Asia's virgin forest has been lost, and of what is left, only one-fifth (a mere 6 percent of virgin forest) can be classified as frontier forest. WRI estimates that 60 percent of Asia's remaining frontier forests are under threat from coastal development.

On mainland Southeast Asia, most frontier forests have disappeared. The most severe losses have been in Bangladesh, India, the Philippines, Sri Lanka, and Vietnam. Most of Asia's remaining frontier forests can be found on the islands of Borneo, Sumatra, Sulawesi, and Irian Jaya. Even here, however,

BOX 12.6

Palm Oil Industry and Indonesia's Forests

Palm oil is a major ingredient of soap, moisturizers, lipsticks, and food stuffs—and growing demand for it is likely to lead to a doubling of the area of oil-palm plantations in Indonesia, threatening the country's already dwindling forests, and the animals that depend on them.

The extent and speed of forest loss in Indonesia is alarming. The country already has one of the highest rates of deforestation in the world. Fifty years ago, the island of Sumatra was covered with millions of hectares of tropical rainforest. Today, most of the lowland forest has disappeared, converted to settlements, oil-palm and pulpwood plantations, and other crops. With two million hectares of lowland forest destroyed each year, the last remaining tracts will also be lost in a few years. The same could happen on the island of Kalimantan by 2010.

The shrinking forest area threatens the existence of thousands of animal and plant species, many of them endemic and already endangered. Sumatra's Tesso Nilo forest, for example, has the highest level of lowland forest plant biodiversity known to science, with over 4,000 plant species recorded so far. It is also home to 3 percent of the world's mammal species, including elephants, rhinos, and tigers.

Forest loss and oil-palm plantations are proving a particularly deadly mix for Sumatra's elephants. As their natural habitat disappears, the animals are increasingly raiding oil-palm plantations surrounding Tesso Nilo for food. However, an agonizing death awaits them. Angry farmers coat the palm fronds with pesticides or lay out poisoned baits. In 2002, seventeen elephant corpses were found in the vicinity of a plantation. An entire family had been wiped out, every one a victim of poisoning. Tigers too are increasingly entering villages to find food, where they are often killed. With the area of oil palm plantations in Indonesia predicted to double to six million hectares by 2020 and logging—both legal and illegal—continuing unabated, the outlook seems bleak for the country's remaining forests and the animals that depend on them.

SOURCE: Emma Duncan and Jamie Grant, "Greening the Palm Oil Industry Could Help Save Indonesia's Forests," in *People & the Planet 2000–2003* (2002), Web site at http://www.peopleandplanet.net.

the forests are under constant threat as illegal loggers exploit the most accessible forests along the coasts and major rivers. Agriculture and poorly planned resettlement programs also take a toll. Between 1969 and 1994, Indonesia's transmigration program moved 8 million people to the nation's forested islands where 1.7 million hectares of tropical forest were soon stripped. Box 12.6 gives a more detailed insight into the deforestation problem in Indonesia.

Threats of forest destruction come not only from commercial logging, but more so from the region's rapidly growing population and its ever-increasing demand for food and agricultural land. Between 1990 and 1995 alone, the region's largely rural population grew by more than 270 million people. The world's most densely populated region, Asia had more than one person for every hectare of land in 1995.

12.4.2   Main Drivers of Environmental Change in Asia

The environment is an integral part of the economy, as it provides inputs to and supports all economic production and consumption activities. The impact of an economy's growth and development on the nation's natural resources cannot be emphasized enough. More specifically, rapid economic growth is predicted to cause environmental degradation as production and consumptions patterns in the economy increase and change with growth. This idea is formally presented in what has been known as the environmental Kuznets' curve—which says that environmental pollution starts low in a low-income economy, accelerates with the increase in per-capita incomes, and then start to diminish after a particular threshold income level. Another way to view this is to say that environmental degradation is low in traditional agrarian economies, fairly high in rapidly industrializing ones, and becomes low again at high-income levels. In Asia, there is much empirical evidence to support this environmental Kuznets' curve[2]—but in this section, we will discuss the underlying forces that cause Asia's growth to be the single most identifiable cause of environmental degradation in the region.

INCREASED PRODUCTION   Asia continues to grow in importance as a global production center. Industrial production increased by 38 percent in the region's developing economies, and 23 percent globally from 1995 to 2002. Regional agricultural production increased by over 60 percent from 1990 to 2002. Many countries in the region derive their incomes from export earnings, but much of the commodities produced for export contribute to pollution and other environmental pressures in the economy.

There is, for example, increasing demand for timber to support the production of wood products for both domestic and export markets. This means that the region's natural forests are under significant pressure from illegal or indiscriminate logging and replacement by plantation forests. Given the difficulty of verifying the origin of wood and wood products, it is highly likely that several countries around the world are significant importers of illegally harvested timber and timber products.

Another resource with increased rates of extraction is the region's minerals. Regional iron ore accounts for a major proportion of mineral production in the region, and this has increased by some 40 percent between 1995 and 2004. In contrast, global production increased only by 30 percent in the same period. Mineral production is growing fastest in Thailand, Vietnam, and Malaysia. Iron ore is exported everywhere around the world, but China and Japan are the two main markets for processed minerals in the region.

INCREASED HOUSEHOLD CONSUMPTION   Rapid economic growth in the region is also fuelled by the demands of an expanding global and regional consumer base. In Asia, household consumption expenditures have been growing at higher than global rates. Between 1995 and 2002, the highest expansion in household consumption occurred in the densely populated economies of Southeast Asia and China. A country analysis by ESCAP shows that improvements in a population's standard of living imply lifestyle changes that tend to be characterized by energy-intensive and waste-producing consumption patterns. Rising incomes, thus, easily translate into increased demand for more cars and means of transport, for new, bigger housing, and for more television sets and other electronic equipments in the house; it also means more non-organic waste production per person. In general, the income and lifestyle change result in smaller, but more energy-intensive households. As an example, the demand for refrigeration has expanded rapidly—per-capita sales of refrigerators increased by as much as sixteen times between 1995 and 2000 in China, and twenty-two times in Thailand and Vietnam (Consumer Asia, 2002).

In general, energy consumption in the region increased by more than 20 percent between 1990 and 2002—twice that of global consumption in the same period. The fast-growing economies of China and India pose the greatest concern. There is still much unmet demand and therefore increasing pressure to pursue environmentally friendly growth policies everywhere (see Figure 12.7).

POVERTY   Much of the environmental degradation in many parts of the world can be directly attributed to the low standard of living that currently exists, especially in developing countries. Low current income makes it very difficult for households to meet daily consumption needs, and thus, environmental resources are unwisely exploited to supplement their incomes. With sustainable harvesting and forest management, the rich forest resources in the Sarawak region of Indonesia, for example, can easily

---

[2] Gangadharan and Valenzuela (2001) provide evidence of this for a cross-section of countries.

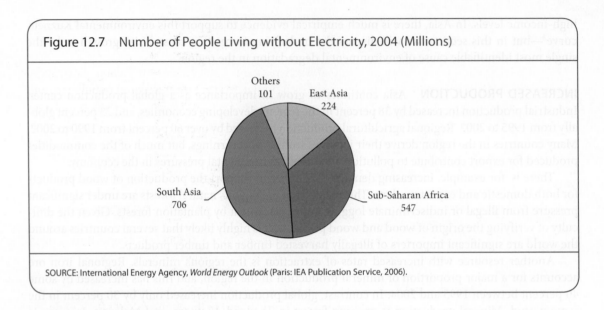

Figure 12.7   Number of People Living without Electricity, 2004 (Millions)

Others
101

East Asia
224

South Asia
706

Sub-Saharan Africa
547

SOURCE: International Energy Agency, *World Energy Outlook* (Paris: IEA Publication Service, 2006).

produce a steady stream of income to local inhabitants over time. However, because current income from farming always seems inadequate for many households, the poor often resort to excessive harvesting of trees to provide a temporary boost to current income, but at the expense of future income flows. In similar fashion, poor farmers tend to cultivate their land more intensively, cattle farmers to overgraze their land, and village fishermen to overharvest fish resources from the open rivers and seas—all as a means of augmenting their current income to meet daily consumption needs.

Poverty thus tends to contribute to environmental degradation where there are market institutional and policy failures. The poor often live in places where land and resource costs are low—areas of heavy pollution or subject to flooding, landslides, or volcanic eruption. They also poach on natural resources, such as fuel wood, fish, wild game, and so forth.

The low income in many poor economies reflects the low level of its factor productivity—both capital and human. Where there is low and insufficient income, there will also be little available for saving. A very low level of savings, in turn, implies that there will not be enough resources to devote to either capital or human investment. As a result, opportunities for increasing productivity will remain constrained, which then perpetuates low incomes overall. This poverty cycle presents a chronic threat to the environment—that as long as people are poor, their short-term dependence on the environment and its resources will not stop. Many poor countries get trapped into this poverty cycle this way, and the high population growth rates simply aggravate the problem. The more rapid rise in current consumption needs relative to the growth in household incomes leads to many unwise decisions on the use of the environment, including poor land management resulting in soil erosion and loss of soil fertility, overfishing, poor forestry management, and growing air pollution in urban areas. This is lamentable because many of these decisions are not reversible and have long-term consequences for the economic future of the nation.

POPULATION FACTOR   The high incidence of poverty is one factor that is directly putting great pressure on environmental resources in many developing countries. Because these countries tend to have high rates of population growth, population is seen as a significant contributor to the rapid degradation of the environment. Indeed, depletion of nonrenewable resources is accelerated by rapid population growth. A comprehensive World Bank (2002) study notes that rising population densities have contributed to deforestation in many parts of the developing world, as rural people move up the hill-sides in search of more agricultural land and firewood. The same study has pointed out the impact of a growing total population on urbanization that brings with it extra costs that society must bear.

The linkages between population growth and environmental degradation are strong, particularly when there are other active factors, such as ill-defined property rights, a largely rural population, and a high incidence of poverty. Most typically, this leads to deforestation in countries where population is increasing rapidly and where it is difficult to restrict encroachment into forestlands. This can occur in two ways. Population pressure forces rural inhabitants to encroach on forest preserves, by cutting trees and clearing land for cultivation. Secondly, rural residents in search of firewood enter the forest and gather firewood by cutting down some trees, as well as collecting dead branches. The latter may create only temporary damage, but if this activity is extensive, partial deforestation can result. Parts of Malaysia, Nepal, Pakistan, the Philippines, Thailand, and Vietnam are prime examples of this kind of deforestation, as well as illegal logging.

In the economic literature, some analysts have cast doubt on the claim that faster population growth retards income and is, therefore, undesirable. Australian economist Colin Clark (1970) was one of the first to note the lack of empirical support for this proposition while subsequent studies point out the positive impact of population growth on agricultural intensification, productivity, and technological growth. In spite of these, the general view, particularly with regard to the circumstances in most developing countries, is that slower population growth would permit per-capita income to rise more rapidly. The experience of the East Asian countries in the past three decades shows how rapid economic growth and falling fertility can interact to create a "virtuous cycle" that is the antithesis of the "vicious cycle" of poverty and high fertility accompanied by high rates of sickness and death. The conclusion here is that addressing the population growth problem in many poor nations will go a long way in relieving the economic pressure on precious environmental resources in the economy.

URBANIZATION   Although Asia and the Pacific, along with Africa, are still among the least urbanized regions in the world, their urban populations have been growing faster than that of other regions during the past decade and a half. In 1990, 33.3 percent of the population of Asia lived in urban areas, compared with 40.9 percent in 2006. The fastest influx of people from the rural areas to cities has occurred in the ASEAN countries, where the share of the urban population rose from 31.6 percent in 1990 to 44.9 percent in 2006. The effects of this rapid urbanization on the region are being felt most acutely in heavily populated slums, which are city areas characterized by substandard housing and poor access to basic services. In Asia, about four out of every ten urban dwellers live in slums. Regional urban populations in Asia are projected to increase by some 352 million people between 2005 and 2015. How these centers use resources will determine future environmental pressures in the region.

12.4.3   Climate Change: Some Implications for Asia

Climate change pertains to any long-term significant change in the expected patterns of weather in the regions of the earth. It reflects abnormal variations to the expected climate within the earth's atmosphere over a period of time. In policy circles, climate change is synonymous with global warming and is associated with rising temperatures that can cause seawater levels to rise, and million-decade masses of ice shelves to break.

Scientific evidence show that increased carbon dioxide levels exacerbate the heating effects of harmful greenhouse gases in the air by reducing the re-radiation of heat from the sun, and therefore increasing the temperature contained in the atmosphere (IPCC, 2001). Scientists point to human activity as the main reason for the rapid changes in world climate in the past several decades. The significant human factors identified in the increase in carbon dioxide levels are emissions from fossil fuel combustion, aerosols, and cement manufacture. Thus, public electricity and heat production are the main sources of greenhouse gas emissions globally, followed by the transport sector. Other factors contributing to heightened carbon dioxide emissions include intensified land use, large-scale irrigation, animal agriculture, and deforestation.

Carbon dioxide emissions in the Asian region increased by almost 30 percent between 1990 and 2000, with most of this growth occurring in India and China. Several fast-growing smaller economies in the region, such as Vietnam and Thailand, also exhibit fast-growing carbon dioxide emission rates, their total contribution pales in comparison with those from their two larger neighbors. However, developed countries in North America and Europe still account for the continued rise in carbon dioxide emissions overall. Developing countries, including China and India, have per-capita carbon dioxide emissions that are eighteen times lower than those of some developed countries.[3] The implications of climate change are far-reaching for many countries in the region. The Pacific Island state of Tuvalu and the Carterets island of Papua New Guinea have already been seriously affected by rising sea levels such that their governments have announced plans for evacuation (UNESCAP, 2006).

A 2001 synthesis report by the Intergovernmental Panal on Climate Change identified a range of impacts that climate change may have on Asia and the Pacific countries. The list includes:

- Increasing food insecurity
- Accelerated extinction rates
- Changing marine productivity, due to coral bleaching, changing conditions on mangroves and sea grass beds
- Extreme weather conditions including serious drought in some areas, excessive rains and flooding in others
- Rising frequency of tropical cyclones
- Increased potential for heat-related and infectious diseases

Accordingly, the Asia and Pacific region is the most disaster-prone area in the world. Around 80 percent of all disasters and 90 percent of deaths from natural disasters around the world have occurred here since 1900. Among the most destructive and frequent hazards have been flash floods, earthquakes, storm surges, and droughts. In the last twenty years alone, the region has been devastated by some of the world's record-breaking disasters, including:

- the June 1991 Mt. Pinatubo volcanic eruption in the Philippines, the second most devastating volcanic eruption of the twentieth century;
- the Boxing Day 2004 tsunami in the Indian Ocean and Southeast Asia, triggered by one of the most severe earthquakes in recorded history, which left 230,000 people killed, and the livelihoods of millions were destroyed in more than ten countries;
- the October 2005 earthquake in Pakistan, which killed 79,000 persons, and
- the May 2008 earthquake in Sichuan, China, which killed 80,000 people and left 5 million homeless.

Deforestation, soil erosion, overgrazing, overcultivation, and other unsustainable agricultural practices and the degradation of natural buffers have amplified the effects of natural hazards. Communities sheltered by coastal buffers, such as sand dunes or mangroves, were found to have suffered substantially less damage in the December 2004 tsunami. Natural disasters cause major loss of life and damage to infrastructure, and impact on future growth prospects. Yet, sufficient investment has not been made to prepare for and mitigate such disasters.

---

[3] Based on International Energy Agency (IEA) data.

12.5   PROMOTING SUSTAINABLE DEVELOPMENT IN ASIA

It is clear that the market, left alone, is not able to deliver efficient and socially optimal outcomes consistent with sustainable growth and development. In Asia and elsewhere, new policy approaches and some government intervention are needed to stop and reverse the rapid rate of environmental degradation in the region. There are a number of policy instruments that governments can use. In this section, we look further into policy options discussed in Section 12.4 by citing actual examples of environmental policies that governments have adopted, and evaluating the impact of these policies on market efficiency.

12.5.1   Command and Control Policies

For many countries in the world, command and control policies were the most popular approach to environmental control. However, such policies and regulations have been criticized as generating more abatement costs than necessary to achieve a given level of emission. For instance, critics of the U.S. environmental policies, which are primarily based on the command and control method, have argued that expenditures on pollution control are excessively high and that policies based on taxation and market permits would be more effective. Notwithstanding, there are circumstances in which command and control policies are more effective.

WHEN MONITORING COSTS ARE HIGH   Alternative methods of pollution control, particularly those that allow firms to pollute up to a certain level, must know exactly how much each polluter emits. In the simple case of littering, it will entail an enormous amount of resources to ensure each individual does not exceed the maximum allowable level of litter. The monitoring costs could be very high, and could easily render the policy useless. In such cases, imposing relatively high fines on those found littering is more likely to bring results.

WHEN ZERO-LEVEL EMISSIONS ARE THE BEST   When pollutants are extremely dangerous and no allowable level can be accepted, it is easier to legislate a ban on this pollutant. An outright ban on radioactive waste, for example, is a clear and simple rule, easily implementable and incurs very little monitoring costs.

DURING EMERGENCIES   Direct controls tend to be highly reliable options in emergency cases, where immediate and drastic action is warranted. In a drought situation, for instance, it is far easier to prohibit the use of water for watering plants and gardens and fine those who violate that rule. Similarly, during smog alerts, it is easier for city governments to order factories to close and stop production temporarily until the air is clearer and the emergency passes.

12.5.2   Economic Incentives

Economic incentives, such as taxes and marketable permits, do equate marginal abatement cost across polluters and therefore, minimize the costs of obtaining the target level of environmental quality. Taxes are preferable to command and control policies since pollution taxes minimize the cost of abatement and provide other desirable incentives. The reaction of polluters to the new taxes is, however, not known until the policy has actually been put in place—so there is some chance that the level of pollution induced by the new tax may differ substantially from the target level of pollution. Marketable permits do not suffer from this problem and can generate the target level of pollution with much more certainty.

Pollution control through economic incentives leaves the polluter (producer or consumer) the choice of how much emission is best for his/her own situation. In places where marketable permits are used, polluters who want to exceed their allowable emission levels can purchase this "right." Correspondingly, some may find that the cost of high pollution emissions is greater than its benefits, in which case, they could sell their "rights" and aim to have zero emissions. Since firms seek to maximize profits over the long term, cost minimization objectives will drive them to seek technologies that are friendlier to the environment. Resources for research and development in this direction will also be encouraged in the long term. By giving producers the flexibility of responding to pollution reduction standards with different technologies, such incentives to reduce pollution can provide long-term benefits for both the individual firm and the wider society as well.

12.5.3   Clarifying Property and Tenure Rights through Tenure Reform

In general, the prescription to clarify property rights where required is not easily implemented mainly because of the inherent nature of environmental resources that are of the open-access types, such as air, forests, and open seas. This prescription is relevant, however, in many developing countries where tenanted farming is still in place. Here, as farmers do not hold titles to the land they till, there is little incentive to conserve resources and to improve efforts to reduce pollution and improve environmental management. Furthermore, there is no guarantee that the current landowner–tenant relationships that have been passed on from the previous generation will continue into the next. The tenant farmers, therefore, have little incentive to maintain the land's long-term viability, especially if it is only for the benefit of the absentee landowner and his family.

This problem is well-recognized by many governments, in Thailand, Indonesia, the Philippines, Brazil, Venezuela, and other agricultural-based developing countries. In the last fifty years alone, government efforts to correct the problem—through numerous land reform packages that seek to redistribute large tracts of farmlands to small farmers—are widespread. These programs have, however, been met with limited success because of the enormous political resistance put up by the landowners, who also often serve as high government officials in these developing countries. Notwithstanding, land tenure reform has had its share of success in other places, and this has made a tremendous difference in promoting sustainable growth and development in some countries. In Mozambique, Tanzania, and Uganda, for instance, new tenure laws were passed to recognize land held under customary or traditional (untitled) tenure as fully and legally tenured (WRI, 2005). This law was included using certification processes based on verbal endorsements (in Mozambique), as well as using a community-administered land recording and titling process (in Tanzania). This new tenure system allows owners to invest in the property and manage the resource for optimum benefit.

For securing property "rights" to open-access resources, the case of the Fiji fishing villages provides a good example. The government of Fiji formally recognizes "customary fishing rights areas" in which villagers have traditionally fished and collected shellfish, in cases where these nearshore zones have been surveyed and accurately mapped by the state. This legally sanctioned system of recognizing traditional ownership includes the right to exclude others, and to manage the resource for optimum benefits. More specifically, the state has granted the local communities the right to draw up their own management plans for these customary use areas, with the aim of restoring these fisheries as a community asset.

12.5.4   Phase-Out Subsidies

For many years, subsidies were seen as important instruments that could be used by governments to influence individuals away from environmentally damaging behavior. This type of incentive pays the polluter a fixed amount of money for each unit of pollution that is reduced. The effectiveness of this policy in practice is, however, in question because people in general find it difficult to accept that polluters are being given a payment, rather than making one. There also tends to be more polluting firms in a subsidy system, compared with a taxation system (Khan, 1998).

Governments generally also provide subsidies to consumers. Energy and water in developing countries are often heavily subsidized. In Southeast Asia, for instance, the average price paid by consumers for electricity is 4 cents per kilowatt hour, while it costs an average of 10 cents to produce. The usual justification given for such policies is to make these utilities more affordable and therefore improve the lives of the citizenry. Closer investigation reveals, however, that this mostly benefits the urban middle class, as they are the ones who are able to pay the high cost of connection to the grid.

Such subsidies have tended to benefit only the producers but are harmful to the environment and the larger society in general. Subsidies effectively set the prices of resources below cost, and therefore encourage overuse. In Asia, the major offenders are often provided with subsidized water for irrigation, energy, and fertilizer use. Low water charges have led to salinity and water logging problems. Energy subsidies result in waste and more extensive levels of air pollution, while fertilizer subsidies encourage the application of fertilizers that can run off and pollute water downstream. Any existing subsidies should be phased out as there are far better and more effective instruments that can be used for the control of environmental damage.

12.5.5 Improve Institutional Capacity

The Asian governments have a very important role to play in resolving much of the issues affecting the environment in the region. Addressing the challenges presented by the continuing degradation of their environmental resources requires the implementation of appropriate, effective, and complementary policies in several areas. For this to work effectively, however, Asian governments must improve their capacity to implement changes. First, they must shift from a top-down management strategy and engage in the devolution of responsibility to local authorities. Instead of using highly centralized regulatory agencies and employing thousands of environmental inspectors, streamlined environmental ministries can serve as coordinators of a highly decentralized approach to policy implementation, which recognizes the value of and provides sufficient participation from the local community authorities and public servants.

12.6 On Efforts by the Beijing Government to Save Water

In general, the central government can form partnerships with the private sector, non-governmental organizations (NGOs), and local communities in its efforts to conserve water. Private firms and NGOs alike have proven to be enthusiastic partners in such projects. NGOs, in particular, appear to be very effective at delivering results at the grassroots level as they avoid the implementation issues associated with huge bureaucratic processes (see Box 12.7). Clearly, greater decentralization and broader participation are moves in the right direction for Asia's environmental policies to work successfully.

At the international and interregional level, there is much room for cooperation. Many environmental problems spill across national boundaries and it is often difficult to get governments to resolve cross-border issues because of unenforceable contracts and different agendas among the different agencies and countries. Specific environmental problems of this type include the transnational costs of damage caused by acid rain, overharvesting of fish resources in coastal fisheries and the ocean, flood

BOX 12.7

Beijing's Efforts to Save Water

As a centuries-old capital city, Beijing was once the scene of interweaving rivers and lakes. It was dotted with wells in the Ming Dynasty (1368–1644), and boats shuttled in the canal between the capital and Huangzhou, 1,000 kilometers away in southeast China.

Although urbanization and population growth devoured most of the rivers and wells, Beijing managed to live on its seemingly abundant groundwater resources and never knew a water crisis until the 1980s.

"The worst water famine came in the summer of 1981," recalls Duan Wenjie, a chief planner of the Beijing Waterworks Company. "The groundwater level had been dropping one or two meters a year, and there wasn't enough rainfall or other surface runoff to replenish it." Between 1949 and 2000, Beijing's daily per-capita water consumption went up from 28 liters to nearly 300 liters.

From the 1981 water famine, the local leaders became more aware of the necessity to reduce consumption while extending sources. Wang Mingming, Deputy Director of the Beijing Municipal Water-Saving Office, says, "We have worked hard to make it known to the public that it is a virtue to treasure water resources and use it economically."

In mid-1999, Beijing municipal workers were busy installing what is known as a *Jieshui Longtou*—a newly-developed "water-saving tap"—at residences and in public places. This, officials point out, can be turned on and off at least 200,000 times without dripping. Earlier in the year, the authorities had banned the use of screw taps, often made in backyard factories in the countryside and with substandard metals, blaming them for causing 15 percent of the city's water leaks.

"Every drop counts," said a Beijing TV anchor-woman when commenting on the ban of the leaky taps. Every year the Chinese capital needs to consume 4 billion cubic meters, yet in 2000, its runoff was no more than 1.82 billion cubic meters, and it has to rely on previous storage to maintain its water supply. "Beijing is now as thirsty as Israel," says an official at the Beijing Municipal Water Resources Administration. In the 1980s, the Municipal People's Congress and government had issued decrees and regulations on water saving, stipulating that all industrial enterprises should recycle their used water, and every household must have a water meter installed. The decrees and regulations also forced all new projects to have water saving facilities designed, installed, and operated simultaneously with the project. An overall plan gives an annual quota for water consumption to each hotel, factory, shop, government office, and other work units.

At the end of 2000, a municipal government mandate put up even more strict regulations, by which enterprises that surpass the water consumption quota may be charged a fee as high as fifteen times the regular rate. According to the new mandate, tanks with a capacity of more than nine liters for flushing toilets are also banned. Only seven years earlier, the popular tank capacity was as much as 17 liters.

Beijing has led other cities in recycling water for industrial use: more than 80 percent of such water is recycled in Beijing, compared with the national average at 50 percent. More and more citizens have taken action to save water in their daily life. Li Shuzhen, a 66-year-old resident in southern Beijing, has learned to save the water left from washing rice and vegetables to use for mopping the floor, to economize on the use of water when operating the washing machine, and to minimize the use of detergents since they are a source of pollution.

According to Zhou Xing, an official in charge of the water saving campaign in the neighborhood, on average, one household of the community, with nearly 700 families, can save 3 to 4 tons of water every month.

SOURCE: Xiong Lei, "Water Challenge for China, Country Report 1: China," in *People & the Planet 2000–2003* (2001), Web site at http://www.people andplanet.net.

control, and river pollution. When the external costs from such situations are borne by third parties who are residents of another country, there is no legal framework to recover such costs. In these cases, governments have acted on behalf of their resident populations and initiated bilateral or multilateral intergovernmental discussions.

In Asia, the ASEAN (Association of Southeast Asian Nations) has developed a plan of action regarding the environment and established a number of working groups to address trans-boundary issues involving pollution of air and water. The Asian Development Bank (ADB) has also provided important and critical support for enhancing cooperation among countries in the region. It has, for

BOX 12.8

Tale of Darewadi Village: Water Management Success

As recently as 1996, Darewadi, a remote, drought-prone village about 600 miles west of Mumbai, was a picture of despair. Its residents lived without any assurance of drinking and irrigation water. It receives only 300 millimeters of annual rainfall. Agricultural production—even in a year of reasonably good rain—was not sufficient even for three or four months, employment opportunities were scarce, and primary education was a distant dream for the children. Women had to toil hard, either in the places to which they had migrated or in their own village to fetch water, fuel, and other basic needs.

The village has since rebuilt its small economy into a vibrant and dynamic one that is full of hope of a bright future for its residents. The transformation has been due to the Watershed Organisation Trust (WOTR), a German NGO operating in India, which funded the watershed restoration project using an approach that managed to convince villagers to give up traditional ways (such as a ban on free grazing). The WOTR also ensured that the process was community-led, involving residents from the lowest to the highest incomes, as well as made sure that women were well-represented in the Darewadi VWC, the community-based watershed management board.

The process was not smooth initially. It took about two years of promoting the project to villagers and one bad monsoon season to convince the villagers to make some sacrifices (no grazing) for better long-term prospects. This was achieved through constant interaction, audio-visual aids, and exposure through visits to areas where people have conserved and mobilized resources for a better life. The next stage was to mobilize and empower the entire community to undertake the responsibility of managing their resources and life. A series of technical initiatives (contour trenches, gully plugs, farm bunds, and contour bunds, check dams, etc.) along with bioregeneration (plantation, grass seeding, etc.) were undertaken. The once degraded landscape was slowly transformed, providing adequate drinking and irrigation water with increased soil moisture for better crop production and sufficient (sometimes even surplus!) fodder and fuel.

Increased agricultural production as a result of increased availability of water and an enhanced soil moisture regime created linkages with markets for selling the surplus. Earlier pearl-millet farmers diversified to the cultivation of vegetables, cotton, onions, improved cereals, and pulses, even selling the surplus in big cities like Pune, Ahmednagar, Mumbai, etc. Employment opportunities increased from two to eight months in a year. This was possible because of farmers' perception of "minimal risk" as a result of the assured availability of water. In order to conserve the developed natural resources, the VWC took some difficult decisions like baning direct lifting of water from storage structures, digging of bore wells, cultivation of water-intensive crops like sugar cane, and other social fencing methods. Just as scarcity leads to competition, abundance leads to greed, and both can create conflicts. In 1999, the villagers themselves collectively approached the district collector to issue a notice banning the digging of bore wells.

Two critical elements of the Darewadi success are (i) accountability, and (ii) transparency. All the works and processes were shared by the villagers; everyone had a role. Detailed accounts of the works done and money spent were publicly known and this transparency motivated the villagers to work collectively. Fr Robert, head of the WOTR in Sangamner, puts it simply this way: social mobilization is not an easy task but the life of the project and of the villagers become really smooth once they get this magic wand.

SOURCE: Centre for Science & Environment, Web site at http//www.rainwaterharvesting.org.au/rural/Darewadi-village.htm.

instance, facilitated the formation of the Greater Mekong Sub-regional Working Group on Environment, which is a forum for cooperation in the joint management of the Mekong River, which is shared by six countries in the region. Important initiatives have been provided by the ADB, the United Nations, and the World Bank in facilitating regional monitoring projects and regional technical projects that can promote further cooperation and coordination among the countries in the region. With the help of these and other international agencies, close cooperation among governments in the region can be intensified, as it is critical for resolving cross-boundary issues and protecting the overall state of the environment in Asia.

REVIEW QUESTIONS

1. How important is the environment to the economy? What economic functions does the environment provide?
2. In what ways does poverty lead to environmental degradation?
3. What types of environmental problems do the rural and urban poor share? What are the differences in the conditions they face?
4. What features of developing countries may constrain the successful implementation of alternative policy options for environmental control?
5. What are property rights? What are the main characteristics of a property rights system?
6. What are the main characteristics of public goods? Give examples.
7. Explain, using economic tools, why there will always be an undersupply of public goods if the market is left to operate by itself?
8. What is market failure? Why do they matter for the development process?
9. What is an externality? Why will there be overconsumption or overproduction when an externality is present? Illustrate with a diagram.
10. What are open-access resources? How do they give rise to external costs?
11. Explain how there can be an optimal level of environmental damage.
12. Compare and contrast the effectiveness of the three broad approaches to intervention: provision of information, command and control, and economic incentives.
13. Show in a diagram how taxes are able to correct for externalities. Show how subsidies can do the same.
14. What is marketable pollution permits and how do they work? What issues must be considered in the development of market pollution systems.
15. What is the vicious cycle of poverty? How does this impact on the environment?

Notes on References and Suggestions for Further Reading

The following Web sites provide rich sources of statistical information on the environment from various international organizations, such as:

Asian Development Bank, http://www.adb.org/
People and Planet, http://www.peopleandplanet.net/
World Bank, http://www.worldbank.org/
World Resources Institute, http://www.wri.org/ or http://earthtrends.wri.org/

Asia-specific sources of information, survey of trends, current situations, and some projections of trends can also be found in publications by the Asian Development Bank (ADB), United Nations Environmental Program (UNEP), United Nations Economic and Social Commission for Asia and the Pacific (UNESCAP), and the World Bank (WB).

For an in-depth discussion on the economic theory of the environment, the following books by these authors are highly recommended: Michael Common (1996); David W. Pearce and R. Kerry Turner (1990), James Kahn (1998), and Thomas H. Tietenberg (1996).

The Political Economy of Development in Asia

13.1 INTRODUCTION

Mainstream or orthodox economic theory likes to think of itself as being "scientific." As part of the scientific method, neoclassical economics is careful to draw a distinction between positive and normative statements. Its theories are carefully couched in terms of utilitarian values, rational action, the hedonist calculus, the power of the market, maximizing behavior, and so on. It is willing to incorporate theories from other disciplines that it believes to be valid, such as attitudes toward risk or aspects of sociobiology, which allows individuals to treat relatives differently from others whom they share few genes with.

There are some economists—call them the heretical or radical school—who are opposed to this rather mechanistic, mathematical, detached view of economic agents as rational actors evaluating all sensory inputs objectively and then proceeding methodically to make an objective decision. These economists are often interested in more interdisciplinary approaches and believe that psychology, ethics, and moral philosophy have an important contribution to make to economic analysis. They are not tied to a fine distinction between positive and normative judgments. They acknowledge the interdependence between economics, psychology, ethics, and politics.

13.2 COOPERATION, ALTRUISM, AND ETHICS

What are some of the aspects of human behavior that might be considered as alternatives to the narrow self-interest that orthodox economics normally considers? One of the most widely discussed ways that behavior departs from the neoclassical norm is the violation of the pure self-interest assumption. Charity and altruism are two aspects which are widely observed but which do not easily fit into the hedonistic framework. When economic agents are charitable or altruistic, they act on the basis of motives that treat others as more or less equal to themselves. Acts of heroism, such as saving a drowning person or rescuing someone from a burning building at the risk of personal safety, are extreme examples. However, there are many other acts of charity and altruism at a more subtle level. Ethics enters into the discussion and involves actions that uphold implicit and often unenforceable contracts or social norms of behavior. Free riders, moral hazard, principle–agent problems are all areas in which these issues of ethical versus pure economic behaviors arise.

An honest and ethical person would be less likely to take advantage of these situations for his own narrow self-interest. Rather, the ethical individual would comply with both the spirit and letter of the law and regulations. He would do that because he realizes that when he takes advantage of the system he raises costs and reduces the welfare of others. In this sense, an ethical person who acts in this way is also following a path of altruistic and cooperative behavior.

13.2.1 Religious and Spiritual Traditions

The model of self-interest gets no support from the world religious and spiritual traditions. "Love your neighbor as yourself," or the golden rule, "Do unto others as you would have them do unto you" are examples of the spiritual or moral imperative to treat others as you would like to be treated—as if they were your twin, your best friend, or closest relative. To get a sense of how a truly altruistic individual might act, we look toward the behavior of the great saints and spiritual giants, such as Buddha, Jesus, Moses, Mohammed, Ghandi, Mother Teresa, Saint Teresa of Avila, Meister Eckart, Saint Francis of Assisi, and a host of others in all the spiritual traditions. These sages lived in a purely selfless manner, following the golden rule and thinking of the welfare of others in their daily lives and in their actions. The actions of these few enlightened beings are the yardstick by which pure altruism or selfless action can be measured. These great beings truly viewed everyone as equal and treated them as such. They went beyond the pettiness of self-interest, seeing everything and everyone as imbued with the same divine origins. When we lose our ego, our narrow interest in our individual lives, we have the opportunity of finding unity with everything.

This is the concept of self-realization that many eastern philosophies, such as Buddhism and Hinduism stress, and also by the Christian, and Sufi (Islamic) mystics. Getting rid of egoistic behavior requires putting other people on an equal footing with oneself. Egocentric behavior is out. Egoism is self-defeating while self-sacrifice actually leads to a higher form of self-realization.

Are we a mixture of self-interest and altruism? How do most of us act in our daily lives? Are we a mixture of higher and baser motives? Do we act with self-interest most of the time? Are there glimpses of the higher actions of the saints? Do we ride the trams for free when there is no one around to watch? Do we tell a few lies now and then to make it easier to get our way? If we know that material in a class is not going to be included on a test, do we forget it completely, even though we know it might be important later on in our careers? Did you ever go out of your way to help someone in trouble with no thought of getting "paid back?" How often are we selfish and how often do we put other people first? For most people, their actions are usually a combination of selfish and selfless behavior. Often we do not even think about it. We just do what comes naturally, what we have been taught, and what seems comfortable. We do not contemplate or consider what is the right or just thing to do in any particular circumstance.

13.3 How Do We Model Altruism?

Altruism can be defined as "unselfish regard for or devotion to the welfare of others." There are several ways that economists have modeled this behavior within the conventional orthodox neoclassical framework.

13.3.1   Altruism as a Preference in the Utility Function

In the simplest model, there are two individuals i and k, and i is an altruist. Then k's utility will be in i's utility function.

$$U_i = (1-a)\ U_i(c_i) + a\ U_k(c_k)$$

Although this model is constructed for two individuals, it could be generalized so that k could be a representative of a group of people all of whom the altruist favors, and a could be a vector of altruism coefficients which relate to each of these people. The way that economists have modeled this kind of altruistic behavior is to assume that a, the altruism parameter, is exogenously determined by taste. Just as people have a "taste" for discrimination, or for sugar or whatever else, they also have a taste for altruism. When a person operates with pure selfishness toward all people then a is zero.

The motivation for a positive a is not discussed in these models. It could be that by looking after others, the ith individual could increase his own utility by being evaluated more positively by his boss, parents, and so forth. There are social pressures to do this. Charitable behavior toward siblings can be rewarded by parents, and negative behavior discouraged.

13.3.2   Altruism as Cooperative Behavior

In the case of a prisoner's dilemma game, both players can be better off if they cooperate. If we view altruism as cooperation, then it can be easily shown that altruistic players are more likely to reach the cooperative solution. The more trust that one player has in the cooperative instincts of others, the more likely it will be that the cooperative strategy will be the dominant strategy. However, when cooperative players meet up with those following self-interest, they are the losers in prisoners' dilemma games and generally in these kinds of real-life situations. Frank (1988) discusses this issue, arguing that there are many situations when cooperation is observed and others when competition prevails. There is a legendary feud in U.S. history between the Hatfields and the McCoys, where generation after generation tries to wipe out the other clan, knowing that if any survived, they would try to do the same. This feud was a "lose/lose" situation for both sides. Yet it continued. On the other hand, there are many examples of cooperation that result in benefits to both sides—amicable management/labor bargaining, maintaining wild-life sanctuaries, and other environmental protection activities by private-interest groups. Generally, economists believe that competition is more common, particularly in the market place, but Frank points out that this need not necessarily be the case.

13.3.3   Altruism as *Quid Pro Quo*

If we think of altruism as being conditional and based on reciprocity, one could argue that it is not really altruism. However, in the literature, this kind of behavior has been called conditional altruism or reciprocal altruism. A common case of this kind of altruism is family investment in children. (Forget for the moment the pure altruism case in which parents have no regard for payback in the future, being only interested in the welfare and happiness of their children). The investment could be in exchange for implicit payback when the child can earn, at a time when parents need financial and logistical support. A purist would argue that this is not altruism at all but self-interest parading as altruism. However, if the payback period is long and unsure, then the conditional relationship may be weak. In such cases, *quid pro quo* may have similar results to a purer form of unconditional altruism.

13.3.4   Altruism as a Genetically or Inherited Trait

This is an argument that sits well with geneticists and biologists, particularly sociobiologists. When are people generally more likely to cooperate than compete? The answer given by geneticists is that there is more cooperative or altruistic behavior when genetic ties are strongest. I may sacrifice my life to save my children and in that way improve the chances that my genes survive. I am unlikely to act the same way with the children of a stranger. Using genetic linkages, this argument can be extended to other relatives. The closer the genetic connection, the greater the chances are that we will observe cooperative or altruistic behavior. Parents sacrifice for their children. Brothers stick by their brothers, and clan members stick together. From this perspective, we are most altruistic toward those with whom we share a large gene pool. To make sure that genes survive, we are most altruistic toward our closest relatives—in a mechanical way I might add. This expands the narrow definition of genetic fitness, or survival of the fittest, as strongest or most competitive, to include the survival of close kin.

Thus, self-interest and genetic selection, in the narrow sense, can exist and lead to altruism. Oded Stark (1995) shows that even in situations where cooperative and altruistic behavior is penalized, such as the prisoner's dilemma (see Box 13.1), altruistic behavior can prevail when individuals share the same role model of altruistic or cooperative behavior. Altruistic behavior can survive wherever altruistic people cluster. It may be for family or cultural reasons. The motivation is the important determinant of this beneficial behavior.

 BOX 13.1

The Prisoner's Dilemma

The prisoner's dilemma is a simple game where two prisoners X and Y are held in separate cells for a crime that they did, in fact, commit. The prosecutor, however, has only enough evidence to convict them of a minor crime that carries a very light sentence. Each prisoner is told that if one confesses while the other remains silent denying the crime, the confessor will go free while the other will spend twenty years in prison. If both confess, they will each get an intermediate sentence of five years. If both remain silent, they each get a sentence of only six months. The two prisoners are not allowed to communicate with each other (see Box Table 13.1 for the payoff matrix).

The preferred strategy is for each prisoner to confess. No matter what prisoner Y does, prisoner X gets a lighter sentence by confessing. If prisoner Y remains silent, he goes free. If prisoner Y also confesses, he gets a five-year sentence. The same is true for prisoner X. However, if both prisoners confess, they get five years, while in the case that they both remain silent, they each get only six months.

The fact that they are not allowed to communicate may seem like it should affect the decision to confess or not (to defect or cooperate). The problem is more fundamental. If prisoner X agrees with prisoner Y to remain silent, sealing the bargain that they both get a very short term for a very big crime, he can still do better if he defects and confesses while Prisoner Y remains silent. So the nub of the prisoners' dilemma puts the issue of cooperation and competition in bold relief. It also highlights the issue of trust, which is fundamental to whether cooperation will take place between parties in any economic or social situation.

Box Table 13.1   The Payoff Matrix

	Prisoner Y	
Prisoner X	**Confesses**	**Remains silent**
Confesses	5 years for each prisoner	20 years for Y, and X is set free
Remains silent	20 years for X, and Y is set free	6 months for both prisoners

Carrying this argument a bit further, it is more likely that people will cooperate with those they know and love, and compete with those they do not know. Gary Becker (1981) uses the phrase "cooperate at home and compete at work."

However, within a firm, creating an atmosphere of cooperation and harmony can foster the same kind of cooperative environment. When the Japanese economy was growing very fast in the 1980s, the practice of life-time employment, singing company songs early in the morning, and "bottoms up" management were studied closely by Western management experts. These Western managers were used to a competitive workplace where employees were pitted against each other for promotion, and management and labor went toe-to-toe in every bargaining situation. Strikes were common in the West but unheard of in Japan.

While the appeal of the Japanese management system has dissipated since the stock and real-estate bubble burst in the late 1980s, the advantages of cooperation to achieve better corporate results and raise labor productivity cannot be denied.

In other situations where people can either cooperate or compete, various research studies have shown that, when there is an opportunity to know the other person, the chances of cooperation rises. One reason is that emotional factors enter into the picture, giving rise to a more cooperative attitude. It is harder to compete with a friend than with someone you do not know. Furthermore, when situations are repeated, as in the prisoner's dilemma type of game, cooperation is more likely because a cooperator has a chance to retaliate if his partner defects and follows a self-interested strategy. Once it becomes obvious that defection invites retaliation, the players settle into a pattern of mutual cooperation. This pattern is also observed among siblings, although often the older sibling will be willing to put up with retaliation since the younger ones cannot mete out as much punishment.

13.3.5   Altruism as a "Kantian" Duty

Writing in 1997, the philosopher Immanuel Kant spoke of a "categorical imperative" whereby rational individuals decide to behave morally and ethically, based on fundamental beliefs and duty as human beings (Kant, 1997). There is much discussion about whether this moral duty is fully consistent with altruism, but it has been used by many writers as a justification for ethical and altruistic behavior. According to Kant, we have a duty as human beings to behave in a moral and ethical fashion. There can be no arguments about this, and it is not subject to the analysis of utility maximization.

13.4   WHAT ARE THE ADVANTAGES OF ALTRUISTIC/COOPERATIVE BEHAVIOR?

There are many situations in which unselfish or altruistic action leads to more satisfactory economic outcomes, as well as provides a more acceptable moral or spiritual foundation for behavior. However, in some of the models that economists have constructed using interactions between selfish individuals and altruists, the altruists are dominated and taken advantage of. This leads to a lower social optimum and an inferior economic solution compared to one that favors self-interest. However, such a solution does not take into account many of the side benefits of altruism or cooperative behavior. The following are some examples.

13.4.1   Altruism Can Raise Overall Levels of Welfare

In situations where others' welfare is in the utility function of an individual, he is motivated to share his income and wealth with them. Under certain fairly general conditions, Stark (1995) shows that this will lead to an increase in welfare.

13.4.2   Altruism in the Form of Intergenerational Transfers Can Increase the Formation of Human Capital and Therefore, Stimulate Economic Growth

If fathers are altruistic in the sense that they leave all their wealth to their children, then an increase in life expectancy will stimulate the children to become more educated (Stark, 1995). This happens because when the father dies at a young age, he will bequeath his wealth to his children while they are still young. Therefore, the incentive to become more educated could fall. (Father dies at forty leaving a twenty-year-old son—born when the father was twenty—all his wealth). Therefore, an exogenous shock, or better health measures resulting in an increase in life expectancy, will create a virtuous cycle of growth, education, and longevity.

13.4.3   Altruism Can, Under Certain Circumstances, Lead to Higher Rates of Savings and Growth

If altruistic people have stronger intergenerational motives to make bequeaths to their children and others, then saving rates could increase. In certain models, such as the Harrod–Domar model, this leads to an increase in the rate of growth. If, however, the lack of altruism individually is offset by the society's saving motives through social security systems, then altruism may have a limited effect (Kapur, 1999).

13.4.4   Altruism Can Improve Family Interactions in Terms of Divorce Rates, Social Disintegration of Families, and Abuse of Children

While altruism says nothing about emotional problems, it is likely that greater social responsibility will flow from situations where individuals are more caring for the welfare of others than in situations where individuals are pursuing pure self-interest.

13.4.5   Caring for the Elderly in a Family

Altruism is likely to result in better and more consistent care of grandparents and parents by their children and grandchildren as their parents and grandparents age.

13.4.6   Financial Support within Families and Extended Families

Altruistic individuals are more likely to bear these financial burdens and to take responsibility for those in the extended family (see Section 13.9 on parent's role on altruism and education).

13.4.7   Moral Hazard

If one party to an agreement pledges to take certain actions which are hard to observe, it is difficult to enforce these pledged actions. Fire insurance is a good example. Once a building has been insured against fire, the owner will have little incentive to install and maintain costly maintenance equipment to prevent fire. Similar results can be seen when there is a high level of insurance on deposits in commercial banks. Other things being equal, this leads bank managers to undertake risky loans. Much time is spent in writing enforceable contracts that make breach of these contract provisions grounds for not paying damages. If people were altruistic, they would value the welfare of others as well as their own. Therefore, they would act in a way that was less likely to present a moral hazard.

13.4.8   Principal–Agent Relationships

Principal–agent theory, which relates a quasi-monopolistic buyer (the principal) to a variety of employees, borrowers, and subcontractors, tenant farmers, potential borrowers from the bank, and so on (the agents). Because of his quasi-monopoly power, the principal is in a position to write performance contracts with the agents. There is a large body of economic theory that discusses how these contracts should be written so that the principal gets the most for his money. The general assumption is that the agent will keep hidden information that might have an adverse effect on the contract. Someone who has gone bankrupt will generally not disclose this information. There may also be hidden actions by the agents that can subvert the goals of the principal. For example, a person with a fixed wage contract may not exert as much effort since the excess production will go to the principal. However, if the person is altruistic, he is more likely to be cognizant of the rights of the principal under the contract and hence abide by it.

13.4.9   Asymmetric Information

When one party to a transaction or a party in a market has access to information that is not available to others, he can profit from it. One of the best examples of this is insider stock trading. This is illegal in most stock markets but hard to prove. It may also extend to the safety of a building or the fact that a car being sold has been in a wreck or had its odometer turned back. Altruistic individuals are less likely to enter into these kinds of agreements since they harm the other party and create unethical gains.

13.4.10   Crime

The rule of law and law enforcement is designed to protect the rights of citizens and their personal property. It stands to reason that a more altruistic/cooperative citizen who has other people's interest in his objective function would be less likely to commit crimes. It does not preclude the commission of crime, however. In fact, in some cases it may increase the chances of crime—a so-called Robin Hood effect. In general, however, evidence from groups or societies with communitarian or shared values where, for example, private property does not exist, show that crimes against property are minimal. These are extreme examples but they do serve to make a point.

13.4.11   Business Ethics and Decision Making

In analyzing corporate behavior, we can draw the distinction between two broad kinds of decisions. First, there are those that have a measurable external impact on the rest of the society or the consumer himself, such as tobacco, unsafe equipment, pollution of the environment, hazardous waste. Secondly, there are those decisions that have a direct impact on the firm and its employees but there is no clear-cut answer as to whether there is an overall benefit or tax on society.

Corporate buyouts and restructuring/sale of assets might fall in the second category. There would be job losses but an increase in overall efficiency. The ethical principles hold more clearly in the first case, which could also involve some of the items mentioned above, such as hidden or asymmetric information and principal/agent problems. Cases which come to mind include the Pinto automobile and tobacco cases in the United States, and the various oil spills by oil companies all over the world. Were there adequate safeguards? Was there a moral hazard? Were they random acts of incompetence?

How would an altruistic and ethical person assess these situations compared with a more self-centered and profit-maximizing individual? The answer to this question is clear from the actions that were taken by the tobacco companies and Ford Motor Company to hide information that could have damaged the sale of their products, yet also cause danger to consumers. In other situations, the distinction between different courses of action may be less clear, yet it would appear that the more ethical the decisions that are taken, keeping in mind the welfare of society and consumers in general, the more beneficial they would be.

There is, nevertheless, the risk that taking the "high ground" of ethics and altruism can lead to situations where the rights of others are ignored. In the case of HIV/AIDS versus military spending discussed in the section on health in Chapter 10, the implicit argument was that more money should be spent on HIV/AIDS and less on military spending. However, if the democratic process results in a different outcome, then individual motives have to be surrendered to the outcome of the political process. This leads to the next point.

13.4.12   Taking Positions on Issues as Informed Citizens

An altruistic person would address these issues from the viewpoint that all members of society are equal. In this way, the value to both those who benefit and those harmed by a particular policy or action can be evaluated more objectively than if the person has only his own self-interest in mind. Often, markets can be developed to resolve these issues, as in the case of some environmental questions. In other cases, there should be government involvement. The following are some instances which come to mind.

EVALUATING NEEDS FOR SCARCE HEALTH CARE   When expensive medical treatments have to be rationed, some method has to be derived to order potential recipients. The expected years of healthy life is one way of making this judgment. This means young, healthy people would rank higher, whereas ill, older people would rank lower. Is this ethical and fair?

SENTENCING OF CRIMINALS   Society and the legal system have to make a judgment regarding the risks to society and the chance of rehabilitation. Society also has to make choices as to the severity of the crime. How are these decisions made and by whom, and what are they based on?

ENVIRONMENTAL ISSUES   Where possible, the "polluter pays principle" can be brought to bear. What about cases where the pollution goes beyond national boundaries, such as pollution of the ocean, acid rain, and overfishing? In these cases, a more altruistic individual is likely to objectively evaluate the damage to other countries in a different way from someone with purely nationalistic interests.

Furthermore, an altruistic person may be less liable to succumb to the free-agent problem when it comes to voting and coming to informed positions on public and corporate issues.

13.4.13   Corporate Issues

The free-rider problem also arises with regard to monitoring the decisions of corporate executives. If you own shares in a company, it is quite likely that the due diligence to make sure the company is acting in the best interest of the shareholders is weak, since the temptation is to free ride on the efforts of the few that are monitoring its activities. In the case of Enron and other recent cases of corporate malfeasance, there was a breakdown in the monitoring function, as a result of a combination of free-rider problems, poor regulation, and various instances of fraud, misuse of private information, and corruption by the top executives.

13.5   How Do These Wider Issues of Altruism and "Agency" Alter Economic Analysis?

In the narrow world of the classical economists, there is no room for anything other than hedonistic calculus. In this system, economic efficiency is the primary goal. If all the other conditions imposed by fundamental theorems of welfare economics, such as no externalities, were to hold, then every agent pursues his or her self-interest. This leads to a Pareto optimal solution. If anyone departs from this narrow self-interest, then the Pareto criterion would be violated. In such a system, there is no reason to abandon self-interest.

This is an artificial, yet very elegant theoretical construct, where everyone is paid the value of his marginal product, all decisions made by consumers are consistent with demand theory, all markets contain perfect information, there is atomistic competition, and the government is basically very limited, supplying some services and the courts.

Yet, this is the kind of theoretical world that economists see as the point from which reality departs. Because economic efficiency, competitive markets, and economic freedom are given such a high standing in such a system, it is difficult for economists to admit the importance of other values except as an exception to this theoretical construct.

Notice that the theory says nothing about the distribution of income, either bad or good. It is ignored completely. It is what it is, and is derived from the marginal productivity conditions and the supply of labor to that market.

One reason for this lack of attention to welfare economics in the classical tradition is the lack of dynamism. It is a static or, at best, a comparative static model. If dynamics had been brought into it at the beginning, perhaps some welfare aspects could have been considered. However, once dynamics were introduced in growth models, the income distribution was not considered in any detail (recall the discussion in Chapters 2 and 9).

To go beyond the conventional analysis, we have to introduce the possibility that economic agents have noneconomic motives. It is only when we include other arguments in the utility function that we can move away from purely economic motives for action. We can still use the same framework for utility maximization. What does matter, however, is that the arguments in this utility function will change. As a result, so will the outcomes, as we saw in the previous sections. Thus, the techniques remain more or less the same, but the focus for their use will change.

13.6   Corruption and Bribery

Corruption and bribery are used to pursue self-interest outside the legal framework. These are behaviors that would be discouraged by an altruistic person because these actions could hurt others in the society. It is important enough to have a separate section devoted to it.

Corruption and bribery are widespread throughout the world, having been around as long as humans have been organized into social groups, where the possibility of corruption can exist. Some believe that it has become worse in the present era in the developing countries. In many of these countries, it is associated with the government. Officials are bribed in order to avoid paying taxes on income, output, exports, or imports. They are bribed in order to avoid taking a driver's test, to register a car, to get your children into school, to get a contract to construct a road, bridge, or some other public works, to get a permit to build a new building, or to open a restaurant or to sell liquor. The list goes on and on.

In the economic analysis of corruption, the principal–agent framework is adopted. The one who is seeking to bribe is the principal, and the official who is bribed is the agent. Generally, corruption is defined as the use of public office for private gain. Contracts are awarded to the principal who offers the agent the largest bribe. In this situation, the contract is awarded openly, although the bribe is given privately. There are other instances where the transaction between the principal and agent is kept secret. These cases of corruption and bribery could include the sale of contraband goods, overlooking tax evasion, and lax enforcement of quality control standards and legal regulations.

There are various other types of corruption and bribery in the private sector, such as ticket scalping, hoarding of scarce goods which are eventually auctioned to the highest bidder, and more general types of corruption where political favors are granted to large campaign contributors.

Most of the economic analysis deals with the first case. In this section, we will examine three aspects of corruption—its effects on economic efficiency, its effects on economic growth, and the dynamics of corruption. How to deal with corruption will be discussed in Section 13.7.

13.6.1   Effects on Efficiency

The overall level of bribery and corruption can only be estimated. Anecdotal evidence suggests that many people in the developing countries pay bribes as part of everyday life, that as much as half of their total income goes unreported for income tax, and tax auditors also accept bribes as a matter of course. In the experience of one of the authors who has lived in several developing Asian countries, confiscated goods were offered for sale by customs officials, and bribes were demanded (said to be a fee) for car registration and drivers license renewal.

All this corruption and bribery result in a loss of revenue to the government. When the violation involves those with a punitive role in the system (such as judges, policemen, etc.), corruption reduces the effectiveness of the legal system. Murder, kidnapping, and extortion are the more sinister forms of corruption.

Other aspects of corruption are subtle. For example, in order to discourage corruption there are elaborate rules and regulations and much red tape—leaving a paper trail as it is called. In cases where countries are trying to attract foreign investors, the bribery requirement can be a significant deterrent, not only because of the ethical overtones but also because of the potential for blackmail and additional bribes and extortion.

In terms of the impact on efficiency and allocation of resources, there are two lines of arguments. The first asserts that corruption speeds up efficiency by bypassing bureaucratic procedures and that a centralized corruption network improves efficiency. Research tends to discount these two arguments since there is much evidence that bureaucratic procedures that are bypassed are themselves a source of economic inefficiency. Furthermore, when bribes are made, there is also the chance that the agent will renege and the principal will not have any recourse.

In economic and political systems where there are many different political constituencies and overlapping jurisdictions and areas of political responsibility, it is more difficult to make corruption effective, since more people need to be bribed.

Generally, then, research seems to support the second line of argument, that corruption and bribery reduce economic efficiency. They also distort the allocation of resources by diverting funds to large investment projects where bidders for the contract can be bribed, and discouraging spending on other kinds of projects, often smaller in nature and less capital-intensive, such as education, health, and repair and maintenance.

13.6.2   Effects on Economic Growth and Investment

Evidence and economic theory both suggest that corruption reduces the incentive to invest, particularly for new businesses and for innovators. This is because all new activities have to be sanctioned by the government and are therefore subject to potential bribery and corruption. There is a corollary reduction in the pace of economic growth as lower investment leads to slower capital formation and speed of economic advancement. Conversely, economic growth seems to eventually reduce corruption since the rewards to entrepreneurship rise, relative to rent-seeking in a society where incomes are growing rapidly. Mauro (1995) presents information from a cross-section of countries for the period of the early 1980s. This evidence suggests that, other things being equal, a one-standard deviation improvement in the index of corruption (he uses the Business International Index, some components of which are reported in Table 13.1) will increase the investment rate by nearly 3 percent of gross domestic product (GDP). He also finds that a one-standard deviation in the index of corruption results in about a 1 percent increase in the GDP per capita. While these results are subject to sampling error, they do suggest that the effect of corruption on aggregate economic activity can be substantial.

In a cross-cultural study of growth in about one hundred countries from 1960 to 1993 containing a number of other explanatory variables, such as the initial levels of GDP and human capital, government spending, fertility, inflation, and the terms of trade, Barro (1997) found that a variable, identified as the "rule of law," was an important determinant of the rate of growth of income. This variable serves as a catch-all for a variety of different attributes of government and society, including the quality of the bureaucracy, political corruption, risk of government expropriation, and repudiation of contracts. An improvement of one rank in the index is estimated to raise the growth rate by 0.5 percentage points, other factors being held equal.

13.6.3 Dynamics of Corruption

Game theory has been used to analyze corruption. In some models, each time a principal tries to bribe an agent, he runs the risk of being arrested or fired by an honest official. As the number of corrupt officials goes up, the chance of being sacked goes down. As time goes on, the level of corruption is bound to increase. Looking at it another way, the subjective probability of meeting a corrupt official increases the more often one is encountered. This causes principals to revise their probabilities of meeting corrupt officials and results in more bribery. Furthermore, news that corruption is rampant will also encourage more corruption. Because of these dynamics, it is possible to have similar economies with different levels of corruption because of a shock that sent them in one direction or the other. Northern and Southern Italy are used as examples of this possibility of multiple equilibria.

IS CORRUPTION AN INVERSE FUNCTION OF ECONOMIC DEVELOPMENT? There has been very little written on this topic. It appears as if the Western societies have less corruption. The rule of law

Table 13.1   Index of Economic Freedom and Average Per-Capita Income, 2001 (US$)

Index	Average Per-Capita Income in US$
Free	$21,000
Mostly free	11,000
Mostly not free	2,800
Repressed	2,900

SOURCE: Kim R. Holmes, Melanie Kirkpatrick, and Gerald P. O'Driscoll, Jr. *The 2001 Index of Economic Freedom* (New York: The Heritage Foundation and Dow Jones & Company, 2001), available at http://www.heritage.org/research/features/index/2001/.

seems to apply most of the time. This is not to say that there are no scandals in every country. However, they do not seem to be as widespread as the network of bribery in the developing Asian countries. Japan has had a number of scandals where politicians have accepted large bribes from businessmen. Perhaps the level of corruption depends upon the social and ethical system of a country. Moreover, richer countries can usually afford to pay their public officials well. This alone will reduce the level of corruption.

One approach would be to use a surrogate measure of corruption. On the surface, it seems that openness could be a useful measure of corruption. When societies are open, there is competition and a free flow of information. As a result, there are fewer opportunities for rent-seeking and corruption. Given human nature, perhaps it is better to keep the opportunities for wrongdoing to a minimum by increasing the openness of the society, while at the same time, promoting more altruistic and coopera-tive motives within the educational system and in society in general.

Certainly, openness and economic freedom seem to be highly correlated with economic devel-opment. Consider, for example, the Index of Economic Freedom reported in Tables 13.1 and 13.2.

Table 13.2   Index of Economic Freedom, 2001

	Ranking (1 = Most Free; 145 = Least Free)
Hong Kong	1
Singapore	2
United States	5
United Kingdom	7
Australia	9
Japan	14
Korea	20
Taiwan	20
Thailand	27
Sri Lanka	48
Malaysia	75
Philippines	81
Pakistan	106
Nepal	110
China	114
Indonesia	114
Bangladesh	132
India	133
Vietnam	144
Myanmar	145

SOURCE: Kim R. Holmes, Melanie Kirkpatrick, and Gerald P. O'Driscoll, Jr. *The 2001 Index of Economic Freedom* (New York: The Heritage Foundation and Dow Jones & Company, 2001), available at http://www.heritage.org/research/features/index/2001/.

The relationship is strong. Free systems have higher per-capita incomes. In Asia, the newly industrialized economies (NIEs) score high while South Asia scores low. Southeast Asia is somewhere in between.

Business International also has developed an index of corruption that was used by Mauro (1995) in his study of the relationship between income and corruption. It is reported for some of the Asian countries in Table 13.3. Furthermore, a recent paper by Boettke and Subrick (2009) and the work of Barro (1997) suggest that the rule of law has a positive impact on economic development. Economic policies and actions that are not in conformity with a rule of law reduce the predictability and stability of the economic environment, whereas policies consistent with the rule of law ensure that economic participants will be able to predict more accurately the behavior patterns of others and achieve more efficient outcomes.

WHAT IS THE PATTERN OF CORRUPTION IN ASIA?   Wei (1999) has surveyed evidence from a number of studies in Asia. These studies show that, other things being equal, corruption tends to reduce the amount of investment, increase the level of poverty, reduce tax revenue, divert money from maintenance to new construction (where bribes are possible) and away from health and education to construction projects. It also tends to reduce economic growth and foreign direct investment from overseas lenders.

In Asia, corruption is inversely correlated with the level of income and the rate of growth in income. This is evident from Table 13.3, which displays three measures of corruption for several Asian

Table 13.3   Corruption Indices, 1999

	Business International	Transparency International	Global Competitiveness Report
Singapore	1.00	2.34	1.77
Japan	2.25	4.43	2.96
Hong Kong	3.00	3.72	2.17
Taiwan	4.25	5.58	4.60
Malaysia	5.00	5.99	5.67
South Korea	5.25	6.71	6.20
India	5.75	8.25	7.30
Philippines	6.50	7.98	7.94
Pakistan	7.00	8.97	n.a.
Bangladesh	7.00	9.20	n.a.
Thailand	9.50	7.94	7.93
Indonesia	9.50	8.28	7.94
China	n.a.	8.12	5.86

The Global Competitiveness (GC) Report was prepared by Political Risk Services, the Transparency International Index (TI) by World Economic Forum, and the Business International Index by Business International. Wei has made some transformations of the original data to make the indices comparable.

SOURCE: Wei Shang Jim, "Corruption in Economic Development, Beneficial Grease, Minor Annoyance, or Major Obstacle?" World Bank Policy Research Working Paper 2048, February 1999.

countries. Japan, Singapore, and Hong Kong rank at the top, while India, Indonesia, Pakistan, and Bangladesh rank near the bottom. These results are consistent with those reported in Tables 13.1 and 13.2. The good results attained by Japan, Singapore, and Hong Kong in resisting and combating corruption are even more astonishing when their comparatively large share of public-sector ownership to that of other developing Asian countries further down the corruption scale, is taken into consideration. The top-twenty companies with state participation greater than 20 percent include Singapore (45 percent), Korea (15 percent), Hong Kong and Japan (5 percent), according to the Singapore Ministry of Trade and Industry. Case studies of corruption in Indonesia and Korea have been provided in the Box 13.2.

Has the pattern of corruption changed over time? The answer is yes. Within Asia, there have been some changes in the ranking of corruption in the last decade, as reflected by the ranking of corruption in the thirteen countries reported in Table 13.3. In Table 13.4, the Philippines has become relatively less honest, as shown in the ranking of the country in both the Transparency International Index and the Global Competitiveness Report, while Korea has become relatively less corrupt than it was in the late 1990s. The other countries have maintained more or less the same positions. This evidence suggests that the pattern of corruption is generally constant, or slowly moving. It takes concerted effort and commitment for a society to reduce the level of corruption in a society. By the same token, only a few countries slip into a more corrupt frame of reference as a result of poor governance and a general attitude that condones corruption.

Table 13.4   Comparison of Corruption Indices Ranking, 1999 and 2009

	TI Rank in Table 13.3	TI Rank in 2008	GC Report Rank in Table 13.3	GC Report Rank in 2008
Singapore	1	1	1	1
Hong Kong	2	2	2	3
Japan	3	3	3	2
Taiwan	4	4	4	5
Malaysia	5	6	5	6
South Korea	6	5	7	4
Thailand	7	8	9	8
Philippines	8	12	10	11
China	9	7	6	7
India	10	9	8	9
Indonesia	11	10	11	10
Pakistan	12	11	n.a.	n.a.
Bangladesh	13	13	n.a.	n.a.

SOURCES: Transparency International, *Transparency International Corruption Perceptions Index*, Table 13.3, Web site at http://www.transparency.org; *Global Competitiveness Report* (2009), Web site at http://www.gcr.weforum.org.

BOX 13.2

Corruption in Indonesia and Korea

Corruption in Indonesia and Korea was particularly widespread during the 1990s, although after the Asian financial crisis, both countries attempted to clean up their acts. Box Figure 13.1 displays the Corruption Perception Index[1] (CPI) for the two countries in 1995, 1997, and 2002. Corruption in Indonesia is perceived to be twice as great as that in Korea.

INDONESIA   Under former President Suharto's rule till 1998, massive public funds were siphoned from charitable organizations (*yayasans*) and joint ventures into gratifying his own personal wants and family comforts. Crony capitalism ruled, as companies owned by the leader's family members or friends were subjected to preferential treatment and granted contracts, exclusive licenses, and loans at favorable terms. One good example was the direct loan of funds to Suharto's daughter's taxi company from Hong Kong's Peregrine Investment Holdings. Furthermore, most major industries, such as telecommunications, manufacturing, electronics, construction, natural gas, etc, were all under the direct control of the Suharto family during that period. However, such state-owned enterprises (SOEs) tend to be poorly managed and running at a loss. Low salaries of government officers created strong rent-seeking incentives on their part. The omnipresence of corruption,

even at the very individual level, was such that the citizens accepted it as a way of life, and considered bribes as a method of getting things done. For instance, graduates who wanted good jobs had to pay contacts for their cooperation; or if civilians wished to be let off the hook for speeding, they had to give the traffic police officer a small token sum of appreciation. On the other hand, if they did not give this goodwill sum, they had to face tedious procedures at the office to pay the fine. The Asian financial crisis put an effective end to Suharto's days of corruption when they were unable to pay off bank loans previously taken, given the sharply declining value of the Indonesian rupiah and their debt-laden SOEs.

Indonesia has enacted new anti-corruption legislations and passed a law requiring civil servants to declare their assets to an independent auditing agency. Other measures to combat corruption include the passing of the decentralization laws on regional government and intergovernment fiscal relation in 1999, so as to reduce central government officials' control over government funding. However, the actual extent of implementation of the various anti-corruption measures discussed above has been highly questionable (Rosser, 2003). Furthermore, the government's intention to privatize the rent-seeking hotbeds, namely, the SOEs, has been faced with strong opposition from government bureaucrats, local businessmen, and SOE workers. Box Figure 13.1 shows

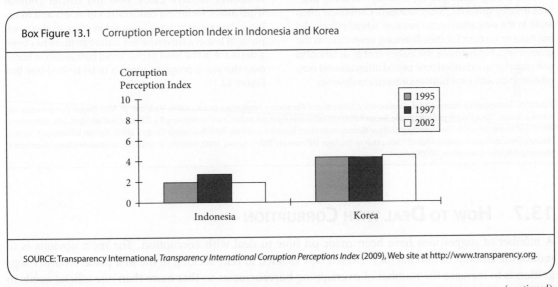

Box Figure 13.1   Corruption Perception Index in Indonesia and Korea

SOURCE: Transparency International, *Transparency International Corruption Perceptions Index* (2009), Web site at http://www.transparency.org.

(continued)

---

[1] The CPI index indicates the perception of businessmen, academics, and risk analysts to the degree of corruption. The higher the CPI, the more "clean" an economy is perceived to be. A value of 10 is regarded as very clean whereas 0 is highly corrupt.

BOX 13.2 *(continued)*

that the CPI fell in 2002. The perceived level of corruption appears to have risen, indicating that Indonesia needs to work harder at reducing corruption.

KOREA Korea has long faced financial scandals and illegal collusion between politicians and local big businesses (*chaebols*) since its transition from an authoritarian nation to a democratic state in 1993. This was primarily due to the strong political control of government ministries over favorable or unfavorable commercial legislations and developments to local business interests. In return for the *chaebols'* continued financial support of the ruling party, the government would grant them special licenses or loans. Blechinger (2000) reported that the top-four donors to former President General Roh Tae-Woo in the "Slush Fund Scandal" in 1995 were Hyundai and Samsung Group (US$32.7 million each), Daewoo Group (US$31.4 million), and Lucky Goldstar (US$27.5 million). In addition, the lack of accountability and clear guidelines in the governance of government operations, as well as the low wages of civil servants were factors contributing to the level of corruption in the public sector. High corruption-prone areas within the public sector included tax administration, police, construction, education, procurement, budget, and policy funds (Korean Information Service, 2000). For instance, the tax system in the past had allowed officials to have control over the selection of taxpayers to be audited, thereby leading to opportunities for *chonji* practices (money given for favors granted). Corruption often arose in the education sector because school officers did not have to account for their financing operations to the government. Furthermore, the assignment of an official to one place for an extended time period often allowed cozy relationships with local business interests to develop.

In order to qualify for the aid assistance offered by the International Monetary Fund (IMF) and the World Bank to deal with the aftermath of the Asian financial crisis, Korea started stronger anti-corruption reforms in 1998. First, it actively introduced an anti-corruption index of each government agency by means of a public poll, so as to diagnose and eradicate corruption in the public sector. Furthermore, in order to combat the lack of accountability and clear guidelines in the governance of government operations, Korea employed the use of ICT in its government administration. It introduced the OPEN (Online Procedures Enhancement for civil applications) system that allowed the public to monitor the progress of various government applications using the Internet. Tax income-related records have since been computerized, doing away with meetings between tax officers and taxpayers. Government procurement procedures have also been simplified and made available online via the EDI (electronic data interchange) system. Secondly, efforts have also been made to put the civil-service salary rates on a scale comparable with the private sector, so that government officers will not be so easily tempted into corrupt practices. Codes of conduct are to be established for civil servants and employees of state-run enterprises. The Korean police have further established a "conscience room" in each police station for police officers to return "gifts" to their respective senders. Lastly, new and stricter criminal legislations, including confiscation of assets and freezing of bank assets, have been set in place to deal with political bribery. Nevertheless, although there has been a decrease in the level of perceived corruption in Korea over the years, progress appears to be limited (see Box Figure 13.1).

SOURCES: Transparency International, *Transparency International Corruption Perceptions Index* (2009), Web site at http://www.transparency.org; Andrew Rosser, "What Paradigm Shift? Public Sector Reform in Indonesia since the Asian Crisis," in Anthony B. L. Cheung and Ian Scott, eds., *Governance and Public Sector Reform in Asia: Paradigm Shifts or Businesses as Usual* (London and New York: Routledge Curzon, 2003); Korean Information Service, "Korea's Second-Phase Fighting Against Corruption in the New Millennium," Policy Series, 2000, Web site at http://www.korea.net/learnaboutkorea/library/publication/corruption_200006.html.

13.7 HOW TO DEAL WITH CORRUPTION

A number of suggestions have been made on how to deal with corruption. The most obvious is to reduce the amount of bureaucracy and red tape that led to rent-seeking in the first place. Another suggestion is to increase the number of overlapping bureaucracies so that more than one official needs to be bribed. The risk here is that the level of red tape will escalate without reducing corruption, although this system seems to have worked well in Singapore, where officials work in pairs.

Another suggestion that has been widely applied with considerable success is to increase the wages of government bureaucrats, while strengthening anti-corruption efforts. By working on both sides of the risk/reward nexus, corruption can be reduced.

Would a greater degree of altruism reduce the extent of corruption and bribery? Theoretically, it probably would. However, when the beneficiaries of reduced corruption or increased tax collections are questionable, then altruistic actions may be less clear-cut. For example, suppose that a person avoids tax because he is not benefiting from the goods derived from the taxes (as he lives overseas, yet is still taxed). He may feel a moral obligation to avoid paying taxes rather that to pay taxes.

Because corruption and bribery are such important aspects of the economic landscape, we will analyzes them further. Later on, we will come back to the issues of ethics, altruism, and cooperative behavior. If we think of bribery as another choice to be made, the reward must be balanced against the cost of being caught. If penalties are stiff and the chances of getting caught are high, the cost of corruption goes up and the return goes down. As a result, there will be less corruption.

Evidence compiled by C. Van Rijckenhem and B. Weder (1997) suggests that this is indeed the case—returns to corruption are balanced against the threat of being caught.

In what follows, a number of suggestions are presented to both increase the costs of corruption by enforcement and other measures, while reducing the benefits of corruption by raising salaries and providing inducements for good performance.

13.7.1 Adequate Financial Rewards

In many countries, there has been a real decline in government salary levels. This is particularly true in Africa, where the interaction between corruption and revenue intake has put many countries on a downward spiral of lower salaries, more corruption, lower salaries, and so on. Evidence from Asia suggests that what is important is the comparison of salaries in the government with the next best alternative, given the same level of education and experience. As seen in Chapter 10, Section 10.3.4, higher salaries relative to manufacturing wages helped the schools in Korea and Taiwan to attract better and more qualified teachers. The same principles apply for recruiting government officials in areas where corruption is a threat.

13.7.2 Better Record Keeping

A better system of recording would make it easier to supervise and to control corruption, particularly if there are secondary checks on the transactions involved. For it to succeed, officials need to be "clean." Otherwise, the pressure to collude is enormous.

13.7.3 Better Quality Bureaucrats and Judges

If there is a small core of incorruptible officials at the top and sprinkled throughout the system, it will be better able to enforce regulations, get rid of those who are corrupt, and so on. This will only work if those doing the hiring are not corrupt. There have been successes. The customs services in Thailand, the Philippines, and Indonesia have been cleaned up. It must begin at the top, because if the reputation of the bureaucracy is one of corruption, then it will be difficult to attract honest workers.

13.7.4 Promotion Based on Performance, Not on Nepotism

If the civil service pays well and is run on a merit system, the opportunities for crony relationships will be minimized. It will also permit more flexible hiring and firing policies so that corrupt officials can be diminished.

13.7.5 Reduce Discretion

When officials have discretion to make exceptions, exclusions, etc., there is scope for corruption. Establishing flat-rate taxes on all goods imported, as Chile has done, would help to eliminate corruption. It would also raise more revenue. There is great reluctance to undertake this process of simplification because of vested interests not only in the corrupt bureaucracies, but also among businessmen who get exemptions through bribery, or the "old boys" network.

13.7.6   Reduce the Scope for Corruption

In general, this involves cutting down the amount of bureaucratic red tape. This can be done by rationing and other procedures where licenses and permits are needed, and also where authority needs to be granted.

13.7.7   Anti-Corruption Agency, Free Press, and International Pressure

There are various other ways to put pressure on the government to reduce corruption, including media coverage of corrupt practices, and the formation of a watchdog agency to monitor reports on corruption and to take action to stop it. International pressure by agencies, such as the World Bank and the Asian Development Bank, can also help to galvanize public opinion and the government.

13.7.8   Tax Farming: A Radical Proposal

Since corruption is so widespread and there have been few successes in dealing with it in the developing countries, one proposal is to legalize corruption. After it is legalized, the government would set the tax rates for various categories of taxpayers and then sell/auction the right to collect taxes for a fixed sum of money. The tax collector winning the bid would then be responsible for determining the liabilities of individual taxpayers, as well as collecting money from them. Taxpayers can file an appeal in a tax court that would be set up by the government. Costs would be incurred for doing this so that the courts would not be overburdened—for example, the loser pays court costs and a fine.

Because of the nature of this system, the incentive to cheat the government is replaced by the possibility of extorting money from taxpayers. This is where the tax court comes in. If the sources of income are unknown to the tax collector and the government, and if taxpayers lie, then this system will yield more revenue than the current system where everyone bribes and some collectors accept the bribes. The tax collector will try to get as much income as possible because he has paid for the right to collect the taxes. Hidden income will then be revealed. However, if a low-income taxpayer is pushed, he can always go to the tax court to appeal. There will be an intense scrutiny of his income, but he has nothing to worry about. On the other hand, the high-income taxpayer will also be subject to intensive investigation if he asks to go to the tax court, and he risks having his tax bill raised even further. The success of the system would depend critically on the tax courts. Can honest judges be found who are incorruptible? This may be difficult, but it is probably an easier solution than finding a large group of honest taxpayers.

13.8   ROLE OF THE EDUCATIONAL SYSTEM

There are examples of economic models that assume that economic agents are altruistic or cooperative. There is also some evidence that altruistic or cooperative behavior leads to more favorable outcomes for society in many cases. It could cut down on the problems inherent in behavior motivated by self-interest alone—principal–agent behavior, corruption, and other dishonest acts, crime, and unethical business practices. Are these values taught in school? Should more time be spent on the teaching of ethics, moral behavior, and spiritual aspects of life? Alternative schools, such as Steiner, Montessori, and other non-traditional educational approaches may be worth evaluating.

13.9 ALTRUISM AND EDUCATION: THE ROLE OF PARENTS

Gary Becker (1981) has developed models of altruistic behavior to be taught by parents to their children. In societies where schooling requires some sacrifice by the parents, either personally or through the political system, the role of altruism is critically important. In one particular model, developed by Casey Mulligan (1997), altruism becomes endogenous. In the model, the amount of altruistic behavior depends on the hours spent together—between the child and parent. The more time spent together, the stronger the altruism.

How does this assumption sit with you? Could it be the other way around? Remember the expression: familiarity breeds contempt? What would happen if various factors in the life of the family change, given the assumption of endogenous altruism? Consider first the effect of an increase in income. This could have the effect of increasing leisure in the leisure/income choice, and so give the parent more time to spend with the child. This would increase altruism and also the transfers to the child from the parent. Consider also a reduction in hours worked. It would have the same effect. What about the increase in the labor-force participation of women? What would it do to altruism and to transfers of income?

In any case, a model where more time spent together increases the possibility of altruism is in keeping with a model of altruism based on sociobiology or genetics. Those you know and spend time with are usually family members, and you bond with them more closely. As your associations with others become more at arm's length, the tendencies of altruism become weaker. One exception to this rule is the hero syndrome: the fireman runs into a burning building to save a child, a soldier single-handedly attacks an enemy position, or a bystander helps to detain a thief.

13.10 SUMMING UP OF ALTRUISM

Those who have developed altruistic behavior, either naturally or by following some spiritual or religious path, or by contemplating their own actions and motivations, are probably more likely to follow behavioral patterns that minimize confrontation with others and lead to more cooperative behavior. While such behavior is probably beneficial within family groups or community groups, it is still looked upon with some skepticism in the business world. Becker (1981) uses the phrase "cooperative at home, competitive at work." However, the great thinkers and spiritual leaders of all generations do not make such a distinction. There are also business firms with a highly developed sense of social responsibility and a culture of looking out for the customer—or putting the customer first. One of the first rules of doing business in Japan is to blindly follow the aphorism, "The customer is always right." In retailing, this makes good sense, but it also makes good sense in doing business generally. Treating subcontractors and suppliers well is good for business. There is a saying: "What goes around comes around." There is something of a virtuous cycle in treating others well. Somehow, it makes us feel good and it also makes the other person feel good. Why not do it more often?

This brings up the question of competitors. What about competitors? How should they be treated? To cooperate with competitors is often illegal and against the tenets of competitive behavior that says that such collusion (monopoly/oligopoly) will lead to higher prices and a lower level of output. On the other hand, we do not have to trash our competitor. We can respect their rights to do business. We simply try to attract customers away from them in an ethical way. This may not be acting altruistically toward them but it is also not overtly competitive either.

13.11 ETHICS AND ECONOMIC ANALYSIS

Still on the subject of altruism and corruption, it is useful to consider the interaction between ethical principles and economics. The discussion will be brief since it takes us into the realm of welfare economics, which is an extensive topic in itself. According to J. S. Mill (1994), the foundation of classical economic analysis is based on the principle of utilitarianism. Economic agents are motivated by the desire to increase their satisfaction. In an economic sense, this satisfaction comes from the consumption of goods and services. It is assumed that the more the better. As this utilitarian theory evolved, indifference analysis and utility maximization were created, showing that an individual will allocate income among competing goods so that utility/satisfaction is maximized subject to an income constraint. Price lines and indifference curves intersect to determine this maximizing value. As the price of goods increase, other goods are substituted for them, and so a demand curve can be drawn.

This microeconomic analysis assumes that consumers are rational and they are always searching for the best way to maximize satisfaction, subject to an income constraint. If the classical theory is extended further, it is assumed that all individuals are paid the value of their marginal product. Put together, the theory of demand and the theory of factor payments lead to an equilibrium that is efficient. This is a very mechanistic view that attempts to replicate the process of decision making by a scientific model that is free of judgment, yet describes how decisions are made. As far as it goes, it can provide many useful insights about the activities of economic agents.

This very brief description of classical microeconomics is just meant to be illustrative of the fact that nothing in the classical model says anything about the distribution of income and whether it is fair or equitable. Thus, classical economics, despite its initial grounding in moral philosophy, became a rather mechanistic, even engineering-orientated, method of theorizing how economic agents and the economy as a whole would act under a set of assumptions grounded in utilitarianism.

How do ethics and moral aspects of life come into economic decision making? There are several different approaches to this question taken by different writers. In the first instance, the initial formulation of welfare economics, as this aspect of the discipline came to be called, used the utilitarian calculus to make some simple decisions based on the concept of decreasing marginal utility. They argued that since marginal utility decreases for nearly everything, the marginal utility of money must decline too. Therefore, if we want to redistribute money from the rich to the poor, we can take money from the rich by way of progressive taxation and redistribute it to the poor. This should bring about an increase in welfare because the money transferred has more utility to the poor than it does to the rich.

As welfare economics evolved, the economics profession decided that this was not such a good criterion since it required making judgments on an interpersonal basis about the marginal utility of money. Economists decided that they did not like making these interpersonal comparisons of utility because it required them to make a value judgment about utility and they were very concerned about this. They thought that economics should be scientific and value free (normative and not positive, to use more familiar terms.) As a result, they were able to devise other methods for deciding whether there was an increase in welfare without having to make such value judgments required in interpersonal comparisons.

Pareto came up with a very useful proposition that we could move from one situation or equilibrium to another and there would be an increase in welfare if at least one person was made better off and no one was worse off. Economists also hit upon the idea of revealed preference, which allowed them to say that if one good or combination of goods was preferred to another in the market, then it gave a higher utility because it was found to be preferred. Therefore, preferences did not have to be determined *a priori*—a very difficult job—as they could be determined from the market through revealed preference.

It turned out that, after much theorizing on the use of the Pareto principle and revealed preferences, the analysis was left with the conclusion that there were usually many equilibrium points on a so-called "Pareto path." However, in order to find the one equilibrium value, one had to know how to make interpersonal comparisons of utility to reach that unique solution (see Box 13.3 for a simple explanation of an Edgeworth box and how this Pareto path is generated.)

BOX 13.3

Edgeworth Box and Paretian Optimum

In Box Figure 13.2, A and B represent two individuals that are about to exchange goods X and Y between them. Suppose we draw indifference curves for each of them, with A starting at the lower left-hand corner and B at the upper right-hand corner. The curves are convex from below. A move toward the upper right represents more of both goods for A, and a move toward the lower left-hand corner means more of both goods for B. You can see the situation from B's point of view by turning the chart around so that the upper-right corner is in the lower-left corner. Suppose we start with an initial distribution of

goods between A and B at W_1. W_1 is a legitimate combination of goods X and Y, whose values are shown on the two axes, because it is on the indifference curve of A, as well as the indifference curve of B. Now consider what happens when we allow A and B to trade goods. They can be better off if the trade along the new equilibrium is a or b, or c or d! If we draw a line through all the possible points where the indifference curves of A and B are at a tangent to each other, then we have what is called the contract curve. However, since we cannot make interpersonal comparisons of utility, we cannot say which of these points is optimal. So we are left in a position of indeterminacy.

Box Figure 13.2　Edgeworth Box and Pareto Optimality

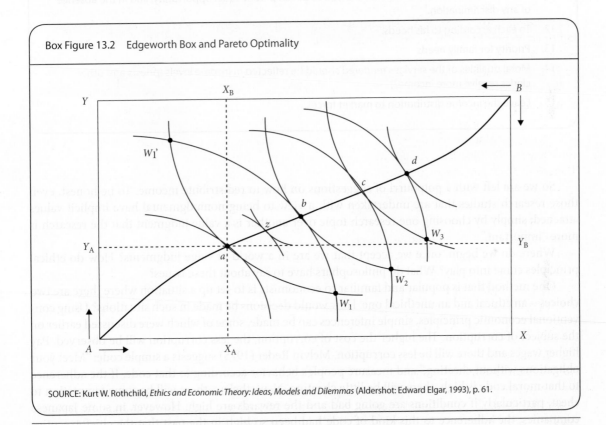

SOURCE: Kurt W. Rothschild, *Ethics and Economic Theory: Ideas, Models and Dilemmas* (Aldershot: Edward Elgar, 1993), p. 61.

It is not that the analysis is back at square one but it looks as if in order to make any reasonable kinds of welfare judgment some form of interpersonal comparisons of utility has to be made, and we are back in the realm of positive economics.

Once we are back in the world of value judgments, and recognizing that we are interested in the intersection of ethics and economics, a whole Pandora's box of possibilities is introduced. Kurt Rothschild (1993) has listed some of them, which are shown in Table 13.5.

Table 13.5   List of Proposals on How to Handle Income Distribution

1. The question of income distribution is unimportant
2. Incomes should be derived only from work (implying that all other income is taxed away)
3. Complete equality of income, modified by age, family size, etc.
4. The highest incomes (say, the top 10 percent) are too high.
5. The lowest incomes (say, the lowest 10 percent) are too low.
6. High and medium incomes are immoral as long as poverty exists.
7. Wage income should comprise a "just" share of total income.
8. Progressive taxes.
9. Easily earned income (windfalls) should be taxed at higher rates.
10. The income distribution should be "fair" and should be based on wide social consensus.
11. The income distribution should be allowed to develop from equal opportunity, and in the absence of any discrimination.
12. To each according to his needs.
13. Priority for family needs.
14. Moral qualities of the services rendered should be reflected in income levels (priests and other clerics receive more income?)
15. Leave the income distribution to market forces.

So we are left with a potpourri of suggestions on how to redistribute income. To be honest, even those research studies that are undertaken with a view to being nonjudgmental have implicit values attached; simply by choosing one research topic over another is a value judgment that the research is more "important."

Where do we begin, once we accept that we are in a world of value judgments? How do ethical principles come into play? What do philosophers have to say about these issues?

One method that is popular and familiar to economists is to set up a situation where there are two choices—an ethical and an unethical one. How would decisions be made in such situations? Using conventional economic principles, simple inferences can be made, some of which were discussed earlier on the subject of corruption. The higher the cost of corruption, the less corruption will be observed. Pay higher wages and there will be less corruption. Melvin Reder (1975) suggests a simple code: "Meet your obligations without cheating," and measure people's behavior according to that code. If the adherence to that moral code is high, there will be little cheating. Nevertheless, there will be some temptation to cheat, particularly if conditions are going bad and the rewards are high. However, in some Japanese companies, the adherence to this kind of code had been so high in the past that the chief executive officers of companies going bankrupt had committed suicide.

Sociologists like to think of ethical principles as being embodied in how society views the actions of individuals, whether they are economic decisions or other kinds of decisions. Therefore, they believe that there are social norms that influence people's behavior in addition to pure self-interest. In their view, action is taken as a result of interaction between self-interest and social norms. If someone lives in a lawless society, with few adhering to ethical principles, then most actions will pay little cognizance to these principles, whatever they may be.

Once we realize how all this determines how ethical standards are applied and enforced in a society, we have to consider the role of the state. The state is critical because it is the mechanism by which ethical principles are applied and enforced. The role of the state can be light on interference with market principles *a la* Milton Friedman (1968) and Friederick von Hayek (1948), or very heavy as in a highly socialist or communist system.

Without getting into all this, there are certain principles that economists have found very attractive as extensions of the idea of Pareto optimality. The philosopher John Rawls (1971) proposed one of these. He deals with a large number of ethical propositions. The one that is most attractive puts great weight on being risk averse, a trait that economists believe is characteristic of many economic decisions.[2] Rawls says that a solution or incremental movement from one equilibrium is just if it is characterized by a change in the income structure so that the income of the least advantaged (poorest) is improved or maximized. Many comparisons with a Rawls solution and a Pareto optimum are possible, and it can be shown that a Rawls solution and a Pareto solution are consistent. However, Rawls pays particular attention to the poorest elements of society and this decision tool often leads to a situation where the poor are made better off, while others are not made worse off.

One aspect of the discussion on ethics and the improvement of income distribution through such government policies as progressive taxation, is the impact that such policies have on work effort. There is a large body of research that has investigated these impacts and has found them not minimal, particularly at high rates of marginal taxation. In formulating public policy, therefore, these adverse impacts have to be taken into account as well as the shift in preferences between work and leisure that occur as a result.

13.12 APPLICATION OF ETHICAL PRINCIPLES OF JUSTICE AND GREATER INCOME EQUALITY TO ASIA

As we saw in Chapter 9, on poverty and income distribution, there have been only very gradual changes in the overall distribution of income in Asia during the past few decades, as measured by the Gini coefficient. It was also concluded in that chapter that it is very difficult to make significant changes in the overall distribution of income without a revolution or war or other cataclysmic event that rearranges the entire social order. Nevertheless, the evidence does support the conclusion that a society that has better income distribution to begin with is more likely to grow more rapidly in the future. This is clear from the evidence from Asia, seen in Chapter 9, and also from the study by Persson and Tabellini (1994). Societies in which income distribution is relatively equitably distributed, such as Korea and Taiwan, had higher rates of income growth compared with those societies where income is less equitably distributed.

The problem is how to move from one distribution pattern to another. As we saw in Chapter 9, it is hard to change the pattern of distribution of income, which has been relatively stable over long periods of time. Therefore, if we are to consider how to change the distribution of income in keeping with the principles of justice, as laid down by Rawls (1971), or based on one of the other methods described in Table 13.5, we have to rely on other ways besides changing the entire income distribution. This involves microeconomic analysis and particular attention to the needs of the poorest members of society. For these approaches, we need to go back to Chapter 9.

---

[2] See the work of experimental economists and psychologists, such as two Nobel Prize winners in economics in 2002.

13.13 Religion, Social Responsibility, and Governmental Attention to Poverty and Basic Needs

In some loose sense, it may be reasonable to argue that societies where ethical values are promoted more fully within the social fabric are more likely to have a sympathetic approach to addressing issues of poverty and basic needs. In this regard, the findings of Bruce E. Moon (1991, p. 252) that Buddhist societies in Asia achieved higher basic needs provision than other countries, based on the average relationship between income and basic needs provision: "It appears that the fine basic needs performance ascribed to Asian countries in general is actually found in only the nine countries coded as Buddhist."

Certainly, there is more to this than meets the eye. Taking a worldview, it can be argued that communist societies supplied a much higher level of basic needs than did capitalist countries at a similar level of income for many years. Furthermore, who is to say that Buddhism carries with it a higher standard for attending to the needs of the poor? There are many anecdotes regarding Thai children who are neglected because society thinks it is their *karma* to be born in this lifetime with a defect because of sins carried over from a past life.

The point is well taken, however, that the social context is very important in determining the way in which the society addresses the need for providing relief as well as basic needs for the poor. Social safety nets are provided in most European countries to a much wider extent than they are in the United States. These differences can be explained by a political consensus that has been arrived at to adopt a more communitarian approach to social justice in Europe than in the United States. Advocates of the U.S. system stress the importance of providing incentives to work, and the flexibility that the system has in adjusting to shifting demand patterns. The period of eurosclerosis in Europe has been identified as a negative side effect of a social system that is characterized by labor markets that are rigid and inflexible, and which protects its citizenry from the time they enter the world until the time they leave it.

This discussion is simply to point out that there are social choices to be made, and how the society makes them will be conditioned by its attitudes toward social justice and economic and political freedom. In Asia, and even in the West, for many years the Japanese system was applauded for its attention to communitarian values and the responsibility that managers had toward their employees. The ability to reach decisions through consensus, wait patiently for a promotion, work ceaselessly to achieve the company's objectives, and the dedication of employees toward their employers, were also recognized as highly desirable communitarian traits. Bottom-up management was applauded and many Western companies copied the practice of caring customer relations.

However, in recent years, as the Japanese economy floundered, these same values were ridiculed for leading to bureaucratic gridlock and a frustrating, even maddening, ability to decide not to decide on any policies that had not been accepted by the society. Policies that could lift the economy out of the doldrums have been rejected because they would fracture the political consensus.

The bottom line is not to let the pendulum swing too much in one direction or the other. The circle of influence where altruism and cooperative motives are strongest begins in the family. There are obvious reasons for this, both from a sociobiological point of view, and from the point of view of getting along with those around us. The strength of these motives diminishes as those we come in contact with are further removed from the family. In earlier times when agriculture was much more important, the village group was probably more central to life than the company now is for most employees in the West. Yet in Asia, loyalty to the firm and to the family is still strong, perhaps as a carryover from the agricultural setting which they had only recently abandoned.

Nevertheless, no matter what the nuances of attachments and relationships there are in individual societies and cultures, there is no doubt that the circle of close altruistic association diminishes as day-to-day contact with a person or group lessens. How individual societies deal with this will depend on a wide array of factors, which will be difficult to pinpoint unless detailed studies are undertaken.

The relevant point for public policy is that many of the values that economists have traditionally relied upon exclusively in the past to make recommendations regarding the thrust and focus of public policy need to be broadened and adjusted to take into account the wider values that incorporate an ethical approach to these issues and problems.

13.14   SUMMARY AND CONCLUSIONS

This chapter has investigated various aspects of behavior of economic agents that are outside the usual limits of economic analysis. We have looked, in particular, at altruistic and cooperative behavior and how such behavior may have a beneficial impact on the allocation of resources and the economic efficiency of an economy. Much of what we have been discussing in this chapter has gone back and forth between normative and positive aspects of economic analysis. What should be and what is are different. When we argue from a normative point of view, we are making individual value judgments and economists do not like to do this. In their view, it destroys the objectivity of the analysis and allows individuals to impose their value judgments on society. On the other hand, there are aspects of a system which allow individuals to make free choices, which sometimes create negative externalities or conflict with general norms of behavior set down by the society in which they reside. These are the areas that have been the focus of this chapter. We have not touched on the political process by which individual preferences are translated into collective action. Rather, we have focused on areas where negative externalities can be offset by a class of actions that can be characterized as cooperative or altruistic, as opposed to selfish. In doing this, we have not made the normative judgment that these actions are preferred to selfish actions. Rather, we have tried to point out the positive social impact of such actions without constraining the actions of other individuals in any way. Nevertheless, some may read into the analysis the conclusion that self-interest is somehow inferior to altruistic or cooperative behavior. This is not the intent of this chapter. The intent is rather to demonstrate that there are other motivations for economic behavior that are not consistent with self-interest. Whether either of these actions, self-interest or altruistic, lead to an increase in well-being or happiness, is another matter altogether.

REVIEW QUESTIONS

1. How would a neoclassical economist incorporate altruistic behavior into a model of consumer choice?
2. Do we have to look at the behavior of great saints to get a sense for the importance of altruistic behavior in some instances? Give an example.
3. The economist might think of altruistic behavior as a kind of taste for helping others in the same way that a consumer has a taste for fast cars. Is there a basic difference between the two?
4. How does the concept of external benefit come into the picture when we are looking at acts of altruism? Give some examples.
5. What do you think of the economist's argument that there is no such thing as altruism? All acts (or demand for goods and services) involve some degree of self-interest. Otherwise, we would not demand the goods or perform the acts.
6. Discuss the concept of duty or social responsibility and how it relates to the concept of hedonism.
7. Why is corruption such a pervasive problem in many developing countries?

8. Most of the recommendations for dealing with corruption are economic in nature—raising salaries, increasing punishment, stepping up surveillance. Are there other ways to deal with corruption from a broader social point of view?

9. How would a libertarian's view of income distribution differ from a state socialist? Is there a way to reconcile these opposing views?

10. How do strictly communitarian or "communist" social organizations distribute the fruits of labor of the workers. What are the risks in such a system?

11. Why have large communist/communal experiments failed while smaller experiments have often been successful?

12. Define the terms "principal/agent," "free rider," "moral hazard," "asymmetric information," "public good," and "externality." How do these terms relate to the issues of the environment and the ethical principles of good governance?

Notes on References and Suggestions for Further Reading

This chapter includes a number of seemingly unrelated topics which come together under the heading of the political economy of economic development. The argument is that if individuals adopt a more altruistic, communitarian, and cooperative view, then many of the difficulties that plague modern economic and social systems would be more easily dealt with. The chapter starts off with a discussion of altruism. Here, the main reference is the book of readings on altruism by Stefano Zamagni (1995).

Building on the concept of altruism, a number of examples are discussed. The volume edited by M. G. Quibria and J. Malcolm Dowling (1996) considers a number of issues outside the normal bounds of economic analysis, including corruption. Basant Kapur (1995) and Robert H. Frank (1988) explore the relationship between communitarian or cooperative values and economics, while Oded Stark (1995) extends the Beckerian framework of altruism to a number of interesting examples.

The chapter shifts to a discussion of corruption and bribery. The IMF, OECD, and World Bank staff have produced interesting papers on this topic. They include Wei Shang Jim (1999), C. van Rijckenhem and B. Weder (1997), and OECD (2000). They all suggest that economic incentives will go a long way toward reducing corruption.

Finally, on the topic of income distribution and civil responsibility, three books are suggested for careful and reflective reading. They are Kurt W. Rothschild (1993), John Rawls (1971), and Amartya Sen (1989).

Bibliography

General Textbook References

Ray, Debraj. *Development Economics*. Princeton, NJ: Princeton University Press, 1998.

Thirlwall, A. P. *Growth and Development, with Special References to Developing Economies*. 7th ed. New York: Palgrave Macmillan, 2003.

Todaro, Michael P., and Stephen C. Smith. *Economic Development*. 8th ed. Boston: Addison Wesley, 2003.

Specialized References Focusing on Developing Countries and Asia

Asian Development Bank (ADB). *Asian Development Outlook*. Web site at http://www.adb.org (A yearly publication; previous issues can be ordered from ADB).

Behrman, Jere R., and T. N. Srinivasan, eds. *Handbook of Development Economics*. 2 vols. Amsterdam, North Holland: Elsevier Science Publishers, 1995.

Chenery, Hollis, and T. N. Srinivasan, eds. *Handbook of Development Economics*. 2 vols. Amsterdam, North Holland: Elsevier Science Publications, 1988.

Drysdale, Peter, ed. *Reform and Recovery in East Asia: The Role of the State and Economic Enterprise*. New York: Routledge, 2000.

International Monetary Fund (IMF). *World Economic Outlook* (a yearly publication).

Masuyama, Seiichi, Donna Vanderbrink, and Chia Siow Yue, eds. *Restoring East Asia's Dynamism*. Tokyo: Nomura Research Institute; Singapore: Institute of Southeast Asian Studies, 2000.

United Nations (UN). *World Investment Report*. Available at http://www.unctad.org/wir.

United Nations Conference on Trade and Development (UNCTAD). *Trade and Development Report* (a yearly publication).

United Nations Economic and Social Commission for Asia and the Pacific (ESCAP). *Economic and Social Survey of Asia and the Pacific* (a yearly publication).

World Bank. *World Development Report* (a yearly publication).

Yanagihara, Toru, and Susumu Sambommatsu, eds. *East Asian Development Experience: Economic System Approach and its Applicability*. Papers and proceedings of the symposium held by the Institute of Developing Economies on January 22, 1997.

Yusuf, Shahid, and Simon J. Evenett. *Can East Asia Compete? Innovation for Global Markets*. Washington, D.C.: World Bank, 2002.

Country Studies

Asian Development Bank (ADB). *East ASEAN Growth Area: Brunei Darussalam, Indonesia, Malaysia and Philippines*. Manila: ADB, 1996.

Hill, Hal. *The Indonesian Economy*. 2nd ed. Cambridge and New York: Cambridge University Press, 2000.

Navaratnam, Ramon V. *Managing the Malaysian Economy: Challenges & Prospects*. Kuala Lumpur: Pelanduk Publications, 1997.

Pebbles, Gavin, and Peter Wilson. *The Singapore Economy*. Cheltenham, UK and Brookfield, VT: Edward Elgar, 1996.

Journals (specializing in Asian topics)

ASEAN Economic Bulletin
Asian Development Review
Asian Pacific Economic Literature
Bulletin of Indonesian Economic Studies
Economic Development and Cultural Change
Journal of Asian Economics
Journal of Asian Studies
Journal of Contemporary Asia
Journal of Developing Areas
Journal of Development Economics
Journal of the Asia Pacific Economy
Malaysian Economic Review
Philippine Economic Journal
Saving and Development (World Bank)
Singapore Economic Review
The Developing Economies
World Bank Economic Review
World Development

Chapter Bibliographies

CHAPTER 1: INTRODUCTION AND OVERVIEW

Repetto, Robert, William Magrath, Michael Wells, Christine Beer, and Fabrizio Rossini. *Wasting Assets: Natural Resources in the National Income Accounts*. Washington, D.C.: World Resources Institute, 1989.

United Nations Development Program (UNDP). *Human Development Report 2002*. New York: Oxford University Press for the United Nations, 2002.

_____. *Human Development Report 2008*. New York: Oxford University Press for the United Nations, 2008.

World Bank. *World Development Indicators* (online database). Washington, D.C.: World Bank, 2009.

World Health Organization (WHO). Statistical Information System (online database). Available at http://www.who.int/whosis/en/index.html (accessed on March 10, 2009).

CHAPTER 2: GROWTH AND THE ASIAN EXPERIENCE

Amsden, Alice H. *Asia's Next Giant: South Korea and Late Industrialization*. New York: Oxford University Press, 1989.

Ardic, Oya P. "The Gap between the Rich and the Poor: Patterns of Heterogeneity in the Cross-Country Data." Paper prepared for the Department of Economics, University of Wisconsin-Madison, 2002. Available at http://www.econ.boun.edu.tr/seminars/spring03/ardic.pdf (accessed on May 5, 2003).

Asian Development Bank. *Asian Development Outlook 2002*. Manila: ADB, 2002.

_____. *Asian Development Outlook 2009*. Manila: ADB, 2009.

_____. *Key Indicators of Developing Asian and Pacific Countries*. Manila: ADB, various issues.

Barro, Robert J., and Xavier Sala-i-Martin. *Economic Growth*. Singapore: McGraw-Hill, 1995.

Behrman, Jere R., and Ryan Schneider. "An International Perspective on Schooling Investments in the Last Quarter Century in Some Fast-Growing East and Southeast Asian Countries." *Asian Development Review* 12 (September 1994): 1–50.

Bhagwati, Jagdish N. "The Miracle That Did Happen: Understanding East Asia in Comparative Perspective." Keynote address in the Conference on Government and Market: The Relevance of the Taiwanese Performance to Development Theory and Policy, in Honor of Professors Liu and Tsang at Cornell University, Ithaca, NY, May 3, 1996.

Bloom, David, and Jeffrey Williamson. "Demographic Transitions and Economic Miracles in Emerging Asia." National Bureau of Economic Research Working Paper 6268, 1999.

Bosworth, Barry P., and Susan M. Collins. "Economic Growth in East Asia: Accumulation versus Assimilation." *Brookings Papers on Economic Activity* 2 (1996): 135–191.

Chenery, Hollis B., and Moises Syrquin. *Patterns of Development, 1950–1970.* London: Oxford University Press, 1975.

Chenery, Hollis B., Sherman Robinson, and Moshe Syrquin. *Industrialization and Growth: A Comparative Study.* Oxford: Oxford University Press, 1986.

Christensen, Scott R., David Dollar, Ammar Siamwalla, and Pakorn Vichyanond. "Thailand: The Institutional and Political Underpinnings of Growth." In *Lessons from East Asia,* edited by Danny M. Leipziger. Ann Arbor: University of Michigan Press, 1997.

Council for International Economic Cooperation and Development, Executive Yuan. *Taiwan Statistical Data Book.* Taipei, 2002.

Domar, Evsey D. "Capital Expansion, Rate of Growth, and Employment." *Econometrica* 14 (1946): 137–147. [Reprinted in Stiglitz and Uzawa, 1969.]

Dowling, John M. *Future Perspectives on the Economic Development of Asia.* Singapore: World Scientific Publishing, 2008.

Dowling, Malcolm, and Peter M. Summers. "Total Factor Productivity and Economic Growth: Issues for Asia." *Economic Record* 74 (June 1998): 170–185.

Easterly, William. *The Elusive Quest for Growth: Economists' Adventures and Misadventures in the Tropics.* Cambridge, MA: MIT Press, 2001.

Fei, John C. H., and Gustav Ranis. *Development of the Labor Surplus Economy: Theory and Policy.* Homewood, Ill: Irwin, 1964.

Grossman, Gene M., and Elhanan Helpman. *Innovations and Growth in the Global Economy.* Cambridge MA: MIT Press, 1991.

Harberger, Arnold C. "Reflections on Economic Growth in Asia and the Pacific." *Journal of Asian Economics* 7 (1996): 365–392.

Harrod, Roy F. "An Essay in Dynamic Theory." *Economic Journal* 49 (1939): 14–33. [Reprinted in Stiglitz and Uzawa, 1996.)

Keynes, John M. *The General Theory of Employment, Interest, and Money.* New York: Harcourt Brace, 1936.

Kim, Jong-Il, and Lawrence. J. Lau. "The Sources of Economic Growth of the East Asian Newly Industrialized Countries." *Journal of the Japanese and International Economics* 8 (September 1994): 235–271.

Krugman, Paul. "The Myth of Asia's Miracle." *Foreign Affairs* 73 (November/December 1994): 62–78.

Lau, Lawrence J. "The Sources of Long-Term Economic Growth: Observations from the Experience of Developed and Developing Countries." In *The Mosaic of Economic Growth,* edited by Ralph Landau, Timothy Taylor, and Gavin Wright. Stanford, CA: Stanford University Press, 1996.

Lewis, W. Arthur. "Economic Development with Unlimited Supplies of Labour." *The Manchester School of Economic and Social Studies* 22 (1954): 139–191.

Little, Ian. "Picking Winners: The East Asian Experience." *Occasional paper.* London: Social Market Foundation, 1996.

Lucas, Robert E., Jr. "Why doesn't Capital Flow from Rich to Poor Countries?" *American Economic Review* 80 (May 1990): 92–96.

Maddison, Angus. *Monitoring the World Economy, 1820–1992.* Paris: OECD Development Centre, 1995.

Mankiw, N. Gregory, and David Romer, eds. *New Keynesian Economics.* 2 vols. Cambridge, MA: MIT Press, 1991.

Mankiw, N. Gregory, David Romer, and David N. Weil. "A Contribution to the Empirics of Economic Growth." *The Quarterly Journal of Economics* 107 (May 1992): 407–437.

Naya, Seiji. *The Asian Development Experience: Overcoming Crises and Adjusting to Change.* Manila: Asian Development Bank, 2002.

Pack, Howard. "Industry Policy: Growth Elixir or Poison?" *World Bank Research Observer* 15 (February 2000): 47–67.

Quibria, M. G. "Growth and Poverty: Lessons from the East Asian Miracle Revised." ADB Institute Research Paper Series 33, 2002. Available at http:www.adbi.org/PDF/wp/rp33.pdf (accessed on January 15, 2003).

Ranis, Gustav, and John C. F. Fei. "A Theory of Economic Development." *American Economic Review* 51 (September 1961): 533–565.

Rostow, Walter W. *The Stages of Economic Development: A Non-Communist Manifesto.* Cambridge: Cambridge University Press, 1960.

Sachs, Jeffrey, and Andrew Warner. "Economic Reforms and the Process of Global Integration." *Brookings Papers on Economic Activity* 26 (1995): 1–118.

Sarel, Michael. "Growth and Productivity in ASEAN Countries." International Monetary Fund Working Paper 97/97, 1997. Available at http://www.imf.org/external/pubs.ft/wp/wp9797.pdf (accessed on January 10, 2003).

Solow, Robert M. "A Contribution to the Theory of Economic Growth." *Quarterly Journal of Economics* 70 (February 1956): 65–94. [Reprinted in Stiglitz and Uzawa, 1969.]

_____. "Technical Change and the Aggregate Production Function." *Review of Economics and Statistics* 39 (August 1957): 312–320.

Stiglitz, J., and H. Uzawa, eds. *Readings in the Modern Theory of Economic Growth.* Cambridge, MA: MIT Press, 1969.

Swan, T. W. "Economic Growth and Capital Accumulation." *Economic Record* 32 (1956): 334–361. [Reprinted in Stiglitz and Uzawa, 1969.]

UNCTAD (United Nations Conference on Trade and Development). *Trade and Development Report.* New York: United Nations, 1997.

_____. *World Investment Report.* New York: United Nations, various years.

United Nations Development Program. *Human Development Report.* New York: Oxford University Press for the United Nations, various years.

World Bank. *The East Asian Miracle: Economic Growth and Public Policy.* New York: Oxford University Press, 1993.

_____. *World Development Indicators* (CD-ROM). Washington, D.C.: World Bank, 2002.

_____. *World Development Indicators* (CD-ROM, network ver.). Washington, D.C.: World Bank, 2003.

_____. *World Development Indicators* (online database). Washington, D.C.: World Bank, 2008.

_____. *World Development Indicators* (online database). Washington, D.C.: World Bank, 2009.

World Economic Forum. *Global Competitiveness Report.* Geneva: World Economic Forum, 1998.

Young, Alwyn. "A Tale of Two Cities: Factor Accumulation and Technical Change in Hong Kong and Singapore." In *NBER: Macroeconomics Annual 1992,* edited by Oliver J. Blanchard and Stanley Fischer, 13–54. Cambridge, MA: MIT Press, 1992.

_____. "The Tyranny of Numbers: Confronting the Statistical Realities of the East Asian Growth Experience." *Quarterly Journal of Economics* 110 (August 1995): 641–680.

CHAPTER 3: THE ASIAN CRISIS AND RECENT DEVELOPMENTS

Asian Development Bank. *Asian Development Outlook 2001.* Manila: ADB, 2001.

_____. *Asian Development Outlook 2002 Update.* Manila: ADB, 2002.

_____. *Asian Development Outlook 2002.* Manila: ADB, 2002.

_____. *Asian Development Outlook 2003.* Manila: ADB, 2003.

_____. *Asian Development Outlook 2008 Update.* Manila: ADB, 2008.

_____. *Asian Development Outlook 2008.* Manila: ADB, 2008.

_____. *Key Indicators of Developing Asian and Pacific Countries.* Manila: ADB, 1999.

Athukorala, Prema-chandra, and Peter G. Warr. "The Vulnerability to a Currency Crisis: Lessons from the Asian Experience." *World Economy* 25 (January 2002): 33–57.

Bank for International Settlements. *Annual Report 67.* Basle: Bank for International Settlements, 1997.

Brooks, Douglas H., and Pilipinas F. Quising. "Dangers of Deflation." ERD Policy Brief Series 12, 2000. Available at http://www.adb.org/Documents/EDRC/Policy_Briefs/PB012.pdf (accessed on January 15, 2003).

Chu, Yun-Peng, and Hall Hill, eds. *The Social Impact of the Asian Financial Crisis.* Cheltenham, UK and Northampton, MA: Elgar, 2001.

Development Bank of Singapore. *Market Outlook and Strategy.* Singapore: DBS Bank, July 2001.

Dowling, John M. *Future Perspectives on the Economic Development of Asia.* Singapore: World Scientific Publishing, 2008.

Dowling, Malcolm, and Juzhong Zhuang. "Causes of the 1997 Financial Crisis: What Can An Early Warning Model System Tell Us?" ERD Policy Brief Series No. 7, 2002. Available at http://www.adb.org/Documents/EDRC/Policy_Briefs/PB007.pdf (accessed on January 15, 2003).

Economic and Social Commission for Asia and the Pacific (ESCAP). *Economic and Social Survey of Asia and the Pacific.* Bangkok: United Nations, 1999.

Economist Intelligent Unit (EIU). EIU CountryData (online database). Web site at http://www.eiu.com (accessed on February 15, 2003).

Federal Reserve Bank of Minneapolis. *The Recession in Perspective.* Available at http://www.minneapolisfed.org/publications_papers/studies/recession_perspective/index.cfm (assessed April 1, 2009).

Fernald, John G., Hali J., Edison, and Prakash Loungani. "Was China the First Domino? Assessing the Links between China and the Rest of Emerging Asia." *Journal of International Money and Finance* 18 (August 1999): 515–536.

Furman, Jason, and Joseph E. Stiglitz. "Economic Crises: Evidence and Insights from East Asia Economic Studies." *Brookings Papers on Economic Activity* 2 (1998): 1–135.

Goldstein, Morris. *The Asian Financial Crisis: Causes, Cures, and Systematic Implications.* Washington, D.C.: Institute for International Economics, 1998.

International Monetary Fund. *World Economic Outlook: Crisis and Recovery.* Washington, D.C.: IMF, April 2009. Available at http://www.imf.org/external/data.htm (accessed February 15, 2009).

International Monetary Fund. *World Economic Outlook: Globalization of Financial Markets and Recent Exchange Market Turmoil in Asia.* Washington, D.C.: IMF, 1997.

Knowles, C., Ernesto Pernia, and Mary Racelis. "Social Consequences of the Financial Crisis in Asia: The Deeper Crisis." Paper presented at the ADB Manila Social Forum, Philippines, November 9–12, 1999.

Merill Lynch. *The Asian Equity Economist*, April 29, 2003.

Ou, Chun Hua. "Emerging Digital Divide between the Northeast and Southeast Asia." Term paper, Singapore Management University, 2003.

Roubini, Nouriel. *The Asian Currency Crisis of 1997.* New York: New York University, 2003. Available at http://www.stern.nyu/~nroubini (accessed on May 5, 2003).

Semiconductor Industry Association. Web site at http://www.sia-online.org (accessed on August 1, 2009).

Shirazi, Javad K. "The East Asian Crisis: Origins, Policy Challenges and Prospects." Paper presented at the National Bureau of Asian Research and the Strategic Studies Institute's conference on East Asia in Crisis, June 10, 1998.

The Economist. London: Economist Newspaper Ltd, various issues.

Tobin, James. "A Proposal for International Reform?" *Eastern Economic Journal* 4 (1978): 153–159.

UNCTAD (United Nations Conference on Trade and Development). *Trade and Development Report.* New York: United Nations, 1996.

_____. *Trade and Development Report.* New York: United Nations, 2000.

World Bank. *World Development Indicators* (CD-ROM, network ver.). Washington, D.C.: World Bank, 2003.

_____. *World Development Indicators Online.* Washington, D.C.: World Bank, 2008.

Yusuf, Shahid, and Simon J. Evenett. *Can East Asia Compete? Innovation for Global Markets.* Washington, D.C.: World Bank, 2002.

CHAPTER 4: AGRICULTURE

Alston, Julian M., Connie Chan-Kang, Michele C. Marra, Philip G. Pardey, and T. J. Wyatt. *A Meta-Analysis of Rates of Return to Agricultural R&D: Ex Pede Herculem?* Washington, D.C.: International Food Policy Research Institute (IFPRI), 2000.

Asian Development Bank. *Asian Development Outlook.* Manila: ADB, 2000.

_____. *Key Indicators of Developing Asian and Pacific Countries.* Manila: ADB, 2001.

Birner, R., and Jock R. Anderson "How to Make Agricultural Extension Demand-Driven: The Case of India's Agricultural Extension Policy." International Food Policy Research Institute Discussion Paper 729, 2007.

Central Intelligence Agency. *The World Factbook.* Washington, D.C.: CIA, 2002.

China Statistical Publishing House. *Rural Statistics Yearbook of China.* Beijing: China Statistical Publishing House, various issues.

Council for International Economic Cooperation and Development, Executive Yuan. *Taiwan Statistical Data Book.* Taipei, various years.

Dixit, R. S., and P. P. Singh. "Impact of High Yielding Varieties on Human Labour Inputs." *Agricultural Situation in India* 24 (1970): 1081–1089.

Economist Newspaper Ltd. *The Economist*, November 1999.

Energy Information Administration (EIA). *Country Analysis Briefs: The People of China*, 2002. Available at http://www.eia.doe.gov/emeu/cabs/china/part1.html (accessed on March 15, 2003).

Food and Agriculture Organization (FAO). "Chinese Accession to the World Trade Organization and Implications for Chinese Agricultural Policies," Part II: Regional Review; Section II: Asia and the Pacific. *The State of Food and Agriculture*, 2002. Available at http://www.fao.org/DOCREP/004/y6000e/y6000e08.htm (accessed on March 15, 2003).

Haan, Cees de, Henning Steinfeld, and Harvey Blackburn. "Livestock & the environment: Finding a balance." Commission of the European Communities; the World Bank; and the governments of Denmark, France, Germany, The Netherlands, United Kingdom, and The United States of America; Food and Agriculture Organization; United States Agency for International Development; and the World Bank, Washington, D.C., 1996.

Hayami, Yujiro, and Vernon W. Ruttan. *Agricultural Development: An International Perspective.* Baltimore: Johns Hopkins University Press, 1985.

Lewis, William A. "Economic Development with Unlimited Supplies of Labour." *The Manchester School of Economic and Social Studies* 22 (May 1954): 139–191.

Mellor, John. W., and Mohinder S. Mudahar. "Agriculture in Economic Development: Theories, Findings and Challenges in an Asian Context." In *A Survey of Agricultural Economics Literature: Agriculture in Economic Development*, Vol. 4, edited by R. Martin Lee. Minneapolis: University of Minnesota Press, 1992.

Oshima, Harry T. *Economic Growth in Moonsoon Asia: A Comparative Survey.* Tokyo: University of Tokyo Press, 1995.

Rosegrant, Mark W., Claudia Ringler, Timothy B. Sulser, Siwa Msangi, Tin gju Zhu, Rowena Valmonte-Santos, and Stanley Wood. "Reducing Poverty and Hunger in Asia; Agriculture in Asia: Challenges and Opportunities." International Food Policy Research Institute Discussion Brief 6, 2008.

Timmer, Peter C. "The Agriculture Transformation." In *Handbook of Development Economics*, Vol. 1, edited by Hollis Chenery and T. N. Srinivasan. Amsterdam: Elsevier Science Publishers, 1988.

Timmer, Peter, ed. *Agriculture and the State: Growth, Employment and Poverty in Developing Countries*. Ithaca, NY: Cornell University Press, 1991.

Tomich, Thomas P., Peter Kilby, and Bruce F. Johnston. *Transforming Agrarian Economies: Opportunities Seized, Opportunities Missed*. Ithaca, NY: Cornell University Press, 1995.

World Bank. *World Development Report 1980*. Washington, D.C.: World Bank, 1980.

_____. *World Development Report 1982*. Washington, D.C.: World Bank, 1982.

_____. *World Development Report 2008*. Washington, D.C.: World Bank, 2008.

World Resources Institute. *World Resources, 1995–1997*. New York: Oxford University Press, 1998.

Zhang, Fusuo, and Li Long. "Using Competitive and Facilitative Interactions in Intercropping Systems Enhances Crop Productivity and Nutrient-Use Efficiency." *Plant and Soil* 248 (2003): 305–312.

CHAPTER 5: INDUSTRIALIZATION AND CULTURAL CHANGE

Amsden, Alice H. *Asia's Next Giant: South Korea and Late Industrialization*. New York: Oxford University Press, 1989.

_____. *The Rise of "the Rest": Challenges to the West from Late-Industrializing Economies*. New York: Oxford University Press, 2001.

Asian Development Bank. *Asian Development Outlook*. Manila: ADB, 2003.

Aswicahyono, Haryo, and Hal Hill. " 'Perspiration' vs. 'Inspiration' in Asian Industrialisation: Indonesia Before the Crises." *Journal of Development Studies* 38 (2002): 138–163.

Balassa, Bela. "Trade Liberalization and 'Revealed' Comparative Advantage." *The Manchester School of Economic and Social Sciences* 33 (1965): 99–123.

Bloom, David E., and Jeffrey G. Williamson. "Demographic Transitions and Economic Miracles in Emerging Asia." National Bureau of Economic Research Working Paper 6268, 1999.

Bosworth, Barry P., and Susan M. Collins. "Economic Growth in East Asia: Accumulation versus Assimilation." *Brookings Papers on Economic Activity* 2 (1996): 135–191.

Bosworth, Barry P., Susan M. Collins, and Yu-chin Chen. "Accounting for Differences in Economic Growth." Paper presented at the conference on Structural Adjustment Policies in the 1990s: Experiences and Prospects, Tokyo, 1995.

Chen, Edward K. Y. "The Total Factor Productivity Debate: Determinants of Economic Growth in East Asia?" *Asian-Pacific Economic Literature* 11 (1997): 18–38.

Chenery, Hollis B., Sherman Robinson, and Moshe Syrquin. *Industrialization and Growth: A Comparative Study*. New York: Oxford University Press for the World Bank, 1986.

Crafts, Nicholas. "East Asian Growth Before and After the Crisis." International Monetary Fund Working Paper 98/137, 1998.

Djankov, S., Rafael La Porta, Florencio Lopez-de-Silanes, and Andrei Shleifer. "The Regulation of Entry." *Quarterly Journal of Economics* 117 (2002): 1–37.

Dowling, Malcolm, and David Ray. "The Structure and Composition of International Trade in Asia: Historical Trends and Future Prospects." *Journal of Asian Economics* 11 (December 2000).

Dowling, Malcolm, and Peter M. Summers. "Total Factor Productivity and Economic Growth: Issues for Asia." *Economic Record* 74 (June 1998): 170–185.

Drysdale, Peter, and Yiping Huang. "Technological Catch-Up and Economic Growth in East Asia and the Pacific." *Economic Record* 73 (September 1997): 201–211.

Fei, John C. H., and Gustav Ranis. *Development of the Labor Surplus Economy: Theory and Policy*. Homewood, Ill: Irwin, 1964.

Findlay, Ronald. "Relative Backwardness, Direct Foreign Investment and the Transfer of Technology: A Simple Dynamic Model." *Quarterly Journal of Economics* 92 (February 1978): 1–16.

Gill, Indermit, and Homi Kharas. *An East Asian Renaissance: Ideas for Economic Growth*. Washington, D.C.: World Bank, 2007.

Harberger, Arnold C. "Reflections on Economic Growth in Asia and the Pacific." *Journal of Asian Economics* 7 (1996): 365–392.

Harris, John R., and Michael P. Todaro. "Migration, Unemployment and Development: A Two-Sector Analysis." *American Economic Review* 60 (1970): 126–142.

Hobday, Michael. *Innovation in East Asia: The Challenge to Japan*. Aldershot, UK: Ashgate Publishing, 1995.

Kawai, H. "International Comparative Analysis of Economic Growth: Trade Liberalization and Productivity." *Developing Economies* 32 (1994): 373–397.

Kim, Linsu, and Richard R. Nelson, eds. *Technology, Learning, and Innovation: Experiences of Newly Industrializing Economies*. Cambridge: Cambridge University Press, 2000.

Krugman, Paul. "The Myth of Asia's Miracle." *Foreign Affairs* (November/December 1994): 62–78.

Lall, Sanjaya. "Meeting the Human Capital Needs of Maturing Asian Economies." In *The Future of Asia in the World Economy*, edited by C. Foy, F. Harrigan and D. O'Connor. Paris: OECD and ADB, 1998.

Lau, Lawrence J. "The Sources of Long-Term Economic Growth: Observations from the Experience of Developed and Developing Countries." In *The Mosaic of Economic Growth*, edited by Ralph Landau, Timothy Taylor, and Gavin Wright. Stanford, CA: Stanford University Press, 1996.

Leung, Hing Man. "The Effects of Learning on Growth-Divergence and Convergence-Club Memberships." Mimeographed. Singapore Management University, 2003.

Lewis, W. Arthur. "Economic Development with Unlimited Supplies of Labour." *The Manchester School of Economic and Social Studies* 22 (1954): 139–191.

Nehru, Vikram, and Ashok Dhareshwar. "New Estimates of Total Factor Productivity Growth for Developing and Industrialised Countries." World Bank Policy Research Working Paper 1313, 1994.

Nelson, R. R., and Howard Pack. "The Asian Miracle and Modern Growth Theory." World Bank Policy Research Working Paper 1881, 1998.

Nelson, Richard R., and Edmund S. Phelps. "Investment in Humans, Technology Diffusion and Economic Growth." *American Economic Review* 56 (1966): 69–75.

Pedersen, Poul O. "Freight Transport Under Globalisation and Its Impact on Africa." *Journal of Transportation Geography* 9 (April 2001): 85–99.

Quibria, M. G. "Growth and Poverty: Lessons from the East Asian Miracle Revisited." ADB Institute Research Paper 33, 2002.

Ranis, Gustav, and John C. H. Fei. "A Theory of Economic Development." *American Economic Review* 51 (1961): 535–565.

Rodrik, Dani. "Getting Interventions Right: How South Korea and Taiwan Grew Rich." *Economic Policy* 20 (1995): 78–91.

Sarel, Michael. "Growth and Productivity in ASEAN Countries." International Monetary Fund Working Paper 97/97, 1997. Available at http://www.imf.org/external/pubs.ft/wp/wp9797.pdf (accessed on January 10, 2003).

Singapore Ministry of Trade and Industry. "Declining Global Market Shares of Singapore's Electronic Products: Is It a Concern?" Occasional paper, February 28, 2002. Available at http://app-stg.mti.gov.sg/data/article/21/doc/NWS_2001Annual_Electronics.pdf (accessed on April 28, 2003).

_____. "Singapore Productivity Performance." Occasional paper, May 18, 2001. Available at http://app-stg.mti.gov.sg/data/article/21/doc/NWS_Productivity.pdf (accessed April 28, 2003).

Temple, Jonathan. "Growth Effects of Education and Social Capital in the OECD Countries." Centre for Economic Policy Research Discussion Paper 2875, 2001.

UNCTAD (United Nations Conference on Trade and Development). *Trade and Development Report*. New York: United Nations, 1996.

World Bank. *The East Asian Miracle: Economic Growth and Public Policy*. Washington, D.C.: World Bank, 1993.

Young, Alwyn. "A Tale of Two Cities: Factor Accumulation and Technical Change in Hong Kong and Singapore." In *NBER Macroeconomics Annual 1992*, edited by Oliver J. Blanchard and Stanley Fischer, 13–54. Cambridge, MA: MIT Press, 1992.

_____. "Accumulation, Exports and Growth in the High Performing Asian Economies: A Comment." Carnegie-Rochester Conference Series on Public Policy 40, 1994, 237–250.

_____. "The Tyranny of Numbers: Confronting the Statistical Realities of the East Asian Growth Experience." *Quarterly Journal of Economics* 109 (1995): 641–680.

Yusuf, Shahid, and Simon J. Evenett. *Can East Asia Compete? Innovations for Global Markets*. Washington, D.C.: World Bank, 2002.

CHAPTER 6: INTERNATIONAL TRADE AND INVESTMENT

Akamatsu, Kaname "A Historical Pattern of Economic Growth in Developing Countries." *Developing Economies* 1 (1962): 3–25.

_____. "A Theory of Unbalanced Growth in the World Economy." *Weltwirtschaftliches Archiv* 86 (1961): 196–217.

Asian Development Bank. "Greater Mekong Sub-region." (April 8, 2009). Available at http://www.adb.org/GMS/ (accessed on March 30, 2003).

_____. *Asian Development Outlook*. Manila: ADB, 2003.

Balassa, Bela. "Trade Liberalization and 'Revealed' Comparative Advantage." *The Manchester School of Economic and Social Sciences* 33 (1965): 99–123.

Bowen, Harry P., Abraham Hollander, and Jean-Marie Viaene. *Applied International Trade Analysis*. Basingstoke: University of Michigan Press, 1998.

Cline, William R. "Can the East Asian Model of Development be Generalized?" *World Development* 10 (February 1982): 81–90.

Council for International Economic Cooperation and Development, Executive Yuan. *Taiwan Statistical Data Book*. Taipei, 2008.

Dollar, David. "Outward-Oriented Developing Economies Really Do Grow More Rapidly: Evidence from 95 LDCs, 1976–1985." *Economic Development and Cultural Change* 40 (April 1992): 523–544.

_____. *Outward-Oriented and Growth: An Empirical Study Using a Price-Based Measure of Openness.* Washington, D.C.: World Bank, East Asia and Pacific Region, Country Department 1, 1990.

Dowling, John M. *Future Perspectives on the Economic Development of Asia.* Singapore: World Scientific Publishing, 2008.

Dowling, M., and Cheang, C. T. "Shifting Comparative Advantage in Asia: New Tests of the 'Flying Geese' Model." *Journal of Asian Economics* 11 (2000): 443–464.

Edwards, Sebastian "Openness, Productivity and Growth: What Do We Really Know?" *Economic Journal* 108 (March 1998): 383–398.

Far Eastern Economic Review (FEER), December 19, 2002.

Gill, Indermit, and Homi Kharas. *An East Asian Renaissance: Ideas for Economic Growth.* Washington, D.C.: World Bank, 2006.

Gould, David M., and William C. Gruben. "The Role of Intellectual Property Rights in Economic Growth." *Journal of Development Economics* 48 (March 1996): 323–350.

Hanson, Gordon H., Raymond J. Mataloni, and Matthew J. Slaughter. "Vertical Production Networks in Multinational Firms." National Bureau of Economic Research Working Paper 9723, 2003.

Hardin, A., and L. Holmes. "Service Trade and Direct Foreign Investment." Australian Industry Commission Staff Research Paper, 1997.

Heckscher, Eli. F. "The Effect of Foreign Trade on the Distribution of Income." In *Heckscher-Ohlin Trade Theory*, edited by Harry Flam and M. June Flanders. Cambridge, MA: MIT Press, 1997.

International Monetary Fund. *International Financial Statistics.* Washington, D.C.: IMF, 2001.

Korhonen, Pekka. "The Theory of the Flying Geese Pattern of Development and Its Interpretations." *Journal of Peace Research* 31 (1994): 93–108.

Naya, Seiji F. *The Asian Development Experience: Overcoming Crises and Adjusting to Change.* Manila: Asian Development Bank, 2002.

Ohlin, Bertil. *Interregional and International Trade.* Cambridge, MA: Harvard University Press, 1933.

Pack, Howard. "Industry Policy: Growth Elixir or Poison?" *World Bank Research Observer* 15 (February 2000): 47–67.

Ricardo, David. *On the Principles of Political Economy and Taxation.* London: John Murray, 1817.

Rybczynski, T. M. "Factor Endowment and Relative Commodity Prices." *Economica* 22 (1955): 336–341. [Reprinted in *Readings in International Economics*, edited by R. E. Caves and H. G. Johnson. London: George Allen and Unwin Ltd., 1986.]

Sachs, Jeffrey, and Andrew Warner. "Economic Reforms and the Process of Global Integration." *Brookings Papers on Economic Activity* 26 (1995): 1–118.

Saggi, Kamal. "Trade, Foreign Direct Investment, and International Technology Transfer: A Survey." *World Bank Research Observer* 17 (September 2002): 191–235.

Samuelson, Paul A. "International Trade and Equalisation of Factor Prices." *Economic Journal* 58 (June 1948): 163–184.

Shirazi, Javad K. "The East Asian Crisis: Policy Challenges and Prospects." Paper presented at the National Bureau of Asian Research and the Strategic Studies' conference on East Asia in Crisis. Seattle, June 10, 1998.

Stolper, Wolfgang, and Paul A. Samuelson. "Protection and Real Wages." *Review of Economic Studies* 9 (1941): 58–73.

UNCTAD (United Nations Conference on Trade and Development). *World Investment Report.* New York: UNCTAD, various issues.

Vernon, Raymond. "International Investment and International Trade in the Product Cycle." *Quarterly Journal of Economics* 80 (1966): 190–207.

World Bank. *The East Asian Miracle: Economic Growth and Public Policy.* New York: Oxford University Press, 1993.

_____. *World Development Indicators* (CD-ROM). Washington, D.C.: World Bank, 2002.

Yamazawa, Ippei. *Economic Development and International Trade: The Japanese Model.* Honolulu: Resource Systems Institute, East-West Center, 1990.

Yusuf, Shahid, and Simon J. Evenett. *Can East Asia Compete? Innovations for Global Markets.* Washington, D.C.: World Bank, 2002.

CHAPTER 7: SAVINGS AND THE FINANCIAL SYSTEM

Asian Development Bank. *Asian Development Outlook.* Manila: ADB, 1996.

_____. *Asian Development Outlook.* Manila: ADB, 1997.

_____. *Asian Development Outlook.* Manila: ADB, 1999.

_____. *Asian Economic Monitor,* October 2002. Web site at http://aric.adb.org (accessed April 15, 2003).

_____. *Regional Economic Monitoring Unit,* 2003. Web site at http://aric.adb.org (accessed on April 15, 2003).

Campbell, J. Y., and N. G. Mankiw. "Consumption, Income, and Interest Rates: Reinterpreting the Time Series Evidence." National Bureau of Economic Research Working Paper 2924, March 1989.

Caprio, Gerard. Jr., William C. Hunter, George G. Kaufman, and Danny M. Leipziger. *Preventing Bank Crises: Lessons from Recent Global Bank Failures*. Washington, D.C.: World Bank, 1998.

Deaton, Angus. "Savings and Liquidity Constraints." *Econometrica* 59 (September 1991): 1221–1248.

_____. "Savings in Developing Countries: Theory and Review." *Proceedings of the World Bank Annual Conference on Development Economics*. Washington, D.C.: World Bank, 1989.

_____. *Understanding Consumption*. New York: Oxford University Press, 1992.

Diaz-Alejandro, C. "Good-bye Financial Repression, Hello Financial Crash." *Journal of Development Economics* 19 (January 1985): 1–24.

Dowling, J. M. *Domestic Resource Mobilization through Financial Development: Korea*. Manila: Asian Development Bank, 1984.

Dowling, John Malcolm "Global recession and Asian growth: Experience and prospects." *Journal of Indonesian Economics and Business* (forthcoming).

Feldstein, Martin S. "Social Security and Saving: New Time Series Evidence." National Bureau of Economic Research Working Paper 5054, March 1995.

Fisher, Irving. *The Theory of Interest*. New York: Macmillan, 1930.

Friedman, Milton. *A Theory of Consumption Function*. Princeton, NJ: Princeton University Press, 1957.

Fry, Maxwell J. Money, *Interest, and Banking in Economic Development*. Baltimore: Johns Hopkins Press, 1988.

_____. *Sequencing Financial Sector Reform and Development in Small Economies*. Birmingham: International Finance Group, University of Birmingham, 1994.

Fry, Maxwell J., Charles A. E. Goodhart, and Alvaro Almeida. *Central Banking in Developing Countries: Objectives, Activities and Interdependency*. London: Routledge, 1996.

Ghate, Prabhu. *Informal Finance: Some Findings for Asia*. Manila: Oxford University Press for Asian Development Bank, 1994.

Hall, Robert E. "Stochastic Implications of the Life-Cycle Permanent Income Hypothesis: Theory and Evidence." *Journal of Political Economy* 86 (1978): 971–987.

Harrigan, F. R. "Asian Savings: Theory, Evidence and Policy." In *East Asian Development: Will the East Asian Growth Miracle Survive?*, edited by F. Gerald Adams and Shinichi Ichimura, 127–158. Westport, Conn. and London: Greenwood, Praeger, 1998.

Higgins, Matthew. "Demography, National Savings, and International Capital Flows." *International Economic Review* 39 (May 1998): 343–369.

International Herald Tribune, December 16, 2002.

International Monetary Fund. *International Financial Statistics*. Washington, D.C.: IMF, 2000.

James, William E., Donghyun Park, Shikha Jha, Juthathip Jongwanich, Akiko Terada-Hagiwara, and Lea Sumulong. "The US Financial Crisis, Global Financial Turmoil, and Developing Asia: Is the Era of High Growth at an End?" Asian Development Bank Economics Working Paper 139, December 2008.

Keynes, J. M. *The General Theory of Employment, Interest and Money*. New York: Harcourt Brace, 1936.

Masson, Paul R., Tamim Bayoumi, and Hossein Samiei. "International Evidence on the Determinants of Private Saving." International Monetary Fund Working Paper 95/51, 1995.

_____. "International Evidence on the Determinants of Private Saving." *World Bank Economic Review* 12 (September 1998): 483–501.

McKinnon, Ronald. "Financial Liberalization in Retrospect: Interest Rates Policy in LDCs." In *The State of Development Economics: Progress and Perspectives*, edited by G. Ranis and T. P. Schultz. Oxford and New York: Basil Blackwell, 1988.

_____. *Money and Capital in Economic Development*. Washington, D.C.: Brookings Institute, 1973.

Modigliani, Franco. "The Life-Cycle Hypothesis of Savings and Intercountry Differences in the Savings Ratio." In *Induction, Growth and Trade: Essays in Honour of Sir Roy Harrod*, edited by W. A. Eltis, M. F. Scott, and J. N Wolfe. Oxford: Clarendon Press, 1970.

Nam, Sang-Woo. "What Determines National Savings?: A Case Study of Korea and the Philippines." World Bank Working Paper 205, 1989.

Neff, Gina. "Microcredit, Microresults." *Left Business Observer* 74 (1996). Available at http://www.panix.com/ (accessed on April 25, 2003).

Obstfeld, Maurice. "Aggregate Spending and the Terms of Trade: Is there a Laursen-Metzler Effect?" The *Quarterly Journal of Economics* 97 (May 1982): 251–270.

Ostry, Jonathan D., and Carmen M. Reinhart. "Private Savings and Terms of Trade Shocks." International Monetary Fund Staff Paper 39, 1992, 495–517.

Page, Sheila. *Monetary Policy in Developing Countries*. London and New York: Routledge, 1993.

Pitt, Mark M., and Shahidur R. Khandker. "The Impact of Group-Based Credit Programs on Poor Households in Bangladesh: Does the Gender of Participants Matter?" *Journal of Political Economy* 106 (October 1998): 958–996.

Ramsay, Frank. "A Mathematical Theory of Savings." *Economic Journal* 38 (1930): 543–559.

Sarker, Abu Elias "The Secrets of Success: The Grameen Bank Experience in Bangladesh." *Labour and Management in Development Journal* 2 (2001): 1–17. Available at http://labour-management.anu.edu.au/prt/voltwo/2-1-abusarker.pdf (accessed on April 20, 2003).

Shahid N. Zahid, ed. *Financial Sector Development in Asia*. Manila: Asian Development Bank, 1995.

Shaw, Edward S. *Financial Deepening in Economic Development*. New York: Oxford University Press, 1973.

Terell, Henry S. "The Role of Foreign Banks in Domestic Banking Markets." *Financial Policy and Reform in Pacific Basin Countries*. Lexington, MA and Toronto: Health, Lexington Books, 1986.

Thomas, J. J. "The Informal Financial Sector: How Does It Operate and Who Are the Customers?" In *Monetary Policy in Developing Countries*, edited by Sheila Page. London and New York: Routledge, 1993.

Westcott, Robert F. "Prospects of World Savings." Paper presented at the ICSEAD conference, Kitakyushu, Japan, July 28, 1995.

World Bank. *World Development Indicators* (online database). Washington, D.C.: World Bank, 2009.

CHAPTER 8: POPULATION

Asian Development Bank. *Key Indicators 2002: Population and Human Resource Trends and Challenges*. Manila: ADB, 2002.

Becker, Gary. *A Treatise on the Family*. Cambridge, MA: Harvard University Press, 1981.

Birdsall, Nancy. "Economic Approaches to Population Growth." In *Handbook of Development Economics*, vol. 1, edited by Hollis B. Chenery and T. N. Srinivasan. Amsterdam: Elsevier Science Publications, 1988.

Bloom, David E., David Canning, and Jaypee Sevilla. *The Demographic Dividend: A New Perspective on the Economic Consequences of Population Change*. Santa Monica: CA: RAND Corporation, 2003. Available at http://www.rand.org/publications/MR/MR1274 (accessed on September 9, 2003).

Bloom, David, and Jeffrey Williamson. "Demographic Transitions and Economic Miracles in Emerging Asia." *World Bank Economic Review* 12 (September 1998): 419–455.

China Internet Information Center. Available at http://www.china.org.cn (accessed on April 26, 2003).

Coale, Ansley J., and Edgar M. Hoover. *Population and Economic Development in Low-Income Countries*. Princeton, NJ: Princeton University Press, 1958.

East-West Center. *The Future of Population in Asia*. Honolulu, Hawaii: East-West Center, 2002.

Economic and Social Commission for Asia and the Pacific (ESCAP). Population Data Sheet 2002. Available at http://www.unescap.org/pop/data_sheet?2002/tab2.htm (accessed on June 11, 2003).

Fei, John C. H., and Gustav Ranis. *Development of the Labor Surplus Economy: Theory and Policy*. Homewood, Ill: Irwin, 1964.

Fogel, Robert. "Catching Up with the Economy." *American Economic Review* 89 (March 1999): 1–21.

Kaufman, Joan. "China's Population Policy: Recent Developments and Prospects for Change." *China in Transition: A Look Behind the Scenes*. Presentation for the National Committee on U.S.-China Relations/Center for Strategic and International Studies, September 25, 2002. Available at http://www.csis.org/china/020925kaufman.pdf (accessed on March 18, 2003).

Kremer, Michael. "Population Growth and Technology Change: One Million B.C. to 1990." *Quarterly Journal of Economics* 108 (August 1993): 681–716.

Lewis, W. Arthur. "Economic Development with Unlimited Supplies of Labour." *The Manchester School of Economic and Social Studies* 22 (1954): 139–191.

Maddison, Angus. *Monitoring the World Economy, 1820–1992*. Paris: OECD, 1995.

Malthus, Thomas R. *An Essay on the Principle of Population, As It Affects the Future Improvement of Society with Remarks on the Speculations of Mr. Godwin, M. Condorcet, and Other Writers*. Harmondsworth: Penguin Books, 1982 [Originally published 1798.]

Mason, Andy. "Population and Economic Growth in East Asia." In *Population Change and Economic Development in East Asia: Challenges Met, Opportunities Seized*, edited by A. Mason. Stanford: Stanford University Press, 2001.

_____. *ADB Key Indicators 2002: Population and Human Resource Trends and Challenges* [theme chapter]. Manila: Asian Development Bank, 2002.

Massimo, Livi-Bacci. *A Concise History of World Population*. 2nd ed. Oxford: Blackwell, 1997.

Olsen, Randall J. "Mortality Rates, Mortality Events, and the Number of Births." *American Economic Review* 73 (1983): 29–32.

People's Republic of China. *China Statistical Yearbook*. 2002.

Ray, Debraj. *Development Economics*. Princeton, NJ: Princeton University Press, 1998.

Sanderson, J. Warne, and Jee-Peng Tan. *Population in Asia*. Washington, D.C.: World Bank Regional and Sector Study, World Bank, 1995.

Solow, Robert M. "A Contribution to the Theory of Economic Growth." *Quarterly Journal of Economics* 70, no. 1 (1956): 65–94. [Reprinted in Stiglitz and Uzawa, 1969.]

Taiwan. *Taiwan Statistical Data Book*. Taipei, various issues.

United Nations Development Program. 1999. Available at http://www.undp.org/popin/wdtrends/a99/a99.htm (accessed on June 20, 2000).

United Nations Population Division. *World Population Prospects: The 2002 Revision*. New York: United Nations, 2002.

_____. *World Population Prospects: The 2006 Revision, Highlights*. New York: United Nations, 2007.

United Nations Population Reference Bureau (UNPRB). *World Population Data Sheet* 2007.

World Bank. *World Development Indicators*. Washington, D.C.: World Bank, 1998.

_____. *World Development Indicators*. Washington, D.C.: World Bank, 2002.

_____. *World Development Indicators*. Washington, D.C.: World Bank, 2003.

_____. *World Development Report*. Washington, D.C.: World Bank, 1984.

CHAPTER 9: POVERTY AND INCOME DISTRIBUTION

Adams, Richard H., and Jane J. He. 1995. *Sources of Income Inequality and Poverty in Rural Pakistan* Washington, D.C.: International Food Policy Research Institute, 1995.

Alesina, Alberto, and Dani Rodrik. "Distributive Politics and Economic Growth." *Quarterly Journal of Economics* 109 (May 1994): 465–490.

Asian Development Bank. *Asian Development Outlook*. Manila: ADB, 2008.

_____. *Key Indicators for Asia and the Pacific 2008*. Manila: ADB, 2008.

Atkinson, Anthony B. *The Economics of Inequality*. Oxford: Oxford University Press, 1975.

Barro, Robert J. *Determinants of Economic Growth: A Cross-Country Empirical Study*. Cambridge, MA: MIT Press, 1997.

Bourguignon, Francois, and Christian Morrison. "Inequality Among World Citizens: 1820–1992." *American Economic Review* 92 (September 2002): 727–744.

Chen, Shaohua, and Martin Ravallion. "The Developing World is Poorer Than We Thought, But No Less Successful in the Fight against Poverty." World Bank Policy Research Paper 4703, 2008.

Chronic Poverty Research Centre (CPRC). *The Chronic Poverty Report 2008–09*, Annex E. Manchester: CPRC, University of Manchester, 2008.

Datt, Gaurav, and Martin Ravallion. "Growth and Redistribution Component of Changes in Poverty Measures: A Decomposition with Applications to Brazil and India in the 1980s." *Journal of Development Economics* 38 (April 1992): 275–295.

Deininger, Klaus, and Lyn Squire. "A New Data Set Measuring Income Inequality." *World Bank Economic Review* 10 (September 1996): 565–591.

_____. "New Ways of Looking at Old Issues: Inequality and Growth." *Journal of Development Economics* 57 (1998): 257–287.

Deolalikar, Anil B., Alex B. Brillantes, Jr., Raghav Gaiha, Ernesto M. Pernia, and Mary Racelis. "Poverty Reduction and the Role of Institutions in Developing Asia." ERD Working Paper Series 10, May 2002.

Dowling, John Malcolm, and Yap Chin-Fang. *Chronic Poverty in Asia: Causes, Consequences and Policies*. Singapore: World Scientific Publishing, 2009.

Forbes, Kristin J. "A Reassessment of the Relationship between Inequality and Growth." *American Economic Review* 90 (September 2000): 869–887.

Gallup, John L., Jeffrey D. Sachs, and Andrew D. Mellinger. "Geography and Economic Development." Harvard University Center of International Development Working Paper 1999. Available at http://www.cid.harvard.edu/cidglobal/economic.htm (accessed on June 1, 2003).

Kakwani, Nanak, and Ernesto M. Pernia. "What is Pro-poor Growth?" *Asian Development Review* 18 (2000): 1–16.

Kuznets, Simon. "Economic Growth and Income Inequality." *American Economic Review* 45 (1955): 1–28.

Lindert, Peter, and Jeffery G. Williamson. "Growth, Equality and History." *Explorations in Economic History* 22 (October 1985): 341–377.

Londono, Juan-Luis. "Comment on 'Globalization and Inequality: Historical Trends,' by Kevin H. O'Rourke, and 'Fear of Globalization: The Human Capital Nexus,' by Daniel Cohen." In *Annual World Bank Conference on Development Economics 2001/2002*, edited by Boris Pleskovic et al., 94–102. Washington, D.C.: World Bank, 2002.

McCulloch, Neil, and Baulch, Bob. "Distinguishing the Chronically from the Transitorily Poor: Evidence from Rural Pakistan," Institute of Development Studies Working Paper 97, 1999.

Pernia, Ernesto M., ed. *Urban Poverty in Asia: A Survey of Critical Issues*. Hong Kong: Oxford University Press, 1994.

Quibria, M. G, ed. *Rural Poverty in Developing Asia*, Vol. 1. Manila: Asian Development Bank, 1994.

_____. *Rural Poverty in Developing Asia*, Vol. 2. Manila: Asian Development Bank, 1996.

Quibria, M. G. "Growth and Poverty: Lessons from the Asian Miracle Revisited." ADB Institute Research Paper 33, February 2002, 1–123.

Sala-i-Martin, Xavier. "The World Distribution of Income: Falling Poverty and . . . Convergence, Period." *Quarterly Journal of Economics* 121 (May 2006): 351–397.

Sen, Amartya K. "Poverty: An Ordinal Approach to Measurement." *Econometrica* 44 (March 1976): 219–231.

United Nations. "World Population Prospects: The 2006 Revision, Highlights." UNPD Working Paper No. ESA/P/WP 202, 2007.

World Bank. *World Development Indicators Online*. Washington, D.C.: World Bank, 2008.

_____. *World Development Report* (CD-ROM). Washington, D.C.: World Bank, 2001.

CHAPTER 10: HUMAN RESOURCE DEVELOPMENT: A FOCUS ON EDUCATION AND HEALTH

Adams, Don, and David Chapman. *The Quality of Education: Dimensions and Strategy*. Vol. 5. Manila: Asian Development Bank, 2002. Available at http://www.adb.org/Documents/Books/Education_NatlDev_Asia (accessed on March 26, 2003).

Armitage, Jane, and Richard Sabot. "Educational Policy and Intergenerational Mobility: Analysis of a Natural Experiment." Paper presented at Northeast Universities' Consortia in Development Economics, Yale University, 1986.

Asian Development Bank. *Key Indicators 2002: Population and Human Resource Trends and Challenges*. Manila: ADB, 2002.

_____. *Key Indicators of Developing Asian and Pacific Countries*. Manila: ADB, 2002.

_____. *Key Indicators of Developing Asian and Pacific Countries: Health and Education*. Manila: ADB, 2008.

Bloom, David E., Ajay Mahal, Larry Rosenberg, Jaypee Sevilla, David Steven, and Mark Weston. *Asia's Economies and the Challenge of AIDS*. Manila: Asian Development Bank, 2004. Available at http://www.adb.org/Documents/Books/Asia-AIDS/asia-eco-aids.pdf.

Bray, Mark. *The Costs and Financing of Education: Trends and Policy Implications* (Education in Developing Asia series). Vol. 3. Manila: Asian Development Bank, 2002.

Cameron, Lisa A., J. Malcolm Dowling, and Christopher Worswick. "Education and Labor Market Participation of Women in Asia: Evidence from Five Countries." *Economic Development and Cultural Change* 49 (April 2001): 459–478.

Cohen, Daniel. "Fear of Globalization: The Human Capital Nexus." In *Annual World Bank Conference on Development Economics 2001/2002*, edited by Boris Pleskovic et al., 94–102. Washington, D.C.: World Bank, 2002.

Dean, Michael, and Stephen J. O'Brien. "In Search of AIDS-Resistance Genes." *Scientific American* 227 (September 1997): 28–35.

Eberstadt, Nicholas. "The Future of AIDS: Grim Toll in Russia, India, and China." *Foreign Affairs* (November/December 2002).

Jimenez, Emmanuel. *Pricing Policy in the Social Sectors: Cost Recovery for Education and Health in Developing Countries*. Baltimore, MD: John Hopkins University Press for the World Bank, 1987.

Lau, Lawrence J. "The Sources of Long-Term Economic Growth: Observations from the Experience of Developed and Developing Countries." In *The Mosaic of Economic Growth*, edited by Ralph Landau, Timothy Taylor, and Gavin Wright. Stanford, CA: Stanford University Press, 1996.

Leroy, C. "Groupement des eleves et efficacite pedagogique." In *Revue Francaise de Pedagogie* [in French]. Place: Publisher, 1995.

Mincer, Jacob A. *Schooling, Experience, and Earnings*. New York: National Bureau of Economic Research, 1974.

Mingat, Alain, and Jee-Peng Tan. "The Mechanics of Progress in Education: Evidence from Cross-Country Data." World Bank Policy Research Working Paper 2015, 1998.

_____. *Education in Asia: A Comparative Study of Cost and Financing*. Washington, D.C.: World Bank, 1992.

Mingat, Alain. "Toward Improving our Understanding of the Strategy of High Performing Asian Economies in the Education Sector." Paper presented at the Asian Development Bank International Conference on Financing Human Resource Development in Advanced Asian Economies, Manila, November 17–18, 1995.

Pritchett, Lant. "Where Has All the Education Gone?" *World Bank Economic Review* 15 (December 2001): 367–391.

Psacharopoulos, George, and A. M. Arriagada. "The Educational Composition of the Labour Force: An International Comparison." *International Labour Review* 125 (September–October 1986): 561–574.

Psacharopoulos, George. "Returns to Investment in Education: A Global Update." *World Development* 22 (September 1994): 1325–1343.

Ravallion, Martin. "Growth, Inequality and Poverty: Looking Beyond Averages." *World Development* 29 (November 2001): 1803–1815.

_____. "Growth, Inequality, and Poverty: Looking Beyond Averages." In *Growth, Inequality, and Poverty: Prospects for Pro-poor Economic Development*, edited by Anthony Shorrocks and Rolph van der Hoeven, 62–80. Oxford and New York: UNU-WIDER Studies in Development Economics, Oxford University Press, 2004.

Schultz, T. Paul. "Education Investments and Returns." In *Handbook of Development Economics*, Vol. 1, edited by Hollis B. Chenery and T. N. Srinivasan. Amsterdam: Elsevier, 1988.

Southeast Asian Medical Information Center and International Medical Foundation of Japan. *SEAMIC Health Statistics 2001*. Tokyo: SEAMIC/IMFJ, 2002.

Taydon, Ajay. "Macroeconomic Impact of the HIV/AIDS in the Asian and Pacific Region." ERD Working Paper Series No 75, 2005.

UNAIDS (Joint United Nations Programme on HIV/AIDS). *AIDS Epidemic Update 2006*. Web site at http://www.unaids.org.

UNESCO (United Nations Educational, Scientific and Cultural Organization). *Global Monitoring Report 2009*. Paris: UNESCO, 2008.

United Nations Development Program (UNDP). *Human Development Report 2007/2008*. New York: Palgrave Macmillan for United Nations, 2007.

_____. *Human Development Report 1992*. New York: Oxford University Press for the United Nations, 1992.

United Nations Population Division, Department of Economic and Social Affairs. "World Population Prospects: 2008 Revision Highlight," Working Paper No ESA/P/WP 210, 2009.

United Nations Population Reference Bureau (UNPRB). *World Population Data Sheet 2007*.

United Nations, Statistics Division. *Millennium Indicators*. Available at http://www.unstats.un.org/unsd/ (accessed on June 15, 2003).

World Bank. *World Development Indicators* (CD-ROM). Washington, D.C.: World Bank, 2002.

_____. *World Development Indicators Online*. Washington, D.C.: World Bank, 2003.

_____. *World Development Report*. Washington, D.C.: World Bank, 1998.

World Health Organization. *Macroeconomics and Health: Investing in Health for Economic Development*. Geneva: WHO, 2001.

_____. Web site at http://www.who.int/en/ (accessed on June 17, 2003).

_____. *World Health Statistics 2008*. Available at http://www.who.int/whosis/whostat/2008/en/index.html.

Yusuf, Shahid, and Simon J. Evenett. *Can East Asia Compete? Innovation for Global Markets*. Washington, D.C.: World Bank, 2002.

CHAPTER 11: GLOBALIZATION AND THE NEW ECONOMY

APEC Economic Committee. *The New Economy in APEC: Innovations, Digital Divide, and Policy*. Singapore: APEC, 2002. Available at http://www.apec.info/NewEconomyNApec2002.pdf (accessed on March 15, 2003).

Asian Development Bank Institute. "New ICT Strategies for Developing Asia." *Executive Summary Series S62/02*. Paper presented at Malaysia Executive Summary of Proceedings, Kota Kinabalu, May 31–June 6, 2002. Available at http://www.adbi.org/PDF/ess/ess62.pdf (accessed on March 18, 2003).

Asian Development Bank. "Asia's Globalization Challenge," *Asian Development Outlook* [special chapter]. Manila: ADB, 2000.

_____. *Asian Development Outlook*. Manila: ADB, 2003.

_____. *Asian Development Outlook*. Manila: ADB, 2008.

Central Intelligence Agency. *The World Factbook*. Washington, D.C.: CIA, 2002.

Common, Richard. "Malaysia: A Case of 'Business as Usual'?" In *Governance and Public Sector Reform in Asia: Paradigm Shifts or Business as Usual?* edited by Anthony B. L. Cheung and Ian Scott. New York: Routledge Curzon, 2003.

Darrow, Duncan N., William R. Campbell, and Marie-Anne J. Birken. *The Silicon Valley Model and Internet Starts-ups in Asia*. Vol. 1, *The Venture Capital Perspective*. 2000. Available at http://www.orrick.com/news/InternetNews/asia.htm (accessed on April 27, 2003).

Digital Opportunity Initiative. "Creating a Development Dynamic: Final Report of the Digital Opportunity Initiative." *Digital Opportunity Initiative Report*. New York: Digital Opportunity Initiative, 2001. Available at http://www.opt-init.org/framework.html (accessed on March 17, 2003).

Dunning, John H. "Globalization and FDI in Asian Developing Countries." In *Global Change: The Impact of Asia in the 21st Century*, edited by Richard Thorpe and Stephen Little. New York: Palgrave, 2001.

_____. *Multinational Enterprises and the Global Economy*. Wokingham, UK: Addison-Wesley, 1993.

Eichengreen, Barry, and Tamim Bayoumi. "Is Asia an Optimum Currency Area? Can It Become One? Regional, Global, and Historical Perspectives on Asian Monetary Relations" In *Exchange Rate Policies in Emerging Asian Countries*, edited by Stefan Collignon, Jean Pisani-Ferry, and Yung Chul Park. London: Routledge, 1999.

Eichengreen, Barry. "Capitalizing on Globalization." ERD Working Paper Series 1, 2002.

EIU (Economist Intelligent Unit). "China: Laws and Regulations" May 8, 2002. Web site at http://www.ebusinessforum.com (accessed on April 16, 2003).

_____. "China; Attempts to Censor Internet Content Increasingly Elaborate," March 7, 2003. Available at http://www.ebusinessforum.com (accessed on April 16, 2003).

_____. "Doing ebusiness in Thailand." *E-readiness ranking (July 2002)*, 2002. Web site at http://www.ebusinessforum.com (accessed on April 16, 2003).

_____. "India: Infrastructure." *Doing ebusiness in India*, December 1, 2000. Web site at http://www.ebusinessforum.com (accessed on April 16, 2003).

_____. "Vietnam: E-business marketplace," August 8, 2002. Web site at http://www.ebusinessforum.com (accessed on April 16, 2003).

_____. "Vietnam: Government unveils programme to develop e-commerce." *Global News Analysis*, August 21, 2001. Web site at http://www.ebusinessforum.com (accessed on April 16, 2003).

_____. Ebusiness.forum.com, 2003. Available at http://www.ebusinessforum.com (accessed on April 16, 2003).

Feenstra, Robert C. "Integration of Trade and Disintegration of Production in the Global Economy." *Journal of Economic Perspectives* 12 (Fall 1998): 31–50.

Hayllar, Mark R. "The Philippines: Paradigm Lost or Paradigm Retained?" In *Governance and Public Sector Reform in Asia: Paradigm Shifts or Businesses as Usual*, edited by Anthony B. L. Cheung and Ian Scott. London and New York: Routledge Curzon, 2003.

Henderson, Clarence. "Philippines Capsule." *Asian Market Research*, 2002. Available at http://www.asiamarketresearch.com/philippines/ (accessed on March 25, 2003).

International Institute for Management. *The World Competitiveness Yearbook*. Lausanne, Switzerland: IIM, 2002.

International Monetary Fund. *World Economic Outlook 2000*. Washington, D.C.: IMF, 2000.

_____. *World Economic Outlook 2008*. Washington, D.C.: IMF, 2008.

International Telecommunications Union. "ICT free statistics homepage," 2003. Available at http://www.itu.int/ITU-D/ict/statistics/ (accessed on March 25, 2003).

James, William E., Donghyun Park, Shikha Jha, Juthathip Jongwanich, Akiko Terada-Hagiwara, and Lea Sumulong. "The US Financial Crisis, Global Financial Turmoil, and Developing Asia: Is the Era of High Growth at an End?" Asian Development Bank Working Paper Series 139, December 2008.

Kennedy, Robert E., and Richard H. K. Vietor. *Globalization and Growth*. Houston: Drysden/Harcourt College Publishers, 2001.

Lewis, Thomas G. "Wiring China For the New Century." In *China's Century: The Awakening of the Next Economic Powerhouse*, edited by L. J. Brahm. Singapore and New York: Wiley, 2001.

Lim, Tiong Pin. "Is China more of a threat than opportunity to ASEAN?" Term paper, Singapore Management University, May 22, 2003.

Madhur, Srinivasa. "Costs and Benefits of a Common Currency for ASEAN." ERD Working Paper Series 12, 2002.

Nomura Securities, *Nomura Economics Asia*, February 2009.

Nua Internet Surveys. "Accenture: Customer Satisfaction Driving egovernment." April 9, 2002. Available at http://www.nua.com/surveys/ (accessed on March 25, 2003).

Obstfeld, Maurice. "The Global Capital Market: Benefactor or Menace." *Journal of Economic Perspectives* 12 (Fall 1998): 9–30.

OECD (Organization for Economic Cooperation and Development). *Trends in International Migration*. Paris: OECD, 2000.

Prakash, Brahm. "Information and Communication Technology in Developing Countries of Asia." In *Technology and Poverty Reduction in Asia and the Pacific*, edited by Jorge Braga de Macedo and Taoda Chino. Paris: OECD Development Centre, 2002.

Rodrik, Dani. "Feasible Globalizations." National Bureau of Economic Research Working Paper 9129, 2002. Available at http://www.nber.org/papers/w9129 (accessed on February 5, 2003).

_____. "Symposium on Globalization in Perspective: An Introduction." *Journal of Economic Perspectives* 12 (Fall 1998): 3–8.

Rosenberg, Tina. "The Free-Trade Fix." *New York Times* (magazine), August 18, 2002.

Smadja, Claudia. "Dealing with Globalization." In *China's Century: The Awakening of the Next Economic Powerhouse*, edited by Lawrence J. Brahm. Singapore and New York: Wiley, 2001.

Stiglitz, Joseph E. *Globalization and Its Discontents*. New York: W. W. Norton, 2002.

_____. *Making Globalization Work*. New York: W.W. Norton, 2006.

Taiwan Government. *Taiwan Statistical Yearbook*. Taipei, 2008.

The Straits Times. April 17, 2003.

UNCTAD (United Nations Conference on Trade and Development). *Trade and Development Report: Capital Flows to Developing Countries*. New York and Geneva: United Nations, 1999a.

_____. *Trade and Development Report 2008*. New York and Geneva: United Nations, 2008.

_____. *World Investment Report*. New York and Geneva: United Nations, 1999b.

_____. *World Investment Report*. New York and Geneva: United Nations, 2002.

_____. *World Investment Report*. New York and Geneva: United Nations, 2008.

Westcott, Clay G. "E-Government in the Asia Pacific Region." Manila: Asian Development Bank, 2001. Available at http://www.adb.org/Documents/Papers/E_Government/default.asp/ (accessed on March 20, 2003).

Williamson, John. "Globalization, Labor Markets and Policy Backlash in the Past." *Journal of Economic Perspectives* 12 (Fall 1998): 51–71.

World Bank. *World Development Finance*. Washington, D.C.: World Bank, 1999.

_____. *World Development Indicators* (CD-ROM). Washington, D.C.: World Bank, 2002.

_____. *World Development Indicators* (CD-ROM, network version). Washington, D.C.: World Bank, 2003.

World Resources Institute. *Earth Trends: Trend in Goods and Services* (Washington, D.C.: WRI, 2009). Available at http://earthtrends.wri.org/searchable_db/index.php?theme=5&variable_ID=658&action=select_countries (accessed March 5, 2009).

World Times/IDC. "Information Society Index Ranking." Boston: World Times, Inc, 2001. Available at http://www.worldpaper.com/2001/Xjan01/ISI/2001%20Information%20Society%20Ranking.html (accessed on March 4, 2003).

Xinhua News Agency, May 17, 2002.

Yusuf, Shahid, and Simon J. Evenett. *Can East Asia Compete? Innovation for Global Markets*. Washington, D.C.: World Bank, 2002.

CHAPTER 12: THE ENVIRONMENT AND SUSTAINABLE DEVELOPMENT IN ASIA

Asian Development Bank. *Emerging Asia: Changes and Challenges*. Manila: ADB, 1997.

Clark, Colin. "The Economics of Population Growth and Control: A Comment." *Review of Social Economy* 28 (March 1970): 449–466.

Coase, Robert H. "The Problem of Social Cost." *Journal of Law and Economics* 3 (1960): 1–44.

Common, Michael. *Environmental and Resource Economics: An Introduction*. 2nd ed. London and New York: Longman, 1996.

Consumer Asia. *Consumer Asia 2002*. London: Euromonitor Plc, 2002.

Duncan, Emma, and Jamie Grant. "Greening the Palm Oil Industry Could Help Save Indonesia's Forests." In *People & the Planet 2000–2003*, December 16, 2002. Web site at http://www.peopleandplanet.net" (accessed on December 16, 2003).

Gangadharan, Lata, and Ma Rebecca Valenzuela. "Interrelationships between Income, Health and the Environment: Extending the Environmental Kuznets Curve Hypothesis." *Ecological Economics* 36 (March 2001): 515–532.

International Energy Agency. *World Energy Outlook*. Paris: IEA Publication Service, 2006.

IPCC (Intergovernmental Panel on Climate Change). "Climate Change 2001: Impacts, Adaptation and Vulnerability." *Report of Working Group II of the Intergovernmental Panel on Climate Change*. Geneva: IPCC, 2001.

Kahn, James. *The Economic Approach to Environmental and Natural Resources*. 2nd ed. San Diego, CA: Dryden Press, 1998.

Pearce, David W., and R. Kerry Turner. *Economics of Natural Resources and the Environment*. New York: Harvester Wheatsheaf, 1990.

People & the Planet, 2000–2003. Web site at http://www.peopleandplanet.net/.

Population Reference Bureau. "World Population Highlights." *Population Bulletin 63* (September 2008).

Tacio, Henrylito D. "Lethal Inhalation in the Philippines." In *People & the Planet, 2000–2003*, 2003. http://www.peopleandplanet.net/doc.php (accessed on January 30, 2003).

Tietenberg, Thomas H. *Environmental and Natural Resource Economics*. 4th ed. New York: Harper Collins, 1996.

UNEP (United Nations Environment Program). *World Resources 1996–97: The Urban Environment*. Washington, D.C.: World Resources Institute, UNEP, and the World Bank, 1996.

_____. *Global Environment Outlook*. New York: Oxford University Press, 2000.

_____. *Global Environment Outlook*. New York: Oxford University Press, 2003.

UNESCAP (United Nations Economic and Social Commission for Asia and the Pacific). *The Statistical Yearbook for Asia and the Pacific*. Bangkok: UNESCAP, 2006.

_____. *The State of the Environment in Asia and the Pacific*. Bangkok: UNESCAP, 1999.

_____. *The State of the Environment in Asia and the Pacific*. Bangkok: UNESCAP, 2000.

World Bank. *World Bank Development Report*. Washington, D.C.: World Bank. Various years.

World Resources Institute (WRI), in collaboration with the United Nations Development Program, United Nations Environment Program, and World Bank. *World Resources 2005: The Wealth of the Poor—Managing Ecosystems to Fight Poverty*. Washington, D.C.: WRI, 2005.

World Resources Institute (WRI). *EarthTrends: Environmental Information*. Washington, D.C.: WRI, 2007. Available at http://earthtrends.wri.org.

Xiong Lei. "Water Challenge for China, Country Report 1: China." In *People & the Planet 2000–2003*, 2001. Available at http://www.peopleandplanet.net/ (accessed on January 11, 2003).

CHAPTER 13: THE POLITICAL ECONOMY OF DEVELOPMENT IN ASIA

Barro, Robert J. *Determinants of Economic Growth: A Cross-Country Empirical Study*. Cambridge, MA: MIT Press, 1997.

Becker, Gary. "Altruism in the Family and Selfishness in the Market Place." *Econometrica* 48 (February 1981): 1–15.

Blechinger, Verena. "Working Paper: Report on Recent Bribery Scandals, 1996–2000." Paper presented at a TI workshop on corruption and political party funding, La Pietera, Italy, October 2000. Available at http://www.transparency.org/working_papers/country/s_korea_paper.html (accessed on March 7, 2003).

Boettke, Peter, and J. Robert Subrick. "Rule of Law, Development and Human Capabilities, " Mimeo, 2009.

Frank, Robert H. *Passions Within Reason: The Strategic Role of the Emotions*. New York: W. W. Norton, 1988.

Friedman, Milton. "The Role of Monetary Policy." *American Economic Review* 58 (March 1968): 1–17.

Global Competitiveness Report Index (2009), Web site at http://www.gcr.weforum.org (accessed on March 21, 2009).

Holmes, Kim R., Melanie Kirkpatrick, and Gerald P. O'Driscoll, Jr. *The 2001 Index of Economic Freedom*. Washington, D.C.: The Heritage Foundation and New York: Dow Jones & Company, 2001. Available at http://www.heritage.org/research/features/index/2001/ (accessed on February 15, 2003).

Kant, Immanuel. *Immanuel Kant: Lectures on Ethics*, edited by Peter Heath and J. B. Schneewind. New York: Cambridge University Press, 1997. [Translated by Peter Heath.]

Kapur, Basant K. "Harmonization Between Communitarian Ethics and Market Economics." *Journal of Markets and Morality* 2 (Spring 1999): 35–52.

_____. *Communitarian Ethics and Economics*. Aldershot, UK and Brookfield, VT: Avebury, 1995.

Korean Information Service. "Korea's Second-Phase Fighting Against Corruption in the New Millennium." Policy Series, 2000. Available at http://www.korea.net/learnaboutkorea/library/publication/corruption_200006.html (accessed on April 3, 2003).

Mauro, Paolo. "Corruption and Growth." *Quarterly Journal of Economics* 110 (August 1995): 681–712.

Mill, John S. *Principles of Political Economy, The World's Classic*. New York: Oxford University Press, 1994. [Originally published 1848.]

Moon, Bruce E. *The Political Economy of Basic Human Needs*. Ithaca, NY: Cornell University Press, 1991.

Mulligan, Casey B. *Parental Priorities and Economic Inequality*. Chicago: University of Chicago Press, 1997.

OECD (Organization for Economic Cooperation and Development). *No Longer Business as Usual, Fighting Bribery and Corruption*. Paris: OECD, 2000.

Persson, Torsten, and Guido Tabellini. "Is Inequality Harmful for Growth?" *American Economic Review* 84 (June 1994): 600–621.

Quibria, M. G., and J. M. Dowling, eds. *Current Issues in Economic Development: An Asian Perspective*. Hong Kong and New York: Oxford University Press for the Asian Development Bank, 1996.

Rawls, John. *A Theory of Justice*. Cambridge, MA: The Belknap Press of Harvard University Press, 1971.

Reder, Melvin. "Corruption as a Feature of Government Organization: Comment." *Journal of Law and Economics* 18 (1975): 607–609.

Rosser, Andrew. "What Paradigm Shift? Public Sector Reform in Indonesia since the Asian Crisis." In *Governance and Public Sector Reform in Asia: Paradigm Shifts or Businesses as Usual*, edited by Anthony B. L. Cheung and Ian Scott. London and New York: Routledge Curzon, 2003.

Rothschild, Kurt W. *Ethics and Economic Theory: Ideas, Models and Dilemmas*. Aldershot, UK: Edward Elgar, 1993.

Sen, Amartya. *Ethics and Economics*. Oxford and Cambridge, MA: Basil Blackwell, 1989.

Stark, Oded. *Altruism and Beyond: An Economic Analysis of Transfers and Exchanges within Families and Groups*. New York: Cambridge University Press, 1995.

Transparency International. *Transparency International Corruption Perceptions Index*, various years. Web site at http://www.transparency.org (accessed on May 7, 2003 and March 2009)

Van Rijckenhem, C., and B. Weder. "Corruption and the Rate of Temptation: Do Low Wages in the Civil Service Cause Corruption?" International Monetary Fund Working Paper 97/73, 1997.

von Hayek, Friederick. *Individualism and Economic Order*. Chicago: University of Chicago Press, 1948.

Wei, Shang Jim. "Corruption in Economic Development, Beneficial Grease, Minor Annoyance, or Major Obstacle?" World Bank Policy Research Working Paper 2048, February 1999.

Zamagni, Stefano, ed. *Economics of Altruism*. Aldershot, UK and Brookfield, VT: Edward Elgar, 1995.

Index